To the Point

▲

ALSO BY ROBERT HARTWELL FISKE

The Dictionary of Unendurable English

The Dimwit's Dictionary

To the Point

A Dictionary of Concise Writing

Robert Hartwell Fiske

W. W. NORTON & COMPANY

NEW YORK • LONDON

For information about permission to reproduce selections from this book, write to Permissions, W. W. Norton & Company, Inc., 500 Fifth Avenue, New York, NY 10110

For information about special discounts for bulk purchases, please contact W. W. Norton Special Sales at specialsales@wwnorton.com or 800-233-4830

Manufacturing by RR Donnelley, Harrisonburg, VA
Book design by BTDnyc
Production manager: Anna Oler

Library of Congress Cataloging-in-Publication Data

Fiske, Robert Hartwell.
  [Dictionary of concise writing]
  To the point : a dictionary of concise writing / Robert Hartwell Fiske.
      pages cm
  "Previous editions published under the Titles: The Dictionary of Concise Writing, The Writer's Digest Dictionary Of Concise Writing, And Guide To Concise Writing."
  ISBN 978-0-393-34717-3 (pbk.)
  1. English language—Rhetoric—Dictionaries. 2. English language—Usage—Dictionaries. 3. Report writing—Dictionaries. I. Title.
  PE1464.F57 2014
  808'.04203—dc23
                        2013046070

W. W. Norton & Company, Inc.
500 Fifth Avenue, New York, N.Y. 10110
www.wwnorton.com

W. W. Norton & Company Ltd.
Castle House, 75/76 Wells Street, London W1T 3QT

1 2 3 4 5 6 7 8 9 0

To Brad and Bruce—my big brothers—

the one as accomplished and caring

as the other.

Contents

Words are like leaves; and where they most abound,
Much fruit of sense beneath is rarely found.

—ALEXANDER POPE, *Essay on Criticism*

POLONIUS: *What do you read, my lord?*
HAMLET: *Words, words, words.*

—WILLIAM SHAKESPEARE, *Hamlet*, act 2, scene 2

A barren superfluity of words.

—SIR SAMUEL GARTH, *The Dispensary, canto 2*

Let thy words be few.

—ECCLESIASTES 5:2

Reckless writers and slipshod speakers use many words where few would do. . . . Yet for all the words, their expression is but impoverished; more words do not necessarily signify more meaning.

Life is measured by its meaning, and a good deal of that meaning is inherent in the words we use. If so many of our words are superfluous—and thus do not signify— so much of our life is, ineluctably, meaningless.

In the end, we are no more superfluous than are the words we use.

—ROBERT HARTWELL FISKE, *The Dimwit's Dictionary*

Foreword

I n a letter to a twelve-year-old boy, Mark Twain wrote, "I notice you use plain, simple language, short words, and brief sentences. That is the way to write English—it is the modern way and the best way. Stick to it; don't let fluff and flowers and verbosity creep in."

Alas, with most of us, as we grow older, fluff and flowers and verbosity do creep in. Writing today often has too much fat, too little muscle—bulk without strength. Much of what we read these days ranges from slightly flabby to grossly obese. As children, we wrote sentences like "See Dick run." As adults, we are more likely to write, "It is imperative that we assiduously observe Richard as he traverses the terrain at an accelerated rate of speed." We gain girth and lose mirth—and so does our prose.

What happens to people's writing in the years between childhood and maturity? For one thing, their reasons for writing change. The child writes for the best of reasons—to tell somebody something that is worth telling. Little Janie Jones wants her friends to know about her dog, Spot. Her only concern is to share her joy that "Spot is the bestest dog in the whole wide world."

Mr. Jones, Janie's dad, also has something worthwhile to write about—his company's new marketing plan, which may or may not be the "bestest" marketing plan in the industry. But his real reason for writing a long memo about the plan is that he wants to be perceived as having had "input" into the plan's development. As he writes, he worries about the impression his writing might make on his colleagues, especially his boss. He chooses his words carefully—the more and the longer, the better. Even if his instinct tells him to write simply, he's afraid to, lest his memo not be taken seriously.

Janie has no such fear. While she uses a simple, clear, unaffected second-grade vocabulary, her dad draws on marketing terms he learned while earning his MBA. Relying heavily on the jargon of his business, he throws in a couple of viable alternatives, a new set of parameters, and a plan for prioritization that should be implemented at this point in time—the bureaucrat's way to use seventeen letters to write *now*. When it's done, he has produced a bloated, tedious, pompous piece of writing full of sound and fury, signifying very little.

As Janie grows older, her writing gradually becomes more like her dad's—lacking in warmth, sincerity, and directness. She begins to worry about impressing her classmates and teachers—or even Dad, just as Dad worries about impressing his boss. In junior high, her teacher assigns the class a theme about summer vacation and insists that the composition be at least 800 words. This encourages Janie to use two or three words where one would do the job, to stretch out her composition to the 800-word minimum set by the teacher. So what might have been an interesting, tightly written 500-word piece about a trip to Disney World turns out to be just another example of dull, flabby, padded prose, wheezing away as it lurches uphill.

In addition, Janie and Mr. Jones read so much bloated writing that they start to emulate the style that seems to be the norm. Even if they were fortunate enough to have good writing instruction in school, they allow hard-learned skills to rust. They lose confidence in their ability to write clearly and convincingly. They underestimate the power and grace of the simple, declarative sentence. To get their points across, they resort to the theory that if one word is good, two words must be twice as good.

Far from contributing to the reader's enlightenment, wordiness enshrouds meaning in a fog of confusion. As William Zinsser, the author, teacher, and journalist, wrote in *On Writing Well*, "Writing improves in direct ratio to the things we can keep out of it that shouldn't be there." Cutting the fat is probably the quickest and surest way to improve. No matter how solid is your grasp of grammar, punctuation, spelling, and other fundamentals, you cannot write well unless you train yourself to write with fewer words.

If you want to create fat-free sentences and paragraphs, you will pay heed to Robert Hartwell Fiske's advice throughout the dictionary you are about to explore. He means what he says, and he says what he means.

RICHARD LEDERER

Preface

This is a reference book and, like all such books, is meant to be referred to, not read through. Although I've long thought works of reference, dictionaries in particular, to be among the most spellbinding books, I cannot expect everyone to agree.

I do wish, as any writer would, that this were a work of creation instead of compilation; still, whether you refer to or read through the book, it will help you write and speak more clearly.

To the Point: A Dictionary of Concise Writing consists of three parts. In the first part, I suggest how to identify and correct wordiness. The second part of the book is a compilation of several thousand wordy phrases followed by concise alternative expressions and real-world examples. I show each sentence example in its original, wordy version and then in a revised, concise version. Part three is a reverse dictionary that shows, in a left-hand column, concise entries alongside, in a right-hand column, wordy ones.

In replacing a wordy phrase with a less wordy one or a single word, or by deleting the phrase altogether, I have tried to show how wordiness can encumber clarity and that it can be corrected. The sentence examples have been edited only to remedy the wordiness diagnosed; rarely are they syntactically and stylistically indefectible.

I don't claim that the entries I've compiled are unfailingly inferior to the alternatives I suggest. All the alternatives are merely proposed; they are not inarguable. You may at times find that an alternative suggested here, though less wordy, does not work as well as your own writing.

Finally, as author of this book, I am solely accountable for any errors or, if I may be so charitable, oversights that these pages may hold. Although I have tried to be as thorough as possible and to include as many entries and alternatives to them as time would allow, I don't doubt that I have overlooked some. Anyone who finds an error or omission is welcome to share his discovery with me, and in a revised edition, I will gladly include any correction.

—RHF

PART ONE

Advice on Writing Concisely

Chapter 1

The Perfectibility of Words

Words are flawed, but they can easily be fixed. Words exist to be thought and then formed, to be written and then revised, and even to be said and then denied. They can be misused and neglected or cared for and corrected.

Inadequate though they may be, words distinguish us from all other living things. Only humans can reflect on the past and plan for the future; it is language that allows us to do so. Indeed, our worth is partly in our words. Effective use of language—clear writing and speaking—is a measure of our humanness.

When they do their work best, words help people communicate; they promote understanding between people. And this, being well understood, is precisely the goal we should all aspire to when writing and speaking. As obvious as this seems, it is not a goal we commonly achieve.

Words often ill serve their purpose. When they do their work badly, words militate against us. Poor grammar, sloppy syntax, abused words, misspelled words, and other infelicities of style impede communication and advance only misunderstanding. But there is another, perhaps less well-known, obstacle to effective communication: too many words.

We often believe that many words are better than few. Perhaps we imagine that the more we say, the more we know or the more others will think we know, or that the more obscure our writing is, the more profound our thoughts are. Seldom, of course, is this so. Wordiness is arguably the biggest obstacle to clear writing and speaking, but it is also more than this.

- *Wordiness is an obstacle to success.* Almost all professional people know that success in business partly depends on good communications skills, on writing and speaking clearly and persuasively. Businesspeople who cannot express themselves well are often at a disadvantage in the corporate world.

- *Wordiness is an obstacle to companionship.* Few of us enjoy being with someone who speaks incessantly or incoherently. Wordiness in others may make us impatient; it may annoy us, and we may think it rude. Worse than that, when we have difficulty understanding someone, sooner or later we may not care what it is that he tries to convey. We lose interest in what a person says and, ultimately, in who a person is.

- *Wordiness is an obstacle to self-knowledge.* A superfluity of words conceals more than it reveals. We need time to be silent and still, time to reflect on the past and think about the future.

Whatever your profession or personality, wordiness is a condition for which we all should seek a cure.

Of Polish and Panache

Usually, in reading someone's writing, we see more words than we need to, and in listening to someone speak, we hear more words than we care to. For example, how often have you heard someone say *at this juncture* or, worse still, *at this moment in the history of my life* when a simple *now* would serve? These two phrases are flawed; they are two and eight words longer than they need be. The extra words are not needed to convey the thought; instead, they interfere with the conveyance of thought.

These are but two of the wordy phrases that we overindulge in when writing and speaking. The English language contains thousands of wordy phrases that dull our understanding of and interest in whatever is being said or written.

Wordiness is a flaw of style—in the way we express language. Today, our style is prevailingly shoddy. In almost everything we read and hear, there is complexity instead of simplicity and obscurity instead of clarity. This is particularly inexcusable in written material, where words can be reworked.

Few of us write well effortlessly. Typically, we have a thought, and then we write it down in whatever form it first occurred to us. Looking at our sentence further, though, we are usually able to improve on it. By reducing the number of words in a phrase, substituting a single word for a phrase, or deleting extraneous words or phrases, we are able to polish our sentence, to simplify and clarify our thought.

Reducing the Number of Words in a Phrase

The real test, however, lies in the degree to which the man's performance at his regular job improves.

▲ The real test, however, lies in how much the man's performance at his regular job improves.

Note: the ▲ is placed before the concise sentence.

<u>Insofar as</u> the implementation of new curricula <u>is concerned</u>, the situation is going back to normal.

▲ <u>As for</u> the implementation of new curricula, the situation is going back to normal.

While interest in mindfulness meditation as a stress reliever has grown through the years, there's been little <u>evidence to support that</u> it helps those suffering from chronic inflammation in which psychological stress plays a significant role.

▲ While interest in mindfulness meditation as a stress reliever has grown through the years, there's been little <u>evidence that</u> it helps those suffering from chronic inflammation in which psychological stress plays a significant role.

The MWRA's decision will allow it to <u>concentrate its energies on</u> rebuilding the region's water and sewer systems.

▲ The MWRA's decision will allow it to <u>concentrate on</u> rebuilding the region's water and sewer systems.

Substituting a Single Word for a Phrase

The practice <u>is in violation of</u> perjury laws requiring candidates to attest that every signature was signed in person.

▲ The practice <u>violates</u> perjury laws requiring candidates to attest that every signature was signed in person.

<u>Despite the fact that</u> her recent mammogram had come back perfect, the ultrasound turned up a suspicious dark spot on her left breast.

▲ <u>Although</u> her recent mammogram had come back perfect, the ultrasound turned up a suspicious dark spot on her left breast.

I think <u>to a large extent</u> this kind of problem is a function of our society's inability to talk about sexuality in a reasonable way.

▲ I think this kind of problem is <u>largely</u> a function of our society's inability to talk about sexuality in a reasonable way.

We're talking about a sports anchor who stands to make <u>in the neighborhood of</u> a half million bucks a year.

▲ We're talking about a sports anchor who stands to make <u>around</u> a half million bucks a year.

Deleting Extraneous Words or Phrases

The three-acre park is <u>located</u> in the center of the village.

▲ The three-acre park is in the center of the village.

He or she must develop strategies to resolve potentially disruptive or dysfunctional conflict <u>situations</u>.

▲ He or she must develop strategies to resolve potentially disruptive or dysfunctional conflicts.

The Japanese government is not supplying much <u>in the way of</u> guidance concerning comparative advantages involved in investments in particular countries.

▲ The Japanese government is not supplying much guidance concerning comparative advantages involved in investments in particular countries.

<u>There are</u> a large number of applications <u>that</u> involve manipulating uncertain knowledge.

▲ A large number of applications involve manipulating uncertain knowledge.

A further benefit of applying some polish, of expressing ourselves more concisely, is that mistakes in grammar and word usage often are corrected as well. For example, we *compare* one person or thing *to* or *with* another, not *against* or *versus* another; *to* and *with* both have one syllable fewer than *against* and *versus*. Fewer syllables count; life is short.

The investigators will analyze the new data and <u>compare</u> them <u>against</u> computer models in an effort to link unequivocally the Arctic's perturbed chemistry to its ozone loss.

▲ The investigators will analyze the new data and <u>compare</u> them <u>with</u> computer models in an effort to link unequivocally the Arctic's perturbed chemistry to its ozone loss.

Likewise, the correct expression is *center on,* not *center around.*

Much of their behavior <u>centers around</u> doing things to please others in an attempt to earn approval.

▲ Much of their behavior <u>centers on</u> doing things to please others in an attempt to earn approval.

The analphabetic *that way there* and *this way here* are incorrect; use *that way* and *this way*.

> <u>That way there</u>, I won't have to worry about someone hitting my car.

> ▲ <u>That way</u>, I won't have to worry about someone hitting my car.

Irregardless, like *irregardless of the fact that,* is as wordy as it is incorrect.

> Marriage proposals from strangers followed her Internet moment, <u>irregardless of the fact that</u> she's a mother of two and married.

> ▲ Marriage proposals from strangers followed her Internet moment, <u>even though</u> she's a mother of two and married.

Instead of *the reason is because,* say *the reason is* or simply *because,* and you are both concise and correct.

> A common <u>reason</u> people join groups <u>is because</u> they work near one another.

> ▲ A common <u>reason</u> people join groups <u>is</u> they work near one another.

The familiar *but rather* or *but instead* is also solecistic. Use *but, rather,* or *instead,* for each alone does the job.

> It was a rare sight in a suburban neighborhood, as federal agents loaded up hundreds of handguns, not from a store <u>but instead</u> from an Albuquerque home.

> ▲ It was a rare sight in a suburban neighborhood, as federal agents loaded up hundreds of handguns, not from a store <u>but</u> from an Albuquerque home.

After a word like *wish,* people nearly always use the wordy and grammatically incorrect *would have* instead of *had.*

> Cosmetology instructors <u>*wish they would have*</u> been involved with the decision to cut the program.

> ▲ Cosmetology instructors <u>*wish they had*</u> been involved with the decision to cut the program.

One final example is using *for example, for instance, like,* or *such as* together with *and others, and so forth, and so on, and such, and the like, et al.,* or *etc.* Use one or the other set, not both sets of expressions, to convey your meaning.

We have to give it the serious attention that we give illicit drugs <u>such as</u> heroin and cocaine, <u>and so on</u>.

▲ We have to give it the serious attention that we give illicit drugs <u>such as</u> heroin and cocaine.

I grumble about grammar because mistakes in it invariably vitiate one's style of writing and, like wordiness, often arrest the reader's flow of thought.

A good writing style starts with polish, but it does not stop with it. Style must also have presence and personality. Along with polish, then, a writing style would be a good deal improved by panache, which is as creative as polish is corrective. Panache means writing with variety as well as with balance, writing heedful of sound as well as of sense, and writing interestingly as well as enthusiastically. All this is panache, and it is far more than this.

With a dollop of polish and a dash of panache our words will approach perfection.

Clues to Concision

There are several clues to realizing a clear and concise writing style. By being vigilant—by rereading and rewriting your material—you will become increasingly adept at identifying superfluous words.

Further, the more words you know and have at your command, the more concise you can be. You will repeatedly discover, in the definition of one word, two or three others that you may have faithfully relied on to express a thought. For example, *like* means *in the same way that*, *never* means *under no conditions*, *halve* means *cut in half*, *share* means *have in common*, *with* means *in the company of*, and *cynosure* means *center of attention*. By becoming well acquainted with the meanings of words, you will see that a single word often says as much as a string of words.

The key is to question. Ask yourself whether each word in every sentence that you write is needed. More than that, is it vital? Does it contribute to or interfere with the meaning of your sentence? Does it add anything to your meaning that another, perhaps adjacent, word does not?

Eventually, this constant questioning becomes second nature. Not only will you start writing better, you will start speaking better. As you question, be especially aware of phrases containing prepositions, verbs, and nouns, and of extraneous adjectives and adverbs. Euphemisms, circumlocutions, clichés, idioms, and polysyllables are also frequent offenders.

Preposition Phrases

Prepositions express spatial relationships (such as *on, in, over*) or suggest semantic ones (such as *of, for, with*). A preposition and its modifiers form a preposition phrase. Many preposition phrases, particularly those longer than two words, can be reduced to a single word—the preposition without its modifiers—or deleted altogether. We depend on these three- and four-word preposition phrases because we are unfamiliar with the meanings of so many one-word prepositions.

Consider a few examples:

> Over the duration of the project, we expect there will be some disruption due to noise, dirt, and dust.

Over the duration of is one of those four-word preposition phrases; it is an excrescence. *During* is all that is needed.

> ▲ During the project, we expect there will be some disruption due to noise, dirt, and dust.

> As a result of last year's ONA process, a host of new network services will become available to providers of enhanced services in the very near future.

In the very near future is certainly a murky preposition phrase. Far better is the more clear *soon* or *shortly*.

> ▲ As a result of last year's ONA process, a host of new network services will soon become available to providers of enhanced services.

> I think it is premature to relinquish our destiny to the hands of fate, for indeed much progress has been made in the past, and much more is still possible in the future.

In the past, like *in the future*, is often needlessly used. The context of the sentence usually makes the tense clear.

> ▲ I think it is premature to relinquish our destiny to the hands of fate, for indeed much progress has been made, and much more is still possible.

> They are people who buy a gun for the purpose of giving it to someone who is legally barred from having a firearm.

For the purpose of -ing is unpardonably wordy. Use the simpler *to*.

> ▲ They are people who buy a gun to give it to someone who is legally barred from having a firearm.

> In the event that you are not sure whether a particular problem is an emergency, we encourage you to call the Plan for advice.

In the event that usually can be reduced to *if* or *should*.

▲ If you are not sure whether a particular problem is an emergency, we encourage you to call the Plan for advice.

We should be moving <u>in the direction of</u> finding psychotherapeutic measures to help correct this sexual disorder whenever the patient wishes it to be corrected.

In the direction of means *toward* in this sentence, though the phrase also can mean *on, to,* or *with.*

▲ We should be moving <u>toward</u> finding psychotherapeutic measures to help correct this sexual disorder whenever the patient wishes it to be corrected.

You can even set these switches <u>in such a way that</u> the RAM area can be read from but not written to.

In such a way that is a long-winded way of saying *so* or *so that.*

▲ You can even set these switches <u>so that</u> the RAM area can be read from but not written to.

There are a number of theories <u>as to</u> how firm value is affected by a firm's capital structure design.

As to, like *as regards, in relation to, with reference to,* and other equally dull devices, usually means an unadorned *about, for, in, of,* or *on.*

▲ There are a number of theories <u>on</u> how firm value is affected by a firm's capital structure design.

Verb Phrases

Many verb phrases are redundant. In them, two or more words (generally, a verb followed by noun) are used instead of one word (the noun made into a verb). For example, *decided* is usually better than *arrived at a decision.*

Be aware of these verb phrases:

to arrive at, to come to, and *to reach* phrases

Space probes are reluctantly <u>reaching the conclusion</u> that there is little likelihood that intelligent life is in the empty spaces beyond our solar system.

▲ Space probes are reluctantly <u>concluding</u> that there is little likelihood that intelligent life is in the empty spaces beyond our solar system.

Several economists predict that the expansion will <u>come to an end</u> in its seventh year.

▲ Several economists predict that the expansion will <u>end</u> in its seventh year.

to be phrases

He <u>is lacking in</u> sensitivity.

▲ He <u>lacks</u> sensitivity.

Unlike computers, which depended on the Cold War and the space race for the funds that drove their development, U.S. biotech <u>is dependent on</u> the flow of various health-care payment streams.

▲ Unlike computers, which depended on the Cold War and the space race for the funds that drove their development, U.S. biotech <u>depends on</u> the flow of various health-care payment streams.

to express and *to voice* phrases

In one letter, dated June 15, 1892, Cather <u>expresses regret</u> that friendships between women are looked upon as unnatural.

▲ In one letter, dated June 15, 1892, Cather <u>regrets</u> that friendships between women are looked upon as unnatural.

The government of Israel <u>voiced disapproval of</u> the decision.

▲ The government of Israel <u>disapproved of</u> the decision.

to give phrases

The rest of the equation is to give people from diverse backgrounds a chance <u>to give expression to</u> their different views of the world.

▲ The rest of the equation is to give people from diverse backgrounds a chance <u>to express</u> their different views of the world.

The continuing demand for our products and improving trends in component costs <u>give us encouragement</u> that this will be another year of significant growth in revenues and earnings.

▲ The continuing demand for our products and improving trends in component costs <u>encourage us</u> that this will be another year of significant growth in revenues and earnings.

to have phrases

This measure <u>has the appearance of</u> reasonableness, but its application would have to be monitored to make sure it did not induce high turnovers by employers to cut labor costs.

▲ This measure <u>appears</u> reasonable, but its application would have to be monitored to make sure it did not induce high turnovers by employers to cut labor costs.

Any further disruption in school operations may <u>have a considerable influence on</u> the holiday schedule.

▲ Any further disruption in school operations may <u>considerably influence</u> the holiday schedule.

to make phrases

University students are <u>making use of</u> the leftover foods at the dining halls on campus to feed the local hungry.

▲ University students are <u>using</u> the leftover foods at the dining halls on campus to feed the local hungry.

The column does not <u>make a distinction</u> between having chronic pain as a symptom and being a "chronic pain patient," that is, having a chronic pain syndrome.

▲ The column does not <u>distinguish</u> between having chronic pain as a symptom and being a "chronic pain patient," that is, having a chronic pain syndrome.

to place and *to put* phrases

The women's groups now <u>put heavy emphasis on</u> fielding candidates for open seats and on identifying incumbents who might be vulnerable.

▲ The women's groups now <u>heavily emphasize</u> fielding candidates for open seats and identifying incumbents who might be vulnerable.

Excess supply within the next few years would <u>place pressure on</u> the cartel to maintain production restraint and keep average prices low.

▲ Excess supply within the next few years would <u>pressure</u> the cartel to maintain production restraint and keep average prices low.

to present, *to provide*, and *to show* phrases

The final section of the chapter <u>provides an explanation of</u> how to use most of MathCAD's more popular features.

▲ The final section of the chapter <u>explains</u> how to use most of MathCAD's more popular features.

The middle third of the screen <u>shows a listing of</u> the jobs available.

▲ The middle third of the screen <u>lists</u> the jobs available.

to take phrases

I would like <u>to take this opportunity</u> to thank all of you who aided my candidacy.

▲ I would like to thank all of you who aided my candidacy.

Their forecasts are best prepared when they <u>take</u> the functional area forecasts <u>into consideration</u>.

▲ Their forecasts are best prepared when they <u>consider</u> the functional area forecasts.

Noun Phrases

These are flaccid phrases that often begin with *a* or *the* followed by a noun and end with *of.* They can easily be made firm, as the following examples show:

(a/the) -ance of and *(a/the) -ence of* phrases

<u>Maintenance of</u> this flow is assured by their willingness to rubber-stamp the decisions of their benefactor.

▲ <u>Maintaining</u> this flow is assured by their willingness to rubber-stamp the decisions of their benefactor.

When a number of investment proposals perform essentially the same function so that <u>the acceptance of</u> one proposal necessarily means rejecting the others, we are dealing with mutually exclusive investments.

▲ When a number of investment proposals perform essentially the same function so that <u>accepting</u> one proposal necessarily means rejecting the others, we are dealing with mutually exclusive investments.

(a/the) -sion of and *(a/the) -tion of* phrases

<u>The inclusion of</u> families is crucial if nurses are to become a source of help rather than an addition to families' difficulties.

▲ <u>Including</u> families is crucial if nurses are to become a source of help rather than an addition to families' difficulties.

The installation and testing of a new product, the conversion of user files, and training users are not small matters.

▲ Installing and testing a new product, converting user files, and training users are not small matters.

(a/the) -ment of phrases

For more than a decade, Motorola invested in the development and marketing of cellular systems and phones around the world.

▲ For more than a decade, Motorola invested in developing and marketing cellular systems and phones around the world.

To the masses, a good government is one that prevents the strong from exploiting the weak, which is best done by the punishment of transgression.

▲ To the masses, a good government is one that prevents the strong from exploiting the weak, which is best done by punishing transgression.

(a/the) -ity of phrases

I am looking for a mutuality of interests and attraction.

▲ I am looking for mutual interests and attraction.

Women's roles in leadership positions in our society often involve a complexity of issues.

▲ Women's roles in leadership positions in our society often involve complex issues.

(a/the) -ing of phrases

Personal computers were meant to give people more flexibility in the processing of information.

▲ Personal computers were meant to give people more flexibility in processing information.

Organizing at the middle level means the making of specific adjustments in the organizational structure and the allocating of the resources acquired by top management.

▲ Organizing at the middle level means making specific adjustments in the organizational structure and allocating the resources acquired by top management.

the . . . of phrases

The president will be expected to secure <u>the judgment of the Senate</u> upon any proposed change in educational policy.

▲ The president will be expected to secure <u>the Senate's judgment</u> upon any proposed change in educational policy.

<u>The task of the writer</u> is not to attain recognition or reward but to meditate upon our passing world.

▲ <u>The writer's task</u> is not to attain recognition or reward but to meditate upon our passing world.

(a/the) . . . of phrases

You have to deal with <u>the issues of</u> betrayal, anger, and rejection.

▲ You have to deal with betrayal, anger, and rejection.

In other situations, <u>the practice of</u> rotating managers of work teams on a normal schedule can stimulate a group.

▲ In other situations, rotating managers of work teams on a normal schedule can stimulate a group.

Adjectives and Adverbs

By coupling adjectives to perfectly good nouns or pronouns, and adverbs to perfectly good verbs or adjectives, we often diminish the force and effectiveness of our writing. Powerful writing is taut; it admits no weak word, no superfluous adjective or adverb.

Look at these examples:

Individual managers need to be <u>actively</u> involved in the human resource planning process.

▲ Individual managers need to be involved in the human resource planning process.

Ideas are exchanged, but there is no <u>real</u> closure or plan of action.

▲ Ideas are exchanged, but there is no closure or plan of action.

My sense is that there is some interest, though it's too early to say how many people will <u>actually</u> sign up for the class.

▲ My sense is that there is some interest, though it's too early to say how many people will sign up for the class.

I was <u>totally</u> overwhelmed by their generosity.

▲ I was overwhelmed by their generosity.

You're one of my favorites in the <u>whole entire</u> competition.

▲ You're one of my favorites in the competition.

There are other examples: *full potential* says no more than *potential; completely eliminate* no more than *eliminate; possibly may* no more than *may; close scrutiny* no more than *scrutiny; firm commitment* no more than *commitment;* and *exactly identical* no more than *identical.*

Other Common Phrases to Watch For

back with *refer, repay, return, revert,* and the like

The second section of the booklet, while occasionally <u>referring back</u> to ideas discussed in the first section, is more or less independent.

▲ The second section of the booklet, while occasionally <u>referring</u> to ideas discussed in the first section, is more or less independent.

Type the new text, and then press Return to <u>return</u> the cursor <u>back</u> to the left margin.

▲ Type the new text, and then press Return to <u>return</u> the cursor to the left margin.

mutual with *and, between, both, two,* and the like

I think this is <u>mutually</u> beneficial to <u>both</u> sides.

▲ I think this is beneficial to <u>both</u> sides.

The receiver must share in these responsibilities if the <u>two</u> parties are to arrive at a <u>mutual</u> understanding.

▲ The receiver must share in these responsibilities if the <u>two</u> parties are to arrive at an understanding.

old with *adage, cliché, maxim, proverb, saying,* and the like

> Children, according to the <u>old adage</u>, are to be seen, not heard.

> ▲ Children, according to the <u>adage</u>, are to be seen, not heard.

> You may have heard the <u>old saying</u>, "the best laid plans of mice and men often go astray."

> ▲ You may have heard the <u>saying</u>, "the best laid plans of mice and men often go astray."

past, previous, or *prior* with *experience, history,* and the like

> From <u>previous experience</u>, we know we will find many typographical errors.

> ▲ From <u>experience</u>, we know we will find many typographical errors.

> <u>Past history</u> is full of people who didn't fit in and were regarded as outcasts.

> ▲ <u>History</u> is full of people who didn't fit in and were regarded as outcasts.

record with *all-time, high, new,* and the like

> He wants to set the <u>all-time record</u> for the fastest 40-yard dash and longest broad jump.

> ▲ He wants to set the <u>record</u> for the fastest 40-yard dash and longest broad jump.

> The number of days in the 90s in Boston and Washington may set a <u>record high</u>.

> ▲ The number of days in the 90s in Boston and Washington may set a <u>record</u>.

relatively with *compared to, contrasted to, in comparison to, in relation to, relative to,* and the like

> Although my proposal has one disadvantage, it is a <u>relatively</u> insignificant one <u>compared to</u> its many advantages.

> ▲ Although my proposal has one disadvantage, it is an insignificant one <u>compared to</u> its many advantages.

> The nature of many businesses means that earnings may be <u>relatively</u> small <u>in comparison to</u> the overall cash generated.

> ▲ The nature of many businesses means that earnings may be small <u>in comparison to</u> the overall cash generated.

separate with *apart, distinct, entity, independent,* and the like

> The public permitting process was <u>separate and distinct</u> from the landlord's approval rights under the contract.
>
> ▲ The public permitting process was <u>separate</u> from the landlord's approval rights under the contract.
>
> In the biological world, there are many instances in which the same adaptation has evolved <u>separately and independently</u>.
>
> ▲ In the biological world, there are many instances in which the same adaptation has evolved <u>independently</u>.

together with *combine, group, join, link,* and the like

> Its many parts are <u>linked together</u> by computers and can respond to changing needs more quickly than their aging counterparts.
>
> ▲ Its many parts are <u>linked</u> by computers and can respond to changing needs more quickly than their aging counterparts.
>
> We're thousands of Americans who have <u>joined together</u> to lower our cost of living and live better on the money we earn.
>
> ▲ We're thousands of Americans who have <u>joined</u> to lower our cost of living and live better on the money we earn.

Euphemisms

Euphemisms are inoffensive or tasteful words and phrases that we use in place of offensive or distasteful ones. Many well-known euphemisms deal with sex or death, topics long thought too delicate for candor. Other euphemisms, less well known, are expressions of politeness or deception. Euphemisms also mask disagreeable situations. It sounds better, for example, for a company to speak of *downsizing* or even *rightsizing* than it does for it to speak of *laying off* or *firing* employees. During wars or dubious governmental policies, euphemisms abound, like *pacification* for *killing, collateral damage* for *wounding or killing civilians,* and *ethnic cleansing* for *genocide.* At other times, euphemisms are less recognizable but only because we are less watchful.

Consider these euphemisms:

INSTEAD OF	USE
differently abled	disabled
economic adjustments	price hikes
involuntary severance	layoff
loss prevention specialist	security guard
made the ultimate sacrifice	died
no longer with us	dead
put to sleep	euthanize
revenue enhancements	taxes
seminal fluid	semen
succumb to injuries	die

Circumlocutions

Circumlocutions are indirect expressions that say in several words what one or two ably would. Circumlocutions are often used to evade an issue. When people do not want to commit themselves to a cause, or when they do not want to be held accountable for either supporting or not supporting a position, they hedge by using ambiguous words. Circumlocutions may mean something far different from what almost anyone would imagine.

Consider these circumlocutions:

INSTEAD OF	USE
a limited number	one
an overwhelming majority of	most
a significant proportion of	some
a sizable percentage of	many
in the near future	soon
is at variance with	differs from
is supportive of	endorses
make a statement saying	say
over the long term	ultimately
to a certain extent	in part

Clichés

We should never become too attached to a term for fear that it be reduced to a cliché. Once people start using a word or phrase excessively, its meaning is blunted and its usefulness lost. Clichés are words or phrases that no longer effectively express thought or sentiment.

Consider these clichés:

INSTEAD OF	USE
alive and kicking	well
at the speed of light	quickly
avoid like the plague	avoid
cute as a kitten	cute
frighten to death	frighten
kinder and gentler	humane
made of money	wealthy
par for the course	typical
sick and tired	annoyed
window of opportunity	opportunity

Idioms

Since idioms have figurative meanings, they seldom make literal sense. Unlike euphemisms and clichés, which usually should be shunned, many popular idioms have their place in the language. Idioms often say clearly and cleverly what other words cannot. Many, however, are wordy expressions for which we can find a more economical phrase or word.

Consider these idioms:

INSTEAD OF	USE
day in and day out	daily
high and mighty	arrogant
in all probability	most likely
in a nutshell	briefly
in place of	for
on the part of	by
put on an act	pretend

INSTEAD OF	USE
take exception	object
take offense to	resent
the long and the short	the gist

Polysyllables

The more words you know and can correctly use, the wider your knowledge and understanding of the world and of yourself. Still, there are polysyllabic words that we can, without fear of unrefinement, do well without.

Consider these polysyllables:

INSTEAD OF	USE
effectuate	effect
eventuality	event
indebtedness	debt
methodology	method
necessitate	require
remunerate	pay
saponaceous	soapy
subsequently	later
supernumerary	extra
substantially	substance

Couples

A couple is two words, on either side of *and,* that have but one meaning. We often feel that two words do the job twice as well as one, that in a couple, the second word reinforces the first. In truth, the second word enfeebles the first. The English language contains scores of couples, and most of them should never have met.

Consider these couples:

INSTEAD OF	USE
aid and abet	aid *or* abet
compare and contrast	compare *or* contrast

INSTEAD OF	USE
fair and equitable	fair *or* equitable
first and foremost	first *or* foremost
new and innovative	new *or* innovative
null and void	null *or* void
peace and quiet	peace *or* quiet
pick and choose	pick *or* choose
plain and simple	plain *or* simple
various and sundry	various *or* sundry

Embarrassments

Embarrassments are found more often in speech than in writing. Of course, these expressions are more embarrassing to the listener than the speaker, who were he embarrassed, wouldn't say them. Embarrassments are best abolished.

Consider these embarrassments:

INSTEAD OF	USE
and everything	*delete*
and stuff like that	*delete*
anyway	*delete*
I'll tell you	*delete*
I mean	*delete*
kind of thing	*delete*
most definitely	yes
or something	*delete*
whatever	*delete*
you know?	*delete*

Chapter 2

The Imperfectibility of People

As the several thousand entries in this dictionary suggest, wordiness is a problem—an omnipresent problem. Though a contagion that nearly all of us suffer from, businesspeople, lawyers, politicians, journalists, and academics seem unusually afflicted with wordiness.

Wordiness Everywhere

Business Jargon

In a survey, 503 top executives at leading U.S. manufacturing and service firms reported that two-thirds of their entry-level managers and professionals wrote unclearly. Entry level or top level, it seems to matter not.

Consider this diffuse phrasing from the president and CEO of a bank, from whom we should expect a style more stately:

> We've enclosed an informative brochure that includes a map and information on the changes occurring February 17. As you will note, you can continue banking just as you have in the past. There is no action required on your part.

Informative and *information* are redundant, *in the past* is superfluous with *as you have,* and *There is no action required on your part* is much inferior to, for example, *You need do nothing.*

From a real-estate professional, we have this unwieldy wording:

> I'm under the impression, due to the fact that I've not heard from the main office, that your application has been accepted.

Had this person written *I believe* instead of *I'm under the impression that* and *since* instead of *due to the fact that,* we might have a bit more confidence in his abilities.

Consider this sentence from a letter written by the president of a business:

> The employees thank you in advance for your past, present, and future business and support.

The phrase *thank you in advance* is an offensive one, but used in this typically "business-like" sentence, it is nescient; *thank you for your business and support* would do.

Here is an "explanation" from a credit card company:

> The Minimum Payment Due each month shall be reduced by the amounts paid in excess of the Minimum Payment Due during the previous three months which have not already been so applied in determining the Minimum Payment Due in such earlier months, unless you have exceeded your line of credit or have paid the entire New Balance shown on your billing statement.

This language is so laborious to understand that many people simply wouldn't bother to try. Of course, the purpose of a statement like this is less to lucidly convey a policy than to legally protect a company.

And here's another typically verbose example of business jargon, also from a credit card company:

> It is vitally imperative that this process be exactly accurate. If you error when inputting, take correctives prior to final handoff.

It means but this:

> This must be done accurately; if you make an error, fix it.

Consider this artful sentence from the chairman and CEO of a well-known consulting firm:

> Management, with the participation and concurrence of key professional staff, has determined that we can best serve our shareowners and ourselves by resisting temptation to pursue all of the interesting challenges we are equipped to handle.

This is typical business bombast. It sounds fairly good, and it is meant to (coming as it does from an annual report). But as often happens in business, sound precedes sense. Though phrases like *participation and concurrence, key professional staff, resisting temp-*

tation, and *all of the interesting challenges we are equipped to handle* may to shareholders sound sweet, the sentence means no more than:

We will focus on only some areas of our expertise.

Among the verbose phrases valued by those in the business world are *a high level of, component part, course of action, from the standpoint of, game plan, have an impact on, in a timely fashion, in the not-too-distant future, is in receipt of, plan of action, please be advised that, prioritize, time frame, valuable asset,* and *window of opportunity.*

Legalese

The language of the law is often complicated and unintelligible, but it could be made less so if lawyers would only choose to communicate with laymen in fewer words and clearer phrases:

Neither party to this Agreement nor any persons to whom either party has disclosed the Proprietary Information pursuant to this paragraph shall disclose the Proprietary Information to any persons, or permit any person access to the Proprietary Information, or use the Proprietary Information or permit it to be used, directly or indirectly, for their own account, or for the account of another, or make any copy of the Proprietary information without the express prior written consent in each instance of the party from whom it originated, with such consent being granted only by an individual with the capacity to authorize copying, except that each party may disclose and grant access to the Proprietary Information to those members of its staff who (a) need such access in order to effectuate the Arrangement and (b) have agreed not to further disclose or allow access to the Proprietary Information, and not to use it or permit it to be used, directly or indirectly for their own account or for the account of another, but to safeguard the Proprietary Information and treat it as the highly confidential, proprietary and trade secret property of the other party and to use it only to effectuate the Arrangement and only so long as the Arrangement remains in effect.

And that's just one sentence. Here are a couple of shorter, though no less bewildering, illustrations of lawyers' language:

This Agreement shall inure to the benefit of the Agent's successors and assigns, and it shall be binding upon Author's successors, assigns, executors, administrators, heirs, and legal representatives.

Boilerplate like this invariably contains the grandiloquent *inure to the benefit of;* in piecing together their contracts, lawyers should one day learn that *inure to* says no less.

> The trust has agreed that in the event the advisory agreement between the invest-ment adviser and the trust is terminated, or if the affiliation between the invest-ment adviser and its parent company is terminated, the trust will eliminate the name "Alltown" from its name if the investment adviser or its parent company so request.

Here the writer exposes the simpler meaning of one of his wordy phrases. *In the event* on the first line means *if,* as the *if* on the second line makes plain.

Lawyers, too, have their preferred words and phrases: *compensate, effectuate, expe-ditiously, in accordance with, in consequence of the fact that, in consideration of, in force and effect, in the absence of, necessitate, notwithstanding, pursuant to, save and except, subsequent to,* and *until such time as.*

Political Cant

In a poll of 1,513 adults, 70 percent of the respondents considered politicians "not so good" or "poor." The prevailing view was that most politicians make campaign promises they do not intend to fulfill, will lie if the truth would hurt them politically, and are mainly concerned with holding on to power.

Indeed, it is often in the interest of politicians and government officials to conceal their thoughts from us. Consider this prize display of evasiveness by a political aide to a city mayor:

> I confirm that I said it, but I will neither confirm nor deny that I meant it.

Of saying as little as possible with as many words as possible, this phrasing by a high-ranking military official is paradigmatic:

> We will benefit from the experience that we've already had about how to imple-ment that, and learning from the lessons of the past in terms of what we've already done.

Or consider this wording by a top presidential aide, the meaning of which is meant to elude us all:

> I think what's important to point out there is that they said they found no evidence of wrongdoing on my part and certainly nothing that indicated anything that he said with evidence to anything that I've done.

Equally unsettling is how politicians are forever devising new expressions or redefining old ones to serve their own interests.

> *"I misspoke,"* explained the politico when the committee asked about his stated opinion on abortion.

The danger here is that *misspeak* will lose its literal meaning and become a euphemism for *lie.* We must all loudly complain, lest euphemisms become synonyms, dictionaries become undone, and minds become mangled.

There are other illustrations of euphemism; for example, the wordy *it remains to be seen* and *that's an open question,* favored by politicians and their sort, so often truly mean the inadmissible *I don't know.*

Allied to euphemism is circumlocution, another stratagem that politicians depend on:

> The senator, who once was seen as wavering, says he now "is supportive of the president's nominee" for secretary of defense.

The verb phrase *is supportive of* is less binding than the verb *supports* and nicely serves the senator's equivocal purpose. Verb phrases are more wordy than verbs, so it seems as though more is being said, but they are less direct and less meaningful. Deception requires more words than truthfulness does.

Consider, too, this ineffectual phrasing by a government bureaucrat:

> It remains my hope and cautiously optimistic expectation that necessary legislation may be enacted prior to October 1.

The phrase *hope and expectation* is redundant, but to qualify *expectation* with *cautiously optimistic* is witless. Moreover, *cautiously optimistic*—one of officialdom's favorite phrases—is oxymoronic. But it is surely the incongruity of the words that so appeals to politicians. Juxtaposed, they mean nothing, and politicians generally prefer saying nothing to saying something. Still uneasy with his pronouncement, the bureaucrat further tempers it with *may* preceding *be enacted.* He might have written his words more capably had he used fewer of them:

> I hope legislation will be enacted before October 1.

Journalese

If politicians are attached to euphemism and circumlocution, journalists are surely attached to cliché and slang: *bear a striking resemblance to, despite the fact that, express concern, in connection with, in the meantime, in the midst of, in the wake of, on the condition that, on the part of, on the verge of, stand in sharp contrast to,* and *the vast majority of* are a few of their frightful phrases.

Moreover, despite the confines of their columns, newspaper and magazine writers have yet to learn much about using the shorter phrase or the single word.

> Oftentimes, the Senate, as well as the White House, struggles with questions involving what is now being described as lifestyle. The problem is that, in effect, the Senate and the White House sometimes are being asked to put their stamp of approval on lifestyles that, while acceptable in Washington, are not acceptable by general standards elsewhere.

If we change *oftentimes* to *often, as well as* to *and, involving what is now being described as* to *of, the Senate and the White House* to *both, put their stamp of approval on* to *approve,* and *by general standards* to *generally* and delete *in effect* and *being,* we lose two lines of text but not a word of meaning:

> Often, the Senate and the White House struggle with questions of lifestyle. The problem is that both sometimes are asked to approve lifestyles that, while acceptable in Washington, are not generally acceptable elsewhere.

Journalists furnish their newspapers and magazines with quantities of verbiage. Here are a few more examples:

> Lack of experience on the part of the firm is also a source of delay and difficulty.

Lack of experience would be better phrased as *the inexperience,* and *on the part* can be deleted:

> The inexperience of the firm is also a source of delay and difficulty.

> If sea levels rise to the extent that scientists predict, the Marshall Islands, which are composed of two chains of coral islands rising no more than 5 feet above the sea, would be submerged.

A more careful journalist might have written *as much as* instead of *to the extent that,* and *comprise* instead of *are composed of*:

> If sea levels rise as much as scientists predict, the Marshall Islands, which comprise two chains of coral islands rising no more than 5 feet above the sea, would be submerged.

In the course of the debate, legislators complained that the vote was futile, because the governor had the power to freeze spending regardless of what legislators did.

In the course of can be replaced by *during,* and *regardless of what* by *despite what*:

During the debate, legislators complained that the vote was futile, because the governor had the power to freeze spending despite what legislators did.

The law created the Occupational Safety and Health Administration, a federal agency charged with the responsibility of ensuring the safety of workers.

The phrase *charged with the responsibility of* is repetitious; either *charged with* or *responsible for* is enough:

The law created the Occupational Safety and Health Administration, a federal agency responsible for ensuring the safety of workers.

Academicspeak

Another area known for its reliance on jargon and gibberish is academia. Academics, both faculty and students, regularly try to give more prestige to their disciplines, and themselves, by breeding their own vocabularies. The author of a recent book on relationships identifies five levels of commitment, including "monogamy plus—you're a couple and everyone around you knows it."

Monogamy plus (which we might reasonably think a euphemism for bigamy) is an unfortunate idiom. Academics create such terms to mystify the obvious. Of course, most of these terms we can happily do without. More than just idioms, academics (and those who would have us think they are) use specialized terminologies to make their disciplines appear difficult and accessible only to the cognoscenti.

From a college preparatory school catalog, here is an entertaining, some might say indecorous, description of a course in human sexuality:

Human sexuality is a required skills course that teaches sexuality topics through the framework of values clarification activities.

I think most parents would like further explanation of *required skills course* and *values clarification activities,* but better yet would be a less ambiguous description.

Disturbingly often, the academics' language belies their intellectual standing. Consider this paragraph from the manuscript of a college text on finance:

> Mutual savings banks have grown steadily, but relatively slowly. A major reason for their relatively slow growth is that they are geographically limited. There are less than 500 of them operating in only 16 states. They primarily are located only in the Northeastern section of the country—with the sole exception of 6 states, and less than 20 mutual savings banks, that operate in the Far West and Midwest.

There's nothing inherently abstruse about the information in this paragraph. It is the wordiness of the writing, the fuzziness of the thinking, that interferes with our understanding. This is clearer:

> Mutual savings banks have grown steadily but slowly. Fewer than 500 of them operate in only 16 states. Except for some 20 mutual savings banks in the Far West and Midwest, they are all in the Northeast.

Here is a lovely example of academicspeak:

> The University in its continuous effort to improve the physical plant, will at this time proceed to implement the window replacement initiative in Coburn Hall.

The university, we can surmise, will have new windows installed.

Regaining Clarity

To say *at this juncture* or *at this moment in the history of my life* instead of *now* signifies more than mere wordiness. It signifies an inability to communicate and a lack of civility.

But why are we wordy? Why do we say seven words where two will do or write three instead of only one? Understanding why we are wordy may help us reclaim our command of the language.

Habit, ignorance, and imitation are among the most common reasons for our wordiness.

Habit. People who write and speak wordily may do so out of habit. Habit, though human, means behaving automatically, without question or deliberation. Many of us write and speak habitually, as we always or long have; few of us pay much attention to how we express ourselves. We neither read what we write nor listen to what we say.

Ignorance. Often people are wordy because they know no better. They are unaware that the concise phrase is preferable to the prolix and the precise word to the vague.

Imitation. As never before, people do as others do, speak as others speak, and think as others think. Nothing is so reviled as individuality. We imitate one another lest we be left alone. We want to fit in, to be part of the crowd. We want groups to engulf us and institutions to direct us.

Habits can be broken, ignorance overcome, and imitation resisted.

PART TWO

Dictionary of Concise Writing

A

about the fact that *because/for/in that/since/ that* delete. • Management is also concerned about the fact that Walco has not developed brand identification within the market. *Management is also concerned that Walco has not developed brand identification within the market.* • Moscow is worried about the fact that the Israeli side has used heavy arms for the first time since the sides, in principle, approved of the ceasefire working plan. *Moscow is worried because the Israeli side has used heavy arms for the first time since the sides, in principle, approved of the ceasefire working plan.* • Are they proud about the fact that over 60% of these students didn't redesignate? *Are they proud that over 60% of these students didn't redesignate?*

about/concerning/in/on/regarding the matter/ subject of *about/as for/as to/concerning/for/in/ of/on/over/regarding/respecting/to/toward/with* delete. • All of these factors assume you have a choice in the matter of where you will hold your meeting. *All of these factors assume you have a choice in where you will hold your meeting.* • He related a passage out of John during which disciples of John the Baptist argued about the matter of ceremonial washing. *He related a passage out of John during which disciples of John the Baptist argued about ceremonial washing.* • Both authors have written widely on the subject of behavioral science research and application. *Both authors have written widely on behavioral science research and application.*

(the) above *that/the/this.* • Please call me if you have any questions concerning the above. *Please call me if you have any questions concerning this.*

above and beyond *above/besides/beyond/more than/over.* • The officers were honored for actions that went above and beyond the call of duty. *The officers were honored for actions that went beyond the call of duty.*

(the) above-mentioned *that/those/the/this (these).*

(a/the) absence of *dis-/having no/il-/im-/in-/ ir-/lacking/-less(ness)/mis-/missing/no/non-/not/ not any/not having/scant/un-/with no/without.* • I wanted to communicate to young people the absence of purpose and how it felt so senseless and wasteful. *I wanted to communicate to young people the purposelessness and how it felt so senseless and wasteful.* • In the absence of progressive and centrist politics, discontent among the oppressed found expression in the Islamic ideology propagated by the religious parties. *Without progressive and centrist politics, discontent among the oppressed found expression in the Islamic ideology propagated by the religious parties.*

absolutely *at all* delete. • Rarely am I dissatisfied with purchases of music I know absolutely nothing about. *Rarely am I dissatisfied with purchases of music I know nothing about.*

absolutely *yes.* • Are you happy with him? Absolutely. *Are you happy with him? Yes.*

absolutely essential/indispensable *essential/ indispensable.* • I abhor government regulations except where absolutely indispensable. *I abhor government regulations except where indispensable.*

absolutely not *by no means/no/not at all.*

absolutely positively *absolutely/positively* delete. • Descartes was an introspective man who probed his meditations for things he could be absolutely, positively sure of. *Descartes was an introspective man who probed his meditations for things he could be absolutely sure of.*

ABS system *ABS.*

(an/the) abundance of *abundant/ample/copious/countless/legion/liberal/many/myriad/numerous/plentiful/plenty of/profuse.* • Among the educated, there is an abundance of people trained in these occupations. *Among the educated, there are plenty of people trained in these occupations.*

acclamation *acclaim.* • Over the years the author has obtained acclamation for the extensive work that she has performed in the industry. *Over the years the author has obtained acclaim for the extensive work that she has performed in the industry.* • I don't necessarily need the acclamation; I just want to know that somewhere out there a kid's getting a bike. *I don't necessarily need the acclaim; I just want to know that somewhere out there a kid's getting a bike.*

acclimatization *acclimation.* • It turns out that cold-weather acclimatization helps determine a game's outcome. *It turns out that cold-weather acclimation helps determine a game's outcome.*

acclimatize *acclimate.* • Perhaps your company has recently hired several Nigerian accountants, and you want to help them successfully acclimatize to your corporate culture. *Perhaps your company has recently hired several Nigerian accountants, and you want to help them successfully acclimate to your corporate culture.* • It's hard to acclimatize myself to the literary world, and I don't want to be a part of it. *It's hard to acclimate myself to the literary world, and I don't want to be a part of it.*

accommodations *rooms.*

accompanied by *along with/and/as well as/combined with/coupled with/joined with/paired*

with/together with/with. • The results are an increase in job satisfaction accompanied by a decrease in turnover and absenteeism. *The results are an increase in job satisfaction coupled with a decrease in turnover and absenteeism.*

(an) accomplished/established fact *accomplished (established)/a fact* delete. • It is an established fact that reaction times and vision deteriorate with age. *It is established that reaction times and vision deteriorate with age.*

accordance *accord.* • The budget proposal is in accordance with the fiscal policy guidelines. *The budget proposal is in accord with the fiscal policy guidelines.*

accordingly *hence/so/then/therefore/thus.* • Accordingly, the board of directors recommends a vote against this stockholder proposal. *Therefore, the board of directors recommends a vote against this stockholder proposal.*

according to *affirm/allege/announce/assert/attest/aver/avow/claim/comment/contend/declare/maintain/note/say/state/suggest/vouch.* • According to various estimates, the measure would translate into a 10-percent trimming of insurance rates next year. *Various estimates suggest the measure would translate into a 10-percent trimming of insurance rates next year.*

according to *by/following/to/under.*

according to plan/projections *as planned (projected).* • If everything goes according to plan, five old-fashioned riverboat casinos should begin operating about a year from now on the Mississippi. *If everything goes as planned, five old-fashioned riverboat casinos should begin operating about a year from now on the Mississippi.*

account for the fact (that) *explain (how).* • And that does not even account for the fact that the working-age population has continued to grow. *And that does not even explain how the work-*

ing-age population has continued to grow. • How do we account for the fact that every action Petruchio performs on Kate he performs in equal degree on himself? *How do we explain every action Petruchio performs on Kate he performs in equal degree on himself?*

accumulate together *accumulate.* • It all accumulated together to cause a significant medical problem. *It all accumulated to cause a significant medical problem.* • When snow forms, hundreds of tiny ice crystals accumulate together to form the snowflakes we are familiar with. *When snow forms, hundreds of tiny ice crystals accumulate to form the snowflakes we are familiar with.*

accumulative *cumulative.* • The proportions reflect accumulative information as one reads the table from left to right. *The proportions reflect cumulative information as one reads the table from left to right.* • A study appearing in *Psychological Science* indicates that negative beliefs about an individual have an accumulative effect on the individual's performance. *A study appearing in* Psychological Science *indicates that negative beliefs about an individual have a cumulative effect on the individual's performance.* • Oak Ridge was third in accumulative points followed by Ponderosa. *Oak Ridge was third in cumulative points followed by Ponderosa.*

accurate and factual *accurate/factual.* • We respect everyone's right to protest but expect that the information used is accurate and factual. *We respect everyone's right to protest but expect that the information used is accurate.*

AC current *AC.*

(an) acknowledged/known fact *acknowledged (known)/a fact* delete. • It is an acknowledged fact that well-trained and highly skilled construction craftsmen are not willing to work for wages less than the prevailing rate. *It is acknowledged that well-trained and highly skilled con-*struction craftsmen are not willing to work for wages less than the prevailing rate.

(all) across/throughout the country/nation *nationwide.*

(all) across/throughout the world *worldwide.*

act in accord/accordance with *act on/comply with/conform to/follow/obey.* • The bankers were responding to a Federal Reserve study that found that they were not acting in accordance with the federal Community Reinvestment Act. *The bankers were responding to a Federal Reserve study that found that they were not complying with the federal Community Reinvestment Act.*

(a/the) . . . action delete. • Jailing Danilov was retaliatory action against the seizure of a Soviet agent in the United States. *Jailing Danilov was retaliation against the seizure of a Soviet agent in the United States.* • We are taking steps to revoke the security clearances of individuals who have been involved in illegal actions. *We are taking steps to revoke the security clearances of individuals who have been involved in illegalities.* • The innovative actions of the European Regional Development Fund are laboratories of ideas for disadvantaged regions. *The innovations of the European Regional Development Fund are laboratories of ideas for disadvantaged regions.* • Thai police increased patrols at international schools in Bangkok after receiving intelligence information about potential terrorist action. *Thai police increased patrols at international schools in Bangkok after receiving intelligence information about potential terrorism.*

action/attack/battle/game plan *course/design/formula/idea/method/plan/policy/procedure/proposal/scheme/strategy.* • The Democratic leadership's action plan is simple: Delay action as long as possible. *The Democratic leadership's strategy is simple: Delay action as long as possi-*

ble.•We believe you will be pleased with the findings and enthusiastic about the action plans that will emerge. *We believe you will be pleased with the findings and enthusiastic about the plans that will emerge.* • A vision, a game plan, and prudent investment are necessary elements in assuring that the Commonwealth maintains its competitive edge in the life sciences. *A vision, a design, and prudent investment are necessary elements in assuring that the Commonwealth maintains its competitive edge in the life sciences.*

active/actively delete. • They are learning to actively participate in their own decisions. *They are learning to participate in their own decisions.* • To counteract this, the nonprofit takes an active role in encouraging new solutions and approaches to problems. *To counteract this, the nonprofit takes a role in encouraging new solutions and approaches to problems.* • Citibank is actively pursuing private banking in numerous domestic markets around the world. *Citibank is pursuing private banking in numerous domestic markets around the world.*

. . . activity delete. • There could be some thunderstorm activity as well. *There could be some thunderstorms as well.* • Unfortunately, countries where counterfeiting activity is widespread are generally not parties to such treaties. *Unfortunately, countries where counterfeiting is widespread are generally not parties to such treaties.* • The majority of unemployed were so by choice or because of childrearing activities. *The majority of unemployed were so by choice or because of childrearing.*

(the) act of delete. • The act of making sketches and writing statements about the problem helps to get the designer off dead center. *Making sketches and writing statements about the problem helps to get the designer off dead center.*

actual/actually delete.

add (on) . . . additional/further/more *add.* • If I can add any additional information, please do not hesitate to contact me. *If I can add any information, please do not hesitate to contact me.* • Please add an additional three days to your schedule if you have oversized images. *Please add three days to your schedule if you have oversized images.* • We will be adding on additional counties during the day. *We will be adding counties during the day.*

added bonus/extra/fillip/perk *bonus/extra/fillip/perk.* • This added fillip heightened the flavor of Friday's elegant performances in a way that called to mind the brilliant French film *Ridicule. This fillip heightened the flavor of Friday's elegant performances in a way that called to mind the brilliant French film* Ridicule. • As an added extra for new bet365 customers, they will receive a 100 percent deposit bonus. *As an extra for new bet365 customers, they will receive a 100 percent deposit bonus.* • Give a friend or loved one a favorite film or TV show for the holidays and it's probably going to come with an added bonus—the freedom to watch it anywhere, anytime. *Give a friend or loved one a favorite film or TV show for the holidays and it's probably going to come with a bonus—the freedom to watch it anywhere, anytime.*

(an) additional . . . added/extra/further/more/other *added/extra/further/more/other.* • He is sending an additional 30,000 more troops. *He is sending 30,000 more troops.*

additionally *also/and/as well/besides/beyond that/this/even/further/furthermore/moreover/more than that/this/still more/then/too/what's more.* • Additionally, he was an authority on butterflies. *He was also an authority on butterflies.*

add together *add/total.* • Add together the first 31 numbers in the sequence 6, 66, 666, 6666, . . . *Add the first 31 numbers in the sequence 6, 66,*

666, 6666, . . . • If you add together the workers in all industries who lose jobs, change jobs, or get their first jobs, 37% of the labor force changes its employment status every year. *If you total the workers in all industries who lose jobs, change jobs, or get their first jobs, 37% of the labor force changes its employment status every year.*

adequate enough *adequate/enough.* • As important as these rewards may be, no one would suggest that they are adequate enough to inspire the changes anticipated. *As important as these rewards may be, no one would suggest that they are enough to inspire the changes anticipated.*

(an/the) adequate number (of) *enough.* • Performance tasks appear quite feasible in classroom use, provided an adequate number of good tasks are available. *Performance tasks appear quite feasible in classroom use, provided enough good tasks are available.*

admit to *admit.* • The General Accounting Office found 16 percent of the employers surveyed admitted to engaging in discriminatory hiring practices. *The General Accounting Office found 16 percent of the employers surveyed admitted engaging in discriminatory hiring practices.* • The "complex" words, which the author admits to having some trouble understanding, are shown in all-capital letters. *The "complex" words, which the author admits having some trouble understanding, are shown in all-capital letters.*

advance ahead/forth/forward/on/onward *advance/continue/go on/move on/proceed/progress.* • Those who exhibit mastery can advance forth/those who need reinforcement would be assigned with repeated practice and advance forth only when ready. *Those who exhibit mastery can advance/those who need reinforcement would be assigned with repeated practice and advance only when ready.* • Advance forward and go with the words and visions I have planted deep within your hearts. *Advance and go with the words and visions I have planted deep within your hearts.*

advanced/along in years *aged/elderly/old.* • She's dating a man who's advanced in years. *She's dating a man who's old.*

advance/prior notice *notice.* • Congress is in the thick of a new stage of the battle over my proposal to require businesses to give advance notice to workers before plants are closed or major layoffs are ordered. *Congress is in the thick of a new stage of the battle over my proposal to require businesses to give notice to workers before plants are closed or major layoffs are ordered.* • Since there is no evidence that unannounced quizzes improve performance, it seems reasonable to provide students with as much advance notice about testing as possible. *Since there is no evidence that unannounced quizzes improve performance, it seems reasonable to provide students with as much notice about testing as possible.*

advance planning/plans *planning/plans.* • The overhead projector is a powerful aid for demonstrations and is simple to use with a minimum of advanced planning. *The overhead projector is a powerful aid for demonstrations and is simple to use with a minimum of planning.*

advance preparation *preparation.* • In a meeting designed to solve problems or make decisions, you should include in your advance preparations a statement of the problem and your recommended solution. *In a meeting designed to solve problems or make decisions, you should include in your preparations a statement of the problem and your recommended solution.*

advance reservations *reservations.* • Participants are strongly advised to make advance reservations for the Athens–Mytilini–Athens leg of their trip, because flights to and from the islands are usually fully booked during this period. *Participants are strongly advised to make reservations for the Athens–Mytilini–Athens leg of their trip, because flights to and from the islands are usually fully booked during this period.*

advance up *advance.* • As the person's needs are met on one level, the person advances up to the next level of needs. *As the person's needs are met on one level, the person advances to the next level of needs.*

advance warning *warning.* • Seismologists generally concur that the science of earthquake prediction is such that a region about to be struck by a major quake would have, at best, only a few days' advance warning. *Seismologists generally concur that the science of earthquake prediction is such that a region about to be struck by a major quake would have, at best, only a few days' warning.*

affiliated with *belongs to/employed by/works for.*

affirmative *yes.* • If the answer is affirmative, selecting an optimal dividend policy is a valid concern. *If the answer is yes, selecting an optimal dividend policy is a valid concern.*

afford/give/offer/present/provide . . . (an/the) opportunity (to) *allow/give . . . (the) chance/let/permit.* • Winning the Boston Marathon provided me with an opportunity to make running my career. *Winning the Boston Marathon allowed me to make running my career.* • Raising cattle gave him an opportunity to practice genetics on a large scale, though the results weren't always what he expected. *Raising cattle let him practice genetics on a large scale, though the results weren't always what he expected.* • Tessa Martin of Surrey said she has always wanted to visit Australia and basketball has presented her with an opportunity to do so. *Tessa Martin of Surrey said she has always wanted to visit Australia and basketball has allowed her to do so.*

(the) aforementioned *that/those/the/this/these.* • Each of the aforementioned techniques can be used to solve a specific employee problem in the workplace. *Each of these techniques can be used to solve a specific employee problem in the workplace.*

(the) aforesaid *that/those/the/this/these.*

after/for/in/over/within a brief/limited/little/short amount of time/length of time/moment of time/period/period of time/span of time/time/while *before long/briefly/directly/momentarily/presently/quickly/shortly/soon/straightaway.* • This anxiety will pass after a short time, and you will then be wondering why you felt it in the first place. *This anxiety will pass quickly, and you will then be wondering why you felt it in the first place.* • It snowed for a brief period of time. *It snowed briefly.* • In a short while, he will be making a speech before the convention delegates. *He will shortly be making a speech before the convention delegates.*

after all is said and done *even so/finally/in the end/still/ultimately/yet* delete.

after . . . first *after.* • Any model relying on deseasonalized data should be built after the modified Census II method of deseasonalization is first applied to the data. *Any model relying on deseasonalized data should be built after the modified Census II method of deseasonalization is applied to the data.*

after . . . later/subsequently *after.* • After you have created and saved a file on the disk, you can retrieve it later for editing. *After you have created and saved a file on the disk, you can retrieve it for editing.*

after . . . next *after.* • After you note the spread, next check your stock's level II screen for the depth of the market makers. *After you note the spread, check your stock's level II screen for the depth of the market makers.*

after the conclusion/end of *after/following.* • And 3.25 million women were pushed or persuaded to leave industrial jobs after the end of World War II. *And 3.25 million women were pushed or persuaded to leave industrial jobs after World War II.*

after the event/incident/occurrence *after/afterward/later/next/then.*

after . . . then *after.* • After making changes, you can then use the transfer command to save the style sheet. *After making changes, you can use the transfer command to save the style sheet.* • Finally, after the additional taxes, if any, are added in, you then arrive at the total tax. *Finally, after the additional taxes, if any, are added in, you arrive at the total tax.*

again and again *frequently/often/recurrently/regularly/repeatedly.*

again re- *re-.* • It's an image that again reinforces my belief that we are more interested in pizzazz than performance. *It's an image that reinforces my belief that we are more interested in pizzazz than performance.*

age/aged delete. • Women reach peak fertility at age 25 and then the ability to get pregnant naturally declines. *Women reach peak fertility at 25 and then the ability to get pregnant naturally declines.*

(the) age of delete. • It predicts a tightening labor market will force the hiring of more people between the ages of 35 and 45. *It predicts a tightening labor market will force the hiring of more people between 35 and 45.*

aggregate together *aggregate.* • The most remarkable aspect of the developmental process of these bacteria is their ability to aggregate together to form a swarm. *The most remarkable aspect of the developmental process of these bacteria is their ability to aggregate to form a swarm.* • Wires from individual homes are aggregated together in a hierarchical manner. *Wires from individual homes are aggregated in a hierarchical manner.*

aggrievance *grievance.* • Another niece of Hume's, Brenda Stephenson said there was a sense of aggrievance among locals. *Another niece of Hume's, Brenda Stephenson said there was a sense of grievance among locals.*

ahead of *before.* • The ambassador departed five minutes ahead of the deadline imposed by the State Department. *The ambassador departed five minutes before the deadline imposed by the State Department.*

ahead of schedule *early/too soon.* • They arrived in the country two hours ahead of schedule. *They arrived in the country two hours early.*

ahead of time *before/beforehand/earlier/in advance/sooner.* • The production manager never knew what was in the pipeline, so he could never prepare the materials ahead of time. *The production manager never knew what was in the pipeline, so he could never prepare the materials beforehand.*

aid and abet *abet/aid/help.* • The NRC, aided and abetted by the industry and most of the press, has chosen to wink at the law. *The NRC, aided by the industry and most of the press, has chosen to wink at the law.*

aid in -ing *help.* • To aid in recharging the groundwater, large basins were constructed along the Santa Ana River. *To help recharge the* *groundwater, large basins were constructed along the Santa Ana River.*

AIDS syndrome *AIDS.*

alas and alack *regrettably/sadly/sorrowfully/ unfortunately/unhappily.*

albeit *although/though.* • His wife is experiencing a craving, albeit an understandable one. *His wife is experiencing a craving, though an understandable one.* • Today will be partly sunny, albeit windy, in Knoxville. *Today will be partly sunny, although windy, in Knoxville.*

all and sundry *all/everybody/everyone/everything.* • He is cheered by all and sundry despite his confession. *He is cheered by all despite his confession.*

all done/finished *complete/done/ended/finished/over/past.* • Are you all done with your homework? *Are you done with your homework?*

alleged suspect *suspect.* • The detective will next attempt to locate and interview the alleged suspect concerning the allegations. *The detective will next attempt to locate and interview the suspect concerning the allegations*

alleviate *lessen/reduce.* • The proposal is designed to alleviate overcrowding at Framingham State Prison. *The proposal is designed to lessen overcrowding at Framingham State Prison.*

all in all *all told/in all/overall.* • All in all, it would be difficult to find a less suitable site. *All told, it would be difficult to find a less suitable site.*

all . . . long *all.* • The president, shop chairman, and entire shop committee of UAW Local 422 worked hard all winter long. *The president, shop chairman, and entire shop committee of UAW Local 422 worked hard all winter.*

all of (the) *all (the).* • Can you do all of the exercises? *Can you do all the exercises?*

all of (us) *(we) all.* • All of us practice singing harmony. *We all practice singing harmony.*

all of a sudden *suddenly.* • All of a sudden, I began getting memos from the corporate office criticizing my performance. *Suddenly, I began getting memos from the corporate office criticizing my performance.*

allow of *allow/permit.* • The museum exhibits do not allow of any interaction. *The museum exhibits do not permit any interaction.* • When one broadcasts an online lecture, it often does not allow of real interaction. *When one broadcasts an online lecture, it often does not allow real interaction.*

allow . . . to *let.* • Do it in a way that allows you to look the consumer straight in the eye. *Do it in a way that lets you look the consumer straight in the eye.*

all/just the same *anyhow/even so/still/yet.*

all the time *always/ceaselessly/constantly/endlessly/everyday/forever.*

all things considered *all in all/all told/altogether/in all/overall.*

all throughout *all through/during/throughout.* • All throughout the 17 days of Turin's Winter Olympics, the excited buzz about China's 2008 Summer Games in Beijing built in volume and intensity. *Throughout the 17 days of Turin's Winter Olympics, the excited buzz about China's 2008 Summer Games in Beijing built in volume and intensity.* • We're trying to make sure that all throughout the process there are people who can help beginners. *We're trying to make sure that all through the process there are people who can help beginners.*

all-time record (high) *record.* • International Falls, Minnesota, sometimes called the nation's icebox, tied its all-time record of 98 degrees. *International Falls, Minnesota, sometimes called the nation's icebox, tied its record of 98 degrees.*

all-time record low *record low.* • Temperatures in Alaska reached 78 degrees below zero, an all-time record low for the area. *Temperatures in Alaska reached 78 degrees below zero, a record low for the area.*

almost without exception *almost all/almost every/most/nearly all/nearly every.* • Almost without exception, those professionals stated that innovation was of major importance to the continued success of the company. *Almost all those professionals stated that innovation was of major importance to the continued success of the company.*

(all) alone by himself/herself *alone/by himself (herself).* • Adam was alone by himself and God gave him Eve. *Adam was alone and God gave him Eve.*

alongside of *alongside/among/beside/next to/ with.* • You will work alongside of experienced dancers and see what joys and frustrations they undergo. *You will work with experienced dancers and see what joys and frustrations they undergo.*

along that/this line *about that (this)/on that (this).* • I don't know what the Twins' thinking was along that line. *I don't know what the Twins' thinking was on that.*

along that/this line *like that/like this.* • I can see using a scanner for work along that line but only if the documents' layouts aren't too complex. *I can see using a scanner for work like that but only if the documents' layouts aren't too complex.*

along the lines of *akin to/close to/like/resembling/similar to/such as.* • They have no interest in publishing anything along the lines of horror stories. *They have no interest in publishing anything similar to horror stories.*

along the same line *alike/likewise/much the same/similar/similarly.* • Along the same line, increasing benefits but not expanding opportunities for promotion would be a serious mistake. *Likewise, increasing benefits but not expanding opportunities for promotion would be a serious mistake.*

along with/and/combined with/coupled with/ plus/together with the fact that *and that.* • U.S. Labor Department figures show that most minimum-wage employees work part time coupled with the fact that 60 percent are between 16 and 24 years old. *U.S. Labor Department figures show that most minimum-wage employees work part time and that 60 percent are between 16 and 24 years old.* • One of the largest impediments to getting chronic fatigue syndrome recognized were the vast and varied symptoms that accompany it, along with the fact that many practitioners refused to accept it as a verifiable disease. *One of the largest impediments to getting chronic fatigue syndrome recognized were the vast and varied symptoms that accompany it, and that many practitioners refused to accept it as a verifiable disease.*

alphabetical *alphabetic.*

alphanumerical *alphameric/alphanumeric.*

also . . . as well *also/as well.* • They also agreed to other demands as well. *They also agreed to other demands.* • Also the content needs to be protected as well. *The content needs to be protected as well.*

also . . . too *also/too.* • We also know that Marilyn Monroe was one of his lovers, too. *We know that Marilyn Monroe was one of his lovers, too.*

alternative choice *alternative.* • Herbs are an alternative choice for modern-day medicines treating stress. *Herbs are an alternative for modern-day medicines treating stress.* • In the event that we are unable to provide you with the hotel room you requested, we reserve the right to provide you with an alternative choice. *In the event that we are unable to provide you with the hotel room you requested, we reserve the right to provide you with an alternative.*

always and forever *always/forever.*

ameliorate *heal/help/improve/make better.* • As medical technology and surgical procedures increase their ability to ameliorate, they unfortunately also increase their ability to harm. *As medical technology and surgical procedures increase their ability to heal, they unfortunately also increase their ability to harm.*

(8:00) a.m. . . . morning *(8:00) a.m./in the morning.* • I want the cost estimates by 9:00 a.m. tomorrow morning. *I want the cost estimates by 9:00 a.m. tomorrow.* • At the start of the week, everyone was predicting strong winds and rain, but who would have thought that at 11 a.m. this morning there would be a pleasant breeze and the April sun burning through the clouds? *At the start of the week, everyone was predicting strong winds and rain, but who would have thought that at 11 a.m. there would be a pleasant breeze and the April sun burning through the clouds?*

(a/the) . . . amount of *delete.* • If you have any amount of intelligence, you know what's right and what's wrong. *If you have any intelligence, you know what's right and what's wrong.* • In reality, it takes a considerable amount of political skill and perseverance to get anything of significance through this process. *In reality, it takes considerable political skill and perseverance to get anything of significance through this process.*

amount/quantity/sum of cash/money *sum.* • When the Soviets spent enormous amounts of money improving their antiaircraft systems, the United States responded by improving its bombers with cruise missiles, electronic jammers, and so on. *When the Soviets spent enormous sums improving their antiaircraft systems, the United States responded by improving its bombers with cruise missiles, electronic jammers, and so on.*

(a/the) . . . amount of time/length of time/period of time/span of time *period/time/while* delete. • They filmed our arguments over a three-month period of time. *They filmed our arguments over three months.* • You can get to know someone very well if you date him or her for a long enough period of time. *You can get to know someone very well if you date him or her for a long enough while.* • Over the same length of time, inflation averaged 3 percent a year. *Over the same period, inflation averaged 3 percent a year.*

amounts to *is/totals.* • The number of prisoners released amounts to less than one-third of those held. *The number of prisoners released is less than one-third of those held.*

analytical *analytic.*

analyze in depth/in detail *analyze/detail.* • He analyzes in detail the three nativist eruptions that occurred during the era of mass immigration. *He details the three nativist eruptions that occurred during the era of mass immigration.*

(a/the) –ance/-ence of *-ing.* • With such asset and liability opportunities, the avoidance of large credit losses was a practical management consideration in ensuring attractive profitability. *With such asset and liability opportunities, avoiding large credit losses was a practical management consideration in ensuring attractive profitability.* • In the performance of their routines, they are acting as extensions of your position. *In performing their routines, they are acting as extensions of your position.* • A recent variation on providing version protection has been liquidation of the product on site by issuance of a credit to the retailer. *A recent variation on providing version protection has been liquidation of the product on site by issuing a credit to the retailer.*

and . . . also *also/and.* • The Winters' models are more complex and also more potentially rewarding. *The Winters' models are more complex and more potentially rewarding.*

and . . . as well *and/as well.* • It is being done by some of the women whose careers you chronicled and by a growing number of working women as well. *It is being done by some of the women whose careers you chronicled and by a growing number of working women.*

and etc./et cetera *and so forth/and so on/and the like/etc.* • He talked to us about the projection lens, the mirror, orientation and parity, the parallel plate, the prism, and etc. *He talked to us about the projection lens, the mirror, orientation and parity, the parallel plate, the prism, and so on.* • Notifications on smartphones are an important feature as they keep us informed of new messages, emails and etc. *Notifications on smartphones are an important feature as they keep us informed of new messages, emails, etc.*

and everything delete.

and everything/stuff/things like that *and so forth/and so on/and the like/etc.* delete.

and . . . further/furthermore/in addition/moreover/what's more *also/and/as well/besides/beyond that/this/even/further/furthermore/in addition/moreover/more than that/this/still more/then/too/what's more.* • And furthermore, the company is seeking to cooperate with other companies with expertise for mutual advancement. *The company is also seeking to cooperate with other companies with expertise for mutual advancement.* • You can restore the database

to its state at the time of any available backup, and in addition you can reapply subsequent committed transactions up to some desired time. *You can restore the database to its state at the time of any available backup; in addition, you can reapply subsequent committed transactions up to some desired time.*

and so *and/so.* • Thank you for submitting your pieces to *Critical Inquiry;* however, they are inappropriate for our journal, and so we are returning them to you. *Thank you for submitting your pieces to* Critical Inquiry; *however, they are inappropriate for our journal, so we are returning them to you.*

and so as a result *as a result/consequently/hence/so/then/therefore/thus.*

and so on and so forth *and so forth/and so on/and the like/etc.* • We believe our neighbor started the conflict with propaganda, espionage, assassinations, bombings, and so on and so forth. *We believe our neighbor started the conflict with propaganda, espionage, assassinations, bombings, and so on.*

and . . . too *and/too.* • I have become acutely aware of the epidemic of abuse suffered by children in this country—and elsewhere, too. *I have become acutely aware of the epidemic of abuse suffered by children in this country—and elsewhere.*

and yet (even so) *even so/yet.* • The cameras were low resolution, often in black-and-white only, and yet even so the machine just couldn't process the end result. *The cameras were low resolution, often in black-and-white only, yet the machine just couldn't process the end result.* • It was something funny, and yet completely innovative. *It was something funny, yet completely innovative.*

annual/yearly anniversary *anniversary/annual.* • Their annual anniversary party is part customer appreciation, part holiday mixer and always a charity fundraiser. *Their anniversary party is part customer appreciation, part holiday mixer and always a charity fundraiser.* • Yearly anniversary gifts are a must when you are wanting to keep your loved one feeling special. *Anniversary gifts are a must when you are wanting to keep your loved one feeling special.*

antecedent to *before/earlier than/preceding.* • It does appear that for many released offenders a definable series of emotional and cognitive events occurs antecedent to new offenses. *It does appear that for many released offenders a definable series of emotional and cognitive events occurs before new offenses.* • Either in or out of time, the decision of a personal agency to commit an action happens antecedent to the action itself. *Either in or out of time, the decision of a personal agency to commit an action happens before the action itself.*

anterior to *before/earlier than/preceding.* • What is now called administrative tutelage was an institution in France anterior to the Revolution. *What is now called administrative tutelage was an institution in France before the Revolution.*

anticipate ahead/ahead of time/in advance *anticipate.* • If you work closely or otherwise deal regularly with an argumentative co-worker, anticipate ahead of time how you're going to handle the situation. *If you work closely or otherwise deal regularly with an argumentative co-worker, anticipate how you're going to handle the situation.* • Each disaster is unique and the challenges each present are hard to anticipate in advance. *Each disaster is unique and the challenges each present are hard to anticipate.*

any and all *any/all.* • This certificate replaces any and all insurance certificates that may have been issued previously to the Insured under the Group Policy and is subject to the terms of the Group Policy. *This certificate replaces all insurance certificates that may have been issued previously to the Insured under the Group Policy and is subject to the terms of the Group Policy.*

anybody/anyone and everybody/everyone *all/ anybody (anyone)/everybody (everyone).* • They told anyone and everyone that you are the one we want to use in our ads. *They told everyone that you are the one we want to use in our ads.*

anyplace/anywhere else *elsewhere.* • This is an invaluable resource that you will not find anywhere else. *This is an invaluable resource that you will not find elsewhere.*

anything and everything *all/all things/anything/anything at all/everything.* • These kids lie about anything and everything. *These kids lie about everything.*

anything/something in the way of *any/ some* delete. • It has yet to accomplish anything in the way of practical benefits. *It has yet to accomplish any practical benefits.*

anyway delete.

anywhere/somewhere between . . . and *between . . . and.* • Upjohn says Minoxidil's success rate ranges anywhere between 24 and 40 percent. *Upjohn says Minoxidil's success rate ranges between 24 and 40 percent.*

anywhere/somewhere in the range of . . . to *in the range of . . . to.*

anywhere near *nearly.* • You are not anywhere near as dumb as some of this material will make you feel. *You are not nearly as dumb as some of this material will make you feel.*

apart from *besides/beyond.* • Apart from looking like the original, the counterfeit product often performs as well as the original. *Besides* *looking like the original, the counterfeit product often performs as well as the original.*

apart from . . . also/as well *apart from/besides/ beyond.* • Apart from being expensive, the international development process is also very risky. *Besides being expensive, the international development process is very risky.*

appear/arrive on/upon the scene *appear/ arrive.* • Several bands will appear on the scene such as Implant and of course a special show by Suicide Commando himself. *Several bands will appear such as Implant and of course a special show by Suicide Commando himself.*

appellation *name/title.*

appertain/appertaining to *pertain to/relate to.* • Moneys therefor having been deposited with the Trustee from and after June 12, 1989, interest thereon shall cease to accrue and coupons appertaining to said bonds payable after that date will be void. *Moneys therefor having been deposited with the Trustee from and after June 12, 1989, interest thereon shall cease to accrue and coupons pertaining to said bonds payable after that date will be void.*

appoint as *appoint.* • Harding was succeeded by Calvin Coolidge, who appointed Harlan Fiske Stone as attorney general. *Harding was succeeded by Calvin Coolidge, who appointed Harlan Fiske Stone attorney general.*

appreciate *admire/applaud/approve of/enjoy/(be) grateful (for)/like/prize/(be) thankful (for)/thank you (for)/value/welcome.* • We appreciate it. *We are grateful.* • I appreciate your coming. *I thank you for coming.* • Your concern is very much appreciated. *Your concern is very much welcomed.*

appreciate in value *appreciate.* • Due to the overall rise of the stock market, many individuals have securities which have appreciated considerably in value. *Due to the overall rise of*

the stock market, many individuals have securities which have appreciated considerably. • Another effective tax strategy is to make a charitable contribution with long-term assets that have substantially appreciated in value. *Another effective tax strategy is to make a charitable contribution with long-term assets that have substantially appreciated.*

apprehend *arrest/capture/catch/seize.* • Daniel Mahoney, 30, was apprehended near Los Lunas shortly before 1:00 a.m. *Daniel Mahoney, 30, was captured near Los Lunas shortly before 1:00 a.m.*

approbation *approval/praise.*

(for) approximately *about/around/close to/ more or less/near/nearly/or so/roughly/say/some.* • It will last for approximately two hours. *It will last about two hours.*

(the) . . . area (of) delete. • The main interest for me is the history area. *The main interest for me is history.* • These teams should be granted broad functions, with key roles being played by representatives from the engineering, manufacturing, marketing, and finance areas. *These teams should be granted broad functions, with key roles being played by representatives from engineering, manufacturing, marketing, and finance.*

(an/the) area/locale/locality/location/place/ point/position/region/site/spot *where/wherever.*

(an/the) area/locale/locality/location/place/ point/position/region/site/spot where *where/ wherever.* • The COMSPEC line will show the place where COMMAND.COM is expected. *The COMSPEC line will show where COMMAND.COM is expected.* • If you click your mouse on the map, it will show you the area where ATM Mega Link Service is available or planned. *If you click your mouse on the map, it will show you where ATM Mega Link Service is available or planned.*

argumentation *argument/debate/dispute.* • Some members may take unyielding positions, leading to unproductive argumentation and bickering. *Some members may take unyielding positions, leading to unproductive arguments and bickering.*

armed gunman/holdup *gunman/holdup.* • An Akron barber was a hero Wednesday when he prevented an armed gunman from robbing the beauty shop next door to his barbershop. *An Akron barber was a hero Wednesday when he prevented a gunman from robbing the beauty shop next door to his barbershop.*

ARM mortgage *ARM.*

around about *about/around.* • It was around about then that he left for East Africa. *It was around then that he left for East Africa.*

(an) array of *assorted/countless/different/ diverse/extensive/many/numerous/scores of/sundry/varied/various/varying* delete. • Lately, however, an array of new troubles has surfaced—troubles like radon. *Lately, however, many new troubles have surfaced—troubles like radon.*

arrive at (an/the) accord (about/as to/concerning/of/on/regarding) *agree/compromise/concur/decide/resolve/settle.* • AT&T and unions representing about 160,000 employees arrived at an accord on a new three-year national contract. *AT&T and unions representing about 160,000 employees agreed on a new three-year national contract.*

arrive at (an/the) agreement (about/as to/concerning/of/on/regarding) *agree/compromise/concur/decide/resolve/settle.* • I'm confident that we will arrive at an agreement on how to proceed jointly on that operation. *I'm confident that we will decide on how to proceed jointly on that operation.* • Several small color sketches may be produced in an effort to arrive at an agreement on the look of the final work. *Several small color sketches may be produced in an effort to agree on the look of the final work.*

arrive/come/occur/at a time when *arrive when/come when/occur when.* • It will arrive at a time when Ford is launching its South American built EcoSport mini SUV as a global model. *It will arrive when Ford is launching its South American built EcoSport mini SUV as a global model.* • The change will come at a time when rice farmers already are struggling. *The change will come when rice farmers already are struggling.*

arrive at (a/the) compromise (about/as to/concerning/of/on/regarding) *agree/compromise/concur/decide/resolve/settle.* • Nearly 10 months since negotiations began, it seems as though the two may not arrive at a compromise any time soon. *Nearly 10 months since negotiations began, it seems as though the two may not agree any time soon.* • Either arrive at a compromise or agree to maintain your differences but respect them. *Either compromise or agree to maintain your differences but respect them.* • It seems highly unlikely that she would want to arrive at a compromise and lose the opportunity to impeach Mr. Wahid. *It seems highly unlikely that she would want to settle and lose the opportunity to impeach Mr. Wahid.*

arrive at (a/the) conclusion (about/as to/concerning/of/on/regarding) *conclude/decide/deduce/determine/infer/judge/reason/resolve/settle.* • I think they have arrived at the conclusion that he is now a neutralized force. *I think they have concluded that he is now a neutralized force.* • Tennessee officials have told him to take all the time he needs to arrive at a conclusion. *Tennessee officials have told him to take all the time he needs to decide.*

arrive at (a/the) decision (about/as to/concerning/of/on/regarding) *conclude/decide/deduce/determine/infer/judge/reason/resolve/settle.* •

The democratic process requires discussion and debate for people to arrive at a decision on a course of action. *The democratic process requires discussion and debate for people to decide on a course of action.* • The details of a particular case must be used to arrive at a decision about what is best for the specific patient being considered. *The details of a particular case must be used to deduce what is best for the specific patient being considered.*

arrive at (a/the) determination (about/as to/ concerning/of/on/regarding) *conclude/decide/ deduce/determine/infer/judge/reason/resolve/ settle.* • Sampling from an elderly population of bereaved spouses, the authors used various psychological measures to arrive at a determination of the principle elements of complicated grief. *Sampling from an elderly population of bereaved spouses, the authors used various psychological measures to determine the principle elements of complicated grief.*

arrive at (an/the) estimate/estimation (about/ as to/concerning/of/on/regarding) *approximate/assess/estimate/evaluate/rate.* • Since information from subsequent steps in an assessment is needed to arrive at an estimate of what the firm's actual marketing effort will be, the assessment from this point on is reiterative. *Since information from subsequent steps in an assessment is needed to estimate what the firm's actual marketing effort will be, the assessment from this point on is reiterative.*

arrive at (an/the) opinion (about/as to/concerning/of/on/regarding) *conclude/decide/deduce/ determine/infer/judge/reason/resolve/settle.* • Through analysis of verbal, physical and sexual behavior, we arrive at an opinion whether a series of crimes was committed by the same offender or not. *Through analysis of verbal, physical and sexual behavior, we conclude whether a series of crimes was committed by the same offender or not.* • Each property is unique, and the appraiser relies on his or her general exper-

tise and specific research to arrive at an opinion of its value. *Each property is unique, and the appraiser relies on his or her general expertise and specific research to decide its value.*

arrive at (a/the) resolution (about/as to/concerning/of/on/regarding) *agree/conclude/ decide/resolve/settle.* • If the parties arrive at a resolution of their dispute, they, with the help of the mediator, typically write an agreement that captures their chosen course of action. *If the parties settle their dispute, they, with the help of the mediator, typically write an agreement that captures their chosen course of action.*

arrive at (an/the) understanding (about/as to/ concerning/of/on/regarding) *agree/compromise/concur/decide/resolve/settle.* • Where the Commission fails to arrive at a settlement of the complaint, the Commission will then request the appointment of a tribunal, referred to as a board of inquiry. *Where the Commission fails to resolve the complaint, the Commission will then request the appointment of a tribunal, referred to as a board of inquiry.*

as a consequence *consequently/hence/so/then/ therefore/thus.* • As a consequence, there are a lot of charlatans, zealots, and incompetents offering their services. *Thus, there are a lot of charlatans, zealots, and incompetents offering their services.*

as a consequence of *after/because of/by/due to/ following/for/from/in/out of/owing to/through/ with.* • As a consequence of the 43 million babies born in the years immediately following World War II, a middle-aged bulge is forming and eventually the 35- to 45-year-old age group will increase by 80 percent. *Owing to the 43 million babies born in the years immediately following World War II, a middle-aged bulge is forming and eventually the 35- to 45-year-old age group will increase by 80 percent.* • He showed that production increased not as a consequence of actual changes in working conditions introduced by the plant's management but because management demonstrated interest in such improvements. *He showed that production increased not because of actual changes in working conditions introduced by the plant's management but because management demonstrated interest in such improvements.*

as a consequence of the fact that *because/considering/for/given/in that/since.* • Expectations were low as a consequence of the fact that screen technology was fairly grim. *Expectations were low because screen technology was fairly grim.* • As a consequence of the fact that the IPA is a global organization, a number of details regarding ethics are viewed differently in different practice locales. *Since the IPA is a global organization, a number of details regarding ethics are viewed differently in different practice locales.*

as against *against/to.* • Total investments in property, plant and equipment amounted to SEK 1,592 m. in 1987, as against SEK 1,643 m. in the preceding year. *Total investments in property, plant and equipment amounted to SEK 1,592 m. in 1987, against SEK 1,643 m. in the preceding year.*

as a general rule *almost all/as a rule/chiefly/commonly/customarily/generally/greatly/in general/largely/mainly/most/mostly/most often/much/nearly all/normally/overall/typically/usually.* • As a general rule, interest payments are made every six months. *Typically, interest payments are made every six months.*

as a matter of course *commonly/customarily/habitually/naturally/normally/ordinarily/regularly/routinely/typically/usually.* • Most veterinarians do it as a matter of course because it is a money-making procedure. *Most veterinarians do it routinely because it is a money-making procedure.*

as a matter of fact *actually/indeed/in fact/in faith/in reality/in truth/really/truly* delete. • As

a matter of fact, there are some rumors of discontent. *In fact, there are some rumors of discontent.*

as a matter of fact *also/and/as well/besides/beyond that/this/even/further/furthermore/moreover/more than that/this/still more/then/too/what's more.*

as a means for/of/to (-ing) *for (-ing)/so as to/to.* • I have found the spelling checker extremely useful as a means for proofreading text. *I have found the spelling checker extremely useful for proofreading text.*

as and when *as/when.* • At the same time, they have substantial outflows, ongoing expenses which cannot be shifted but must be paid as and when they become due. *At the same time, they have substantial outflows, ongoing expenses which cannot be shifted but must be paid as they become due.*

as an example *for example/for instance.*

as . . . apply to *about/as for/as to/concerning/for/in/of/on/over/regarding/respecting/to/toward/with* delete. • I've always been intrigued by the concept of marketing as it applies to health care. *I've always been intrigued by the concept of health care marketing.*

as a result *consequently/hence/so/then/therefore/thus.* • The IDA was working to make jobs available to the graduates of these schools, and as a result, the educational climate in Ireland has changed dramatically. *The IDA was working to make jobs available to the graduates of these schools, and thus, the educational climate in Ireland has changed dramatically.*

as a result of *after/because of/by/due to/following/for/from/in/out of/owing to/through/with.* • More people die as a result of drinking alcohol than as a result of smoking marijuana. *More people die from drinking alcohol than from* *smoking marijuana.* • Much pain and resentment was rekindled as a result of recent political maneuverings between the Turkish and U.S. governments. *Much pain and resentment was rekindled following recent political maneuverings between the Turkish and U.S. governments.* • Other citizens have closed minds to rehabilitation programs as a result of what they refer to as its failures. *Other citizens have closed minds to rehabilitation programs because of what they refer to as its failures.*

as a result of the fact that *because/considering/for/given/in that/since.* • This is clearly an area of growing importance to BOCs, particularly as a result of the fact that a recent court decision allows them to enter in certain segments of enhanced services. *This is clearly an area of growing importance to BOCs, particularly since a recent court decision allows them to enter in certain segments of enhanced services.* • As a result of the fact that this law was not passed earlier, the judge had to return the confiscated photos. *Because this law was not passed earlier, the judge had to return the confiscated photos.*

as a rule *almost all/chiefly/commonly/generally/greatly/in general/largely/mainly/most/mostly/most often/much/nearly all/normally/overall/typically.* • As a rule, I wouldn't dream of doing something like this. *Normally, I wouldn't dream of doing something like this.*

as a way for/of/to (-ing) *for (-ing)/so as to/to.* • More and more professionals are using dating services as a way of meeting the perfect mate. *More and more professionals are using dating services to meet the perfect mate.* • Many of them embrace their Jewishness through baseball as a way to distinguish themselves from the legions of right-handed relievers and utility infielders. *Many of them embrace their Jewishness through baseball to distinguish themselves from the legions of right-handed relievers and utility infielders.*

as a whole *complete/entire/whole* delete. • It's an embarrassment to the administration as a whole. *It's an embarrassment to the administration.*

ascend up *ascend.* • As you ascend up the status hierarchy, you get to select more expensive furnishings. *As you ascend the status hierarchy, you get to select more expensive furnishings.*

as compared to/with *against/alongside/beside/compared to/with/-(i)er than/less/less than/more/more than/next to/over/than/to/versus/vis-à-vis.* • The governments of developing countries give low priority to these skills as compared to technological skills and knowledge. *The governments of developing countries give lower priority to these skills than to technological skills and knowledge.* • The Japanese can design and build a car in about 3½ years as compared to U.S. auto makers' average of 5 years. *The Japanese can design and build a car in about 3½ years against U.S. auto makers' average of 5 years.* • Data communications is not very familiar ground to the operating companies as compared to their expertise in voice. *Data communications is not very familiar ground to the operating companies compared to their expertise in voice.*

as compared to/with . . . relatively *compared to/with/-(i)er than/less than/more than/than.* • As compared to Western Europeans and the Japanese, Americans save a relatively small proportion of their disposable income. *Compared to Western Europeans and the Japanese, Americans save a small proportion of their disposable income.*

as concerns *about/as for/as to/concerning/for/in/of/on/over/regarding/respecting/to/toward/with.* • As concerns the judicial control of the proceedings of a selection board, the commission stated that one has to distinguish between two kinds of decisions. *As for the judicial control of the proceedings of a selection board, the com-*

mission stated that one has to distinguish between two kinds of decisions.

as contrasted to/with *against/alongside/beside/ compared to/with/-(i)er than/less/less than/ more/more than/next to/over/than/to/unlike/ versus/vis-à-vis.* • Epidemiologists find that people who eat a lot of fish have much lower rates of both cholesterol-caused heart disease and cholesterol gallstones as contrasted to people who don't. *Epidemiologists find that people who eat a lot of fish have much lower rates of both cholesterol-caused heart disease and cholesterol gallstones than people who don't.*

ascribable to *because of/caused by/due to/owing to/resulting from.* • Likewise, WIG may not be held liable for any loss or damage ascribable to computer viruses when users call up or download data from this website. *Likewise, WIG may not be held liable for any loss or damage due to computer viruses when users call up or download data from this website.*

as (the) days/decades/months/weeks/years go on *at length/eventually/in time/later/one day/ over the months (years)/over time/someday/ sometime/ultimately/with time/yet* delete. • As the years go on, customers will look to Nynex and others to give them more than just the transmission of information—they'll also need the software and the systems integration to run their businesses and homes more efficiently. *Over time, customers will look to Nynex and others to give them more than just the transmission of information—they'll also need the software and the systems integration to run their businesses and homes more efficiently.*

as/so far as . . . (goes/is concerned) *about/as for/ as to/concerning/for/in/of/on/over/regarding/ respecting/to/toward/with* delete. • The effect of lead is particularly traumatic as far as young children are concerned. *The effect of lead is particularly traumatic on young children.* • In fact, as far as the "secrets of entrepreneurial success"

go, it's impossible to recognize that a little bit of luck helps and a lot of luck is even better. *In fact, concerning the "secrets of entrepreneurial success," it's impossible to recognize that a little bit of luck helps and a lot of luck is even better.* • The general view seems to be that infectious agents transmitted by rodents are not of particular relevance as far as public health goes. *The general view seems to be that infectious agents transmitted by rodents are not of particular relevance to public health.* • As far as fish are concerned, the optimal Hct theory appears to be too simplistic to account for our present state of knowledge. *As for fish, the optimal Hct theory appears to be too simplistic to account for our present state of knowledge.*

as follows delete. • The quote is as follows: "I never met a man who had better motives for all the trouble he's causing." *The quote is "I never met a man who had better motives for all the trouble he's causing."*

as . . . for example/for instance *as/for example/ for instance/like/say/such as.* • No such close match is necessary if the intent of the assessment is to monitor the general state of student knowledge and competence in science, as for example in past assessments conducted by NAEP. *No such close match is necessary if the intent of the assessment is to monitor the general state of student knowledge and competence in science, as in past assessments conducted by NAEP.*

as for/in/with the case of *as for (in/with)/like.* • Even when countries adopt state religions, as in the cases of the United Kingdom, Spain, and Italy, the religious context of the country is not necessarily monolithic. *Even when countries adopt state religions, as in the United Kingdom, Spain, and Italy, the religious context of the country is not necessarily monolithic.*

as how *that.* • He allowed as how he could further explore the idea. *He allowed that he could further explore the idea.* • Not having a mistress I explained as how I didn't see the problem. *Not having a mistress I explained that I didn't see the problem.*

aside from *besides/beyond.* • Aside from the lack of restraints, there are other differences a foreign investor must get used to. *Besides the lack of restraints, there are other differences a foreign investor must get used to.*

aside from . . . also/as well *aside from/besides/ beyond.*

as, if, and when *if/when.* • The Company will be deemed to have purchased tendered Shares as, if, and when it gives oral and written notice to the Depositary of its acceptance for payment of such Shares. *The Company will be deemed to have purchased tendered Shares when it gives oral and written notice to the Depositary of its acceptance for payment of such Shares.*

(even) as I/we speak *(just/right) now* delete. • As we speak, New York state is starting a drug education program. *New York state is now starting a drug education program.*

as is the case *as/like.* • As is the case with all of our new words, they sound terribly impressive at cocktail parties. *Like all of our new words, they sound terribly impressive at cocktail parties.*

as it turned out *by chance/luckily/unluckily.*

ask (a/the) question (on) *ask.* • We need to ask ourselves the question if animals are necessary for medical training. *We need to ask ourselves if animals are necessary for medical training.* • If you would like to ask a question on how magnets may possibly help a condition, we will do our best to answer your question as soon as possible. *If you would like to ask how magnets may possibly help a condition, we will do our best to answer your question as soon as possible.*

as long as/so long as (that) *if.* • This program, as well as others like it, will make a difference as long as we have strong public support for changing the plight of these children. *This program, as well as others like it, will make a difference if we have strong public support for changing the plight of these children.*

as luck would have it *by chance/luckily/ unluckily.*

as many/much as *up to.* • There are nearly 300 individual fund managers, ranging from those with a single fund to the very large mutual fund families that offer as many as 100 different funds. *There are nearly 300 individual fund managers, ranging from those with a single fund to the very large mutual fund families that offer up to 100 different funds.*

as of *on* delete. • The plant will shut down as of November 1. *The plant will shut down November 1.*

as often as not *commonly/customarily/generally/normally/often/ordinarily/typically/usually.*

as opposed to *against/alongside/beside/compared to/with/-(i)er than/less/less than/more/ more than/next to/over/than/to/unlike/versus/ vis-à-vis.* • Thanks to the recent strength of the dollar, the U.S. markets remain attractive, as opposed to their foreign counterparts. *Thanks to the recent strength of the dollar, the U.S. markets remain more attractive than their foreign counterparts.* • You should experience better results with the cool white as opposed to the warm white because the cool white approximates natural sunlight. *You should experience better results with the cool white than the warm white because the cool white approximates natural sunlight.* • The court of law, as opposed to the food court in the mall, remains a bastion of decorum. *The court of law, unlike the food court in the mall, remains a bastion of decorum.*

as opposed to *instead of/not/rather than/ whereas.* • Why do customers choose one brand as opposed to another? *Why do customers choose one brand rather than another?* • This typically includes name, e-mail address, and home address, as opposed to anonymous demographic information such as country, gender, and Web service preferences. *This typically includes name, e-mail address, and home address, not anonymous demographic information such as country, gender, and Web service preferences.*

as opposed to . . . relatively *compared to/with/-(i)er than/less than/more than/than.* • As opposed to the organization and access rules of network and hierarchical data models, those of the relational model are relatively simple. *Compared to the organization and access rules of network and hierarchical data models, those of the relational model are simple.*

as regards *about/as for/as to/concerning/for/in/of/on/over/regarding/respecting/to/toward/with.* • He promises to be less tightfisted in the future as regards training. *He promises to be less tightfisted in the future about training.* • There are significant differences across countries as regards the use of on-site and off-site supervisory techniques. *There are significant differences across countries regarding the use of on-site and off-site supervisory techniques.*

assemble in a group *assemble.* • Students assemble in a group and pretend that the teacher is an alien from another world. *Students assemble and pretend that the teacher is an alien from another world.*

assemble together *assemble.* • Proteins are constructed by assembling together several modules or domains. *Proteins are constructed by assembling several modules or domains.*

assistance *aid/help/succor.*

assist in -ing *help.* • This view assists you in visualizing the problem. *This view helps you visualize the problem.*

associated with *belongs to/employed by/works for.*

associated with *for/in/linked to/of/related to/-'s/with.* • The greater the required accuracy, the greater the cost associated with generating a plan. *The greater the required accuracy, the greater the cost of generating a plan.* • Because of the rugged terrain associated with mountainous areas, you will frequently encounter fractures and sprains. *Because of the rugged terrain of mountainous areas, you will frequently encounter fractures and sprains.* • One of the essential reasons for this is the high cost associated with owning and maintaining the infrastructure required to create a common global platform. *One of the essential reasons for this is the high cost of owning and maintaining the infrastructure required to create a common global platform.*

association *connection/link/relation/tie.* • The CDC study concluded there was no association between use of the pill and breast cancer. *The CDC study concluded there was no link between use of the pill and breast cancer.*

as soon as *once/when.* • I'll call you as soon as I can. *I'll call you when I can.*

(most/very) assuredly *yes.*

assure/ensure/insure . . . guarantee *ensure/guarantee.* • There must be a way to ensure that their privacy is guaranteed. *There must be a way to ensure their privacy.*

as the basis for (-ing) *for (-ing)/so as to/to.* • Data is any information used as the basis for discussing or deciding something. *Data is any information used to discuss or decide something.* • The purpose of the course is to provide an understanding of physics as a basis for successfully launching new high-tech ventures. *The purpose of the course is to provide an understanding of physics so as to successfully launch* *new high-tech ventures.* • We can use their modern ecological requirements as a basis for interpreting what past environments must have been like. *We can use their modern ecological requirements to interpret what past environments must have been like.*

as the case/situation may be delete. • When both are used on the same drawing, the parts list is placed directly above and in contact with the title block or the title strip, as the case may be. *When both are used on the same drawing, the parts list is placed directly above and in contact with the title block or the title strip.*

as the need arises/develops *as needed.* • Corrections and adjustments can be made as the need arises. *Corrections and adjustments can be made as needed.*

as the saying goes delete.

as time goes on *at length/in due time/in time/later/one day/over time/someday/sometime/ultimately/with time/yet* delete. • As time goes on, maintenance revenues will rise for the average distributor. *Maintenance revenues will yet rise for the average distributor.*

as time progresses/forward/on/onward *at length/eventually/in due time/in time/later/one day/over the months (years)/over time/someday/sometime/ultimately/with time/yet* delete. • As time progressed, she decided to divorce him. *At length, she decided to divorce him.*

as to *about/by/for/from/in/of/on/over/to/with* delete. • I'm curious as to why you would choose to be in that situation. *I'm curious why you would choose to be in that situation.* • People have different ideas as to what is sexually acceptable to them. *People have different ideas on what is sexually acceptable to them.* • Once you know your skills, aptitudes, interests, and motivations, you will have a good idea as to what you have going for you and what you

want. *Once you know your skills, aptitudes, interests, and motivations, you will have a good idea of what you have going for you and what you want.* • We were bewildered as to what was taking place. *We were bewildered by what was taking place.* • Different or missing sounds can be a clue as to what's malfunctioning. *Different or missing sounds can be a clue to what's malfunctioning.*

as to whether *whether.* • It's too early to speculate as to whether the two stabbings are connected. *It's too early to speculate whether the two stabbings are connected.* • In the past, Internet Explorer used to guess as to whether data stored in the cache was actually stale. *In the past, Internet Explorer used to guess whether data stored in the cache was actually stale.*

as well as *and.* • Banks have added to their capital by retaining a higher share of current earnings, in some cases selling their undervalued real estate as well as business assets. *Banks have added to their capital by retaining a higher share of current earnings, in some cases selling their undervalued real estate and business assets.*

as (of) yet *yet* delete. • I haven't mastered the sport as of yet. *I haven't mastered the sport.* • Listen to a tape, or jot down ideas that you haven't put on paper as yet. *Listen to a tape, or jot down ideas that you haven't yet put on paper.*

at about/around *about/around.* • We got there at about 7:00. *We got there about 7:00.*

at a certain/any/one/some point in my history/point in my life/point in the history of my life/point in time *at one time/ever/once/one day/someday/sometime* delete. • At one point in the history of my life, I was a high school English teacher. *I was once a high school English teacher.*

at/for a/the cost/price/sum of *at/for.* • The Tower was built from 1970 to 1974 at a cost of more than $150 million. *The Tower was built from 1970 to 1974 for more than $150 million.*

at a/some future/later/subsequent date/ time *at length/eventually/in due time/in time/ later/one day/over the months (years)/over time/ someday/sometime/ultimately/with time/yet.* • These guidelines also apply to other reading materials that you will need to reread and study at a later date. *These guidelines also apply to other reading materials that you will later need to reread and study.*

at a/the juncture/juncture in time/moment/ moment in time/period/period in time/point/ point in time/stage/stage in time/time *when.* • At the point in time this book was published, several other titles were also available. *When this book was published, several other titles were also available.*

at a/the juncture/juncture in time/moment/ moment in time/period/period in time/point/ point in time/stage/stage in time/time when *when.* • On a computer, the design is created on the screen, and the scale can be decided, and changed, at the time when the final drawing is printed out on a printer or plotter. *On a computer, the design is created on the screen, and the scale can be decided, and changed, when the final drawing is printed out on a printer or plotter.*

at all delete. • You're unwilling to make any sort of compromise at all. *You're unwilling to make any sort of compromise.*

at an/some earlier/former/past/previous date/ time *before/earlier/formerly/once.* • It seems we are becoming dependent on these tricks that would simply be solved with learning how to go to bed at an earlier time. *It seems we are becoming dependent on these tricks that would simply be solved with learning how to go to bed earlier.* • It was evident the coffin had been disturbed at some previous date. *It was evident the coffin had been disturbed before.*

at/from/in/on/to an/the area/locale/locality/ location/place/point/position/region/site/ spot *where/wherever.* • The program is temporarily interrupted, and can be restarted any time at the exact place it left off. *The program is temporarily interrupted, and can be restarted any time exactly where it left off.*

at/from/in/on/to an/the area/locale/locality/ location/place/point/position/region/site/ spot where *where/wherever.* • The voodoo doctor told me to put them in a location where no one would ever find them. *The voodoo doctor told me to put them where no one would ever find them.*

at an/some earlier/former/past/previous date/ time *before/earlier/formerly/once.* • It seems we are becoming dependent on these tricks that would simply be solved with learning how to go to bed at an earlier time. *It seems we are becoming dependent on these tricks that would simply be solved with learning how to go to bed earlier.* • It was evident the coffin had been disturbed at some previous date. *It was evident the coffin had been disturbed before.*

at an end *complete/done/ended/finished/over/ past.* • Barring the unexpected, the 25-year search for a new arena is at an end. *Barring the unexpected, the 25-year search for a new arena is over.*

at/from/in/on/to any/each/every/some area/ locale/locality/location/place/point/position/ region/site/spot *anyplace/anywhere/ever/ everyplace/everywhere/one day/someday/some- place/sometime/somewhere/where/wherever.* • If at any point I felt I was an embarrassment to the president, I would resign. *If I ever felt I was an embarrassment to the president, I would resign.*

at/from/in/on/to any/each/every/some area/ locale/locality/location/place/point/position/ region/site/spot where *anyplace/anywhere/ ever/everyplace/everywhere/one day/someday/*

someplace/sometime/somewhere/where/wherever. • At every place where food was available, people went hungry for lack of dry fuel. *Wherever food was available, people went hungry for lack of dry fuel.*

at any date/hour/time *any time.*

at any minute/moment *directly/momentarily/momently/presently/soon.*

at any rate *anyhow/even so/still/yet.*

at every turn *always/ceaselessly/consistently/constantly/endlessly/eternally/everyday/forever/unfailingly.*

at frequent/periodic/regular intervals/periods *frequently/periodically/regularly.* • At periodic intervals, the entries made in the journals are posted to the general ledger. *Periodically, the entries made in the journals are posted to the general ledger.*

at (a/the) . . . level *-(al)ly* delete. • Prices at the wholesale level will go up 6 cents per gallon. *Wholesale prices will go up 6 cents per gallon.*

at long last *at last/finally.*

ATM machine *ATM.*

at/for no charge/cost *free.* • It will be available at no charge through Avatar dealers nationwide. *It will be available free through Avatar dealers nationwide.*

at no time *never.* • At no time was it this union's position to oppose the Emerson College proposal or deprive fellow workers of jobs made available by this project. *Never was it this union's position to oppose the Emerson College proposal or deprive fellow workers of jobs made available by this project.*

at one time (in the past) *once.* • His name was being used in connection with Brittney Jones,

one of Vivid's film actresses, who claims she had slept with Kutcher at one time in the past. *His name was being used in connection with Brittney Jones, one of Vivid's film actresses, who claims she had once slept with Kutcher.*

atop of *atop.*

at (a/the) . . . pace (of) *at/by/-(al)ly* delete. • We've had fairly stable interest rates and an economy that continues to grow at a moderate pace. *We've had fairly stable interest rates and an economy that continues to grow moderately.*

at (the) present *(just/right) now/nowadays/these days/today/(just) yet* delete. • At present, nothing indicates that South Africa is prepared to completely dismantle apartheid. *Nothing yet indicates that South Africa is prepared to completely dismantle apartheid.*

at (a/the) . . . rate (of) *at/by/-(al)ly* delete. • Crime on college campuses is growing at a geometric rate. *Crime on college campuses is growing geometrically.* • Bank of America advertises the 7/1 ARM at a rate of 2.750 percent. *Bank of America advertises the 7/1 ARM at 2.750 percent.*

at some point/time along the line/the way *at some point/at some time.*

at specific/specified/timed intervals/periods *periodically/regularly.*

at (a/the) . . . speed (of) *at/by/-(al)ly* delete. • Loosened by rain or melting snow, ordinary soil on a steep hillside can suddenly turn into a lethal wave sweeping downward at speeds of more than 30 miles per hour. *Loosened by rain or melting snow, ordinary soil on a steep hillside can suddenly turn into a lethal wave sweeping downward at more than 30 miles per hour.*

attach together *attach.* • There are four separate graphics panels which attach together to form a display. *There are four separate graphics panels which attach to form a display.*

attack by assailants *assail/assault/attack.* • They were departing a local discotheque and entering their vehicle when they were attacked by assailants. *They were departing a local discotheque and entering their vehicle when they were attacked.*

attempt *try.* • My ex-wife and I attempted to have a child for six years. *My ex-wife and I tried to have a child for six years.*

attempt/endeavor/strive/try to emulate *emulate.* • I admire you so much I thought I would try to emulate you. *I admire you so much I thought I would emulate you.*

attention . . . focused on/upon *attention on/focus on.* • In presidential politics, everyone's attention is now focused on the South. *In presidential politics, everyone is now focused on the South.*

attest to the fact (that) *attest/confirm/corroborate/demonstrate/prove/substantiate/verify.* • Most of you that know me can attest to the fact that the holidays are my most cherished time of the year. *Most of you that know me can attest that the holidays are my most cherished time of the year.* • I am sure Kyle will attest to the fact that we want to win the game. *I am sure Kyle will corroborate that we want to win the game.*

at that/this juncture *at present/at that/this time/current/currently/(just/right) now/nowadays/present/presently/then/these days/today/(just) yet* delete. • For nimble investors, a little buying may be appropriate at this juncture. *For nimble investors, a little buying may now be appropriate.*

at that/this juncture/juncture in time/moment/moment in time/period/period in time/point/point in time/stage/stage in time/time in my history/in my life/in the history of my life *at present/at that/this time/current/currently/(just/right) now/nowadays/present/presently/then/these days/today/(just) yet* delete. • At that point in my life, death seemed vague and romantic. *Death seemed vague and romantic then.* • At this point in time in our history, that can be a subtle and tricky distinction. *Today, that can be a subtle and tricky distinction.* • At this point in time, it is much easier to start with an inch than to break things down into as yet unknown pixel requests or percentages of an inch. *It is much easier to start with an inch than to break things down into as yet unknown pixel requests or percentages of an inch.*

at that/this juncture/moment/period/point/stage in time *at present/at that/this time/current/currently/(just/right) now/nowadays/present/presently/then/these days/today/(just) yet* delete. • At this moment in time, he must abide by the way I want things to be. *He now must abide by the way I want things to be.*

at that/this moment *at present/at that/this time/current/currently/(just/right) now/nowadays/present/presently/then/these days/today/(just) yet* delete. • Did you know at that moment that your father had killed the rest of the family? *Did you know then that your father had killed the rest of the family?*

at that/this point *at present/current/currently/(just/right) now/nowadays/present/presently/then/these days/today/(just) yet* delete. • At that point, we will discontinue our aid to them. *We will then discontinue our aid to them.*

at that/this stage *at present/at that/this time/current/currently/(just/right) now/nowadays/present/presently/then/these days/today/(just) yet* delete. • It's hard to tell at this stage. *It's hard to tell now.*

at that/this time *at present/current/currently/(just/right) now/nowadays/present/presently/then/these days/today/(just) yet* delete. • The potential return on the investment is uncertain at this time. *The potential return on the invest-ment is presently uncertain.*

at/in the blink of an eye *abruptly/apace/ briskly/directly/fast/forthwith/hastily/hurriedly/ posthaste/presently/promptly/quickly/rapidly/ right away/shortly/soon/speedily/straightaway/ swiftly/wingedly.* • All this happens at the blink of an eye, as it would with a standard desktop application. *All this happens swiftly, as it would with a standard desktop application.*

at/on the brink of *about to/approaching/close to/near/nearly/verging on.* • Some 10,000 Suda-nese are on the brink of starving to death in a southern town under siege by armed guerrillas. *Some 10,000 Sudanese are close to starving to death in a southern town under siege by armed guerrillas.*

at the corner/intersection of *at.* • The site is located at the intersection of Buffum and Blake Streets in the Central Square Historic District. *The site is located at Buffum and Blake Streets in the Central Square Historic District.*

at the current/present time *at present/at this time/current/currently/(just/right) now/nowa-days/present/presently/these days/today/(just) yet* delete. • What is the value of Digital's stock at the present time? *What is the current value of Digital's stock?*

at the current/present time in my life *at pres-ent/at this time/current/currently/(just/right) now/nowadays/present/presently/these days/ today/(just) yet* delete. • I live alone at the pres-ent time in my life. *I live alone now.*

at the end of the day *all in all/all told/alto-gether/finally/in all/in the end/overall/ulti-mately* delete. • At the end of the day, though, there's a straightforward set of criteria you should apply before taking the plunge with any mutual fund. *In the end, though, there's a straightforward set of criteria you should apply*

before taking the plunge with any mutual fund. • It's up to parents to take a more active role because at the end of the day it will be them who will have to foot medical bills if something goes wrong. *It's up to parents to take a more active role because ultimately it will be them who will have to foot medical bills if something goes wrong.*

at the hands of *by/from/through.* • I am enraged by the second-class treatment we are receiving at the hands of those who legislate for and govern us. *I am enraged by the second-class treatment we are receiving from those who leg-islate for and govern us.*

at the (very) minimum *at least.*

at the (current/present) moment *at present/ current/currently/(just/right) now/nowadays/ present/presently/these days/today/(just) yet* delete. • At the moment, this effort is being left largely to individual state colleges and uni-versities to initiate. *This effort is now being left largely to individual state colleges and universi-ties to initiate.*

at/on the point of *about to/approaching/close to/near/nearly/verging on.*

at the same time *as one/at once/collectively/ concurrently/jointly/together.* • If too many things happened at the same time, data would be lost in the process. *If too many things hap-pened at once, data would be lost in the process.*

(and) at the same time (as/that) *as/while.* • In many cases, Soviet interest in smoothing East-West relations has been complicated by con-flicting diplomatic priorities, such as improving ties with China and maintaining relations with Vietnam at the same time. *In many cases, Soviet interest in smoothing East-West relations has been complicated by conflicting diplomatic pri-orities, such as improving ties with China while maintaining relations with Vietnam.* • A similar dilemma faces Cray Research Inc., which relies on Japanese-made chips at the same time it fends off Japanese challenges to its role as the world's leading maker of supercomputers. *A similar dilemma faces Cray Research Inc., which relies on Japanese-made chips as it fends off Japanese challenges to its role as the world's leading maker of supercomputers.*

attired *dressed.*

(a/the) . . . attitude (of) delete. • He had a very cavalier attitude about money. *He was very cavalier about money.*

at/on (the) top (of) *atop/on.* • It removes the dead cells that accumulate on top of the skin. *It removes the dead cells that accumulate on the skin.*

attributable to *because of/caused by/due to/ owing to/result from.* • These increases were primarily attributable to a variety of merchant banking activities. *These increases were primarily caused by a variety of merchant banking activities.*

attributable to the fact that *because/considering/for/given/in that/since.* • The differing performance of black and white incomes is primarily attributable to the fact that white-married-couple families did significantly better last year than black-married-couple families. *The differing performance of black and white incomes is primarily because white-married-couple families did significantly better last year than black-married-couple families.* • The low recovery rate in these cases is largely attributable to the fact that the nature of art theft will involve thieves who know both their art and where to find markets for the sale of stolen works. *The low recovery rate in these cases is largely because the nature of art theft will involve thieves who know both their art and where to find markets for the sale of stolen works.*

at what/which juncture/juncture in time/ moment/moment in time/period/period in time/point/point in time/stage/stage in time/ time *when.* • At what point will you know if the business is profitable? *When will you know if the business is profitable?* • A term to age 65 policy provides protection to age 65, at which time the policy expires. *A term to age 65 policy provides protection to age 65, when the policy expires.* • My research of racial oppression began over 50 years ago, at which time I experienced a traumatic incident that left me with the first of many racial scars that have not healed until this day. *My research of racial oppression began over 50 years ago, when I experienced a traumatic incident that left me with the first of many racial scars that have not healed until this day.*

at your earliest convenience *as soon as possible/at once/presently/quickly/right away/shortly/ soon/without delay* delete. • Please return the signed and completed application to this office at your earliest convenience. *Please return the signed and completed application to this office.*

audible to the ear *audible.* • CDRs burned below this standard are very likely to be rejected by the CD manufacturing facility on account of too many "uncorrectable errors" (data flow inconsistencies that are not audible to the ear but could result in glitches on replicated discs). *CDRs burned below this standard are very likely to be rejected by the CD manufacturing facility on account of too many "uncorrectable errors" (data flow inconsistencies that are not audible but could result in glitches on replicated discs).*

authentic replica *replica.* • These archaeology kits contain an authentic replica of an artifact representing an ancient culture. *These archaeology kits contain a replica of an artifact representing an ancient culture.*

author *(v)* write.

authoress *author.*

(the/this) author/reader/writer *I/he/her/him/ me/she/them/they/us/we* delete. • Every word processing manual the authors have seen assumes you know what a hanging indent, widow, and running header are. *Every word processing manual we have seen assumes you know what a hanging indent, widow, and running header are.* • The athletic Springsteen is back in this new tour, judging from the opening night this writer caught at the Meadowlands. *The athletic Springsteen is back in this new tour, judging from the opening night I caught at the Meadowlands.* • The author is unaware if any such experiments have been performed. *She is unaware if any such experiments have been performed.* • This book is meant to help the reader learn how to program in C. *This book is meant to help you learn how to program in C.* • This reader was dismayed by his cynical and narrow view of the public sector. *I was dismayed by his cynical and narrow view of the public sector.*

avail herself/themselves of *use.* • Please avail yourself of your Constitutionally protected right to vote. *Please use your Constitutionally protected right to vote.* • Now you can avail yourself of the union's collective bargaining efforts and other benefits for nothing. *Now you can use the union's collective bargaining efforts and other benefits for nothing.*

B

background (of) experience *background/experience.* • It is, then, from a background of experience in communication that I want to present two ideas. *It is, then, from a background in communication that I want to present two ideas.* • They both have background experience in doing this kind of work. *They both have experience in doing this kind of work.*

back in *in/last* delete. • My daughter disappeared back in January. *My daughter disappeared last January.*

back/before in the past *before/earlier/formerly/ in the past/once* delete. • Dealing with irrational people is something my father has done well back in the past and is something he'll do well in the future. *Dealing with irrational people is something my father has done well in the past and is something he'll do well in the future.*

backward and forward *completely/entirely/ fully/thoroughly/totally/utterly/wholly.*

badge/mark/sign/symbol of authenticity/distinction/honor/prestige/rank *cachet.* • Basler says the bumps, which appear on the foot and are regarded as a badge of distinction among serious surfers, result from long hours spent in contact with a surfboard. *Basler says the bumps, which appear on the foot and are regarded as a cachet among serious surfers, result from long hours spent in contact with a surfboard.*

balance out *balance.* • Because seasonal forces are relative, they balance each other out by the completion of a full year. *Because seasonal forces are relative, they balance each other by the completion of a full year.*

bald-headed *bald.*

-based *from/in/of/-'s* delete. • Sharon Howard, an Atlanta-based attorney, has given a lot of thought to the way she is treated in the courtroom. *Sharon Howard, an Atlanta attorney, has given a lot of thought to the way she is treated in the courtroom.*

based in *from/in/of/-'s* delete. • PCE is a privately held company based in Portland, Oregon. *PCE is a privately held company in Portland, Oregon.*

based on/upon *after/by/for/from/in/on/through/ with* delete. • Based on what I hear, everyone thinks Fan Pier has lost its moment of opportunity. *From what I hear, everyone thinks Fan Pier has lost its moment of opportunity.*

based on/upon my personal judgment/opinion *I assert/I believe/I claim/I consider/I contend/I feel/I hold/I judge/I maintain/I regard/I say/I think/I view/to me* delete. • Based on my personal judgment, I think tax revenues will grow by 8.3 percent. *I think tax revenues will grow by 8.3 percent.*

based on the fact that *because/considering/for/given/in that/since.* • I'm not in favor of it based on the fact that a lot of small businesses will suffer. *I'm not in favor of it because a lot of small businesses will suffer.* • Based on the fact that no single timing rule works well all the time, AIQ incorporates many rules that work together in a powerful synergism to signal when the overall market, and individual securities, are ready to move. *Since no single timing rule works well all the time, AIQ incorporates many rules that work together in a powerful synergism to signal when the overall market, and individual securities, are ready to move.*

baseless/groundless/unfounded/unsubstantiated rumor *hearsay/rumor.* • A Foreign Ministry spokesman characterized the reports as unfounded rumors. *A Foreign Ministry spokesman characterized the reports as rumors.*

basic delete. • In this section, we introduce you to the basic procedures to control page breaks and page numbers. *In this section, we introduce you to the procedures to control page breaks and page numbers.*

basically *chiefly/largely/mainly/most/mostly* delete. • Basically, the social service groups involved are either indifferent or corrupt. *The social service groups involved are either indifferent or corrupt.* • The rest of the day will be basically partly cloudy. *The rest of the day will be partly cloudy.* • What basically began as an experiment to determine whether a family-type YMCA would survive quickly evolved into a challenge to serve a very enthusiastic community. *What began as an experiment to determine whether a family-type YMCA would survive quickly evolved into a challenge to serve a very enthusiastic community.* • Basically, the next step is adding the molasses. *The next step is adding the molasses.*

basic (and) fundamental *basic/fundamental.* • Our basic, fundamental values are the same. *Our fundamental values are the same.* • At the same time, by advancing basic and fundamental research and development, MEXT strives to ensure the promotion of research throughout the nation. *At the same time, by advancing fundamental research and development, MEXT strives to ensure the promotion of research throughout the nation.*

basic principle *principle.* • We feel there are two basic principles to successful advertising. *We feel there are two principles to successful advertising.*

basis in fact/reality/truth *basis/fact/reality/reason/truth/veracity.* • About the only statement in the article that has any basis in fact is "I want to build the biggest film group in the world." *About the only statement in the article that has any truth is "I want to build the biggest film group in the world."*

bathroom facilities *bathroom/john/loo/toilet.*

(please) be advised/informed that delete. • Please be advised that we must be notified at least two weeks prior to your closing date in order to issue your 6(d) certificate. *We must be notified at least two weeks prior to your closing date in order to issue your 6(d) certificate.* • However, please be advised that this person is out of town until next week; I am sure she will then respond to you at her earliest possible convenience. *However, this person is out of town* *until next week; I am sure she will then respond to you at her earliest possible convenience.*

bear/have/hold a grudge (against) *dislike/resent.* • He and Latin America aide Janice O'Connell bear a grudge against the Cuban-American. *He and Latin America aide Janice O'Connell resent the Cuban- American.*

(please) bear in mind *consider/heed/note/realize.*

bear (a/the) . . . resemblance/similarity to *be like/be similar to/look like/resemble.* • The Lumina's body bears a similarity to Chevrolet's Corsica and Beretta. *The Lumina's body resembles Chevrolet's Corsica and Beretta.* • Jay argues that the protesters of the '60s and today's campus left bear a resemblance to the deranged militias of today. *Jay argues that the protesters of the '60s and today's campus left resemble the deranged militias of today.*

bear witness to *affirm/attest to/certify to/declare/testify to/verify.* • A splendid perennial garden surrounds the house and bears witness to the collaboration in the family. *A splendid perennial garden surrounds the house and attests to the collaboration in the family.*

because of *after/by/for/from/in/out of/through/with.* • Such a model would be inappropriate because of two reasons. *Such a model would be inappropriate for two reasons.*

because of the fact that *because/considering/for/given/in that/since.* • Because of the fact that they are still monopoly suppliers of local exchange, I also see a discouraging prospect for the operating companies in this area. *Since they are still monopoly suppliers of local exchange, I also see a discouraging prospect for the operating companies in this area.* • I discounted these things because of the fact that I cared so much for you. *I discounted these things because I cared so much for you.* • We know there is a game because of the fact that there are a lot of people waiting in line. *We know there is a game because there are a lot of people waiting in line.*

because why *why.* • You say you are a submissive wife, but you are that way because why? *You say you are a submissive wife, but why are you that way?*

become known *emerge/surface/transpire.*

before/earlier/previously -ed/-en *-ed/-en.* • As we previously noted, the high-cost load funds distributed through a salesperson have dominated the industry. *As we noted, the high-cost load funds distributed through a salesperson have dominated the industry.*

before . . . first *before.* • Before you use the delete option, first extract the records you are considering deleting. *Before you use the delete option, extract the records you are considering deleting.*

before (very) long *shortly/soon.*

begin and commence *begin/commence.* • So now, free agents will wait for their time to begin and commence the unceremonious task of picking through NFL draftees' leftovers. *So now, free agents will wait for their time to begin the unceremonious task of picking through NFL draftees' leftovers.*

begin/start at . . . and end/finish at *(be) between . . . and/range from . . . to.* • Price tags for the condos will start at $350,000 and end at $1.75 million. *Price tags for the condos will range from $350,000 to $1.75 million.*

begin . . . first *begin.* • You should begin by sketching the centerline and guidelines first. *You should begin by sketching the centerline and guidelines.*

behavior pattern *behavior.*

(a/the) . . . being delete. • What sets teachers apart from other mortal beings is that they never have first names. *What sets teachers apart from other mortals is that they never have first names.*

being (as/as how/that) *because/considering/for/given/in that/since.* • They usually deliver by noontime, and being that you're local, it'll probably be before noon. *They usually deliver by noontime, and because you're local, it'll probably be before noon.* • I'm afraid that is an impossibility being as how we don't have a copying machine. *I'm afraid that is an impossibility since we don't have a copying machine.*

besides . . . also/as well *besides/beyond.* • Besides providing the high-end AI tools, they have shells for Apple Macs and compatibles as well. *Besides providing the high-end AI tools, they have shells for Apple Macs and compatibles.*

beside the point *immaterial/inapt/irrelevant/not pertinent.*

best/biggest/fastest/greatest/largest/most/slowest . . . single *best/biggest/fastest/greatest/largest/most/slowest.* • Great Britain, where annual production capacity was increased to 700,000 lines a year, is the largest single market. *Great Britain, where annual production capacity was increased to 700,000 lines a year, is the largest market.*

be that as it may *all (just) the same/anyhow/even so/still/still and all/yet.*

(the) better part (of) *almost (all)/close to/most (of)/near/nearly (all).* • An adaptation of the play has been in the works for the better part of a decade. *An adaptation of the play has been in the works for nearly a decade.*

between . . . as compared to/as opposed to/compared to/versus *between . . . and.* • The difference between using nonnested tags as opposed to those from the nested library is that using the nested version allows the tags to relate to each other in a nested hierarchy. *The difference between using nonnested tags and those from the nested library is that using the nested version allows the tags to relate to each other in a nested hierarchy.* • Is there much difference between the taste of fresh turkey compared to flash frozen turkeys? *Is there much difference between the taste of fresh turkey and flash frozen turkeys?* • Although it may be interesting to know if there's an observable difference between people who visit often versus people who visit and buy your products, you need to stay focused on your target audience choices. *Although it may be interesting to know if there's an observable difference between people who visit often and people who visit and buy your products, you need to stay focused on your target audience choices.* • What's the difference between Clinton's health care proposal as opposed to John Edwards' proposal? *What's the difference between Clinton's health care proposal and John Edwards' proposal?*

between the two of them/us *between them/us.*

between you and me/us *between us.* • Enclosed is a basic proposal which should lay the groundwork for future discussions between you and us. *Enclosed is a basic proposal which should lay the groundwork for future discussions between us.*

betwixt and between *in between/undecided.*

beverage *drink.*

beyond a/the shadow of a doubt *assuredly/certainly/doubtless/indisputably/irrefutably/no doubt/surely/undoubtedly/unquestionably.*

beyond number *countless/endless/infinite/millions (of)/myriad/numberless/untold.*

beyond/outside the realm of possibility *impossible/inconceivable/undoable/unthink-*

able. • So it's not beyond the realm of possibility that corporate performance could be improved if directors surveyed other areas of corporate activity, like manufacturing and marketing. *So it's not inconceivable that corporate performance could be improved if directors surveyed other areas of corporate activity, like manufacturing and marketing.*

biased opinion *bias/prejudice.* • It merely expressed a biased opinion about a so-called problem without any indication of the extent and consequences of the problem. *It merely expressed a bias about a so-called problem without any indication of the extent and consequences of the problem.*

(a) bigger/greater/higher/larger degree/ extent (of) *further/more.* • Politicians and public officials should be required to tolerate a greater degree of criticism than ordinary citizens since, unlike such citizens, they have willingly taken on a public role in a democratic context where their actions are subject to the scrutiny of the public. *Politicians and public officials should be required to tolerate more criticism than ordinary citizens since, unlike such citizens, they have willingly taken on a public role in a democratic context where their actions are subject to the scrutiny of the public.* • One can speculate whether concentrating all the army special forces units in one regiment is the most appropriate solution or if rather a bigger degree of force diversification would contribute to achieving more specialization and introduce a competitive factor among the units. *One can speculate whether concentrating all the army special forces units in one regiment is the most appropriate solution or if rather more force diversification would contribute to achieving more specialization and introduce a competitive factor among the units.* • A bigger extent of improvement was prevented by the HUF 197 million of cash contribution made by BC Rt. to promote the development of its subsidiaries. *Further*

improvement was prevented by the HUF 197 million of cash contribution made by BC Rt. to promote the development of its subsidiaries.

(the) biggest/greatest/highest/largest amount/degree/extent/number/part/percentage/portion/ proportion/quantity (of) *(the) most.* • The concept of calories has been well embedded in the minds of people throughout the largest portion of the twentieth century. *The concept of calories has been well embedded in the minds of people throughout most of the twentieth century.* • So where will the biggest number of Muslims call home? *So where will most Muslims call home?*

big, huge/large *big/huge/large.* • I packed a big, huge picnic lunch for us. *I packed a huge picnic lunch for us.*

biographical *biographic.*

biological *biologic.*

biometrical *biometric.*

biophysiological *biophysiologic.*

bit by bit *gradually/slowly.*

bits and pieces *bits/pieces.* • Bits and pieces of segregation have been jettisoned or have rotted away. *Bits of segregation have been jettisoned or have rotted away.*

blend of both *blend.* • Management is a blend of both science and art. *Management is a blend of science and art.*

blend together *blend.* • Blend this WordStar expertise together in a book, and you have the definitive resource to the most widely used word processing software. *Blend this WordStar expertise in a book, and you have the definitive resource to the most widely used word processing software.*

block out *block.* • Other conversations, the sound of machinery, and traffic noises can block out messages from being received. *Other conversations, the sound of machinery, and traffic noises can block messages from being received.*

bode ill/well for the future *bode ill/well.* • The fact that electric companies had to institute such emergency procedures does not bode well for the future. *The fact that electric companies had to institute such emergency procedures does not bode well.*

borrowed loan *loan.* • Provided that borrowers repay the borrowed loan on the payment date, these plans may be an excellent source of immediate cash. *Provided that borrowers repay the loan on the payment date, these plans may be an excellent source of immediate cash.*

botch up *botch.* • In my first transplant session, the doctor botched up the job. *In my first transplant session, the doctor botched the job.*

both . . . alike *alike/both.* • The adherence of career-oriented women to the masculine prototype has led both men and women alike to undermine the value of female qualities and responsibilities. *The adherence of career-oriented women to the masculine prototype has led men and women alike to undermine the value of female qualities and responsibilities.*

both . . . as well as *as well as/both . . . and.* • He was both brilliant as well as eccentric. *He was both brilliant and eccentric.* • Both the source .PAS file as well as the compiled .PEN file are available. *Both the source .PAS file and the compiled .PEN file are available.* • This failure to remember encompasses both product consumption as well as product purchase. *This failure to remember encompasses both product consumption and product purchase.* • Crosswords encourage people to use dictionaries, both specialized crossword dictionaries as well as collegiate and unabridged volumes. *Crosswords encourage people to use dictionaries, both specialized crossword dictionaries and collegiate and unabridged volumes.*

both equally *both/equally.* • We're both equally attractive. *We're equally attractive.* • The poem speaks of two paths, both equally beautiful in their nature and both equally tempting to take; however a decision was made by the traveler to take the road that was less traveled. *The poem speaks of two paths, equally beautiful in their nature and equally tempting to take; however a decision was made by the traveler to take the road that was less traveled.*

both . . . in combination *both/in combination.* • Both analytic techniques and judgmental methods might be used in combination to verify each other. *Analytic techniques and judgmental methods might be used in combination to verify each other.*

both of (the) *both.* • Both of the boys suffer from Tourette Syndrome. *Both boys suffer from Tourette Syndrome.*

(the) both of *both.* • I saw the both of them on a talk show today. *I saw both of them on a talk show today.* • It is uncomfortable for the both of us. *It is uncomfortable for both of us.* • He followed the both of them. *He followed both of them.*

both share *both/share.* • We both share a deep commitment to the welfare of the American people. *We share a deep commitment to the welfare of the American people.*

both together *both/together.* • Both of the products together cost $117.95. *Together, the products cost $117.95.*

bound and determined *determined/resolute/resolved.* • We are still bound and determined that we are going to build a new arena. *We are* *still determined that we are going to build a new arena.*

bouquet of flowers *flowers.* • Every year, millions of us purchase a bouquet of flowers to honor the mothers in our lives. *Every year, millions of us purchase a bouquet to honor the mothers in our lives.*

brand new *new.* • With a brand new product, there is a significant educational need. *With a new product, there is a significant educational need.*

breadth and depth *ambit/area/breadth/compass/degree/extent/field/magnitude/range/reach/scope/sphere/sweep.*

briefly in passing *briefly/in passing.* • Let me say briefly in passing that I am opposed to women not having control of their own bodies. *Let me say briefly that I am opposed to women not having control of their own bodies.*

brief/concise/short/small/succinct snippet *snippet.* • I was constantly overhearing brief snippets of conversation. *I was constantly overhearing snippets of conversation.*

brief/concise/short/small/succinct summary *summary.* • A concise summary of the scope of the international product manager's task has been provided by Wind. *A summary of the scope of the international product manager's task has been provided by Wind.*

brief/concise/short/small/succinct synopsis *synopsis.* • I just wondered if I could give you a brief synopsis of the long-distance services that MCI offers. *I just wondered if I could give you a synopsis of the long-distance services that MCI offers.*

bring about *begin/cause/effect/occasion/produce.* • Rather than bring about the death of

Yellowstone, the fires triggered natural processes of change that are a normal part of the ecosystem. *Rather than cause the death of Yellowstone, the fires triggered natural processes of change that are a normal part of the ecosystem.*

bring (to) a close (to) *cease/close/complete/conclude/end/finish/halt/settle/stop.* • How would you bring this meeting to a close? *How would you close this meeting?*

bring (to) a completion (to) *cease/close/complete/conclude/end/finish/halt/settle/stop.* • In their final year at St. Valentine's Middle School, students bring to a completion their academic and spiritual foundation for high school and beyond. *In their final year at St. Valentine's Middle School, students complete their academic and spiritual foundation for high school and beyond*

bring (to) a conclusion (to) *cease/close/complete/conclude/end/finish/halt/settle/stop.* • In December 1997, First Ministers requested that Social Services Ministers bring to a conclusion the development of a vision statement and national framework to guide future collaborative work in this area. *In December 1997, First Ministers requested that Social Services Ministers conclude the development of a vision statement and national framework to guide future collaborative work in this area.*

bring (to) a halt (to) *cease/close/complete/conclude/end/finish/halt/settle/stop.* • The timber industry said the decision could bring logging to a halt throughout much of the Pacific Northwest within 30 days and cause the loss of as many as 160,000 jobs. *The timber industry said the decision could halt logging throughout much of the Pacific Northwest within 30 days and cause the loss of as many as 160,000 jobs.*

bring (to) an end (to) *cease/close/complete/conclude/end/finish/halt/settle/stop.* • That comment well describes the work that is yet to be done to bring an end to the pain and suffering. *That comment well describes the work that is yet to be done to end the pain and suffering.*

bring attention to *advertise/announce/blazon/ broadcast/disclose/divulge/expose/herald/indi- cate/make known/make public/mention/point out/point to/present/proclaim/promote/publi- cize/reveal/show/tell/uncover/unveil.* • They were demonstrating at the bank branch in order to bring attention to community lending and banking service issues. *They were demonstrating at the bank branch in order to disclose commu- nity lending and banking service issues.*

bring/give forth *bear/effect/produce/yield.*

bring into being/existence *conceive/conjure/ create/devise/fashion/forge/form/invent/make/ mold/plan/produce/shape.* • He says that reason itself is a ladder that can now be dispensed with—and should be dispensed with—to help bring the liberal utopia into existence. *He says that reason itself is a ladder that can now be dispensed with—and should be dispensed with— to help fashion the liberal utopia.*

bring into question *challenge/contradict/dis- pute/doubt/question.* • The issue goes beyond sexual politics and brings into question how the orthodox verities of an ancient religion fit into the modern world. *The issue goes beyond sexual politics and challenges how the orthodox verities of an ancient religion fit into the modern world.*

bring into the open *advertise/announce/blazon/ broadcast/disclose/divulge/expose/herald/indi- cate/make known/make public/mention/point out/point to/present/proclaim/promote/publicize/ reveal/show/tell/uncover/unveil.* • These experi- ences are designed to bring into the open some of the students' preconceptions and enable the students to explore ideas related to the topics under discussion. *These experiences are designed to uncover some of the students' preconceptions*

and enable the students to explore ideas related to the topics under discussion.

bring into the world *bear/give birth to/produce.*

bring pressure to bear on/upon *coerce/compel/ force/press/pressure.* • No matter who is presi- dent, the international community must bring pressure to bear on the government to end apartheid. *No matter who is president, the inter- national community must pressure the govern- ment to end apartheid.*

bring to a standstill *cease/close/complete/con- clude/end/finish/halt/settle/stop.* • It should seek to bring to a standstill the international flow of arms to the various Khmer factions. *It should seek to halt the international flow of arms to the various Khmer factions.*

bring to . . . attention (of) *advertise/announce/ blazon/broadcast/disclose/divulge/expose/her- ald/indicate/make known/make public/men- tion/point out/point to/present/proclaim/ promote/publicize/reveal/show/tell/uncover/ unveil.* • He was determined to bring to the world's attention the devastation of the inno- cents. *He was determined to publicize the dev- astation of the innocents.*

bring to bear (on/upon) *apply/employ/exercise/ exert/influence/use.* • Whether such influence can be brought to bear now is of vital impor- tance to the bottom half in the schools. *Whether such influence can be applied now is of vital importance to the bottom half in the schools.*

bring together *ally/bond/connect/join/unite.*

bring together *amass/assemble/collect/gather/ join.*

bring to light *advertise/announce/blazon/ broadcast/disclose/divulge/expose/herald/indi- cate/make known/make public/mention/point out/point to/present/proclaim/promote/publi-*

cize/reveal/show/tell/uncover/unveil. • Many uncertainties are brought to light when a bank makes a number of changes. *Many uncertainties are revealed when a bank makes a number of changes.*

bring (back) to mind *recall/recollect.*

bring to pass *begin/cause/start.*

(a/the) broad/extensive/great/vast/wide array of *an array of/assorted/broad/countless/different/diverse/extensive/many/numerous/scores of/sundry/untold/varied/various/varying/vast* delete. • In any domestic market, a wide array of official and unofficial sources provides information about the chosen market segments. *In any domestic market, numerous official and unofficial sources provide information about the chosen market segments.*

(a/the) broad/extensive/great/vast/wide range of *a range of/assorted/broad/countless/different/diverse/extensive/many/numerous/scores of/sundry/untold/varied/various/varying/vast* delete. • A wide range of products is sold by NTIS as subscriptions or standing orders. *Various products are sold by NTIS as subscriptions or standing orders.*

(a/the) broad/extensive/great/vast/wide spectrum of *a spectrum of/assorted/broad/countless/different/diverse/extensive/many/numerous/scores of/sundry/untold/varied/various/varying/vast* delete.

(a/the) broad/extensive/great/vast/wide variety of *a variety of/assorted/broad/countless/different/diverse/extensive/many/numerous/scores of/sundry/untold/varied/various/varying/vast* delete. • A wide variety of templates are available for drawing nuts and bolts. *Various templates are available for drawing nuts and bolts.*

build a bridge across/between *bridge.* • Is it not time for you to use these tools to build a bridge across the gulf of knowledge that separates the Islamic world from the West? *Is it not time for you to use these tools to bridge the gulf of knowledge that separates the Islamic world from the West?*

(the) bulk (of) *almost all/most/nearly all.* • Unfortunately for the startups, though, a few major players have secured the bulk of the orders. *Unfortunately for the startups, though, a few major players have secured most of the orders.*

(a/the) burgeoning/growing/increasing/rising amount/degree/extent/number/part/percentage/portion/proportion/quantity (of) *increasingly/more/more and more.* • A growing number of attorneys are bringing this up of their own initiative in the course of estate planning reviews. *Increasingly, attorneys are bringing this up of their own initiative in the course of estate planning reviews.* • A burgeoning number of HIV/AIDS clients require frequent primary medical visits to stay healthy. *More and more HIV/AIDS clients require frequent primary medical visits to stay healthy.*

but all (just) the same *all (just) the same/but.*

but . . . however *but/however.* • But however, this is what we do on an everyday basis. *However, this is what we do on an everyday basis.*

but instead *but/instead.* • A child's mind is not a tabula rasa but instead is filled with ideas generated through continuous interaction with the environment. *A child's mind is not a tabula rasa but is filled with ideas generated through continuous interaction with the environment.*

but nevertheless *but/nevertheless.*

but nonetheless *but/nonetheless.*

but on the other hand *but/on the other hand.*

but rather *but/rather.* • Behavior is not an isolated event, but rather it is influenced by the past, present, and future. *Behavior is not an isolated event; rather it is influenced by the past, present, and future.*

but whereas *but/whereas.*

by and large *chiefly/commonly/generally/ largely/mainly/most/mostly/normally/typically/ usually.* • But members involved argue the furor is by and large a phony one. *But members involved argue the furor is largely a phony one.*

by any means *at all.*

by/in comparison *but/however/whereas/ yet* delete. • In comparison, about one-third of the patients whose vessels remained partly blocked showed late potentials on their EKGs. *Whereas about one-third of the patients whose vessels remained partly blocked showed late potentials on their EKGs.*

by comparison (to/with) . . . relatively *compared to/with/-(i)er than/less than/more than/than.* • By comparison with the rational method, the incremental method uses relatively little quantitative analysis. *Compared to the rational method, the incremental method uses little quantitative analysis.* • The figures are prominent even by comparison to the relatively high accident rate for Glasgow as a whole. *The figures are prominent even compared to the high accident rate for Glasgow as a whole.*

by comparison to/with *against/alongside/ beside/compared to/with/-(i)er than/less/less than/more/more than/next to/over/than/to/versus/vis-à-vis.* • By comparison with the electronic speed of computers, the postal service and the telephone are slow. *Compared with the electronic speed of computers, the postal service and the telephone are slow.*

by consequence of *after/because of/by/due to/ following/for/from/in/out of/owing to/through/ with.*

by (a/the) considerable/good/great/huge/ large/overwhelming/sizable/vast/wide margin *by far/far and away/much.* • The leader by a considerable margin was the deep-water lake trout. *The leader by far was the deep-water lake trout.*

by/in contrast *but/however/whereas/yet* delete. • Post-modernism, by contrast, is indifferent to consistency and continuity altogether. *Yet post-modernism is indifferent to consistency and continuity altogether.*

by contrast to/with *against/alongside/beside/ compared to/with/-(i)er than/less/less than/ more/more than/next to/over/than/to/unlike/ versus/vis-à-vis.* • And, by contrast with the governor and some younger politicians, Crane has always seen politics as an essential part of the job. *And, unlike the governor and some younger politicians, Crane has always seen politics as an essential part of the job.*

by definition delete. • Collaboration, by definition, is a two-way venture. *Collaboration is a two-way venture.*

(all) by itself/themselves *alone.* • Each microcomputer has its own computational ability, so it can function either by itself or as a part of the network. *Each microcomputer has its own computational ability, so it can function either alone or as a part of the network.*

by (a/the) little narrow/nominal/slender/slight/ slim/small/tiny margin *marginally/narrowly/ nominally/slightly.* • Blue-chip stocks closed higher by a small margin in a listless session as many participants were absent because of the Jewish New Year holiday. *Blue-chip stocks closed marginally higher in a listless session as many* *participants were absent because of the Jewish New Year holiday.*

by (a/the) . . . margin (of) *by/-(al)ly* delete. • Advancing issues outpaced losers by a margin of more than 2 to 1 among issues listed on the New York Stock Exchange. *Advancing issues outpaced losers by more than 2 to 1 among issues listed on the New York Stock Exchange.*

by (the) means of *by/from/in/on/over/through/with.* • It retains control over product decisions and generally markets a standardized product and attempts to influence local decisions by means of persuasion. *It retains control over product decisions and generally markets a standardized product and attempts to influence local decisions through persuasion.* • He was convicted of assault and battery by means of a dangerous weapon. *He was convicted of assault and battery with a dangerous weapon.* • To rappel means to descend a mountain, building, wall, or other vertical surface by means of a rope. *To rappel means to descend a mountain, building, wall, or other vertical surface by rope.*

by (its/their) (very) nature delete. • The truth is that genuine debt crises are, by their nature, almost impossible to predict. *The truth is that genuine debt crises are almost impossible to predict.* • The best way to start a speech is not with a joke, but with an arresting, unexpected fact—a fact so intriguing by its very nature that your audience sits spellbound for a moment, weighing its impact. *The best way to start a speech is not with a joke, but with an arresting, unexpected fact—a fact so intriguing that your audience sits spellbound for a moment, weighing its impact.*

by no means *far from/hardly/scarcely.* • Though this advice is extremely helpful to many families, it is by no means the only thing they need to know. *Though this advice is extremely helpful to many families, it is far from the only thing they need to know.*

by occupation delete. • He's a day laborer by occupation. *He's a day laborer.*

by one means or another *anyhow/anyway/by some means/however/in any way/in some way/in whatever way/somehow/somehow or another/someway(s).*

by reason of *after/because of/by/due to/following/for/from/in/out of/owing to/through/with.* • Nomura, by reason of its size, capital, research abilities, and leading position in the largest creditor nation, should certainly be in the top group. *Nomura, because of its size, capital, research abilities, and leading position in the largest creditor nation, should certainly be in the top group.*

by reason of the fact that *because/considering/for/given/in that/since.* • Property the decedent had interest in includes dividends payable to the decedent by reason of the fact that, on or before the date of death, the decedent was a shareholder of record. *Property the decedent had interest in includes dividends payable to the decedent because, on or before the date of death, the decedent was a shareholder of record.* • This was made inevitable by reason of the fact that the IWW was the result of a later and more mature period of industrial development. *This was made inevitable given that the IWW was the result of a later and more mature period of industrial development.*

(all) by -self/-selves *alone.* • She lives all by herself. *She lives alone.*

by . . . standards *-(al)ly* delete. • By historical standards, these relative prices for thrifts are extremely low. *Historically, these relative prices for thrifts are extremely low.*

by the fact that *because/considering/for/given/in that/since.* • By the fact that they are using state capital, there can be no free competition.

Considering they are using state capital, there can be no free competition.

by the result of *after/based on/because of/by/ due to/following/for/from/in/on/owing to/ through/with.* • In the United States, policies are determined mainly by the result of discussion and debate, whereas in Europe they are determined on the basis of authority and position. *In the United States, policies are determined mainly from discussion and debate, whereas in Europe they are determined on the basis of authority and position.*

by the same token *also/and/as well/besides/ beyond that/this/even/further/furthermore/like- wise/moreover/more than that/this/similarly/still more/then/too/what's more* delete. • By the same token, northeastern and southeastern banks, which have been the fastest growing, could witness slower loan growth. *Similarly, northeastern and southeastern banks, which have been the fastest growing, could witness slower loan growth.*

by/in virtue of *after/because of/by/due to/fol- lowing/for/from/in/out of/owing to/through/ with.* • The U.S. hockey team is up by one by virtue of their win over Austria. *The U.S. hockey team is up by one following their win over Austria.* • The immiscible units attempt to sep- arate, but by virtue of their connectivity they can never get very far from each other. *The immiscible units attempt to separate, but because of their connectivity they can never get very far from each other.*

by/in virtue of the fact that *because/consider- ing/for/given/in that/since.* • People who can be helpful to you are attracted to you by virtue of the fact that you're a person who is doing inter- esting things and initiating activity yourself. *People who can be helpful to you are attracted to you because you're a person who is doing interest- ing things and initiating activity yourself.* • Enter- prise programmers have the most control over

their environment by virtue of the fact that they have personal access to every machine that will use the program they create. *Enterprise program- mers have the most control over their environment because they have personal access to every machine that will use the program they create.*

by way of (-ing) *by (-ing)/for (-ing)/so as to/ through (-ing)/to.* • All of this is by way of mak- ing a point. *All of this is to make a point.* • It is today possible to cure the disease by way of performing a bone marrow transplant. *It is today possible to cure the disease through per- forming a bone marrow transplant.* • We would do this by way of creating more awareness in your communities and through grants. *We would do this by creating more awareness in your communities and through grants.*

by (the) way of *by/from/in/on/over/through/ with* delete. • By way of conclusion, here are four salient facts. *In conclusion, here are four salient facts.* • We will not be ambushed by way of impromptu telephone calls for the purposes of any interview. *We will not be ambushed by impromptu telephone calls for the purposes of any interview.*

by way of being *by being/for being/so as to be/ through being/to be* delete. • Today's column is by way of being a commentary on a column that appeared in this space a week ago. *Today's col- umn is a commentary on a column that appeared in this space a week ago.* • James is going out to SLAC pretty straight after the Edinburgh meet- ing, so it's by way of being a farewell party as well. *James is going out to SLAC pretty straight after the Edinburgh meeting, so it's a farewell party as well.* • Yesterday I met with Gregg, a new acquaintance; this was by way of being a blind date. *Yesterday I met with Gregg, a new acquaintance; this was a blind date.*

by way of comparison/contrast *but/however/ whereas/yet.* • The volume directory for a Pro- DOS-formatted disk can hold up to 51 files, and by way of contrast, a DOS 3.3 directory can hold 105 files. *The volume directory for a ProDOS-formatted disk can hold up to 51 files, whereas a DOS 3.3 directory can hold 105 files.*

by way of example/illustration *for example/to illustrate.* • By way of illustration, here are the main points of a speech about Thailand given by a Thai student. *To illustrate, here are the main points of a speech about Thailand given by a Thai student.* • By way of illustration, existentialism could be considered a humanistic form of individualism. *For example, existentialism could be considered a humanistic form of individualism.*

by whatever/whichever manner/means *despite how/however.* • By whatever means they have been brought to our attention, they have been corrected. *However they have been brought to our attention, they have been corrected.* • By logging on to our site, by whichever manner you choose, you accept these terms and conditions. *By logging on to our site, however you choose, you accept these terms and conditions.*

by what/which means/mechanism *how.* • Still a mystery is by what mechanism insulin resistance might cause heart disease. *Still a mystery is how insulin resistance might cause heart disease.* • By what means does the church secure financial support? *How does the church secure financial support?*

C

cacophony of noise/sound *cacophony.* What you end up with is a cacophony of sound that is hard to decipher and doesn't accomplish anything. *What you end up with is a cacophony that is hard to decipher and doesn't accomplish anything.*

call a halt to *cease/close/complete/conclude/end/finish/halt/settle/stop.* • We asked them to call a halt to the violence and harassment. *We asked them to stop the violence and harassment.*

call an end to *cease/close/complete/conclude/end/finish/halt/settle/stop.* • We should call an end to the national ID card debate. *We should end the national ID card debate.*

call a stop to *cease/close/complete/conclude/end/finish/halt/settle/stop.* • We must call a stop to this madness now. *We must stop this madness now.*

call . . . attention to *advertise/announce/blazon/broadcast/disclose/divulge/expose/herald/indicate/make known/make public/mention/point out/point to/present/proclaim/promote/publicize/reveal/show/tell/uncover/unveil.* • She said the sole purpose of the program was to call attention to what happened in Mexico. *She said the sole purpose of the program was to disclose what happened in Mexico.* • Today, many fire fighters are marching in Philadelphia to call attention to this serious, and deadly, occupational disease. *Today, many fire fighters are marching in Philadelphia to publicize this serious, and deadly, occupational disease.*

called *delete.* • A set is a collection of objects, and the objects in the set are called the elements. *A set is a collection of objects, and the objects in the set are the elements.*

call into being/existence *conceive/create/devise/fashion/forge/form/invent/make/mold/plan/produce/shape.* • This new future requires people to call into existence a new humanity. *This new future requires people to create a new humanity.*

call into question *challenge/contradict/dispute/doubt/question.* • Whether the magazine has accurately interpreted what those interests are is a point some former staffers call into question. *Whether the magazine has accurately interpreted what those interests are is a point some former staffers dispute.*

call to . . . attention (of) *advertise/announce/ blazon/broadcast/disclose/divulge/expose/herald/indicate/make known/make public/mention/ point out/point to/present/proclaim/promote/ publicize/reveal/show/tell/uncover/unveil.* • The results were called to the attention of the town's building inspector, who forced the ferry service to shut down. *The results were shown to the town's building inspector, who forced the ferry service to shut down.*

call to mind *recall/recollect.*

call up *call.*

calm, cool, and collected *calm/collected/cool.* • She is calm, cool, and collected now, but you should have seen her Friday night. *She is calm now, but you should have seen her Friday night.*

cameo appearance *cameo.*

candor and frankness *candor/frankness.*

capability *ability.* • No two managers are equal in their abilities, and their subordinates will have differing capabilities and levels of experience. *No two managers are equal in their abilities, and their subordinates will have differing abilities and levels of experience.*

capacity *job/position.*

capital city *capital.* • Funds raised by the golf tournament will help build an orphanage, school and clinic to help 300 children in Rwanda's capital city of Kigali. *Funds raised by the golf tournament will help build an orphanage, school and clinic to help 300 children in Rwanda's capital of Kigali.*

capitol building *capitol.* • Our capitol building is a one of the key features in the memorable Denver skyline. *Our capitol is a one of the key features in the memorable Denver skyline.*

(the) case *right/so/true* delete. • I think that's probably the case. *I think that's probably true.* • Such companies are often durable goods manufacturers, but this is not always the case. *Such companies are often durable goods manufacturers, but this is not always so.*

(a) case in point *(an/one) example/for example/ for instance.* • Teachers in the trades and industry program at Queen Anne's County High School are a case in point. *Teachers in the trades and industry program at Queen Anne's County High School are an example.*

cast about for *look for/search for/seek.* • Toymakers have been casting about for something exciting enough to pull parents and children back into the toy stores. *Toymakers have been searching for something exciting enough to pull parents and children back into the toy stores.*

cast doubt on/upon *challenge/contradict/dispute/doubt/question.*

catch by surprise *startle/surprise.* • He says the association was caught by surprise by the House's action. *He says the association was surprised by the House's action.*

cause . . . (to) delete. • Protease inhibitors have the ability to cause damage to liver cells if they are used for long periods of time. *Protease inhibitors have the ability to damage liver cells if they are used for long periods of time.* • After controversies last October, I'm afraid that the document might cause embarrassment to us all. *After controversies last October, I'm afraid that the document might embarrass us all.* • We cannot possibly cause harm to God's most magnificent creation. *We cannot possibly harm God's most magnificent creation.* • The defendant angrily shouted that he was going to look for his wife and warned that he would cause harm to his wife or to any person who had helped his wife. *The defendant angrily shouted that he was going to look for his wife and warned that he* *would harm his wife or any person who had helped his wife.*

caused because of/due to/owing to *because of/caused by/due to/owing to.* • Night blindness is caused due to a disorder of the cells in the retina of the eye. *Night blindness is due to a disorder of the cells in the retina of the eye.* • Close to 50 percent of family bankruptcies are caused because of a health care crisis. *Close to 50 percent of family bankruptcies are caused by a health care crisis.*

cause . . . to be/become *make/render.* • Reading his performance appraisal caused him to become angry. *Reading his performance appraisal made him angry.*

cause to happen/occur/take place *bring about/cause/effect/produce.* • Although policy cannot in and of itself cause improvement to happen in the classroom, it can impede or facilitate improvement. *Although policy cannot in and of itself cause improvement in the classroom, it can impede or facilitate improvement.*

CD-ROM disc *CD-ROM.*

cease and desist *cease/desist.*

center around *center on.* • All these fears center around the loss of control, which may result in being embarrassed or ridiculed by others. *All these fears center on the loss of control, which may result in being embarrassed or ridiculed by others.* • The USER subsystem includes a lot of new input options, many of which appear to center around the mouse. *The USER subsystem includes a lot of new input options, many of which appear to center on the mouse.*

center of attention/attraction *cynosure/focus.*

(of) central/critical/vital importance *central/critical/important/vital.* • Although these contextual factors are often ignored by domestic

firms, they are of central importance to international firms. *Although these contextual factors are often ignored by domestic firms, they are central to international firms.* • This information will be critically important to researchers and to the quality of health care for all Americans well into the next century. *This information will be critical to researchers and to the quality of health care for all Americans well into the next century.*

(a/the) central . . . in/of/to *central to.* • His experience is a central part of the resume on which he is running for office. *His experience is central to the resume on which he is running for office.* • As such, religion (or its traces) is a central element of a culture. *As such, religion (or its traces) is central to a culture.*

(a) certain amount of *much/some* delete. • There's a certain amount of truth to what you say. *There's much truth to what you say.*

characterize as *call/name/term.* • What percentage of your work would you characterize as consulting? *What percentage of your work would you call consulting?*

(the) character of delete. • He played the character of a picaro. *He played a picaro.*

charge with the responsibility for/of *charge with/responsible for.* • The organization might have a management information system that is charged with the responsibility for gathering and processing data. *The organization might have a management information system that is responsible for gathering and processing data.* • Does it matter if the people we charge with the responsibility of protecting our nation believe in God? *Does it matter if the people we charge with protecting our nation believe in God?*

check to see *check/examine/inspect/look/see.* • You should also check to see if the original warranty is still in effect. *You should also check if* the original warranty is still in effect. • When you've done that, check to see that the verbs and pronouns that depend on it agree with it in person and number. *When you've done that, check that the verbs and pronouns that depend on it agree with it in person and number.*

christen as *christen.* • She was later raised by the Confederates, covered with armor plating, and rechristened as the C.S.S. *Virginia. She was later raised by the Confederates, covered with armor plating, and rechristened the C.S.S. Virginia.*

(the) city/town of delete. • In the city of Chicago, there are a lot of counseling centers. *In Chicago, there are a lot of counseling centers.*

clear, free, and unencumbered *clear/free/unencumbered.* • The title to all the Trust Property is clear, free and unencumbered. *The title to all the Trust Property is clear.* • Peak experiences are our healthiest moments, clear, free and unencumbered, living at our optimum potential. *Peak experiences are our healthiest moments, unencumbered, living at our optimum potential.*

climb up *climb.* • Young Americans have become increasingly disillusioned with their ability to successfully climb up the corporate ladder. *Young Americans have become increasingly disillusioned with their ability to successfully climb the corporate ladder.*

close/near/rough approximation/estimate/ estimation *approximation/estimate/estimation.* • Powers of two roughly approximate powers of ten. *Powers of two approximate powers of ten.*

close/near at hand *close by/close to/near/ nearby.*

close down *close.* • Both health plans will close down as of December 31 because of projected financial losses. *Both health plans will close as*

of December 31 because of projected financial losses.

close scrutiny *scrutiny.* • The interest deduction is likely to receive close scrutiny when the chairman of the House Ways and Means Committee looks into the matter this month. *The interest deduction is likely to receive scrutiny when the chairman of the House Ways and Means Committee looks into the matter this month.*

cluster together *cluster.* • Groups of chapters in textbooks may be clustered together into units or parts. *Groups of chapters in textbooks may be clustered into units or parts.*

cobble together *cobble.* • This might scan articles on a computerized news service to cobble together a personalized daily news bulletin containing articles of interest to a particular individual. *This might scan articles on a computerized news service to cobble a personalized daily news bulletin containing articles of interest to a particular individual.*

cohabitate *cohabit.* • Statistically, people are much more likely to get a divorce if they cohabitate first. *Statistically, people are much more likely to get a divorce if they cohabit first.* • Couples who cohabitate have characteristics different from non-cohabitating couples. *Couples who cohabit have characteristics different from non-cohabiting couples.*

cohabit together *cohabit.* • Studies show that people who cohabit together first and then get married have a higher rate of getting divorced than people who don't live together first. *Studies show that people who cohabit first and then get married have a higher rate of getting divorced than people who don't live together first.*

collaborate together *collaborate.* • Generally, a gang can be considered to be a loosely organized group of individuals who collaborate together for social reasons. *Generally, a gang* can be considered to be a loosely organized group of individuals who collaborate for social reasons.

collect together *collect*. • Collect together your word processing, desktop publishing, document conversion, and text search programs under one main menu entry. *Collect your word processing, desktop publishing, document conversion, and text search programs under one main menu entry.* • A comprehensive set of papers that cover the multiplexing standards, network topologies, and performance and management is collected together in SS96. *A comprehensive set of papers that cover the multiplexing standards, network topologies, and performance and management is collected in SS96.*

(the) color delete. • I noticed the predominance of the color green in their costumes. *I noticed the predominance of green in their costumes.*

(a/the) combination (of) *both* delete. • Architects use a combination of feet and inches, but the inch units are omitted (e.g., 7'2). *Architects use feet and inches, but the inch units are omitted (e.g., 7'2).*

(a/the) combination of . . . along with/combined with/coupled with/joined with/paired with/together with *along with/combined with/coupled with/joined with/paired with/together with*. • The combination of the Relaxation Response coupled with the person's particular belief will work. *The Relaxation Response coupled with the person's particular belief will work.*

(a/the) combination of both *both (of them)/combination*. • A combination of both whites and blacks are members of these groups. *Both whites and blacks are members of these groups.* • Even when children understand questions, they may be reluctant to answer out of fear, misguided love, or a combination of both. *Even when children understand questions, they may be reluctant to answer out of fear, misguided love, or both.*

(a/the) combination of the two *both (of them)/combination*. • You may use either technique or a combination of the two. *You may use either or both techniques.* • The investigation may be done by corporate security personnel, by a private investigator, or by a combination of the two. *The investigation may be done by corporate security personnel, by a private investigator, or by both of them.*

combine both *combine*. • The latest development is to combine both record and programming so you can record and then edit macros. *The latest development is to combine record and programming so you can record and then edit macros.*

combine into one *combine*. • The single justice noted that combining the two motions into one was a minor procedural discrepancy. *The single justice noted that combining the two motions was a minor procedural discrepancy.*

combine together *combine/join*. • The mixed chart allows you to combine different types of charts together. *The mixed chart allows you to combine different types of charts.* • No one has yet been able to produce a lichen in the laboratory by combining the two partners together. *No one has yet been able to produce a lichen in the laboratory by combining the two partners.*

come about *befall/happen/occur/result/take place*.

come as a disappointment (to) *disappoint*. • I know this may come as a disappointment to some of you, but my husband is not going to be running for office. *I know this may disappoint some of you, but my husband is not going to be running for office.*

come as a relief (to) *relieve*. • The pronunciation system of the former OED, a frequent source of criticism, has been replaced by the International Phonetic Alphabet, which should come as a relief to many. *The pronunciation system of the former OED, a frequent source of criticism, has been replaced by the International Phonetic Alphabet, which should relieve many.*

come as a surprise (to) *startle/surprise.* • It came as a surprise to all the women who work with the senator to learn that his wife left him. *It surprised all the women who work with the senator to learn that his wife left him.*

come close/near to *approach/resemble.* • The results of a true national probability sample would most likely come close to these findings. *The results of a true national probability sample would most likely approach these findings.*

come equipped/furnished with *come with.* • All computers come equipped with a keyboard. *All computers come with a keyboard.*

come in contact (with) *come across/contact/ discover/encounter/find/locate/meet (with)/spot/ touch.* • If the part is designed to come in contact with another surface, the rough surface must be machined. *If the part is designed to touch another surface, the rough surface must be machined.*

come into/to (a/the) . . . (of) delete. • Eventually they came to the recognition that the supercomputer business is a high stakes poker game. *Eventually they recognized that the supercomputer business is a high stakes poker game.* • It neither glosses over the true historical picture nor attempts to come to the defense of any individuals. *It neither glosses over the true historical picture nor attempts to defend any individuals.*

come into being *appear/arise/evolve/exist.*

come into existence *appear/arise/evolve/exist.* • In the chain network, the possibility of screening by levels comes into existence. *In the chain network, the possibility of screening by levels arises.*

come into play *appear/arise/come about/ develop/emerge/happen/occur/result/surface/ take place/turn up/unfold.* • When they act out their depression, thoughts of suicide can come into play. *When they act out their depression, thoughts of suicide can surface.*

come out and delete. • It's one thing to come out and make a statement like that now that he's shot the film and gotten paid. *It's one thing to make a statement like that now that he's shot the film and gotten paid.* • I think it's good that folks come out and volunteer and get stuff done. *I think it's good that folks volunteer and get stuff done.* • Man what I would pay to hear just one politician come out and talk real, no BS, no lies. *Man what I would pay to hear just one politician talk real, no BS, no lies.* • Whoever hit him needs to come out and face the facts that you don't hit a kid and keep on driving. *Whoever hit him needs to face the facts that you don't hit a kid and keep on driving.*

come to a close *cease/close/complete/conclude/ end/finish/halt/stop.*

come to a/the compromise (about/as to/concerning/of/on/regarding) *agree/compromise/ concur/decide/resolve/settle.* • The best situation would be to come to a compromise now so both arties can salvage what is left of the Traveler heritage. *The best situation would be to compromise now so both parties can salvage what is left of the Traveler heritage.*

come to a/the conclusion (about/as to/concerning/of/on/regarding) *cease/close/complete/ conclude/end/finish/halt/stop.* • We came to the conclusion that she should start with antibiotics. *We decided that she should start with antibiotics.*

come to a/the decision (about/as to/concerning/of/on/regarding) *conclude/decide/deduce/ determine/infer/judge/reason/resolve/settle.* • It was during the counseling session that we came to the decision to let Allison move in with us.

It was during the counseling session that we decided to let Allison move in with us.

come to a/the determination (about/as to/concerning/of/on/regarding) *conclude/decide/deduce/determine/infer/judge/reason/resolve/settle.* • While the Board has not come to a determination on the viability of the TPA baseline under current funding scenarios, limited consideration of alternatives is warranted. *While the Board has not determined the viability of the TPA baseline under current funding scenarios, limited consideration of alternatives is warranted.*

come to a halt *cease/close/complete/conclude/end/finish/halt/stop.* • Suddenly, all activity came to a halt. *Suddenly, all activity stopped.*

come to an accord (about/as to/concerning/of/on/regarding) *agree/compromise/concur/decide/resolve/settle.* • Croatia, Bosnia-Herzegovina and Yugoslavia have come to an accord on how to deal with the still remaining 1.2 million refugees and displaced persons in their countries. *Croatia, Bosnia-Herzegovina and Yugoslavia have resolved how to deal with the still remaining 1.2 million refugees and displaced persons in their countries.*

come to an agreement (about/as to/concerning/of/on/regarding) *agree/compromise/concur/decide/resolve/settle.* • The parents and the school board have not yet come to an agreement on whether the child should be in regular classes. *The parents and the school board have not yet agreed on whether the child should be in regular classes.*

come to an end *cease/close/complete/conclude/end/finish/halt/stop.* • He sees himself as the last survivor of the so-called Bengal Renaissance, the cultural movement that came to an end with the death of Rabindranath Tagore in 1941. *He sees himself as the last survivor of the so-called Bengal Renaissance, the cultural movement that ceased with the death of Rabindranath Tagore in 1941.*

come to an/the estimate/estimation (about/as to/concerning/of/on/regarding) *approximate/assess/estimate/evaluate/rate.* • Thanks to radiometric dating, scientists have come to an estimate that the earth is 4.65 billion years old. *Thanks to radiometric dating, scientists have estimated that the earth is 4.65 billion years old.*

come to an/the opinion (about/as to/concerning/of/on/regarding) *conclude/decide/deduce/determine/infer/judge/reason/resolve/settle.* • I came to the opinion that it was an electrical fire, not arson. *I deduced that it was an electrical fire, not arson.*

come to an/the understanding *agree/compromise/concur/decide/resolve/settle.*

come to an/the understanding (about/as to/concerning/of/on/regarding) *appreciate/comprehend/grasp/understand.* • Through this, we will come to an understanding of our own concepts of the primitive and industrial worlds. *Through this, we will understand our own concepts of the primitive and industrial worlds.*

come to a/the resolution (about/as to/concerning/of/on/regarding) *agree/conclude/decide/determine/resolve/settle.* • I don't understand why they did what they did, and I hope we can come to a resolution about it. *I don't understand why they did what they did, and I hope we can resolve it.*

come to a/the settlement (about/as to/concerning/of/on/regarding) *agree/conclude/decide/resolve/settle.*

come to a standstill *cease/close/complete/conclude/end/finish/halt/stop.* • A spokesman for the Export-Import Bank of Japan said talks with China have come to a standstill. *A spokesman for the Export-Import Bank of Japan said talks with China have halted.*

come together *assemble/congregate/converge/gather.* • In the days before mass immunizations when compulsory education began, disease could spread quickly as large numbers of children came together in unsanitary, poorly heated, poorly ventilated buildings. *In the days before mass immunizations when compulsory education began, disease could spread quickly as large numbers of children gathered in unsanitary, poorly heated, poorly ventilated buildings.*

come to grips with *accept/comprehend/cope with/deal with/face/struggle with/understand.* • The systems software maker is now coming to grips with a period of rapid growth. *The systems software maker is now struggling with a period of rapid growth.*

come to light *emerge/surface/transpire.* • In the past year, a few new clues have come to light. *In the past year, a few new clues have transpired.*

come to pass *befall/happen/occur/result/take place.* • If this should come to pass, it would benefit everybody. *If this should happen, it would benefit everybody.*

come to terms (about/as to/concerning/of/on/regarding) *agree/arbitrate/compromise/concur/decide/settle.* • What they can't come to terms on is whether selling the profitable Eastern Shuttle will cure the airline or kill it. *What they can't agree on is whether selling the profitable Eastern Shuttle will cure the airline or kill it.*

come to terms with *accept/comprehend/cope with/deal with/face/struggle with/understand.* • Fitzwater said the president has come to terms with the constant press attention. *Fitzwater said the president has accepted the constant press attention.*

come up with *craft/create/design/devise/draft/fashion/find/form/make/map (out)/mold/plan/plot/prepare/produce/propose/shape/sketch/suggest.* • The NRC has given the nuclear plant a month to come up with a workable plan. *The NRC has given the nuclear plant a month to devise a workable plan.*

comfortably ensconced *ensconced.* • He is comfortably ensconced as head of the national guard of Panama. *He is ensconced as head of the national guard of Panama.*

comfort facilities *bathroom/john/loo/toilet.* • It seems to me that the required visitor-information services, tour departments, and comfort facilities could be provided in a leased ground-floor space in an existing nearby building. *It seems to me that the required visitor-information services, tour departments, and bathrooms could be provided in a leased ground-floor space in an existing nearby building.*

comical *comic.*

commence *begin/start.* • If the candidate accepts the employment offer, the next phase commences. *If the candidate accepts the employment offer, the next phase begins.*

commencement *start.* • Investment of the net proceeds will take place during a period which will not exceed six months from the commencement of operations. *Investment of the net proceeds will take place during a period which will not exceed six months from the start of operations.*

commit (a/the) . . . (of) delete. • You could not give it to your spouse without committing a violation of federal law. *You could not give it to your spouse without violating federal law.*

common (and) everyday *common/everyday.*

communicate (with) *call/call or write/phone/speak (with)/talk (to)/write (to).* • Please communicate with us at your first opportunity. *Please call us at your first opportunity.*

communicate in writing *communicate/write.* • To communicate in writing is a very complex process and represents the capturing of an abstract thought in a permanent manner in space and time. *To write is a very complex pro-*

cess and represents the capturing of an abstract thought in a permanent manner in space and time. • Be sure to communicate in writing to the Village Communities staff regarding withdrawal of an application and/or cancellation of an agreement. *Be sure to write to the Village Communities staff regarding withdrawal of an application and/or cancellation of an agreement.*

communication *dialogue/letter/message/note/report/speech/talk/text/words.* • Nurses frequently make the assumption that their communication has been listened to and understood by patients. *Nurses frequently make the assumption that their words have been listened to and understood by patients.*

(the) . . . company delete. • In 1986, the Hitachi company displaced General Electric as the firm receiving the most U.S. patents. *In 1986, Hitachi displaced General Electric as the firm receiving the most U.S. patents.*

comparatively *-(i)er/less/more.* • Computing what happens to stars and gas in a galactic cube, 100 cells on a side, turns out to be comparatively straightforward. *Computing what happens to stars and gas in a galactic cube, 100 cells on a side, turns out to be more straightforward.*

comparatively . . . compared/contrasted to *compared to/contrasted to/-(i)er than/less than/more than.* • The muscle mass is comparatively small compared to other ruminants. *The muscle mass is small compared to other ruminants.* • Although FFWs increased 71 percent, this was comparatively small compared to other short-fuse warnings. *Although FFWs increased 71 percent, this was smaller than other short-fuse warnings.*

comparatively -(i)er than/less than/more than *-(i)er than/less than/more than.* • U.S. experts say the Soviet budget deficit that Moscow has finally acknowledged is comparatively larger than that of America. *U.S. experts say the Soviet budget deficit that Moscow has finally*

acknowledged is larger than that of America. • Comparatively, Benin is slightly smaller than the state of Pennsylvania. *Benin is slightly smaller than the state of Pennsylvania.*

compare against/versus *compare to/with.* • Compare the printout carefully against Figure 50. *Compare the printout carefully with Figure 50.*

compare and contrast (versus) *compare to/contrast to.* • Perhaps it should have appeared in the Living section, where lifestyles of women from other Arab populations could be compared and contrasted to those living in the occupied territories under Israeli control. *Perhaps it should have appeared in the Living section, where lifestyles of women from other Arab populations could be contrasted to those living in the occupied territories under Israeli control.* • Compare and contrast logical versus physical organization. *Compare logical to physical organization.*

compared to/with *against/alongside/beside/-(i)er than/less/less than/more/more than/next to/over/than/to/versus.* • Smoking prevalence has declined across all educational groups, but the decline has occurred five times faster among the higher educated compared with the less educated. *Smoking prevalence has declined across all educational groups, but the decline has occurred five times faster among the higher educated than the less educated.* • Volume on the Big Board averaged 153.57 million shares a day compared to 153.39 million in the first week of 1989. *Volume on the Big Board averaged 153.57 million shares a day against 153.39 million in the first week of 1989.* • Heavy buying of dollars by traders, or governments, on exchange markets drives up its price, making it strong compared to other currencies. *Heavy buying of dollars by traders, or governments, on exchange markets drives up its price, making it stronger than other currencies.* • Star networks have better link budget characteristics compared to bus networks. *Star networks have better link budget characteristics than bus networks.* • There is an expectation that electronic books should be considerably less expensive compared to print editions. *There is an expectation that electronic books should be considerably less expensive than print editions.*

compared/contrasted to/with . . . relatively *compared to/contrasted to/-(i)er than/less than/more than.* • Compared to the advantages, there are relatively few disadvantages for a sole proprietorship. *Compared to the advantages, there are few disadvantages for a sole proprietorship.* • The primary effect appears to be a loss of plutonium from a diseased liver with possible redistribution to the skeleton when compared to relatively healthy individuals. *The primary effect appears to be a loss of plutonium from a diseased liver with possible redistribution to the skeleton when compared to healthy individuals.*

compartmentalize *compartment.* • People who compartmentalize their feelings can be trustworthy, dependable, wise, and trusted. *People who compartment their feelings can be trustworthy, dependable, wise, and trusted.*

compensate *pay.*

compensation *cash/fee/money/pay/payment/reward/wage.*

competency *competence.* • I feel this would be a good way of assessing his competency. *I feel this would be a good way of assessing his competence.*

compile together *compile.* • A database is a compilation of data that compiles all psychological journal abstracts together. *A database is a compilation of data that compiles all psychological journal abstracts.* • Even while busy with these duties, he found time to compile together the legal statements of the popes and councils. *Even while busy with these duties, he found time to compile the legal statements of the popes and councils.*

complete and utter *complete/utter.* • It is going to be a complete and utter mess for people to figure out. *It is going to be an utter mess for people to figure out.*

completely *delete.* • The car was completely destroyed in the fire. *The car was destroyed in the fire.*

completely and totally/utterly *completely/totally/utterly/wholly.* • This was a feel-good story, and it was completely and totally false. *This was a feel-good story, and it was completely false.*

completely/entirely/exclusively/fully/solely/thoroughly/totally/utterly/wholly dedicated to *dedicated to.* • SDS recently moved into a new facility exclusively dedicated to EWSD development for the U.S. market. *SDS recently moved into a new facility dedicated to EWSD development for the U.S. market.*

completely/entirely/exclusively/fully/solely/thoroughly/totally/utterly/wholly devoted to *devoted to.* • The store was devoted entirely to consumer-oriented systems of racks, shelves, bins and hooks, largely of European manufacture, all designed to make a small space more serviceable. *The store was devoted to consumer-oriented systems of racks, shelves, bins and hooks, largely of European manufacture, all designed to make a small space more serviceable.*

completely/entirely/fully/thoroughly/totally/utterly/wholly eliminate *eliminate.* • Computer specialists at MIT said it would take several more days to entirely eliminate the virus. *Computer specialists at MIT said it would take several more days to eliminate the virus.* • In some cases, you may even want to completely eliminate certain log entries simply because you don't want to monitor them. *In some cases, you may even want to eliminate certain log entries simply because you don't want to monitor them.*

completely/entirely/fully/thoroughly/totally/ utterly/wholly **eradicate** *eradicate.* • Dr. Carlos said he expects the trend to continue, although completely eradicating the decay is probably not possible. *Dr. Carlos said he expects the trend to continue, although eradicating the decay is probably not possible.*

completely/entirely/fully/thoroughly/totally/ utterly/wholly **unanimous** *unanimous.*

complete monopoly *monopoly.*

component *part.* • Two-tier coverage was cited as an important component of successful marketing. *Two-tier coverage was cited as an important part of successful marketing.*

component part/piece *component/part/piece.* • The plants manufacture electrical appliances or component parts for the appliances. *The plants manufacture electrical appliances or parts for the appliances.*

concatenate together *concatenate/connect/ link.* • Input lines are concatenated together until a semicolon is encountered, and the result is handled as one statement. *Input lines are concatenated until a semicolon is encountered, and the result is handled as one statement.* • Strings can easily be concatenated together using the + operator. *Strings can easily be concatenated using the + operator.*

concentrate . . . attention on/upon *concentrate on/focus on.* • Eastern has decided to concentrate most of its attention on keeping its shuttle going. *Eastern has decided to concentrate on keeping its shuttle going.*

concentrate (media/people's/public) attention on/upon *advertise/announce/blazon/ broadcast/disclose/divulge/expose/herald/indicate/make known/make public/mention/point out/point to/present/proclaim/promote/publicize/reveal/show/tell/uncover/unveil.* • She

never became president of the American Economics Association—perhaps because of her relentless work concentrating attention on the low status of women in the profession. *She never became president of the American Economics Association—perhaps because of her relentless work exposing the low status of women in the profession.*

concentrate . . . effort on/upon *concentrate on/focus on.* • If we concentrate our effort on the areas of most need, we might be able to make a difference. *If we concentrate on the areas of most need, we might be able to make a difference.*

concentrate . . . energy on/upon *concentrate on/focus on.* • Students need to concentrate their energies on their studies, extracurricular activities, and work. *Students need to focus on their studies, extracurricular activities, and work.*

concentrate . . . time and energy on/upon *concentrate on/focus on.* • We still have 10 million gallons of oil in the water, and we ought to be concentrating our time and energy on minimizing the damage that that does. *We still have 10 million gallons of oil in the water, and we ought to be concentrating on minimizing the damage that that does.*

(the) concept of delete. • The following example illustrates the concept of correlation. *The following example illustrates correlation.*

concerning *about/as for/as to/for/in/of/on/ over/to/toward/with* delete. • The Federal Reserve Board makes available various indexes, including one concerning industrial production. *The Federal Reserve Board makes available various indexes, including one about industrial production.*

conclusive end *conclusion/end.*

concurrently *as one/at once/jointly/together.*

concurrently . . . while *while.* • Schools need better tools to help them concurrently diagnose their level of functioning while establishing developmental plans for improvement. *Schools need better tools to help them diagnose their level of functioning while establishing developmental plans for improvement.*

concurrent with *while/with.* • Concurrent with rejecting the tender offer, Prime's directors approved a series of defensive measures. *While rejecting the tender offer, Prime's directors approved a series of defensive measures.*

(a/the) . . . condition *delete.* • Congruency is a necessary condition for clients to develop trust in nurses. *Congruency is necessary for clients to develop trust in nurses.*

(the) condition of *delete.* • British companies do not hesitate to go to the market with a share issue when the condition of the balance sheet warrants it. *British companies do not hesitate to go to the market with a share issue when the balance sheet warrants it.* • The condition of his health has deteriorated. *His health has deteriorated.*

conduct (a/the) . . . (into/of/on/to/with) *delete.* • We conducted interviews with EFT industry experts early in the study. *We interviewed EFT industry experts early in the study.* • Another method of collecting information is to conduct research on hunters' opinions about the merits of introducing a hunting seat on the market. *Another method of collecting information is to research hunters' opinions about the merits of introducing a hunting seat on the market.* • They should conduct an investigation into how these scholarships were awarded with no set criteria for selection, and explain why linguistic minorities are seemingly underrepresented. *They should investigate how these scholarships were awarded with no set criteria for selection, and explain why linguistic minorities are seemingly underrepresented.* • I am grateful to you for agreeing to conduct an inquiry into the circumstances giving rise to the current situation at the Equitable Life Assurance Society. *I am grateful to you for agreeing to inquire into the circumstances giving rise to the current situation at the Equitable Life Assurance Society.*

confer together *confer.* • The Virginia deputies meet and confer together two or three hours every day. *The Virginia deputies meet and confer two or three hours every day.*

congregate together *congregate.* • We feel that the five baby dinosaurs were congregating together behind a sand dune in a sandstorm. *We feel that the five baby dinosaurs were congregating behind a sand dune in a sandstorm.*

connected with *for/in/linked to/of/-'s/with.* • Obviously, the most profitable method of investing would be to buy low and sell high; however, there are several problems connected with this method. *Obviously, the most profitable method of investing would be to buy low and sell high; however, there are several problems with this method.*

connect together *connect/link.* • A network is two or more computers connected together with cables so that they can exchange files and share resources. *A network is two or more computers connected with cables so that they can exchange files and share resources.* • The nuclear material appears as fibrous patches scattered about the cytoplasm; however, it is all connected together. *The nuclear material appears as fibrous patches scattered about the cytoplasm; however, it is all connected.*

connotate *connote.* • The very words "deep sleep" connotated rest, restoration, the likelihood of awakening energized. *The very words "deep sleep" connote rest, restoration, the likelihood of awakening energized.* • Certain signs connotate larger and generalized cultural meanings. *Certain signs connote larger and generalized cultural meanings.*

consecutive/continuous days/weeks/months in a row *consecutive/continuous.* • The same holds true when markets make higher highs or lower lows on consecutive days in a row or when markets rise or fall on continuous days in a row. • *The same holds true when markets make higher highs or lower lows on consecutive days or when markets rise or fall on continuous days.*

consensus (of) opinion *consensus.* • There is a consensus of opinion in this country against executing our young. *There is a consensus in this country against executing our young.*

consequence *import/moment.*

consequence *effect/outcome/result.*

(a/the) consequence of *because of/caused by/due to/owing to/resulting from.* • The increase is almost entirely the consequence of rising economic activity. *The increase is almost entirely caused by rising economic activity.*

consequence/effect/outcome resulting from *consequence/effect/outcome of/result of.* • The potential long-term outcomes resulting from their reactions are destroyed creativity and stifled initiative. *The potential long-term outcomes of their reactions are destroyed creativity and stifled initiative.*

consequently *hence/so/then/therefore/thus.* • They were victims of misfortune or of circumstances beyond their control, and consequently, they live in shelters or on the streets. *They were victims of misfortune or of circumstances beyond their control, and thus, they live in shelters or on the streets.*

(a/the) considerable/good/great/huge/large/sizable/vast amount (of) *a good (great) deal (of)/a good (great) many (of)/almost all (of)/considerable/many (of)/most (of)/much (of)/nearly all (of)/vast* delete. • It's operationally complex and requires a large amount of resources. *It's operationally complex and requires vast resources.*

(a/the) considerable/good/great/huge/large/sizable/vast degree (of) *a good (great) deal (of)/considerable/great/much (of)/vast* delete. • They now realize they showed a considerable degree of insensitivity toward small businesses. *They now realize they showed great insensitivity toward small businesses.*

(a/the) considerable/good/great/huge/large/sizable/vast element (of) *a good (great) deal (of)/considerable/great/much (of)/vast* delete. • True to the spirit of covert operations, there was a large element of deception and dissembling in this struggle. *True to the spirit of covert operations, there was much deception and dissembling in this struggle.*

(a/the) considerable/good/great/huge/large/overwhelming/sizable/vast/wide majority (of) *a good (great) deal (of)/a good (great) many (of)/almost all (of)/many (of)/most (of)/much (of)/nearly all (of)* delete. • The two own the vast majority of the stock. *The two own almost all the stock.*

(a/the) considerable/good/great/huge/large/overwhelming/sizable/vast number (of) *a good (great) many (of)/almost all (of)/countless/dozens (of)/hundreds (of)/many (of)/millions (of)/most (of)/nearly all (of)/numerous/scores (of)/thousands (of).* • The language provides a large number of primitive data types. *The language provides dozens of primitive data types.*

(a/the) considerable/good/great/huge/large/sizable/vast part (of) *a good (great) deal (of)/a good (great) many (of)/almost all (of)/many (of)/most (of)/much (of)/nearly all (of)* delete. • A large part of this analysis is within your reach at little or no cost. *Much of this analysis is within your reach at little or no cost.*

(a/the) considerable/good/great/huge/large/ overwhelming/sizable/vast percentage (of) *a good (great) deal (of)/a good (great) many (of)/ almost all (of)/many (of)/most (of)/much (of)/ nearly all (of)* delete. • We know that a large percentage of IRA contributors had been saving little before IRAs were created. *We know that many IRA contributors had been saving little before IRAs were created.*

(a/the) considerable/good/great/huge/large/ sizable/vast portion (of) *a good (great) deal (of)/a good (great) many (of)/almost all (of)/ many (of)/most (of)/much (of)/nearly all (of)* delete. • It will be unseasonably cool over a considerable portion of the United States today. *It will be unseasonably cool over much of the United States today.*

(a/the) considerable/good/great/huge/large/ sizable/vast proportion (of) *a good (great) deal (of)/a good (great) many (of)/almost all (of)/many (of)/most (of)/much (of)/nearly all (of)* delete. • They may squander huge proportions of their purchasing power by paying high instead of low prices on each purchase. *They may squander much of their purchasing power by paying high instead of low prices on each purchase.*

(a/the) considerable/good/great/huge/large/ sizable/vast quantity (of) *a good (great) deal (of)/a good (great) many (of)/almost all (of)/doz-ens (of)/hundreds (of)/many (of)/millions (of)/ most (of)/much (of)/nearly all (of)/scores (of)/ thousands (of).* • Students often fail to remember or understand large quantities of their elementary calculus. *Students often fail to remember or understand much of their elementary calculus.*

considerably *a good (great) deal/amply/far/ greatly/largely/mostly/much/vastly.* • This is con-siderably different from the past, when information was printed and approved before being passed up the hierarchy. *This is far different from the past, when information was printed and approved before being passed up the hierarchy.*

consider as *consider.* • It could be considered as false advertising. *It could be considered false advertising.* • Do you have an estimation which mean rate per hour, day or month you would consider as a reasonable fee for your services? *Do you have an estimation which mean rate per hour, day or month you would consider a reasonable fee for your services?*

consider as being *consider.* • In many ways, software engineering may be considered as being similar to various other sciences and branches of engineering. *In many ways, software engineering may be considered similar to various other sciences and branches of engineering.*

considering the fact that *because/considering/ for/given/in that/since/when.* • Considering the fact that the average person uses 77 gallons of water a day, we can estimate that each person uses close to 26 gallons of water every day simply by flushing the toilet. *Since the average person uses 77 gallons of water a day, we can estimate that each person uses close to 26 gallons of water every day simply by flushing the toilet.* • Considering the fact that some 6,400 hospitals endured a lengthy and intensive evaluation, analyzing everything from new technology to nurse-to-bed ratio, our ranking is something to be proud of. *Because some 6,400 hospitals endured a lengthy and intensive evaluation, analyzing everything from new technology to nurse-to-bed ratio, our ranking is something to be proud of.* • This strikes me as nothing other than laziness, especially considering the fact that there are numerous bodies of water that begin with the letter Z. *This strikes me as nothing other than laziness, especially since there are numerous bodies of water that begin with the letter Z.*

consolidate together *consolidate.* • Cooperatives are independent firms that have consolidated parts of their operations together into one organization. *Cooperatives are independent firms that have consolidated parts of their operations into one organization.*

constitute *be/compose/form/make up.* • Corporate debt issues constitute the largest segment, totaling more than $341 billion in 2006. *Corporate debt issues make up the largest segment, totaling more than $341 billion in 2006.*

consult with *consult.* • Blair consulted with Bush. *Blair consulted Bush.* • The government of Canada will continue to consult with industry stakeholders. *The government of Canada will continue to consult industry stakeholders.*

contact *call/phone/reach/write (to).* • She contacted the state agency that helps welfare recipients. *She called the state agency that helps welfare recipients.*

contain (a/the) . . . of delete. • Chapter 15 contains a formal discussion of the theoretical underpinnings of these formulas. *Chapter 15 formally discusses the theoretical underpinnings of these formulas.* • Table 4-3 contains a list of all 26 ProDOS commands and command numbers. *Table 4-3 lists all 26 ProDOS commands and command numbers.*

(the) continent of (the . . . continent) delete. • Despite droughts, floods, wars, and low oil and commodity prices, the African continent as a whole is better off now than a year ago. *Despite droughts, floods, wars, and low oil and commodity prices, Africa as a whole is better off now than a year ago.*

continue in existence/to exist *continue/endure/exist/last/persevere/persist/prevail/remain/survive.* • The possibility of becoming an independent company continues to exist. *The possibility of becoming an independent company persists.*

continue into the future *continue.* • The rate of growth in the market is expected to continue into the future. *The rate of growth in the market is expected to continue.*

continue on *continue.* • If he doesn't raise enough money, he won't be able to continue on. *If he doesn't raise enough money, he won't be able to continue.* • Her business is going to continue on. *Her business is going to continue.*

continue to be *be still/remain/stay.* • This was the case before the New York state law and continues to be the case after the New York state law. *This was the case before the New York state law and remains the case after the New York state law.*

continue to remain *be still/remain/stay.* • Sex stereotypes continue to remain a problem in the military. *Sex stereotypes remain a problem in the military.*

continuously/incessantly and without interruption *continuously/incessantly/without interruption.* • Central makes no representations, warranties or guarantees that the Site will be accessible continuously and without interruption, or error free. *Central makes no representations, warranties or guarantees that the Site will be accessible continuously, or error free.* • You save continuously and without interruption until age 67. *You save without interruption until age 67.*

contractual agreement *agreement/contract.* • Contractual agreements with independent distributors in Indonesia are required by law to be for a minimum of three years. *Contracts with independent distributors in Indonesia are required by law to be for a minimum of three years.*

contrariwise *but/conversely/however/instead/not so/rather/still/whereas/yet.*

contrary to *after all/apart (from)/aside (from)/despite/even with/for all/with all.* • Contrary to some of the things you've heard, I am the same man I was when I came to Washington. *Despite some of the things you've heard, I am the same man I was when I came to Washington.*

contrasted to/with *against/alongside/beside/ compared to/with/-(i)er than/less/less than/ more/more than/next to/over/than/to/unlike/ versus/vis-à-vis.*

contribute to *add to.*

converge together *converge.* • We both could not tell the resolution reading since the lines seemed to converge together. *We both could not tell the resolution reading since the lines seemed to converge.*

(in) conversation *talk.*

converse *speak/talk.* • She has multiple personalities, and I was able to converse with all of them. *She has multiple personalities, and I was able to talk with all of them.*

convicted felon *felon.* • There are concerns over the fact that the bank loaned money to convicted felons. *There are concerns over the fact that the bank loaned money to felons.*

cooperate together *cooperate.* • And there's no question in my mind that as we cooperate together, the people of both our countries will benefit. *And there's no question in my mind that as we cooperate, the people of both our countries will benefit.*

core essence *core/crux/essence/gist/pith/substance.* • Issues are supposed to be the core essence of a political convention. *Issues are supposed to be the core of a political convention.*

correctional/prison facility *jail/prison.* • Opponents complained that a prison facility for 500 inmates and several hundred staff members would overwhelm the town of barely 800 people. *Opponents complained that a prison for 500 inmates and several hundred staff members would overwhelm the town of barely 800 people.*

correspond back and forth *correspond.* • I'd like to meet someone who is open-minded and who would like to correspond back and forth with me. *I'd like to meet someone who is open-minded and who would like to correspond with me.*

correspondence *letter/memo/note/report.*

(a/the) countless number (of) *countless/endless/infinite/millions (of)/myriad/numberless/ untold.* • The congestion has resulted in interminable delays and countless numbers of accidents for motorists. *The congestion has resulted in interminable delays and countless accidents for motorists.*

(the) country of delete. • Revelation was first written for Christians living in seven cities in Asia Minor, in what today is the country of Turkey. *Revelation was first written for Christians living in seven cities in Asia Minor, in what today is Turkey.*

(a) couple of *a few/two.*

(a) couple three/two/two or three *a couple of/a few/two/two or three/three.* • I've known her for a couple two or three years, and never has she said anything like that to me before. *I've known her for a few years, and never has she said anything like that to me before.*

couple together *along with/couple (with).* • Channels up to 150 THz (125 nm) apart will be coupled together with SRS. *Channels up to 150 THz (125 nm) apart will be coupled with SRS.* • The National Rifle Association's extremist positions coupled together with last year's shooting at an elementary school in Newtown have really inflamed things lately. *The National Rifle Association's extremist positions along with last year's shooting at an elementary school in Newtown have really inflamed things lately.*

course of action *action/course/direction/intention/method/move/plan/policy/procedure/route/scheme/strategy.* • The coalition has urged a boycott of tuna, but strengthening existing laws—and enforcing them—would be a better course of action. *The coalition has urged a boycott of tuna, but strengthening existing laws—and enforcing them—would be a better course.*

cover over *cover.*

criminal act *crime.* • Certainly if a public official commits a criminal act, he or she must face full consequences. *Certainly if a public official commits a crime, he or she must face full consequences.*

criminal offense *crime/offense.* • Mr. Hurd said he had misgivings about making drinking on the streets a criminal offense. *Mr. Hurd said he had misgivings about making drinking on the streets an offense.*

criminal record *record.*

criminal wrongdoing *crime/wrongdoing.* • McNamara may not be guilty of any criminal wrongdoing, but he is a terrible U.S. attorney. *McNamara may not be guilty of any crime, but he is a terrible U.S. attorney.*

critically/crucially/vitally important *critical/crucial/important/vital.* • This is crucially important to the investigators since any compromise of the scene lessens its investigative value. *This is crucial to the investigators since any compromise of the scene lessens its investigative value.*

(a/the) critical . . . in/of/to *critical to.* • A critical ingredient in a manager's philosophy of change is how much emphasis is placed on trust in the work environment. *Critical to a manager's philosophy of change is how much emphasis is placed on trust in the work environment.* • Active cooperation between all industry groups is a critical factor to the success of EFT and POS. *Active cooperation between all industry groups is critical to the success of EFT and POS.* • The entire landscape of faculty will change, and a critical part of our strategy is bringing new faces to U of T. *The entire landscape of faculty will change, and critical to our strategy is bringing new faces to U of T.*

(a/the) crucial . . . in/of/to *crucial to.* • He believes hostility is a crucial component of the Type A personality and a potent predictor of heart trouble. *He believes hostility is crucial to the Type A personality and a potent predictor of heart trouble.* • Although a crucial part of the equation, this limited view fails to take into account the large number of high achievers who also possess chronic low self-esteem. *Although crucial to the equation, this limited view fails to take into account the large number of high achievers who also possess chronic low self-esteem.*

current/present incumbent *incumbent.* • The present incumbent, Kathryn Colvin, leaves the post in September after completing her three-year tenure. *The incumbent, Kathryn Colvin, leaves the post in September after completing her three-year tenure.*

currently *(just/right) now/today/(just) yet* delete. • It's the only spreadsheet currently on the market that has the look and feel of WordPerfect. *It's the only spreadsheet now on the market that has the look and feel of WordPerfect.*

current/present status *status.* • Nothing material to date can be reported on the current status of these negotiations. *Nothing material to date can be reported on the status of these negotiations.*

custom-built *custom/tailored.* • At least one vendor uses a custom-built database system in addition to a commercial one to speed up operations. *At least one vendor uses a custom database system in addition to a commercial one to speed up operations.*

custom-made *custom/tailored.* • Our courses are custom-made to meet the training needs of each client. *Our courses are tailored to meet the training needs of each client.*

custom-tailored *custom/customized/tailored.* • Customers today demand custom-tailored solutions to communications problems. *Customers today demand customized solutions to communications problems.*

cut by/in half *halve.* • A cooperative agreement was announced that could cut by half the amount of ozone-destroying chemicals released in the service and repair of auto air conditioners. *A cooperative agreement was announced that could halve the amount of ozone-destroying chemicals released in the service and repair of auto air conditioners.*

cute/handsome/pretty/ugly looking *cute/handsome/pretty/ugly.* • Kim is pretty looking but remember our women are also pretty. *Kim is pretty but remember our women are also pretty.* • The species, named Nycticebus kayan, is a small, cute-looking animal that is more closely related to bushbabies and lemurs than to monkeys. *The species, named Nycticebus kayan, is a small, cute animal that is more closely related to bushbabies and lemurs than to monkeys.*

cyclical *cyclic.* • The lengths of time within cyclical periods tend to vary. *The lengths of time within cyclic periods tend to vary.*

D

date back to *date from/date to.* • Rogation Days date back at least to the 13th century and probably to the days before the Norman Conquest. *Rogation Days date to at least the 13th century and probably to the days before the Norman Conquest.* • "Dog eat dog" dates back from the sixteenth century. *"Dog eat dog" dates from the sixteenth century.*

(the) date of *delete.* • The paper illustrated this definition with examples supplemented by the speaker on the date of September 26, 2012. *The paper illustrated this definition with examples supplemented by the speaker on September 26, 2012.*

day in (and) day out *always/ceaselessly/consistently/constantly/daily/endlessly/eternally/everlastingly/every day/forever/invariably/never ending/perpetually/routinely/unfailingly.* • I was doing portraits day in and day out. *I was doing portraits every day.*

day-to-day routine *routine.* • I am greatly tired of the day-to-day routine. *I am greatly tired of the routine.*

DC current *DC.*

dead body *body.* • Lying next to him as he wrote was the dead body of his son, who had been killed in the first day of battle. *Lying next to him as he wrote was the body of his son, who had been killed in the first day of battle.*

deadly killer *killer.* • There is no cure for this deadly killer, which has spread across the southwestern United States. *There is no cure for this killer, which has spread across the southwestern United States.*

(the) decade/period/period of time/span of time/time/years between . . . and *between . . . and/from . . . through/to/to.*

(the) decade/period/period of time/span of time/time/years from . . . through/till/to/until *between . . . and/from . . . through/to/to.* • The United Nations General Assembly recently declared the decade from 1990 to 2000 to be the International Decade of Natural Disaster Reduction. *The United Nations General Assembly recently declared 1990 to 2000 to be the International Decade of Natural Disaster Reduction.*

decapitate . . . (the) head (of) *behead/decapitate.* • I never could watch my father decapitate the heads of our chickens. *I never could watch my father decapitate our chickens.*

decide on what/when/where/whether/which/why *decide what/when/where/whether/which/why.* • Dog-friend will help you decide on what pet is right for you. *Dog-friend will help you decide what pet is right for you.* • And it helps end users decide on which electronic product to buy when they enter a shopping mall. *And it helps end users decide which electronic product to buy when they enter a shopping mall.*

(a/the) declining/decreasing/diminishing/dwindling amount/degree/extent/part/percentage/portion/proportion (of) *decreasingly/less/less and less.*

(a/the) declining/decreasing/diminishing/dwindling number/quantity (of) *decreasingly/few/fewer and fewer.*

(a/the) decreased/decreasing amount of *less.* • Overture has a decreasing share of the traffic and therefore advertisers are spending a decreasing amount of time managing bids. *Overture has a decreasing share of the traffic and therefore advertisers are spending less time managing bids.* • There is a decreased amount of swelling and healing is much faster. *There is less swelling and healing is much faster.*

(a/the) decreased/decreasing number of *fewer.* • The financial position of the healthcare system has become more strained, and has resulted in a decreased number of hospital beds. *The financial position of the healthcare system has become more strained, and has resulted in fewer hospital beds.*

decrease down *decrease.* • Density of water increases as temperature decreases down to 4°C. *Density of water increases as temperature decreases to 4°C.*

decreasing in *decreasingly.*

deductive reasoning *deduction.*

deem as *deem.* • Values are preferences, or what we deem as good. *Values are preferences, or what we deem good.* • The interior is comfortable and complete with numerous antiques, as well as conveniences that most modern travelers would deem as necessary. *The interior is comfortable and complete with numerous antiques, as well as conveniences that most modern travelers would deem necessary.*

defer back *defer.* • Although you might be able to defer back to your accountant, the best impression will be left by you if you are in command of the information. *Although you might be able to defer to your accountant, the best impression will be left by you if you are in command of the information.*

(most/very) definitely *yes.*

(a/the) . . . degree of *delete.* • He provides a healthy and thoughtful degree of skepticism about prospects for positive change at the national level. *He provides a healthy and thoughtful skepticism about prospects for posi-*

tive change at the national level. • Competitor reaction cannot be predicted with any degree of accuracy. *Competitor reaction cannot be predicted with any accuracy.* • This is sophisticated, suicidal, and there's a degree of ruthlessness that we haven't ever seen in the use of terrorism before. *This is sophisticated, suicidal, and there's a ruthlessness that we haven't ever seen in the use of terrorism before.*

(the) degree of *how much/the* delete. • The closer the value of *r* to either extreme, the greater the degree of association. *The closer the value of r to either extreme, the greater the association.* • I am concerned with the degree of difficulty they're having getting the product out. *I am concerned with how much difficulty they're having getting the product out.*

(a/a certain/some) degree (of) *a certain/much (of)/some (of)/somewhat* delete. • The best results will likely be obtained by firms that exercise some degree of restraint in their offshore activities. *The best results will likely be obtained by firms that exercise some restraint in their offshore activities.* • Each of us has a planning method that works with some degree of effectiveness. *Each of us has a planning method that works somewhat effectively.*

(the) degree to which *how/how far/how much/ how often.* • The GOP's principal concern is the degree to which the law would regulate child-care facilities nationwide. *The GOP's principal concern is how much the law would regulate child-care facilities nationwide.*

delimitate *delimit.* • You can use the hammer tool to hear how a chord (or any zone you delimitate) sounds. *You can use the hammer tool to hear how a chord (or any zone you delimit) sounds.* • In order to delimitate the kind of genres present in our text, I also took into account the kind of multidimensional approach proposed by Biber. *In order to delimit the kind of genres present in our text, I also took into*

account the kind of multidimensional approach proposed by Biber.

demise *death/end.* • That access is hastening the demise of many U.S. industries. *That access is hastening the end of many U.S. industries.*

denotate *denote.* • Rhythm and cadence primarily denotate the genre and the speech act. *Rhythm and cadence primarily denote the genre and the speech act.* • In the Arabic language, we find the general term Allah, which is used to denotate God and it is used as such also by Arabic speaking Christians. *In the Arabic language, we find the general term Allah, which is used to denote God and it is used as such also by Arabic speaking Christians.*

depart *leave.* • The president departs for Moscow this morning. *The president leaves for Moscow this morning.*

dependency *dependence.* • It may also be difficult for these people to make the decision to marry because of the dependency and commitment required in an intimate relationship. *It may also be difficult for these people to make the decision to marry because of the dependence and commitment required in an intimate relationship.*

depreciate in value *depreciate.* • He was carrying several hundred condos which depreciated between 10 and 30 percent in value. *He was carrying several hundred condos which depreciated between 10 and 30 percent.*

derive benefit (from) *benefit.* • This suggests that many people would derive benefit from "stand-up and stretch" workbreaks. *This suggests that many people would benefit from "stand-up and stretch" workbreaks.*

derive enjoyment from *admire/delight in/ enjoy/rejoice in/relish/savor.* • Although badgers and other mammals are trapped so that their pelts can be sold, the hunters also derive enjoyment from their activities. *Although badgers and other mammals are trapped so that their pelts can be sold, the hunters also enjoy their activities.*

derive pleasure from *admire/appreciate/delight in/enjoy/rejoice in/relish/savor.* • We derived great pleasure from their performance. *We delighted in their performance.* • You derive pleasure from traditional climbing, we derive pleasure from making sure you'll be well outfitted with the protection you need. *You enjoy traditional climbing, we enjoy making sure you'll be well outfitted with the protection you need.* • Most people in the industry derive pleasure from working with their horses, whether it's for a hobby or profit. *Most people in the industry relish working with their horses, whether it's for a hobby or profit.*

derive satisfaction from *admire/appreciate/ delight in/enjoy/rejoice in/relish/savor.* • If you derive genuine satisfaction from being in a leadership role, you will obviously bring that attitude to your role as a meeting leader. *If you genuinely enjoy being in a leadership role, you will obviously bring that attitude to your role as a meeting leader.*

descend down *descend.* • The summer months of December through February hit the mid-80s and descend down to the mid-60s at night. *The summer months of December through February hit the mid-80s and descend to the mid-60s at night.* • The ball will descend down at 11:59 tonight and take one minute to do so. *The ball will descend at 11:59 tonight and take one minute to do so.*

describe/explain in . . . detail *detail.* • The proposal should describe in detail the procedure to be used to obtain data. *The proposal should detail the procedure to be used to obtain data.*

desideratum *need.*

designate as *designate.* • Designating schools as failed or unsatisfactory could do more damage than the label of success would do good. *Designating schools failed or unsatisfactory could do more damage than the label of success would do good.* • It is standard convention to designate counterclockwise moment directions as positive and those in the clockwise direction as negative. *It is standard convention to designate counterclockwise moment directions positive and those in the clockwise direction negative.*

despite the fact that *although/but/even though/ still/though/yet.* • Despite the fact that all the charts are on paper rather than on-line, the bank reports that departments competed to improve their performance. *Although all the charts are on paper rather than on-line, the bank reports that departments competed to improve their performance.* • Despite the fact that often they're the only green spot in a concrete and asphalt jungle, golf courses are still targeted as threats to the environment. *Though often they're the only green spot in a concrete and asphalt jungle, golf courses are still targeted as threats to the environment.* • Schumer wants to break the law despite the fact that Bush administration officials say the current stockpile of Cipro is adequate. *Schumer wants to break the law even though Bush administration officials say the current stockpile of Cipro is adequate.*

detailed/in-depth analysis *analysis/detail.* • Apparently there are some who would discourage any detailed analysis of these weaknesses. *Apparently there are some who would discourage any analysis of these weaknesses.*

determine the truth/truthfulness/validity/ veracity of *verify.* • Consumers cannot easily inspect software to determine the truth of a manufacturer's claims about a product's expected behavior. *Consumers cannot easily inspect software to verify a manufacturer's claims about a product's expected behavior.*

devoid of *dis-/il-/im-/in-/ir-/lack/-less(ness)/ mis-/no/non-/not/un-/want/with no/without.* • Your editorial makes the term censorship somewhat devoid of meaning. *Your editorial makes the term censorship somewhat meaningless.*

diametrical *diametric/diametral.*

(five/many/several) different *(five/many/several)/different.* • My parents own five different homes. *My parents own five homes.*

different and distinct *different/distinct.* • The idea that each person's fingerprints were different and distinct from everyone else's was based on the work of Sir Francis Galton. *The idea that each person's fingerprints were different from everyone else's was based on the work of Sir Francis Galton.*

(a/the) difficult/hard/tough slog/task *slog/ task.* • It will still be a tough slog for them. *It will still be a slog for them.* • The difficult task of obtaining information for marketing decisionmaking presents two challenges. *The task of obtaining information for marketing decision-making presents two challenges.*

difficulty in/of -ing *difficulty -ing.* • She has great difficulty in falling asleep. *She has great difficulty falling asleep.*

diminish down *diminish.* • As this century advances, the difficulties that a writer of one gender has with portraying characters of the other gender will continue to diminish down. *As this century advances, the difficulties that a writer of one gender has with portraying characters of the other gender will continue to diminish.*

direct . . . attention to *advertise/announce/blazon/broadcast/disclose/divulge/expose/herald/ indicate/make known/make public/mention/point out/point to/present/proclaim/promote/publicize/ reveal/show/tell/uncover/unveil.* • The Draper award is seen by some engineering leaders as a way of directing attention to the profession and making sure engineers share the spotlight with scientists. *The Draper award is seen by some engineering leaders as a way of promoting the profession and making sure engineers share the spotlight with scientists.*

disassociate *dissociate.* • It set off calls by the faculty for nationally known conservatives to disassociate themselves from alleged Jew-baiting by the *Review,* which in the past has been accused of race-baiting and unfair characterization of women and homosexuals. *It set off calls by the faculty for nationally known conservatives to dissociate themselves from alleged Jew-baiting by the* Review, *which in the past has been accused of race-baiting and unfair characterization of women and homosexuals.* • Since a man does not disassociate responsibility and blame, he often refuses both. *Since a man does not dissociate responsibility and blame, he often refuses both.* • All you have to do is highlight the text—a range of characters if you want to disassociate them from the applied character style or one or more paragraphs if you want to disassociate it/them from the applied paragraph style. *All you have to do is highlight the text—a range of characters if you want to dissociate them from the applied character style or one or more paragraphs if you want to dissociate it/them from the applied paragraph style.*

discomfiture *discomfit/discomfort.*

(in) discussion *speaking/talking.* • At Honda, managers spend up to 50 percent of their time in discussions with dealers and distributors. *At Honda, managers spend up to 50 percent of their time talking with dealers and distributors.*

disenfranchise *disfranchise.* • Do we want to disenfranchise those voters? *Do we want to disfranchise those voters?*

display (a/the) . . . (for/of/to) delete. • The Task Manager displays a list of the programs that are currently running. *The Task Manager lists the programs that are currently running.* • All kids display a tendency to show minor misbehavior with their parents and other siblings. *All kids tend to show minor misbehavior with their parents and other siblings.* • It is not only individuals who display a liking for the word tabi, but companies too. *It is not only individuals who like the word tabi, but companies too.*

distinct difference (distinctly different) *different/distinct/distinction.* • We wanted to do something distinctly different. *We wanted to do something distinct.*

(a/the) diversity of different *assorted/a variety of/broad/countless/different/diverse/extensive/ many/numerous/scores of/sundry/varied/various/varying.* • The diversity of different types of music that the Society now offers would have been unheard of 20 years ago. *The diverse types of music that the Society now offers would have been unheard of 20 years ago.*

divide in half *halve.* • Divide in half and fold into the chocolate and vanilla pastry cream. *Halve and fold into the chocolate and vanilla pastry cream.*

divide up *divide.* • He suggested we divide up the money between us. *He suggested we divide the money between us.*

do (a/the) . . . (about/in/of/on/to) *-(al)ly* delete. • We did a thorough search of the area and found nothing. *We thoroughly searched the area and found nothing.* • They'd rather build a roadway than provide a program that prevents someone from doing harm to someone else. *They'd rather build a roadway than provide a program that prevents someone from harming someone else.* • Are we supposed to be doing the underlining of the title twice? *Are we supposed to be underlining the title twice?* • I don't think it took place, but we're going to do an investigation. *I don't think it took place, but we're going to investigate.* • I

don't think it would be a smart thing to let that team leave because it would really do damage to that city and the mentality of that city. *I don't think it would be a smart thing to let that team leave because it would really damage that city and the mentality of that city.*

do away with *cancel/destroy/end/kill/stop.*

doctorate degree *doctorate.* • While a number of people on Taiwan claim to be spirit mediums or shamans, it is rare that a shaman here has a doctorate degree. *While a number of people on Taiwan claim to be spirit mediums or shamans, it is rare that a shaman here has a doctorate.*

does not . . . any *no/none/nothing.* • I do not understand any of this. *I understand none of this.*

does not have to *need not.* • You do not have to specify extensions when you save or load files. *You need not specify extensions when you save or load files.* • Of course the article does not have to be this long. *Of course the article need not be this long.*

does not necessarily *need not.* • A long waiting time does not necessarily mean that your doctor is smart, successful, busy, dedicated, or involved in saving lives. *A long waiting time need not mean that your doctor is smart, successful, busy, dedicated, or involved in saving lives.*

does not pay attention to *ignores.* • We are pleased that the survey has emphasized that the existing practice of budgeting does not pay attention to its impact on women. *We are pleased that the survey has emphasized that the existing practice of budgeting ignores its impact on women.*

does not remember *forgets.*

$ . . . dollars *$ . . .* • A single day of downtime for one of these huge generators can cost up to

$1 million dollars. *A single day of downtime for one of these huge generators can cost up to $1 million.* • The maximum state award generally ranges between $10,000 and $25,000 dollars. *The maximum state award generally ranges between $10,000 and $25,000.*

dollar amount delete. • The daily maximum price change is 50 basis points, which is equivalent to a dollar amount of $1,250. *The daily maximum price change is 50 basis points, which is equivalent to $1,250.*

dollar value *value.*

domicile (*n*) *home/house.*

domicile (*v*) *dwell/live/reside.*

done/finished/over with *done/finished/over.*

doomed to fail/failure *doomed.* • The governor said the president's strategy is doomed to fail. *The governor said the president's strategy is doomed.*

dosage *dose.* • If the recommended dosage does not provide relief of symptoms or symptoms become worse, seek immediate medical attention. *If the recommended dose does not provide relief of symptoms or symptoms become worse, seek immediate medical attention.*

doubt but that *doubt that.* • Who can doubt but that those conditions are now met? *Who can doubt that those conditions are now met?*

(going) down the line/pike/road/way *at length/from now/in/in time/later/soon* delete. • Ten years down the line where are you going to be? *Ten years from now where are you going to be?* • A job may become available a few months down the road. *A job may become available in a few months.* • That will be a huge challenge going down the road. *That will be a huge challenge.*

down to a minimum of *down to.*

dramatical *dramatic.*

draw attention to *advertise/announce/blazon/broadcast/disclose/divulge/expose/herald/indicate/make known/make public/mention/point out/point to/present/proclaim/promote/publicize/reveal/show/tell/uncover/unveil.* • Our goal is to draw attention to what has been accomplished in improving the world food situation. *Our goal is to point out what has been accomplished in improving the world food situation.*

draw (a/the) conclusion (of) *conclude/deduce/draw/infer/reason.* • What conclusions were you able to draw from your experience? *What were you able to conclude from your experience?* • I drew the conclusion that competent readers make competent students and that competent students generally stay out of prison. *I concluded that competent readers make competent students and that competent students generally stay out of prison.*

draw (a/the) inference (of) *conclude/deduce/draw/infer/reason.* • If it does not find the employer's explanation adequate then it is entitled but not compelled to draw an inference of sex discrimination. *If it does not find the employer's explanation adequate then it is entitled but not compelled to infer sex discrimination.*

draw to a close/end *cease/close/complete/conclude/end/finish/halt/stop.* • Scientists expect to feel in the next few days a real sense of letdown as the first phase of humanity's exploration of the Earth's neighborhood draws to a close. *Scientists expect to feel in the next few days a real sense of letdown as the first phase of humanity's exploration of the Earth's neighborhood concludes.*

draw to a conclusion *cease/close/complete/conclude/end/finish/halt/stop.* • As these tasks draw to a conclusion, the panel needs to consider the contents of their report to the LGA Executive. *As these tasks conclude, the panel needs to consider the contents of their report to the LGA Executive.*

driving force *drive/energy/force/impetus/motivation/power.* • He is especially concerned about young people and is the driving force behind Catholic Schools United. *He is especially concerned about young people and is the impetus behind Catholic Schools United.*

drop down *down/drop.*

dualistic *dual.* • They have dualistic meanings. *They have dual meanings.*

due and payable *due/payable.* • The child support debt will be due and payable at particular periods. *The child support debt will be due at particular periods.* • The pension becomes due and payable 30 days after the retirement date. *The pension becomes payable 30 days after the retirement date.*

due to the fact that *because/considering/for/given/in that/since.* • This procedure is impractical due to the fact that the game tree for any interesting games is extremely large. *This procedure is impractical because the game tree for any interesting games is extremely large.* • We are unable to accept returns or issue refunds for any order due to the fact that this is a prescription medication. *We are unable to accept returns or issue refunds for any order since this is a prescription medication.*

duplicate copy *copy/duplicate.* • When you want a duplicate copy of one or more files, you use the COPY command. *When you want a copy of one or more files, you use the COPY command.*

during a/the juncture/juncture in time/ moment/moment in time/period/period in time/point/point in time/stage/stage in time/
time when *when.* • He had supported my friends and I during the time when we retrieved the abusive pictures from the Marine in Mississippi. *He had supported my friends and I when we retrieved the abusive pictures from the Marine in Mississippi.*

during the course/length of *during/for/in/over/throughout/when/while/with.* • During the course of the analysis, we suppose the array or list contains *n* elements. *Throughout the analysis, we suppose the array or list contains n elements.* • During the course of trying to negotiate with the gunmen, her husband was shot and killed. *While trying to negotiate with the gunmen, her husband was shot and killed.* • In addition, all regional students must attend one colloquium during the length of their enrollment. *In addition, all regional students must attend one colloquium during their enrollment.* • I wish to have my sheets replaced on a daily basis during the length of my stay. *I wish to have my sheets replaced on a daily basis during my stay.*

during/for/over the decade/period/period of time/span of time/time/years (from) . . . through/till/to/until *between . . . and/from . . . through/to.* • The fees and expenses of the non-interested Trustees for the period November 26, 1996, to October 31, 1997, amounted to $3,731. *The fees and expenses of the non-interested Trustees from November 26, 1996, to October 31, 1997, amounted to $3,731.*

during the period/period of time/span of time/ time/years (that) *while.* • You are not required to work during the period of time that you are enrolled as a full-time student. *You are not required to work while you are enrolled as a full-time student.* • What did M.C. Escher produce during the years that he lived in Belgium before the war? *What did M.C. Escher produce while he lived in Belgium before the war?*

during the rule of *under.* • It was turned into a Roman colony during the rule of Augustus, around the year 20 B.C. *It was turned into a Roman colony under Augustus, around the year 20 B.C.*

dwindle down *dwindle.* • A $10,000 gross bonus can dwindle down to a surprisingly small amount with income tax deductions. *A $10,000 gross bonus can dwindle to a surprisingly small amount with income tax deductions.*

dynamical *dynamic.*

E

each and every (one) *all/each/every (one).* • Each and every one of these crimes was committed by a pathological killer. *Each of these crimes was committed by a pathological killer.*

each one *each.* • My method is to introduce the key elements of office automation and explain each one in concrete terms. *My method is to introduce the key elements of office automation and explain each in concrete terms.*

(from) each other *delete.* • The two dates on the printout differ from each other because the first was entered as text and the second as a code. *The two dates on the printout differ because the first was entered as text and the second as a code.*

early beginnings *beginnings.*

-ed/-en before/earlier/previously *-ed/-en.* • Actually the term was used previously by Thomas Edison. *Actually the term was used by Thomas Edison.*

edifice *building.*

educational institution *college/school/university.* • Locate and identify a newsgroup available at your educational institution related to mar-

keting. *Locate and identify a newsgroup available at your school related to marketing.*

effectuate *achieve/bring about/carry out/effect/execute/realize.* • In order to effectuate this policy, the legislature imposed strict liability for all damages resulting from a failure to remove such materials on the owners of residential premises. *In order to effect this policy, the legislature imposed strict liability for all damages resulting from a failure to remove such materials on the owners of residential premises.*

efficacity *efficacy.*

e.g. . . . and others/and so forth/and so on/and such/and the like/et al./etc. *and others/and so forth/and so on/and such/and the like/e.g./et al./etc./for example/for instance.* • They typically have unpredictable ranges of occurrences, and they usually have related attributes (e.g., skill category, detailed skill description, etc.) that are of interest to the organization. *They typically have unpredictable ranges of occurrences, and they usually have related attributes (skill category, detailed skill description, etc.) that are of interest to the organization.* • Analyze the resulting circuit to determine the required quantities (e.g., voltage gain, input resistance, etc.). *Analyze the resulting circuit to determine the required quantities (e.g., voltage gain, input resistance).*

egoistical/egotistical *egoistic/egotistic.*

either one *either.* • The vice president doesn't like either one of them. *The vice president doesn't like either of them.*

elect as *elect.* • Whom will you elect as president? *Whom will you elect president?*

electrical *electric.*

(a/the) . . . element (in/of/to) *some* delete. • There will always be an element of doubt. *There will always be some doubt.* • The florid phrases and poor editing suggest some element of haste in the booklet's concoction. *The florid phrases and poor editing suggest some haste in the booklet's concoction.* • A common element to any system is the need for continuous top-management involvement. *Common to any system is the need for continuous top-management involvement.*

ellipses dots/marks/periods *ellipses.* • In my printout, the ellipses dots were the only item on the last line. *In my printout, the ellipses were the only item on the last line.*

elliptical *elliptic.*

emblematical *emblematic.*

emerge out *emerge.* • Part (d) corresponds to a time when the reflected shock waves have emerged out from the dust cloud. *Part (d) corresponds to a time when the reflected shock waves have emerged from the dust cloud.*

empathetic *empathic.*

employ *use.* • Fewer than one-tenth of the small business prospects worldwide employ computers today. *Fewer than one-tenth of the small business prospects worldwide use computers today.*

employment *use.* • The consistent employment of particular defenses leads to the development of personality traits. *The consistent use of particular defenses leads to the development of personality traits.*

employment opportunities *jobs.*

enable . . . to *let.* • This enables analysts to sense the need for changes in methods. *This lets analysts sense the need for changes in methods.*

encapsulate *encapsule.* • The responses provide a snapshot view of current U.S. efforts to use Japanese information and encapsulate some of the challenges faced by both providers and users. *The responses provide a snapshot view of current U.S. efforts to use Japanese information and encapsule some of the challenges faced by both providers and users.*

encircle *circle.*

enclosed herein/herewith is/please find *enclosed is/here is.* • Enclosed herewith please find a letter from our client, Mr. Edward Price, which is self-explanatory. *Here is a letter from our client, Mr. Edward Price, which is self-explanatory.* • Enclosed herein please find a really funny romantic comedy, submitted for your perusal. *Enclosed is a really funny romantic comedy, submitted for your perusal.*

enclosed in parentheses *in parentheses.* • The simplest sort of example is one in which the entire sentence is enclosed in parentheses. *The simplest sort of example is one in which the entire sentence is in parentheses.*

enclosed is *here is.*

encounter *find/have/meet* delete. • This support usually consists of a technical representative you can call if you encounter a problem. *This support usually consists of a technical representative you can call if you have a problem.*

endeavor *try.*

endorse on the back (of) *endorse.* • These are calculated on forms that resemble actual paychecks, which the students and their parents must endorse on the back. *These are calculated on forms that resemble actual paychecks, which the students and their parents must endorse.*

end product *product.* • Each writer has his or her own process because there are different ways to make the end product. *Each writer has his or her own process because there are different ways to make the product.*

end/final/net/ultimate result *result.* • The end result was a series of consolidations that lasted until a single company was left to serve the market. *The result was a series of consolidations that lasted until a single company was left to serve the market.*

engage in . . . (a/the) delete. • I appreciate the straightforward way in which you've engaged in this discussion. *I appreciate the straightforward way in which you've discussed this.* • Known as an active force in the labor movement, the unions at the Gillette France plant are engaged in a nationwide campaign to shape public opinion. *Known as an active force in the labor movement, the unions at the Gillette France plant are campaigning nationwide to shape public opinion.* • Keeping older people engaged in activity can give them a sense of self and wellbeing. *Keeping older people active can give them a sense of self and wellbeing.*

enter a bid *bid.* • Go to sfgoodwill.org and you can enter a bid for any of the 40 or so suits, shirts and ties that I didn't wear this past year. *Go to sfgoodwill.org and you can bid for any of the 40 or so suits, shirts and ties that I didn't wear this past year.*

enter into an agreement/contract *agree/contract.* • Courier Dispatch Group Inc. said it has entered into an agreement in principle to acquire the assets of J.A. Finn Inc. *Courier Dispatch Group Inc. said it has agreed in principle to acquire the assets of J.A. Finn Inc.* • The department may enter into an agreement with more than one association if the services provided by the associations are complementary. *The department may contract with more than one association if the services provided by the associations are complementary.*

entirely delete. • Our competition introduced an entirely new product. *Our competition introduced a new product.*

entitle *title.* • The report is entitled "Outlook for EFTPOS: An Executive Summary." *The report is titled "Outlook for EFTPOS: An Executive Summary."*

enumerate *count/list/name/numerate.*

epidemical *epidemic.*

epidemiological *epidemiologic.*

epigrammatical *epigrammatic.*

epigraphical *epigraphic.*

(the) equal/equivalent of *equal to/equivalent to/like.* • The loss of 1 high-value customer was the equivalent of losing the business of 36 small-value customers. *The loss of 1 high-value customer was equivalent to losing the business of 36 small-value customers.*

equally as *equally/as.* • It was equally as difficult for me. *It was equally difficult for me.* • Newer categories of antidepressant drugs are equally as effective as older generation antidepressants. *Newer categories of antidepressant drugs are as effective as older generation antidepressants.*

equitable *fair.*

eristical *eristic.*

(the) -(i)er . . . of the two *(the) -(i)er/(the) more.* • Sunday will probably be the better of the two days. *Sunday will probably be the better day.* • Their client is the younger of the two brothers. *Their client is the younger brother.*

-(i)er . . . rather than *-(i)er . . . than.* • It is quicker to multiply both sides by the reciprocal of the fraction rather than by the common denominator. *It is quicker to multiply both sides by the reciprocal of the fraction than by the common denominator.*

essential core *core/crux/essence/gist/pith/substance.* • The reviewer let himself be diverted by the book's feminist frame and missed its essential core. *The reviewer let himself be diverted by the book's feminist frame and missed its essence.*

(an/the) essential . . . for/in/of/to *essential to.* • Homeownership is an essential part of the American dream. *Homeownership is essential to the American dream.* • His point is that physical contact is an essential element in everyone's life, and most people don't get enough. *His point is that physical contact is essential to everyone's life, and most people don't get enough.* • Toughness is not an essential ingredient for getting ahead, and it isn't the same as resolve. *Toughness is not essential to getting ahead, and it isn't the same as resolve.*

essential prerequisite *essential/prerequisite.* • Categorizing a given product is an essential prerequisite for a successful marketing effort. *Categorizing a given product is essential for a successful marketing effort.*

establish *set up.*

establish conclusive evidence/proof of *prove.*

established standard *standard.* • Over the past few years, a number of spreadsheet, database, and word processing programs have become established standards in their areas of application. *Over the past few years, a number of spreadsheet, database, and word processing programs have become standards in their areas of application.*

established tradition *tradition.* • IBM broke established traditions and set up a special group at Boca Raton, Florida, to develop their own microcomputer. *IBM broke traditions and set up a special group at Boca Raton, Florida, to develop their own microcomputer.*

establishment *business/club/company/firm/shop/store.* • The state supreme court will decide whether to allow nude dancing to continue at that establishment. *The state supreme court will decide whether to allow nude dancing to continue at that club.*

-est ever *-est.* • That amount is the largest ever paid by the city in a civil right's action. *That amount is the largest paid by the city in a civil right's action.*

(an) estimated *about/around/close to/more or less/near/nearly/or so/roughly/some.* • An estimated 50,000 people lined up yesterday to register to vote. *Nearly 50,000 people lined up yesterday to register to vote.*

et cetera, et cetera, et cetera (etc., etc., etc.) *and so forth/and so on/and the like/etc.* • It quickly becomes confusing as you open one, copy what you want, find the application you want to paste it into, do the paste, go to the next application you need to copy something from, return to the one into which you're pasting, etc., etc., etc. *It quickly becomes confusing as you open one, copy what you want, find the application you want to paste it into, do the paste, go to the next application you need to copy something from, return to the one into which you're pasting, and so on.* • Others call the cameras by other names: deer cams, trail cams, game cams, etc., etc. *Others call the cameras by other names: deer cams, trail cams, game cams, etc.*

eventuality *consequence/ending/event/occurrence/outcome/result* delete. • Kodak should have prepared for this eventuality. *Kodak should have prepared for this.* • The best inoculation against such an eventuality is to decide, as a party, what risks we are ready to take and what fights we are willing to have. *The best inoculation against such an outcome is to decide, as a party, what risks we are ready to take and what fights we are willing to have.*

eventuate *arise/befall/come about/happen/occur/result/take place.* • What crises erupt and decisions eventuate from the moment your eyelids flutter open until the hour you fall asleep? *What crises erupt and decisions come about from the moment your eyelids flutter open until the hour you fall asleep?*

ever and anon *at times/now and again/now and then/occasionally/once in a while/on occasion/sometimes.*

every day/month/week/year *daily/monthly/weekly/yearly.*

every now and then *at times/from time to time/now and again/now and then/occasionally/once in a while/on occasion/sometimes.*

every once in a while *at times/from time to time/now and again/now and then/occasionally/once in a while/on occasion/sometimes.* • Every once in a while, I was struck by how hot it was. *Now and then, I was struck by how hot it was.*

every single (solitary) *all/every.* • Every single solitary juvenile in these four states was examined. *Every juvenile in these four states was examined.*

evidence in/to support (of/that) *evidence for (of/that).* • The great pay-raise debate is on, and the spectator sees very little evidence to support that higher salaries will attract and keep higher-quality candidates. *The great pay-raise debate is on, and the spectator sees very little evidence that higher salaries will attract and keep higher-quality candidates.* • This discovery provided evidence in support of the Copernican system and showed that everything did not revolve around the Earth. *This discovery provided evidence of the Copernican system and showed that everything did not revolve around the Earth.*

evolve over time *evolve.* • Long experience shows that our first accounts of terrorist attacks and other tragedies often evolve over time. *Long experience shows that our first accounts of terrorist attacks and other tragedies often evolve.*

exact/exactly duplicate *duplicate/exact/identical/match/(the) same.* • Nothing could exactly duplicate what we just heard. *Nothing could match what we just heard.*

exact/exactly equivalent *duplicate/equivalent/exact/identical/match/(the) same.* • This situation is exactly equivalent to our usual neglect of the Earth's rotation when we do experiments in laboratories. *This situation is equivalent to our usual neglect of the Earth's rotation when we do experiments in laboratories.*

exact/exactly identical *duplicate/exact/identical/match/(the) same.* • This pattern, though not exactly identical, tends to recur every year. *This pattern, though not identical, tends to recur every year.*

exactly sure *sure.* • I'm not exactly sure of her name. *I'm not sure of her name.*

exact/exactly match *duplicate/exact/identical/match/(the) same.* • When you enter a value that doesn't exactly match one of those listed on the lookup table, the function will find the value equal to or less than the value being looked up. *When you enter a value that doesn't match one of those listed on the lookup table, the function will find the value equal to or less than the value being looked up.*

exact/exactly (the) same *duplicate/exact/identical/just/match/(the) same.* • He used those exact same words. *He used those exact words.*

examination *exam.*

(an) example that illustrates/to illustrate *example (of)/(to) illustrate.* • Here are some examples to illustrate the benefits of word processing on a network. *Here are some examples of the benefits of word processing on a network.*

except when *unless.* • Jessie rarely saw him, except when he came home to sleep. *Jessie rarely saw him, unless he came home to sleep.*

excerption *excerpt.*

(a/the) excessive amount (of) *excessive/too much.*

(a/the) excessive number (of) *excessive/too many.* • If your failure to detect errors in the proofing stage results in a published text that contains an excessive number of errors, the costs of making these corrections in a subsequent printing will be charged against your royalties. *If your failure to detect errors in the proofing stage results in a published text that contains excessive errors, the costs of making these corrections in a subsequent printing will be charged against your royalties.*

excess verbiage *verbiage.* • Excess verbiage befogs language. *Verbiage befogs language.*

excruciatingly painful *excruciating/painful.* • It has been an excruciatingly painful experience for the town's 8,000 residents. *It has been an excruciating experience for the town's 8,000 residents.*

(the) existence of delete. • The existence of even one extra, undocumented Write statement in a module may change what appears on a user's terminal. *Even one extra, undocumented Write statement in a module may change what appears on a user's terminal.*

(that) exist to . . . delete. • Ample evidence exists to support the differences in investment tax shields across industries. *Ample evidence supports the differences in investment tax shields across industries.* • Believe it or not, it is freely admitted even within the ranks of psychiatry that no conclusive evidence exists to show that any form of mental illness is biologically caused. *Believe it or not, it is freely admitted even within*

the ranks of psychiatry that no conclusive evidence shows that any form of mental illness is biologically caused. • County attorneys have broad discretion in this area, and generally do not file charges unless they are satisfied that sufficient evidence exists to prove the crime beyond a reasonable doubt. *County attorneys have broad discretion in this area, and generally do not file charges unless they are satisfied that sufficient evidence proves the crime beyond a reasonable doubt.*

expect/expectation and hope *expect/expectation/hope/trust.* • We're pleased with our progress and expect and hope that it will continue as our initiatives take hold. *We're pleased with our progress and expect that it will continue as our initiatives take hold.*

expediency *expedience.*

expeditiously *abruptly/apace/briskly/directly/ fast/forthwith/hastily/hurriedly/posthaste/presently/promptly/quickly/rapidly/right away/ shortly/soon/speedily/straightaway/swiftly/ wingedly.* • This problem must be dealt with expeditiously. *This problem must be dealt with quickly.*

expenditure (of money) *cost/expense.* • He deplored the long electoral campaigns that involved heavy expenditures of money and brought the country to a virtual standstill for months. *He deplored the long electoral campaigns that involved heavy costs and brought the country to a virtual standstill for months.*

expenses and costs *costs/expenses.*

(a/the) . . . experience delete. • Just getting up in the morning is a painful experience for her. *Just getting up in the morning is painful for her.* • I wasn't afraid; it wasn't a nightmare, but it was a rather startling experience. *I wasn't afraid; it wasn't a nightmare, but it was rather startling.*

experience delete. • This magazine has experienced tremendous growth in the past two years. *This magazine has grown tremendously in the past two years.* • Today, nearly 50 years after I had experienced reading "colored need not apply," job segregation and discrimination still exist for African-Americans who are not trained for the better-paying jobs. *Today, nearly 50 years after I had read "colored need not apply," job segregation and discrimination still exist for African-Americans who are not trained for the better-paying jobs.*

experience *feel/find/go through/have/know/see/sense/suffer.* • According to this book, many people have experienced boredom and alienation. *According to this book, many people have known boredom and alienation.* • The goal was to show people all over the world laughing and having fun, and to emphasize the fact that all human beings are born with the ability to experience joy. *The goal was to show people all over the world laughing and having fun, and to emphasize the fact that all human beings are born with the ability to feel joy.*

exploitative *exploitive.* • New research reveals how to spot a sexually exploitative man no matter how famous, respected or "safe" he appears. *New research reveals how to spot a sexually exploitive man no matter how famous, respected or "safe" he appears.*

express . . . (about/for/of/to) delete. • He expressed doubt whether the issue would be much of a headache on the campaign trail this fall. *He doubted whether the issue would be much of a headache on the campaign trail this fall.* • Many express open admiration for women who are healthy, well-groomed, and confident. *Many openly admire women who are healthy, well-groomed, and confident.* • Most top executives seem to believe strongly in the need for better human relations, but they often express distrust of the training program itself. *Most top executives seem to believe strongly in the need for better human relations, but they often distrust the training program itself.* • We wish to express our sincere thanks to our special representative for her responsiveness. *We wish to sincerely thank our special representative for her responsiveness.*

express concern (about) *agonize (over/about)/brood (on/over)/dread/fear/fret (about/over)/regret/stew (about/over)/worry (about/over).* • Some scientists express concern about the implications of splicing the genes for certain insecticides into plants. *Some scientists worry about the implications of splicing the genes for certain insecticides into plants.*

express opposition to *contest/criticize/disagree with/disapprove of/dispute/object to/oppose/protest.*

express skepticism (about) *disbelieve/distrust/doubt/mistrust/question.* • But others express skepticism about those results, with some scientists' questions verging upon accusations of exaggeration. *But others distrust those results, with some scientists' questions verging upon accusations of exaggeration.*

express sorrow (about) *bemoan/deplore/grieve/lament/moan/mourn/regret.* • At a press conference earlier in the day, he had expressed sorrow that American writers and American politics seem to occupy two different worlds. *At a press conference earlier in the day, he had bemoaned that American writers and American politics seem to occupy two different worlds.*

extend/issue an invitation to *invite.* • The Open Software Foundation would like to extend an invitation to you to explore the OSF/Motif user environment. *The Open Software Foundation would like to invite you to explore the OSF/Motif user environment.*

(after/for/in/over/within) (an) extended/lengthy/long/prolonged/protracted amount of time/length of time/period/period of time/span of time/time/while *after (for/in/over/*

within) (one) month (year)/at last/at length/even-tually/finally/in due time/in time/over the months (years)/over time/ultimately/with time delete. • If you truly want to sell your home and you aren't getting offers within an extended amount of time, you may need to drop the price. *If you truly want to sell your home and you aren't getting offers within four months, you may need to drop the price.* • After a prolonged period of time we finally have the next batch of episodes ready for your viewing pleasure. *We finally have the next batch of episodes ready for your viewing pleasure.* • Who knows, after a lengthy span of time, we might actually get to know what we are doing. *Who knows, in time, we might actually get to know what we are doing.*

extend out *extend.* • Press the right arrow until the highlight extends out to cell F4, and then press Return. *Press the right arrow until the highlight extends to cell F4, and then press Return.*

extensively throughout *all through/extensively in (through)/throughout.* • Our reporter has traveled extensively throughout South America. *Our reporter has traveled throughout South America.*

(an/a certain/some) extent of *a certain/much/some/somewhat* delete.

(an/the) . . . extent of delete. • The opening of the first permanently located fair was September 24, 1894, and it ran for an extent of six days. *The opening of the first permanently located fair was September 24, 1894, and it ran for six days.* • And between Coney Island and Rockaway inlet there is an extent of some five miles of beach that could be used for re-embarkations. *And between Coney Island and Rockaway inlet there is some five miles of beach that could be used for re-embarkations.*

(the) extent of *how much/the* delete. • Most people know something about Social Security, but few know the extent of the monthly benefits

they will eventually receive when they retire. *Most people know something about Social Security, but few know the monthly benefits they will eventually receive when they retire.* • Despite early campaign rhetoric, the extent of actual change a new treasurer would attempt is of course unknown. *Despite early campaign rhetoric, how much actual change a new treasurer would attempt is of course unknown.*

(the) extent to which *how/how far/how much/how often.* • The extent to which these facilitating and reconciling capabilities are needed, and how they are developed and structured, depends on the company's involvement in exporting or foreign marketing. *How much these facilitating and reconciling capabilities are needed, and how they are developed and structured, depends on the company's involvement in exporting or foreign marketing.* • Eastern cannot predict the extent to which its operations and financial results will continue to be affected by the negative public perception generated by the investigations. *Eastern cannot predict how its operations and financial results will continue to be affected by the negative public perception generated by the investigations.*

extricate . . . out *extricate.* • His brother jumped into the hole to try to extricate him out. *His brother jumped into the hole to try to extricate him.*

F

face up to *face.* • The men face up to 10 years in prison if found guilty. *The men face 10 years in prison if found guilty.*

facilitate *ease/help/promote/simplify.*

facility *bathroom/building/factory/hospital/jail/office/place/plant/prison/school/site* delete. • In 1986, hospital executives estimated that 21 percent of their facilities might close. *In 1986, hos-*

pital executives estimated that 21 percent of their hospitals might close.

(a/the) . . . fact delete. • This is an alarming fact, considering that these workers make up the foundation of our service-sector economy. *This is alarming, considering that these workers make up the foundation of our service-sector economy.*

(the) fact is (that) *actually/indeed/in fact/in faith/in truth/really/truly* delete. • The fact is we have to deal with the public every day. *We have to deal with the public every day.* • The fact is that Mrs. Eddy doesn't advocate any kind of a positive thinking or "think good, feel good" philosophy. *Indeed, Mrs. Eddy doesn't advocate any kind of a positive thinking or "think good, feel good" philosophy.*

(the) (simple) fact of the matter is (that) *actually/indeed/in fact/in faith/in reality/in truth/really/truly* delete. • The fact of the matter is you cannot copyright an idea. *You cannot copyright an idea.*

(a/the) . . . factor (in/of/to) delete. • The fact that we could not have children was a contributing factor to our divorce. *The fact that we could not have children contributed to our divorce.* • Knowing the consequences of obesity should be a motivating factor in losing weight. *Knowing the consequences of obesity should be a motivation in losing weight.* • Researchers indicate, however, that after age 50 lifestyle becomes a less influential factor in physiological change than aging itself. *Researchers indicate, however, that after age 50 lifestyle becomes less influential in physiological change than aging itself.*

(the) fact remains (that) delete. • The fact remains we have the overwhelming support of the Christian and Jewish religions. *We have the overwhelming support of the Christian and Jewish religions.*

facts and information *facts/information.* • Request a full disclosure statement highlighting all the pertinent facts and information about the franchisor. *Request a full disclosure statement highlighting all the pertinent facts about the franchisor.*

(the) fact that *that.* • This ignores the fact that increased use of kilowatts has significantly decreased our use of oil. *This ignores that increased use of kilowatts has significantly decreased our use of oil.*

factual and accurate *accurate/factual.*

factual basis *basis/fact/reason/truth.* • People who know me know there's no factual basis to the story. *People who know me know there's no truth to the story.*

fail to comply with *break/disobey/violate.* • The Federal Trade Commission is readying a crackdown on commercial sites that fail to comply with the law. *The Federal Trade Commission is readying a crackdown on commercial sites that violate the law.* • In the future, farmers and drivers who fail to comply with the biosecurity requirements are likely to be reported for prosecution. *In the future, farmers and drivers who disobey the biosecurity requirements are likely to be reported for prosecution.*

fair/just and equitable *fair/just/equitable.* • I support fair and equitable taxes to insure human services are funded. *I support equitable taxes to insure human services are funded.*

fair and square *fair/honest/just/square.*

false and misleading *deceptive/false/misleading.*

false illusion *illusion.*

false pretense *pretense.*

far and away *by far/much.* • The judgment was for $10.3 billion, far and away the biggest ever in American commerce. *The judgment was for*

$10.3 billion, by far the biggest ever in American commerce.

far and wide *broadly/widely.*

far away from *far from.* • These blocks are usually physically located far away from the file's data blocks. *These blocks are usually physically located far from the file's data blocks.*

(what is) (the) fashion/manner/way in which/ that *how.* • What do you think about the fashion in which this testing program was introduced into the plant? *What do you think about how this testing program was introduced into the plant?* • More important than the sample's size is the manner in which the sample is taken. *More important than the sample's size is how the sample is taken.*

fasten shut *fasten.* • *Bulletin* signified the seal on a message, often a warm ball of wax pressed flat by a metal seal and used to fasten shut an important short document. Bulletin *signified the seal on a message, often a warm ball of wax pressed flat by a metal seal and used to fasten an important short document.* • Use strips of self-sticking Velcro to fasten shut your fridge or cabinets. *Use strips of self-sticking Velcro to fasten your fridge or cabinets.*

fasten together *fasten.* • Screw threads provide a fast and easy method of fastening two parts together and of exerting a force that can be used for adjustment of movable parts. *Screw threads provide a fast and easy method of fastening two parts and of exerting a force that can be used for adjustment of movable parts.*

favor . . . as opposed to/instead of/rather than *favor . . . over/favor . . . to.* • Lager is a pale, American-style beer favored by the young as opposed to the dark, traditional "bitter" English beer. *Lager is a pale, American-style beer favored by the young over the dark, traditional "bitter" English beer.* • He is armed, like his men, with a cut-down musket and a tomahawk, which the

Rangers favored instead of traditional European edged weapons. *He is armed, like his men, with a cut-down musket and a tomahawk, which the Rangers favored over traditional European edged weapons.*

fear and trembling *anxiety/dismay/dread/fear/ foreboding/horror/terror/trembling.*

(a/the) . . . feeling(s) (of) delete. • We describe the intensity of the feeling of anger along a four-point scale. *We describe the intensity of anger along a four-point scale.* • Neither of us has any guilt feelings about it. *Neither of us has any guilt about it.*

feel inside *feel.* • What's most important is how you feel inside about it. *What's most important is how you feel about it.*

(the) female/male gender/sex *females/males/ men/women.* • I like talking to the female gender. *I like talking to women.*

fervency *fervor.*

few and far between *exiguous/few/infrequent/ meager/rare/scant/scanty/scarce/scattered/sel-dom/sparse/uncommon/unusual.* • Since then the shooting stars have been few and far between. *Since then the shooting stars have been infrequent.*

few/small in number *exiguous/few/infrequent/ limited/meager/not many/rare/scant/scanty/ scarce/sparse/uncommon.* • Although the clinical trials are few in number and have small patient populations, the response rates are higher than those reported with intravenous chemotherapy. *Although the clinical trials are few and have small patient populations, the response rates are higher than those reported with intravenous chemotherapy.* • New projects are too small and few in number to make up for the shrinking volumes. *New projects are too small and scarce to make up for the shrinking volumes.*

fictional novel *novel.* • Among the sports memorabilia Levy will be auctioning online is an autographed copy of the fictional novel he wrote, *Between the Lies. Among the sports memorabilia Levy will be auctioning online is an autographed copy of the novel he wrote,* Between the Lies.

(the) field of delete. • This process became known as Boolean algebra and is widely used in the fields of computing and philosophy. *This process became known as Boolean algebra and is widely used in computing and philosophy.*

fiery conflagration *conflagration/fire.* • In 1993, after a 51 day siege with federal law-enforcement agencies, Koresh and 81 members of his sect died in a fiery conflagration. *In 1993, after a 51 day siege with federal law-enforcement agencies, Koresh and 81 members of his sect died in a conflagration.*

fifty/50 percent (of) *half (of)/one-half (of).* • Nearly fifty percent of the town's population is associated with the university. *Nearly half the town's population is associated with the university.*

figuratively speaking *as it were/in a sense/in a way/so to speak.*

(a/the) . . . figure delete. • Alan Paton has become something of a legendary figure. *Alan Paton has become something of a legend.*

fill to capacity *fill.* • The auditorium was filled to capacity with the singer's adoring fans. *The auditorium was filled with the singer's adoring fans.*

fill up *fill.* • Fill up the tank when you're in town. *Fill the tank when you're in town.*

filter out *filter.* • It's very hard to filter out fact from fiction. *It's very hard to filter fact from fiction.*

filthy dirty *dirty/filthy.*

final and irrevocable *final/irrevocable.* • His decision not to seek a fourth term as governor is final and irrevocable. *His decision not to seek a fourth term as governor is final.*

final/ultimate completion *completion.* • Because the order, timing, and costs of the individual tasks are interrelated, they all affect the total cost of the project and its final completion date. *Because the order, timing, and costs of the individual tasks are interrelated, they all affect the total cost of the project and its completion date.*

final/ultimate conclusion *conclusion.* • I haven't yet come to a final conclusion about what we should do. *I haven't yet come to a conclusion about what we should do.*

final/ultimate culmination *culmination.* • The Graduation Review serves as the final culmination of the MA Program in terms of review, reflection, summative integration and completed documentation. *The Graduation Review serves as the culmination of the MA Program in terms of review, reflection, summative integration and completed documentation.*

finalize *complete/conclude/finish.* • After five or ten successful projects, you should review guidelines and begin to finalize the procedure. *After five or ten successful projects, you should review guidelines and begin to complete the procedure.*

final/ultimate outcome *outcome.* • We were saddened by the final outcome. *We were saddened by the outcome.*

final/ultimate resolution *resolution.* • The ultimate resolution of such matters will not have a material adverse impact on AT&Ts financial position. *The resolution of such matters will not have a material adverse impact on AT&T's financial position.*

final/ultimate settlement *settlement.*

financial/monetary resources *assets/capital/finances/funds/money/resources.*

financial wherewithal *assets/capital/cash/finances/funds/means/money/wherewithal.* • The commission also is considering whether owners have the financial wherewithal to operate the plant. *The commission also is considering whether owners have the money to operate the plant.*

find out *find/learn.* • We found out that today's teenagers are very anxious about the future. *We learned that today's teenagers are very anxious about the future.*

(all) fine/good and good/well *all right/fine/good/great/nice/pleasant/pleasing/welcome/well.* • It's all fine and good to settle into a comfortable routine. *It's fine to settle into a comfortable routine.*

finish off *finish.* • But though I could have finished off the final thirty-nine pages fairly easily before going to bed, I decided not to. *But though I could have finished the final thirty-nine pages fairly easily before going to bed, I decided not to.*

finish up *finish.*

firm/strong commitment *commitment.* • Voters are not firmly committed to any of the candidates. *Voters are not committed to any of the candidates.*

firm/strong conviction *conviction.* • This participative process has enabled us to develop a strong conviction throughout the Company that our strategy is the right one. *This participative process has enabled us to develop a conviction throughout the Company that our strategy is the right one.*

firmly establish *establish/firm.* • We should have resolved them earlier in the implementation of the reorganization, before structure and behavior patterns became firmly established. *We should have resolved them earlier in the implementation of the reorganization, before structure and behavior patterns became firm.*

firm/strong resolution *resolution.*

first and foremost *chief/chiefly/first/foremost/main/mainly/mostly/primarily/primary/principal/principally* delete. • Football is first and foremost a running game. *Football is primarily a running game.*

first and last *only/sole.*

first and only *only/sole.* • Was he the first and only person to have superheated ice, yet whose work has fallen into obscurity? *Was he the only person to have superheated ice, yet whose work has fallen into obscurity?*

first . . . before *before.* • You cannot print a document on the disk that has been fast-saved unless you first positioned the cursor at the end of the document before you saved it. *You cannot print a document on the disk that has been fast-saved unless you positioned the cursor at the end of the document before you saved it.* • The only way to prevent such occurrences is to ensure that the nodes performing the restoration first determine the type of failure before invoking their restoration mechanisms. *The only way to prevent such occurrences is to ensure that the nodes performing the restoration determine the type of failure before invoking their restoration mechanisms.* • Complications due to sampling and disease need to be first eliminated before firm conclusions can be made. *Complications due to sampling and disease need to be eliminated before firm conclusions can be made.*

first begin *begin/start.* • If you note the appropriate framework when you first begin your assignment, you will be able to relate what you know from these broader areas to the text at hand. *If you note the appropriate framework when you begin your assignment, you will be able to relate what you know from these broader areas to the text at hand.*

first/initially coined *coined.* • The term *psychic distance* was initially coined by Swedish researchers at the University of Uppsala. *The term* psychic distance *was coined by Swedish researchers at the University of Uppsala.*

first come into being *arise/begin/start.* • When Social Security first came into being, relatively few people lived to the retirement age of 65, so the many were supporting the few. *When Social Security began, relatively few people lived to the retirement age of 65, so the many were supporting the few.*

first created *created.*

first ever *first.* • This was the first-ever congressional review of the condition of wilderness areas protected from development under a landmark 1964 law. *This was the first congressional review of the condition of wilderness areas protected from development under a landmark 1964 law.*

first initially *first/initially.* • When he first initially got the complaint, he wrote a letter to the Human Rights Commission admitting his guilt. *When he first got the complaint, he wrote a letter to the Human Rights Commission admitting his guilt.*

first introduced *introduced.* • He built on some ideas first introduced by Leibniz almost 200 years earlier. *He built on some ideas introduced by Leibniz almost 200 years earlier.*

first invented *invented.* • The idea of a sweet treat was first invented by cavemen who ate honey from bee hives. *The idea of a sweet treat was invented by cavemen who ate honey from bee hives.*

firstly *first.* • Firstly, Brookside Estates is a privately managed and maintained housing complex. *First, Brookside Estates is a privately managed and maintained housing complex.* • Firstly, the users of system A may be convinced that system A is far superior to the universal standard. *First, the users of system A may be convinced that system A is far superior to the universal standard.*

first of all *first.* • I would first of all ask how many of you are going to help us. *I would first ask how many of you are going to help us.*

first off *first.* • First off, these price and yield figures are for multimillion-dollar dealer-to-dealer negotiated transactions at any given hour or day. *First, these price and yield figures are for multimillion-dollar dealer-to-dealer negotiated transactions at any given hour or day.*

first start *begin/start.* • The market share of Searle's Calan was fairly low when we first started. *The market share of Searle's Calan was fairly low when we began.*

first time ever *first time.* • It's the first time ever that disabled skiers were represented at the Olympics. *It's the first time that disabled skiers were represented at the Olympics.*

fly in the face of *challenge/contradict/defy/dispute/disregard/go against/ignore/neglect/overlook.* • Although it may be morally reassuring, this tale flies in the face of historical fact. *Although it may be morally reassuring, this tale defies historical fact.*

focal point *center/focus.* • The U.S.-Canada trade agreement has been the focal point of the campaign. *The U.S.-Canada trade agreement has been the focus of the campaign.*

focus (media/people's/public) attention on/upon *advertise/announce/blazon/broadcast/disclose/divulge/expose/herald/indicate/make* known/make public/mention/point out/point to/ present/proclaim/promote/publicize/reveal/ show/tell/uncover/unveil. • All this has helped us focus attention on the problem. *All this has helped us publicize the problem.*

focus . . . attention on/upon *concentrate on/ focus on.* • It's time we focus our attention on the plight of the poor. *It's time we focus on the plight of the poor.* • I was too wrapped up in my own concerns to be able to focus my attention on him. *I was too wrapped up in my own concerns to be able to concentrate on him.*

focus . . . effort on/upon *concentrate on/focus on.* • He said the crew would focus efforts on saving baby penguins. *He said the crew would concentrate on saving baby penguins.*

focus . . . energy on/upon *concentrate on/focus on.* • If production focuses its energies on manufacturing a product at the lowest possible cost, but the sales department is willing to accept unprofitable orders, conflict will arise. *If production focuses on manufacturing a product at the lowest possible cost, but the sales department is willing to accept unprofitable orders, conflict will arise.*

focus in *focus.* • We're focusing in on what we have to do to achieve this. *We're focusing on what we have to do to achieve this.*

focus of attention *cynosure/focus.*

focus . . . time and energy on/upon *concentrate on/focus on.* • With Bonney managing all aspects of our temporary staffing program, our HR staff is able to focus time and energy on other responsibilities. *With Bonney managing all aspects of our temporary staffing program, our HR staff is able to focus on other responsibilities.*

fold up *fold.* • The commission folded up because the voters implicitly voted to have it fold up. *The commission folded because the voters implicitly voted to have it fold.*

follow after *follow.* • Your META tags should follow after your <TITLE></TITLE> tags. *Your META tags should follow your <TITLE></ TITLE> tags.* • The company's marketing manager explained that more celebration activities would follow after the basketball tournament. *The company's marketing manager explained that more celebration activities would follow the basketball tournament.*

follow along the lines of *ape/copy/be like/duplicate/imitate/look like/match/mimic/replicate/ resemble.* • There might be a settlement on rates by the end of this year; however, we doubt it will follow along the lines of the New York rate case moratorium. *There might be a settlement on rates by the end of this year; however, we doubt it will resemble the New York rate case moratorium.* • If you are looking for a good vampire novel that doesn't follow along the lines of authors past, try wrapping your fangs around the on-going saga of "The Red Fang." *If you are looking for a good vampire novel that doesn't imitate authors past, try wrapping your fangs around the on-going saga of "The Red Fang."*

follow . . . below *below/follow.* • Look at the following sentences below. *Look at the following sentences.*

food fare *fare/food.* • As we went from line to line, we couldn't believe how many were willing to wait so long for just a small portion of the food fare being offered. *As we went from line to line, we couldn't believe how many were willing to wait so long for just a small portion of the fare being offered.*

foot pedal *pedal.* • Investigators believe a thick metal foot pedal in the helicopter stopped the bullet from striking the pilot. *Investigators believe a thick metal pedal in the helicopter stopped the bullet from striking the pilot.*

for all intents and purposes *effectively/essentially/in effect/in essence/practically/virtually.* • Following the treatment with interleukin-2, the nodule for all intents and purposes disappeared. *Following the treatment with interleukin-2, the nodule virtually disappeared.*

for all practical purposes *effectively/essentially/in effect/in essence/practically/virtually.* • For all practical purposes, there will be no expansion in existing programs. *There will be virtually no expansion in existing programs.* • For all practical purposes, there are but two ways to get this information. *In essence, there are but two ways to get this information.*

for a long time/while *long.* • She has wanted to travel to Europe for a long time. *She has long wanted to travel to Europe.*

for (an) extended/prolonged/protracted amount of time/length of time/period/period of time/span of time/time/while *awhile/for a long time/while/for a time/while/for days (hours/weeks/years)/long.* • We had observed this family for a prolonged period of time. *We had long observed this family.*

for another (thing) *second.* • For another thing, there is still ample legal precedent for highly effective affirmative action programs that stop short of specific quotas. *Second, there is still ample legal precedent for highly effective affirmative action programs that stop short of specific quotas.*

forasmuch as *because/considering/for/given/in that/since.* • Forasmuch as Brian and Laura have consented together in wedlock, and have pledged themselves each to the other in the presence of this company, I do now pronounce that they are husband and wife. *In that Brian and Laura have consented together in wedlock, and have pledged themselves each to the other in the presence of this company, I do now pronounce that they are husband and wife.*

for a while *awhile.* • After this program executes for a while, procedure B is called. *After this program executes awhile, procedure B is called.*

for awhile *awhile.* • If the program continues to run for awhile, the answer may not be so clear. *If the program continues to run awhile, the answer may not be so clear.*

forebearer *forebear.* • Episodic reform movements were separated by long periods when many citizens, much like their Colonial forebearers, fantasized that Americans had created a near-utopian society. *Episodic reform movements were separated by long periods when many citizens, much like their Colonial forebears, fantasized that Americans had created a near-utopian society.*

forecast . . . future *forecast/foretell/predict.* • After a model is identified as being a good predictor, it is used to forecast future sales. *After a model is identified as being a good predictor, it is used to forecast sales.*

(the) foregoing *that/those/the/this (these).* • On top of the foregoing, the recent legislation on extending mandatory retirement further heightens the concern about job performance in the later years. *On top of this, the recent legislation on extending mandatory retirement further heightens the concern about job performance in the later years.*

foreign import *import.* • Of course he's against foreign imports, the Mariners don't have the money to bring in top overseas players. *Of course he's against imports, the Mariners don't have the money to bring in top overseas players.* • Norman farmers have even set fire to live lambs in a dispute over cheap foreign imports. *Norman farmers have even set fire to live lambs in a dispute over cheap imports.*

(the) forenamed *that/those/the/this (these).*

foretell . . . future *forecast/foretell/predict.* • If you choose to believe that the cards do foretell future events, the obvious follow-up question is whether events suggested by the cards are set in stone, or whether they can be avoided. *If you choose to believe that the cards do foretell events, the obvious follow-up question is whether events suggested by the cards are set in stone, or whether they can be avoided.*

forever and a day *always/ceaselessly/consistently/constantly/endlessly/eternally/everlastingly/everyday/forever/invariably/never ending/perpetually/routinely/unfailingly.*

forevermore *always/evermore/forever.* • I am not naive enough to think that we will forevermore walk hand in hand with the business community to clean the environment. *I am not naive enough to think that we will forever walk hand in hand with the business community to clean the environment.*

forewarn *warn.* • We do, however, forewarn the authorities in charge of our planet's destiny against decisions which are supported by pseudoscientific arguments or false and nonrelevant data. *We do, however, warn the authorities in charge of our planet's destiny against decisions which are supported by pseudoscientific arguments or false and nonrelevant data.*

for example/for instance *say.* • When the scanner reads the bar code on, for example, a can of beans, the computer looks up the product number the bar code represents and returns its name and price to the register. *When the scanner reads the bar code on, say, a can of beans, the computer looks up the product number the bar code represents and returns its name and price to the register.*

for example . . . and others/and so forth/and so on/and such/and the like/et al./etc./or whatever *and others/and so forth/and so on/and such/and the like/et al./etc./or/e.g./for example/for instance.* • Many other examples of the influence religion has on buyer behavior—for example, on values and norms, time, sense of self, and so forth—will be found in the following sections. *Many other examples of the influence religion has on buyer behavior—on values and norms, time, sense of self, and so forth—will be found in the following sections.*

for fear (that/of) . . . (can/could/may/might/shall/should/will/would) *lest.* • Few of us know what to say to friends who are mourning, so we may avoid them for fear we'll say the wrong thing. *Few of us know what to say to friends who are mourning, so we may avoid them lest we say the wrong thing.* • The Arab League has meanwhile refused to transfer millions of dollars in aid to the PA for fear that top officials would lay their hands on the money. *The Arab League has meanwhile refused to transfer millions of dollars in aid to the PA lest top officials lay their hands on the money.*

for free *free.* • Purchasers of 1.0 versions will receive 1.1 upgrades for free from IBM. *Purchasers of 1.0 versions will receive free 1.1 upgrades from IBM.*

for/in/to (the) furtherance of *for/to advance/to foster/to further/to promote.* • Neither the conspiracy itself nor the overt acts allegedly done in furtherance of it were directed toward Boisjoly. *Neither the conspiracy itself nor the overt acts allegedly done to foster it were directed toward Boisjoly.* • This is done in furtherance of the principle that all witness identifications be made independently. *This is done to advance the principle that all witness identifications be made independently.* • In furtherance of its corporate purposes, the corporation shall have all the general powers enumerated in Article 1396-2.02. *To further its corporate purposes, the corporation shall have all the general powers enumerated in Article 1396-2.02.*

for (an) indefinite/indeterminate amount of time/length of time/period/period of time/span of time/time/while *briefly/for a time/for a while/indefinitely/temporarily.* • We are freezing prices and wages for an indefinite period. *We are freezing prices and wages temporarily.*

for instance . . . and others/and so forth/and so on/and such/and the like/et al./etc./or whatever *and others/and so forth/and so on/and such/and the like/et al./etc./or/e.g./for example/for instance.* • Use one of these labels to assign a number and perhaps a descriptive title to each disk, for instance, Disk 1: Letters, Disk 2: Spreadsheet Files, Disk 3: Reports, and so on. *Use one of these labels to assign a number and perhaps a descriptive title to each disk, for instance, Disk 1: Letters, Disk 2: Spreadsheet Files, and Disk 3: Reports.*

for long *long.* • If top executives cannot control their responsibilities, they usually do not remain in their positions for long. *If top executives cannot control their responsibilities, they usually do not remain long in their positions.*

form (a/the) judgment (about/as to/concerning/of/on/regarding) *assess/conclude/decide/deduce/determine/evaluate/infer/judge/reason/resolve/settle.* • Voters cannot form a judgment unless the candidates say what they mean. *Voters cannot decide unless the candidates say what they mean.* • The Stock Selection Guide helps you to learn the facts about a company's past and present and form a judgment as to its likely value in the future. *The Stock Selection Guide helps you to learn the facts about a company's past and present and assess its likely value in the future.*

form (an/the) opinion (about/as to/concerning/of/on/regarding) *assess/conclude/decide/deduce/determine/evaluate/infer/judge/reason/resolve/settle.* • Just as you should not form an opinion of a person you meet based upon a fragment (first impression), so you should not form an opinion of the market. *Just as you should not*

judge a person you meet based upon a fragment *(first impression), so you should not judge the market.*

form (a/the) resolution (about/as to/concerning/of/on/regarding) *conclude/decide/determine/resolve/settle.* • When you rise in the morning, form a resolution to make the day a happy one for a fellow creature. *When you rise in the morning, resolve to make the day a happy one for a fellow creature.* • Then bring the two sides together to form a resolution to peacefully and equitably end the conflict. *Then bring the two sides together to determine to peacefully and equitably end the conflict.*

formulate *devise/form/make.* • Have you formulated no opinion about her? *Have you formed no opinion about her?*

for obvious reasons *obviously.* • For obvious reasons, he wants to announce his choice at the convention. *Obviously, he wants to announce his choice at the convention.*

for one (thing) *first.* • For one thing, a national program would have to be tailored to each state because the delivery of health care services can differ significantly. *First, a national program would have to be tailored to each state because the delivery of health care services can differ significantly.*

for one . . . (be) an example/an instance *(be) an example (an instance)/for one/one example (one instance).* • The Massachusetts Industrial Services Program, for one, is an example of the kind of broad industrial extension service we think is needed to retool manufacturing facilities. *The Massachusetts Industrial Services Program is one example of the kind of broad industrial extension service we think is needed to retool manufacturing facilities.*

for . . . purposes (of) *for/so as to/to.* • The money we receive from licensing John Wayne's image is used entirely for charitable purposes. *The money we receive from licensing John Wayne's image is used entirely for charity.*

for reasons of *after/because of/by/for/from/in/ out of/through.* • When airlines have replaced older planes, they have done so primarily for reasons of economics—newer aircraft cost less to inspect and repair. *When airlines have replaced older planes, they have done so primarily because of economics—newer aircraft cost less to inspect and repair.*

for some time (now) *long.* • I have enjoyed reading your articles for some time now. *I have long enjoyed reading your articles.*

for that matter *also/and/as well/besides/beyond that/this/even/further/furthermore/moreover/ more than that/this/still more/then/too/what's more* delete. • How can they speak up and tell the South Africans what they should do with their people or, for that matter, what the Soviet Union should do with its Jewish population? *How can they speak up and tell the South Africans what they should do with their people, or even what the Soviet Union should do with its Jewish population?*

for that/this reason *consequently/hence/so/ then/therefore/thus.* • For that reason, I wouldn't do it again. *I therefore wouldn't do it again.*

for the duration/length of *during/throughout.* • The company intends to maintain silence for the duration of the sale process. *The company intends to maintain silence during the sale process.*

for the first/last time *first/last.* • The series of studies were presented for the first time at the three-day conference. *The series of studies were first presented at the three-day conference.*

for the foreseeable future *for a time/for a while/for now/for many (several) months (years)/ for some time/for the present/for the time being/ temporarily.* • He is one of those who believes that a recession can be avoided for the foreseeable future. *He is one of those who believes that a recession can be avoided for now.*

for the immediate future *for a time/for a while/ for now/for many (several) months (years)/for some time/for the present/for the time being/ temporarily.* • Several said they were canceling planned business trips for the immediate future. *Several said they were canceling planned business trips for the present.*

for the most part *almost all/chiefly/commonly/ generally/greatly/in general/largely/mainly/most/ mostly/most often/much/nearly all/normally/ overall/typically/usually.* • Those problems for the most part have been overcome. *Those problems have been largely overcome.*

for the (very) near future *for a time/for a while/ for now/for many (several) months (years)/for some time/for the present/for the time being/ temporarily.* • While the analysts expected Kraft and General Foods to exist as separate entities for the near future, they said they did not expect the honeymoon to last forever. *While the analysts expected Kraft and General Foods to exist as separate entities for now, they said they did not expect the honeymoon to last forever.*

for the not-so-distant/not-too-distant future *for a time/for a while/for now/for many (several) months (years)/for some time/for the present/for the time being/temporarily.*

for the present *for now* delete. • Perhaps one day we shall find an Etruscan library, buried deep in the Italian countryside, but for the present, we have to make do with what we have, which is precious little. *Perhaps one day we shall find an Etruscan library, buried deep in the Italian countryside, but for now, we have to make do with what we have, which is precious little.*

for the purpose of (-ing) *for (-ing)/so as to/to.* • All deposited items are received for the purpose of collection, and all credits for deposited items are provisional. *All deposited items are received for collection, and all credits for deposited items are provisional.* • The mission of the Deaf Dog Education Action Fund is to provide education and funding for the purpose of improving and/or saving the lives of deaf dogs. *The mission of the Deaf Dog Education Action Fund is to provide education and funding so as to improve and/or save the lives of deaf dogs.* • Trade Council of Iceland was established in 1986 for the purpose of promoting exports and increasing marketing awareness among Icelandic companies. *Trade Council of Iceland was established in 1986 to promote exports and increase marketing awareness among Icelandic companies.*

for the (simple) reason that *because/considering/for/given/in that/since.* • Normally, short-term Treasuries yield less than longer-term Treasuries, for the simple reason that investors demand to be rewarded for tying up their money in longer-term instruments. *Normally, short-term Treasuries yield less than longer-term Treasuries since investors demand to be rewarded for tying up their money in longer-term instruments.* • It's not a bestseller for the simple reason that people aren't brave enough to read it. *It's not a bestseller because people aren't brave enough to read it.*

for the sake of *for/so as to/to.* • I have never found it necessary to practice "defensive medicine," if that means doing that which would not otherwise be done solely for the sake of protecting oneself against possible legal action. *I have never found it necessary to practice "defensive medicine," if that means doing that which would not otherwise be done solely to protect oneself against possible legal action.*

for the time/while being *for now/for the moment/for the present* delete. • For the time being, look at the current PLOT ORIGIN and the SCALE. *For the moment, look at the current PLOT ORIGIN and the SCALE.*

for (decades) . . . to come *for (decades) . . .* • This can go on for generations to come. *This can go on for generations.* • We think it'll act as a model for future elections to come. *We think it'll act as a model for future elections.* • If the contaminants end up in the marine sediments/muds, then they will remain there for decades to come. *If the contaminants end up in the marine sediments/muds, then they will remain there for decades.*

forward in/into the future *forward/in/into the future.* • He misleads those who may be truly seeking to understand where the Jews come from and how, as Jews, they can best carry their traditions forward into the future. *He misleads those who may be truly seeking to understand where the Jews come from and how, as Jews, they can best carry their traditions forward.* • AgriVision will take a real and practical look at how to take UK farming forward into the future. *AgriVision will take a real and practical look at how to take UK farming into the future.*

forward planning/progress *planning/progress.* • Such a relationship can shift the emphasis onto future events and encourage better forward planning. *Such a relationship can shift the emphasis onto future events and encourage better planning.* • Gannett Co., Inc. convinces investors it is making forward progress and has improved. *Gannett Co., Inc. convinces investors it is making progress and has improved.*

for (many/several) years (now) *long.* • The few policies I was able to get from SBLI have, for many years now, paid me an annual dividend, with no payment of any premium. *The few policies I was able to get from SBLI have long paid me an annual dividend, with no payment of any premium.*

for your information delete. • For your information, links may not appear underlined, but will appear in this color. *Links may not appear underlined, but will appear in this color.*

fourthly *fourth.*

frame of mind *attitude/belief/opinion/position/posture/stand/standpoint/vantage/view/viewpoint* delete.

fraught with meaning/moment/consequence/significance *consequential/meaningful/momentous/significant.* • If nothing else, the question is fraught with significance for Democrats trying to figure out whether to mount a campaign today that will peak three years from now. *If nothing else, the question is significant for Democrats trying to figure out whether to mount a campaign today that will peak three years from now.* • Silly or not, the prices we settle for are fraught with meaning for they either substantiate our travel savvy or betray our gullibility. *Silly or not, the prices we settle for are meaningful for they either substantiate our travel savvy or betray our gullibility.*

free and clear *clear/free.* • Section 363(f) authorizes sale of property free and clear of any interest in the property held by another entity if certain conditions exist. *Section 363(f) authorizes sale of property free of any interest in the property held by another entity if certain conditions exist.*

free and gratis *free.* • All the applications found in this Web site are free and gratis. *All the applications found in this Web site are free.* • You receive, free and gratis, the assistance, help, company and conversation of the princess whenever she is staying with you. *You receive, free, the assistance, help, company and conversation of the princess whenever she is staying with you.*

free, complimentary *complimentary/free.* • If you would like to receive a free, complimentary copy of the Samplers for each of these courses, return the enclosed self-addressed, postage-paid card and mail it today. *If you would like to receive a complimentary copy of the Samplers for each of these courses, return the enclosed self-addressed, postage-paid card and mail it today.*

free gift *gift.* • For your free gift, fill out this form today. *For your gift, fill out this form today.*

free of charge *free.* • All meetings are free of charge and open to the public. *All meetings are free and open to the public.*

free pass *pass.*

free up *free.* • On some programs, rows and columns can be deleted to free up memory for new data on a model. *On some programs, rows and columns can be deleted to free memory for new data on a model.* • Dropping a basic skill would free children's minds up to use high-level thinking skills. *Dropping a basic skill would free children's minds to use high-level thinking skills.* • Perhaps the biggest sense of freedom came from feeling freed up from my own bitterness and resentment. *Perhaps the biggest sense of freedom came from feeling freed from my own bitterness and resentment.*

freezing cold *cold/freezing.* • It's freezing cold outside. *It's freezing outside.*

frightening scare *scare.*

from (a/the) . . . aspect (of) *as (does)/as for/as to/for/from/in/in that/-(al)ly/since/to* delete. • From a legal aspect, the joint venture falls under local company or corporation law when participation is in the form of equity. *Legally, the joint venture falls under local company or corporation law when participation is in the form of equity.*

from beginning to end *all through/completely/entirely/thoroughly/throughout/totally/*

wholly delete. • I listened to the whole song, from beginning to end. *I listened to the whole song.* • Our surety bonding software is custom designed to meet your specific needs from beginning to end. *Our surety bonding software is custom designed to meet your specific needs completely.*

from (a/the) . . . distance of *from/from . . . away.* • Most of the spectators watched from a distance of 1,300 feet, while the Soviet observers viewed the firings from a concrete bunker. *Most of the spectators watched from 1,300 feet away, while the Soviet observers viewed the firings from a concrete bunker.*

from hence *hence.*

from minute/moment to minute/moment *directly/momentarily/momently/presently/soon.* • I expect them from moment to moment. *I expect them momentarily.*

from now (on) *hence.*

from . . . on/onward *since.* • Other researchers had already confirmed that from 200 A.D. onward there had been human sacrifices of varying kinds. *Other researchers had already confirmed that since 200 A.D. there had been human sacrifices of varying kinds.*

from one . . . to another *between.* • Moving your funds from one institution to another is easy to do, and there is no tax liability or IRS penalty at all, if you follow the correct procedures. *Moving your funds between institutions is easy to do, and there is no tax liability or IRS penalty at all, if you follow the correct procedures.*

from (a/the) . . . perspective (of) *as (does)/as for/as to/for/from/in/in that/-(al)ly/since/to* delete. • From my perspective, trashing my system makes a lot of sense. *Trashing my system makes a lot of sense to me.* • From a historical perspective, there have been more than a few

cases where decisions that have been rendered seem to fly in the face of the evidence. *Historically, there have been more than a few cases where decisions that have been rendered seem to fly in the face of the evidence.*

from (a/the) . . . point of view (of) *as (does)/as for/as to/for/from/in/in that/-(al)ly/since/to* delete. • You've got to look at it from an optimistic point of view. *You've got to look at it optimistically.* • I try to see things from the customer's point of view. *I try to see things as the customer does.*

from (a/the) . . . standpoint (of) *as (does)/as for/as to/for/from/in/in that/-(al)ly/since/to* delete. • From a statistical standpoint, who is most vulnerable to colon-rectal cancer? *Statistically, who is most vulnerable to colon-rectal cancer?* • I have had some experience with grief from a personal standpoint. *I have had some personal experience with grief.* • The proposed purchase price is indeed a good value from the city's standpoint. *The proposed purchase price is indeed a good value for the city.* • A move to Jacksonville will be highly profitable for the club and would be smart from a business standpoint. *A move to Jacksonville will be highly profitable for the club and would be smart business.* • From a medical standpoint, we don't have any evidence that the senator abuses alcohol. *We don't have any medical evidence that the senator abuses alcohol.*

from start to finish *all through/completely/entirely/thoroughly/throughout/totally/wholly.*

from that day/moment/point/time forward/on/onward *from then (on)/since/since then* delete. • From that point on, she hasn't said a word to me. *Since then, she hasn't said a word to me.*

from the beginning/start *always.* • From the start, it has been a haven for those whose religions or political beliefs were not tolerated in their homelands. *It has always been a haven for those whose religions or political beliefs were not tolerated in their homelands.*

from the fact that *because/considering/for/ given/in that/since.*

from/in the following year *from/in (1991).*

from/in the preceding year *from/in (1989).* • At year-end 1987, 70,893 persons were employed within Ericsson, a decrease of 1,682 from the preceding year. *At year-end 1987, 70,893 persons were employed within Ericsson, a decrease of 1,682 from 1986.*

from the time of . . . (on) *since.* • From the time of the Elizabethan settlement on, the Church of England attempted, with varying degrees of success, to consolidate its position both as a distinctive middle way between Catholicism and Puritanism and as the national religion of England. *Since the Elizabethan settlement, the Church of England attempted, with varying degrees of success, to consolidate its position both as a distinctive middle way between Catholicism and Puritanism and as the national religion of England.*

from this day/moment/point/time forward/on/ onward *from now (on)/hence/henceforth/hence- forward* delete. • From this point on, elected students and faculty will be running the affairs of the school. *Henceforth, elected students and faculty will be running the affairs of the school.*

from . . . until *from . . . to.* • This book is intriguing because it also concerns the role of that on-again, off-again colonial revival in pop- ular culture from 1876 until the present. *This book is intriguing because it also concerns the role of that on-again, off-again colonial revival in popular culture from 1876 to the present.*

from (a/the) . . . viewpoint (of) *as (does)/as for/ as to/for/from/in/in that/-(al)ly/since/to* delete.

• From a business viewpoint, it makes good sense to free brain power from the drudgery of processing data and to engage it in finding new ways to apply that data. *It makes good sense for business to free brain power from the drudgery of processing data and to engage it in finding new ways to apply that data.*

from whence *whence.* • From whence did he draw his strength? *Whence did he draw his strength?*

full capacity *capacity.* • Demand for petroleum products was so strong that refineries were operating at or near full capacity. *Demand for petroleum products was so strong that refineries were operating at or near capacity.*

full/maximum potential/potentiality *potential/ potentiality.* • If we are to achieve our full poten- tial, we must see beyond the routine. *If we are to achieve our potential, we must see beyond the routine.*

full satisfaction *satisfaction.*

(the) function of delete. • The function of set- tling disputes requires the exercise of tact and concern for resolution of conflicts. *Settling dis- putes requires the exercise of tact and concern for resolution of conflicts.*

fundamental *basic* delete.

fundamental (and) basic *basic/fundamental.* • These are fundamental and basic rights. *These are basic rights.*

fundamental basis *basis.* • The fundamental basis of any relationship is truth. *The basis of any relationship is truth.*

fundamental principle *principle.*

furiously angry *angry/furious.* • She's furiously angry. *She's furious.*

further *more.* • For further information, or free form samples, contact Deluxe at their toll-free number. *For more information, or free form samples, contact Deluxe at their toll-free number.*

furthermore *also/and/as well/besides/even/further/still more/then/too.* • Furthermore, some of the changes may reduce the extent to which issuers may issue tax-exempt bonds. *Further, some of the changes may reduce the extent to which issuers may issue tax-exempt bonds.*

fuse together *fuse.* • Most metals, except for low- and medium-carbon steels, require fluxes to aid in the process of melting and fusing the metals together. *Most metals, except for low- and medium-carbon steels, require fluxes to aid in the process of melting and fusing the metals.*

future developments *developments.* • Please check back regularly for updates and future developments. *Please check back regularly for updates and developments.*

future plans *plans.* • He said future plans call for the introduction of 20-Mbs service by 2012. *He said plans call for the introduction of 20-Mbs service by 2012.*

future projections *projections.*

future prospects *prospects.* • Proponents of the information center concept, Smith Consultants are not overly hopeful about its future prospects. *Proponents of the information center concept, Smith Consultants are not overly hopeful about its prospects.*

G

gather together *gather.* • In Dubai, about 400 relatives of the dead and their supporters gathered together for a memorial service at a large Shiite mosque. *In Dubai, about 400 relatives of the dead and their supporters gathered for a memorial service at a large Shiite mosque.*

general consensus *consensus.* • The general consensus among corporations is to be cautious about 1989. *The consensus among corporations is to be cautious about 1989.*

general public *public.*

general vicinity *vicinity/area.*

gentleman *man.* • Nothing would give me greater pleasure than to see these gentlemen put out of business. *Nothing would give me greater pleasure than to see these men put out of business.*

geographical *geographic.* • Several large commercial banks provide economic data and forecasts for the geographical area they serve. *Several large commercial banks provide economic data and forecasts for the geographic area they serve.*

geological *geologic.* • On-site geological studies would be needed to confirm an impact origin. *On-site geologic studies would be needed to confirm an impact origin.*

geometrical *geometric.*

get across *convey/explain.* • There's an important element here that we need to get across. *There's an important element here that we need to convey.*

get in touch with *call/contact/phone/reach/visit/write (to).* • Agency representatives with reports to enter can get in touch with him at (703) 323-5711. *Agency representatives with reports to enter can reach him at (703) 323-5711.*

get married *marry.* • We plan to get married in the fall. *We plan to marry in the fall.*

give (a/the) . . . (for/of/to) delete. • Give an estimate on the amount of time it will take and the number of people you will need. *Estimate the amount of time it will take and the number of people you will need.* • The Book of Leviticus gives a list of the women who are not available to marry certain men. *The Book of Leviticus lists the women who are not available to marry certain men.* • The main purpose of choosing an outside auditor is to guarantee to insiders and interested outsiders that the financial data presented in financial documents give an accurate representation of events. *The main purpose of choosing an outside auditor is to guarantee to insiders and interested outsiders that the financial data presented in financial documents accurately represent events.* • They work hard; they deserve to be given compensation. *They work hard; they deserve to be compensated.* • Did he give any indication of what he plans to do? *Did he indicate what he plans to do?* • I'll give you a call at the end of the week. *I'll call you at the end of the week.* • I hope you will give me consideration for diverse projects. *I hope you will consider me for diverse projects.* • Many small businesses and private individuals are giving serious consideration to their energy and resource needs for the year ahead. *Many small businesses and private individuals are seriously considering their energy and resource needs for the year ahead.* • Thanks to Craig for taking the time out of his busy schedule to give this book a read. *Thanks to Craig for taking the time out of his busy schedule to read this book.*

give birth to *bear.* • The prospect that the princess might give birth to a girl has already sparked speculation that there will be pressure to change the law. *The prospect that the princess might bear a girl has already sparked speculation that there will be pressure to change the law.* • This dilemma gave birth to an idea that was to revolutionize the road building industry. *This dilemma bore an idea that was to revolutionize the road building industry.*

given at/in *at/in.* • Since all limits are given in thousandths, the values can be converted by moving the decimal point three places to the left. *Since all limits are in thousandths, the values can be converted by moving the decimal point three places to the left.*

given the fact that *because/considering/for/given/in that/since/when.* • Given the fact that she only read 400 pages of the book, she didn't do too badly. *Considering she only read 400 pages of the book, she didn't do too badly.* • Given the fact that more than 90 percent of information is still in paper form, this is indeed a tall order. *Since more than 90 percent of information is still in paper form, this is indeed a tall order.*

give offense to *offend.* • Ask them to develop a set of labels that does not give offense to any group of countries. *Ask them to develop a set of labels that does not offend any group of countries.*

give rise to *bear/cause.* • The researchers concluded that abnormalities in the neurotransmitter system may give rise to the depression in demented patients. *The researchers concluded that abnormalities in the neurotransmitter system may cause the depression in demented patients.*

go along with *agree with/back/endorse/favor/support.* • He was unwilling to say whether he would go along with such a recommendation. *He was unwilling to say whether he would support such a recommendation.*

(just) goes to show *attests/proves/reveals/shows/supports/verifies* delete. • It just goes to show that safety in driving is most important. *It shows that safety in driving is most important.*

(it) goes without saying (that) *clearly/naturally/obviously/of course/plainly* delete. • This may go without saying, but I also look at a person's motivation, commitment, and energy.

Naturally, I also look at a person's motivation, commitment, and energy.

go fetch *fetch.* • Some rural communities may be asked to go fetch their mail from the post office rather than have it delivered. *Some rural communities may be asked to fetch their mail from the post office rather than have it delivered.* • He sent someone else to go fetch his truck, with Favre taunting with a friendly wave as he jumps in and drives away. *He sent someone else to fetch his truck, with Favre taunting with a friendly wave as he jumps in and drives away.*

go forward *advance/continue/go on/happen/ move on/occur/proceed/progress.* • We want the project to go forward as soon as possible, and we are confident that these issues can be addressed. *We want the project to proceed as soon as possible, and we are confident that these issues can be addressed.* • McVeigh prosecutors predict execution will go forward. *McVeigh prosecutors predict execution will occur.*

good and sufficient *adequate/good/sufficient.* • We think that the safety of present plants is good and sufficient. *We think that the safety of present plants is adequate.*

go through . . . experience *experience/go through.* • I think I'm a much better person for having gone through that experience. *I think I'm a much better person for having experienced that.*

GPS system *GPS.*

grateful thanks *gratitude/thanks.*

(a/the) greater/larger number (of) *more.* • Usually the greater number of services offered, the larger the margin needed on each side to maintain profitability. *Usually the more services offered, the larger the margin needed on each side to maintain profitability.*

(a/the) great/large fraction (of) *a good (great) deal (of)/a good (great) many (of)/almost all (of)/ many (of)/most (of)/much (of)/nearly all (of)/ three-fourths (two-thirds) (of).* • Of the numerous complete fossils discovered in this quarry, a large fraction are either babies or mothers carrying young. *Of the numerous complete fossils discovered in this quarry, most are either babies or mothers carrying young.*

group together *group.* • The Chapter command divides your Notepad pages into chapters and groups together related information. *The Chapter command divides your Notepad pages into chapters and groups related information.* • There have been debates for decades regarding the best ways for employees to be grouped together. *There have been debates for decades regarding the best ways for employees to be grouped.*

H

had . . . then *had.* • Had he exhibited the kind of behavior that would have warranted such a recommendation, then it would have been made. *Had he exhibited the kind of behavior that would have warranted such a recommendation, it would have been made.*

hale and hearty *hale/healthy/hearty/well.*

half (a) dozen *six.*

half of *half.* • The menus occupy almost half of the screen display. *The menus occupy almost half the screen display.*

happens to be *is.* • The G sedan happens to be the first model to go through this nameplate metamorphosis. *The G sedan is the first model to go through this nameplate metamorphosis.* • He's an evangelical Christian Tea Partier with impeccable social-conservative bona fides—and he happens to be black. *He's an evangelical Christian Tea Partier with impeccable social-conservative bona fides—and he is black.*

harbinger of the future/of things to come *harbinger/omen/sign.* • I hope it is a harbinger of the future. *I hope it is an omen.* • This made 1989 the most stable year in terms of oil prices since 1984, and was widely interpreted as a harbinger of things to come: a more prosperous era for OPEC. *This made 1989 the most stable year in terms of oil prices since 1984, and was widely interpreted as a harbinger: a more prosperous era for OPEC.*

hard and fast *firm/fixed/steadfast/strict.*

has (a/the) . . . (about/for/of/on/over) delete. • If you have intentions of going, you should make your reservations now. *If you intend to go, you should make your reservations now.* • He has control over the entire program. *He controls the entire program.* • Boston has the need for a new harbor tunnel. *Boston needs a new harbor tunnel.* • The strategic partnering lawyer must have a firm grasp of the fundamentals of the legal principles in Europe and in the Far East. *The strategic partnering lawyer must firmly grasp the fundamentals of the legal principles in Europe and in the Far East.* • Applicants should have knowledge of intersections of race, ethnicity, class, and sexualities in feminist studies. *Applicants should know intersections of race, ethnicity, class, and sexualities in feminist studies.*

has a bearing on/upon *acts on/affects/bears on/influences.* • What we are learning about primates and other social species has a direct bearing on our own species. *What we are learning about primates and other social species directly bears on our own species.*

has (an/the) ability to *can/is able to.* • Eighty percent of the retail deposit accounts have the ability to be accessed by a debit card even though actual usage is much less. *Eighty percent of the retail deposit accounts can be accessed by a debit card even though actual usage is much less.*

has a/the capability to *can/is able to.*

has a difference of opinion with *differs/disagrees with/disputes/objects to/opposes.* • We have a difference of opinion with the decision the judge made. *We disagree with the decision the judge made.*

has a/the habit of (-ing) *tends to/will.* • He has a habit of biting his nails. *He tends to bite his nails.*

has (an/the) appreciation for *appreciates/approves of/cherishes/enjoys/esteems/likes/prizes/treasures/understands/values.* • Most people don't have an appreciation for esoteric beliefs. *Most people don't appreciate esoteric beliefs.*

has a/the preference for *favors/prefers.* • By now, you will have gathered that I have a strong preference for organization along functional lines. *By now, you will have gathered that I strongly prefer organization along functional lines.* • He plays piano and has a preference for Mozart and Beethoven. *He plays piano and prefers Mozart and Beethoven.* • Segregated or pooled accounts will be considered but the client has a preference for segregated accounts. *Segregated or pooled accounts will be considered but the client favors segregated accounts.*

has a/the tendency (to) *tends to/will.* • As a community, the Basques have a tendency to be healthy and long-lived. *As a community, the Basques tend to be healthy and long-lived.* • Roth is a similar type player who has a tendency to lose his temper. *Roth is a similar type player who tends to lose his temper.* • He said mankind has a tendency to think that anything enjoyable must be bad for us. *He said mankind tends to think that anything enjoyable must be bad for us.*

has (a) . . . effect on/upon *acts on/affects/bears on/influences* delete. • Over the past twenty years, the U.S. economy has had a significant effect on the Amish way of life. *Over the past twenty years, the U.S. economy has significantly influenced the Amish way of life.* • Human activity is changing the composition of the atmosphere in ways that could have profound effects upon life on the Earth. *Human activity is changing the composition of the atmosphere in ways that could profoundly affect life on the Earth.*

has got *has/must.* • A woman has got to love a bad man once or twice in her life, to be thankful for a good one. *A woman has to love a bad man once or twice in her life, to be thankful for a good one.*

has (a) . . . impact on/upon *acts on/affects/bears on/influences* delete. • It has a direct impact on the majority of the American people. *It directly affects the majority of the American people.* • Your tone of voice, expression, and apparent receptiveness to others' responses all have a tremendous impact upon those you wish to reach. *Your tone of voice, expression, and apparent receptiveness to others' responses all tremendously influence those you wish to reach.*

has (a) . . . influence on/upon *acts on/affects/ bears on/influences* delete. • Management was alerted to the fact that the social environment of employees had a great influence on productivity. *Management was alerted to the fact that the social environment of employees greatly affected productivity.*

has occasion to be *is.* • The ombudsman often has occasion to be aware of problems arising between levels and units. *The ombudsman often is aware of problems arising between lev-*

els and units. • If he has occasion to be in Washington, the president likes to spend time with him. *If he is in Washington, the president likes to spend time with him.* • Some fifty years later I had occasion to be in the vicinity of that church and I went in, just to see. *Some fifty years later I was in the vicinity of that church and I went in, just to see.* • If you have ever had occasion to be deprived of your normal sleep, you know how hard it is to function when you haven't had enough rest. *If you have ever been deprived of your normal sleep, you know how hard it is to function when you haven't had enough rest.*

has only to *need only.* • To view any of the channels available, you have only to switch between channels. *To view any of the channels available, you need only switch between channels.*

has reference to *concerns/deals with/is about/ pertains to/regards/relates to.* • Abase has reference to a bringing down in condition or feelings; debase has reference to the bringing down of a thing in purity; degrade has reference to a bringing down from some higher grade or from some standard. *Abase pertains to a bringing down in condition or feelings; debase pertains to the bringing down of a thing in purity; degrade pertains to a bringing down from some higher grade or from some standard.* • This letter has reference to the outstanding series of articles in your esteemed daily appearing in the column "Without Malice." *This letter concerns the outstanding series of articles in your esteemed daily appearing in the column "Without Malice."*

has the effect of -ing *-s* delete. • Such a slowdown would have the effect of easing inflationary fears. *Such a slowdown would ease inflationary fears.* • The Seven of Diamonds is called the Ugly Card, and has the effect of doubling the negative value of any Jacks collected by the player who wins a trick containing this card. *The Seven of Diamonds is called the Ugly*

Card, and doubles the negative value of any Jacks collected by the player who wins a trick containing this card. • The decision has the effect of legalizing same-sex marriage in Maine's neighboring province. *The decision legalizes same-sex marriage in Maine's neighboring province.*

has (got) to *must.* • I have to be going. *I must be going.* • He understands that he has to do as I say. *He understands that he must do as I say.*

(that) has to do with *concerns/deals with/is about/pertains to/regards/relates to.* • The first has to do with the relative merits of CD versus analog. *The first pertains to the relative merits of CD versus analog.*

have a conversation (about) *chat/communicate/confer/converse/discuss/speak/talk.* • We need to have a conversation about that. *We need to talk about that.* • It's almost as if they are afraid to have a conversation about an issue when disagreement is present. *It's almost as if they are afraid to converse about an issue when disagreement is present.*

have/take a listen *listen.* • Take a listen to the interview and check out this cool technology. *Listen to the interview and check out this cool technology.* • The New Year's shows are sold out, but take a listen to his 1994 album "Dream" and you'll be sure to get tickets well in advance next time around. *The New Year's shows are sold out, but listen to his 1994 album "Dream" and you'll be sure to get tickets well in advance next time around.* • Let's take a listen to what the prime minister said. *Let's listen to what the prime minister said.* • Have a listen. *Listen.*

have/take a look *look.* • Have a look at her. *Look at her.* • Yesterday, we took a look at NBC's new sitcom slate. *Yesterday, we looked at NBC's new sitcom slate.*

have/possess . . . in common *share.* • We have no interests in common. *We share no interests.*

have . . . in (my) possession *have/possess.* • We now have in our possession a class of machines that are right around energy breakeven. *We now possess a class of machines that are right around energy breakeven.* • Many of the tombstone pictures I now have in my possession represent a unique record because the original tombstones have been replaced with newer ones. *Many of the tombstone pictures I now have represent a unique record because the original tombstones have been replaced with newer ones.*

head up *direct/head/lead.* • Bush headed up the committee that eliminated those regulations. *Bush headed the committee that eliminated those regulations.*

(the) heart of the matter *center/core/crux/essence/gist/heart/pith/substance/sum.*

heat up *heat.* • I just threw it all together and then heated it up. *I just threw it all together and then heated it.*

(a/the) height of delete. • The stratosphere is one of the middle layers of the atmosphere that starts some 15 kilometers above Earth's surface and extends to a height of about 50 kilometers. *The stratosphere is one of the middle layers of the atmosphere that starts some 15 kilometers above Earth's surface and extends to about 50 kilometers.*

help assist *assist/help.* • Is there anything else I can help assist you with? *Is there anything else I can help you with?* • The study would touch on the health issues raised by the community to help assist in better understanding the structure and its effects. *The study would touch on the health issues raised by the community to assist in better understanding the structure and its effects.* • For us, it's not a money-making thing; it's trying to help assist the city. *For us, it's not a money-making thing; it's trying to help the city.*

help in/of -ing *help (-ing).* • Those who have no diversions or hobbies may need help in selecting appropriate activities. *Those who have no diversions or hobbies may need help selecting appropriate activities.* • The work may also help in tracking down inherited influences in mental diseases. *The work may also help track down inherited influences in mental diseases.*

help out *help.* • They're very eager to help out. *They're very eager to help.*

help . . . to *help.* • Following these guidelines may help to cut down on the amount of aspirin you need. *Following these guidelines may help cut down on the amount of aspirin you need.*

henceforth/henceforward *hence.*

henceforth and forevermore *forevermore/ henceforth.* • And let this be the end of him as a subject of discussion between us or even correspondence, *henceforth and forevermore.* And let this be the end of him as a subject of discussion between us or even correspondence, *forevermore.* • I pray fervently "that the world is going to be stuck with" you from henceforth and forevermore! *I pray fervently "that the world is going to be stuck with" you from henceforth!*

hereafter *hence.*

(the) here and now *(just/right) now/presently/ the present.*

hereinafter (referred to as) delete. • A limited partnership (hereinafter "the Partnership") is under contract with a political subdivision of the State of Connecticut (hereinafter "the Agency") to operate, manage and maintain the Agency's facility (hereinafter "the Facility"). *A limited partnership ("the Partnership") is under contract with a political subdivision of the State of Connecticut ("the Agency") to operate, manage and maintain the Agency's facility ("the Facility").* • Under a nonrenewable ground lease (hereinafter referred to as "the Ground Lease")

with a term of 99 years, a landlord (hereinafter referred to as "the Landlord") leased premises (hereinafter referred to as "the Leased Premises") located in Connecticut to a general partnership (hereinafter referred to as "the Tenant"). *Under a nonrenewable ground lease ("the Ground Lease") with a term of 99 years, a landlord ("the Landlord") leased premises ("the Leased Premises") located in Connecticut to a general partnership ("the Tenant").*

high and dry *alone/helpless/powerless.*

high and low *everywhere.*

high and mighty *arrogant/disdainful/dogmatic/ domineering/haughty.*

(a/the) high degree (of) *abundant/a good (great) deal (of)/a good (great) many (of)/ample/ broad/enormous/extensive/great/high/huge/ large/many (of)/marked/most (of)/much (of)/ salient/signal/significant/sizable/striking/substantial/vast* delete. • Tuesday's federal budget placed a high degree of importance on improving learning in Canada. *Tuesday's federal budget placed much importance on improving learning in Canada.* • Drug development involves a high degree of risk. *Drug development involves significant risk.* • One of the distinguishing characteristics of the Eurobond market is its high degree of competitiveness. *One of the distinguishing characteristics of the Eurobond market is its marked competitiveness.* • In 2012 U.S. exports to Canada are likely to increase on the strength of the high degree of integration that exists between the Canadian and U.S. pork markets. *In 2012 U.S. exports to Canada are likely to increase on the strength of the broad integration that exists between the Canadian and U.S. pork markets.*

(a/the) high level (of) *abundant/a good (great) deal (of)/a good (great) many (of)/ample/broad/ enormous/extensive/great/high/huge/large/ many (of)/marked/most (of)/much (of)/salient/*

signal/significant/sizable/striking/substantial/ vast delete. • The London merchant banks have a very high level of expertise. *The London merchant banks have vast expertise.*

(a/the) high number (of) *a good (great) many (of)/almost all/countless/dozens (of)/hundreds (of)/ many (of)/millions (of)/most (of)/nearly all (of)/ numerous/scores (of)/thousands (of).* • Hampton's high number of published recordings further supports the idea that he has spent several decades sharing his vibe playing with those who would listen. *Hampton's numerous published recordings further supports the idea that he has spent several decades sharing his vibe playing with those who would listen.* • A high number of Dominicans migrate to the United States from the Dominican mountains. *Thousands of Dominicans migrate to the United States from the Dominican mountains.* • Even now it appears that a high number of the viewers of the film are members of the Latino communities in the United States. *Even now it appears that many of the viewers of the film are members of the Latino communities in the United States.*

(a/the) high percentage (of) *a good (great) deal (of)/a good (great) many (of)/almost all (of)/ many (of)/most (of)/much (of)/nearly all (of)/ three-fourths (two-thirds) (of).* • That probably is excellent advice, if these bonds represent a high percentage of your total investments. *That probably is excellent advice, if these bonds represent much of your total investments.*

(a/the) high proportion (of) *a good (great) deal (of)/a good (great) many (of)/almost all (of)/ many (of)/most (of)/much (of)/nearly all (of)/ three-fourths (two-thirds) (of).* • In the pharmaceutical industry, most companies devote a high proportion of their budgets to R&D expenditures. *In the pharmaceutical industry, most companies devote much of their budgets to R&D expenditures.*

hired mercenary *mercenary.*

historical experience *experience/history.* • The quote could be misconstrued to leave the impression that we made an explicit assumption that was at odds with recent historical experience. *The quote could be misconstrued to leave the impression that we made an explicit assumption that was at odds with recent experience.*

historically . . . in the past *historically/in the past.* • I didn't have any anxiety about being paid because I know that historically the government always has in the past. *I didn't have any anxiety about being paid because I know that historically the government always has.*

historical precedent *history/precedent.* • We are unaware of any historical precedent that has seen a nation indefinitely borrow and consume its way to prosperity. *We are unaware of any precedent that has seen a nation indefinitely borrow and consume its way to prosperity.*

historical record *history/record.* • Mr. Macdonald is too young to have known this, but neither youth nor filial piety justifies distorting the historical record. *Mr. Macdonald is too young to have known this, but neither youth nor filial piety justifies distorting the record.*

(the) history of delete. • For the first time in the history of this century, the death penalty is extended beyond the borders of a single country, in spite of the laws of other countries. *For the first time in this century, the death penalty is extended beyond the borders of a single country, in spite of the laws of other countries.*

HIV virus *HIV.*

hoist up *hoist.*

hold a meeting *meet.*

hold (to) the opinion (that) *assert/believe/ claim/consider/contend/feel/hold/judge/maintain/regard/say/think/to/view.*

hold (to) the view (that) *assert/believe/claim/ consider/contend/feel/hold/judge/maintain/ regard/say/think/to/view.* • Most utility regulators and economists hold to the view that electric utilities are "natural monopolies." *Most utility regulators and economists hold that electric utilities are "natural monopolies."*

hold true *hold.* • As we age, our muscles become weaker and more easily tired, and the same holds true for polio victims. *As we age, our muscles become weaker and more easily tired, and the same holds for polio victims.* • If these preliminary data hold true a sample size of 2500 may be insufficient to detect a 25% change with 90% confidence. *If these preliminary data hold a sample size of 2500 may be insufficient to detect a 25% change with 90% confidence.*

hollow tube *tube.*

honestly and truly/truthfully *honestly/truly/ truthfully* delete. • I tell people what I honestly and truthfully believe. *I tell people what I honestly believe.*

(the) honest truth *honestly/truly/(the) truth/ truthfully.* • The person you're interviewing doesn't want you to discover the honest truth. *The person you're interviewing doesn't want you to discover the truth.*

hope and expect/expectation *expect/expectation/hope/trust.* • It is my hope and expectation that these cuts won't take effect. *It is my hope that these cuts won't take effect.* • We hope and expect that donors will increase their support. *We expect that donors will increase their support.*

hopeful optimist *optimist.*

hopefully *(I/we) hope/let's hope* delete. • Today, hopefully, we have some answers to these problems. *Today, I hope, we have some answers to these problems.* • We're looking forward to

working with you on this project (and hopefully others later). *We're looking forward to working with you on this project (and we hope others later).* • Hopefully women's magazines will help to empower our society's females. *Let's hope women's magazines will help to empower our society's females.*

(a) (whole) host of *many/numerous.* • There are a whole host of reasons why these people resigned from their jobs. *There are many reasons why these people resigned from their jobs.*

how do (you) go about (-ing) *how do (you).* • How do you go about getting an income tax extension? *How do you get an income tax extension?*

how in God's/heaven's name *however/how ever.*

how in the world/on earth *however/how ever.* • How in the world did you manage that? *However did you manage that?*

how is it (that) *how come/why.*

(the) hows and (the) whys *aims/causes/goals/ motives/purposes/reasons.* • Our association has attempted to encourage proactive lending in low-income communities by working with the Fed to educate banks about the hows and whys of these investment opportunities. *Our association has attempted to encourage proactive lending in low-income communities by working with the Fed to educate banks about the aims of these investment opportunities.*

howsoever *however.*

HTML language *HTML.*

hue and cry *clamor/hubbub/outcry.* • He moved to stem the hue and cry by saying that the House would vote next week on trimming the raise to 30 percent. *He moved to stem the outcry by say-*

ing that the House would vote next week on trimming the raise to 30 percent.

huge/large throng *throng.* • At the hotel, Sitting Bull welcomed large throngs of people who simply wanted to see him. *At the hotel, Sitting Bull welcomed throngs of people who simply wanted to see him.* • Even before winning the U.S. presidency, he spoke outdoors to a huge throng in Berlin last summer. *Even before winning the U.S. presidency, he spoke outdoors to a throng in Berlin last summer.*

human being *being/female/human/male/man/ person/woman.* • Such a statement is beneath the dignity of any civilized human being. *Such a statement is beneath the dignity of any civilized person.*

human resources *employees/people/persons/ workers.* • If the company does not have enough human resources to meet future needs, it must begin hiring them. *If the company does not have enough employees to meet future needs, it must begin hiring them.*

humongous *big/giant/grand/great/huge/ immense/large/mammoth/mighty/monstrous.* • It's a humongous amount, oceans and oceans of material. *It's a huge amount, oceans and oceans of material.*

hurry up *hurry.*

I

(the) idea of delete. • A large number of today's teens have actually thought about the idea of suicide. *A large number of today's teens have actually thought about suicide.*

(an/the) identical/identically match *duplicate/ exact/identical/match/(the) same.* • Make sure

you have two forms of identification that are an identical match to your ticket documentation. *Make sure you have two forms of identification that are identical to your ticket documentation.*

(an/the) identical/identically (the) same *duplicate/exact/identical/match/(the) same.* • The operating system assumes they are the same file because the first eight characters are identically the same. *The operating system assumes they are the same file because the first eight characters are identical.*

I do not think so *I think not.* • Has there been a bloodier stain on our country's honor and reputation than the Shock and Awe Show he premiered in Iraq a year ago? I do not think so. *Has there been a bloodier stain on our country's honor and reputation than the Shock and Awe Show he premiered in Iraq a year ago? I think not.* • Certainly the former CEO's personal improprieties are embarrassing, but do they indicate a deep flaw in the business? I don't think so. *Certainly the former CEO's personal improprieties are embarrassing, but do they indicate a deep flaw in the business? I think not.*

I don't think *I doubt/I think* delete. • If Dole doesn't act more civilized, he's not going to make it, I don't think. *If Dole doesn't act more civilized, he's not going to make it.* • Technology is not now being taxed, and I don't think it will ever be taxed in the supply of these services. *Technology is not now being taxed, and I doubt it will ever be taxed in the supply of these services.*

if and only if *if/only if.* • It is agreed that the premiums stated in the Coverage Selections page are subject to recomputation if, and only if, the rates fixed and established are found not to meet the requirements of state law. *It is agreed that the premiums stated in the Coverage Selections page are subject to recomputation only if* *the rates fixed and established are found not to meet the requirements of state law.*

if and/or when *if/when.* • To use a program, it is not necessary for you to know all the commands because many of them are for advanced features that you learn if and when you need them. *To use a program, it is not necessary for you to know all the commands because many of them are for advanced features that you learn if you need them.*

if by way of hypothesis/supposition *assuming (that)/supposing (that).*

if . . . had *had.* • If you had run a large number of trials, the results would be very similar. *Had you run a large number of trials, the results would be very similar.*

if it were not for *but for/except for.* • The loss would have been $261 million if it were not for an accounting change related to the treatment of income taxes. *The loss would have been $261 million but for an accounting change related to the treatment of income taxes.*

ifs, ands, or buts *absolutely/conditions* delete. • Money in an FDIC-insured account is absolutely safe—no ifs, ands, or buts. *Money in an FDIC-insured account is absolutely safe.*

if . . . should *should.* • We will be alert to other opportunities if this one should collapse. *We will be alert to other opportunities should this one collapse.*

if that/this is the case/situation *if so.* • If that is the situation, please contact me for detailed information on costs and time required. *If so, please contact me for detailed information on costs and time required.*

if that/this is true *if so.*

if . . . then *if.* • If he tells you he doesn't ever want to have children, then you will have to make a

decision. *If he tells you he doesn't ever want to have children, you will have to make a decision.* • If so, then you would most likely have the learning style of doing or active experimentation. *If so, you would most likely have the learning style of doing or active experimentation.*

if . . . were *should/were.* • If that were the only penalty, I would settle for keeping 22 cents on the dollar. *Were that the only penalty, I would settle for keeping 22 cents on the dollar.*

I'll/let me tell you (something) delete.

illustrative example *example/illustration.* • From the Software Library, you can download illustrative code examples and the latest technical specifications. *From the Software Library, you can download code examples and the latest technical specifications.*

I'm curious why *why (do).* • I'm curious why you want to see him. *Why do you want to see him?*

I mean delete.

immunological *immunologic.*

impact (on/upon) *(v) act on/affect/bear on/influence.* • It's the numbers that impact on all of us. *It's the numbers that influence all of us.* • This ABC program enables U.S. non-profit or public institutions to support current and future collaborative training-related research on infectious diseases that impact upon people living in tropical countries. *This ABC program enables U.S. non-profit or public institutions to support current and future collaborative training-related research on infectious diseases that affect people living in tropical countries.*

implement *achieve/complete/effect/fulfill/make/perform/produce/realize/set.*

implode on itself *implode.* • It seems as if it'd be so obvious for the whole thing to implode on itself, so natural for everything to just fall apart. *It seems as if it'd be so obvious for the whole thing to implode, so natural for everything to just fall apart.*

importance *import/moment.* • I trust you understand the importance and implication of what he is saying. *I trust you understand the import and implication of what he is saying.* • It was of great importance to the United States to effect a treaty of this kind with Great Britain. *It was of great moment to the United States to effect a treaty of this kind with Great Britain.*

important essentials *essentials.* • There are six important essentials to having a good quality compost heap. *There are six essentials to having a good quality compost heap.*

(an/the) important . . . for/in/of/to *important for/to.* • Because decision making is an important element of a manager's job, we need to discover anything that can improve the quality of decision making. *Because decision making is important to a manager's job, we need to discover anything that can improve the quality of decision making.* • Their willingness to commit capital was an important factor for success. *Their willingness to commit capital was important for success.* • Certainly, overall physical health is an important component in any society. *Certainly, overall physical health is important to any society.*

in a bad mood *angry/dejected/depressed/displeased/downcast/glum/grouchy/sad/unhappy/vexed.*

in accord/accordance with *according to/at one with/by/compliant with/consistent with/consonant with/following/in keeping with/in line with/in step with/to/under.* • This document shall be governed and construed in accordance with the laws of the State of Utah. *This document shall be governed and construed under the laws of the State of Utah.*

in a class by herself/itself *matchless/novel/peerless/singular/special/unequaled/unique/*

unmatched/unrivaled/without equal/without peer.* • Now you can see why SFT is the most recommended actor-training center in the city and why The School for Film and Television is in a class by itself. *Now you can see why SFT is the most recommended actor- training center in the city and why The School for Film and Television is unequaled.* • Eric Moulds is in a class by himself; he's one of the best receivers we'll face this year, no question about it. *Eric Moulds is peerless; he's one of the best receivers we'll face this year, no question about it.*

in a/the . . . condition delete. • The Tenant must keep the Apartment in a clean and sanitary condition, free of garbage, rubbish, and other filth. *The Tenant must keep the Apartment clean and sanitary, free of garbage, rubbish, and other filth.*

in actual fact *actually/indeed/in fact/in faith/in reality/in truth/really/truly* delete. • And, in actual fact, the copywriter who created the spots and several other people who worked on it are also Catholic. *And, in fact, the copywriter who created the spots and several other people who worked on it are also Catholic.*

in actuality *actually/indeed/in fact/in faith/in truth/really/truly* delete. • In actuality, such a situation seldom occurs. *In fact, such a situation seldom occurs.*

in addition *also/and/as well/besides/beyond that/this/even/further/furthermore/moreover/more than that/this/still more/then/too/what's more.* • In addition, we reviewed several net present value models. *We even reviewed several net present value models.*

in addition to *besides/beyond.* • In addition to using words to communicate, all of us talk with our body poses and facial expressions. *Besides using words to communicate, all of us talk with our body poses and facial expressions.*

in addition to . . . additionally/also/as well/too *besides/beyond/in addition to.* • In addition to measuring a computer in terms of its memory and processing speed, we must also analyze the computer's ability to handle list processing. *In addition to measuring a computer in terms of its memory and processing speed, we must analyze the computer's ability to handle list processing.* • In addition to the methods defined in Table 13-1, each property has both a get and set method as well. *In addition to the methods defined in Table 13-1, each property has both a get and set method.*

in a/the . . . direction delete. • Vertical lines are drawn along the left side of a triangle in an upward direction. *Vertical lines are drawn upward along the left side of a triangle.* • It was definitely a move in the positive direction. *It was definitely a positive move.* • Stocks were sliding in a negative direction during the opening half of the trading session today. *Stocks were sliding during the opening half of the trading session today.*

in advance *before/beforehand/earlier/sooner* delete. • If I'd known in advance that out of every 100 books published, only one becomes a best seller, I wouldn't have started a book. *If I'd known sooner that out of every 100 books published, only one becomes a best seller, I wouldn't have started a book.*

in advance of *ahead of/before.* • In advance of our first break, let me introduce Thomas Armstrong, Ph.D., a learning and education specialist. *Before our first break, let me introduce Thomas Armstrong, Ph.D., a learning and education specialist.*

inadvertent/unintended/unintentional oversight *oversight.* • It was an unintentional oversight that the material was not provided to the members of the Board of Massage Therapy. *It was an oversight that the material was not provided to the members of the Board of Massage Therapy.*

in a/the fashion/manner/way (in which/ that) *as/like.* • Zeus allows you to work intuitively in the way that you think best. *Zeus allows you to work intuitively as you think best.* • But such a scientific inquiry already took place years ago, in the manner provided for by law. *But such a scientific inquiry already took place years ago, as provided for by law.* • Science fiction and mystery are often mixed, but not in the fashion that Roberts has managed. *Science fiction and mystery are often mixed, but not as Roberts has managed.*

in a/the fashion/manner/way characteristic of *alike/as/like/much as/much like/much the same (as)/rather like/resembling/similar to/similarly to.* • In a fashion characteristic of his other work, the paintings are on scrap wood panels and other flat, rectangular materials that Young salvages from the streets. *Like his other work, the paintings are on scrap wood panels and other flat, rectangular materials that Young salvages from the streets.*

in a/the fashion/manner/way similar to *alike/as/like/much as/much like/much the same (as)/rather like/resembling/similar to/similarly to.* • In a manner similar to modern-day whales, ichthyosaurs seem to have frequented breeding or birthing areas. *Like modern-day whales, ichthyosaurs seem to have frequented breeding or birthing areas.*

in a few minutes/moments/seconds *briefly/directly/momently/presently/quickly/shortly/soon/straightaway.* • Press any key, and in a few moments, the spreadsheet will appear on the screen. *Press any key, and the spreadsheet will directly appear on the screen.*

in a good mood *cheerful/glad/gleeful/happy/joyful/joyous/merry/pleased.*

in agreement with *according to/at one with/by/compliant with/consistent with/consonant with/following/in keeping with/in line with/in step with/to/under.*

in (almost) all/every cases/circumstances/instances/situations *all/almost all/almost* *always/always/consistently/constantly/invariably/ nearly all/nearly always/unfailingly.* • The actual percentage should be given in all cases. *The actual percentage should always be given.*

in all likelihood *likely/most (very) likely/probably/most (very) probably.* • In all likelihood, it will get extended until there is a determination of the ESOP litigation. *Most likely, it will get extended until there is a determination of the ESOP litigation.*

in all probability *likely/most (very) likely/probably/most (very) probably.* • A telephone call to the coordinator keeps the bank from stepping on its own toes by duplicating efforts and, in all probability, makes the call more effective. *A telephone call to the coordinator keeps the bank from stepping on its own toes by duplicating efforts and, most probably, makes the call more effective.*

in a lot of cases/circumstances/instances/situations *frequently/most often/often/sometimes/ usually.* • In a lot of cases, serial killers seek power over others. *Often, serial killers seek power over others.*

in a/the majority of cases/circumstances/ instances/situations *frequently/most often/ often/usually.* • Taking less than half the lung does not appear to be an adequate cancer operation in the majority of circumstances. *Taking less than half the lung does not usually appear to be an adequate cancer operation.* • In a majority of cases, those who join cults do not necessarily hold to the beliefs of the cult. *Most often, those who join cults do not necessarily hold to the beliefs of the cult.*

in a manner of speaking *as it were/in a sense/ in a way/so to speak.*

in a (some) measure *partially/partly/somewhat.*

in a minute/moment/second *briefly/directly/ momently/presently/quickly/shortly/soon/ straightaway.*

in an attempt/effort/endeavor to *in trying to/ to try to.* • In an attempt to satisfy the informal group, the employee may come in conflict with the formal organization. *In trying to satisfy the informal group, the employee may come in conflict with the formal organization.*

in an attempt/effort/endeavor to try to *in trying to/to try to.* • In an effort to try to contain the spiraling cost of automobile insurance, a number of legislative changes have been proposed. *In trying to contain the spiraling cost of automobile insurance, a number of legislative changes have been proposed.* • Police administrators have begun to get law enforcement to explore alliances with private security professionals in an attempt to try to find the community roots of crime. *Police administrators have begun to get law enforcement to explore alliances with private security professionals to try to find the community roots of crime.* • In an endeavor to try to make more dramatic progress for these youngsters, I want to turn your attention to something that has not happened before in our school system. *To try to make more dramatic progress for these youngsters, I want to turn your attention to something that has not happened before in our school system.*

in and of itself *as such/in itself.* • The mere claim of protection asserted by a witness of his constitutional rights does not in and of itself constitute the admission of a crime. *The mere claim of protection asserted by a witness of his constitutional rights does not in itself constitute the admission of a crime.*

in a nutshell *briefly/concisely/succinctly/tersely.* • That, in a nutshell, explains the financial community's attitude toward the crash. *That briefly explains the financial community's attitude toward the crash.*

in any case/event *all (just) the same/anyhow/ even so/still/still and all/yet.*

in any fashion/manner/way *at all/in the least* delete. • And he personally is not obligated in any way to stand behind the $675 million bond offering, or any other debt of the project. *And he personally is not at all obligated to stand behind the $675 million bond offering, or any other debt of the project.*

in any way, shape, or form/fashion *at all/in any way/in the least/in the slightest* delete. • Can that evidence be used in any way, shape, or form? *Can that evidence be used in any way?* • I will never discuss this issue with you in any way, shape, form, or fashion again. *I will never discuss this issue with you again.*

in a position to *able to/ready to.* • By the end of the year, we will be in a position to hire another person. *By the end of the year, we will be ready to hire another person.* • This year, only 11 players are currently in camp, but with eight players back from last season, the Titans should be in a position to get stronger. *This year, only 11 players are currently in camp, but with eight players back from last season, the Titans should be able to get stronger.*

in appearance delete. • They may look different in appearance, but each is built essentially with the same type of components that perform the same functions. *They may look different, but each is built essentially with the same type of components that perform the same functions.*

in a row *straight.* • Whether the bill dies on Beacon Hill for the third year in a row or becomes law in some form, the advocates of acupuncture are pressing their case with a gentle insistence. *Whether the bill dies on Beacon Hill for the third straight year or becomes law in some form, the advocates of acupuncture are pressing their case with a gentle insistence.*

in arrears *late/overdue.*

in (a/the) . . . sense *-(al)ly* delete. • In a broad sense, office automation is the incorporation of technology to help people manage information. *Broadly, office automation is the incorporation*

of technology to help people manage information. • Although there is a significant relationship in a statistical sense, the association is not strong. *Although there is a significant statistical relationship, the association is not strong.* • I don't mean this in a pejorative sense. *I don't mean this pejoratively.* • There was really nothing which could be called communication in any genuine sense. *There was really nothing which could be called genuine communication.*

in a similar fashion/manner/way (to) *alike/as/like/much as/much like/much the same (as)/rather like/resembling/similar (to)/similarly (to).* • My guess is 99 percent of the customers will behave in a similar manner. *My guess is 99 percent of the customers will behave similarly.*

inasmuch/insomuch as *as far as/as much as/so far as/so much as.* • Inasmuch as we can tell, you need to be direct. *So far as we can tell, you need to be direct.*

inasmuch/insomuch as *because/considering/for/given/in that/since.* • All seemed to share the conviction that the American educational system is far superior inasmuch as it focuses on the individual student. *All seemed to share the conviction that the American educational system is far superior because it focuses on the individual student.* • There are limitations to their work inasmuch as they do not have access to all the same resources that are available to federal and state police agencies. *There are limitations to their work since they do not have access to all the same resources that are available to federal and state police agencies.*

in association with *along with/and/as well as/combined with/coupled with/joined with/paired with/together with/with.*

in a/the . . . state (of) . . . *in* delete. • I'm in a state of uncertainty about how to travel. *I'm uncertain about how to travel.* • But while men's wear has been doing pretty well, women's wear storeowners are in a state of shock. *But while* *men's wear has been doing pretty well, women's wear storeowners are in shock.* • So we are left to walk the earth like robots or zombies, telling ourselves and others that everything's fine while we are actually numb, cut off from our emotions, entrenched in a state of denial. *So we are left to walk the earth like robots or zombies, telling ourselves and others that everything's fine while we are actually numb, cut off from our emotions, entrenched in denial.*

in a timely fashion/manner/way *by next week (tomorrow)/fast/in (within) a day (year)/in/on time/promptly/quickly/rapidly/right away/shortly/soon/speedily/swiftly/timely.* • Please give me your response in a timely manner. *Please give me your response by tomorrow.* • Many larger and more complex companies are able to provide audited reports in a timely fashion. *Many larger and more complex companies are able to provide audited reports speedily.*

in attendance *present.* • Also in attendance were key attorneys and representatives on both sides of the lawsuit. *Also present were key attorneys and representatives on both sides of the lawsuit.*

in a way *rather/somehow/someway(s)/somewhat.* • In a way, I find it intimidating. *I somehow find it intimidating.*

in back of *after/behind.*

in . . . behalf (of) *by/for.*

(something/somewhere) in between *between/in/within.* • The bonds are selling at $2 bid, $4 offered for a $100 face value bond, which means that the selling price would probably fall somewhere in between that range. *The bonds are selling at $2 bid, $4 offered for a $100 face value bond, which means that the selling price would probably fall in that range.*

in (a/the) bigger/greater/higher/larger amount/degree/number/quantity *more/more*

often/more so. • Apple must wait until high-quality flat-panel screens are available in greater numbers before it can release a lap-top Macintosh. *Apple must wait until more high-quality flat-panel screens are available before it can release a lap-top Macintosh.*

in big/great/high/huge/large/overwhelming/ sizable/vast numbers *a good (great) many/ almost all/dozens (of)/hundreds (of)/many/millions (of)/most/nearly all/scores (of)/thousands (of).* • Riot police in large numbers were called in to stop the protestors. *Scores of riot police were called in to stop the protestors.*

in both cases/circumstances/instances/situations *both/for (in) both* delete. • In both cases, about 10 percent of the sales force accounted for about 90 percent of the revenues. *For both, about 10 percent of the sales force accounted for about 90 percent of the revenues.*

in brief/concise/succinct summary *briefly (concisely/succinctly)/in brief/in fine/in short/ in sum.* • In brief summary, those are some of the reasons why original intention cannot be a neat solution to the problem of expounding our Constitution—and living under it. *In sum, those are some of the reasons why original intention cannot be a neat solution to the problem of expounding our Constitution—and living under it.*

in (a/the) . . . capacity/function/position/role (as/of) *as (a/the).* • In my capacity as chairman of the Arab group, I would like to express our deep regret for the steps taken by the United States in this regard. *As chairman of the Arab group, I would like to express our deep regret for the steps taken by the United States in this regard.* • In his capacity as the vice president at Mindware, Mr. Chatterjee has successfully sold to and signed multiyear contracts with large to medium-size firms. *As the vice president at Mindware, Mr. Chatterjee has successfully sold to and signed multiyear contracts with large to medium-size firms.*

incarcerate *jail.*

in case *if/lest/should.* • In case you've just joined us, we're talking about men's perception of the Women's Movement. *If you've just joined us, we're talking about men's perception of the Women's Movement.*

in (a/the) . . . case/circumstance/instance/situation *-(al)ly.* • In a typical situation, the MLI command will have stored important information in an MLI data area that is used by all MLI commands. *Typically, the MLI command will have stored important information in an MLI data area that is used by all MLI commands.*

in (the) . . . case (of) *about/as for/as to/concerning/for/in/of/on/over/regarding/respecting/to/toward/with* delete. • In the case of the airport, that role is performed by the air traffic controller and each airline's operations center. *As to the airport, that role is performed by the air traffic controller and each airline's operations center.* • In contrast, in the case of a married working couple without children, premature death of one income earner is not likely to cause serious financial problems for the surviving spouse. *In contrast, for a married working couple without children, premature death of one income earner is not likely to cause serious financial problems for the surviving spouse.*

in cases/circumstances/instances/situations in which *if/when/where.* • In cases in which improperly tested blood products had been released, Dr. Sandler said the donors were contacted for retesting to assure that no tainted blood had been transmitted. *Where improperly tested blood products had been released, Dr. Sandler said the donors were contacted for retesting to assure that no tainted blood had been transmitted.*

in cases when/where *if/when/where.* • In cases where one topic requires knowledge of another, the required topic is cross-referenced. *Where one topic requires knowledge of another, the required topic is cross-referenced.*

in certain/some cases *at times/now and then/occasionally/on occasion/some/sometimes* delete. • In some cases, smoking does affect mental acuity. *Smoking sometimes does affect mental acuity.*

in certain/some circumstances *at times/every so often/now and again/now and then/occasionally/on occasion/some/sometimes* delete. • In some circumstances, the computer can augment or replace many of the engineer's other tools. *Now and then, the computer can augment or replace many of the engineer's other tools.*

in certain/some instances *at times/every so often/now and again/now and then/occasionally/on occasion/some/sometimes* delete. • In some instances, we lost the customer to the competition. *We lost some customers to the competition.*

in certain/some regards *rather/somehow/someway(s)/somewhat.*

in certain/some respects *rather/somehow/someway(s)/somewhat.* • The finding is somewhat surprising since auditory information processing seems in some respects quite different from the operations required to sense visual patterns. *The finding is somewhat surprising since auditory information processing seems somehow quite different from the operations required to sense visual patterns.*

in certain/some situations *at times/every so often/now and again/now and then/occasionally/on occasion/some/sometimes* delete. • In some situations, change threatens security. *Sometimes change threatens security.*

in character delete. • As the market becomes more institutional in character, it will be easier for foreign companies to enter the U.S.

market. *As the market becomes more institutional, it will be easier for foreign companies to enter the U.S. market.* • His conduct was so outrageous in character as to go beyond all possible bounds of decency. *His conduct was so outrageous as to go beyond all possible bounds of decency.*

in . . . circumstances/conditions *-(al)ly* delete. • The attack was a carefully planned military operation that ended in tragic circumstances. *The attack was a carefully planned military operation that ended tragically.*

in circumstances when/where *if/when/where.* • Independent counsel might well be required prior to accepting a defendant's waiver of important constitutional rights in circumstances where there is reason to believe that independent legal advice is necessary in order to permit the defendant to decide whether to waive or to exercise his rights. *Independent counsel might well be required prior to accepting a defendant's waiver of important constitutional rights where there is reason to believe that independent legal advice is necessary in order to permit the defendant to decide whether to waive or to exercise his rights.*

in close proximity (to) *close by/close to/in proximity/near/nearby.* • Some who have worked in close proximity to the Oval Office in recent years support his major propositions. *Some who have worked close to the Oval Office in recent years support his major propositions.*

including everything *in all/overall.*

in color delete. • Chalkboards are commonly black or green in color. *Chalkboards are commonly black or green.* • If he or she is pale, ashen (gray), or cyanotic (bluish) in color and appears anxious, frightened, or restless, suspect shock. *If he or she is pale, ashen (gray), or cyanotic (bluish) and appears anxious, frightened, or restless, suspect shock.*

in combination with *along with/and/as well as/combined with/coupled with/joined with/paired with/together with/with.* • This risk is now avoided by using estrogen in combination with progesterone. *This risk is now avoided by using estrogen along with progesterone.*

in/over (the) coming days/decades/months/weeks/years *at length/before long/eventually/in time/later/one day/over time/presently/quickly/shortly/someday/sometime/soon/ultimately/with time/yet* delete. • Other schemes could emerge in coming months. *Other schemes could emerge before long.*

in common with *like.* • You are quite right in pointing out that I, in common with other cultural historians, have singled out but one out of several possible Adams lines. *You are quite right in pointing out that I, like other cultural historians, have singled out but one out of several possible Adams lines.*

in company with *along with/and/as well as/together with/with.* • If anything, the Reagan administration, in company with the Kremlin and the other big powers, waited too long to denounce the use of chemical weapons. *If anything, the Reagan administration, as well as the Kremlin and the other big powers, waited too long to denounce the use of chemical weapons.*

in comparison to/with *against/alongside/beside/compared to/with/-(i)er than/less/less than/more/more than/next to/over/than/to/versus/vis-à-vis.* • The reunion's turnout was large in comparison to other reunions. *The reunion's turnout was larger than other reunions.* • U.S. students are inferior in their spelling ability in comparison to the other nations' students. *U.S. students are inferior in their spelling ability to the other nations' students.* • Dutch auction issues experience less price volatility in comparison to ARPS. *Dutch auction issues experience less price volatility compared to ARPS.*

in comparison/in contrast to/with . . . relatively *compared/contrasted to/with/in comparison/in contrast to/with/relatively.* • In comparison to earlier years, inflation has been relatively moderate over the last half decade. *Compared to earlier years, inflation has been moderate over the last half decade.* • America may never be a perfectly safe place to be, but it is in comparison, relatively the safest as well as the freest. *America may never be a perfectly safe place to be, but it is in comparison the safest as well as the freest.* • In comparison, relatively little is known about how developing RGCs acquire these characteristics. *Relatively little is known about how developing RGCs acquire these characteristics.* • In contrast, relatively little is known about the gender-specific changes in body composition that characterize AIDS wasting in women. *In contrast, little is known about the gender-specific changes in body composition that characterize AIDS wasting in women.*

incompetency *incompetence.* • Hospitalization often makes clients vulnerable to thoughts of inadequacy and incompetency. *Hospitalization often makes clients vulnerable to thoughts of inadequacy and incompetence.*

in compliance with *according to/at one with/by/compliant with/consistent with/consonant with/following/in keeping with/in line with/in step with/to/under.* • In compliance with the new order, participants now receive a 2 percent discount from market prices on shares made available directly from the company. *Under the new order, participants now receive a 2 percent discount from market prices on shares made available directly from the company.*

in conclusion *finally/in closing/lastly.*

in conformance to/with *according to/at one with/by/compliant with/consistent with/consonant with/following/in keeping with/in line with/in step with/to/under.* • Certain terms of the Agreement shall be completed in conformance to the terms of the successful proposal. *Certain terms of the Agreement shall be completed according to the terms of the successful proposal.*

in conformity to/with *according to/at one with/by/compliant with/consistent with/consonant with/following/in keeping with/in line with/in step with/to/under.* • The law says a product is presumed to be free of defects when it is produced in conformity to government standards. *The law says a product is presumed to be free of defects when it is produced to government standards.*

in conjunction *combined/together.* • The primary evidence with which the Warren Report failed to deal consists of the ballistics report, the Zapruder film, and the autopsy report, taken in conjunction. *The primary evidence with which the Warren Report failed to deal consists of the ballistics report, the Zapruder film, and the autopsy report, taken together.*

in conjunction with *along with/and/as well as/combined with/coupled with/joined with/paired with/together with/with.* • The results of the interviews in conjunction with other supporting data are contained in the report. *The results of the interviews and other supporting data are contained in the report.*

in connection with *along with/and/as well as/combined with/coupled with/joined with/paired with/together with/with.*

in connection with *about/as for/as to/concerning/for/in/of/on/over/regarding/respecting/to/toward/with delete.* • The bank with sufficient presence and skills may be asked to work with the client's own local advisors in connection with purely domestic transactions. *The bank with sufficient presence and skills may be asked to work with the client's own local advisors on purely domestic transactions.*

in consequence *consequently/hence/so/then/ therefore/thus.*

in consequence of *after/because of/by/due to/ following/for/from/in/out of/owing to/through/ with.* • The defendants cannot claim to have suffered damage in consequence of the plaintiffs' early entry onto premises they had already vacated pursuant to a notice to quit for nonpayment of rent. *The defendants cannot claim to have suffered damage from the plaintiffs' early entry onto premises they had already vacated pursuant to a notice to quit for nonpayment of rent.*

in consequence of the fact that *because/considering/for/given/in that/since.* • In consequence of the fact that the Personal Suitability scores were arrived at without the consensus of all Board members, there is some doubt as to whether the assessment of Personal Suitability was conducted in accordance with merit. *Since the Personal Suitability scores were arrived at without the consensus of all Board members, there is some doubt as to whether the assessment of Personal Suitability was conducted in accordance with merit.* • I believe that we are subject to the law of habit in consequence of the fact that we have bodies. *I believe that we are subject to the law of habit because we have bodies.*

in consideration of *because of/due to/for/in return for/in view of/on account of/owing to/ through.* • In consideration of the foregoing and of the mutual promises contained herein, the parties mutually agree as follows. *In view of the foregoing and the mutual promises contained herein, the parties mutually agree as follows.*

in consideration of the fact that *because/considering/for/given/in that/since.* • In consideration of the fact that Medicare payments are already deducted from my Social Security checks, am I entitled to a credit for this further deduction? *Since Medicare payments are already deducted from my Social Security checks, am I entitled to a credit for this further deduction?* • In consideration of the fact that Ownertrades.com has no credit card transaction capabilities, and maintains no credit card information or database, and in consideration of the fact that all credit card payments to Ownertrades.com and its principals are made through PayPal using their secure transaction processes, you agree to hold Ownertrades.com and its principals harmless from any losses, claims, or damages related to your credit card. *Since Ownertrades.com has no credit card transaction capabilities, and maintains no credit card information or database, and since all credit card payments to Ownertrades.com and its principals are made through PayPal using their secure transaction processes, you agree to hold Ownertrades.com and its principals harmless from any losses, claims, or damages related to your credit card.*

in consonance to/with *according to/at one with/by/compliant with/consistent with/consonant with/following/in keeping with/in line with/ in step with/to/under.*

in contrast to/with *against/alongside/beside/ compared to/with/-(i)er than/less/less than/ more/more than/next to/over/than/to/unlike/ versus/vis-à-vis.* • In contrast to last month, September sales of government debt are expected to be light. *Compared to last month, September sales of government debt are expected to be light.*

in conversation with *conversing with/speaking to/with/talking to/with.* • I don't know what happened/I was in conversation with my friend. *I don't know what happened/I was talking with my friend.*

in copious profusion *copiously/in profusion.* • As naturally and spontaneously as the notes that issue from the throat of a thrush, the melodies poured forth from Schubert's pen in copious profusion. *As naturally and spontaneously as the notes that issue from the throat of a thrush, the melodies poured forth from Schubert's pen in profusion.*

incorporate in(to) *add/contain/have/include.*

in correspondence to/with *according to/at one with/by/compliant with/consistent with/consonant with/following/in keeping with/in line with/in step with/to/under.*

(an/the) increased/increasing amount of *increasing/more.* • As the world's leisure time expands, an increasing amount of time and money is spent on all forms of entertainment. *As the world's leisure time expands, more time and money is spent on all forms of entertainment.* • There is an increasing amount of industrialization and urban development throughout the area. *There is increasing industrialization and urban development throughout the area.*

(an/the) increased/increasing number of *increasing/more.* • An increased number of grants and other contributions have been made available for event funding. *More grants and other contributions have been made available for event funding.* • Robots are taking an increasing number of jobs, a new UN report says. *Robots are taking more jobs, a new UN report says.*

(a) . . . increase over *more than.* • That's a 33-percent increase over last year. *That's 33 percent more than last year.*

increase up *increase.* • Cash Consideration may increase up to a maximum of $466.67. *Cash Consideration may increase to a maximum of $466.67.*

increasing in *increasingly.* • The seaweed treatments are increasing in popularity with both men and women. *The seaweed treatments are*

increasingly popular with both men and women.

increasingly more *increasingly/more/more and more.* • Information processing is becoming increasingly more automated through the use of machines. *Information processing is becoming increasingly automated through the use of machines.* • As the size and complexity of software systems increase, the task of building and maintaining these systems becomes increasingly more arduous. *As the size and complexity of software systems increase, the task of building and maintaining these systems becomes more arduous.*

in/over (the) days/decades/months/weeks/years ahead *at length/before long/eventually/in time/later/one day/over time/presently/quickly/shortly/someday/sometime/soon/ultimately/with time/yet* delete. • We expect prospects will improve over the years ahead. *We expect prospects will improve in time.*

in (the) days/decades/months/weeks/years gone by *before/earlier/formerly/once/over the (years)/over time* delete. • In years gone by, much has been written about perceived gains in the powers of the presidency compared with the powers of the Congress and vice versa. *Much has been written about perceived gains in the powers of the presidency compared with the powers of the Congress and vice versa.*

in (the) days/decades/months/weeks/years of old *before/earlier/formerly/once/over the (years)/over time* delete. • The world must have seemed a larger place in days of old. *The world must have once seemed a larger place.*

in (the) days/decades/months/weeks/years past *before/earlier/formerly/once/over the (years)/over time/previously* delete. • Police academy training is more extensive for new officers, providing extensive computer training, whereas in years past only a few officers would have had any experience with computers. *Police academy training is more extensive for new officers, providing extensive computer training, whereas before only a few officers would have had any experience with computers.*

in (the) days/decades/months/weeks/years since *since/since then.* • However, in the years since 1970, the same continent has experienced precipitation levels above the mean measurements for the reference period. *However, since 1970, the same continent has experienced precipitation levels above the mean measurements for the reference period.*

in/over . . . days'/decades'/hours'/minutes'/months'/weeks'/years' time *in/over . . . days/decades/hours/minutes/months/weeks/years.* • I'm going to be visiting some Navy bases in a few months' time. *I'm going to be visiting some Navy bases in a few months.* • In three days' time it'll be your turn. *In three days it'll be your turn.*

in/over (the) days/decades/months/weeks/years to come *at length/before long/eventually/in time/later/one day/over time/presently/quickly/shortly/someday/sometime/soon/ultimately/with time/yet* delete. • We are deadly serious about making changes that will allow us to remain a viable competitor in the years to come. *We are deadly serious about making changes that will allow us to remain a viable competitor.*

indebtedness *debt(s).* • Sales tax revenues are down because people are spending less, paying off their indebtedness, and saving more. *Sales tax revenues are down because people are spending less, paying off their debts, and saving more.*

in defense of *for/with.* • May I please put in a word in defense of poor Livia Budai, who has been lambasted out of all proportion in your articles? *May I please put in a word for poor Livia Budai, who has been lambasted out of all proportion in your articles?*

in defiance of *against/despite.* • Responsibility for the tragedy rests exclusively on the war criminals in the Iranian government who have elected, in defiance of the rules of warfare established for many centuries, to make regular murderous attacks on neutral merchant ships on the high seas. *Responsibility for the tragedy rests exclusively on the war criminals in the Iranian government who have elected, despite the rules of warfare established for many centuries, to make regular murderous attacks on neutral merchant ships on the high seas.*

in degree/extent delete. • In all cases, the hearing loss is prelingual, symmetric, and moderate to severe in degree. *In all cases, the hearing loss is prelingual, symmetric, and moderate to severe.* • Yucca House National Monument contains the unexcavated remains of an ancient pueblo, dating from 1200 to 1300 AD and quite large in extent. *Yucca House National Monument contains the unexcavated remains of an ancient pueblo, dating from 1200 to 1300 AD and quite large.*

in depth *deep.*

in despite of *after all/apart/aside/despite/even with/for all/with all.* • In despite of his good looks, he has never married. *For all his good looks, he has never married.*

indicate *feel/hint/mention/say/show/suggest/tell.* • He indicated that he would be fine. *He said that he would be fine.*

indication *clue/cue/hint/inkling/sign.* • There are indications that Iran may have its own chemical weapons. *There are clues that Iran may have its own chemical weapons.*

individual *(adj)* delete. • I think there are individual exceptions. *I think there are exceptions.*

individual(s) *(n) anybody/anyone/everybody/everyone/man/men/people/person/somebody/someone/those/woman/women/you* delete. • The dominant behavioral characteristic of phobic individuals is avoidance. *The dominant behavioral characteristic of phobic persons is avoidance.*

inductive reasoning *induction.*

in due course/time *at length/in time/later/one day/over time/someday/sometime/with time/yet.* • We will consider your statement in due time. *We will yet consider your statement.*

in duration *last/long* delete. • Girls are at far greater risk for sexual abuse than boys, and their sexual abuse apparently is more common and longer in duration than the abuse boys are likely to experience. *Girls are at far greater risk for sexual abuse than boys, and their sexual abuse apparently is more common and lasts longer than the abuse boys are likely to experience.*

in each/every case/circumstance/instance/situation *all/always/consistently/constantly/each/each time/for (in) each/for (in) every/every one/every time/invariably/unfailingly* delete. • In every instance, the acquirer selected is the one with the best bid. *The acquirer selected is always the one with the best bid.*

in earlier/former/prior times *before/earlier/formerly/once.* • There was plenty of weekend ticketing in prior times. *There once was plenty of weekend ticketing.*

in either/neither case/circumstance/instance/situation *either/neither way* delete. • In either case, a veto would have provided Democratic opponents with powerful rhetorical ammunition in light of the 80 percent approval for the legislation in public opinion polls. *Either way, a veto would have provided Democratic opponents with powerful rhetorical ammunition in light of the 80 percent approval for the legislation in public opinion polls.*

in either/neither event *either/neither way* delete. • In either event, you have a few options. *Either way, you have a few options.*

in error *wrong.* • He will not listen, nor will he back down even when he knows he is in error. *He will not listen, nor will he back down even when he knows he is wrong.*

in (the) event (of/that) *if (there were)/if . . . should/in case (of)/should (there)/were (there/. . . to)/when* delete. • In the event that any liquid or solid object falls into the cabinet, unplug the unit and have it checked by qualified personnel. *Should any liquid or solid object fall into the cabinet, unplug the unit and have it checked by qualified personnel.* • Such information would be vital in the event they choose to have children. *Such information would be vital if they choose to have children.*

in evidence *apparent/conspicuous/evident/obvious/plain.* • Little of that has been in evidence among the thrifts. *Little of that has been evident among the thrifts.*

in excess of *above/better than/beyond/faster than/greater than/larger than/more than/over/stronger than.* • Annually, retailers lose in excess of $1.5 billion, and only about 30 percent of those losses are to shoplifters and other outsiders. *Annually, retailers lose more than $1.5 billion, and only about 30 percent of those losses are to shoplifters and other outsiders.*

in exchange (for) *for.* • The deal would involve his gaining credibility with the administration in exchange for his helping Nicaraguan Contras in their fight against the Sandinistas. *The deal would involve his gaining credibility with the administration for his helping Nicaraguan Contras in their fight against the Sandinistas.*

in (the) face of *after all/apart/aside/despite/even with/for all/with all.* • He persevered in the face of strong pressure within his agency. *He persevered despite strong pressure within his agency.*

in fact delete. • Women not able to have power in the external world have in fact developed a secondary power. *Women not able to have power* *in the external world have developed a secondary power.*

in (a/the) . . . fashion *-(al)ly* delete. • It is true that the records are stored in a sequential fashion. *It is true that the records are stored sequentially.* • I don't think I was treated in a loyal fashion by the president. *I don't think I was treated loyally by the president.* • Your story quotes antismokers 11 times and tobacco industry representatives only twice—and then in a disdainful fashion. *Your story quotes antismokers 11 times and tobacco industry representatives only twice—and then disdainfully.*

in favor (of) *for/with.* • Five circuit courts of appeal have ruled in favor of testing without individualized suspicion. *Five circuit courts of appeal have ruled for testing without individualized suspicion.*

(an/the) infinite number (of) *countless/endless/infinite/millions (of)/myriad/numberless/untold.* • The voice is capable of an infinite number of sounds and pitches. *The voice is capable of countless sounds and pitches.*

inflammable *flammable.*

in force and effect *active/at work/effective/in action/in effect/in force/in play/working.* • Tenant agrees to pay Landlord at the rate of $1200 per month on the first day of each and every month in advance so long as this lease is in force and effect. *Tenant agrees to pay Landlord at the rate of $1200 per month on the first day of each and every month in advance so long as this lease is in effect.*

in (a/the) . . . form *in/-(al)ly* delete. • An analyst must be able to state the assumption in explicit form. *An analyst must be able to explicitly state the assumption.* • Specifications of a patent must be attached to the application in written form describing the invention in detail so that a person skilled in the field can produce the item. *Written specifications of a patent must*

be attached to the application describing the invention in detail so that a person skilled in the field can produce the item.

inform *tell/write.* • She informed me that she wants a divorce. *She told me that she wants a divorce.*

in . . . from now *from now/in.* • In about six to seven years from now, OPEC will once again be able to capture 50 percent of the world market. *In about six to seven years, OPEC will once again be able to capture 50 percent of the world market.*

in front of *before.* • We have tough challenges in front of us. *We have tough challenges before us.*

in fulfillment of *to complete/to finish/to fulfill/to satisfy.* • In fulfillment of its open-ended agreement, Saatchi & Saatchi will also advise the Soviets on how much they should charge for TV spots that could reach some 180 million Soviet citizens and another 30 million viewers in Eastern Europe. *To fulfill its open-ended agreement, Saatchi & Saatchi will also advise the Soviets on how much they should charge for TV spots that could reach some 180 million Soviet citizens and another 30 million viewers in Eastern Europe.*

in furtherance of *to advance/to further/to help/toward.* • PTG is providing information and services on the Internet as a benefit and service in furtherance of PTG's nonprofit and tax-exempt status. *PTG is providing information and services on the Internet as a benefit and service to further PTG's nonprofit and tax-exempt status.*

in general delete. • Women in general have a responsibility to one another. *Women have a responsibility to one another.*

(a/the) -ing of *-ing.* • The taking of drugs is bad for people. *Taking drugs is bad for people.* • Often the initial development of a program focuses on the obtaining of some correct solution to the given problem. *Often the initial* *development of a program focuses on obtaining some correct solution to the given problem.* • It has several verification problems that can only be appreciated by a careful reading of the treaty. *It has several verification problems that can only be appreciated by carefully reading the treaty.*

in good time *at length/in time/later/one day/ over time/someday/sometime/with time/yet.*

in great/large measure *almost all/chiefly/commonly/generally/greatly/in general/largely/ mainly/most/mostly/most often/much/nearly all/ normally/overall/typically/usually.* • Your today is in large measure a result of your yesterdays. *Your today is largely a result of your yesterdays.*

in great/large part *almost all/chiefly/commonly/generally/greatly/in general/largely/ mainly/most/mostly/most often/much/nearly all/ normally/overall/typically/usually.* • The lower cost of U.S. labor was due in large part to the drop in value of the dollar compared with most other currencies. *The lower cost of U.S. labor was largely due to the drop in value of the dollar compared with most other currencies.*

in great/large quantities *a good (great) deal (of)/a good (great) many (of)/almost all/dozens (of)/hundreds (of)/many/millions (of)/most/ nearly all/scores (of)/thousands (of).* • The $2 bills are not being ordered by area banks even though the Federal Reserve has them in large quantities. *The $2 bills are not being ordered by area banks even though the Federal Reserve has millions of them.*

. . . in height *high* delete. • They should be at least 18 inches in height, not encircled, and placed close to the parts they apply to. *They should be at least 18 inches high, not encircled, and placed close to the parts they apply to.* • Bald cypress is the sentinel of the Southern swamp, reaching over one hundred feet tall in height. *Bald cypress is the sentinel of the Southern swamp, reaching over one hundred feet tall.* •

These patients are short in height and severely affected by joint laxity and dislocations. *These patients are short and severely affected by joint laxity and dislocations.*

in (the) history (of the world) *ever.* • Original plans called for a fleet of 132 bombers with the cost of each plane estimated at $500 million, making it the most expensive plane in history. *Original plans called for a fleet of 132 bombers with the cost of each plane estimated at $500 million, making it the most expensive plane ever.*

in honor of *after/for/to.*

in imitation of *after/following.*

in instances when/where *if/when/where.* • In instances where the products and services being traded within the firm are unique, the cost-plus method seems appropriate. *When the products and services being traded within the firm are unique, the cost-plus method seems appropriate.*

in isolation (from) *alone/apart (from)/by itself/ separate (from).* • It makes no sense to discuss one issue in isolation from the other. *It makes no sense to discuss one issue separate from the other.*

initial/initially *at first/first.* • Initially, the key was successfully marketing the fund to commercial banks. *At first, the key was successfully marketing the fund to commercial banks.*

initially . . . begin/start *begin/start.* • I believe he initially started as a stand-up comic. *I believe he started as a stand-up comic.*

in its/their entirety *all (the)/(the) complete/completely/(the) entire/entirely/every/(the) full/fully/ (the) whole/wholly* delete. • When you read the book in its entirety, you will understand my position. *When you read the entire book, you will understand my position.*

(be) in jeopardy *endangered/imperiled/jeopardized.* • None of us can avoid the responsibility of working in all ways open to us to shore up the democracy that is so clearly in jeopardy. *None of us can avoid the responsibility of working in all ways open to us to shore up the democracy that is so clearly jeopardized.*

in length *last/long* delete. • The panel discussion itself will be two hours in length. *The panel discussion itself will last two hours.* • The first is genuine trading courses, usually lasting three to five days in length. *The first is genuine trading courses, usually lasting three to five days.*

in (the) light of the fact that *because/considering/for/given that/in that/since/when.* • Perhaps the notion that information has some value is a misguided one, particularly in light of the fact that most popular websites merely drag you in under the pretense of providing information, while in reality they are setting you up for a sales pitch. *Perhaps the notion that information has some value is a misguided one, particularly given that most popular websites merely drag you in under the pretense of providing information, while in reality they are setting you up for a sales pitch.* • Now, why would teams who are doing miserably not give him a shot, especially in light of the fact that he led his defense to the lowest points ever allowed, and followed it up with a Super Bowl Championship? *Now, why would teams who are doing miserably not give him a shot, especially since he led his defense to the lowest points ever allowed, and followed it up with a Super Bowl Championship?*

in like fashion/manner *likewise/similarly.* • In like fashion, managers need to know how they are doing from the viewpoints of those they are paid to serve. *Likewise, managers need to know how they are doing from the viewpoints of those they are paid to serve.*

in (a/the) . . . manner *-(al)ly* delete. • I hope future stories dealing with sensitive issues such as this will be handled in a more responsible and accurate manner. *I hope future stories dealing with sensitive issues such as this will be handled more responsibly and accurately.* • According to CAREI, studies have found that some families were affected in a positive manner by the start changes and some were negatively affected. *According to CAREI, studies have found that some families were positively affected by the start changes and some were negatively affected.* • All writing on labels must be printed in a clear and legible manner and should be in Spanish unless authorized otherwise by the DFC. *All writing on labels must be printed clearly and legibly and should be in Spanish unless authorized otherwise by the DFC.*

in many/most cases *almost all/almost always/commonly/frequently/many/many times/most/most often/much/nearly all/nearly always/normally/often/typically/usually.* • In most cases, the pitch can be approximated or laid off with a scale or dividers. *Usually, the pitch can be approximated or laid off with a scale or dividers.*

in many/most circumstances *almost all/almost always/commonly/frequently/many/many times/most/most often/much/nearly all/nearly always/normally/often/ordinarily/typically/usually.* • RISC microprocessors operate faster than CISC microprocessors in many circumstances. *RISC microprocessors often operate faster than CISC microprocessors.*

in many/most instances *almost all/almost always/commonly/frequently/many/many times/most/most often/much/nearly all/nearly always/normally/often/ordinarily/typically/usually.* • In many instances, the family is in a state of dysfunction and disrepair. *Often, the family is in a state of dysfunction and disrepair.*

in many/most regards *almost always/largely/many/most/mostly/most often/nearly always/often/usually.*

in many/most respects *almost always/largely/ many/most/mostly/most often/nearly always/ often/usually.* • In most respects, competition among banks has been polite. *Competition among banks has been largely polite.*

in many/most situations *almost all/almost always/commonly/frequently/many/many times/most/most often/much/nearly all/nearly always/normally/often/ordinarily/typically/ usually.* • The speed with which a modem can transmit and receive data is important in many situations. *The speed with which a modem can transmit and receive data is usually important.*

in (our) midst *among (us).*

in much the same fashion/manner/way (as/ that) *much as/much like.* • Though similar in size, material, and color and fabricated in much the same way as their plainer cousins, the new tokens bore various kinds of surface markings and showed a greater variety of shapes. *Though similar in size, material, and color and fabricated much like their plainer cousins, the new tokens bore various kinds of surface markings and showed a greater variety of shapes.* • In much the same fashion as it had done two weeks earlier when scuttling a chance to knock off Saint Mary's, a team that boasted the No. 2 RPI in the nation, SDSU again shot itself out of the game by connecting on just 32.2 percent of its field-goal attempts. *Much as it had done two weeks earlier when scuttling a chance to knock off Saint Mary's, a team that boasted the No. 2 RPI in the nation, SDSU again shot itself out of the game by connecting on just 32.2 percent of its field-goal attempts.* • The second stanza proceeded in much the same manner as the first. *The second stanza proceeded much like the first.*

in my assessment *I assert/I believe/I claim/I consider/I contend/I declare/I feel/I hold/I judge/I maintain/I regard/I say/I think/I view/ to me* delete. • In my assessment, the most desirable changes for commercial banks to

incorporate are as follows. *To me, the most desirable changes for commercial banks to incorporate are as follows.*

in my estimation *I assert/I believe/I claim/I consider/I contend/I declare/I feel/I hold/I judge/I maintain/I regard/I say/I think/I view/ to me* delete. • In my estimation, the treatment is suitable to Mr. Ross's case. *I feel the treatment is suitable to Mr. Ross's case.*

in my judgment *I assert/I believe/I claim/I consider/I contend/I declare/I feel/I hold/I judge/I maintain/I regard/I say/I think/I view/to me* delete. • The most critical issue confronting America, in my judgment, is how we match educational accessibility and opportunity to the demographic change. *The most critical issue confronting America, I contend, is how we match educational accessibility and opportunity to the demographic change.*

in my (own) mind(s) *for myself* delete. • I had to find out in my own mind if quiet diplomacy would work. *I had to find out for myself if quiet diplomacy would work.*

(to) . . . in my (own) mind's eye *envisage/envision/imagine/visualize* delete. • Once you get to the gate, you need to review in your mind's eye where the engines are. *Once you get to the gate, you need to visualize where the engines are.*

in my opinion *I assert/I believe/I claim/I consider/I contend/I declare/I feel/I hold/I judge/I maintain/I regard/I say/I think/I view/to me* delete. • In my opinion, the cruelest aggression is nonverbal, passive aggression. *To me, the cruelest aggression is nonverbal, passive aggression.*

in my view *I assert/I believe/I claim/I consider/I contend/I declare/I feel/I hold/I judge/I maintain/I regard/I say/I think/I view/to me* delete. • In my view, most of these principles were narrow in scope. *I believe most of these principles were narrow in scope.*

in nature delete. • Christianity is theistic and revelatory in nature; the New Age is humanistic and generally solipsistic in nature. *Christianity is theistic and revelatory; the New Age is humanistic and generally solipsistic.*

in no case *never/not/not ever/not once.* • In no case would I recommend anything that could lead to the situation at Agawam. *Never would I recommend anything that could lead to the situation at Agawam.*

in normal/ordinary/typical/usual practice *commonly/customarily/normally/ordinarily/typically/usually.* • In normal practice, the party chairman is nominated, and the voting delegation then stands in unison to express its support. *Normally, the party chairman is nominated, and the voting delegation then stands in unison to express its support.*

in no small measure *almost all/chiefly/commonly/generally/greatly/in general/largely/mainly/most/mostly/most often/much/nearly all/normally/overall/typically/usually.* • Our continued success is due in no small measure to their contribution on a daily basis. *Our continued success is greatly due to their contribution on a daily basis.*

in no small part *almost all/chiefly/commonly/generally/greatly/in general/largely/mainly/most/mostly/most often/much/nearly all/normally/overall/typically/usually.* • And I continue to feel that his lifelong feelings of inadequacy and frustration stemmed in no small part from the limitations that he imposed upon his work. *And I continue to feel that his lifelong feelings of inadequacy and frustration stemmed largely from the limitations that he imposed upon his work.*

in no time (at all) *promptly/quickly/rapidly/right away/shortly/soon/speedily/swiftly.*

innovative new *innovative/new.* • An innovative new product combining the latest in communications technology is being installed in courthouses and recording offices throughout the country for public use. *A new product combining the latest in communications technology is being installed in courthouses and recording offices throughout the country for public use.*

in no way *never/not/not ever/not once.* • In no way are they meant to represent the official position of NYNEX. *They are not meant to represent the official position of NYNEX.*

in no way, shape, or form *in no way/never/not/not ever/not once.* • In no way, shape, or form did we aid anyone or offer incentives to anyone to go to the town meeting. *Never did we aid anyone or offer incentives to anyone to go to the town meeting.* • In no way, shape or form am I trying to disparage our opponent. *I am not trying to disparage our opponent.*

in number delete. • Nineteenth-century sweatshops are once again increasing in number. *Nineteenth-century sweatshops are once again increasing.*

innumerable *countless/endless/infinite/millions (of)/myriad/numberless/untold.*

in (March) of (2013) *(March) (2013).* • The second moving year begins in February of 2010 and extends through January of 2011. *The second moving year begins February 2010 and extends through January 2011.*

in (the) olden days *before/earlier/formerly/once.*

in operation *active/functioning/in place/running/set up/working* delete. • A large midwestern bank has had a performance monitoring program in operation since 1981. *A large midwestern bank has had a performance monitoring program since 1981.*

in opposition to *against/opposed to/with.* • Lenin set himself in opposition to the blundering, indecisive czar; Khomeini against the blundering, indecisive shah. *Lenin set himself against the blundering, indecisive czar; Khomeini against the blundering, indecisive shah.*

in . . . order *-(al)ly* delete. • We examine, in alphabetical order, all the MLI commands that make up ProDOS 8. *We examine, alphabetically, all the MLI commands that make up ProDOS 8.*

in order for *for.* • Is it necessary that animals die in order for humans to live? *Is it necessary that animals die for humans to live?*

in order that *for/so/so that/that.* • The overall dimension and the radii are given in order that their centers may be located. *The overall dimension and the radii are given so that their centers may be located.*

in order to *so as to/to.* • In order to qualify for a heart transplant, certain criteria must be met, one of which is having less than a year to live. *To qualify for a heart transplant, certain criteria must be met, one of which is having less than a year to live.*

in other cases/circumstances/instances/situations *at times/other/(at) other times/some/sometimes* delete. • In other cases, the application may be more mundane, like helping users set up newly delivered microcomputers. *Other applications may be more mundane, like helping users set up newly delivered microcomputers.*

in other words *namely/that is/to wit.* • The directory names in the chain must define a continuous path; in other words, each directory specified must be contained within the preceding directory. *The directory names in the chain must define a continuous path; that is, each directory specified must be contained within the preceding directory.*

in partial fulfillment of *to advance/to further/ to help/toward.*

in/over (the) past days/decades/months/weeks/ years *before/earlier/formerly/once/previously.*

in payment for/of *for.* • Connoisseurs of the region cannot help wondering what Assad could offer Washington in payment for such a favor. *Connoisseurs of the region cannot help wondering what Assad could offer Washington for such a favor.*

in perpetuity *always/ceaselessly/constantly/ endlessly/eternally/everlastingly/forever/never ending/perpetually.* • It promised to preserve the rest of the farm in perpetuity as farm or forest. *It promised to preserve the rest of the farm forever as farm or forest.*

in place of *for.* • No reasonably literate person of my acquaintance says "sunk" in place of "sank." *No reasonably literate person of my acquaintance says "sunk" for "sank."*

in point of *about/as for/as to/concerning/for/in/ of/on/over/regarding/respecting/to/toward/ with* delete.

in point of fact *actually/indeed/in fact/in faith/ in reality/in truth/really/truly* delete. • The U.S. government said he wasn't working for them, but in point of fact, he was a military attache. *The U.S. government said he wasn't working for them, but in truth he was a military attache.*

in preference to *over.* • Mile's new product emphasis is on performance in preference to fashion. *Mile's new product emphasis is on performance over fashion.*

in proportion to *for/with.*

in proximity (to) *close by/close to/near/nearby.* • The property is in proximity to metropolitan Boston. *The property is near metropolitan Boston.*

in punishment for/of *for.*

in pursuit of *exploring/probing/pursuing/searching/seeking.* • One would think they could better spend their time in pursuit of the pressing problems which beset the Redevelopment Authority and the city's development plans. *One would think they could better spend their time pursuing the pressing problems which beset the Redevelopment Authority and the city's development plans.*

input *clout/pull/say/voice.* • I have a lot of input into what I'll wear on the set. *I have a lot of say about what I'll wear on the set.*

input *thoughts/views.* • These style alternatives do not solicit employee input. *These style alternatives do not solicit employee views.*

(the) . . . in question *the/that/this* delete. • Neither Phillips nor any of its subsidiaries has ever sold the chemical in question to Libya. *Neither Phillips nor any of its subsidiaries has ever sold this chemical to Libya.*

in quick/short order *abruptly/apace/briskly/directly/fast/forthwith/hastily/hurriedly/posthaste/presently/promptly/quickly/rapidly/right away/shortly/soon/speedily/straightaway/swiftly/wingedly.* • Surely a motivated work force could whip us back into shape in short order. *Surely a motivated work force could whip us back into shape quickly.*

inquire (about/of) *ask.* • I inquired of the doctor why these children have distended stomachs. *I asked the doctor why these children have distended stomachs.*

in reaction to *after/because of/by/due to/following/for/from/in/out of/owing to/through/with.*

in reality *actually/indeed/in fact/in faith/in truth/really/truly* delete.

in recent days/decades/months/weeks/years *lately/of late/recent/recently* delete. • But events have not been kind to the university in recent weeks. *But recent events have not been kind to the university.*

in recent history/memory/times *in days/months/weeks/years/lately/of late/recent/recently* delete. • It is the largest drop in auto insurance rates in recent memory. *It is the largest drop in auto insurance rates in years.*

in recorded history *on record/recorded.* • Though final figures aren't yet in, as of November 1 this has been the hottest year in recorded history. *Though final figures aren't yet in, as of November 1 this has been the hottest year on record.*

in reference to *about/as for/as to/concerning/for/in/of/on/over/regarding/respecting/to/toward/with* delete. • Never make any assumptions or promises in reference to product flaws, but report all instances either to customer service or the appropriate management personnel for corrective action. *Never make any assumptions or promises about product flaws, but report all instances either to customer service or the appropriate management personnel for corrective action.*

in regard to *about/as for/as to/concerning/for/in/of/on/over/regarding/respecting/to/toward/with* delete. • They questioned me in regard to a 1986 bank robbery. *They questioned me about a 1986 bank robbery.*

in relation to *about/as for/as to/concerning/for/in/of/on/over/regarding/respecting/to/toward/with* delete. • The researchers interviewed the survivors in relation to six areas of postwar life. *The researchers interviewed the survivors regarding six areas of postwar life.*

in relation/relationship to *against/alongside/beside/compared to/with/-(i)er than/less/less than/more/more than/next to/over/than/to/versus/vis-à-vis.* • What has been done is very small in relationship to what needs to be done. *What has been done is very small compared to what needs to be done.*

in repetition *again/over.*

in resistance to *against/with.*

in respect of/to *about/as for/as to/concerning/ for/in/of/on/over/regarding/respecting/to/ toward/with* delete. • Some additional perspective is needed in respect to South Korea. *Some additional perspective is needed on South Korea.*

in response to *after/because of/by/due to/following/for/from/in/out of/owing to/through/ with.* • The dollar yesterday fell against most major currencies in response to renewed dollar sales by central banks. *The dollar yesterday fell against most major currencies following renewed dollar sales by central banks.*

in return for *for.* • Switch traders are willing, in return for a fee, to find buyers for countertraded goods. *Switch traders are willing, for a fee, to find buyers for countertraded goods.*

(the) ins and (the) outs *details/features/particulars/specifics.*

in scale delete.

in scope delete. • Smokeless tobacco is becoming a problem large in scope. *Smokeless tobacco is becoming a large problem.*

. . . in shape delete. • The true-size surface is elliptical in shape. *The true-size surface is elliptical.* • The Japanese (Akoya) cultured pearls are round in shape and are a very good match. *The Japanese (Akoya) cultured pearls are round and are a very good match.*

in short supply *meager/rare/scant/scarce/sparse.*

inside of *inside.* • I continued to pack my gear, with pain and anger burning inside of me. *I continued to pack my gear, with pain and anger burning inside me.*

inside (and) out *completely/thoroughly.*

inside the boundaries/limits/parameters of *within.*

in/on/with (a/the) . . . -sion/-tion of/that/ to *-ing (that).* • In the 1980s, many people made plans on the assumption that oil prices would exceed $75 per barrel by 1990. *In the 1980s, many people made plans assuming that oil prices would exceed $75 per barrel by 1990.* • These same people are making significant international dispositions on the expectation that Japan will continue to be the world's largest creditor. *These same people are making significant international dispositions expecting that Japan will continue to be the world's largest creditor.*

in situations when/where *if/when/where.* • In situations where market heterogeneity limits opportunity for uniformity, the firm should actively promote global convergence of market segments. *Where market heterogeneity limits opportunity for uniformity, the firm should actively promote global convergence of market segments.*

. . . in size delete. • The sides range from 4 to 24 inches in size. *The sides range from 4 to 24 inches.* • The Provento potato, round to oval and medium to large in size, has light yellow flesh and is of consistently good quality for a variety of preparations. *The Provento potato, round to oval and medium to large, has light yellow flesh and is of consistently good quality for a variety of preparations.* • Because panfish are not big in size, the use of very light line by anglers has several advantages. *Because panfish are not big, the use of very light line by anglers has several advantages.*

insofar as *as far as/as much as/so far as/so much as.* • As a historian, Mr. Chaudhuri is useful insofar as he recounts personal experience—for example, his accounts of the Bose brothers. *As a historian, Mr. Chaudhuri is useful so far as he* *recounts personal experience—for example, his accounts of the Bose brothers.*

insofar as *because/considering/for/given/in that/ since.* • Insofar as more than 98 percent of House incumbents were returned to office in the last election, it shouldn't surprise anyone that the members are turning Congress into a family business. *Since more than 98 percent of House incumbents were returned to office in the last election, it shouldn't surprise anyone that the members are turning Congress into a family business.*

insofar as . . . (goes/is concerned) *about/as for/ as to/concerning/for/in/of/on/over/regarding/ respecting/to/toward/with* delete. • The president's position, insofar as negotiations are concerned, has never changed. *The president's position on negotiations has never changed.* • Intent, an element of the offense, may also be a factor insofar as a vehicle's recovery and condition are concerned. *Intent, an element of the offense, may also be a factor in a vehicle's recovery and condition.* • The ruling clarifies that the "orthotics" benefit in section 1861(s)(9) of the Act, insofar as braces are concerned, is limited to leg, arm, back, and neck braces that are used independently rather than in conjunction with, or as components of, other medical or non-medical equipment. *The ruling clarifies that the "orthotics" benefit in section 1861(s)(9) of the Act, regarding braces, is limited to leg, arm, back, and neck braces that are used independently rather than in conjunction with, or as components of, other medical or non-medical equipment.*

in some fashion/manner/way *somehow/some-way(s).* • He considers it an idea that will be adopted in some fashion to meet the spiraling demands on air travel. *He considers it an idea that will somehow be adopted to meet the spiraling demands on air travel.*

in spite of *after all/apart/aside/despite/even with/for all/with all.* • In spite of his malady, he wrote music with great skill and creativity. *Even with his malady, he wrote music with great skill and creativity.*

in spite of the fact that *although/but/even though/still/though/yet.* • The number of deaths from asthma has doubled in the past decade in spite of the fact that treatments have improved. *The number of deaths from asthma has doubled in the past decade, yet treatments have improved.* • Some commentators claim that careful writers avoid the adverb *slow* in spite of the fact that it has over four centuries of usage behind it. *Some commentators claim that careful writers avoid the adverb* slow *even though it has over four centuries of usage behind it.*

instantaneous/instantaneously *at once/from the start/instant/instantly/straightaway.* • We fell in love with her instantaneously. *We fell in love with her at once.*

institute *found/launch/set up.*

institution *building/factory/hospital/institute/ jail/office/place/plant/prison/school* delete.

institution of higher learning *college/school/ university.* • Mitchell Scholars may study or conduct research at institutions of higher learning. *Mitchell Scholars may study or conduct research at universities.*

in such a fashion/manner/way as to/so as to *so as to/to.* • The light fixture had to be designed in such a manner so as to provide the maximum light to the operating area. *The light fixture had to be designed to provide the maximum light to the operating area.* • Further, we do not authorize any organization to use the Association's name in such a way as to imply that such a relationship exists. *Further, we do not authorize any organization to use the Association's name so as to imply that such a relationship exists.*

in such a fashion/manner/way so/so that *so/so that/such that.* • Only meter stamped, return address labels may be used on single piece, special fourth-class rate or library rate mail, and these labels must adhere in such a manner so they will not come off in one piece. *Only meter stamped, return address labels may be used on single piece, special fourth-class rate or library rate mail, and these labels must adhere so that they will not come off in one piece.*

in such a fashion/manner/way that *so/so that.* • Export business may be structured in such a way that the buyer bears most of the risks. *Export business may be structured so that the buyer bears most of the risks.* • The first was the "store," designed in such a manner that numbers could be stored in 1,000 "registers," each capable of storing 50 digits. *The first was the "store," designed so that numbers could be stored in 1,000 "registers," each capable of storing 50 digits.*

in such (a/the) . . . fashion/manner/way *so -(al)ly* delete.

insufficient *dis-/il-/im-/in-/ir-/lack of/-less(ness)/ mis-/no/non-/not/not enough/scant/too few/too little/un-.* • There is insufficient reason for joy. *There is not enough reason for joy.*

in sufficient amount *enough.* • If radon gas enters your lungs in sufficient amounts, it can emit alpha particles that attack tissue and lead to lung cancer. *If enough radon gas enters your lungs, it can emit alpha particles that attack tissue and lead to lung cancer.*

(a/the) insufficient amount (of) *not enough/too little.*

in sufficient number *enough.* • I hope you heard from people in sufficient number to alert you to the possibility of a nationwide constituency for extended incarceration of violent felons. *I hope you heard from enough people to alert you to the possibility of a nationwide constituency for extended incarceration of violent felons.*

(a/the) insufficient number (of) *not enough/too few.* • Within two years, other American cities expect a similar gridlock of hospital beds, largely because of AIDS and an insufficient number of health-care workers. *Within two years, other American cities expect a similar gridlock of hospital beds, largely because of AIDS and too few health-care workers.*

in sufficient quantity *enough.* • Libya doesn't have the industrial capacity to make toxic agents in sufficient quantities to conduct warfare. *Libya doesn't have the industrial capacity to make enough toxic agents to conduct warfare.*

in summary/summation *in brief/in fine/in short/in sum.* • In summary, it is apparent that a country's comparative advantage situation will be vitally affected by the productivity of available factor inputs. *In sum, it is apparent that a country's comparative advantage situation will be vitally affected by the productivity of available factor inputs.*

in support of *for/with.* • Radical environmentalists are already demanding that legal and ethical protection be extended to all of nature, and a few of them have demonstrated a willingness to fight, break the law, and even die in support of this conviction. *Radical environmentalists are already demanding that legal and ethical protection be extended to all of nature, and a few of them have demonstrated a willingness to fight, break the law, and even die for this conviction.*

(an) integral part of *a part of/integral to.* • Keeping abreast of these developments is an integral part of successful EFT strategy development. *Keeping abreast of these developments is integral to successful EFT strategy development.*

integrate together *integrate/join.* • The cost of the transmitters can be significantly reduced if all the lasers can be integrated together on a single substrate. *The cost of the transmitters can* *be significantly reduced if all the lasers can be integrated on a single substrate.*

intellectual ability/capacity *ability/capacity/ intellect/intelligence.* • Tools and other remains left by Neanderthals show no indication that these creatures possessed the intellectual capacity for symbolic thought or language. *Tools and other remains left by Neanderthals show no indication that these creatures possessed the capacity for symbolic thought or language.*

interact with each other/one another *interact.* • Sites like Facebook and Twitter have revolutionized the Web, altered how we interact with each other, and even changed the way news is gathered and delivered. *Sites like Facebook and Twitter have revolutionized the Web, altered how we interact, and even changed the way news is gathered and delivered.* • Valve has fixed the effects of some items and abilities and the way they interact with each other. *Valve has fixed the effects of some items and abilities and the way they interact.*

interdependency *interdependence.*

interestingly (enough) delete. • Interestingly enough, in about 50 percent of the cases involved, the professional offering an opinion believed abuse had occurred. *In about 50 percent of the cases involved, the professional offering an opinion believed abuse had occurred.*

(the) interesting thing is (that) *interestingly* delete. • The interesting thing is that he never realized what he had done. *He never realized what he had done.*

interlocutor *speaker/talker.*

in . . . terms *-(al)ly* delete. • They both spoke in optimistic terms. *They both spoke optimistically.*

in terms of *about/as/as for/as to/by/concerning/ for/in/of/on/regarding/respecting/through/under/ with* delete. • In terms of safety, honesty, and

trust, banks consistently score higher than life insurance companies. *In safety, honesty, and trust, banks consistently score higher than life insurance companies.* • How would you say you are different in terms of your personas? *How would you say your personas are different?* • She's more aggressive in terms of what she wants. *She's more aggressive about what she wants.* • Women are looking for help in terms of PMS. *Women are looking for help with PMS.* • Other doctors have criticized IL-2 therapy in terms of its toxicity. *Other doctors have criticized IL-2 therapy for its toxicity.* • The forecast level should be judged in terms of its reasonableness. *The forecast level should be judged on its reasonableness.*

interpretate *interpret.* • I realized they were both inspired by *Alice in Wonderland,* but there are different ways to interpretate it. *I realized they were both inspired by* Alice in Wonderland, *but there are different ways to interpret it.*

interpretative *interpretive.* • Strategically placed U.S. nationals play an important interpretative role between the host country and the U.S. headquarters. *Strategically placed U.S. nationals play an important interpretive role between the host country and the U.S. headquarters.* • To provide this for students makes the experience more "active"—encouraging students to use the dictionary for productive as well as interpretative purposes. *To provide this for students makes the experience more "active"—encouraging students to use the dictionary for productive as well as interpretive purposes.*

interpret to mean *interpret as.* • Achieving a desired standard of living must be interpreted to mean finding the pattern of consumption expenditures that yields maximum satisfaction. *Achieving a desired standard of living must be interpreted as finding the pattern of consumption expenditures that yields maximum satisfaction.*

in that/this case/circumstance/instance/situation *here/now/then/there* delete. • No ampersand is required in this case because the argument will not be modified. *No ampersand is required now because the argument will not be modified.*

in that/this connection *about (for/in/on/to) that/this* delete.

in that/this day and age *in that/this age/in that/this day/in that/this time/(just/right) now/nowadays/then/these (those) days/today.* • In this day and age of global violence, I find it interesting that the *Globe Magazine* would publish articles about two international terrorists. *In this age of global violence, I find it interesting that the Globe Magazine would publish articles about two international terrorists.*

in that/this direction *toward that/this.* • That means any push in this direction would require guidance from officials of the new administration. *That means any push toward this would require guidance from officials of the new administration.*

in that/this fashion/manner/way *like this (that)/so/thus.* • What can she expect if she continues to behave in this manner? *What can she expect if she continues to behave like this?*

in that/this general vicinity *around (near) here (there)/thereabouts (hereabouts).* • There have been a lot of crimes in this general vicinity. *There have been a lot of crimes near here.*

in/on that/this matter *about (for/in/on/to) that/this* delete. • Rothko's views on this matter were very well known among his circle of friends. *Rothko's views on this were very well known among his circle of friends.*

in that/this regard *about (for/in/on/to) that/this* delete. • There will be no change at all in that regard. *There will be no change at all in that.*

in that/this respect *about (for/in/on/to) that/this* delete.

in the absence of *absent/failing/having no/lacking/minus/missing/not having/with no/without.* • In the absence of any other form of security, the shareholders of the contractor might be willing to let the company go out of business in the face of a serious problem. *Absent any other form of security, the shareholders of the contractor might be willing to let the company go out of business in the face of a serious problem.* • In the absence of quality, employees may face an "unclean" environment, which can lead to dissatisfaction for the workforce. *Lacking quality, employees may face an "unclean" environment, which can lead to dissatisfaction for the workforce.* • So in the absence of widespread XML+CSS rendering support, what is the importance of CSS in an XML developer's toolkit? *So without widespread XML+CSS rendering support, what is the importance of CSS in an XML developer's toolkit?* • The surface of the Earth is warmer than it would be in the absence of an atmosphere because it receives energy from two sources: the Sun and the atmosphere. *The surface of the Earth is warmer than it would be with no atmosphere because it receives energy from two sources: the Sun and the atmosphere.*

in the act of -ing *-ing/while -ing.* • Archaeological investigations uncovered idols of women in the act of giving birth or praying, figures of animals, neolithic shells and tools. *Archaeological investigations uncovered idols of women giving birth or praying, figures of animals, neolithic shells and tools.* • The student need not be caught in the act of using for it to be recorded as "use." *The student need not be caught using for it to be recorded as "use."* • If you preach fiscal responsibility to your kids, they'll certainly catch you in the act of straying. *If you preach fiscal responsibility to your kids, they'll certainly catch you straying.* • If she crossed a physical line in the act of protesting, she will have to face the consequences of her actions. *If she crossed a physical line while protesting, she will have to face the consequences of her actions.*

in the affirmative *affirmatively/favorably/positively/yes.* • Eight members having voted in the affirmative, the vote carries. *Eight members having voted yes, the vote carries.*

in the aftermath of *(just/right) after/(close) behind/ensuing/following/succeeding.* • In the aftermath of the assault-rifle mass murder, Americans should remain rational and not legislate away the right to own any type of firearm. *Following the assault-rifle mass murder, Americans should remain rational and not legislate away the right to own any type of firearm.*

in the altogether *naked/nude.*

in the amount/sum of *for/of* delete. • Enclosed is a check in the amount of $900.00. *Enclosed is a check for $900.00.* • We are in the process of researching your claim and have issued credit in the amount of $31.49 to your above referenced account. *We are in the process of researching your claim and have issued credit for $31.49 to your above referenced account.*

(something/somewhere) in the area (of) *about/around/close to/more or less/near/nearly/or so/roughly/some* delete. • The trial is expected to run in the area of nine months. *The trial is expected to run some nine months.*

in the area of *about/as for/as to/concerning/for/in/of/on/over/regarding/respecting/to/toward/with* delete. • The secondary gains for the phobic partner may be in the area of fulfilling nurturing needs. *The secondary gains for the phobic partner may be in fulfilling nurturing needs.* • In the area of politics, women gained the right to control their earnings, own property, and, in the case of divorce, take custody of their children. *Regarding politics, women gained the right to control their earnings, own property, and, in the case of divorce, take custody of their children.* • He was treated as an expert witness in the area of forensic pathology. *He was treated as an expert witness in forensic pathology.*

in the assessment of *assert/believe/claim/consider/contend/feel/hold/judge/maintain/regard/say/think/to/view/with.*

in/within the boundaries/limits/parameters of *in/within.*

in the capacity of *as/as such.* • Thus, a specialized or programmatic accrediting agency may also function in the capacity of an institutional accrediting agency. *Thus, a specialized or programmatic accrediting agency may also function as an institutional accrediting agency.*

in the company of *alongside/among/beside/during/in/with.* • These children are here in the company of their fathers. *These children are here with their fathers.*

in the context of *in.* • In the context of personal financial planning, the application of controls is even more important. *In personal financial planning, the application of controls is even more important.*

(somewhere) in the course of *during/for/in/over/throughout/when/while/with.* • There were several suspects that came up in the course of our investigation, but Nancy Douglas was not one of them. *There were several suspects that came up during our investigation, but Nancy Douglas was not one of them.* • In the course of doing these exercises, students are introduced to almost all of their word processing program's features. *When doing these exercises, students are introduced to almost all of their word processing program's features.*

in the course of events/things/time *at length/eventually/in due time/in the end/in time/later/one day/over the months (years)/over time/someday/sometime/ultimately/with time/yet.* • Continued observation of such men indicates that this is exactly what happens in many cases, and more evidence of this may show up in the course of time. *Continued observation of such men indicates that this is exactly what happens* *in many cases, and more evidence of this may show up over time.*

in the days/decades/months/weeks/years before/prior to *before.* • In the days before LANs, if you wanted a coworker to add to a report you were writing, you copied the file to a disk and delivered it by hand. *Before LANs, if you wanted a coworker to add to a report you were writing, you copied the file to a disk and delivered it by hand.*

in the direction of/toward *at/for/in/on/ through/to/toward/with.* • It appears it's headed in the direction of becoming a more conventional school that focuses on finances. *It appears it's headed toward becoming a more conventional school that focuses on finances.*

in the distant future *eventual/eventually/ future/in many months (years)/in time/later/ much later/next month (year)/one day/over time/ someday/sometime/ultimately/with time/ yet* delete. • In the distant future, the German people may regain unity through self-determination. *In time, the German people may regain unity through self-determination.*

in the distant past *before/earlier/formerly/long ago/long since/many months (years) ago/once/ previously* delete.

in the estimation of *assert/believe/claim/consider/contend/feel/hold/judge/maintain/regard/ say/think/to/view/with.*

in the eventuality of (that/this) *if (there were)/ if . . . should/in case (of)/should (there)/were (there/. . . to)/when* delete. • In the eventuality that someone decides not to follow a court order, what do you do? *If someone should decide not to follow a court order, what do you do?*

in the extreme *extremely/highly/hugely/mightily.* • All three theories seem unlikely in the extreme. *All three theories seem highly unlikely.*

in the face of *against/before/confronted by (with)/confronting/faced with/facing.* • In the face of those developments, the off-farm work movement was inevitable. *Faced with those developments, the off-farm work movement was inevitable.*

in the final/last analysis *all in all/all told/altogether/finally/in all/in the end/overall/ultimately.* • In the final analysis, we are still grappling with the inherent problems of being human. *In the end, we are still grappling with the inherent problems of being human.*

in the first place *first/first of all* delete. • We found ourselves troubleshooting the immediate need, not addressing the larger issues that caused the problem in the first place. *We found ourselves troubleshooting the immediate need, not addressing the larger issues that first caused the problem.*

in the following fashion/manner/way *as follows.* • The value of *M* can be substituted in the equation in the following manner. *The value of M can be substituted in the equation as follows.*

in the foreseeable future *before long/directly/ in a month (week)/next month (year)/presently/ quickly/shortly/soon/this month (year)/tomorrow* delete. • I expect in the foreseeable future we will see them looking inward and opening up to the world. *I expect we will presently see them looking inward and opening up to the world.*

in the form of *as* delete. • I offer these comments in the form of advice, not criticism. *I offer these comments as advice, not criticism.* • A proforma may be created in the form of a profit and loss statement or a cash flow statement. *A proforma may be created as a profit and loss statement or a cash flow statement.*

in the fullness of time *at length/before long/ eventually/in time/later/one day/over time/presently/quickly/shortly/someday/sometime/soon/*

ultimately/with time/yet delete. • These slip-ups on the part of most of the teams ahead of Arsenal in the table could in the fullness of time come to be crucial. *These slip-ups on the part of most of the teams ahead of Arsenal in the table could in time come to be crucial.* • It has the potential to evolve in the fullness of time into a Family Code for Muslim Indians. *It has the potential to evolve into a Family Code for Muslim Indians.* • It is at once a celebratory, elegiac, profoundly inspired, and at the very end troublingly flawed triptych which in the fullness of time will be compared fairly and favorably to Carl Sandburg's meditations on Abraham Lincoln. *It is at once a celebratory, elegiac, profoundly inspired, and at the very end troublingly flawed triptych which one day will be compared fairly and favorably to Carl Sandburg's meditations on Abraham Lincoln.*

in the function of *as.* • They focused on a group of 61 of these genes that had unknown roles in the function of blood stem cells. *They focused on a group of 61 of these genes that had unknown roles as blood stem cells.*

in/into the future *at length/before long/eventually/in a month (week)/in due time/in time/later/next month (year)/one day/over time/someday/sometime/ultimately/with time/yet* delete. • All indications are that these patterns of change will continue into the future. *All indications are that these patterns will continue.*

in the future going/moving forward *in the future.* • That doesn't mean there won't be questions about using them in the future going forward. *That doesn't mean there won't be questions about using them in the future.* • This generic pressure is going to affect how the company is hiring in the future moving forward. *This generic pressure is going to affect how the company is hiring in the future.*

(is) in the habit of *given to/inured to/prone to/tend to/used to/will (would).* • When I was younger, I was in the habit of reading a book a week. *When I was younger, I would read a book a week.* • If you're a frugal shopper, you're probably in the habit of scouring the weekly advertisements from the area's grocery stores. *If you're a frugal shopper, you're probably prone to scouring the weekly advertisements from the area's grocery stores.*

(condemn) in the harshest/strongest possible terms delete. • Although this paper is generally supportive of President Bush, we now feel morally compelled to condemn him in the harshest possible terms. *Although this paper is generally supportive of President Bush, we now feel morally compelled to condemn him harshly.* • Vladimir Putin condemned in the strongest possible terms this barbaric act of killing the innocent and the young. *Vladimir Putin strongly condemned this barbaric act of killing the innocent and the young.* • UNRWA will protest this violation of the sanctity of its school in the strongest possible terms to the Israeli authorities. *UNRWA will strongly protest this violation of the sanctity of its school to the Israeli authorities.*

in the immediate future *at once/before long/directly/immediately/in a month (week)/momentarily/next month (year)/(just/right) now/presently/quickly/shortly/soon/straightaway/this month (year)/tomorrow* delete. • I don't anticipate any layoffs in the immediate future. *I don't anticipate any layoffs immediately.*

in the immediate past *a few months (years) ago/formerly/lately/not long ago/of late/previously/recent/recently* delete. • Computer software consulting firms constitute a growth node that will probably continue, but alone it cannot generate the numbers of jobs that have been generated in the immediate past. *Computer software consulting firms constitute a growth node that will probably continue, but alone it cannot generate the number of jobs that have been recently generated.*

in/on the inside of *inside.* • An undercut could also be a recessed neck on the inside of a cylindrical hole. *An undercut could also be a recessed neck inside a cylindrical hole.* • Now let's turn to what goes on in the inside of the paragraphs in a section. *Now let's turn to what goes on inside the paragraphs in a section.*

in the interest of (-ing) *for/so as to/to.* • The secretary took this action in the interest of ensuring an equitable investigation. *The secretary took this action to ensure an equitable investigation.*

in the interim *meantime/meanwhile.* • In the interim, law enforcement agencies are bracing for the worst. *Meanwhile, law enforcement agencies are bracing for the worst.*

in the interval *meantime/meanwhile.*

in the judgment of *assert/believe/claim/consider/contend/feel/hold/judge/maintain/regard/say/think/to/view/with.* • In the judgment of these scientists, it has hurt the effort. *These scientists believe it has hurt the effort.*

in/over the long run *at length/eventually/in the end/in time/later/long-term/one day/over the months (years)/over time/someday/sometime/ultimately/with time/yet.* • In the long run, presumably fewer citizens would require Medicaid. *In time, presumably fewer citizens would require Medicaid.*

in/over the long term *at length/eventually/in the end/in time/later/long-term/one day/over the months (years)/over time/someday/sometime/ultimately/with time/yet.* • How will the two investments compare over the long term? *How will the two investments compare over time?*

in the main *almost all/chiefly/commonly/generally/greatly/in general/largely/mainly/most/mostly/most often/much/nearly all/normally/overall/typically/usually.* • In the main, politi-cians have become contemptuous of voters. *Generally, politicians have become contemptuous of voters.*

in the making *brewing/developing/forming/stirring.* • The teams go into action when computers at the National Weather Service foresee a disturbance in the making. *The teams go into action when computers at the National Weather Service foresee a disturbance brewing.*

in the meantime *meantime/meanwhile.* • In the meantime, I will discuss the software potential with our people and see if we can come up with some preliminary conclusions. *Meantime, I will discuss the software potential with our people and see if we can come up with some preliminary conclusions.*

in the middle of *amid/among/during/in/in between/inside/through/within.* • Charles said that Britain was in the middle of another building boom and the important question was "whether we can get it right this time." *Charles said that Britain was amid another building boom and the important question was "whether we can get it right this time."*

in the middle/midst of -ing *-ing.* • We are currently in the middle of improving these signs with new panels and brighter lighting. *We are currently improving these signs with new panels and brighter lighting.*

in the midst of *amid/among/during/in/in between/inside/through/within.* • Federal and state authorities are in the midst of a criminal investigation of whether an unreported series of leaks and spills was linked to groundwater polluted by more than 55 chemicals. *Federal and state authorities are amid a criminal investigation of whether an unreported series of leaks and spills was linked to groundwater polluted by more than 55 chemicals.* • In the midst of steady decline in departments of English, creative writing has proven an area of exuberant growth. *Amid steady* decline in departments of English, creative writing has proven an area of exuberant growth.

in the month/year of delete • In the month of November 2007 alone, almost an entire issue of *Armed Forces Journal* was devoted to the subject of robots as war weapons. *In November 2007 alone, almost an entire issue of* Armed Forces Journal *was devoted to the subject of robots as war weapons.*

(something/somewhere) in the nature (of) *about/around/close to/more or less/near/nearly/ or so/roughly/some* delete. • The owners anticipate production to be in the nature of 3,000 gallons weekly. *The owners anticipate production to be around 3,000 gallons weekly.*

in the nature of *akin to/close to/like/resembling/ similar to/such as.* • These days it takes something in the nature of a reception with the Queen Mother to get the Maxwells together. *These days it takes something like a reception with the Queen Mother to get the Maxwells together.*

in the (very) near future *before long/directly/in a month (week)/next month (year)/presently/ quickly/shortly/soon/this month (year)/tomorrow* delete. • I will visit my mother's grave site in the near future. *I will visit my mother's grave site next week.*

in the (very) near past *a few months (years) ago/ before/earlier/formerly/lately/not long ago/of late/once/previously/recent/recently* delete.

in/over the near term *at first/at present/before long/currently/directly/for now/in/over a month (week)/initially/next month (year)/now/presently/short-term/this month (year)* delete. • That, perhaps, best sums up what to expect from AI in the near term. *That, perhaps, best sums up what to expect from AI for now.*

in the negative *negatively/no/unfavorably.*

(something/somewhere) in the neighborhood (of) *about/around/close to/more or less/near/ nearly/or so/roughly/some* delete. • We have somewhere in the neighborhood of 6 million illegal aliens in this country. *We have about 6 million illegal aliens in this country.*

in the neighborhood (of) *close by/close to/near/ nearby/neighboring.* • "Everything around here shook," said a young woman who works at a restaurant in the neighborhood. *"Everything around here shook," said a young woman who works at a nearby restaurant.* • Joy Demark says she's saved in the neighborhood of $20 a month on her electricity bill by changing her habits. *Joy Demark says she's saved $20 or so a month on her electricity bill by changing her habits.*

in the next place *also/and/as well/besides/ beyond that/this/further/furthermore/in addition/moreover/more than that/this/next/second/ still more/too/what's more.*

in the normal/ordinary/typical/usual course of business/events/things *as usual/commonly/ customarily/normally/ordinarily/typically/usually* delete. • In the ordinary course of events, they wouldn't go to court over something like this. *Ordinarily, they wouldn't go to court over something like this.* • In the normal course of business, the company's segments enter into transactions with one another. *Typically, the company's segments enter into transactions with one another.* • In the normal course of things, it is rare for an island to be hit twice or three times in any one season. *Normally, it is rare for an island to be hit twice or three times in any one season.* • Vesta stated in a news release this week that it will be able to handle the claims in the normal course of business. *Vesta stated in a news release this week that it will be able to handle the claims.*

in the not-so-distant/not-too-distant future *before long/directly/in a month (week)/next month (year)/presently/quickly/shortly/soon/this* *month (year)/tomorrow* delete. • We'll be coming out with some new communications products in the not-too-distant future. *We'll be coming out with some new communications products shortly.* • In the not-too-distant future, everything from a writing sample to a student exhibition could be part of the portfolio. *Before long, everything from a writing sample to a student exhibition could be part of the portfolio.* • Capt. Jeff Richardson hopes to see the pile disappear in the not too distant future. *Capt. Jeff Richardson hopes to see the pile disappear next month.*

in the not-so-distant/not-too-distant past *a few months (years) ago/before/earlier/formerly/ lately/not long ago/of late/once/previously/ recent/recently* delete. • In the not-so-distant past, people could have dropped out of high school and gotten a decent-paying job in manufacturing. *Not long ago, people could have dropped out of high school and gotten a decent-paying job in manufacturing.* • Look a little closer and you'll find that those controls appeared in an OCX listing in the not-too-distant past. *Look a little closer and you'll find that those controls once appeared in an OCX listing.*

in the opinion of *assert/believe/claim/consider/ contend/feel/hold/judge/maintain/regard/say/ think/to/view/with.* • The Wall Street inside-information scandal could pull in yet another circle of white-collar criminals in the opinion of criminal lawyers and securities specialists. *Criminal lawyers and securities specialists contend the Wall Street inside-information scandal could pull in yet another circle of white-collar criminals.*

in the opposite direction from/of *against.* • Many bicyclists do not observe traffic signals, ride in the opposite direction of motor traffic, and fail to signal when overtaking pedestrians. *Many bicyclists do not observe traffic signals, ride against motor traffic, and fail to signal when overtaking pedestrians.*

in the overall scope/sphere of things *all in all/ all told/in all/overall* delete. • In the overall sphere of things, a vast majority of tax problems never reach the courts, particularly not as criminal prosecutions. *Overall, a vast majority of tax problems never reach the courts, particularly not as criminal prosecutions.*

in the past *before/earlier/formerly/once/previously* delete. • You said, in the past, that you weren't interested in the vice presidency. *Earlier you said that you weren't interested in the vice presidency.*

in/over the past few/several days/decades/ months/weeks/years *lately/of late/recent/ recently.* • Neural networks have generated much interest, not to mention hype, in the past few years. *Neural networks have lately generated much interest, not to mention hype.*

in the position of *as.*

in the presence of *alongside/among/beside/ during/in/with.* • On only one occasion was I in the presence of Jack and Sam at the same time. *On only one occasion was I with Jack and Sam at the same time.*

in the process of *in/while.* • In the process of doing so, he threw out some good material. *In doing so, he threw out some good material.* • Answers to these and many other questions had to be resolved in the process of developing and implementing the new system of student assessment. *Answers to these and many other questions had to be resolved while developing and implementing the new system of student assessment.* • It is easy to damage or destroy evidence in the process of looking for it. *It is easy to damage or destroy evidence while looking for it.*

in the process of -ing *-ing.* • I'm in the process of cleaning the house. *I'm cleaning the house.* • The company is in the process of changing the regulatory framework in most of its states. *The* *company is changing the regulatory framework in most of its states.* • No publication date has been set for the book, which is in the process of being written. *No publication date has been set for the book, which is being written.* • Out of the parent survey have come many ideas and from those ideas, many projects, which we are currently in the process of putting into action. *Out of the parent survey have come many ideas and from those ideas, many projects, which we are currently putting into action.* • We are currently in the process of reviewing the resumes of all applicants. *We are currently reviewing the resumes of all applicants.* • iCAST Corporation has closed down its website and is in the process of winding down the business. *iCAST Corporation has closed down its website and is winding down the business.*

in the proximity (of) *close by/close to/near/nearby.* • Cosmic gamma ray bursts appear to originate in the proximity of neutron stars, but the sources have never been pinned down. *Cosmic gamma ray bursts appear to originate near neutron stars, but the sources have never been pinned down.*

(something/somewhere) in the . . . range (of) *about/around/close to/more or less/near/nearly/or so/roughly/some* delete. • The price tag on the three-city shuttle was in the range of $200 million. *The price tag on the three-city shuttle was about $200 million.*

(something/somewhere) in the range from (of) . . . through/to *between . . . and/from . . . to/to* delete. • According to a recent study by Arthur Andersen & Co., the cost of drilling new wells is in the range of $6 to $8 a barrel. *According to a recent study by Arthur Andersen & Co., the cost of drilling new wells is between $6 and $8 a barrel.*

(something/somewhere) in the realm (of) *about/around/close to/more or less/near/nearly/or so/roughly/some* delete. • The company expects to employ somewhere in the realm of 300 people there by 1993. *The company expects to employ around 300 people there by 1993.*

in the realm of *about/as for/as to/concerning/for/in/of/on/over/regarding/respecting/to/toward/with* delete. • Furthermore, in the realm of strategic nuclear weapons, he has overseen not reductions but improvements. *Furthermore, in strategic nuclear weapons, he has overseen not reductions but improvements.*

in/within the realm of possibility *conceivable/doable/possible/thinkable.* • She said having a child is still within the realm of possibility. *She said having a child is still possible.*

in/within the recent past *a few months (years) ago/before/earlier/formerly/lately/not long ago/of late/once/previously/recent/recently* delete. • The belief that we have an open society in which anyone can get ahead is less true than in the recent past. *The belief that we have an open society in which anyone can get ahead is less true than before.*

(something/somewhere) in the region (of) *about/around/close to/more or less/near/nearly/or so/roughly/some* delete. • That's on top of an additional estimated increase in food prices somewhere in the region of 4 percent. *That's on top of an additional estimated increase in food prices of about 4 percent.*

in the right *blameless/correct/justified/right.* • With everybody thinking they are in the right, not much unity can develop. *With everybody thinking they are right, not much unity can develop.*

in the role of *as/as such.*

in the same fashion/manner/way (as/that) *as (be)/like/likewise/much like/so/the same as.* • Though not necessarily displayed on the screen, hard carriage returns are much like other characters you enter in a document; therefore, you delete them in the same way you would other characters. *Though not necessarily displayed on the screen, hard carriage returns are much like other characters you enter in a document; therefore, you delete them as you would other characters.* • This strengthens the brain, in the same way that lifting weights strengthens muscles. *This strengthens the brain, much like lifting weights strengthens muscles.* • In the same way, the truths of our religion are strewn across the world, on two distant continents. *Similarly, the truths of our religion are strewn across the world, on two distant continents.*

in the second place *also/and/as well/besides/ beyond that/this/further/furthermore/in addi- tion/moreover/more than that/this/next/second/ still more/too/what's more.*

in the sense of *that is* delete. • He is in a pecu- liar—in the sense of unusual—position. *He is in a peculiar—that is, unusual—position.*

in the sense that *because/considering/for/given/ in that/since.* • Foreign and domestic marketing are the same in the sense that the purpose is to create and manage profitable exchange relation- ships. *Foreign and domestic marketing are the same in that the purpose is to create and manage profitable exchange relationships.*

in/over the short run *at first/at present/before long/currently/directly/for now/in/over a month (week)/initially/next month (year)/now/pres- ently/short-term/this month (year)* delete. • The tax-cut proposal is the nutritional equivalent of a diet of beer: in the short run, it fills you up and gives you a buzz, but eventually it devas- tates the body. *The tax-cut proposal is the nutri- tional equivalent of a diet of beer: at first, it fills you up and gives you a buzz, but eventually it devastates the body.*

in/over the short term *at first/at present/before long/currently/directly/for now/in/over a month (week)/initially/next month (year)/now/pres-* *ently/short-term/this month (year)* delete. • People who can withstand fluctuations over the short term are virtually guaranteed a profit in the stock market. *People who can withstand short-term fluctuations are virtually guaranteed a profit in the stock market.*

in the support of (-ing) *for/so as to/to.*

in the . . . terms *-(al)ly.* • He has denied the charges in the strongest terms. *He has strongly denied the charges.*

in the third place *also/and/as well/besides/ beyond that/this/further/furthermore/in addi- tion/moreover/more than that/this/next/still more/third/too/what's more.*

in the . . . through/to . . . range *between . . . and/from . . . to/to.* • Whether they will be will- ing to pay a base price rumored to be in the $3,000 to $6,000 range is one of the many ques- tions to be answered. *Whether they will be will- ing to pay a base price rumored to be between $3,000 and $6,000 is one of the many questions to be answered.*

in the unexpected/unlikely event of/that *if (there were)/if . . . should/in case (of)/should (there)/were (there/. . . to)* delete. • In the unex- pected event that those costs exceed $30 mil- lion, other joint owners would be obligated. *Should those costs exceed $30 million, other joint owners would be obligated.*

(something/somewhere) in the vicinity (of) *about/around/close to/more or less/near/ nearly/or so/roughly/some* delete. • On its best day, my corporation earned in the vicinity of $2 million. *On its best day, my corporation earned around $2 million.*

in the vicinity (of) *close by/close to/near/nearby.* • It was last seen in the vicinity of the Abbot Street Bridge. *It was last seen near the Abbot Street Bridge.*

in the view of *assert/believe/claim/consider/ contend/feel/hold/judge/maintain/regard/say/ think/to/view/with.* • *In the view of some strategists, he may lose the election unless he can reverse his fortunes on this issue.* *Some strategists think he may lose the election unless he can reverse his fortunes on this issue.*

in the wake of *(just/right) after/because of/ (close) behind/due to/ensuing/following/from/ owing to/succeeding.* • *In the wake of an office and shopping-center boom comes an employment boom in business custodians.* *Following an office and shopping-center boom comes an employment boom in business custodians.*

in the way of delete. • This step requires that you research jobs to determine what they call for in the way of education, skills, and aptitudes. *This step requires that you research jobs to determine what education, skills, and aptitudes they call for.* • There is little motivation for long periods of foolishness, and there is much in the way of market discipline to prevent it. *There is little motivation for long periods of foolishness, and there is much market discipline to prevent it.* • A sentence such as "It is 93 million miles to the sun" does not generate much in the way of questions; it is too specific. *A sentence such as "It is 93 million miles to the sun" does not generate many questions; it is too specific.* • As parents, we got little in the way of help, a good deal in the way of confusion, and an infinite amount in the way of worry. *As parents, we got little help, a good deal of confusion, and an infinite amount of worry.*

in the wrong *at fault/guilty/incorrect/mistaken/ to blame/wrong.* • I suspect she chose to remain anonymous because she realizes she is in the wrong. *I suspect she chose to remain anonymous because she realizes she is at fault.* • From the reaction of you, many believe the lab and newspaper to be quite clearly in the wrong irrespective of the lab results. *From the reaction of you, many believe the lab and newspaper to be quite clearly wrong irrespective of the lab results.*

in thickness *thick* delete. • In their theoretical analysis, Gaylord and Brennan consider a filter consisting of nine layers, each layer a quarter or a half of the electron wavelength in thickness. *In their theoretical analysis, Gaylord and Brennan consider a filter consisting of nine layers, each layer a quarter or a half of the electron wavelength thick.*

intimately familiar *familiar/intimate.*

in (the) time(s) of *amid/during/in/over/throughout.* • The substantial risk of investment in junk bonds, particularly in times of economic uncertainty, is often disregarded by small investors. *The substantial risk of investment in junk bonds, particularly amid economic uncertainty, is often disregarded by small investors.*

in . . . tones *-(al)ly* delete. • Police officers trooped into every grammar school in the city to talk with kids, explaining in dispassionate tones the use and abuse of crack. *Police officers trooped into every grammar school in the city to talk with kids, explaining dispassionately the use and abuse of crack.*

in trade (for) *for.*

introduce (a/the) new *introduce.* • In 1983, Apple introduced a new, easier-to-use computer called the Lisa. *In 1983, Apple introduced an easier-to-use computer called the Lisa.*

inure to the benefit of *inure to.* • This agreement shall be binding upon and inure to the benefit of the executors, administrators, and assigns of the Author and of the Client. *This agreement shall be binding upon and inure to the executors, administrators, and assigns of the Author and of the Client.*

in/on/to/with various/varying degrees/extents *in part/in some way/more or less/partially/ partly/rather/some/somehow/someway(s)/ somewhat/to some degree/extent/various/var-*

iously/varying/varyingly delete. • Four masters of the art of stretch management rely on varying degrees on a set of nuts-and-bolts techniques. *Four masters of the art of stretch management rely varyingly on a set of nuts-and-bolts techniques.*

invidious discrimination *discrimination/invidiousness.* • Few would deny that ferreting out this kind of invidious discrimination is a great if not compelling governmental interest. *Few would deny that ferreting out this kind of invidiousness is a great if not compelling governmental interest.* • A lawyer shall not hold membership in any organization that practices invidious discrimination on the basis of sex, race, religion, or national origin. *A lawyer shall not hold membership in any organization that practices discrimination on the basis of sex, race, religion, or national origin.*

in view of the fact that *because/considering/for/given/in that/since/when.* • These results are particularly interesting in view of the fact that Christian Scientists are forbidden to either smoke or drink. *These results are particularly interesting considering Christian Scientists are forbidden to either smoke or drink.* • In view of the fact that power supplies are being steadily reduced, this can be a serious design limitation. *Since power supplies are being steadily reduced, this can be a serious design limitation.* • Colon cancer is the second-leading cause of cancer deaths in the U.S. for both men and women, so in view of the fact that packaged breakfast cereals are so convenient, this is very good news. *Colon cancer is the second-leading cause of cancer deaths in the U.S. for both men and women, so given that packaged breakfast cereals are so convenient, this is very good news.*

in view of the fact that *whereas.*

invited guest *guest.*

involve *for/in/mean/of/with* delete. • Census II involves using several different types of moving averages to identify trends and outliers within a data set. *Census II uses several different types of moving averages to identify trends and outliers within a data set.* • The operation is self-sustaining and has operated with no public-sector funding involved. *The operation is self-sustaining and has operated with no public-sector funding.*

involved in *in/of/within* delete. • The costs involved in refurbishing the building are prohibitive. *The costs of refurbishing the building are prohibitive.*

in (a/the) . . . way *-(al)ly* delete. • Each of these variations can be revised in a different way. *Each of these variations can be revised differently.* • Computer systems differ in a significant way from stereos. *Computer systems differ significantly from stereos.* • Every group that has scrutinized this product in an impartial way agrees it is safe. *Every group that has impartially scrutinized this product agrees it is safe.*

in whatever/whichever fashion/manner/way *despite how/however.* • In whatever way it comes, the decision will be an important one. *Despite how it comes, the decision will be an important one.*

in what/which fashion/manner/way *how.* • In what fashion does imaging technology offer potential competitive advantage? *How does imaging technology offer potential competitive advantage?* • In what ways does it create a communication problem for you? *How does it create a communication problem for you?*

in what/which regard/respect *how.* • In what respect was this investment "tax free"? *How was this investment "tax free"?*

in width *wide* delete. • In high-performance hard disks, these tracks are roughly 1 micrometer in width. *In high-performance hard disks, these tracks are roughly 1 micrometer wide.*

I, personally *I.* • My unique style self-expresses who I personally am. *My unique style self-expresses who I am.* • I personally believe in team orders, but I think Ferrari made the wrong call at the German Grand Prix. *I believe in team orders, but I think Ferrari made the wrong call at the German Grand Prix.* • Personally, I have a strong bias in favor of short sentences. *I have a strong bias in favor of short sentences.*

IRA account *IRA.*

ironical *ironic.*

irregardless of *despite (what)/no matter what/regardless of/whatever.* • Irregardless of the cause, the pressure of the spinal fluid with the ventricles must be relieved to prevent damage to the brain. *Regardless of the cause, the pressure of the spinal fluid with the ventricles must be relieved to prevent damage to the brain.* • We want every hospitality establishment to have the opportunity to list on our directory irregardless of their size or wealth. *We want every hospitality establishment to have the opportunity to list on our directory whatever their size or wealth.*

irregardless of the fact that *although/but/even though/still/though/yet.* • Irregardless of the fact that she was raised by someone else, she is still my daughter. *Although she was raised by someone else, she is still my daughter.* • Charges resulting from Procard expenditures may be transferred from Local to State Account irregardless of the fact that the original voucher may be greater than $2,000. *Charges resulting from Procard expenditures may be transferred from Local to State Account even though the original voucher may be greater than $2,000.*

irrelevancy *irrelevance.*

irrespective of (what) *despite (what)/no matter what/regardless of/whatever.* • The product-first approach meant marketing the same product to all customers, irrespective of their profiles. *The product-first approach meant marketing the same product to all customers, regardless of their profiles.* • Irrespective of the reasons, the voters simply do not want to participate in a collaborative project. *No matter what the reasons, the voters simply do not want to participate in a collaborative project.*

irrespective of how *despite how/however/no matter how/regardless of how.* • The margins are retained irrespective of how many characters are printed per inch. *The margins are retained despite how many characters are printed per inch.*

irrespective of the fact that *although/but/even though/still/though/yet.* • Ireland Under 21 coach Ciaran Fitzgerald spoke of the value of keeping together his charges for tonight's game in Musgrave Park, irrespective of the fact that the only doubt surrounding the outcome is the final margin of victory. *Ireland Under 21 coach Ciaran Fitzgerald spoke of the value of keeping together his charges for tonight's game in Musgrave Park, even though the only doubt surrounding the outcome is the final margin of victory.* • Irrespective of the fact that the proposed regulations apply only to foreign workers, it means that for the first time it will be stipulated in law that those relying on social assistance lose their claim to a fundamental democratic right. *Although the proposed regulations apply only to foreign workers, it means that for the first time it will be stipulated in law that those relying on social assistance lose their claim to a fundamental democratic right.*

irrespective of when *despite when/no matter when/regardless of when/whenever.* • In other words, the operation of the Reserve benefits all members irrespective of when they join or leave the Scheme. *In other words, the operation of the Reserve benefits all members despite when they join or leave the Scheme.*

irrespective of where *despite where/no matter where/regardless of where/wherever.* • A successful company must have the necessary skill sets to meet the needs and wants of its customers irrespective of where they may do business. *A successful company must have the necessary skill sets to meet the needs and wants of its customers wherever they may do business.*

irrespective of (the fact) whether . . . (or) *despite whether/no matter whether/regardless of whether/whether . . . or (not).* • One delegate said his parish would continue to raise money for its diocese irrespective of whether the archdiocesan assessment is met. *One delegate said his parish would continue to raise money for its diocese whether or not the archdiocesan assessment is met.* • You need to procure the visas for all the countries, even the ones that the trains are passing through, irrespective of the fact whether the trains are stopping in those countries. *You need to procure the visas for all the countries, even the ones that the trains are passing through, whether or not the trains are stopping in those countries.* • Every client has a right to discharge his or her lawyer at any time for any reason or no reason at all, irrespective of the fact whether or not any money is owed. *Every client has a right to discharge his or her lawyer at any time for any reason or no reason at all, regardless of whether any money is owed.* • Kundalini is present in the body of all persons irrespective of the fact whether they are ordinary persons or highly spiritual persons. *Kundalini is present in the body of all persons whether they are ordinary persons or highly spiritual persons.*

irrespective of which *despite which/no matter which/regardless of which/whichever.* • We oppose foreign control, irrespective of which country it involves. *We oppose foreign control, whichever country it involves.*

irrespective of who *despite who/no matter who/regardless of who/whoever.* • Irrespective of who leads the group, one fact remains. *Whoever leads the group, one fact remains.*

irrespective of whom *despite whom/no matter whom/regardless of whom/whomever.*

. . . is . . . (that/which/who/whom) delete. • Batch files are files that contain commands that are executed automatically when you turn on your computer or type the batch file's name. *Batch files contain commands that are executed automatically when you turn on your computer or type the batch file's name.* • Domestic corporations are corporations that do business in the state in which they are chartered, and foreign corporations are corporations that do business outside their chartered state. *Domestic corporations do business in the state in which they are chartered, and foreign corporations do business outside their chartered state.*

is able to *can.* • Investors are able to buy and sell any quantity of securities. *Investors can buy and sell any quantity of securities.*

is accredited/credited to *charges to/accredits to/ascribes to/assigns to/attributes to/imputes to.*

is accustomed to (-ing) *given to/inured to/prone to/tend to/used to/will (would).* • I am accustomed to her sinful ways. *I am inured to her sinful ways.* • We have become accustomed to associating toughness with coarseness. *We tend to associate toughness with coarseness.* • They are accustomed to talking until late into the night. *They will talk until late into the night.*

is a consequence of *arises from/results from/stems from.* • The East African Rift is a consequence of tectonic motion between the African and Eurasian plates. *The East African Rift stems from tectonic motion between the African and Eurasian plates.*

is a contribution to *contributes to.* • This is a continuing contribution to a company's profitability. *This continually contributes to a company's profitability.*

is acquainted with *knows.*

is a demonstration of *demonstrates/shows/ proves.*

is a description of *describes.* • The attached proposal is a brief description of what I have in mind. *The attached proposal briefly describes what I have in mind.*

is a deterrent to *blocks/deters/hinders/impedes/ prevents/stops/thwarts.*

is advantageous for (to) *aids/benefits/favors/ helps.*

is afraid of/to *dreads/fears/frets (about/over)/ stews (about/over)/worries (about/over).*

is a function of *depends on/relates to.* • The popularity of fixed-rate versus adjustable-rate mortgages seems to be a function of the level of interest rates. *The popularity of fixed-rate versus adjustable-rate mortgages seems to depend on the level of interest rates.*

is a hindrance to *blocks/deters/hinders/impedes/ prevents/stops/thwarts.* • A problem is any organizational issue that could be a hindrance to organizational success. *A problem is any organizational issue that could hinder organizational success.* • The National Organization for Women is a hindrance to reproductive-health-care clinics' efforts to protect their patients and employees from anti-choice. *The National Organization for Women hinders reproductive-health-care clinics' efforts to protect their patients and employees from anti-choice.*

is an acquaintance of *knows.* • Mr. Branch was an acquaintance of Miss Gregory. *Mr. Branch knew Miss Gregory.*

is an illustration of *illustrates.* • I believe that these moves by Texaco are a perfect illustration of the precept that a clear and closer relation-

ship between active ownership and management will increase productivity. *I believe that these moves by Texaco perfectly illustrate the precept that a clear and closer relationship between active ownership and management will increase productivity.*

is an impediment to *blocks/deters/hinders/ impedes/prevents/stops/thwarts.*

is an indication/indicator of *argues/attests to/ bespeaks/betokens/indicates/shows/signals/signifies/suggests/testifies to/witnesses.* • The Roman holiday atmosphere reportedly surrounding the event may be an indicator of the level of civilized intercourse we have attained in this so-called advanced industrial nation. *The Roman holiday atmosphere reportedly surrounding the event may signify the level of civilized intercourse we have attained in this so-called advanced industrial nation.*

is an obstacle to *blocks/deters/hinders/impedes/ prevents/stops/thwarts.*

is applicable in/to *applies in/to/bears on/concerns/pertains to/relates to.* • Regardless, the autocratic style is applicable in some situations. *Regardless, the autocratic style applies in some situations.*

is appreciative of *appreciates/approves of/cherishes/enjoys/esteems/likes/prizes/treasures/ understands/values/welcomes.* • We are especially appreciative of the item which appeared in the paper citing our need for volunteers. *We especially appreciate the item which appeared in the paper citing our need for volunteers.*

is apprehensive of *dreads/fears/frets (about/ over)/stews (about/over)/worries (about/over).* • My parents were apprehensive of my going to Iran. *My parents dreaded my going to Iran.*

is appropriate in/to *applies in/to/bears on/concerns/pertains to/relates to.*

is approving of *approves of.* • They are approving of how he is handling health care. *They approve of how he is handling health care.*

is a/the process that delete. • Anxiety is a process that alerts people to possible dangers. *Anxiety alerts people to possible dangers.*

is a reflection of/on/upon *reflects (on).* • Could it be that they felt the actions by the school would be a bad reflection on them? *Could it be that they felt the actions by the school would badly reflect on them?*

is a representation of *represents.*

is a result of *arises from/results from/stems from.*

is associated to/with *correlates to/with/equates with/relates to.* • The development of interest and confidence and infusions of practical, useful applications seem to be associated with success in mathematics. *The development of interest and confidence and infusions of practical, useful applications seem to relate to success in mathematics.*

is at loggerheads (with) *clashes with/conflicts with/contradicts/differs from/disagrees with/quarrels with/varies with.* • He ran unsuccessfully for the Florida house and has frequently been at loggerheads with state and federal authorities. *He ran unsuccessfully for the Florida house and has frequently quarreled with state and federal authorities.*

is at odds over/with *clashes with/conflicts with/contradicts/differs from/disagrees with/quarrels with/varies with.* • She said the strong credit figures were at odds with a stream of government reports pointing toward a slowdown and did not reflect the health of the economy. *She said the strong credit figures contradicted a stream of government reports pointing toward a slowdown and did not reflect the health of the economy.*

is attentive to *attends to/heeds.*

is attributable to *charges to/accredits to/ascribes to/assigns to/attributes to/imputes to.* • The expected growth is attributable to the improved quality of our products and services. *The expected growth accredits to the improved quality of our products and services.*

is at variance with *clashes with/conflicts with/contradicts/differs from/disagrees with/quarrels with/varies with.* • Although some of its particulars are at variance with what U.S. officials have heard, most key details tend to coincide. *Although some of its particulars clash with what U.S. officials have heard, most key details tend to coincide.*

is a variant of *departs from/deviates from/differs from/diverges from/varies from.* • Endowment insurance policies are a variant of whole life in that, if the insured dies within a specified period, the insurance will be paid to a designated beneficiary. *Endowment insurance policies vary from whole life in that, if the insured dies within a specified period, the insurance will be paid to a designated beneficiary.*

is aware of/that *comprehends/knows/realizes/recognizes/sees/understands.* • If you are in the same position as most consumer borrowers, you should be aware that time is not on your side. *If you are in the same position as most consumer borrowers, you should realize that time is not on your side.*

is based on/upon *rests on.* • This policy is based upon three fundamental principles of competitive behavior. *This policy rests on three fundamental principles of competitive behavior.*

is based on the assumption *assumes.* • Capitalism is based on the assumption that you can win. *Capitalism assumes that you can win.* • The annual percentage yield is based on the assumption that dividends will remain on deposit until maturity. *The annual percentage yield assumes that dividends will remain on deposit until maturity.* • This proposal is based on the assumption that qualitative research can add new insight into the real life issues that contribute to the health disparities. *This proposal assumes that qualitative research can add new insight into the real life issues that contribute to the health disparities.*

is beneficial to *aids/benefits/favors/helps.* • Congress needs to make important decisions that will be beneficial to all Americans on a long-range basis. *Congress needs to make important decisions that will benefit all Americans on a long-range basis.*

ISBN number *ISBN.*

is capable of -ing *can/is able to.* • Obsolescence exists when a person or machine is no longer capable of performing to standards or management's expectations. *Obsolescence exists when a person or machine is no longer able to perform to standards or management's expectations.*

is characteristic of *characterizes/depicts/describes/designates/illustrates/pictures/portrays.* • The protein tangles in brain tissue are characteristic of advanced Alzheimer's, and he speculates that A68 may be a precursor of the tangles. *The protein tangles in brain tissue characterize advanced Alzheimer's, and he speculates that A68 may be a precursor of the tangles.*

is cognizant of/that *comprehends/knows/realizes/recognizes/sees/understands.*

is coherent with *agrees with/coheres with/concurs with/conforms to/with/corresponds to/with.*

is comparable to/with *compares to/with/contrasts to/with/corresponds to/with/equates with/likens to/relates to/resembles.* • This revolution in medicine is comparable in certain ways to the computer boom, but is more epochal. *This*

revolution in medicine corresponds in certain ways to the computer boom, but is more epochal.

is compatible with *agrees with/coheres with/concurs with/conforms to/with/corresponds to/with.*

is competitive with *competes with.*

is complementary to *complements.* • Banking is an obvious area for Nomura's diversification since it is complementary to the firm's securities business. *Banking is an obvious area for Nomura's diversification since it complements the firm's securities business.*

is compliant with *complies with.* • Our emphasis is supporting the customers who have been fully compliant with the export regulations. *Our emphasis is supporting the customers who have fully complied with the export regulations.*

is composed of *comprises/consists of/contains/includes.* • The informal organization is composed of all the informal groupings of people within a formal organization. *The informal organization consists of all the informal groupings of people within a formal organization.*

is comprised of *comprises/consists of/contains/includes.* • The marketing infrastructure is comprised of several elements that change as a country develops its industrial and service sectors. *The marketing infrastructure comprises several elements that change as a country develops its industrial and service sectors.* • The sample is comprised of three modules. *The sample consists of three modules.*

is concerned (about) *brood (on/over)/dread/fear/fret (about/over)/regret/stew (about/over)/worry (about/over).* • Company analysts are concerned about the level of debt that the combined companies would carry if the hostile bid succeeds. *Company analysts worry about the* *level of debt that the combined companies would carry if the hostile bid succeeds.*

is concerned with *concerns/deals with/is about/ pertains to/regards/relates to.* • The first two complications are external and are concerned with the environment within which the company competes. *The first two complications are external and concern the environment within which the company competes.*

is conditional/conditioned on/upon *depends on/hinges on/turns on.* • The willingness of VSS to proceed with the transaction is conditioned upon such an agreement. *The willingness of VSS to proceed with the transaction depends on such an agreement.*

is conducive to *conduces to.*

is connected to/with *correlates to/with/equates with/relates to.*

is conscious of/that *comprehends/knows/realizes/recognizes/sees/understands.*

is consistent with *agrees with/coheres with/ concurs with/conforms to/with/corresponds to/ with.* • This approach is consistent with earlier rulings requiring actual proof even where overwhelming numerical evidence allows a reasonable assumption of bias. *This approach conforms to earlier rulings requiring actual proof even where overwhelming numerical evidence allows a reasonable assumption of bias.*

is contemptuous of *despises/disdains/scorns.*

is contingent on/upon *depends on/hinges on/ turns on.* • Success is contingent upon careful, continuous, global market research. *Success depends on careful, continuous, global market research.* • The resolution approved by the BOS and BOF is contingent upon obtaining state funding. *The resolution approved by the BOS and BOF turns on obtaining state funding.*

is contributory to *contributes.* • Patients should also be warned of the cardiovascular and neoplastic liabilities of smoking that along with estrogens may be contributory to these disorders. *Patients should also be warned of the cardiovascular and neoplastic liabilities of smoking that along with estrogens may contribute to these disorders.*

is conversant with *knows.* • I wonder whether he knows any of the Asian languages or is conversant with the sources I consulted. *I wonder whether he knows any of the Asian languages or the sources I consulted.*

is critical of *complains about/condemns/criticizes.* • It's easy to be critical of others if they don't agree with you. *It's easy to criticize others if they don't agree with you.*

is dangerous to *endangers/imperils/jeopardizes.*

is deficient in *lacks/wants.* • In perhaps the most troubling of its recent reports, NAEP showed that while few adults in their early 20s are wholly illiterate, most are deficient in necessary skills. *In perhaps the most troubling of its recent reports, NAEP showed that while few adults in their early 20s are wholly illiterate, most lack necessary skills.*

is defined as *is/means.* • Management is defined as the process of setting and achieving goals through the execution of five basic management functions that utilize human, financial, and material resources. *Management is the process of setting and achieving goals through the execution of five basic management functions that utilize human, financial, and material resources.*

is deleterious to *damages/harms/hurts/ impairs/injures/mars/wrongs.*

is dependent on/upon *depends on/hinges on.* • You shouldn't be dependent upon anyone else for your happiness. *You shouldn't depend on anyone else for your happiness.* • The position of the object of a phrasal verb is dependent on whether or not the phrasal verb is separable or inseparable. *The position of the object of a phrasal verb depends on whether or not the phrasal verb is separable or inseparable.*

is descriptive of *characterizes/depicts/describes/ designates/illustrates/pictures/portrays.* • The model is descriptive of human behavior across all cultures that we have encountered. *The model describes human behavior across all cultures that we have encountered.*

is deserving of *deserves.* • I would like to believe that the trading company concept is deserving of serious treatment by a magazine as exemplary as yours. *I would like to believe that the trading company concept deserves serious treatment by a magazine as exemplary as yours.* • I think we're all deserving of a rain-free weekend. *I think we all deserve a rain-free weekend.*

is desirous of -ing *desires to/longs to/wants to/ wishes to.* • She is desirous of resolving this as soon as possible, so I respectfully request that you have your client consider the proposals. *She wants to resolve this as soon as possible, so I respectfully request that you have your client consider the proposals.* • If a person is desirous of quitting, then don't buy cigarettes, buy the patch instead. *If a person wants to quit, then don't buy cigarettes, buy the patch instead.*

is destructive of/to *damages/destroys/harms/ hurts/impairs/injures/mars/ruins.* • It is a fact that some cats are destructive of property. *It is a fact that some cats destroy property.*

is detrimental to *damages/harms/hurts/ impairs/injures/mars/wrongs.* • The concern of the EEC is that these powerful drugs would be detrimental to the children. *The concern of the EEC is that these powerful drugs would injure the children.*

is different from/than *departs from/deviates from/differs from/diverges from/varies from.* • If a phrase in the file on the disk is different from a phrase in the document on the screen, the command marks the entire phrase in the document on the screen. *If a phrase in the file on the disk differs from a phrase in the document on the screen, the command marks the entire phrase in the document on the screen.*

is dismissive of *dismisses/rejects.* • The president is dismissive of the Republican accusations. *The president dismisses the Republican accusations.*

is disposed to *tends to.*

is disrespectful of/toward *disesteems/disrespects.* • We will not accept any story that is disrespectful toward any member of the Beatles, their families, or their associates. *We will not accept any story that disrespects any member of the Beatles, their families, or their associates.*

is disruptive of *disrupts.* • Chapter 774 is disruptive of any sense of community because all control over its future has been removed. *Chapter 774 disrupts any sense of community because all control over its future has been removed.*

is distinguished from *departs from/deviates from/differs from/diverges from/varies from.*

is distrustful about/of *disbelieves/distrusts/ doubts/mistrusts/questions.* • Until students have assimilated these attitudes, they will be distrustful of scientific information. *Until students have assimilated these attitudes, they will distrust scientific information.*

is doubtful about/of *disbelieves/distrusts/ doubts/mistrusts/questions.* • Many officials are doubtful about the effectiveness of Shultz's Mideast plan. *Many officials doubt the effectiveness of Shultz's Mideast plan.*

is dubious about/of *disbelieves/distrusts/ doubts/mistrusts/questions.* • The A320 and the Concorde are the only commercial aircraft that use exclusively fly-by-wire controls, in part because U.S. aircraft companies are dubious about giving up tried-and-true cables. *The A320 and the Concorde are the only commercial aircraft that use exclusively fly-by-wire controls, in part because U.S. aircraft companies question giving up tried-and-true cables.*

is duplicative of *duplicates.* • The Odyssey team's responsibilities are duplicative of the nursing team's. *The Odyssey team's responsibilities duplicate the nursing team's.* • The ownership of equipment will create a reluctance to try new services that require additional hardware that is partially duplicative of what has already been purchased. *The ownership of equipment will create a reluctance to try new services that require additional hardware that partially duplicates what has already been purchased.*

is emblematic of *emblemizes/indicates/represents/signifies/stands for/symbolizes/typifies.* • The kind of comprehensive care the Clinic can provide to its cancer patients is emblematic of the Clinic's overall approach to medicine. *The kind of comprehensive care the Clinic can provide to its cancer patients typifies the Clinic's overall approach to medicine.*

is (the) equal to *amounts to/duplicates/equals/ is/matches/rivals.* • The value of the emperor's palace in the center of Tokyo is equal to the value of the entire state of California. *The value of the emperor's palace in the center of Tokyo equals the value of the entire state of California.*

is equipped/furnished with *comes with.* • The server normally is equipped with a large-capacity hard disk drive that acts as the central file depository for everyone on the network. *The server normally comes with a large-capacity hard disk drive that acts as the central file depository for everyone on the network.*

is (the) equivalent of/to *amounts to/duplicates/ equals/is/matches/rivals.* • Ideally, the amount of this fund should be the equivalent of at least three months' income. *Ideally, the amount of this fund should equal at least three months' income.*

is (a/the) –er/-or of delete. • She was the originator of the company program. *She originated the company program.* • You should be a helper and encourager of your child's writing efforts. *You should help and encourage your child's writing efforts.*

is evidence of/that *evinces/indicates/proves/ reveals/shows/signifies/testifies (to).* • The calls are evidence of the strong temptation in the judicial arena to seize on an array of recent findings on brain chemistry and behavior. *The calls testify to the strong temptation in the judicial arena to seize on an array of recent findings on brain chemistry and behavior.*

is exploitative/exploitive of *abuses/cheats/ deceives/exploits/ill treats/mistreats/misuses/ uses/victimizes/wrongs.* • Surcharging is unfair and exploitative of customers. *Surcharging is unfair and exploits customers.*

is faced with *faces.* • Dynamic high-technology strategy companies are faced with few national competitors. *Dynamic high-technology strategy companies face few national competitors.*

is familiar with *knows.* • European participants in the computer industry know Europe extremely well, and they are familiar with the U.S. market. *European participants in the computer industry know Europe extremely well, and they know the U.S. market.*

is favorable to *aids/benefits/favors/helps.* • In the five years during which the leveraged buyout has blossomed, the business environment has been particularly favorable to this type of transaction. *In the five years during which the lever-*

aged buyout has blossomed, the business environment has particularly favored this type of transaction.

is fearful (about/of/that) *dreads/fears/frets (about/over)/stews (about/over)/worries (about/over).* • These leaders tend to be fearful of external forces because they may create a middle class or threaten the existing social structure. *These leaders tend to fret about external forces because they may create a middle class or threaten the existing social structure.*

is focused on/upon *focuses on.* • Although most of the chapters in this volume are focused on incentives for educators, several authors remind us that students are the chief agent of their own learning. *Although most of the chapters in this volume focus on incentives for educators, several authors remind us that students are the chief agent of their own learning.*

is for certain/sure *is certain/sure.* • One thing is for certain: they'll have to deal with the governor when all this is over. *One thing is certain: they'll have to deal with the governor when all this is over.*

is founded on/upon *rests on.*

is frightened of/to *dreads/fears/frets (about/over)/stews (about/over)/worries (about/over).*

is going to *shall/will.* • We think that is a trend that is going to continue for several years to come. *We think that is a trend that will continue for several years to come.* • That simply means that you are going to need effective human relations skills. *That simply means that you will need effective human relations skills.*

is harmful to *damages/harms/hurts/impairs/injures/mars/wrongs.* • It will ultimately be harmful to the state's economy in that it will make some products more expensive than anywhere else. *It will ultimately harm the state's economy in that it will make some products more expensive than anywhere else.*

is helpful in (-ing) *aids in/assists in/helps.* • Intelligent market research will be helpful in settling which product lines to offer. *Intelligent market research will help settle which product lines to offer.*

is hopeful *expects/hopes/relies on/trusts.* • I am hopeful that all will go well. *I expect that all will go well.*

is identical to/with *amounts to/duplicates/equals/is/matches/rivals.* • The objective, of course, is to ensure that directors' interests are identical with those of the company and its longer term stockholders. *The objective, of course, is to ensure that directors' interests match those of the company and its longer term stockholders.*

is illustrative of *characterizes/depicts/demonstrates/describes/designates/exemplifies/illustrates/pictures/portrays/represents.* • Some American Feminists is illustrative of the nearly universal nature of the issues the studio examines. *Some American Feminists exemplifies the nearly universal nature of the issues the studio examines.*

is imitative of *imitates.*

is in accord/accordance on/with *agrees with/coincides with/complies with/concurs with/conforms to/with/corresponds to/with.* • We feel that the activities of our diplomats in Nicaragua were in strict accordance with normal patterns of diplomatic behavior. *We feel that the activities of our diplomats in Nicaragua strictly conformed with normal patterns of diplomatic behavior.*

is in agreement (on/with) *agrees (on/with)/coincides (with)/complies (with)/concurs (with)/conforms (to/with)/corresponds (to/with).* • The client should be in agreement with the goals set. *The client should concur with the goals set.* • He said his views were in agreement with those of the conferees on all subjects on which a consensus had been reached. *He said his views agreed with those of the conferees on all subjects on which a consensus had been reached.* • Seldom am I in agreement with *Florida Today*'s editorial opinions, but Friday's was an exception. *I seldom agree with* Florida Today's *editorial opinions, but Friday's was an exception.*

is in attendance (at) *attends.* • Three presidents were in attendance at the graduation ceremonies. *Three presidents attended the graduation ceremonies.* • I was in attendance at the 1996 International Association of Applied Linguistics (AILA) Congress in Jyväskylä, Finland. *I attended the 1996 International Association of Applied Linguistics (AILA) Congress in Jyväskylä, Finland.*

is incapable of -ing *cannot/is unable to.* • All three companies were incapable of managing their prizes and two of them, Hershey and CBS, eventually discarded their acquisitions in dismay. *All three companies were unable to manage their prizes and two of them, Hershey and CBS, eventually discarded their acquisitions in dismay.*

is in charge of *controls/directs/governs/manages.*

is inclined to *tends to.*

is inclined to believe (that) *asserts/believes/claims/contends/feels/holds/maintains/says/thinks/to.* • I am inclined to believe that we will receive a lot more calls when budgets make clear what cuts and fees public schools will institute. *I believe that we will receive a lot more calls when budgets make clear what cuts and fees public schools will institute.*

is inclined to think (that) *asserts/believes/claims/contends/feels/holds/maintains/says/thinks/to.* • I am inclined to think that Windows 95 is in many ways inferior to Windows 3.1. *I think Windows 95 is in many ways inferior to Windows 3.1.*

is in competition with *competes with.* • The WI is in competition with many other organizations that could also satisfy the needs women have for friendship, learning and all the other things our aims and objects describe. *The WI competes with many other organizations that could also satisfy the needs women have for friendship, learning and all the other things our aims and objects describe.*

is in compliance with *complies with/conforms to/with.* • No register of deeds shall accept a deed for recording unless it is in compliance with the requirements of this section. *No register of deeds shall accept a deed for recording unless it complies to the requirements of this section.*

is in concurrence with *agrees with/coheres with/concurs with/conforms to/with/corresponds to/with.* • I suppose everybody is in concurrence with this. *I suppose everybody agrees with this.* • The position is in concurrence with recommendations from the American Heart Association and the National High Blood Pressure Education Program. *The position concurs with recommendations from the American Heart Association and the National High Blood Pressure Education Program.*

is in conflict with *clashes with/conflicts with/contradicts/differs from/disagrees with/quarrels with/varies with.* • The NTIA petition refers to the information services prohibition in the Modification of Final Judgment as "a cumbersome, unnecessary layer of regulation that is in irreconcilable conflict with the Communications Act." *The NTIA petition refers to the information services prohibition in the Modification of Final Judgment as "a cumbersome, unnecessary layer of regulation that irreconcilably conflicts with the Communications Act."*

is in conformance to/with *agrees with/coincides with/complies with/concurs with/conforms to/with/corresponds to/with.* • *A Basic Guide to Fair Housing Accessibility* is an indispensable resource for architects, builders, contractors, site engineers, and developers who need to know that their work is in conformance with federal guidelines. A Basic Guide to Fair Housing Accessibility *is an indispensable resource for architects, builders, contractors, site engineers, and developers who need to know that their work conforms with federal guidelines.*

is in conformity to/with *agrees with/coincides with/complies with/concurs with/conforms to/with/corresponds to/with.* • As long as they're in conformity with the law, they can do business with whomever they like. *As long as they conform to the law, they can do business with whomever they like.*

is in contempt of *defies.* • A parent who is in contempt of a custody order is playing with fire. *A parent who defies a custody order is playing with fire.*

is in (marked/sharp) contrast to *clashes with/conflicts with/contests/contradicts/contrasts with/differs from/disagrees with/disputes/opposes.* • The findings are in contrast to those of the Higher Education Research Institute, which conducts an annual national survey of freshmen. *The findings conflict with those of the Higher Education Research Institute, which conducts an annual national survey of freshmen.*

is in control of *controls/directs/governs/manages.* • Risk-takers feel that they are in control of their own destiny. *Risk-takers feel that they control their own destiny.*

is in defiance of *defies.* • They are in defiance of my orders. *They defy my orders.* • This, too, is in defiance of all expert estimates, including that of the one physician in the Senate, the Republican Bill Frist. *This, too, defies all expert*

estimates, including that of the one physician in the Senate, the Republican Bill Frist.

is indicative of *argues/attests to/bespeaks/betokens/indicates/shows/signals/signifies/suggests/testifies to/witnesses.* • Current sales figures are indicative of a management problem. *Current sales figures indicate a management problem.*

is in disagreement (about/on/with) *clashes with/conflicts with/contradicts/differs from/disagrees with/quarrels with/varies with.* • In the most important and urgent political debates of recent years involving science, a major difficulty has been that scientists of equal distinction and accomplishment have been in disagreement. *In the most important and urgent political debates of recent years involving science, a major difficulty has been that scientists of equal distinction and accomplishment have disagreed.*

is in doubt about/of *disbelieves/distrusts/doubts/mistrusts/questions.* • For anyone who is in doubt about whether ministers are ordinary mortals, Mr. Wangerin makes clear that this is the case. *For anyone who doubts whether ministers are ordinary mortals, Mr. Wangerin makes clear that this is the case.*

is in error *errs.* • She was in error. *She erred.*

is in excess of *exceeds.* • The size of the droplets produced by the unit is in excess of 8 microns. *The size of the droplets produced by the unit exceeds 8 microns.*

is in existence *exists.* • More than 1,000 successful AI applications are in existence today. *More than 1,000 successful AI applications exist today.*

is in favor of *backs/endorses/favors/prefers/supports.* • We are in favor of reform, but we don't like the way it is being implemented. *We favor reform, but we don't like the way it is being implemented.* • The Federalists were in favor of a strong, centralized oligarchic form of government. *The Federalists supported a strong, centralized oligarchic form of government.*

is in fear for/of *dreads/fears (for)/frets (about/over)/stews (about/over)/worries (about/over).* • I was in fear for my life. *I feared for my life.*

is influential in (-ing) *affects/influences.* • The problem with this generalization is that other factors can be influential in determining how many subordinates a manager has. *The problem with this generalization is that other factors can influence how many subordinates a manager has.*

is -ing delete. • What the kids are wanting is to be loved. *What the kids want is to be loved.* • We have gained a much better understanding of what providers are seeking from our networks, and we are looking forward to presenting our plan. *We have gained a much better understanding of what providers seek from our networks, and we look forward to presenting our plan.* • Today, millions of Americans with disabilities are engaging in productive, gratifying endeavors. *Today, millions of Americans with disabilities engage in productive, gratifying endeavors.* • Some are speculating that Apple's new device is a digital music product for its iTunes software, while others think Apple may unveil a PDA, a Web pad—or even a set top box. *Some speculate that Apple's new device is a digital music product for its iTunes software, while others think Apple may unveil a PDA, a Web pad— or even a set top box.*

is in harmony with *agrees with/coheres with/ concurs with/conforms to/with/corresponds to/ with.*

is injurious to *damages/harms/hurts/impairs/ injures/mars/wrongs.*

is in keeping with *agrees with/coheres with/ concurs with/conforms to/with/corresponds to/ with.* • This is in keeping with MicroPro Inter-national's focus and marketing. *This conforms to MicroPro International's focus and marketing.*

is in line with *agrees with/coheres with/concurs with/conforms to/with/corresponds to/with.* • The figures are in line with recent years, when the number of taxpayers filing early in the season declined each year. *The figures conform with recent years, when the number of taxpayers filing early in the season declined each year.*

is in need of *needs/wants.* • Thousands of people are in need of medical attention that private insurance does not offer. *Thousands of people need medical attention that private insurance does not offer.* • This section seems to be in need of a good deal of updating. *This section seems to need a good deal of updating.*

is in opposition to *conflicts with/contests/disagrees with/disapproves of/disputes/objects to/ opposes/protests/resists.* • They are in opposition to the United States. *They oppose the United States.*

is in possession of *has/possesses.* • They were in possession of a large quantity of cocaine. *They possessed a large quantity of cocaine.*

is in receipt of *receives.* • I am in receipt of your impressive resumé and references. *I received your impressive resumé and references.*

is insistent on *demands on/insists on.* • If people are insistent on keeping the Electoral College, why not make it fair? *If people insist on keeping the Electoral College, why not make it fair?*

is in step with *agrees with/coheres with/concurs with/conforms to/with/corresponds to/with.*

is instrumental in (-ing) *aids in/assists in/helps.* • Far from being the marginal movement they are perceived as being today, 19th-century evangelicals were instrumental in setting the political and social agenda for the century. *Far from being the marginal movement they are perceived as being today, 19th-century evangelicals helped set the political and social agenda for the century.* • He was instrumental in helping them put together a financial plan. *He helped them put together a financial plan.*

is in support of *backs/endorses/favors/prefers/ supports.* • I myself am in support of women's rights. *I myself support women's rights.*

is in violation of *desecrates/infringes on/violates.* • My job is solely to determine whether conduct is in violation of the federal criminal law. *My job is solely to determine whether conduct violates the federal criminal law.*

is in want of *needs/wants.* • I would recommend it to anyone who is in want of a good laugh. *I would recommend it to anyone who wants a good laugh.* • But the handing over of the land has not been finalized yet, and the Army is in want of funds to do the construction. *But the handing over of the land has not been finalized yet, and the Army needs funds to do the construction.* • She is an older woman and is in want of a young man. *She is an older woman and wants a young man.*

is it possible for *can.* • Is it possible for you to tell us about your relationship with your child? *Can you tell us about your relationship with your child?*

is knowledgeable about (in/of) *comprehends/ knows/understands.* • We also favor choosing directors who have worked in a company's industry at some point in their careers or are knowledgeable in some collateral industry. *We also favor choosing directors who have worked in a company's industry at some point in their careers or understand some collateral industry.*

island (completely) surrounded by water *island.* • White, racist American servicemen

had struck again, this time on an island surrounded by water away from all civilization. *White, racist American servicemen had struck again, this time on an island away from all civilization.*

is mindful of/that *comprehends/knows/realizes/ recognizes/sees/understands.* • We should be mindful of the benefits of free trade while finding ways to limit it. *We should realize the benefits of free trade while finding ways to limit it.*

is mistrustful about/of *disbelieves/distrusts/ doubts/mistrusts/questions.* • The two sides are deeply mistrustful of each other after an estimated 1 million casualties. *The two sides deeply mistrust each other after an estimated 1 million casualties.*

is needful of *needs/wants.* • Ball State's quaint little paper, *The Daily News*, is needful of inspiring columnists and diligent reporters. *Ball State's quaint little paper, The Daily News, needs inspiring columnists and diligent reporters.* • In terms of her physical well-being she is needful of extensive dental treatment. *In terms of her physical well-being she needs extensive dental treatment.*

is of assistance in (-ing) *aids in (-ing)/assists in (-ing)/helps.* • Huge expenditures are required for EFRAT's activities, and every contribution is of assistance in expanding its efforts. *Huge expenditures are required for EFRAT's activities, and every contribution helps expand its efforts.*

is of benefit to *aids/benefits/favors/helps.* • He agrees that companies need to take caution when choosing a system, but adds that the technology can be of great benefit to a company. *He agrees that companies need to take caution when choosing a system, but adds that the technology can greatly benefit a company.*

is of concern to *bothers/concerns/disturbs/ interests/upsets/worries.* • Since these factors vary considerably from one country to another, they are of particular concern to the global company interested in a new foreign market. *Since these factors vary considerably from one country to another, they particularly concern the global company interested in a new foreign market.*

is offensive to *insults/offends.* • Halloween represents spiritist forces that are offensive to three of the world's major religions, Judaism, Christianity, and Islam. *Halloween represents spiritist forces that offend three of the world's major religions, Judaism, Christianity, and Islam.*

is of interest to *appeals to/attracts/concerns/ excites/interests.* • Although it is most helpful when read from the beginning to end, you can start with any section that is of interest to you. *Although it is most helpful when read from the beginning to end, you can start with any section that appeals to you.*

is of the belief (that) *asserts/believes/claims/ contends/feels/holds/maintains/says/thinks/to.* • The vast majority of physicians are of the belief that Ritalin is a safe drug for children. *To the vast majority of physicians, Ritalin is a safe drug for children.*

is of the opinion (that) *asserts/believes/claims/ contends/feels/holds/maintains/says/thinks/to.* • I am of the opinion that the Celtics are far better off this year than last. *I believe the Celtics are far better off this year than last.* • Management is of the opinion that within three years from the inception of this financing, it will be prepared to undertake an IPO. *Management contends that within three years from the inception of this financing, it will be prepared to undertake an IPO.*

is of the same opinion (as) *agrees (with)/concurs (with).* • Don't assume the person at the receiving end of your email is of the same opinion as you. *Don't assume the person at the receiving end of your email agrees with you.*

is of the view (that) *asserts/believes/claims/ contends/feels/holds/maintains/says/thinks/to.* • He is of the view that a person between the ages of 30 and 40 is more susceptible to tuberculosis than a person between 60 and 70. *He maintains that a person between the ages of 30 and 40 is more susceptible to tuberculosis than a person between 60 and 70.*

is one (that/which/who/whom) delete. • A European option is one which can be exercised only at maturity. *A European option can be exercised only at maturity.* • This situation is one that ought not to be forgotten. *This situation ought not to be forgotten.* • The issue of legal or illegal, documented or undocumented immigrant status is one that is still being argued. *The issue of legal or illegal, documented or undocumented immigrant status is still being argued.* • A multitasking system is one that can perform several tasks simultaneously. *A multitasking system can perform several tasks simultaneously.*

is on (a) par (with) *equals.* • U.S. factory wages are already at least 20 percent below comparable German wages, on a dollar basis, and virtually on a par with Japanese levels. *U.S. factory wages are already at least 20 percent below comparable German wages, on a dollar basis, and virtually equal Japanese levels.*

is operative (in) *appears/applies/exists/occurs/ operates/runs/takes place/works.* • All these issues and prejudices are operative in this story. *All these issues and prejudices appear in this story.* • SIX is operative in four business areas and is organized in six divisions. *SIX operates in four business areas and is organized in six divisions.* • Who first proposed that gravity is operative in space? *Who first proposed that gravity exists in space?* • Darcy's law is operative in porous flow environments. *Darcy's law applies in porous flow environments.*

is opposed to *conflicts with/contests/disagrees with/disapproves of/disputes/objects to/opposes/ protests/resists.* • I would not be opposed to doing that. *I would not object to doing that.*

is outrageous to *outrages.* • The idea that Florida can collect taxes on cigarettes made in Virginia and sold in California is outrageous to me. *The idea that Florida can collect taxes on cigarettes made in Virginia and sold in California outrages me.*

is persistent in *perseveres in/persists in.* • Friends must be persistent in helping the griever come out of himself. *Friends must persist in helping the griever come out of himself.*

is pertinent to *applies to/bears on/concerns/ pertains to/regards/relates to.* • This online manual was written to gather information that is pertinent to the students enrolled in the degree programs of the Department of Electrical Engineering. *This online manual was written to gather information that pertains to the students enrolled in the degree programs of the Department of Electrical Engineering.*

is predicated on the assumption (that) *assumes/ supposes.* • The whole idea is predicated on the assumption that the Missouri River has excess water. *The whole idea supposes that the Missouri River has excess water.* • Of course, this is predicated on the assumption that test scores are of great importance to the college admissions process. *Of course, this assumes that test scores are of great importance to the college admissions process.*

is predictive of *forecasts/foretells/predicts/presages/portends.* • It offers a classification system that may be predictive of the outcome. *It offers a classification system that may predict the outcome.* • It follows then that they can be predic-

tive of a wide variety of behaviors. *It follows then that they can predict a wide variety of behaviors.*

is proof of/that *confirms/evinces/indicates/ proves/reveals/shows/signifies/testifies (to).* • Legendary silent film director Cecil B. DeMille didn't much alter the way he made movies after sound came in, and this 1956 biblical drama is proof of that. *Legendary silent film director Cecil B. DeMille didn't much alter the way he made movies after sound came in, and this 1956 biblical drama shows that.*

is prone to *tends to.* • Company managers are prone to underestimate loyalty and their employees' need for it. *Company managers tend to underestimate loyalty and their employees' need for it.*

is protective against (of) *defends/guards/insulates/protects/shelters/shields.* • A diet high in complex carbohydrates may be protective against the development of chronic diseases like heart disease and cancer. *A diet high in complex carbohydrates may protect against the development of chronic diseases like heart disease and cancer.*

is receptive to *welcomes.* • While lawmakers are generally receptive to his ideas, the feeling is not mutual. *While lawmakers generally welcome his ideas, the feeling is not mutual.*

is (a/the) recipient of *receives.* • The University of South Florida was the recipient of a $600,000 grant from a Florida bank to endow a professorship in banking and finance. *The University of South Florida received a $600,000 grant from a Florida bank to endow a professorship in banking and finance.*

is reflective of *epitomizes/exemplifies/mirrors/ reflects/typifies.* • Films receiving Oscar nominations are reflective of the image that the film industry wants to convey of itself. *Films receiving Oscar nominations mirror the image that the* film industry wants to convey of itself. • Morbid obesity is reflective of a metabolic endocrine disorder. *Morbid obesity reflects a metabolic endocrine disorder.*

is regretful about/of/that *regrets.* • Now I'm regretful that I didn't work harder this week. *Now I regret I didn't work harder this week.*

is related to *correlates to/with/equates with/ relates to.* • It is generally assumed that a species-wide tendency to favor one hand over the other is related to the development of brain hemispheres with specialized functions. *It is generally assumed that a species-wide tendency to favor one hand over the other relates to the development of brain hemispheres with specialized functions.*

is relevant to *applies to/bears on/concerns/pertains to/regards/relates to.*

is reliant on/upon *counts on/depends on/relies on.* • South Korean builders are heavily reliant upon the Mideast market. *South Korean builders rely heavily on the Mideast market.*

is reminiscent of *recalls.* • The apparatus is reminiscent of some Asian musical performances emphasizing the gestures used to play instruments. *The apparatus recalls some Asian musical performances emphasizing the gestures used to play instruments.*

is representative of *emblemizes/indicates/represents/signifies/stands for/symbolizes/typifies.* • For the reader to assume that this is representative of the norm is unfortunate. *For the reader to assume that this represents the norm is unfortunate.*

is required to *has to/must.* • Managers are required to be able to perform certain roles. *Managers must be able to perform certain roles.*

is resentful of *resents.* • He speaks in metaphors and is resentful of the modern media (which, we can safely assume, ignores him). *He speaks in metaphors and resents the modern media (which, we can safely assume, ignores him).*

is resistant to *contests/disagrees with/disapproves of/disputes/objects to/opposes/protests/ resists.* • In fact, they are resistant to measuring learning and performance in meaningful terms. *In fact, they resist measuring learning and performance in meaningful terms.*

is respectful of/toward *respects.* • The two skaters are friends and respectful of each other. *The two skaters are friends and respect each other.*

is restrictive in/to *restricts.* • Even before the *Sheppard* decision, law enforcement officers and prosecuting attorneys were restrictive in the release of certain information to the news media. *Even before the* Sheppard *decision, law enforcement officers and prosecuting attorneys restricted the release of certain information to the news media.*

is revealing of *reveals.* • Both models are revealing of the dynamics of organizational decision making, and they may be related. *Both models reveal the dynamics of organizational decision making, and they may be related.*

is ruinous to *damages/destroys/harms/hurts/ impairs/injures/mars/ruins.* • The closeups are ruinous to the performances of Aprile Millo as Aida and Dolora Zajick as Amneris. *The closeups ruin the performances of Aprile Millo as Aida and Dolora Zajick as Amneris.*

is scared of/to *dreads/fears/frets (about/over)/ stews (about/over)/worries (about/over).*

is scornful of *despises/disdains/scorns.* • Many scientists are scornful of him because of his claims that fluoride causes everything from cancer to AIDS. *Many scientists scorn him because of his claims that fluoride causes everything from cancer to AIDS.*

is similar to/with *compares to/with/corresponds to/with/equates with/relates to/resembles.* • These commands are similar to English sentences, and most of them make sense to the casual reader. *These commands resemble English sentences, and most of them make sense to the casual reader.*

is skeptical about/of/that *disbelieves/distrusts/doubts/mistrusts/questions.* • Immigration officials often are skeptical of businesses' claims that they didn't know a worker was illegal or that they weren't aware of the new immigration law. *Immigration officials often disbelieve businesses' claims that they didn't know a worker was illegal or that they weren't aware of the new immigration law.*

is still to be seen *do not know/is not (now/yet) known/is uncertain/is unclear/is unknown/is unsure.* • They priced it like a Mercedes/whether it's engineered like a Mercedes is still to be seen. *They priced it like a Mercedes/whether it's engineered like a Mercedes is not yet known.*

is stimulative to *stimulates.* • None of this is stimulative to the economy. *None of this stimulates the economy.* • It's said that such an object is stimulative to living beings. *It's said that such an object stimulates living beings.*

issuance *issue.* • Municipal bonds and municipal notes are debt obligations of states, cities, municipalities, and municipal agencies which generally have maturities, at the time of their issuance, of either one year or more or from six months to three years. *Municipal bonds and municipal notes are debt obligations of states, cities, municipalities, and municipal agencies which generally have maturities, at the time of*

their issue, of either one year or more or from six months to three years.

is subject to *depends on/hinges on.* • Completion of the transactions is subject to a definitive agreement and the approval of both boards. *Completion of the transactions hinges on a definitive agreement and the approval of both boards.*

(a/the) . . . issue delete. • The question of whether a firm's financing decisions affect its value remains an unresolved issue. *The question of whether a firm's financing decisions affect its value remains unresolved.* • I was doing well enough so that money was no longer an issue of concern. *I was doing well enough so that money was no longer a concern.*

(the) issue/problem/question/thing is, is *is.* • The question is, is he in the racing business or is it a hobby? *Is he in the racing business or is it a hobby?* • The thing is, is it going to be enough to inspire confidence? *Is it going to be enough to inspire confidence?* • The problem is, is the young offensive line good enough to do that? *Is the young offensive line good enough to do that?*

(the) issue of delete. • We shall first consider the issue of plotting the historical series we want to analyze. *We shall first consider plotting the historical series we want to analyze.*

is suggestive of *argues/attests to/bespeaks/betokens/indicates/shows/signals/signifies/suggests/testifies to/witnesses.* • Any breast mass that is suggestive of malignancy by mammography or on physical examination should be biopsied. *Any breast mass that suggests malignancy by mammography or on physical examination should be biopsied.* • This response is suggestive of the fact that there is more truth to what transpires in this book than either author knows. *This response signals there is more truth to what transpires in this book than either author knows.*

is suitable to *applies to/bears on/concerns/pertains to/regards/relates to.*

is supportive of *endorses/fosters/nurtures/supports/upholds.* • This report is supportive of our findings. *This report supports our findings.* • Predictably, many measurement experts are supportive of such tests. *Predictably, many measurement experts support such tests.*

is symbolic/symbolical of *emblemizes/indicates/represents/signifies/stands for/symbolizes/typifies.* • The contrast, stark and dramatic, is symbolic of what has happened across California. *The contrast, stark and dramatic, symbolizes what has happened across California.*

is symptomatic of *indicates/signals/signifies/symptomizes.* • The small dip is symptomatic of a pause in the housing market in October, as buyers, sellers, and lenders tried to figure out what was occurring in the financial markets. *The small dip indicates a pause in the housing market in October, as buyers, sellers, and lenders tried to figure out what was occurring in the financial markets.*

is tantamount to *amounts to/duplicates/equals/is/matches/rivals.*

is (a) testament to *affirms/attests to/certifies to/declares/testifies to/verifies.* • An excellent credit card rating is a testament to your success in business. *An excellent credit card rating attests to your success in business.*

is (a) testimony to *affirms/attests to/certifies to/declares/testifies to/verifies.* • The high level of business and consumer confidence is testimony to the success of this Fed policy. *The high level of business and consumer confidence testifies to the success of this Fed policy.*

is there . . . (that/who) *is* delete. • Are there different types of restitution available in your jurisdiction? *Are different types of restitution available in your jurisdiction?*

is trustful of *trusts.* • Even when a woman is trustful of her physicians, the gravity of the situation demands that she feel fully confident with the diagnosis before beginning any treatment. *Even when a woman trusts her physicians, the gravity of the situation demands that she feel fully confident with the diagnosis before beginning any treatment.*

is typical of *exemplifies/symbolizes/typifies.* • This kind of comment is typical of the Democrat's campaign. *This kind of comment exemplifies the Democrat's campaign.*

is under the assumption (that) *assumes/believes/feels/supposes/thinks.* • I am under the assumption that the *Globe* is trying to ameliorate the situation. *I assume the* Globe *is trying to ameliorate the situation.*

is under the impression (that) *assumes/believes/feels/supposes/thinks.* • It was fine the first few times, but now he's under the impression I am his grandson. *It was fine the first few times, but now he thinks I am his grandson.*

is what delete. • While consistency is the mainstay of our program, diversity and change are what keep it exciting. *While consistency is the mainstay of our program, diversity and change keep it exciting.* • The person–machine interface is what must be retained if security is not to become a purely mechanical effort. *The person–machine interface must be retained if security is not to become a purely mechanical effort.* • Another major group is what Ogbu calls "autonomous minorities." *Another major group Ogbu calls "autonomous minorities."* • This type of learning process is what is suggested for this preliminary activity. *This type of learning process is suggested for this preliminary activity.* • The daily behavior of good citizens is what holds society together. *The daily behavior of good citizens holds society together.*

is when *in* delete. • Content area reading is when students are not learning to read but are reading to learn information. *In content area reading, students are not learning to read but are reading to learn information.* • Sexual intercourse is when a boy's hard penis goes inside a girl's vagina, and he then ejaculates sperm through his penis. *In sexual intercourse, a boy's hard penis goes inside a girl's vagina, and he then ejaculates sperm through his penis.*

is where *at/in* delete. • PayPalSucks.com is where you will learn about the PayPal class action lawsuit, abuse, fraud and evil behind the PayPal system! *At PayPalSucks.com you will learn about the PayPal class action lawsuit, abuse, fraud and evil behind the PayPal system!* • An analogy is where you use a more well understood concept or situation to explain a more complex one. *In an analogy, you use a more well understood concept or situation to explain a more complex one.*

is witness to *affirms/attests to/certifies to/ declares/testifies to/verifies.* • Poet Kahlil Gibran's popularity in America is witness to the presence of an essential moral and artistic quality in his work. *Poet Kahlil Gibran's popularity in America testifies to the presence of an essential moral and artistic quality in his work.*

is (a) witness to *sees/witnesses.* • He was a witness to the Chinese government's crackdown on students. *He witnessed the Chinese government's crackdown on students.*

it has been called to (my) attention *(I) have been told/(I) have learned/(I) understand* delete.

it has come to (my) attention (I) have been told/ (I) have learned/(I) understand delete. • It has come to our attention that some people are not aware of how to operate the intercom properly. *We have learned that some people are not aware of how to operate the intercom properly.*

it is . . . (that/who) *is/-(al)ly* delete. • It is our intent to share ideas, thoughts, and methods with GEM users. *Our intent is to share ideas, thoughts, and methods with GEM users.* • It is my feeling that it is a human obligation to create meaning. *My feeling is that it is a human obligation to create meaning.*

it is a fact that delete. • Regardless of whether the promiscuous mode operation is legitimate or the work of an intruder, it is a fact that all transmissions are subject to reception by stations other than the intended receiver. *Regardless of whether the promiscuous mode operation is legitimate or the work of an intruder, all transmissions are subject to reception by stations other than the intended receiver.*

it is apparent that *apparently/clearly/evidently/manifestly/obviously/patently/plainly* delete. • It is apparent that management needs to take into account a wide range of variables when devising international product development policies. *Clearly, management needs to take into account a wide range of variables when devising international product development policies.*

it is essential that *must/should.* • It is essential that remaining barriers to women's entrepreneurship be eliminated. *Remaining barriers to women's entrepreneurship must be eliminated.*

it is evident that *apparently/clearly/evidently/ manifestly/obviously/patently/plainly* delete. • It is evident that service industries are more exposed to protectionism in international markets than are most other industries. *Clearly, service industries are more exposed to protectionism in international markets than are most other industries.*

it is (to be) hoped *I (we) hope/let us hope.* • It is to be hoped that your exposé will help prevent this kind of performance by others. *Let's hope that your exposé will help prevent this kind of performance by others.*

it is imperative that *must/should.* • It is imperative that managers and researchers try to assess the value of the information before the research is undertaken. *Managers and researchers should try to assess the value of the information before the research is undertaken.*

it is important to keep in mind *keep in mind/remember* delete. • It is important to keep in mind that these applications address only today's problems. *Keep in mind that these applications address only today's problems.*

it is important to mention/say/state (that) delete. • It is important to mention that a group of auxiliary verbs called modals can also express the disposition and attitude of the speaker. *A group of auxiliary verbs called modals can also express the disposition and attitude of the speaker.*

it is important to note *note* delete. • It is important to note that different stores in a chain may perform differently. *Different stores in a chain may perform differently.*

it is important to realize/recognize *realize/recognize* delete. • It is important to realize that many Chinese willingly remain in their country despite the violence. *Many Chinese willingly remain in their country despite the violence.*

it is important to remember *keep in mind/remember* delete. • It is important to remember that social security reserves are expected to build to about $12 trillion in the next century. *Remember that social security reserves are expected to build to about $12 trillion in the next century.*

it is important to . . . that delete. • It is important to emphasize that the incidence of breast cancer has been rising. *The incidence of breast cancer has been rising.*

it is important to understand *understand* delete. • It is important to understand that not all pressures are the result of marketplace changes, nor do they necessarily affect the marketing activity. *Not all pressures are the result of marketplace changes, nor do they necessarily affect the marketing activity.*

it is interesting to note *interestingly/note* delete. • It is interesting to note that an early meaning of the Spanish word *algebrista* was bonesetter or reuniter of broken bones. *Interestingly, an early meaning of the Spanish word* algebrista *was bonesetter or reuniter of broken bones.*

it is my assessment (that) *I assert/I believe/I claim/I consider/I contend/I declare/I feel/I hold/I judge/I maintain/I regard/I say/I think/I view* delete. • It is my assessment that ufology has failed to recognize the importance of how the Extraterrestrial presence profoundly threatens all terrestrial elites. *I maintain that ufology has failed to recognize the importance of how the Extraterrestrial presence profoundly threatens all terrestrial elites.*

it is my belief(that) *I assert/I believe/I claim/I consider/I contend/I declare/I feel/I hold/I judge/I maintain/I regard/I say/I think/I view* delete. • It is my belief that CFS is an opportunistic disease that preys on bodies that are compromised. *I contend that CFS is an opportunistic disease that preys on bodies that are compromised.*

it is my estimation (that) *I assert/I believe/I claim/I consider/I contend/I declare/I feel/I hold/I judge/I maintain/I regard/I say/I think/I view* delete. • It is my estimation that the vast majority of students who do poorly in this class do so because they fall behind. *I think the vast majority of students who do poorly in this class do so because they fall behind.*

it is my expectation (that) *I anticipate/I expect.* • Next year, it is my expectation that I will be able to report to all of you that we have achieved our membership goals. *Next year, I expect that I will be able to report to all of you that we have achieved our membership goals.*

it is my intention (that) *I intend/I plan.* • It is my intention to sit and play video games for several hours. *I intend to sit and play video games for several hours.*

it is my judgment (that) *I assert/I believe/I claim/I consider/I contend/I declare/I feel/I hold/I judge/I maintain/I regard/I say/I think/I view* delete. • It is my judgment that, from your actions, being on time for our appointments is not important to you, and that my time is not important to you. *I say that, from your actions, being on time for our appointments is not important to you, and that my time is not important to you.*

it is my observation (that) *I discern/I note/I notice/I observe/I perceive/I see.* • While there are certainly many sexually adventurous people out there, it is my observation that sex in multiples is still not perceived as mainstream behavior. *While there are certainly many sexually adventurous people out there, sex in multiples is still not perceived as mainstream behavior.*

it is my opinion (that) *I assert/I believe/I claim/I consider/I contend/I declare/I feel/I hold/I judge/I maintain/I regard/I say/I think/I view* delete. • It is my opinion that a woman can make a successful president. *I believe a woman can make a successful president.*

it is my preference (that) *I fancy/I favor/I prefer.* • It is my preference not to comment on the

report until you have all had a chance to spend some time with it. *I prefer not to comment on the report until you have all had a chance to spend some time with it.*

it is my recommendation (that) *I advise/I advocate/I propose/I recommend/I suggest/I urge.* • It is my recommendation that all students taking my courses be fluent in English reading and writing at college-level proficiency. *I urge that all students taking my courses be fluent in English reading and writing at college-level proficiency.*

it is my suggestion (that) *I advise/I advocate/I propose/I recommend/I suggest/I urge.* • It is my suggestion that you get a hold of some software like PhotoShop and use it to doctor up some of your childhood pictures. *I suggest that you get a hold of some software like PhotoShop and use it to doctor up some of your childhood pictures.*

it is my understanding (that) *I appreciate/I comprehend/I grasp/I realize/I recognize/I understand.* • It is my understanding that there are two types of processes for applying. *I understand that there are two types of processes for applying.*

it is my view (that) *I assert/I believe/I claim/I consider/I contend/I declare/I feel/I hold/I judge/I maintain/I regard/I say/I think/I view* delete. • But when it comes to analysis, it is my view that all ought to be under one umbrella. *But when it comes to analysis, I believe that all ought to be under one umbrella.*

it is necessary (for/that/to) *must/need to.* • It is necessary for this causality to be realistic for the model to be useful. *This causality must be realistic for the model to be useful.*

it is often the case/circumstance/situation (that) *frequently/most often/often/sometimes/usually.* • In applications, it is often the case that descriptive analyses of the individual trajectories, rates of improvement, etc. are of the greatest substantive value. *In applications, frequently descriptive analyses of the individual trajectories, rates of improvement, etc. are of the greatest substantive value.* • As with vanity publishing, it is often the case that the amount you pay for the production of the book hardly ever is returned from the sales. *As with vanity publishing, often the amount you pay for the production of the book hardly ever is returned from the sales.*

it is significant to note *note* delete. • It is significant to note that this land is owned by the city and leased to Harvard. *This land is owned by the city and leased to Harvard.*

it is useful/worthwhile to mention/say/state (that) delete. • It is useful to state that most of the modernization in steel production has occurred as part of a general shift toward all-electric steelmaking. *Most of the modernization in steel production has occurred as part of a general shift toward all-electric steelmaking.*

it is useful/worthwhile to note (that) delete. • It is worthwhile to note that in this outline the results specified in step III could refer to any of several results. *In this outline the results specified in step III could refer to any of several results.*

it must/should be mentioned/remarked/said/ stated (that) delete. • It should be remarked, however, that for both methods success is largely dependent on devising an appropriate method for representing the problem. *However, for both methods success is largely dependent on devising an appropriate method for representing the problem.*

it must/should be noted *note* delete. • It should be noted that people with gastrointestinal disorders share a number of traits. *People with gastrointestinal disorders share a number of traits.*

it must/should be pointed out (that) delete. • It should be pointed out that Boston Technical students have recently received notices of acceptance from institutions such as Princeton, Tufts, Boston College, and the University of California at Berkeley. *Boston Technical students have recently received notices of acceptance from institutions such as Princeton, Tufts, Boston College, and the University of California at Berkeley.*

it must/should be remembered *keep in mind/ remember* delete. • It must be remembered that even though this course deals with an easily measurable good, money, you must make personal value judgments concerning how money is best used. *Even though this course deals with an easily measurable good, money, you must make personal value judgments concerning how money is best used.*

it must/should be understood *understand* delete. • It must be understood that we have a very complex, interrelated economy. *We have a very complex, interrelated economy.*

it (just) so happens *by chance/luckily/unluckily.*

(a/the) -ity of delete. • Its purposes can only be attained through a rationality of communication. *Its purposes can only be attained through rational communication.* • The Taliban is a viciously fundamentalist organization which shares a consanguinity of interests with the equally vicious, revanchist, Islamist Osama group. *The Taliban is a viciously fundamentalist organization which shares consanguine interests with the equally vicious, revanchist, Islamist Osama group.*

I (we) would appreciate it if *please.*

J

(a/the) . . . job of delete. • When the banks offer investments with a high market profile, the job of introducing the funds to bank customers is much easier. *When the banks offer investments with a high market profile, introducing the funds to bank customers is much easier.*

joint agreement *agreement.* • EarthShell Corporation and DuPont Polyester announced today they have entered into a joint agreement to develop and market additional new forms of environmentally friendly packaging for the food service industry. *EarthShell Corporation and DuPont Polyester announced today they have entered into an agreement to develop and market additional new forms of environmentally friendly packaging for the food service industry.*

joint cooperation *cooperation.*

join together *combine/join.* • All of these can be joined together by soldering, brazing, or welding. *All of these can be joined by soldering, brazing, or welding.*

judge as *judge.* • For an invention to be judged as novel, there must be no information available in the public domain. *For an invention to be judged novel, there must be no information available in the public domain.* • Each subject area was judged as excellent, satisfactory or unsatisfactory. *Each subject area was judged excellent, satisfactory or unsatisfactory.*

just about *about/almost/nearly.*

just as (more/most) importantly *just as (more/most) important.* • But perhaps most importantly, they offer trustworthiness. *But perhaps most important, they offer trustworthiness.*

just as (more/most) significantly *just as (more/most) significant.* • Most significantly, the product champion must have the drive to get the work done and the decisions made. *Most significant, the product champion must have the drive to get the work done and the decisions made.*

just exactly *exactly/just.* • He's just exactly what I'm looking for. *He's just what I'm looking for.*

just recently *just/recently.* • We just recently went to England. *We recently went to England.*

just simply *just/simply.*

just the same as *just like/the same as.* • The DEL command works just the same as the ERASE command. *The DEL command works just like the ERASE command.*

K

keep in mind *remember* delete. • Keep in mind that few people, if any, match a job perfectly, and few employers look for a perfect fit. *Few people, if any, match a job perfectly, and few employers look for a perfect fit.*

(a/the) key . . . in/of/to *(a) key to.* • Market segmentation is a key aspect to strategic planning at the corporate and business levels. *Market segmentation is a key to strategic planning at the corporate and business levels.* • In contrast, individualism was the key ingredient to the rise of Greece. *In contrast, individualism was key to the rise of Greece.* • Our continued commitment to quality is a key component of our success. *Our continued commitment to quality is a key to our success.*

kinder (and) gentler *amiable/compassionate/ gentle/humane/kind/tender/tolerant.*

kind of delete. • I kind of stumbled onto the job. *I stumbled onto the job.*

(a) ... kind/sort/type (of) thing *like* delete. • It became a competition type of thing. *It became like a competition.* • This type of thing happens often. *This happens often.*

know for a fact *know.* • We know for a fact that this firm is trying to swindle consumers. *We know that this firm is trying to swindle consumers.*

knowledge base *knowledge.*

known as *called/named/termed* delete. • The three most common knowledge representations in expert system shells are known as rules, frames, and semantic networks. *The three most common knowledge representations in expert system shells are rules, frames, and semantic networks.*

L

label as *label.* • The product is labeled as a cosmetic, not a medication. *The product is labeled a cosmetic, not a medication.*

lackadaisical *idle/languid/lazy/listless.*

lack for *lack.*

lacking in *dis-/il-/im-/in-/ir-/lack/-less(ness)/ mis-/no/non-/not/un-/want/with no/without.* • The defense's case was so often lacking in credibility. *The defense's case was so often incredible.*

(a/the) lack of *dis-/few/il-/im-/in-/ir-/-less(ness)/ mis-/no/non-/not/scant/un-/with no/without.* • This is a result of a lack of cooperation between retailers and financial institutions. *This is a result of noncooperation between retailers and financial institutions.* • Many a computer programming project has failed because of a lack of careful problem analysis and poor program design techniques. *Many a computer programming project has failed because of careless problem analysis and poor program design techniques.* • Jackson concerns me because of his lack of experience in foreign policy and defense. *Jackson concerns me because of his inexperience in foreign policy and defense.*

(the) language of (the ... language) delete. • Twelve of his novels have been translated into the Russian language. *Twelve of his novels have been translated into Russian.*

(a/the) large/overwhelming/sizable/vast plurality (of) *a good (great) deal (of)/a good (great) many (of)/almost all (of)/many (of)/most (of)/ much (of)/nearly all (of)/three-fourths (two-thirds) (of).* • Large pluralities feel Mr. Bush would do about as well as Mr. Reagan. *Most feel Mr. Bush would do about as well as Mr. Reagan.*

large-size(d) *large.*

lasting legacy *legacy.*

last of all *last.*

(the) last time *last.* • A fifth bit acts as a flag indicating whether the file has been modified since the last time it was backed up. *A fifth bit acts as a flag indicating whether the file has been modified since it was last backed up.*

later in time *at length/eventually/from now/in time/later/ultimately.* • Usually the stock will trade lower later in time. *Usually the stock will trade lower in time.*

later on *later.* • I will see you later on. *I will see you later.*

later on down the line/pike/road/way *at length/eventually/from now/in time/later/ulti-*

mately. • Later on down the line, there will have to be a settlement. *In time, there will have to be a settlement.*

latter part of *last half of/late.*

laugh out loud *laugh.* • I still laugh out loud whenever I hear Boone's sappy rendition of the Fats Domino classic, "Blueberry Hill." *I still laugh whenever I hear Boone's sappy rendition of the Fats Domino classic, "Blueberry Hill."*

law enforcement/police officers *authorities/cops/officers/police.*

legitimatize *legitimate/legitimize.* • Unattended operation is being legitimatized by the major hardware and software vendors. *Unattended operation is being legitimized by the major hardware and software vendors.*

lend out *lend.*

(a/the) length of delete. • While adults typically grew to a length of about 30 feet, the embryos measured only about 1.2 feet from head to tail and fit into 7-inch-long eggs. *While adults typically grew to about 30 feet, the embryos measured only about 1.2 feet from head to tail and fit into 7-inch-long eggs.*

(the) length of time *how long/the time.* • The purpose of a network is to show all activities needed to complete a project and to enable the planner to calculate the length of time a project will take from start to finish. *The purpose of a network is to show all activities needed to complete a project and to enable the planner to calculate the time a project will take from start to finish.*

lengthy *long.* • Communists must go through a lengthy selection process and ideological training before being granted membership in the party. *Communists must go through a long selection process and ideological training before being granted membership in the party.*

less . . . (as) compared to/with *than.* • The winds will be a little less active tomorrow as compared to today. *The winds will be a little less active tomorrow than today.* • Service tax in India was much less as compared to international standards. *Service tax in India was much less than international standards.*

(a) lesser/lower/smaller degree/extent (of) *less.* • Transparent WDM systems offer a lesser degree of monitoring than TDM systems. *Transparent WDM systems offer less monitoring than TDM systems.* • They gave uncommon plants a smaller degree of treatment because of their limited use in food production. *They gave uncommon plants less treatment because of their limited use in food production.* • Most land areas in China have a lower extent of soil degradation. *Most land areas in China have less soil degradation.*

less . . . relative to *than.* • So why is it that women became less happy relative to men? *So why is it that women became less happy than men?*

less than (enthusiastic) *dis-/il-/im-/in-/ir-/mis-/non-/un-.* • You can refinance with us even if your credit is less than perfect. *You can refinance with us even if your credit is imperfect.* • This book reveals the sometimes less-than-elegant design of DOS by walking through the source code. *This book reveals the sometimes inelegant design of DOS by walking through the source code.* • The lack of consistent definition and the paucity of carefully designed drug studies of PMS have led to less than satisfactory treatment. *The lack of consistent definition and the paucity of carefully designed drug studies of PMS have led to unsatisfactory treatment.*

(a/the) . . . level (of) delete. • Each organization must assess its level of willingness to take risks. *Each organization must assess its willingness to take risks.* • When a relationship reaches a certain level of intensity, the church should have some way of recognizing that commitment.

When a relationship reaches a certain intensity, the church should have some way of recognizing that commitment. • Random access implies that any piece of information can be read with an equal level of difficulty and delay. *Random access implies that any piece of information can be read with equal difficulty and delay.*

level to the ground *demolish/destroy/level/raze/ruin.* • Numerous historical churches and monasteries were leveled to the ground in severe bombardments and attacks. *Numerous historical churches and monasteries were razed in severe bombardments and attacks.*

lift up *lift.*

like . . . also/as well *like.* • Like 401(k) plans, 403(b) plans also have various investment alternatives: common stocks, bonds, money-market funds, and so on. *Like 401(k) plans, 403(b) plans have various investment alternatives: common stocks, bonds, money-market funds, and so on.*

like . . . and others/and so forth/and so on/and such/and the like/et al./etc. *and others/and so forth/and so on/and such/and the like/et al./etc./like/such as.* • Sheet sizes are specified by letters like Size A, Size B, and so forth. *Sheet sizes are specified by letters like Size A and Size B.* • It can be printed on any printer, but it will not have formats such as boldfacing, underlining, and so on. *It can be printed on any printer, but it will not have formats such as boldfacing and underlining.* • Prosecutors may support the service style of policing by agreeing not to prosecute law violators who seek psychiatric help or who voluntarily participate in programs like Alcoholics Anonymous, family counseling, drug treatment, and the like. *Prosecutors may support the service style of policing by agreeing not to prosecute law violators who seek psychiatric help or who voluntarily participate in programs like Alcoholics Anonymous, family counseling, and drug treatment.* • The hotels where the Afri-can-American girls worked were forbidden to join the union and didn't have any benefits like sick leave, vacation, health insurance et cetera. *The hotels where the African-American girls worked were forbidden to join the union and didn't have any benefits like sick leave, vacation, health insurance.*

like . . . for example/for instance *as/for example/for instance/like/such as.* • The drug is good for ailments like insomnia for example. *The drug is good for ailments like insomnia.* • It is not that fascinating, as it uses a standard approach to computing in XSLT, but its advantage is that it works also with XSLT processors (like, for instance, James Clark's XT) that do not have the "node-set" extension function implemented. *It is not that fascinating, as it uses a standard approach to computing in XSLT, but its advantage is that it works also with XSLT processors (for instance, James Clark's XT) that do not have the "node-set" extension function implemented.*

limitation *limit.* • There is no overall limitation on the percentage of the trust's portfolio securities which may be subject to a hedge position. *There is no overall limit on the percentage of the trust's portfolio securities which may be subject to a hedge position.*

(very) limited *bare/few/little/meager/rare/scant/scanty/scarce/short/slight/small/spare/sparse.* • While opportunities for broad-scale consumer advertising may be limited for a while, there are lots of opportunities for commercial communications. *While opportunities for broad-scale consumer advertising may be scarce for a while, there are lots of opportunities for commercial communications.*

(a/the) limited number of *a couple/a few/little/meager/not many/scant/scanty/(only) so many/some/spare/sparse.* • A surgeon can only do a limited number of operations. *A surgeon can only do so many operations.*

(a/the) limited selection (of) *a couple/a few/ little/meager/not many/scant/scanty/(only) so many/some/spare/sparse.*

linger on *linger.* • Memories of GTV and Smart TV still linger on. *Memories of GTV and Smart TV still linger.*

linkage *link.* • Particular attention needs to be given to the linkage among the various strategic levels within and across national markets. *Particular attention needs to be given to the link among the various strategic levels within and across national markets.*

link together *connect/link.* • It's natural to link the two of them together. *It's natural to link the two of them.*

(the) lion's share *almost all/most/nearly all.*

liquid refreshment *beer/coffee/drink/juice/milk/ soda/tea/water/wine.* • Plan your menu, which should include liquid refreshment. *Plan your menu, which should include wine.*

listen in *listen.*

(a) little bit *a bit/a little/fairly/rather/slightly/ somewhat* delete. • They're a little bit hesitant. *They're hesitant.*

little by little *gradually/slowly.*

little/small child *child.* • How do you tell a little child that his father isn't coming home again? *How do you tell a child that his father isn't coming home again?*

little/small/tiny iota *iota.* • I don't care one little iota less than you do about homelessness in America. *I don't care one iota less than you do about homelessness in America.*

locality *area/city/district/locale/place/point/ region/site/spot/state/town/zone.* • Today, modern water wells are drilled and in some localities are more than 300 meters deep. *Today, modern water wells are drilled and in some sites are more than 300 meters deep.*

located delete. • The school, which is located in an old, poorly cared for building, further added to our misgivings. *The school, which is in an old, poorly cared for building, further added to our misgivings.*

lodge a complaint (with) *complain/to.* • He threatened to lodge a complaint with the management if he wasn't reimbursed for his losses. *He threatened to complain to the management if he wasn't reimbursed for his losses.*

logical reason *reason.*

(the) long and (the) short *center/core/crux/ essence/gist/heart/pith/substance/sum.*

long suit *forte.*

(a) long time/while ago *long ago.* • These Star Wars pages were created a long time ago. *These Star Wars pages were created long ago.*

look ahead/forward to the future *look ahead/ look forward/look to the future.* • We have to look ahead to the future and plan accordingly. *We have to look ahead and plan accordingly.* • The second part will look forward to the future for libraries and publishers and the important challenges that they must address. *The second part will look to the future for libraries and publishers and the important challenges that they must address.*

looking back (on it) in retrospect *in retrospect/ looking back.*

look/observe to see *check/examine/inspect/ look/observe/see.* • Look to see where you have been and where you might go next. *Examine where you have been and where you might go next.*

lose out on *lose.*

(a) lot *much.* • The larger type makes the book a lot easier to read. *The larger type makes the book much easier to read.*

(a) lot of *many/much/numerous.* • In a lot of people's minds, there was no question of his guilt. *In many people's minds, there was no question of his guilt.*

(a) lot of (the) time *frequently/often.* • We went into the city a lot of times. *We went into the city often.*

loudly bellow/holler/howl/roar/scream/shout/ shriek/yell *bellow/holler/howl/roar/scream/ shout/shriek/yell.* • In the early days of VCRs, movie companies howled loudly at the advent of movie rentals and attempted blocking legislation. *In the early days of VCRs, movie companies howled at the advent of movie rentals and attempted blocking legislation.*

-(al)ly enough *-(al)ly* delete. • Ironically enough, many states have loosened their registration laws in the last decade, but turnout still declines. *Ironically, many states have loosened their registration laws in the last decade, but turnout still declines.*

-(al)ly speaking *-(al)ly* delete. • All four of their parents would be the same, genetically speaking. *All four of their parents would be genetically the same.* • Although there may be small differences between the jobs, they are, relatively speaking, inconsequential. *Although there may be small differences between the jobs, they are relatively inconsequential.* • Personally speaking, I belonged to the Howdy Doody generation. *I belonged to the Howdy Doody generation.*

M

made of delete. • The only data show small vestiges of threads made of cotton. *The only data show small vestiges of cotton threads.*

made to measure *custom/customized/custom-made/tailored/tailor-made.*

made to order *custom/customized/custom-made/tailored/tailor-made.*

made up out of *made of* delete. • To keep the spar caps straight, they are made up out of several layers of spruce. *To keep the spar caps straight, they are made of several layers of spruce.*

magnitude *import/moment/scope/size.* • Nothing is unthinkable when you try to solve a problem of this magnitude. *Nothing is unthinkable when you try to solve a problem of this size.*

major delete. • If the vice president comes in third, it's a major disaster. *If the vice president comes in third, it's a disaster.* • Combining these two world-class companies represents a major milestone for the plastics industry. *Combining these two world-class companies represents a milestone for the plastics industry.* • It's going to take a couple of years to shake out, but it won't result in a major calamity. *It's going to take a couple of years to shake out, but it won't result in a calamity.*

(a/the) majority (of) *almost all (of)/many (of)/ more (of)/most (of)/nearly all (of)/three-fourths (two-thirds) (of).* • Surveys reveal that the majority of chronic fatigue syndrome victims are between 22 and 45. *Surveys reveal that 60 percent of chronic fatigue syndrome victims are between 22 and 45.*

(a/the) major part/percentage/portion/proportion (of) *a good (great) deal (of)/a good (great)* *many (of)/almost all (of)/many (of)/more (of)/most (of)/nearly all (of)/three-fourths (two-thirds) (of).* • Murdoch could borrow a major portion of the purchase price using Triangle's assets as collateral. *Murdoch could borrow most of the purchase price using Triangle's assets as collateral.*

make . . . (a/the) . . . (about/for/of/to) delete. • Why make that admission to them? *Why admit that to them?* • We made an agreement that she would keep the stereo for me. *We agreed that she would keep the stereo for me.* • The company's management may not see any reason for making a shift from their current approach. *The company's management may not see any reason for shifting from their current approach.* • Make an estimate of what the person might find if the process were revamped to operate as well as is conceivable. *Estimate what the person might find if the process were revamped to operate as well as is conceivable.* • He must graduate before he can make a design for such a machine. *He must graduate before he can design such a machine.* • In so doing, the findings make a contribution to furthering the ongoing process of the development of a language for spirituality through research. *In so doing, the findings contribute to furthering the ongoing process of the development of a language for spirituality through research.* • Children are expected to use the subject that they are reading about, picture captions, the story title, and other clues to make predictions about what will happen in the story. *Children are expected to use the subject that they are reading about, picture captions, the story title, and other clues to predict what will happen in the story.* • Make a visit to your local elementary school to see what magazines they carry. *Visit your local elementary school to see what magazines they carry.*

make . . . acquaintance *meet.* • I was very pleased to make your acquaintance. *I was very pleased to meet you.*

make allowance for *allow for/arrange for/consider/prepare for/provide for.* • You must make

allowance for quilting shrinkage, and there is no way of telling how much that is. *You must allow for quilting shrinkage, and there is no way of telling how much that is.*

make an appearance *appear/arrive/attend/come/show up/visit.* • She will make an appearance on *The Simpsons* in fully animated form performing the uplifting song "To Hell And Back." *She will appear on* The Simpsons *in fully animated form performing the uplifting song "To Hell And Back."* • Four directors were scheduled to make an appearance, and only one canceled because shooting had begun on his new feature. *Four directors were scheduled to attend, and only one canceled because shooting had begun on his new feature.*

make an attempt/effort/endeavor *try.* • We are going to make an effort to hold prices or even reduce them. *We are going to try to hold prices or even reduce them.*

make available *afford/furnish/provide/supply.* • Paralleling a business school course of study, our curriculum makes available a stable, inclusive, and continuing transmittal of practices and perspectives to those working managers who want to continue their education in management. *Paralleling a business school course of study, our curriculum affords a stable, inclusive, and continuing transmittal of practices and perspectives to those working managers who want to continue their education in management.*

make believe *feign/pretend.*

make concession for *allow for/arrange for/consider/prepare for/provide for.*

make contact (with) *call/contact/discover/encounter/find/locate/meet (with)/phone/reach/speak (to)/talk (to)/visit/write.* • In Sturgis, we made contact with the Sons of Silence. *In Sturgis, we encountered the Sons of Silence.*

make conversation *chat/communicate/converse/speak/talk.* • It was easy to make conversation with him. *It was easy to talk with him.*

make (a/the) decision/determination (about/as to/concerning/of/on/regarding) *conclude/decide/determine/resolve.* • I made the decision to keep on good terms with all the candidates. *I decided to keep on good terms with all the candidates.*

make (a/the) determined decision (about/as to/concerning/of/on/regarding) *conclude/decide/determine/resolve.* • She made a determined decision to overcome her drug dependency. *She resolved to overcome her drug dependency.*

make (a/the) distinction *distinguish.* • For some years, economists have enjoyed making a distinction between "salt water" and "fresh water" approaches to economics. *For some years, economists have enjoyed distinguishing between "salt water" and "fresh water" approaches to economics.*

make false statements *lie.* • He did this by using a false Social Security number and making false statements on his application. *He did this by using a false Social Security number and lying on his application.*

(to) make matters worse *what is worse/worse still/worse yet.* • Making matters worse, a boom in the herring export market has turned to bust. *Worse yet, a boom in the herring export market has turned to bust.*

make mention of *mention.* • You made mention of the fact that S&Ls insure you only up to $100,000. *You mentioned the fact that S&Ls insure you only up to $100,000.*

make provision for *allow for/arrange for/consider/prepare for/provide for.* • No family can attempt to establish a budget without making provision for these "unexpected" but forever recurring expenses. *No family can attempt to establish a budget without allowing for these "unexpected" but forever recurring expenses.*

make (a/the) statement saying/stating *comment/declare/remark/say/state.* • I think it's important for us to make a statement saying that this veto should be overridden. *I think it's important for us to state that this veto should be overridden.*

made/paid the ultimate sacrifice *be killed/died.* • The news reached me this morning that another one of our best has paid the ultimate sacrifice in this war. *The news reached me this morning that another one of our best has died in this war.* • These Marines have been giving their all and sadly some of them made the ultimate sacrifice. *These Marines have been giving their all and sadly some of them were killed.*

make up (my) mind *decide.* • King said he will make up his mind by mid-September on whether to seek the GOP nomination for governor. *King said he will decide by mid-September on whether to seek the GOP nomination for governor.*

make (my) way *driving/proceeding/running/walking.* • The vice president is now making his way to the platform. *The vice president is now walking to the platform.*

(the) manifestation of delete. • Looking first at managers, one once again sees the manifestation of the tendency toward caution with age. *Looking first at managers, one once again sees the tendency toward caution with age.*

(what is) (a/the) manner/means/mechanism/method/procedure/process/technique by which *how.* • What is the means by which a nation can increase investment? *How can a nation increase investment?* • We will now examine the process by which natural and global marketing activities are controlled. *We will now examine how natural and global marketing activities are controlled.* • The answer should describe a process by which all players are equally likely to be chosen. *The answer should describe how all players are equally likely to be chosen.*

manually by hand *by hand/manually.* • Pick the door up manually by hand making sure not to put your fingers between the sections. *Pick the door up by hand making sure not to put your fingers between the sections.*

many and varied *diverse/manifold/multifaceted/multifarious/multifold/multiform/multiple/varied/various.* • Robberies tend to fall into one of three categories, but their targets are many and varied. *Robberies tend to fall into one of three categories, but their targets are manifold.*

many but not all *many.*

many times over *frequently/often/recurrently/regularly/repeatedly.*

marry (the two) together *combine/join/marry/unite.* • We were initially concerned about trying to marry together our 1920's architectural styles with advanced vinyl window products. *We were initially concerned about trying to marry our 1920's architectural styles with advanced vinyl window products.*

mass exodus *exodus.* • The mass exodus to Penturbia is the result of a declining quality of life. *The exodus to Penturbia is the result of a declining quality of life.*

mass extinction *extinction.* • A comet striking Earth with the power of 300 million Hiroshima-sized atomic bombs may be the cause of mass extinction 11 million years ago. *A comet striking Earth with the power of 300 million Hiroshima-sized atomic bombs may be the cause of extinction 11 million years ago.*

match exactly *duplicate/match.* • To find strings that match your case exactly, enter the appropriate characters in uppercase when specifying the string to be searched for. *To find strings that match your case, enter the appropriate characters in uppercase when specifying the string to be searched for.*

match perfectly *duplicate/match.* • The fluctuations of the one variable match perfectly the fluctuations of the other variable. *The fluctuations of the one variable duplicate the fluctuations of the other variable.*

match up *match.*

materialize *develop/evolve/form/happen/occur/result/take place.*

(a) matter of *a* delete. • Automobile insurance has been a matter of concern to me since I got a car. *Automobile insurance has been a concern to me since I got a car.*

(a) matter of *a few/some* delete. • In a matter of seconds, the detergent gets the stain out. *In a few seconds, the detergent gets the stain out.*

matter-of-course *common/customary/habitual/natural/normal/ordinary/regular/routine/typical/usual.*

matter-of-fact *businesslike/factual/literal/plain/prosaic/straightforward/unfeeling.*

maximal *biggest/greatest/highest/largest/longest/most/top.*

maximize *add to/broaden/enlarge/greaten/increase/raise.*

(a/the) maximum . . . of *biggest/greatest/highest/largest/longest/most/top.* • It is necessary to get the maximum mileage out of existing and new products as rapidly as possible. *It is necessary to get the most mileage out of existing and new products as rapidly as possible.*

(a/the) maximum amount (of) *biggest/greatest/highest/largest/longest/most/top.*

(a/the) maximum number (of) *biggest/greatest/highest/largest/longest/most/top.* • Set up your fields for the maximum number of lines. *Set up your fields for the most lines.*

may or may not *may/may not.* • Your assessment of Houston's nascent ascent from the urban graveyard may or may not prove to be on the mark, but your classification of its metropolitan area as the nation's fourth largest was not. *Your assessment of Houston's nascent ascent from the urban graveyard may prove to be on the mark, but your classification of its metropolitan area as the nation's fourth largest was not.*

may/might perhaps *may/might.* • Rome has always had some sort of a Pope, and that ambition and wickedness may perhaps have characterized certain persons high in ecclesiastical affairs. *Rome has always had some sort of a Pope, and that ambition and wickedness may have characterized certain persons high in ecclesiastical affairs.*

may/might possibly *may/might.* • She said Concord Academy might possibly be too difficult. *She said Concord Academy might be too difficult.*

meander back and forth *meander.* • The result is a snaking pattern as the stream meanders back and forth across its down-valley axis. *The result is a snaking pattern as the stream meanders across its down-valley axis.*

meaningful delete. • This slope can represent miles per hour, weight versus length, or a number of other meaningful rates that are import-ant to the analysis of data. *This slope can represent miles per hour, weight versus length, or a number of other rates that are important to the analysis of data.*

meaningless gibberish *gibberish.* • Byrne deftly makes everything clear in context, using many words and expressions that would, out of context, seem like meaningless gibberish. *Byrne deftly makes everything clear in context, using many words and expressions that would, out of context, seem like gibberish.*

(a/a certain/some) measure (of) *a certain/much/some* delete. • With the employer-employee relationship should come a certain measure of understanding. *With the employer-employee relationship should come a certain understanding.*

measured against *against/alongside/beside/compared to/with/-(i)er than/less/less than/more/more than/next to/over/than/to/versus/vis-à-vis.* • Retrieving data from disks is slow measured against the speed of processing the records once they are in memory. *Retrieving data from disks is slower than the speed of processing the records once they are in memory.*

measure up to *meet.* • Because many teachers expect children from the same family to behave in the same manner, it can be particularly difficult for temperamentally different siblings to measure up to their expectations. *Because many teachers expect children from the same family to behave in the same manner, it can be particularly difficult for temperamentally different siblings to meet their expectations.*

mechanical mechanism *mechanical/mechanism.* • The final result was the Pascaline, a polished brass box containing a sophisticated, mechanical calculating mechanism composed of gears. *The final result was the Pascaline, a polished brass box containing a sophisticated calculating mechanism composed of gears.*

(the) medium of delete. • Novelists interpret experience through the medium of plot and character, poets through the medium of rhythm and metaphor, and critics through the medium of other texts. *Novelists interpret experience through plot and character, poets through rhythm and metaphor, and critics through other texts.*

meet together *meet.* • The shores of the sea meet together. *The shores of the sea meet.* • Did the parties ever refuse to meet together? *Did the parties ever refuse to meet?*

meet with (our) approval *approve.* • Our managers are able to use the directory knowing that all vendors have been prescreened and meet with our approval. *Our managers are able to use the directory knowing that all vendors have been prescreened and approved.*

memorandum *memo/note.* • This memorandum is for informative purposes only. *This memo is for informative purposes only.*

mental ability/capacity *ability/capacity.*

mental telepathy *telepathy.*

(a/the) -ment of *-ing.* • The assignment of retirement assets to a money manager may entail a lengthy process of evaluation by the corporate client. *Assigning retirement assets to a money manager may entail a lengthy process of evaluation by the corporate client.* • Meetings do not contribute to the attainment of individual objectives. *Meetings do not contribute to attaining individual objectives.* • The treatment of these items as expenses results in lower rents and more available apartments. *Treating these items as expenses results in lower rents and more available apartments.*

merge into one *merge.* • The two departments are being merged into one. *The two departments are being merged.*

merge together *merge.* • First, create the files to be merged together. *First, create the files to be merged.*

mesh together *mesh.* • Gears are toothed wheels that mesh together to transmit force and motion from one gear to the next. *Gears are toothed wheels that mesh to transmit force and motion from one gear to the next.*

metaphorically speaking *as it were/in a sense/ in a way/so to speak.*

methodology *method.* • When developing estimates of market size, data extrapolation methodologies may be useful. *When developing estimates of market size, data extrapolation methods may be useful.*

metropolis *city.*

(with) might and main *force/power/strength.*

might or might not *might/might not.*

mingle together *mingle.* • An invitation-only crowd of some 40 people met at Kate's Mystery Books, though many in the crowd apparently did not want to mingle together. *An invitation-only crowd of some 40 people met at Kate's Mystery Books, though many in the crowd apparently did not want to mingle.*

minimal *brief/least/lowest/minor/not much/ scant/short/slight/smallest.* • We expect the delay will be minimal. *We expect the delay will be brief.*

(a/the) minimal number (of) *a couple (of)/(a) few (of)/a handful (of)/fewer than half (of)/ hardly any (of)/less than half (of)/not many (of)/ (of)/scarcely any (of).* • Smith said a minimal number of people have irreconcilable differences with the roommate they selected. *Smith said hardly any people have irreconcilable differences with the roommate they selected.*

minimize *decrease/lower/reduce.*

(a/the) minimum (of) *at least/(the) least/little/lowest/minimum/scant/shortest/slightest/smallest/tiniest.* • Most oxyacetylene welding is done manually with a minimum of equipment. *Most oxyacetylene welding is done manually with minimum equipment.*

(a/the) minority (of) *a couple (of)/(a) few (of)/a handful (of)/fewer than half (of)/hardly any (of)/less than half (of)/not many (of)/ (of)/scarcely any (of).* • A minority of those who are comfortable financially are good givers, but some of the country's wealthiest give dramatically large sums. *Few who are comfortable financially are good givers, but some of the country's wealthiest give dramatically large sums.*

minutely detail *detail.* • Given a problem, engineers and computer scientists, accustomed to working with mathematical procedures, would write a program—a list of minutely detailed instructions logically guiding the computer step by step through its assigned task. *Given a problem, engineers and computer scientists, accustomed to working with mathematical procedures, would write a program—a list of detailed instructions logically guiding the computer step by step through its assigned task.*

mix and mingle *mingle/mix.*

mix together *mix.* • The capability to mix text and graphics together in the same document makes it easy to produce newsletters, instructional materials, and other documents where figures, logos, or pictures are needed. *The capability to mix text and graphics in the same document makes it easy to produce newsletters, instructional materials, and other documents where figures, logos, or pictures are needed.*

modern, state-of-the-art *modern/state-of-the-art.* • Today, with modern, state-of-the-art technologies, breast cancer can be detected at very early stages of development. *Today, with modern technologies, breast cancer can be detected at very early stages of development.*

(a/the) modicum of *few/little/some/tiny/trifle.*

(the) month of delete. • Between the months of July and September, only three more ventured-financed firms went public. *Between July and September, only three more ventured-financed firms went public.*

months of age *months.* • At 14 months of age, these children showed fear and shyness when taken into a room with strangers. *At 14 months, these children showed fear and shyness when taken into a room with strangers.*

more . . . (as) compared to/with *than.* • Startup times of apps are usually more as compared to the 32-bit versions. *Startup times of apps are usually more than the 32-bit versions.* • Korea wins thanks to its leader Ahn, who gave more compared to the others also in the team competition. *Korea wins thanks to its leader Ahn, who gave more than the others also in the team competition.*

more . . . relative to/versus *than.* • More high school seniors are now using marijuana versus cigarettes. *More high school seniors are now using marijuana than cigarettes.*

more -(i)er *-(i)er/more.* • Watching television is more easier than reading. *Watching television is easier than reading.* • Watch "Nightstand," where comedy doesn't get any more better. *Watch "Nightstand," where comedy doesn't get any better.* • A reduction in engineering expenses of $100,000 to $150,000 would be appropriate and bring the department to a more healthier expense to sales ratio. *A reduction in engineering expenses of $100,000 to $150,000 would be appropriate and bring the department to a more healthy expense to sales ratio.* • I think it's more subtler than that. *I think it's subtler* *than that.* • Some people are taller, more curvier. *Some people are taller, more curvy.*

more extended/lengthy/prolonged/protracted *longer.* • Even the IRS has been testing itself over a more prolonged period. *Even the IRS has been testing itself over a longer period.*

more improved *improved.*

more inferior *inferior.* • These two lobes are separated by a major fissure, identical to that seen on the right side, although often slightly more inferior in location. *These two lobes are separated by a major fissure, identical to that seen on the right side, although often slightly inferior in location.*

(the) more/most *more (most).* • Testing can answer which of these two models is the more appropriate. *Testing can answer which of these two models is more appropriate.*

more often than not *almost always/commonly/customarily/generally/most often/nearly always/normally/typically/usually.*

(the) more . . . of the two *(the) -(i)er/(the) more.* • Objectivity is certainly the more difficult of the two to sustain. *Objectivity is certainly the more difficult to sustain.*

more preferable *preferable.* • We have never said any one group is more preferable to another. *We have never said any one group is preferable to another.* • Reorganization of the health care industry still remains one of the alternatives being considered because structural and procedural changes are often more preferable than basic, radical changes in the philosophy behind such a system. *Reorganization of the health care industry still remains one of the alternatives being considered because structural and procedural changes are often preferable to basic, radical changes in the philosophy behind such a system.*

more superior *superior.* • It upsets me to think of her with a man more superior to me. *It upsets me to think of her with a man superior to me.*

more than exceeded/surpassed *exceeded/surpassed.* • From all sides, there is little disagreement that while business more than exceeded its component goals, the schools fell short of theirs. *From all sides, there is little disagreement that while business exceeded its component goals, the schools fell short of theirs.*

most but not all *almost all/many/most/nearly all/three-fourths (two-thirds).* • Most, but not all, accounting programs store the data you enter in a database. *Almost all accounting programs store the data you enter in a database.*

most -(i)est *-(i)est/most.* • You missed two of the most simplest questions. *You missed two of the simplest questions.* • This is probably the most happiest moment in my life. *This is probably the happiest moment in my life.* • That was the most stupidest picture I have ever seen. *That was the stupidest picture I have ever seen.*

most favorite *favorite/most favored.* • When I was a kid, this was one of my most favorite jobs. *When I was a kid, this was one of my favorite jobs.*

most important *above all.* • Most important, the system that files are designated by should be consistent and understood by everyone. *Above all, the system that files are designated by should be consistent and understood by everyone.* • Recent studies have shown that for most investors, retiring comfortably is their most important financial goal. *Recent studies have shown that for most investors, retiring comfortably is their foremost financial goal.* • The most important factor in determining the amount of pension plan income you receive is your longevity with one company. *The key factor in determining the amount of pension plan income you receive is your longevity with one company.*

most important *central/chief/critical/crucial/
foremost/key/leading/main/major/pivotal/prin-
cipal/seminal.* • The company's most important
product, Mechanical Advantage, began shipping in early 1987. *The company's leading product, Mechanical Advantage, began shipping in
early 1987.*

most . . . one *most.* • It's fairly obvious that the
third approach will get the best results, but it is
also the most difficult one to employ. *It's fairly
obvious that the third approach will get the best
results, but it is also the most difficult to employ.*

most recent *latest/newest.*

most (of the) time(s) *almost always/commonly/
generally/most often/nearly always/normally/
typically/usually.*

most well known *best known.* • Although
George is the most well known of the family,
his brother Ira was also a successful lyricist.
*Although George is the best known of the fam-
ily, his brother Ira was also a successful lyricist.*
• David Ohanian has been one of the most well
known horn players in the world for many
years. *David Ohanian has been one of the best-
known horn players in the world for many
years.*

motion picture *film/movie.*

motivating force *drive/energy/force/impetus/
motivation/power.* • The primary motivating
force behind their behavior is the need to shock
others. *The primary motivation behind their
behavior is the need to shock others.*

motivation *motive.* • There is doubt about the
ethical standards of life insurance companies
as well as the motivations and practices of the
agents selling their products. *There is doubt
about the ethical standards of life insurance companies as well as the motives and practices of the
agents selling their products.*

move forward *advance/continue/go on/happen/
move on/occur/proceed/progress.* • We urge all
involved to move forward with whatever plans
make the most sense for both the city and the
college. *We urge all involved to proceed with
whatever plans make the most sense for both the
city and the college.* • It will not be possible move
forward with the program without the understanding and support of the general public. *It
will not be possible continue with the program
without the understanding and support of the
general public.*

move forward into the future *advance/con-
tinue/go on/move on/proceed/progress.* • These
questions and many others should be pondered and discussed among us as we prepare
to move forward into the future. *These questions and many others should be pondered and
discussed among us as we prepare to advance.*
• The open industry format will greatly benefit us as we move forward into the future. *The
open industry format will greatly benefit us as
we progress.*

muchly *much.*

multiple *many/several.* • You are taking in data
on multiple levels. *You are taking in data on
many levels.*

(a/the) multiplicity of *a good (great) many/
countless/endless/infinite/many/millions (of)/
numberless/numerous/thousands (of)/untold.* •
She suffers from a multiplicity of moods and
personalities. *She suffers from many moods and
personalities.*

(a/the) multitude of *a good (great) many/count-
less/endless/infinite/many/millions (of)/number-
less/numerous/thousands (of)/untold.* • How do
our customers and prospects view us given the
multitude of changes in customers' needs and
behaviors? *How do our customers and prospects
view us given the many changes in customers'
needs and behaviors?*

multitudinous *a good (great) many/countless/ endless/infinite/many/millions (of)/numberless/ numerous/thousands (of)/untold.*

must necessarily/of necessity *inevitably/must/ necessarily/of necessity/unavoidably.* • Texts organized around specific topics must of necessity limit their discussion to the features contained in those programs. *Texts organized around specific topics must limit their discussion to the features contained in those programs.*

mutual agreement (mutually agree) *agreement/agree.* • The NATO leaders proclaimed mutual agreement about reducing the missile systems. *The NATO leaders proclaimed agreement about reducing the missile systems.*

mutual . . . and/between/both/each other/one another/two *and/between/both/each other/one another/two.* • I think all three news directors in town have a mutual respect for one another. *I think all three news directors in town have a respect for one another.* • Understanding exists when both parties involved in the communication mutually agree not only on the information but also on the meaning of the information. *Understanding exists when both parties involved in the communication agree not only on the information but also on the meaning of the information.* • You can live with many differences of opinion and personal style if you and your partner have mutual respect for each other's abilities. *You can live with many differences of opinion and personal style if you and your partner have respect for each other's abilities.* • It's time to begin the healing process, time to bridge the gap of miscommunication, and time to cultivate an atmosphere of mutual respect between law enforcement and our communities. *It's time to begin the healing process, time to bridge the gap of miscommunication, and time to cultivate an atmosphere of respect between law enforcement and our communities.* • The attached document presents the essential elements of a statement of mutual cooperation between

supervisors. *The attached document presents the essential elements of a statement of cooperation between supervisors.*

mutual communication *communication.* • In this way, mutual communication is established, and some type of agreement becomes much more possible. *In this way, communication is established, and some type of agreement becomes much more possible.*

mutual cooperation *cooperation.*

mutual friendship *friendship.*

mutual understanding *understanding.* • Marketing executives and financial managers must strive to develop a mutual understanding of each others' viewpoints. *Marketing executives and financial managers must strive to develop an understanding of each others' viewpoints.*

mythological *mythologic/mythical/mythic.*

N

name as *name.* • They would more aptly be named as request and execute entry points. *They would more aptly be named request and execute entry points.* • The Georgetown senior has been named as one of five finalists for the award. *The Georgetown senior has been named one of five finalists for the award.*

. . . nature delete. • The ashes are a reminder of the transitory nature of life. *The ashes are a reminder of the transitoriness of life.*

(the) nature of *like* delete. • Disagreement on the viability of standardization strategies also reflects varying interpretations on the nature of the environment facing the international company. *Disagreement on the viability of stan-*

dardization strategies also reflects varying interpretations of the environment facing the international company.

neat and tidy *clean/neat/orderly/organized/tidy.*

necessarily have to *have to.* • It doesn't necessarily have to be a bad place to go. *It doesn't have to be a bad place to go.*

necessary *needed/needful/pressing/urgent/vital.* • The symbol is often in a more simple form when all the specifications are not necessary. *The symbol is often in a more simple form when all the specifications are not needed.*

necessary essential *essential/necessary.* • Therefore, we have 10–15 years to take the necessary essential steps to reform the current situation. *Therefore, we have 10–15 years to take the necessary steps to reform the current situation.*

necessary prerequisite *necessary/prerequisite.* • Detailed knowledge of the people on the beat is undeniably a necessary prerequisite to achieving economy in the use of police force. *Detailed knowledge of the people on the beat is undeniably a prerequisite to achieving economy in the use of police force.* • In most cases, readiness tests emphasize the prerequisites necessary for reading instruction. *In most cases, readiness tests emphasize the prerequisites for reading instruction.*

necessary requirement *necessary/requirement.* • Naturally, we are complying with any necessary reporting requirements. *Naturally, we are complying with any reporting requirements.*

necessary requisite *necessary/requisite.* • He said he has the "toughness and resolve" to bring government spending under control as a necessary requisite to restoring the public's confidence. *He said he has the "toughness and resolve"*

to bring government spending under control as a requisite to restoring the public's confidence.

necessitate *demand/exact/must/need/require.* • Your husband's job necessitates a great deal of independence and a lot of latitude in his hours. *Your husband's job demands a great deal of independence and a lot of latitude in his hours.* • Divided quotations are actually comma splices that necessitate the writer to insert the correct punctuation between the questions or statements. *Divided quotations are actually comma splices that require the writer to insert the correct punctuation between the questions or statements.*

necessity *need.* • The emphasis on technical expertise is being balanced by a necessity for good interpersonal skills. *The emphasis on technical expertise is being balanced by a need for good interpersonal skills.*

needless to say *clearly/naturally/obviously/of course/plainly* delete.

need not necessarily/of necessity *need not.* • This need not necessarily mean that the regime must fall before it can be studied. *This need not mean that the regime must fall before it can be studied.*

needs hardly be said *clearly/naturally/obviously/of course/plainly* delete. • It needs hardly be said in the very patriarchal states of Africa, most gender injustice is perpetrated against women, rather than the other way round. *Obviously, in the very patriarchal states of Africa, most gender injustice is perpetrated against women, rather than the other way round.*

need to have *need.* • We felt in order to support the nugget we needed to have an overall precious metals plan. *We felt in order to support the nugget we needed an overall precious metals plan.* • It's a skill they may need to have to get a good job. *It's a skill they may need to get a good job.*

negative feelings *anger/annoyance/discomfort/ disfavor/dislike/displeasure/disregard/distaste/ frustration/hate/hatred/indifference/resentment.* • I have nothing but negative feelings for her. *I have nothing but hatred for her.* • Why do so many people so often take out their negative feelings on others? *Why do so many people so often take out their frustrations on others?*

neither here nor there *immaterial/inapt/irrelevant/not pertinent.*

neither one *neither.* • Neither one of us wanted to admit it. *Neither of us wanted to admit it.*

never at any time *never/not ever/not once.*

never ever *never/not ever/not once.* • You never ever make concessions to terrorists. *You never make concessions to terrorists.*

nevertheless *anyhow/even so/still/yet.* • There are nagging questions, nevertheless. *Still, there are nagging questions.*

new and improved *improved/new.* • The original design goals may not have been much different than to create a new and improved version of an earlier operating system. *The original design goals may not have been much different than to create an improved version of an earlier operating system.*

new and innovative *innovative/new.* • The health care industry is marketing many new and innovative products. *The health care industry is marketing many innovative products.*

(brand) new baby *baby.*

new construction *construction.* • Both firms predict the vacancy rate will fall, if only because of a lack of new construction. *Both firms predict the vacancy rate will fall, if only because of a lack of construction.*

new creation *creation.*

new departure *departure.* • The environmental community is hopeful that he will represent a new departure in environmental protection. *The environmental community is hopeful that he will represent a departure in environmental protection.*

new innovation *innovation.* • There is now ample evidence that the United States is lagging behind Japan in new innovations. *There is now ample evidence that the United States is lagging behind Japan in innovations.*

new introduction *introduction.*

new (high) record *record.* • This computer, introduced in 1981, set a new record for sales and quickly became the standard around which most other manufacturers designed their machines. *This computer, introduced in 1981, set a record for sales and quickly became the standard around which most other manufacturers designed their machines.*

new recruit *recruit.*

next of all *also/and/as well/besides/further/furthermore/moreover/next/second/still more/too.*

no basis in fact *baseless/groundless/unfounded.* Other senior defense officials, after reviewing Pentagon intelligence reports, said Shaw's remarks had no basis in fact. *Other senior defense officials, after reviewing Pentagon intelligence reports, said Shaw's remarks were baseless.*

no better (than) *best.* • This last point is perhaps no better illustrated than by the recent acquisition of Applied Data Research by Computer Associates. *This last point is perhaps best illustrated by the recent acquisition of Applied Data Research by Computer Associates.*

nod (her) head *nod.* • When asked if she knew what had happened to the children in Newtown, Gia nodded her head and said, "That's bad." *When asked if she knew what had happened to the children in Newtown, Gia nodded and said, "That's bad."*

no longer in existence *dead/deceased/defunct/ departed/extinct.* • The American Alumni Search allows you to quickly and easily find the Alumni Web Sites for all 106,000 K-12 schools in America including the 20,000 schools that are no longer in existence. *The American Alumni Search allows you to quickly and easily find the Alumni Web Sites for all 106,000 K-12 schools in America including the 20,000 schools that are defunct.*

no longer with us *dead/fired/gone.*

no matter (what) *despite (what)/whatever.* • No matter what the period to maturity, they are accepted for payment of taxes due at face or par value. *Whatever the period to maturity, they are accepted for payment of taxes due at face or par value.*

no matter how *despite how/however.* • She was determined, no matter how long it took, to find out the truth. *She was determined, however long it took, to find out the truth.*

no matter when *despite when/whenever.* • No matter when you use them, voice-mail messages are usually a lot briefer and more efficient than the give-and-take of ordinary conversation. *Despite when you use them, voice-mail messages are usually a lot briefer and more efficient than the give-and-take of ordinary conversation.*

no matter where *despite where/wherever.* • From the state's point of view, the collider will be a boon no matter where it is located. *From the state's point of view, the collider will be a boon wherever it is located.*

no matter whether . . . (or) *despite whether/ whether . . . or (not).* • It was unwise to make the purchase and consumption of alcohol illegal no matter whether or not all or some of that purchase and consumption was immoral. *It was unwise to make the purchase and consumption of alcohol illegal whether or not all or some of that purchase and consumption was immoral.*

no matter which *despite which/whichever.* • No matter which way I decide, I will be blamed for making the wrong decision. *Whichever way I decide, I will be blamed for making the wrong decision.*

no matter who *despite who/whoever.* • It is still a good idea and should be adopted, no matter who wins the presidency. *It is still a good idea and should be adopted, whoever wins the presidency.*

no matter whom *despite whom/whomever.* • No matter whom the voters choose, investors will be contemplating the first change of presidents since 1980, with all the questions about future economic policies that implies. *Whomever the voters choose, investors will be contemplating the first change of presidents since 1980, with all the questions about future economic policies that implies.*

no more (and) no less *exactly/just/precisely.*

no more than *but/merely/only.*

nonetheless *anyhow/even so/still/yet.*

noontime *noon.* • The meeting on the 29th will be held at noontime in room 901. *The meeting on the 29th will be held at noon in room 901.*

notable luminary *luminary/notable.*

not anything *nothing.* • There's not anything wrong with this housing code. *There's nothing wrong with this housing code.*

not anywhere *nowhere.* • But this total is not anywhere near the level of demand. *But this total is nowhere near the level of demand.*

not a one *none/no one.*

not . . . at any time *never/not ever/not once.* • My mother was not in a coma at any time; her last few weeks were the only period of very serious pain. *My mother was never in a coma; her last few weeks were the only period of very serious pain.*

notation *memo/note.* • Read the entire chapter carefully and methodically, underlining key points and making marginal notations as you go. *Read the entire chapter carefully and methodically, underlining key points and making marginal notes as you go.*

note how/that *delete.* • Note how in this case, the pathname is not preceded by a slash. *In this case, the pathname is not preceded by a slash.*

(does) not ever *never.* • This routine is called only when a known internal command is executed, so it does not ever attempt to mediate command line switches for program calls. *This routine is called only when a known internal command is executed, so it never attempts to mediate command line switches for program calls.*

not hardly/scarcely *hardly/scarcely.*

notice how/that *delete.* • Notice how the message line indicates how many characters were saved on the disk. *The message line indicates how many characters were saved on the disk.*

notification *notice.*

not in favor of *disagree (with)/oppose.*

(the) notion of *delete.* • While not necessarily new, the notion of live-work developments is

seeing a revival. *While not necessarily new, live-work developments are seeing a revival.*

notwithstanding *after all/apart/aside/despite/even with/for all/with all.* • These misfortunes notwithstanding, the numbers of gorillas are believed to be growing. *These misfortunes aside, the numbers of gorillas are believed to be growing.*

notwithstanding the fact that *although/but/even though/still/though/yet.* • Of what relevance to usage (notwithstanding the fact that the topic is interesting) is an entry on eponyms? *Of what relevance to usage (though the topic is interesting) is an entry on eponyms?* • Unless a confession is given freely and rationally, it will be inadmissible notwithstanding the fact that it is reliable. *Unless a confession is given freely and rationally, it will be inadmissible even though it is reliable.*

null and void *invalid/not binding/null/void/worthless.*

(a/a fair/any) number (of) *a few/almost all/dozens (of)/hundreds (of)/many/most/nearly all/scores (of)/several/sixty-seven (twenty)/some* delete. • A fair number of stores were either sited incorrectly or in the wrong markets and weren't producing the kind of profits they needed to. *Some stores were either sited incorrectly or in the wrong markets and weren't producing the kind of profits they needed to.*

number-one *central/chief/foremost/key/leading/main/major.* • That slow start-up is often the number-one reason why many financial analysts consider biotechnology companies to be a gamble. *That slow start-up is often the main reason why many financial analysts consider biotechnology companies to be a gamble.*

numerical *numeric.*

numerous in number *countless/endless/many/numerous/untold.* • These lines are lower voltage than the high power lines, but they are much more numerous in number. *These lines are lower voltage than the high power lines, but they are much more numerous.* • The lesions may be few or numerous in number, reddish or brownish in color, with a surface that is usually smooth and shiny, but may sometimes be dry and rough with scales. *The lesions may be few or numerous, reddish or brownish in color, with a surface that is usually smooth and shiny, but may sometimes be dry and rough with scales.*

observe *see.*

obstetrical *obstetric.*

obtain (a/the) . . . (for/of/to) delete. • Using the first number less than 3.257 and the first number greater than 3.257, it is possible to obtain an approximation for log 3.257 by using linear interpolation. *Using the first number less than 3.257 and the first number greater than 3.257, it is possible to approximate log 3.257 by using linear interpolation.* • In order to obtain an understanding of the antiquity of Clan MacKay, we must first look at Ireland's history, which according to many historians, makes the history of all other countries look infantile by comparison. *In order to understand the antiquity of Clan MacKay, we must first look at Ireland's history, which according to many historians, makes the history of all other countries look infantile by comparison.*

obviate the necessity/need for/of/to *obviate (-ing).* • Of course, an awareness of this uncertainty doesn't obviate the need to make decisions based on your best guess about what the future holds. *Of course, an awareness of this uncertainty doesn't obviate making decisions based on your best guess about what the future*

holds. • NAS 4 and its support for Enterprise Java Beans obviates the need for the solution proposed in this chapter. *NAS 4 and its support for Enterprise Java Beans obviates the solution proposed in this chapter.* • The Active Directory support obviates the need to register a component locally for use on a remote server. *The Active Directory support obviates registering a component locally for use on a remote server.*

occasionally *at times/now and again/now and then/sometimes.* • Getting to the actual command you want to execute occasionally means you must select a series of commands from the displayed submenus. *Getting to the actual command you want to execute sometimes means you must select a series of commands from the displayed submenus.*

occur again *recur.* • No resident should place items having any value in these bins without being aware that a theft may occur again. *No resident should place items having any value in these bins without being aware that a theft may recur.*

of (a/the) . . . delete. • I'd like to ask a question of the senator. *I'd like to ask the senator a question.* • The article failed to mention that a two-year-old investigation concluded that any irregularities were minor and of no significance. *The article failed to mention that a two-year-old investigation concluded that any irregularities were minor and insignificant.* • Both of these options draw the reader's attention to data of importance. *Both of these options draw the reader's attention to important data.*

(a/the) . . . of *-ing.* • For most American families, this means an analysis of the costs of operating and financing their automobiles. *For most American families, this means analyzing the costs of operating and financing their automobiles.* • Even more important is a knowledge of the costs of consumption in terms of the alternative consumption opportunities that are given up because of the particular choices made. *Even more important is knowing the costs of consumption in terms of the alternative consumption opportunities that are given up because of the particular choices made.*

of all delete. • A cyclical pattern is the most difficult of all to predict. *A cyclical pattern is the most difficult to predict.*

of (a/the) . . . character delete. • A license may be revoked if a meter is used in operating any scheme or enterprise of an unlawful character, for nonuse during any consecutive 12 months, or for any failure of the licensee to comply with the regulations governing the use of postage meters. *A license may be revoked if a meter is used in operating any scheme or unlawful enterprise, for nonuse during any consecutive 12 months, or for any failure of the licensee to comply with the regulations governing the use of postage meters.* • Sellers of such chemicals also are required to report any sale of a suspicious character to the Drug Enforcement Administration. *Sellers of such chemicals also are required to report any suspicious sale to the Drug Enforcement Administration.*

of (a) different opinion *at odds.*

of . . . dimensions/magnitude/proportions/ size delete. • It was a success of monumental dimensions. *It was a monumental success.* • The mess surrounding our president is a tragedy of substantial proportions. *The mess surrounding our president is a substantial tragedy.* • Manny Ramirez hit a homerun of historic proportions. *Manny Ramirez hit a historic homerun.* • If He did not return when He said He would, we have a dilemma of huge proportions. *If He did not return when He said He would, we have a huge dilemma.* • A storm of monstrous proportions developed in the Atlantic that year and several ships were caught in its fury. *A monstrous storm developed in the Atlantic that year and several ships were caught in its fury.* • For those of you

who don't know, World War II was an event of immense magnitude in world history. *For those of you who don't know, World War II was an immense event in world history.*

offer (a/the) . . . (at/of/to) delete. • In this column, we offer a brief look at five organizations that have found methods of reducing the burden. *In this column, we briefly look at five organizations that have found methods of reducing the burden.* • This author offers an examination of the research findings on age and performance. *This author examines the research findings on age and performance.*

offer up *offer.* • We were disappointed in all of the ideas he offered up. *We were disappointed in all of the ideas he offered.*

official business *business.*

off of *from/off.* • She lived one block off of campus. *She lived one block off campus.*

of from . . . to *from . . . to/of . . . to.*

of (a/the) . . . importance (that/to) *important/-(al)ly important* delete. • Information service issues are of vital importance to the telecommunications industry as well as to the general public. *Information service issues are vital to the telecommunications industry as well as to the general public.* • Since increased involvement is generally associated with increased management and financial costs, not all foreign markets are of equal importance. *Since increased involvement is generally associated with increased management and financial costs, not all foreign markets are equally important.*

of (a/the) . . . nature delete. • First-level management deals with day-to-day operations of a repetitive nature. *First-level management deals with repetitive day-to-day operations.* • This type of analysis is of recent origin and is primarily of a conceptual rather than analytical nature. *This type of analysis is of recent origin and is primarily conceptual rather than analytical.* • It was found that the material in his shoe was of an explosive nature. *It was found that the material in his shoe was explosive.* • Volunteer members of the group are trained by the police to patrol neighborhoods looking for anything of a suspicious nature. *Volunteer members of the group are trained by the police to patrol neighborhoods looking for anything suspicious.*

of/to no avail *unsuccessful.*

of one form/kind/sort/type or another *in some way/some form (kind; sort; type)/somehow/someway(s)* delete. • About 15 percent of all U.S. and Soviet missions involving nuclear reactors have suffered failures of one sort or another. *About 15 percent of all U.S. and Soviet missions involving nuclear reactors have suffered some sort of failure.*

of . . . own accord/free will *gladly/readily/willingly.*

of (a/the) . . . persuasion delete. • A physician of liberal persuasion agonized over the senator's fall from grace. *A liberal physician agonized over the senator's fall from grace.*

of such *so.* • The personal balance sheet is of such simplicity that anyone who can add and subtract can also develop the entries. *The personal balance sheet is so simple that anyone who can add and subtract can also develop the entries.*

oftentimes/ofttimes *often.* • Oftentimes, bacteria is present in food when you buy it. *Bacteria is often present in food when you buy it.*

of that/this kind/sort/type *like that/this.* • For an accident of this kind, you can't help blaming yourself. *For an accident like this, you can't help blaming yourself.*

of that/this nature *like that/this.* • The Boston Juvenile Court deals with cases of this nature. *The Boston Juvenile Court deals with cases like this.*

of that/this year *(2010)* delete. • In July of this year, the three-month Treasury stood at 6.73 percent. *In July, the three-month Treasury stood at 6.73 percent.*

of the/them/these delete. • Each of the binomial random variables tends toward *v*. *Each binomial random variable tends toward* v.

of the fact that *that* delete. • She was jealous of the fact that I could do these things. *She was jealous that I could do these things.*

of the first magnitude *best/central/chief/finest/foremost/key/leading/main/major/most important/principal/superior.*

of the first/highest order *best/central/chief/finest/first-class/foremost/great/key/leading/main/major/most important/principal/superior.* • She called it a tragedy of the first order. *She called it a major tragedy.*

of the (-ing) *of . . . 's (-ing).* • This is a collection of the writing of H. L. Mencken. *This is a collection of H. L. Mencken's writing.* • In reading, there is the logic of the thinking of the author and the logic of the thinking of the reader. *In reading, there is the logic of the author's thinking and the logic of the reader's thinking.* • O'Leary's acid chronicle of the ineptitude of the Bush administration is, if anything, too generous. *O'Leary's acid chronicle of the Bush administration's ineptitude is, if anything, too generous.* • Fear was part of the character of Daniel. *Fear was part of Daniel's character.*

of the same opinion *at one.*

of (a/the) . . . variety delete. • Snow of the heavy variety is now falling. *Heavy snow is now falling.*

(a/the) . . . of which *whose.* • It is one of the few gifts the value of which can be juggled successfully to get greater leverage. *It is one of the few gifts whose value can be juggled successfully to get greater leverage.* • Wisdom collected over the course of a lifetime is a wealth the loss of which cannot be borne. *Wisdom collected over the course of a lifetime is a wealth whose loss cannot be borne.*

old adage *adage.* • As the old adage says, "Patriotism is the last refuge of a scoundrel." *As the adage says, "Patriotism is the last refuge of a scoundrel."*

old cliché *cliché.* • Must you always rely on such old clichés? *Must you always rely on such clichés?*

old maxim *maxim.* • Your analysis of that proposal vividly demonstrates an old maxim: For every complex problem, there is an answer that is absolutely obvious, absolutely simple, and absolutely wrong. *Your analysis of that proposal vividly demonstrates a maxim: For every complex problem, there is an answer that is absolutely obvious, absolutely simple, and absolutely wrong.*

old proverb *proverb.* • He referred to the old proverb: If I give you a fish, you will eat for a day/if I teach you to fish, you will eat for a lifetime. *He referred to the proverb: If I give you a fish, you will eat for a day/if I teach you to fish, you will eat for a lifetime.*

old relic *relic.* • There is a gaiety of line which captures, in black and white, the golden opulence of the magnificent old relic. *There is a gaiety of line which captures, in black and white, the golden opulence of the magnificent relic.*

old saw *saw.* • The essence of marginal utility boils down to the old saw that pearls don't cost a lot because men have to dive for them, but rather men dive for them because they command a high price. *The essence of marginal utility boils down to the saw that pearls don't cost a lot because men have to dive for them, but rather men dive for them because they command a high price.*

old saying *saying.* • The old saying "a picture is worth a thousand words" appropriately applies to computer graphics. *The saying "a picture is worth a thousand words" appropriately applies to computer graphics.*

on a/the . . . basis *-(al)ly* delete. • Every exchange has a clearinghouse that transfers funds from losers to winners on a daily basis. *Every exchange has a clearinghouse that transfers funds daily from losers to winners.* • Our sole interest in the report is to be sure that each application is evaluated on a fair basis. *Our sole interest in the report is to be sure that each application is evaluated fairly.* • It has been estimated that, on a worldwide basis, banks and credit card companies lose $3 million annually. *It has been estimated that, worldwide, banks and credit card companies lose $3 million annually.* • Questions as complex as the ones contained in this collection cannot be graded on a right or wrong basis. *Questions as complex as the ones contained in this collection cannot be graded right or wrong.* • We will continue to add features to the site and update information on a frequent basis. *We will continue to add features to the site and update information frequently.*

on account of *after/because of/by/due to/following/for/from/in/out of/owing to/through/with.* • There are millions of women in this country who have been discriminated against on account of their sex. *There are millions of women in this country who have been discriminated against because of their sex.*

on account of the fact that *because/considering/for/given/in that/since.* • Brown suggests that this might be on account of the fact that it posed little challenge to the homosocial order. *Brown* *suggests that this might be because it posed little challenge to the homosocial order.*

on a couple of/a few occasions *a few times/once or twice/twice/two or three times.* • On a couple of occasions, the entire system shut down. *Once or twice, the entire system shut down.*

on a/the . . . note *-(al)ly* delete. • On a disconcerting note, 18 percent of the children surveyed said they had been approached to buy or use drugs. *Disconcertingly, 18 percent of the children surveyed said they had been approached to buy or use drugs.* • The market began the week on a cautious note. *The market began the week cautiously.*

on a number of /any number of/frequent/many/ numerous/several occasions *frequently/many times/numerous times/often/regularly/repeatedly/ several times.* • They have done that on a number of occasions. *They have often done that.*

on a regular basis *bimonthly/biweekly/daily/ hourly/monthly/regularly/weekly/yearly* delete. • Does it mean we should all start taking aspirin on a regular basis? *Does it mean we should all start taking aspirin regularly?*

on a/the . . . scale/scope *-(al)ly* delete. • We can do projects on a much larger scale today. *We can do much larger projects today.*

on a/the . . . scene *-(al)ly* delete. • On the national scene, here's what's happening. *Here's what's happening nationally.*

on a timely basis *by next week (tomorrow)/fast/ in (within) a day (year)/in/on time/promptly/ quickly/rapidly/right away/shortly/soon/speedily/ swiftly/timely.* • It is important that you pay your premiums on a timely basis. *It is important that you pay your premiums on time.*

on (an/the) average *commonly/customarily/ generally/normally/often/ordinarily/typically.*

on . . . behalf (of) *for.* • Nobody is authorized to speak on my behalf. *Nobody is authorized to speak for me.*

once (and) for all *conclusively/decisively/ finally* delete. • Analysts expect their questions about Raytheon's nondefense subsidiaries to be answered once and for all when Phillips' successor makes known his intentions. *Analysts expect their questions about Raytheon's nondefense subsidiaries to be finally answered when Phillips' successor makes known his intentions.*

once in a (great) while *at times/now and again/ now and then/on occasion/sometimes.*

on certain/some occasions *at times/now and again/now and then/occasionally/sometimes.* • On some occasions, the treatment may retard progression of the disease. *Sometimes, the treatment may retard progression of the disease.*

once . . . then *once.* • Once this analysis is done, then special attention may be paid to various short pieces of code that consume the most time. *Once this analysis is done, special attention may be paid to various short pieces of code that consume the most time.* • Once you determine what you want to tell people, you then need to figure out what's in it for them. *Once you determine what you want to tell people, you need to figure out what's in it for them.*

on (the) condition (of/that) *as long as/if/provided/so long as.* • The Maynard computer maker will offer a generous financial support package to 700 employees on condition that they agree to leave the company. *The Maynard computer maker will offer a generous financial support package to 700 employees provided that they agree to leave the company.*

on -day *-day.* • All that the police know is the bank was robbed sometime on Monday morning. *All that the police know is the bank was robbed sometime Monday morning.*

(a/the) . . . one delete. • It remains to be seen, however, if this view will turn out to be the correct one. *It remains to be seen, however, if this view will turn out to be correct.*

(the) one (that) delete. • The one that seems to be the most popular is the use of the pull-down Mac menus for function keys. *The most popular seems to be the use of the pull-down Mac menus for function keys.*

on each/every occasion *all/always/consistently/ constantly/each/each time/for (in) each/for (in) every/every time/invariably/unfailingly* delete.

one and all *all/everyone.*

one and only *one/only/sole.* • Is that the one and only time you have engaged in group counseling? *Is that the only time you have engaged in group counseling?*

one and the same *identical/one/the same.* • We do not believe that computers and communications are going to converge and become one and the same business. *We do not believe that computers and communications are going to converge and become the same business.*

on earlier/former/previous/prior occasions *before/earlier/formerly/previously.* • I asked Governor Cuomo for his support, as I have on prior occasions. *I asked Governor Cuomo for his support, as I have before.*

(the) one best *the best.* • The emphasis of scientific management was to try to find the one best way by examining the way work was done, the sequence of steps, and the skills of the workers. *The emphasis of scientific management was to try to find the best way by examining the way work was done, the sequence of steps, and the skills of the workers.*

one best/most *best/most.* • Each alternative needs to be evaluated to determine which one best achieves the objective. *Each alternative needs to be evaluated to determine which best achieves the objective.*

one-half/one-third *half/third.* • The data is derived from the first one-third of the observations. *The data is derived from the first third of the observations.*

one-half/seven-eighths of an inch *one-half inch/seven-eighths inch.* • Alternate pages are offset from the left margin by an additional one-half of an inch. *Alternate pages are offset from the left margin by an additional one-half inch.*

one more time *again/once more/re-.* • If you position the highlight over the first or last choice on the menu and then press the arrow key one more time, the highlight wraps around to the other end of the menu. *If you position the highlight over the first or last choice on the menu and then press the arrow key again, the highlight wraps around to the other end of the menu.*

(the) one of delete. • In the United States, such a gesture is merely one of politeness. *In the United States, such a gesture is merely politeness.* • The strategy then shifts from one of consolidation to one of integration. *The strategy then shifts from consolidation to integration.*

one-of-a-kind *matchless/novel/peerless/singular/special/unequaled/unique/unmatched/unrivaled.* • "Learn C Now" is a one-of-a-kind course that's designed to make beginning programmers productive quickly. *"Learn C Now" is a unique course that's designed to make beginning programmers productive quickly.*

one single *one/(a) single.* • Not one single college president has ever attempted to lay off a single high-paid administrator. *Not one college president has ever attempted to lay off a single high-paid administrator.*

one/two time(s) *once (twice).* • We visited them two times in two days. *We visited them twice in two days.*

(in) one way or another *anyhow/anyway/by some means/however/in any way/in some way/in whatever way/somehow/somehow or another/someway(s).* • He seemed deranged in one way or another. *He seemed deranged somehow.*

(in) one way or the other *at all/either way/in the least/in the slightest* delete. • It didn't change my religious beliefs one way or the other. *It didn't change my religious beliefs in the least.*

on . . . grounds *about/-(al)ly/on* delete. • The proposed increase in rapid transit fares may be justified on economic grounds. *The proposed increase in rapid transit fares may be economically justified.*

on (the) grounds that *because/considering/for/given/in that/since.* • Democratic leaders oppose the tax cut on grounds that it benefits mainly the rich. *Democratic leaders oppose the tax cut since it benefits mainly the rich.*

on its (the) face (of it/of things) *apparently/appear (to)/outwardly/seem (to)/seemingly/superficially.* • On the face of it, no term fits the Parisian beau monde of the late 18th century better than the one invented 200 years later by Tom Wolfe. *No term seems to fit the Parisian beau monde of the late 18th century better than the one invented 200 years later by Tom Wolfe.*

on its (the) face (of it/of things) . . . appear/seem *appear/seem.* • On the face of it, this would appear to be a simple evaluation to make. *This would appear to be a simple evaluation to make.*

on (a/the) . . . level *-(al)ly* delete. • On a personal level, I cannot stand how he behaves. *Personally, I cannot stand how he behaves.* • I feel it's not possible to have a relationship with a man on a spiritual and emotional level. *I feel it's not possible to have a spiritual and emotional relationship with a man.* • In the past year, the media has gotten to know her, at least on a superficial level. *In the past year, the media has gotten to know her, at least superficially.*

on more than one occasion *a few times/frequently/many times/more than once/often/several times.* • I've been asked that question on more than one occasion. *I've been asked that question more than once.*

on no consideration *never/not ever/not once.*

on no occasion *never/not ever/not once.*

on (the) one hand . . . on the other (hand) delete. • Another way of looking at the basic strategic tradeoffs that Bell Operating Companies are facing is to look at the relationship between their competitiveness on one hand and the need to avoid conflict with various players on the other. *Another way of looking at the basic strategic tradeoffs that Bell Operating Companies are facing is to look at the relationship between their competitiveness and the need to avoid conflict with various players.*

on one/two/three occasion(s) *a few times/once/once or twice/one time/several times/three times/twice/two times.* • On only one occasion in the three years of our negotiations were the Angels and Dick unable to come to a satisfactory agreement. *Only once in the three years of our negotiations were the Angels and Dick unable to come to a satisfactory agreement.*

on . . . part *among/by/for/from/of/-'s* delete. • To beat them will take a great effort on our part. *To beat them will take a great effort by us.* • I think it's foolhardy on your part. *I think it's foolhardy of you.* • The shorter work hours logged by women had more to do with their heavy concentration in retail trade and service-oriented industries than a reluctance on their part to work longer hours. *The shorter work hours logged by women had more to do with their heavy concentration in retail trade and service-oriented industries than their reluctance to work longer hours.* • It was the first time I felt a real commitment on his part. *It was the first time I felt a real commitment from him.* • Hattie always spells this word "ricksha"; I thought it was an error on her part, but the Wikipedia accepts this as a legitimate variant spelling. *Hattie always spells this word "ricksha"; I thought it was an error, but the Wikipedia accepts this as a legitimate variant spelling.*

on . . . terms delete. • We are no longer on speaking terms with each other. *We are no longer speaking with each other.*

on that/this (particular) occasion *at present/at that/this time/currently/(just/right) now/presently/then/today/(just) yet* delete.

on the assumption (that) *assuming (that)/supposing (that).* • On the assumption that the baptism took place within a few days of birth, Shakespeare's birthday is celebrated on 23rd April, which is the feast day of Saint George, Patron Saint of England. *Assuming the baptism took place within a few days of birth, Shakespeare's birthday is celebrated on 23rd April, which is the feast day of Saint George, Patron Saint of England.*

on the basis of *after/based on/because of/by/due to/following/for/from/in/on/owing to/through/with.* • The other guards said the vehicle was a minivan, a fact confirmed on the basis of the tire tracks found at the scene. *The other guards said the vehicle was a minivan, a fact confirmed by the tire tracks found at the scene.* • Employees do not act on the basis of what management thinks, or what management thinks they think; they act on their own opinions. *Employees do not act on what management thinks, or what management thinks they think; they act on their own opinions.* • Its managers

should be selected on the basis of their ability to further the company's goals and maximize its earnings. *Its managers should be selected for their ability to further the company's goals and maximize its earnings.*

on the basis of the fact that *because/considering/for/given/in that/since.* • Everybody knew that Beijing was the leader on the basis of the fact that they'd been the runner up in the 1993 vote that gave Sydney the 2000 Games. *Everybody knew that Beijing was the leader given that they'd been the runner up in the 1993 vote that gave Sydney the 2000 Games.* • This is justifiable on the basis of the fact that the Bible was produced, like Islam, in the Middle East and thus the two may share common factors. *This is justifiable since the Bible was produced, like Islam, in the Middle East and thus the two may share common factors.*

on the bottom of *below/beneath/under/underneath.*

on the contrary *but/conversely/however/instead/not so/rather/still/whereas/yet.*

on the decline *abating/declining/decreasing/waning.* • Heavy metals in the marine sediments of lower Budd Inlet and elsewhere in Puget Sound are on the decline. *Heavy metals in the marine sediments of lower Budd Inlet and elsewhere in Puget Sound are declining.*

on the decrease *abating/declining/decreasing/waning.* • While many crimes are on the decrease, violent crime, according to the latest figures, remains worryingly high. *While many crimes are decreasing, violent crime, according to the latest figures, remains worryingly high.*

on/upon the heels of *(just/right) after/(close) behind/ensuing/following/succeeding.* • On the heels of an FBI investigation, a federal grand jury has indicted five people on charges they defrauded ComFed Savings Bank. *Following an*

FBI investigation, a federal grand jury has indicted five people on charges they defrauded ComFed Savings Bank.

on the increase *booming/flourishing/growing/increasing/rising.* • The Department of Revenue recently released a report on the state's economic indicators that showed personal savings are on the increase. *The Department of Revenue recently released a report on the state's economic indicators that showed personal savings are increasing.*

on the occasion of *if (there were)/if . . . should/in case (of)/should (there)/were (there/. . . to)/when* delete. • The machinists' union has agreements that members of other unions will not do their work on the occasion of a strike. *The machinists' union has agreements that members of other unions will not do their work if there were a strike.*

(something/somewhere) on the order (of) *about/around/close to/more or less/near/nearly/or so/roughly/some* delete. • Typically, the ratio of injury to mortality is something on the order of three or four to one. *Typically, the ratio of injury to mortality is some three or four to one.* • I counted something on the order of 50 interruptions for applause. *I counted 50 or so interruptions for applause.* • For software whose development time is on the order of two years, there are two possible arrangements. *For software whose development time is around two years, there are two possible arrangements.*

on the order of *akin to/close to/like/resembling/similar to/such as.* • What you won't see in Chatham is anything on the order of the commercial changes going on in other Cape towns. *What you won't see in Chatham is anything resembling the commercial changes going on in other Cape towns.* • Have you ever been in a situation where you ask friends what they want to do tonight, and their response is something on the order of, "Oh, it doesn't matter, surprise us"? *Have*

you ever been in a situation where you ask friends what they want to do tonight, and their response is something like, "Oh, it doesn't matter, surprise us"?

on the other hand *but/by/in contrast/conversely/however/whereas/yet* delete. • A parallel device, on the other hand, sends or receives information in packets all at once over many data lines. *A parallel device, in contrast, sends or receives information in packets all at once over many data lines.*

on the outside of *outside.* • The fan blades are on the outside of the engine like a propeller, and all the air that passes inside the engine goes through the combustion chamber as in the earliest jets. *The fan blades are outside the engine like a propeller, and all the air that passes inside the engine goes through the combustion chamber as in the earliest jets.* • Either elemental sulfur is formed outside of the cell or the sulfide is oxidized all the way to sulfate. *Either elemental sulfur is formed outside the cell or the sulfide is oxidized all the way to sulfate.*

on the part of *among/by/for/from/in/of/-'s* delete. • Though deliberate discrimination on the part of the Japanese is often charged, it isn't necessary to prove a discriminatory intent. *Though deliberate discrimination by the Japanese is often charged, it isn't necessary to prove a discriminatory intent.* • The effective teaching of language arts requires a commitment to excellence on the part of the classroom teacher. *The effective teaching of language arts requires a commitment to excellence from the classroom teacher.* • His apt observations point out the need for greater awareness on the part of the public of the architecture that surrounds them. *His apt observations point out the need for greater public awareness of the architecture that surrounds them.* • How has the practice of these concepts on your part affected the way you live, and how has the practice of these concepts on the parts of other people affected the way you perceive the world? *How has your practice of these concepts affected the way you live, and how has other people's practice of these concepts affected the way you perceive the world?*

on the rise *booming/flourishing/growing/increasing/rising.* • Interest rates are on the rise in the United States, Europe, and Japan. *Interest rates are rising in the United States, Europe, and Japan.*

on the . . . side *among/in/-(al)ly* delete. • How would you assess the progress that she has made on the artistic side? *How would you assess the artistic progress that she has made?* • There will be some job losses on the manufacturing side, but some employees will be transferred. *There will be some job losses in manufacturing, but some employees will be transferred.* • The file we would receive is on the large side—10,424 lines long. *The file we would receive is large—10,424 lines long.* • Increased competition for programming and talent has increased our costs on the network side significantly. *Increased competition for programming and talent has significantly increased our network costs.*

on the side of *for/with.* • The second factor working on the side of savings is the president and his wife. *The second factor working for savings is the president and his wife.*

on the surface (of it/of things) *apparently/appear (to)/outwardly/seem (to)/seemingly/superficially* delete. • On the surface of things, one might be tempted to think, if Lacy has one clear advantage it has to be hitting power. *One might be tempted to think, if Lacy has one clear advantage it has to be hitting power.* • On the surface of it, the proposition is a good deal. *The proposition appears to be a good deal.*

on the surface (of it/of things) . . . appear/seem *appear/seem.* • On the surface, a firm may appear to be sound—its balance sheet contains an impressive amount of current assets. *A firm may appear to be sound—its balance sheet contains an impressive amount of current assets.*

on the surface of *on.* • To gain entry, a virus binds to receptors on the surface of the host cell, and is taken up into a vesicle, or sphere, inside the cell. *To gain entry, a virus binds to receptors on the host cell, and is taken up into a vesicle, or sphere, inside the cell.* • Didn't they know that as many Englishmen (none) have walked on the surface of the Moon as on the surface of the final green with the Wanamaker Trophy in hand? *Didn't they know that as many Englishmen (none) have walked on the Moon as on the final green with the Wanamaker Trophy in hand?*

on the threshold of *about to/approaching/close to/near/nearly/verging on.* • We are on the threshold of real educational quality and achievement. *We are verging on real educational quality and achievement.*

on the verge of *about to/approaching/close to/near/nearly/verging on.* • Is he or is he not on the verge of producing chemical weapons? *Is he or is he not about to produce chemical weapons?*

on the whole *all told/in all/overall.*

on/upon the whole *almost all/chiefly/commonly/generally/greatly/in general/largely/mainly/most/mostly/most often/much/nearly all/normally/overall/typically/usually.* • On the whole, Boston's registered nurses were more likely to describe themselves as satisfied with their earnings than their counterparts in other cities. *Overall, Boston's registered nurses were more likely to describe themselves as satisfied with their earnings than their counterparts in other cities.*

on top of (that/this) *also/and/as well/besides/beyond that/this/even/further/furthermore/moreover/more than that/this/still more/then/too/what's more.* • On top of that, interest rates went up to 18 percent or more. *What's more, interest rates went up to 18 percent or more.*

on (the) top of *atop.* • It may not be necessary to develop an emergency plan for flooding if the facility is on the top of a well-drained hill. *It may not be necessary to develop an emergency plan for flooding if the facility is atop a well-drained hill.*

on (the) understanding (of/that) *as long as/if/ provided/so long as.* • The North Koreans agreed to return on the understanding that bilateral talks would take place. *The North Koreans agreed to return provided that bilateral talks would take place.*

OPEC countries *OPEC.*

(an/the) open question *a/the question/arguable/debatable/disputable/doubtful/dubious/in doubt/in question/moot/open/questionable/ uncertain/unclear/undecided/unknown/unsettled/unsure.* • That remains an open question. *That remains questionable.*

open to doubt *arguable/debatable/disputable/ doubtful/dubious/in doubt/in question/moot/ questionable.*

open to question *arguable/debatable/disputable/doubtful/dubious/in doubt/in question/ moot/questionable/uncertain/unclear/undecided/unknown/unsettled/unsure.* • His clout on Capitol Hill remains open to question. *His clout on Capitol Hill remains in doubt.*

open up *open.* • When you use the Note command, a window opens up. *When you use the Note command, a window opens.*

(a/the) . . . operation *delete.* • With the measurement of quality and quantity, process control is a fairly automatic operation. *With the measurement of quality and quantity, process control is fairly automatic.* • While this has been

programmed correctly, it is a dangerous operation. *While this has been programmed correctly, it is dangerous.*

operational *active/live/running/working.*

operative *active/at work/effective/in action/in effect/in force/in play/working.*

(of) (the) opposite sex *female/male/man/ woman.* • He is abandoning his hemline indicator because it tended to offend too many investors of the opposite sex. *He is abandoning his hemline indicator because it tended to offend too many female investors.*

optimal/optimum *best.* • It will be the responsibility of the company's tax advisors to provide counseling on the optimal tax structure for a variety of arrangements. *It will be the responsibility of the company's tax advisors to provide counseling on the best tax structure for a variety of arrangements.*

or anything *delete.*

ordered and adjudged *adjudged/decreed/ ordered.* • It is ordered and adjudged that the defendant forthwith deliver to the plaintiff or as the plaintiff directs possession of the mortgaged property, or of such part of it as is in the possession of the defendant. *It is ordered that the defendant forthwith deliver to the plaintiff or as the plaintiff directs possession of the mortgaged property, or of such part of it as is in the possession of the defendant.* • It is additionally ordered and adjudged that the plaintiff Delta Airlines, Inc. recover of the defendants Elite Travel, Inc., Mileage Club, Inc., Ruth Ashton and Van F. Cleverly its cost of action. *It is additionally decreed that the plaintiff Delta Airlines, Inc. recover of the defendants Elite Travel, Inc., Mileage Club, Inc., Ruth Ashton and Van F. Cleverly its cost of action.*

(an) order of magnitude *delete.* • While the first CD-ROM copy costs an order of magnitude more than a WORM disk, subsequent copies cost much less. *While the first CD-ROM copy costs more than a WORM disk, subsequent copies cost much less.* • The MFC development cycle remains an order of magnitude faster and still represents the better development method to use for desktop application components. *The MFC development cycle remains faster and still represents the better development method to use for desktop application components.*

or else *or.* • Two pathnames must be specified, or else the first letter parameter will be incorrectly interpreted as a pathname. *Two pathnames must be specified, or the first letter parameter will be incorrectly interpreted as a pathname.*

orientate(d) *orient(ed).* • I didn't have a family-orientated family. *I didn't have a family-oriented family.* • Our site contains sexual-orientated material and is intended for adults only. *Our site contains sexual-oriented material and is intended for adults only.* • A more politically orientated analysis was required to understand OPEC. *A more politically oriented analysis was required to understand OPEC.* • Ninety-five percent of Textron's business is defense orientated. *Ninety-five percent of Textron's business is defense oriented.*

oriented delete. • Some depressed people become more activity oriented. *Some depressed people become more active.*

original coiner/originally coined *coiner/coined.* • Usually the identity of the original coiner of a new word is lost in the mists of history. *Usually the identity of the coiner of a new word is lost in the mists of history.*

original creator/originally created *creator/created.* • An impressive number of neologisms can be traced to their original creators. *An impressive number of neologisms can be traced to their creators.*

original founder/originally founded *founder/founded.*

original invention/inventor *invention/inventor.* • The courts determined the patents were invalid on the grounds that Atanasoff was the original inventor. *The courts determined the patents were invalid on the grounds that Atanasoff was the inventor.* • This approach to children's radio is not Disney's original invention, according to Children's Broadcasting Corp. *This approach to children's radio is not Disney's invention, according to Children's Broadcasting Corp.*

original source *source.*

origination *origin.*

or something delete. • Wouldn't it be cheaper for them to fly to Wisconsin and tape the show in Madison or something? *Wouldn't it be cheaper for them to fly to Wisconsin and tape the show in Madison?*

or something like that delete. • If you think about it, that's quite a population and there's quite a lot of drinking, and usually it's a heart attack or an asthma attack or something like that. *If you think about it, that's quite a population and there's quite a lot of drinking, and usually it's a heart attack or an asthma attack.*

or thereabouts *or so.*

or whatever delete.

oscillate back and forth *oscillate.* • In my career of number crunching, I've oscillated back and forth between favoring each of them. *In my career of number crunching, I've oscillated between favoring each of them.*

other people/persons *others.* • Elizabeth Taylor, among other people, has written about this topic. *Elizabeth Taylor, among others, has written about this topic.*

other similar *similar.* • In addition, the order permits the companies to provide electronic mail, voice messaging, and other similar services. *In addition, the order permits the companies to provide electronic mail, voice messaging, and similar services.*

other than *besides.*

other than . . . also/as well *besides/beyond/other than.*

other than to *but to.*

(the) other way around/round *the opposite/the reverse.*

otherwise *other.* • In many competitions, athletic and otherwise, the Finns and Swedes excel. *In many competitions, athletic and other, the Finns and Swedes excel.*

out in *in.* • I have several relatives out in the Springfield area. *I have several relatives in the Springfield area.*

out loud *aloud.*

out of *in/of.* • Three out of every four parents never visit their child's school. *Three of every four parents never visit their child's school.*

(just) out of curiosity *delete.* • Just out of curiosity, is Alexander Haig on the Minnesota ballot? *Is Alexander Haig on the Minnesota ballot?*

out of favor *deprecate/disapprove/disfavor/dislike/disparage.* • But he goes on to say, the time to buy them is when they are out of favor. *But he goes on to say, the time to buy them is when they are disfavored.*

out of fear (of/that) . . . can/could/may/might/shall/should/will/would *lest.* • No one would be so foolish as to sell one's house out of fear that it might someday burn to the ground. *No one would be so foolish as to sell one's house lest it someday burn to the ground.*

out of focus *blurred/indistinct.*

(something) out of the ordinary *curious/different/exceptional/extraordinary/irregular/novel/odd/rare/singular/strange/uncommon/unusual.* • Will you give me a call if anything out of the ordinary happens? *Will you give me a call if anything curious happens?* • Tomorrow's show is going to be something out of the ordinary. *Tomorrow's show is going to be extraordinary.*

out of the question *impossible/inconceivable/undoable/unthinkable.* • Returning to college was out of the question, so with nothing to do, she signed up for oil painting lessons. *Returning to college was unthinkable, so with nothing to do, she signed up for oil painting lessons.*

outside of *outside.* • Chase Manhattan and Bank of America are following a similar strategy, with less emphasis on domestic markets outside of the United States. *Chase Manhattan and Bank of America are following a similar strategy, with less emphasis on domestic markets outside the United States.*

out/outside (of) the realm of possibility *impossible/inconceivable/undoable/unfeasible/unthinkable.* • It is not out of the realm of possibility that Exxon could be facing a billion dollars or more in punitive damages. *It is not impossible that Exxon could be facing a billion dollars or more in punitive damages.* • The offer hinged on their father's ability to furnish the original receipt, a feat that seemed outside the realm of possibility. *The offer hinged on their father's ability to furnish the original receipt, a feat that seemed unfeasible.*

over again *again/afresh/anew/once more/over/re-.* • They asked me to do it over again. *They asked me to do it over.*

overall look/view *overview.* • The introduction gives the readers an overall view of your business and what you want to achieve. *The introduction gives the readers an overview of your business and what you want to achieve.*

over and above *besides/beyond/more than/over.* • Anesthesia doesn't add to the risk over and above that of the surgery itself and the extent of the medical problem the patient already has. *Anesthesia doesn't add to the risk more than that of the surgery itself and the extent of the medical problem the patient already has.*

over and done with *complete/done/ended/finished/over/past.* • I just want this to be over and done with. *I just want this to be over.*

over and over (again) *frequently/often/recurrently/regularly/repeatedly.* • Professor Sommers refers over and over to a "bag of virtues." *Professor Sommers refers often to a "bag of virtues."*

overexaggerate *exaggerate.* • Those countries that do not join might start to overexaggerate the perceived threat from NATO, and may seek closer cooperation with Russia. *Those countries that do not join might start to exaggerate the perceived threat from NATO, and may seek closer cooperation with Russia.*

overly *over-.* • We thought he was overly enthusiastic about winning. *We thought he was overenthusiastic about winning.* • Many supermarkets through the U.S. place overly sexualized magazines, notably *Cosmopolitan* and *Glamour*, in their checkout aisles. *Many supermarkets through the U.S. place oversexualized magazines, notably* Cosmopolitan *and* Glamour, *in their checkout aisles.*

over the course/duration/length of *during/for/in/over/throughout/when/while/with.* • Over the duration of the project, we expect there will be some disruption due to noise, dirt, and dust. *During the project, we expect there will be some disruption due to noise, dirt, and dust.* • It does demonstrate that individuals in need of palliative care often have new and different issues that need attention over the course of time. *It does demonstrate that individuals in need of palliative care often have new and different issues that need attention over time.*

over the fact that *because/for/in that/since/that* delete. • I am concerned over the fact that they made us work so hard. *I am concerned that they made us work so hard.* • The public is feeling betrayed and resentful over the fact that illegal wiretapping continued under President Kim. *The public is feeling betrayed and resentful that illegal wiretapping continued under President Kim.* • We became a little resentful over the fact that we couldn't buy, or even hear about, the music that we were into. *We became a little resentful because we couldn't buy, or even hear about, the music that we were into.*

over the long haul *at length/eventually/in the end/in time/later/long-term/one day/over the months (years)/over time/someday/sometime/ultimately/with time/yet.* • Over the long haul, I still believe that housing is a good investment. *I still believe that housing is a good long-term investment.*

over the short haul *at first/at present/before long/currently/directly/for now/in/over a month (week)/initially/next month (year)/(just/right) now/presently/quickly/shortly/short-term/soon/straightaway/this month (year)/tomorrow* delete. • Industry analysts say they expect the new rules to have little impact, at least over the short haul. *Industry analysts say they expect the new rules to have little impact, at least initially.*

(a/the) overwhelming/vast consensus (of opinion) *consensus.*

(a/the) overwhelming/vast preponderance (of) *a good (great) deal (of)/a good (great) many (of)/almost all (of)/many (of)/most (of)/much* *(of)/nearly all (of)* delete. • A recent poll showed that a vast preponderance of city councilors oppose the relocation. *A recent poll showed that almost all city councilors oppose the relocation.*

(all) over with *complete/done/ended/finished/ over/past.*

owing to the fact that *because/considering/for/ given/in that/since.* • However, owing to the fact that NRDC is a well-thought-of organization, capable of good quality research, we're clearly going to go through their report carefully. *However, since NRDC is a well-thought-of organization, capable of good quality research, we're clearly going to go through their report carefully.* • Elementary Afrikaans is quite easy, owing to the fact that the base grammar structure is simple, and words are generally written the way they are pronounced. *Elementary Afrikaans is quite easy, because the base grammar structure is simple, and words are generally written the way they are pronounced.*

P

pack together *pack.* • Recent advances have made it possible to pack thousands, even millions, of transistors together on a single silicon chip. *Recent advances have made it possible to pack thousands, even millions, of transistors on a single silicon chip.*

paired in twos *paired.* • Paired in twos, they complement any bibliophile's literature collection. *Paired, they complement any bibliophile's literature collection.*

(a) pair of twins *twins.* • Such a proximity is literalized in the documentation of the plight of Viet and Duc, a pair of twins joined at the abdomen and sharing a leg. *Such a proximity is literalized in the documentation of the plight of Viet and Duc, twins joined at the abdomen and sharing a leg.*

panacea for all ills *panacea.* • Finally, law is not a panacea for all ills (real or perceived). *Finally, law is not a panacea (real or perceived).*

paradisiacal *paradisal/paradisiac.*

parameter *boundary/limit.*

par for the course *customary/normal/standard/ typical/usual.* • From drawing up war plans to snubbing an army's worth of scientists when it comes to global warming, an isolated and arrogant White House is par for the course. *From drawing up war plans to snubbing an army's worth of scientists when it comes to global warming, an isolated and arrogant White House is typical.* • It was hectic in the afternoon, but that's par for the course. *It was hectic in the afternoon, but that's normal.*

(a/a certain/some) part (of) *almost all (of)/ many (of)/most (of)/much (of)/nearly all (of)/(a) part (of)/some (of).*

part and parcel *part.* • This generalized tendency to place conflicts in the outside world is part and parcel of a well-known mechanism of the mind called projection. *This generalized tendency to place conflicts in the outside world is part of a well-known mechanism of the mind called projection.*

partially *partly.* • My difficulty with her is partially due to a clash of personalities. *My difficulty with her is partly due to a clash of personalities.*

particular delete. • We would hope that you have already found a new church home that you can serve and that can meet your needs at this particular time in your life. *We would hope that you have already found a new church home that you can serve and that can meet your needs at this time in your life.*

(the) passage of time *time.* • Meanwhile, the passage of time has made it increasingly apparent that last year's stock market crash was not the immediate precursor of a corresponding plunge for the economy. *Meanwhile, time has made it increasingly apparent that last year's stock market crash was not the immediate precursor of a corresponding plunge for the economy.*

pass away/on/over *die.*

passing craze/fad/fancy *craze/fad/fancy.*

passing phase *phase.*

pass judgment/sentence on/upon *judge/sentence.* • Passing judgment on one's potential earnings is even more painful than passing judgment on a former colleague. *Judging one's potential earnings is even more painful than judging a former colleague.*

past previous/prior *past/previous/prior.* • In the past previous two tests that they made they were sanctioned by the Security Council. *In the past two tests that they made they were sanctioned by the Security Council.* • I think this team, the past previous games especially, we haven't been intimidated. *I think this team, the previous games especially, we haven't been intimidated.* • For comparison the average actual reading over the past six months is a 201,000 increase and the past previous two readings beat expectations by 17,000 and 144,000 respectively. *For comparison the average actual reading over the past six months is a 201,000 increase and the previous two readings beat expectations by 17,000 and 144,000 respectively.*

past/previous/prior accomplishment *accomplishment.* • It is startling that he supposes some imagined past accomplishment of his should exempt him from paying rent. *It is startling that he supposes some imagined accomplishment of his should exempt him from paying rent.*

past/previous/prior achievement *achievement.*

past/previous/prior experience *experience.* • A shortage of workers for jobs requiring little skill is forcing some employers to hire people without considering their references, past experience, or education. *A shortage of workers for jobs requiring little skill is forcing some employers to hire people without considering their references, experience, or education.* • I have no prior experience working with children. *I have no experience working with children.* • Ava-Quest's principals have extensive previous experience working with clients in both the government and commercial sectors. *Ava-Quest's principals have extensive experience working with clients in both the government and commercial sectors.*

past/previous/prior history *history.* • Even though forecasts deal with the future, past history is not irrelevant. *Even though forecasts deal with the future, history is not irrelevant.*

past/previous/prior performance *performance.* • Normally, one judges the ability to succeed based on past performance. *Normally, one judges the ability to succeed based on performance.*

past/previous/prior practice *practice.* • But in keeping with past practice for such flights, the Pentagon is expected to announce a three-hour launch-window early this week. *But in keeping with practice for such flights, the Pentagon is expected to announce a three-hour launch-window early this week.*

past/previous/prior precedent *precedent.* • Based on past precedent, Mr. Indelicato would likely serve between 12 and 18 months in prison. *Based on precedent, Mr. Indelicato would likely serve between 12 and 18 months in prison.*

past/previous/prior record *record.* • Both the summer's drought and the fire's extent surpassed all previous records in the park. *Both the* *summer's drought and the fire's extent surpassed all records in the park.*

patchwork quilt *patchquilt/patchwork.* • The question then becomes how to organize this patchwork quilt of topics. *The question then becomes how to organize this patchwork of topics.*

pathetical *pathetic.*

pathological *pathologic.* • Even though this response is accompanied by redness, warmth, and pain, it is not naturally a pathological process. *Even though this response is accompanied by redness, warmth, and pain, it is not naturally a pathologic process.*

pathological disease *disease/pathology.* • Doctors and biological scientists study pathological disease processes knowing that a clear understanding of what goes wrong and how it occurs opens the door to new avenues of medical intervention and healing. *Doctors and biological scientists study disease processes knowing that a clear understanding of what goes wrong and how it occurs opens the door to new avenues of medical intervention and healing.*

pay attention to *attend to/consider/hearken to/ heed/listen to/mind/note/notice/observe/regard/ see/tend to/watch/witness.* • We need to pay attention to the image we're projecting. *We need to consider the image we're projecting.*

pay (them) a visit (to) *visit (them).* • Pay a visit to your nearest McDonald's. *Visit your nearest McDonald's.* • You can pay them a visit at these addresses. *You can visit them at these addresses.*

pay heed to *attend to/consider/hearken to/ heed/listen to/mind/note/notice/observe/regard/ see/tend to/watch/witness.* • Many Americans have paid heed to the results of research and changed their ways of living remarkably. *Many Americans have heeded the results of research and changed their ways of living remarkably.*

peace and quiet *peace/quiet.* • South Korea's four major parties declared a one-month political truce yesterday to assure peace and quiet during this month's Summer Olympics. *South Korea's four major parties declared a one-month political truce yesterday to assure peace during this month's Summer Olympics.*

penetrate into *penetrate.* • Nonprofits are working to deploy comprehensive high-speed networks that penetrate into areas lacking even basic dial-up access. *Nonprofits are working to deploy comprehensive high-speed networks that penetrate areas lacking even basic dial-up access.* • In my opinion, it did not penetrate into their consciousness, and it is important for us to stress this point, in light of the Palestinian festivities. *In my opinion, it did not penetrate their consciousness, and it is important for us to stress this point, in light of the Palestinian festivities.*

people that/who are (doctors) *(doctors).* • These are people that are musicians that I enjoy listening to. *These are musicians that I enjoy listening to.* • He recognizes that people who are physicians and rulers commonly make mistakes. *He recognizes that physicians and rulers commonly make mistakes.* • The fact of the matter is, that if what is happening to the world today is criminal, then there are people who are criminals doing it. *The fact of the matter is, that if what is happening to the world today is criminal, then there are criminals doing it.* • Just because the world's ending doesn't mean that people who are idiots stop being idiots. *Just because the world's ending doesn't mean that idiots stop being idiots.*

per *a.* • According to this study, the average executive spends 11 weeks per year reading memos. *According to this study, the average executive spends 11 weeks a year reading memos.*

(a/a certain/some) percentage (of) *almost all (of)/many (of)/most (of)/much (of)/nearly all* *(of)/(a) part (of)/some (of).* • I own a certain percentage of Caesar's Palace. *I own some of Caesar's Palace.*

percentage point/unit *percent/point/unit.* • The U.S. Labor Department reported that the September unemployment rate fell 0.2 percentage points, to 5.4 percent. *The U.S. Labor Department reported that the September unemployment rate fell 0.2 points, to 5.4 percent.*

per each/every *per.* • NYNEX will deliver your message for just ten cents per each message. *NYNEX will deliver your message for just ten cents per message.* • On a busy summer weekend, emergency room workers average more than 100 patients per every 24 hours. *On a busy summer weekend, emergency room workers average more than 100 patients per 24 hours.*

perfect/perfectly match *duplicate/exact/identical/match/(the) same.* • Spreadsheets and television may seem unlikely partners, but if what's going on at the Tulsa, Oklahoma, offices of United Video is anything to go by, they are a perfect match. *Spreadsheets and television may seem unlikely partners, but if what's going on at the Tulsa, Oklahoma, offices of United Video is anything to go by, they are a match.*

perform (a/the) . . . of *do* delete. • He performed an extensive analysis of the financing patterns of U.S. corporations. *He extensively analyzed the financing patterns of U.S. corporations.* • Then perform a comparison of the two disks. *Then compare the two disks.* • If an order is executed, the database performs the "clearing" of the trade within an escrow account. *If an order is executed, the database "clears" the trade within an escrow account.* • In the first part of the book, Gray offers strategies for empowering staff, boards, volunteers, and clients to perform an evaluation of their organization. *In the first part of the book, Gray offers strategies for empowering staff, boards, volunteers, and clients to evaluate their organi-*

zation. • For example, you could perform a study of the EMF/leukemia link with animals. *For example, you could study the EMF/leukemia link with animals.*

perhaps . . . may/might *may/might/perhaps.* • Perhaps you may want to reread our introductions and note places where we have traded in our role as guides for one as "tour directors." *You may want to reread our introductions and note places where we have traded in our role as guides for one as "tour directors."*

(a/the) . . . period (of) delete. • The FBI conducted its investigation over a two-year period. *The FBI conducted its investigation over two years.* • Total contract value, excluding database licensing fees, was approximately $2 million over a six-year period. *Total contract value, excluding database licensing fees, was approximately $2 million over six years.*

periodical *periodic.*

(a/the) period/time of delete. • After the shock comes a period of doubt and resignation. *After the shock comes doubt and resignation.*

permit . . . to *let.* • Before we dive into the issues at hand, permit us to formally introduce the Council we represent to you. *Before we dive into the issues at hand, let us formally introduce the Council we represent to you.*

(a/the) . . . person delete. • You do not need to be a gourmet cook or model housecleaner to be a worthwhile person. *You do not need to be a gourmet cook or model housecleaner to be worthwhile.*

personal belief/opinion/point of view/view/viewpoint *belief/opinion/point of view/view/viewpoint.* • My personal opinion is that he should be publicly scolded for his actions. *My opinion is that he should be publicly scolded for his actions.*

personal bias *bias.* • Some experts do inject personal bias into the process. *Some experts do inject bias into the process.*

personal charm *charm.*

personal feeling *feeling.* • What are your personal feelings about this? *What are your feelings about this?*

personal friend/friendship *friend/friendship.* • She is a personal friend of mine. *She is a friend of mine.*

personal rapport *rapport.* • Account managers are advised to develop a personal rapport with their clients. *Account managers are advised to develop a rapport with their clients.*

pertain/pertaining to *about/as for/as to/concerning/for/in/of/on/over/regarding/to/toward/with.* • An assets management system can answer these what-if budget questions pertaining to equipment. *An assets management system can answer these what-if budget questions about equipment.*

pharmacological *pharmacologic.*

phone up *phone.*

physiological *physiologic.* • It is believed that anxiety is expressed through physiological processes rather than symbolically through coping mechanisms. *It is believed that anxiety is expressed through physiologic processes rather than symbolically through coping mechanisms.*

pick and choose *choose/cull/pick/select.* • Its organization into independent topics that you can pick and choose from allows you to use it in a one-semester course. *Its organization into independent topics that you can pick from allows you to use it in a one-semester course.*

pick up the phone/telephone and call *call/phone.* • Buying or selling ownership in a corporation is simply a matter of picking up the phone and calling a stockbroker, who can, within minutes, buy or sell stock listed on a stock exchange. *Buying or selling ownership in a corporation is simply a matter of calling a stockbroker, who can, within minutes, buy or sell stock listed on a stock exchange.*

PIN number *PIN.*

place/put (a) . . . (in/into/on/under/upon) delete. • In determining the relative quality of municipal securities, many investors place great reliance on the rating provided by the two major rating agencies. *In determining the relative quality of municipal securities, many investors greatly rely on the rating provided by the two major rating agencies.* • The Act only covers the actual cost of cleaning up pollution damage, and does not put a limit on compensation claims from third parties. *The Act only covers the actual cost of cleaning up pollution damage, and does not limit compensation claims from third parties.* • AT&T was built around the telephone, but with emerging technology, the company is shifting gears to put emphasis on the wireless product. *AT&T was built around the telephone, but with emerging technology, the company is shifting gears to emphasize the wireless product.*

place/put a burden on/upon *burden/encumber/hamper/hinder/oppress/overtax/strain/tax/weigh down.* • The result can be the gradual accumulation of policies and practices that, like a bad diet, overload the organs and place burdens on the members struggling to keep it alive. *The result can be the gradual accumulation of policies and practices that, like a bad diet, overload the organs and burden the members struggling to keep it alive.*

place/put a premium on/upon *appreciate/cherish/esteem/favor/highly regard/prefer/prize/rate highly/respect/treasure/value.* • Like our staff members, who place a premium on their intellectual and professional independence, our clients made it clear that they consider it essential to be able to work with us without concern about any conflicting interests. *Like our staff members, who prize their intellectual and professional independence, our clients made it clear that they consider it essential to be able to work with us without concern about any conflicting interests.*

place/put a priority on/upon *appreciate/cherish/esteem/favor/highly regard/prefer/prize/rate highly/respect/treasure/value.* • We need to place a priority on education at all levels. *We need to prize education at all levels.* • Look for developers who put a priority on producing the best product for you and your customers. *Look for developers who value producing the best product for you and your customers.* • We urge newsroom managers to place a priority on diversity as hiring opportunities present themselves. *We urge newsroom managers to favor diversity as hiring opportunities present themselves.* • We will always place a priority on simplifying the learning process and motivating educators. *We will always highly regard simplifying the learning process and motivating educators.*

place/put a strain on/upon *burden/encumber/hamper/hinder/oppress/overtax/strain/tax/weigh down.* • Hot weather puts a strain on the heart and can lead to exhaustion, heart failure, and stroke. *Hot weather overtaxes the heart and can lead to exhaustion, heart failure, and stroke.*

place/put a value on/upon *appreciate/cherish/esteem/prize/respect/treasure/value.*

place/put credence in *accept/believe/credit.* • A physical model of health and illness was emphasized that didn't place credence in the idea that our thinking and health were related. *A physical model of health and illness was emphasized that didn't accept the idea that our thinking and health were related.*

place/put . . . in danger *endanger/imperil/jeopardize.* • I would prefer a plan that doesn't put people in danger. *I would prefer a plan that doesn't endanger people.*

place/put . . . in jeopardy *endanger/imperil/jeopardize.* • The opposition Liberal Party, two weeks away from a crucial general election, has strengthened its position among voters and placed the U.S.-Canada trade agreement in serious jeopardy. *The opposition Liberal Party, two weeks away from a crucial general election, has strengthened its position among voters and seriously endangered the U.S.-Canada trade agreement.*

place/put . . . in/into peril *endanger/imperil/jeopardize.* • To do otherwise would invite serious trouble and even place our nation in great peril. *To do otherwise would invite serious trouble and even greatly imperil our nation.*

place/put into question *challenge/contradict/dispute/doubt/question.*

place of business/employment/work *business/company/firm/job/office/work/workplace.* • The defendant indicated that he intended to call two witnesses to testify to having overheard Janice yelling at the defendant at his place of employment, a restaurant where the witnesses also worked. *The defendant indicated that he intended to call two witnesses to testify to having overheard Janice yelling at the defendant at his workplace, a restaurant where the witnesses also worked.*

place/put restrictions on/upon *bind/compel/force/obligate/restrict.*

place/put stress on/upon *strain/stress.* • Fasting places great stress on your body. *Fasting greatly stresses your body.*

place/put under obligation *bind/compel/force/obligate/restrict.*

plain and simple *clear/obvious/plain/simple.* • Associating tobacco with the pastoral joy of watching a baseball game or a golf or tennis tournament is plainly and simply false advertising. *Associating tobacco with the pastoral joy of watching a baseball game or a golf or tennis tournament is clearly false advertising.*

plan ahead *plan.* • If people would plan ahead, they wouldn't be confronted by these crisis situations. *If people would plan, they wouldn't be confronted by these crisis situations.*

plan in advance *plan.* • Plan carefully in advance so that you know exactly when to start and stop the tape. *Plan carefully so that you know exactly when to start and stop the tape.*

plan of action/attack/battle *action/course/ direction/intention/method/move/plan/policy/ procedure/route/scheme/strategy.* • Environmentalists say their failure to agree on a plan of battle raises doubts about whether they are up to the challenge. *Environmentalists say their failure to agree on a strategy raises doubts about whether they are up to the challenge.*

plan out *plan.* • It pays in the long run to plan out your career. *It pays in the long run to plan your career.*

plans and specifications *plans/specifications.* • A contractor entered into a written agreement to construct a building according to plans and specifications prepared by the architect. *A contractor entered into a written agreement to construct a building according to plans prepared by the architect.*

plummet down *down/plummet.* • I can provide a litany of cases where competition has brought prices plummeting down. *I can provide a litany of cases where competition has brought prices plummeting.*

plunge down *down/plunge.*

(a/the) plurality (of) *almost all (of)/many (of)/ more (of)/most (of)/nearly all (of)/three-fourths (two-thirds) (of).* • The poll also found that 89 percent of Americans would not want to be president, and a plurality would not want their children to be. *The poll also found that 89 percent of Americans would not want to be president, and 60 percent would not want their children to be.*

(3:00) p.m. . . . afternoon/evening/night *afternoon/evening/night/(3:00) p.m.* • It was 2 p.m. in the afternoon before we got to see her. *It was 2 p.m. before we got to see her.* • On public and bank holidays the Cathedral closes at 5.30 p.m. in the afternoon. *On public and bank holidays the Cathedral closes at 5.30 in the afternoon.* • In Victoria and ACT you can only be involved in this particular study if you call after 8.30 pm at night. *In Victoria and ACT you can only be involved in this particular study if you call after 8.30 pm.*

poetical *poetic.*

(a/the) . . . point (a/the) delete. • Identifying a need is the beginning point of the process. *Identifying a need is the beginning of the process.*

(a/the) point of (a/the) delete. • Is this a point of concern for the rest of the pack? *Is this a concern for the rest of the pack?*

point of departure *starting point.*

point of view *attitude/belief/opinion/position/ posture/stand/standpoint/vantage/view/viewpoint.* • In the United States, there is an increase in sympathy for the Palestinian point of view. *In the United States, there is an increase in sympathy for the Palestinian viewpoint.*

point to the conclusion *indicate/show/signal/ signify/suggest.*

polish up *polish.*

polite euphemism *euphemism.* • Even its fans call it "difficult" and "uningratiating," polite euphemisms for off the wall, a very appropriate pun to describe this museum-proof collection of dirt piles, rusted girders and "conceptual" creations. *Even its fans call it "difficult" and "uningratiating," euphemisms for off the wall, a very appropriate pun to describe this museum-proof collection of dirt piles, rusted girders and "conceptual" creations.* • The word was initially coined as a polite euphemism for "obsolete." *The word was initially coined as a euphemism for "obsolete."*

popular consensus *consensus.* • The opportunity to conduct a rigorous drug trial can only come early in a drug's life, before a popular consensus develops. *The opportunity to conduct a rigorous drug trial can only come early in a drug's life, before a consensus develops.*

(a/a certain/some) portion (of) *almost all (of)/ many (of)/most (of)/much (of)/(a) part (of)/ nearly all (of)/some (of).* • To print only a portion of the document, select the block. *To print only part of the document, select the block.* • Analysts say that the high employment in the state deserves a portion of the credit. *Analysts say that the high employment in the state deserves some of the credit.*

position *job.*

(a/the) . . . position delete. • In the mid-1980s, they began a succession of investments in Telerate, which had a monopoly position in the distribution of quotations on U.S. government securities. *In the mid-1980s, they began a succession of investments in Telerate, which had a monopoly in the distribution of quotations on U.S. government securities.*

positive assurance *assurance.* • Through the end of last week, we received positive assurances the vote would go through, which makes this doubly frustrating. *Through the end of last week,* *we received assurances the vote would go through, which makes this doubly frustrating.*

positive benefit *benefit.* • The Hass Avocado Board is supporting research to improve understanding of the unique, positive benefits of consuming fresh avocados to human health and nutrition. *The Hass Avocado Board is supporting research to improve understanding of the unique benefits of consuming fresh avocados to human health and nutrition.* • Bamman said most people begin to see positive benefits from exercise within about a month. *Bamman said most people begin to see benefits from exercise within about a month.*

positive feelings *admiration/affection/attraction/confidence/esteem/faith/favor/fondness/ hope/interest/liking/love/regard/respect/tenderness/trust.* • I'm anticipating this launch with positive feelings. *I'm anticipating this launch with confidence.* • Business executives interviewed have positive feelings toward the United Nations. *Business executives interviewed have regard for the United Nations.*

positive optimism *optimism.* • With an optimistic outlook on life we not only help ourselves be healthier, we also spread this positive optimism to those around us. *With an optimistic outlook on life we not only help ourselves be healthier, we also spread this optimism to those around us.*

possess (a/the) . . . (about/for/of/on/over) *have/own* delete. • If teachers do not possess a firm understanding of both science content and science curriculum goals, even the best of assessments will not be sufficient to guide their classroom instruction. *If teachers do not firmly understand both science content and science curriculum goals, even the best of assessments will not be sufficient to guide their classroom instruction.*

possibly may/might *may/might.* • Swaggart possibly may decide to start his own church. *Swaggart may decide to start his own church.*

posterior to *after/behind/following/later.*

postpone until later *postpone.* • An anesthesiologist will discuss with the parents whether it is appropriate to proceed with the procedure or postpone it until later. *An anesthesiologist will discuss with the parents whether it is appropriate to proceed with the procedure or postpone it.*

potentiality *potential.* • All these tools have the same power sources, materials, and styling, and most important, each has identical market potentiality. *All these tools have the same power sources, materials, and styling, and most important, each has identical market potential.* • Anarchy is the opening up of boundless potentiality, not a social, political, economic, or moral program for an ideal society. *Anarchy is the opening up of boundless potential, not a social, political, economic, or moral program for an ideal society.* • It also offers common platform to revamp their research and writing potentiality. *It also offers common platform to revamp their research and writing potential.*

pouring (down) rain *pouring.* • It'll probably be pouring down rain at the lake. *It'll probably be pouring at the lake.*

(the) practice of delete. • Japan shares the United States' concern about the practice of using aid funds for export promotion. *Japan shares the United States' concern about using aid funds for export promotion.*

predicate on/upon *base on.*

predict ahead of time/beforehand/in advance *predict.* • I'm not privy to the secret of how to predict ahead of time who will succeed. *I'm not privy to the secret of how to predict who will succeed.* • Since the impedance change may vary with frequency, there is no way of predicting in advance how the modulation percentage will vary across the spectrum. *Since the impedance change may vary with frequency, there is no way of predicting how the modulation per-* centage will vary across the spectrum. • You can't predict beforehand what special grace it will bring to your garden or what distinctive taste to your table. *You can't predict what special grace it will bring to your garden or what distinctive taste to your table.*

predict . . . future *forecast/foretell/predict.* • No one, not the fund manager, not the investor, can predict the future course of financial markets. *No one, not the fund manager, not the investor, can predict the course of financial markets.*

predominant/predominantly *almost all/chief/ chiefly/generally/in general/largely/main/ mainly/most/mostly/most often/nearly all.* • The social structure of this country is predominantly white. *The social structure of this country is largely white.*

prefer . . . as opposed to/instead of/rather than *prefer . . . over/prefer . . . to.* • Most people in any way connected to tourism speak English and prefer to do so rather than deal with a foreigner's French. *Most people in any way connected to tourism speak English and prefer doing so to dealing with a foreigner's French.* • Nurses who prefer listening and comprehension as opposed to verbalization generally experience the most productive and satisfying interactions. *Nurses who prefer listening and comprehension over verbalization generally experience the most productive and satisfying interactions.*

prejudicial opinion *bias/prejudice.* • Contrary to the prejudicial opinion of most women libbers, physical attractiveness has been and will always be a definite asset. *Contrary to the prejudice of most women libbers, physical attractiveness has been and will always be a definite asset.*

preliminary draft *draft.* • He gave me the preliminary draft of their report to review. *He gave me the draft of their report to review.*

preliminary to *before.* • Preliminary to publication of "Sidereus Nuncius," Galileo obtained these images by using the telescope in the observations of this planet. *Before publication of "Sidereus Nuncius," Galileo obtained these images by using the telescope in the observations of this planet.*

premises *building/house/office/site/store.*

preparation/prepare . . . ahead of time/before/ beforehand/in advance *preparation/prepare . . . for.* • We did not prepare these people for this ahead of time. *We did not prepare these people for this.*

prepare (for) . . . ahead of time/before/beforehand/in advance *prepare (for).* • Try to anticipate problems and prepare for them in advance. *Try to anticipate problems and prepare for them.*

preplan *plan.* • In short programs, much of the cognitive input or preplanning takes place on the trainees' own time, thus keeping the seminar to the shortest possible number of hours. *In short programs, much of the cognitive input or planning takes place on the trainees' own time, thus keeping the seminar to the shortest possible number of hours.*

(a/the) preponderance (of) *almost all (of)/many (of)/more (of)/most (of)/nearly all (of)* delete. • The preponderance of short selling is done by market professionals engaged in the day-to-day provision of liquidity to the market. *Almost all short selling is done by market professionals engaged in the day-to-day provision of liquidity to the market.*

(the) presence of delete. • Mammography uses an X-ray technique to detect the presence of lesions, such as tumors, within the breast. *Mammography uses an X-ray technique to detect lesions, such as tumors, within the breast.*

present (a/the) . . . (of/on/to) *(v)* delete. • We present a summary of the key trends that are important to monitor in the future. *We summarize the key trends that are important to*

monitor in the future. • Increased competition, shrinking profit margins, and escalating costs are presenting challenges to management. *Increased competition, shrinking profit margins, and escalating costs are challenging management.*

(of) (the) present *here/this* delete. • In the present chapter, we introduce capital structure theories. *In this chapter, we introduce capital structure theories.*

(the) present day *(just/right) now/nowadays/ the present/these days/today.* • Ever since MIT economist Rudiger Dornbusch first firmly broached the suggestion, the financial world has been absorbed in the resemblance between 1968 and the present day in macroeconomic terms. *Ever since MIT economist Rudiger Dornbusch first firmly broached the suggestion, the financial world has been absorbed in the resemblance between 1968 and today in macroeconomic terms.*

(the) present-day *nowaday's/the present's/ today's.* • Discoveries, innovations, surprises, and complexities of the present-day South multiply beyond what it seemed possible for him to cover. *Discoveries, innovations, surprises, and complexities of today's South multiply beyond what it seemed possible for him to cover.*

present everywhere *all over/everywhere/omnipresent/ubiquitous/widespread.* • Talk about sex is present everywhere. *Talk about sex is ubiquitous.*

presently *(just/right) now/today/(just) yet* delete. • No one is presently available to answer your call. *No one is available just yet to answer your call.*

presently *quickly/shortly/soon.*

present with *give.* • The disabled people met with James O'Leary, MBTA general manager, and presented him with a list of 19 demands.

The disabled people met with James O'Leary, MBTA general manager, and gave him a list of 19 demands.

pressurize *pressure.* • The Indian government is pressurizing Bangladesh to create a separate homeland for 23 million Hindus within its borders. *The Indian government is pressuring Bangladesh to create a separate homeland for 23 million Hindus within its borders.*

pretty delete. • It's pretty awesome to think of a single gene abnormality that can accelerate the age for a heart attack by 50 years. *It's awesome to think of a single gene abnormality that can accelerate the age for a heart attack by 50 years.*

preventative *preventive.* • The idea of preventative training seems to be a necessity in any educational program. *The idea of preventive training seems to be a necessity in any educational program.*

previous/previously *ago/before/earlier* delete. • We are no closer to resolution than we were three years previously. *We are no closer to resolution than we were three years ago.*

previous to *before.* • Previous to yesterday, there was no reason to sound an alarm. *Before yesterday, there was no reason to sound an alarm.* • It was later shown that some of the young men had committed crimes both previous to and after the subway incident. *It was later shown that some of the young men had committed crimes both before and after the subway incident.*

price point *charge/cost/fee/price.* • At the steep $125 price point for 1.7 oz, we feel the previous products offer more and are a better value. *At the steep $125 price for 1.7 oz, we feel the previous products offer more and are a better value.*

primary/primarily *almost all/chief/chiefly/ largely/main/mainly/most/mostly/most often/*

nearly all. • The assumption is that foreign customers are primarily interested in product availability. *The assumption is that foreign customers are mainly interested in product availability.*

principal/principally *almost all/chief/chiefly/ largely/main/mainly/most/mostly/most often/ nearly all.*

(the) principle of delete.

prior approval/consent *approval/consent.* • This Software is licensed only to you, the Licensee, and may not be transferred to anyone without the prior written consent of Microsoft. *This Software is licensed only to you, the Licensee, and may not be transferred to anyone without the written consent of Microsoft.*

prioritize *arrange/list/order/rank/rate.* • By prioritizing your objectives, devising your plan, and controlling your expenditures, you should be able to build your net worth over the course of your career. *By ranking your objectives, devising your plan, and controlling your expenditures, you should be able to build your net worth over the course of your career.*

prior to *before.* • Prior to the sixteenth century, unknown quantities were represented by words. *Before the sixteenth century, unknown quantities were represented by words.*

prior to . . . first *before/prior to.* • Prior to treating external warts in the anogenital region, it is important to first find and treat internal adjacent condyloma. *Prior to treating external warts in the anogenital region, it is important to find and treat internal adjacent condyloma.*

prior to that/the/this time (of) *before/before now (then).* • We will not pay for transportation expenses incurred prior to that time. *We will not pay for transportation expenses incurred before then.*

probability *chance/likelihood/prospect.* • Others may be less familiar with the model or unfamiliar with the program, thus increasing the probability of mistakes. *Others may be less familiar with the model or unfamiliar with the program, thus increasing the likelihood of mistakes.*

problematical *problematic.* • Since the U.K. banking industry was both mature and increasingly competitive, the clear differentiation of services was becoming problematical. *Since the U.K. banking industry was both mature and increasingly competitive, the clear differentiation of services was becoming problematic.*

(the) problem of delete. • Of all the approaches that can be taken to address the problem of fraud, the most important may be a demonstrated intolerance for the problem. *Of all the approaches that can be taken to address fraud, the most important may be a demonstrated intolerance for the problem.*

(a/the) . . . procedure delete. • Autocorrelation analysis is a useful procedure for identifying the existence and shape of a trend. *Autocorrelation analysis is useful for identifying the existence and shape of a trend.*

(the) procedure of delete. • Let's now look at the procedure of how teams are eliminated. *Let's now look at how teams are eliminated.*

proceed *go/move/run/walk.*

(then) . . . proceed (to) *later/next/then* delete. • He took my number, which he proceeded to lose. *He took my number, which he later lost.* • When you are ill, you don't read the medical encyclopedia, diagnose your case, and then proceed to doctor yourself. *When you are ill, you don't read the medical encyclopedia, diagnose your case, and then doctor yourself.* • In 1998, the Colts drafted QB Peyton Manning with the first pick and proceeded to take offensive players with their next three picks. *In 1998, the Colts drafted QB Peyton Manning with the first pick and took offensive players with their next three picks.*

proceed ahead/forth/forward/on/onward *advance/continue/go on/move on/proceed/progress.* • We ran into a brick wall on getting the kind of commitment from a big player that we felt was necessary to proceed ahead. *We ran into a brick wall on getting the kind of commitment from a big player that we felt was necessary to proceed.*

(a/the) . . . process delete. • It's been a gradual process. *It's been gradual.* • The assessment process involves rigorously examining the methods used. *The assessment involves rigorously examining the methods used.* • Getting into the honesty business, in short, can be an expensive and arduous process. *Getting into the honesty business, in short, can be expensive and arduous.* • Doctors should not dismiss complaints of incontinence as an inevitable part of the aging process. *Doctors should not dismiss complaints of incontinence as an inevitable part of aging.* • It is an extremely frustrating process to define a new exception in a low-level class and then have to edit and recompile all the classes that use this class. *It is extremely frustrating to define a new exception in a low-level class and then have to edit and recompile all the classes that use this class.*

(the) process of delete. • The process of selecting the proper school for your child can be hugely exciting. *Selecting the proper school for your child can be hugely exciting.* • For many people, trading in their current car plays an important role in the process of purchasing a new car. *For many people, trading in their current car plays an important role in purchasing a new car.*

procure *get.*

produce (a/the) . . . (of/to) delete. • The model is an analytic framework that produces estimates of future sales. *The model is an analytic framework that estimates future sales.*

proffer *give/offer.* • An interesting response to the pricing dilemma has been proffered by several traditional broker-distributed fund sponsors. *An interesting response to the pricing dilemma has been offered by several traditional broker-distributed fund sponsors.*

profitability/profitableness *profits.* • The strategy for achieving higher profitability was simple: organize our businesses around the customer, not the product. *The strategy for achieving higher profits was simple: organize our businesses around the customer, not the product.*

progress ahead/forward/on/onward *advance/continue/go on/move on/proceed/progress.*

project out *project.* • The movement of endolymph in the cochlea results in displacement of tiny hairs projecting out from specialized sensory cells. *The movement of endolymph in the cochlea results in displacement of tiny hairs projecting from specialized sensory cells.*

(a/a certain/some) proportion (of) *almost all (of)/many (of)/most (of)/much (of)/nearly all (of)/(a) part (of)/some (of).*

protestation *protest.* • Despite Solomon's protestation, the five-member board is expected to consider changing its rules, which also prohibit CPAs from taking commissions. *Despite Solomon's protest, the five-member board is expected to consider changing its rules, which also prohibit CPAs from taking commissions.*

protrude out *protrude.* • These are not the varicose veins that protrude out from the skin. *These are not the varicose veins that protrude from the skin.*

proven *(v) proved.* • The exact number of data points has not yet been proven. *The exact number of data points has not yet been proved.*

proven fact *fact/proof.* • That's a proven fact. *That's a fact.*

prove of benefit to *benefit.* • The service provided is accessible and convenient, and we hope it will prove of benefit to the staff and the company. *The service provided is accessible and convenient, and we hope it will benefit the staff and the company.*

provide (a/the) . . . (for/of/to) delete. • This book provides a review of those techniques. *This book reviews those techniques.* • Nurses check with other members of the health team when they are unable to provide answers to questions. *Nurses check with other members of the health team when they are unable to answer questions.* • The size of the resulting MSE provides an indication of whether additional information is needed. *The size of the resulting MSE indicates whether additional information is needed.* • Even if we were to provide assistance to Syria, it is unreasonable to expect 100% success. *Even if we were to assist Syria, it is unreasonable to expect 100% success.* • The following statements provide a summary of certain estimates for full-year 2005 based on current forecasts. *The following statements summarize certain estimates for full-year 2005 based on current forecasts.* • Practical action is advised to provide a remedy for the complaint if at all possible. *Practical action is advised to remediate the complaint if at all possible.*

provided/providing (that) *if.* • You can use the same filename more than once provided that the files are stored in different directories. *You can use the same filename more than once if the files are stored in different directories.*

provides that *under.* • Section 106(b)(2) provides that life support may be removed upon notice of intent by the spouse to the hospital. *Under Section 106(b)(2), life support may be removed upon notice of intent by the spouse to the hospital.* • FAR 16.505(b)(1) provides that each contractor shall be given fair opportunity to be considered for each order exceeding $3,000. *Under FAR 16.505(b)(1), each contractor shall be given fair opportunity to be considered for each order exceeding $3,000.*

provide . . . with *give.* • It provides us with a starting point for our analysis. *It gives us a starting point for our analysis.*

proximity *closeness/nearness.* • Its proximity to the edge of the street and the limits of one's field of vision restrict how much of it one can see. *Its nearness to the edge of the street and the limits of one's field of vision restrict how much of it one can see.*

psychiatrical *psychiatric.*

psychical *psychic.*

psychoanalytical *psychoanalytic.*

psychobiological *psychobiologic.*

psychometrical *psychometric.*

psychopathological *psychopathologic.*

psychophysiological *psychophysiologic.*

purchase *buy.* • Why would a sensitive, intelligent woman purchase a handgun? *Why would a sensitive, intelligent woman buy a handgun?*

pure and simple *pure/simple.*

pure (and) unadulterated *pure/simple/unadulterated.* • This movie is pure, unadulterated blasphemy. *This movie is pure blasphemy.*

(the) purpose of . . . is to delete. • The purpose of this view is to allow you to work on the outline's organization. *This view allows you to work on the outline's organization.*

pursuant to *by/following/under.* • Licenses issued pursuant to this Article shall be issued

for terms not exceeding one year. *Licenses issued under this Article shall be issued for terms not exceeding one year.*

put a halt to *cease/close/complete/conclude/end/finish/halt/settle/stop.* • Before things get out of hand again this year, let's try to put a halt to it now. *Before things get out of hand again this year, let's try to halt it now.*

put an end to *cease/close/complete/conclude/end/finish/halt/settle/stop.* • In the last century, liberals fought to put an end to the cruel traffic in human flesh known as slavery. *In the last century, liberals fought to end the cruel traffic in human flesh known as slavery.*

(to) put (it) another way *namely/that is/to wit.*

put a stop to *cease/close/complete/conclude/end/finish/halt/settle/stop.* • I want you to put a stop to all of this nonsense. *I want you to stop all of this nonsense.*

put . . . finger on/upon *identify.*

put forth *advance/exert/give/offer/present/propose/submit/suggest.* • Their employees, free to put forth their best efforts, thrive in this environment. *Their employees, free to give their best efforts, thrive in this environment.*

put forward *advance/give/offer/present/propose/submit/suggest.*

put in alphabetical order *alphabetize.* • Suppose we have a list of words that we want to put in alphabetical order. *Suppose we have a list of words that we want to alphabetize.*

put in an appearance *appear/arrive/attend/come/show up/visit.*

put into effect *activate/cause/create/effect/initiate/launch/make/perform/produce/realize/trigger.* • Quaker Fabrics Corp. said it would put into effect cost-cutting measures that specifically exclude personnel reductions. *Quaker Fabrics Corp. said it would effect cost-cutting measures that specifically exclude personnel reductions.* • The visa policy was put into effect on February 1, 2004. *The visa policy was initiated on February 1, 2004.*

put on an act *feign/pretend.*

put together *assemble/build/construct/create/ devise/fashion/form/mold/set up/shape.* • Thus far, KKR has put together four of the largest leveraged buyouts in history. *Thus far, KKR has fashioned four of the largest leveraged buyouts in history.*

put to sleep *destroy/kill.*

put two and two together *conclude/deduce/ draw/infer/reason.*

put up with *abide/bear/endure/stand/suffer/ tolerate.*

puzzlement *puzzle.*

to play this week. "It's a question mark." *"It's up in the air,"* Poole said when asked if he would attempt to play this week. *"It's uncertain."*

(the) question of delete. • Corporate dividend policy deals with the question of how much of the firm's earnings should be paid to its stockholders in cash dividends. *Corporate dividend policy deals with how much of the firm's earnings should be paid to its stockholders in cash dividends.* • I'm here because I've been assigned to write a story on the question of whether caffeine makes you smarter. *I'm here because I've been assigned to write a story on whether caffeine makes you smarter.*

(a/the) question to answer *question.* • The question to answer is what value should be used for the beginning periods in the series. *The question is what value should be used for the beginning periods in the series.*

quickly expedite *expedite.*

quixotical *quixotic.*

Q

qualified expert *expert.*

(a/a certain/some) quantity (of) *almost all (of)/ many (of)/most (of)/much (of)/nearly all (of)/(a) part (of)/some (of).*

question mark *enigma/mystery/puzzle/question/uncertain/unknown/unsure.* • For scientists trying to forecast how the world will react to the burgeoning burden of greenhouse gases, clouds pose a vexing question mark. *For scientists trying to forecast how the world will react to the burgeoning burden of greenhouse gases, clouds pose a vexing question.* • "It's up in the air," Poole said when asked if he would attempt

R

radiate out *radiate.* • Tracks run in concentric circles around the disk, and sectors radiate out from the center in pie-shaped wedges. *Tracks run in concentric circles around the disk, and sectors radiate from the center in pie-shaped wedges.*

raise doubts about/on *challenge/contradict/ dispute/doubt/question.*

raise for discussion *bring up/broach/introduce/ mention/raise.* • As you prepare your program you will probably think of other important questions that would be both interesting and valuable to raise for discussion. *As you prepare* *your program you will probably think of other important questions that would be both interesting and valuable to introduce.* • It will raise for discussion a number of issues that the Task Force proposes to pursue. *It will raise a number of issues that the Task Force proposes to pursue.* • At any time, Commissioners may raise for discussion any matter that is within the competence of the Commission. *At any time, Commissioners may broach any matter that is within the competence of the Commission.*

raise objections about/on/to *challenge/complain about/criticize/demur/deprecate/differ in/disagree with/disapprove of/dispute/find fault with/object to/oppose/protest/question/resent.* • Government employees raised objections to the bill, saying they were worried about getting jobs after leaving government. *Government employees objected to the bill, saying they were worried about getting jobs after leaving government.*

raise opposition about/on/to *challenge/complain about/criticize/demur/deprecate/differ in/disagree with/disapprove of/dispute/find fault with/object to/oppose/protest/question/resent.* • One longs to get a wider view of the times and the people she presents, particularly the women of the period who were raising strong opposition to male authority. *One longs to get a wider view of the times and the people she presents, particularly the women of the period who were strongly deprecating male authority.*

raise questions about/on *challenge/contradict/dispute/doubt/question.* • Congressional critics have raised questions about the plane's future, particularly as cost estimates have increased. *Congressional critics have questioned the plane's future, particularly as cost estimates have increased.*

raise up *raise.*

RAM memory *RAM.*

range anywhere/somewhere from . . . to *range from . . . to.* • Estimates of sales growth in the industry this year range anywhere from 12 to 50 percent. *Estimates of sales growth in the industry this year range from 12 to 50 percent.*

range from . . . all the way to/all the way up to/up to *range from . . . to.* • The cost ranges from $500 up to $10,000. *The cost ranges from $500 to $10,000.*

range from a low of . . . to a high of *range from . . . to.* • The 1987 rates range from a low of 14.8 percent at St. Vincent's Hospital to a high of 35.8 percent at St. Joseph's Hospital. *The 1987 rates range from 14.8 percent at St. Vincent's Hospital to 35.8 percent at St. Joseph's Hospital.*

(a) range of *assorted/countless/different/diverse/extensive/many/numerous/scores of/sundry/varied/various/varying* delete. • It has been tested in a range of working situations in large manufacturing plants. *It has been tested in diverse working situations in large manufacturing plants.*

rant and rave *rant/rave.*

rarely/seldom ever *rarely/seldom.*

(a) . . . ratio (of) delete. • When you add in those with subsyndromal SAD, the figure is closer to one in four, with women outnumbering men by a ratio of three or four to one. *When you add in those with subsyndromal SAD, the figure is closer to one in four, with women outnumbering men by three or four to one.*

rationale *reason/thinking.* • The primary rationale is that it is a necessary condition for an otherwise attractive business deal. *The primary reason is that it is a necessary condition for an otherwise attractive business deal.*

rational reason *reason.* • There's no rational reason for astrology to work. *There's no reason for astrology to work.*

raze to the ground *demolish/destroy/level/raze/ruin.* • A BBC correspondent saw Serbs raze to the ground another ethnic Albanian village. *A BBC correspondent saw Serbs raze another ethnic Albanian village.*

reach (a/the) . . . (about/of/on/upon/with) delete. • The dividends question is part of the union's proxy fight with the company that is expected to reach a culmination at next week's annual meeting. *The dividends question is part of the union's proxy fight with the company that is expected to culminate at next week's annual meeting.* • We tried to reach an accommodation with both parties. *We tried to accommodate both parties.*

reach (an/the) accord (about/of/on/upon/with) *agree/compromise/concur/decide/resolve/settle.* • An attorney representing Eastern said the airline wants to reach an accord with the American Society of Travel Agents. *An attorney representing Eastern said the airline wants to settle with the American Society of Travel Agents.*

reach (an/the) agreement (about/of/on/upon/with) *agree/compromise/concur/decide/resolve/settle.* • Both he and Chandler said the two sides had reached a tentative agreement on an educational trust fund demanded by the union. *Both he and Chandler said the two sides had tentatively agreed on an educational trust fund demanded by the union.*

reach (a/the) compromise (about/of/on/upon/with) *agree/compromise/concur/decide/resolve/settle.* • The tribe, however, appears eager to reach a compromise and expects the game to be online soon. *The tribe, however, appears eager to compromise and expects the game to be online soon.*

reach (a/the) conclusion (about/of/on/upon/with) *conclude/decide/deduce/determine/infer/judge/reason/resolve/settle.* • The Japanese did not reach that conclusion by engaging in abstract reasoning but by observing England's industrial relations. *The Japanese did not deduce that by engaging in abstract reasoning but by observing England's industrial relations.* • I've not reached a conclusion about whether I'll run in 2012. *I've not decided whether I'll run in 2012.*

reach (a/the) decision (about/of/on/upon/with) *conclude/decide/deduce/determine/infer/judge/reason/resolve/settle.* • He said the committee also is weighing the issue of who was responsible for the overstatement and probably will reach a decision within a few weeks. *He said the committee also is weighing the issue of who was responsible for the overstatement and probably will decide within a few weeks.*

reach (a/the) determination (about/of/on/upon/with) *conclude/decide/deduce/determine/infer/judge/reason/resolve/settle.* • If they are unable to reach a determination of the truth of the matter with a sufficient degree of certainty they may nonetheless make recommendations to the Church authority concerning its response to the complainant. *If they are unable to determine the truth of the matter with a sufficient degree of certainty they may nonetheless make recommendations to the Church authority concerning its response to the complainant.*

reach (an/the) estimate/estimation (about/of/on/upon/with) *approximate/assess/estimate/evaluate/rate.* • These amounts must be added back to taxable income to reach an estimate of the equivalent salary income earned by the plaintiff. *These amounts must be added back to taxable income to estimate the equivalent salary income earned by the plaintiff.*

reach (an/the) opinion (about/of/on/upon/with) *conclude/decide/deduce/determine/infer/judge/reason/resolve/settle.* • Social Care and Health will reach an opinion about whether the child is disabled and will also assess whether the child has a need for services. *Social Care and Health will decide whether the child is dis-*

abled and will also assess whether the child has a need for services. • In order to reach an opinion that the individual is under the influence of a specific category of drugs, DREs utilize a 12 step, systematic and standardized process. *In order to conclude that the individual is under the influence of a specific category of drugs, DREs utilize a 12 step, systematic and standardized process.*

reach (a/the) resolution (about/of/on/upon/ with) *agree/conclude/decide/determine/resolve/ settle.* • It is expected that the parties will reach a resolution in one session. *It is expected that the parties will agree in one session.*

reach (a/the) settlement (about/of/on/upon/ with) *agree/conclude/decide/resolve/settle.* • One union source said that the Justice Department and the union leadership were not likely to reach an out-of-court settlement before the start of the racketeering trial. *One union source said that the Justice Department and the union leadership were not likely to settle out of court before the start of the racketeering trial.* • The traditional policy pursued all along by Pakistan has been that it would not recognize Israel or establish any contacts with other Jewish entities until the Arabs reach a settlement of the Middle East question. *The traditional policy pursued all along by Pakistan has been that it would not recognize Israel or establish any contacts with other Jewish entities until the Arabs settle the Middle East question.*

reach (an/the) understanding (about/of/on/ upon/with) *agree/compromise/concur/decide/ resolve/settle.*

re- again *re-.* • That film will make addicts want to reexperience taking crack again. *That film will make addicts want to reexperience taking crack.* • This week, Wright's amazing life is being revisited again, this time on television. *This week, Wright's amazing life is being revisited, this time on television.*

real/really delete. • We know the governor has really serious budget problems this year. *We know the governor has serious budget problems this year.*

(a/the) real fact *fact/truth.*

(the) reality of delete. • Patients facing an ileostomy, colostomy, or urostomy must come to terms with the reality of the disease. *Patients facing an ileostomy, colostomy, or urostomy must come to terms with the disease.*

real live delete. • This is a real live medical problem. *This is a medical problem.*

really (and) truly *actually/indeed/in fact/in faith/in reality/in truth/really/truly* delete. • They really truly did have a very unique product. *They truly did have a very unique product.*

(the) realm of delete. • Brainstorming has broadened its appeal to the business world and has found widespread acceptance in the realm of business meetings. *Brainstorming has broadened its appeal to the business world and has found widespread acceptance in business meetings.*

(after/for/in/over/within) (a) reasonable amount of time/length of time/period/period of time/span of time/time/while *by next week (tomorrow)/fast/in (within) a day (year)/ promptly/quickly/rapidly/shortly/soon/speedily/ swiftly* delete. • Unlike corporate sales, which can be tied up in a relatively reasonable period of time, government sales tend to be drawn out. *Unlike corporate sales, which can be tied up relatively quickly, government sales tend to be drawn out.*

reason as to why *reason (why).* • At last, we come to the reason as to why our generation is so duped into supporting things like redistribution of wealth. *At last, we come to the reason our generation is so duped into supporting things* *like redistribution of wealth.* • It was clear that the struggling Frogs wouldn't be the reason as to why. *It was clear that the struggling Frogs wouldn't be the reason.* • Wilson said the board never gave him a reason as to why they wouldn't renew. *Wilson said the board never gave him a reason they wouldn't renew.*

reason being is *reason is.* • There are a few reasons to add email forms to your website; the best reason being is so you can get information from your guests to you through email. *There are a few reasons to add email forms to your website; the best reason is so you can get information from your guests to you through email.* • The reason being is that most of the teachers are going to the war. *The reason is that most of the teachers are going to the war.*

(the) reason (why) . . . is because *because/reason is (that).* • The reason the business failed was because it was undercapitalized. *The business failed because it was undercapitalized.* • Another reason why the example fails as a good strategic goal is because it violates the rule of accountability. *Another reason the example fails as a good strategic goal is it violates the rule of accountability.* • The reason why statistics work is because for large numbers of molecules some events are overwhelmingly more likely than others. *Statistics work because for large numbers of molecules some events are overwhelmingly more likely than others.*

reason (why) . . . is due to (the fact that) *because of/due to/reason is (that).* • The reason the flooding is so bad this year is due to torrential rains and soil erosion. *The flooding is so bad this year because of torrential rains and soil erosion.* • Part of the reason why we've had a growing economy over the last 2½ years nationwide is due to the fact that we raised the minimum wage, which put more money in people's pockets and they went out and spent it. *Part of the reason we've had a growing economy over the last 2½ years nationwide is that we raised the*

minimum wage, which put more money in people's pockets and they went out and spent it.

reason (why) . . . is that *because.* • The reason we're so successful is that the projects we work with are good ones and we're good at working with community groups. *We're so successful because the projects we work with are good ones and we're good at working with community groups.*

reason why *reason.* • It's one of the reasons why we have so much misconduct, so much scandal, in government. *It's one of the reasons we have so much misconduct, so much scandal, in government.*

rebound back *rebound.* • How long do you think it will take for the stock to rebound back to its 52-week high? *How long do you think it will take for the stock to rebound to its 52-week high?*

recall back *recall.* • Please drop me a line if you would so I can help you recall back those memories at COM. *Please drop me a line if you would so I can help you recall those memories at COM.*

recede back *recede.* • When they flood, the velocity in the overbank water may be very low, and the floodwaters may be weeks in receding back into the channel. *When they flood, the velocity in the overbank water may be very low, and the floodwaters may be weeks in receding into the channel.*

receive back *receive.* • People express doubt that they will receive back as much in benefits as they paid in Social Security taxes. *People express doubt that they will receive as much in benefits as they paid in Social Security taxes.*

recite back *recite.* • You're not asking them to recite back what you said; you're asking them to tell you what they heard. *You're not asking them to recite what you said; you're asking them to tell you what they heard.*

recoil back *recoil.* • When the guard stops, the tube will recoil back to the guard for easy access, instead of the guard searching for the strap and pulling it in. *When the guard stops, the tube will recoil to the guard for easy access, instead of the guard searching for the strap and pulling it in.*

record-breaking (high) *record.* • The Cape is burdened with a record-breaking number of houses for sale. *The Cape is burdened with a record number of houses for sale.* • As record-breaking temperatures continue to assault the nation, people may find themselves snarling where they used to smile and being grouchy when they used to grin. *As record temperatures continue to assault the nation, people may find themselves snarling where they used to smile and being grouchy when they used to grin.*

record high *record.* • Young adults are returning home to live with their parents in record-high numbers. *Young adults are returning home to live with their parents in record numbers.*

record-setting *record.* • That should mean a blessed end to record-setting heat and a host of problems that arose from or probably interacted with it. *That should mean a blessed end to record heat and a host of problems that arose from or probably interacted with it.*

record size *record.* • It appears we've had a record-size turnout at the polls. *It appears we've had a record turnout at the polls.*

recover back *recover.* • How can I recover back my data? *How can I recover my data?*

rectify *correct/fix/improve.* • Why can't they rectify the conditions at Danvers State Hospital? *Why can't they improve the conditions at Danvers State Hospital?*

recur again (and again) *recur.* • The lapse has already been corrected within our systems to insure that the problem will not recur again. *The lapse has already been corrected within our systems to insure that the problem will not recur.*

reduce by/to half *halve.* • The inventor believes this may reduce by half the average doses needed for EPO. *The inventor believes this may halve the average doses needed for EPO.*

reduce down *reduce.* • Reduce the number of paid sick days from 20 down to some lower number. *Reduce the number of paid sick days from 20 to some lower number.* • We'd be happy to accept the number of concurrent users reduced down to 50 for the $500 per year price. *We'd be happy to accept the number of concurrent users reduced to 50 for the $500 per year price.*

refer back *refer.* • The reader may find it helpful to refer back to this diagram after we have completed our discussion. *The reader may find it helpful to refer to this diagram after we have completed our discussion.*

refer to as *call/name/term* delete. • Unconscious attempts to manage anxiety are referred to as defense mechanisms. *Unconscious attempts to manage anxiety are termed defense mechanisms.*

reflect back *reflect.* • Reflecting back on my years at BB&N, I tried to understand why neither the school nor the parents were willing to give this case the publicity it deserved. *Reflecting on my years at BB&N, I tried to understand why neither the school nor the parents were willing to give this case the publicity it deserved.* • Because the use of your news server reflects back on your organization, you also want to teach your users good netiquette when it comes to participating in newsgroups. *Because the use of your news server reflects on your organization, you also want to teach your users good netiquette when it comes to participating in newsgroups.*

regard/regarding *about/as for/as to/for/in/of/ on/over/to/toward/with.* • New Jersey has no law regarding traffic circles. *New Jersey has no law on traffic circles.*

regard as being *regard as.* • Cults usually have some literature that they regard as being holy, with which they back up their beliefs. *Cults usually have some literature that they regard as holy, with which they back up their beliefs.*

regardless of (what) *despite (what)/no matter what/whatever.* • Regardless of what women may accomplish one on one, the most effective agent for change is the company itself. *No matter what women may accomplish one on one, the most effective agent for change is the company itself.*

regardless of how *despite how/however/no matter how.* • All lines and lettering must be absolutely black regardless of how fine the lines may be. *All lines and lettering must be absolutely black despite how fine the lines may be.*

regardless of the fact that *although/but/even though/still/though/yet.* • Because the aquarium is a private enterprise—regardless of the fact that it is nonprofit—such a transfer is not supposed to take place. *Because the aquarium is a private enterprise—although it is nonprofit—such a transfer is not supposed to take place.*

regardless of when *despite when/no matter when/whenever.* • Both proposals would cover all capital assets regardless of when taxpayers bought them. *Both proposals would cover all capital assets despite when taxpayers bought them.*

regardless of where *despite where/no matter where/wherever.* • Visible soft hyphens appear on the screen and print out regardless of where they fall in the document. *Visible soft hyphens appear on the screen and print out wherever they fall in the document.*

regardless of whether . . . (or) *despite whether/ no matter whether/whether . . . or (not).* • Men's masculinity, looks, and concern about their appearance were rated the same regardless of whether lunch was a salad and coffee or a five-course extravaganza. *Men's masculinity, looks, and concern about their appearance were rated the same whether lunch was a salad and coffee or a five-course extravaganza.* • Regardless of whether the reason is internal or external, it has an important bearing on the market-presence alternatives investigated. *Whether the reason is internal or external, it has an important bearing on the market-presence alternatives investigated.*

regardless of which *despite which/no matter which/whichever.* • Regardless of which happens, you can change the result. *Whichever happens, you can change the result.*

regardless of who *despite who/no matter who/ whoever.* • Regardless of who we may be, we all have the right to economic opportunity. *Whoever we may be, we all have the right to economic opportunity.* • The country will survive, regardless of who is in the White House. *The country will survive, no matter who is in the White House.*

regardless of whom *despite whom/no matter whom/whomever.* • Regardless of whom these books are meant for, I think they should be designed and developed to look and feel more accessible. *Whomever these books are meant for, I think they should be designed and developed to look and feel more accessible.*

(the) region of *delete.* • The native of the region of Andalucia got to see her son for a moment and then never again. *The native of Andalucia got to see her son for a moment and then never again.* • As a result, Liverpool will be looking to make around the region of twenty million off of his sale. *As a result, Liverpool will be looking to make around twenty million off of his sale.*

regress back *regress.* • Over time, growth stocks tend to regress back to reality, while cheaper stocks tend to move higher on a relative basis. *Over time, growth stocks tend to regress to reality, while cheaper stocks tend to move higher on a relative basis.*

regular habit *habit.* • Let's make this a regular habit. *Let's make this a habit.*

regular -(al)ly *-(al)ly.* • We attend the regular monthly meeting of the BCS. *We attend the monthly meeting of the BCS.*

regular routine *routine.* • Hiring, training, and record-keeping are part of the regular routine for running any business. *Hiring, training, and record-keeping are part of the routine for running any business.*

reiterate *iterate/repeat.* • Baker also reiterated his insistence that Bush would not debate before September 22. *Baker also repeated his insistence that Bush would not debate before September 22.*

reiterate again (and again) *iterate/reiterate/repeat.* • I have stated in recent press releases, and reiterate again now, that our revenue guidance has increased as a result of these new distribution agreements. *I have stated in recent press releases, and reiterate now, that our revenue guidance has increased as a result of these new distribution agreements.*

relate (to) *say/tell.* • One executive related to us that in Chile he had almost single-handedly stopped a strike. *One executive told us that in Chile he had almost single-handedly stopped a strike.*

relate back *relate.* • This involves the activation of cognitive processes in your brain in which you think about the meaning of the words, weigh ideas, correlate new ideas with your experiences, and relate the ideas back to former material. *This involves the activation of cognitive* processes in your brain in which you think about the meaning of the words, weigh ideas, correlate new ideas with your experiences, and relate the ideas to former material.

-related delete. • This division provides telemarketing-related and other direct marketing services for clients in four areas. *This division provides telemarketing and other direct marketing services for clients in four areas.*

relate/relating to *about/as for/as to/concerning/for/in/of/on/over/regarding/to/toward/with.* • We may add to the basic rental price any taxes or other governmental assessments relating to the use or operation of the postage meter or scale. *We may add to the basic rental price any taxes or other governmental assessments on the use or operation of the postage meter or scale.*

relationship *bond/connection/link/relation/tie.* • The photograph had no relationship to any of the elements of the story. *The photograph had no relation to any of the elements of the story.*

relatively *-(i)er/less/more.* • Lawyer Dukakis repeatedly has expressed disdain for the merger and acquisition; oil man Bush seems to harbor relatively few such concerns. *Lawyer Dukakis repeatedly has expressed disdain for the merger and acquisition; oil man Bush seems to harbor fewer such concerns.*

relatively . . . as/when compared to/with *compared to/with/-(i)er than/less than/more than/than.* • Housing is relatively inexpensive and affordable when compared to Boston and other higher-priced nearby housing markets. *Housing is inexpensive and affordable compared to Boston and other higher-priced nearby housing markets.*

relatively . . . compared/contrasted to/with *compared to/with/contrasted to/with/-(i)er than/less than/more than/than.* • Shrinkage remains relatively low compared to mass retailing standards. *Shrinkage remains low compared to mass retailing standards.* • They tend to have a relatively high loss and PDL, and are relatively expensive compared to mechanical switches. *They tend to have a relatively high loss and PDL, and are more expensive than mechanical switches.* • In fact, Mathers and Bank still stay in close contact with other cast members, and their lives are relatively stable compared with those of other former child stars. *In fact, Mathers and Bank still stay in close contact with other cast members, and their lives are stable compared with those of other former child stars.* • Although the UK is relatively small when compared with the United States, its landscape and people are varied and dramatic. *Although the UK is smaller than the United States, its landscape and people are varied and dramatic.*

relatively -(i)er than/less than/more than *-(i)er than/less than/more than.* delete. • This country is in relatively better shape than other major industrialized nations. *This country is in better shape than other major industrialized nations.* • Its real estate portfolio grew relatively faster than anybody else's. *Its real estate portfolio grew faster than anybody else's.*

relatively . . . in comparison/in contrast to/with *compared to/with/contrasted to/with/-(i)er than/less than/more than/in comparison to/with/in contrast to/with.* • Solving the legal problems of partnerships is relatively simple in comparison to solving the problems of other types of ownership. *Solving the legal problems of partnerships is simple compared to solving the problems of other types of ownership.*

relatively . . . in relation to *compared to/with/contrasted to/with/-(i)er than/less than/more than/in relation to.* • The price or delivery time on a product may be relatively unimportant in relation to overall quality for your Asian customer. *The price or delivery time on a product*

may be unimportant in relation to overall quality for your Asian customer.

relatively . . . relative to *compared to/with/contrasted to/with/-(i)er than/less than/more than/relative to.* • These potential limitations for CO_2 excretion may be partially offset by the relatively high blood volume in these animals relative to other vertebrates. *These potential limitations for CO_2 excretion may be partially offset by the high blood volume in these animals relative to other vertebrates.*

relative to *about/concerning/for/on/regarding.* • We want to talk to him relative to his wife's death. *We want to talk to him about his wife's death.*

relative to *against/alongside/beside/compared to/with/-(i)er than/less/less than/more/more than/next to/over/than/to/versus/vis-à-vis.* • Relative to other societies, Brazil and the United States place considerable emphasis on youth. *Brazil and the United States place considerably more emphasis on youth than do other societies.*

relevancy *relevance.* • Define the term *system*, and explain its relevancy to the study of mass communication. *Define the term* system, *and explain its relevance to the study of mass communication.*

relic of the past *relic.* • But for most people today, CPM is an all-but-forgotten relic of the past which is just a few years old. *But for most people today, CPM is an all-but-forgotten relic which is just a few years old.*

reluctancy *reluctance.* • The reluctancy is something a lot of veterans feel. *The reluctance is something a lot of veterans feel.* • However, there is a measure of reluctancy to share all of the horrifying details. *However, there is a measure of reluctance to share all of the horrifying details.*

remainder *remains/rest.* • No economic indicators are due for the remainder of the week. *No economic indicators are due for the rest of the week.*

remains to be seen *do not know/is not (now/yet) known/is uncertain/is unclear/is unknown/is unsure.* • It remains to be seen if he can sustain a housing partnership. *It's not yet known if he can sustain a housing partnership.*

remand back *remand.* • The case was decided and remanded back to the Court of Appeals which remanded it back to the District Court. *The case was decided and remanded to the Court of Appeals which remanded it to the District Court.*

remember again *remember.* • Remember again, ten dollars times thirty million is three hundred million dollars. *Remember, ten dollars times thirty million is three hundred million dollars.*

remember back *remember.* • One of the easiest ways to understand this operator is to remember back to elementary school mathematics. *One of the easiest ways to understand this operator is to remember elementary school mathematics.*

reminisce about the past *reminisce.* • NostalgiaStreet.com's mission is to provide a friendly place where people can reminisce about the past while enjoying today and preparing for tomorrow. *NostalgiaStreet.com's mission is to provide a friendly place where people can reminisce while enjoying today and preparing for tomorrow.*

remit back *remit.* • You are required to remit back to the plan any reimbursements made for ineligible expenses. *You are required to remit to the plan any reimbursements made for ineligible expenses.*

remittance *cash/fee/money/pay/payment/wage.*

remunerate *pay.*

remuneration *cash/fee/money/pay/payment/reward/wage.*

render *act/do/give/make.* • The biggest question remaining about the use of phenethanolamines is whether the drugs will contaminate meat and render it unsafe for human consumption. *The biggest question remaining about the use of phenethanolamines is whether the drugs will contaminate meat and make it unsafe for human consumption.*

render assistance to *aid/assist/help.* • I hereby pledge to render assistance to fellow jugglers. *I hereby pledge to assist fellow jugglers.* • If possible, render assistance to victims and attempt to limit further injury and property/equipment damage. *If possible, aid victims and attempt to limit further injury and property/equipment damage.*

reoccur *recur.* • This behavior tends to reoccur every year. *This behavior tends to recur every year.* • Let us examine briefly each of the specific areas in which test bias is a reoccurring concern. *Let us examine briefly each of the specific areas in which test bias is a recurring concern.* • Failure to remember is a reoccurring theme of consumer behavior. *Failure to remember is a recurring theme of consumer behavior.*

reoccurrence *recurrence.* • It is even more important that more be done to protect them from the occurrence and reoccurrence of that which precipitates these disorders: sexual abuse. *It is even more important that more be done to protect them from the occurrence and recurrence of that which precipitates these disorders: sexual abuse.*

repatriate back *repatriate.* • With talk of forced repatriation of Hmong back to Laos, where they feared for their lives, additional refugees were admitted into the United States. *With talk of forced repatriation of Hmong to Laos, where they feared for their lives, additional refugees were admitted into the United States.* • The reason that the black man is in the United States today is because his ancestors were not one of those who took the initiative and opportunity to repatriate back to Africa. *The reason that the black man is in the United States today is because his ancestors were not one of those who took the initiative and opportunity to repatriate to Africa.*

repay back *repay.* • How can they claim they won when their client has to repay back the money plus interest? *How can they claim they won when their client has to repay the money plus interest?*

repeat again (and again) *repeat.* • All of this is based on predictable behaviors that are repeated again and again in rather exact ways. *All of this is based on predictable behaviors that are repeated in rather exact ways.*

repeat back *repeat.* • Repeat back the answers you hear so you can make sure you understand them. *Repeat the answers you hear so you can make sure you understand them.* • These are very intelligent people, and they are being bombarded with monotonous detail that a parrot could repeat back after a few sessions with it owner. *These are very intelligent people, and they are being bombarded with monotonous detail that a parrot could repeat after a few sessions with it owner.*

repeat occurrence *recurrence.* • What should he do so as not to have a repeat occurrence of this? *What should he do so as not to have a recurrence of this?*

repeat over (and over) *repeat.* • A loop is a sequence of commands, the last of which refers the program back to the first so that the commands repeat over and over until stopped. *A loop is a sequence of commands, the last of which refers the program back to the first so that the commands repeat until stopped.*

reply back *reply.* • I sent her a letter and then waited two weeks for a reply back. *I sent her a letter and then waited two weeks for a reply.*

report back *report.* • The Insurance Division will report back to the high court within 30 days on whether to rehabilitate them in some ways or declare them insolvent. *The Insurance Division will report to the high court within 30 days on whether to rehabilitate them in some ways or declare them insolvent.* • Most Cobol programs will validate the end user's input and report back any invalid input to the end user. *Most Cobol programs will validate the end user's input and report any invalid input to the end user.*

represents *is.* • These numbers represent the washer's inside diameter, outside diameter, and thickness. *These numbers are the washer's inside diameter, outside diameter, and thickness.* • We believe that our offer represents a fair price and is in the best interest of Pennwalt's shareholders. *We believe that our offer is a fair price and is in the best interest of Pennwalt's shareholders.*

require *need.*

requirement *need.*

requisite *need.*

reside *dwell/live.* • I am now residing in New York City. *I am now living in New York City.*

residence *home/house.*

residual trace *trace.* • She is still beautiful despite residual traces of three massive strokes suffered when she was three-months pregnant. *She is still beautiful despite traces of three massive strokes suffered when she was three-months pregnant.*

resiliency *resilience.* • He has demonstrated extraordinary resiliency. *He has demonstrated extraordinary resilience.*

respective/respectively delete. • Microsoft hereby limits the duration of any implied warranty(ies) on the disk or such hardware to the respective periods stated above. *Microsoft hereby limits the duration of any implied warranty(ies) on the disk or such hardware to the periods stated above.*

respond back *respond.* • I was disappointed the governor did not respond back to me personally. *I was disappointed the governor did not respond to me personally.*

respond in the affirmative *agree/say yes.* • We hope he will respond in the affirmative. *We hope he will say yes.*

respond in the negative *decline/disagree/say no.* • You will be asked if you want to proceed, and if you respond in the negative, the submission is aborted and the previous submission remains unaltered. *You will be asked if you want to proceed, and if you say no, the submission is aborted and the previous submission remains unaltered.* • Members who respond in the negative will not be considered for summer employment but will maintain their relative position on the rotation list. *Members who decline will not be considered for summer employment but will maintain their relative position on the rotation list.*

restore back *restore.* • If something happens to the files on the disk that you back up, you can use the backup copies to restore files back onto it. *If something happens to the files on the disk that you back up, you can use the backup copies to restore files onto it.* • She was optimistic her loving, green thumb could restore the foliage back to health. *She was optimistic her loving, green thumb could restore the foliage to health.*

rest up *rest.* • So, along those lines, the idea for the starters would be to rest up and get ready for the regular season. *So, along those lines, the idea for the starters would be to rest and get ready for the regular season.*

resultant *(n) effect/result.*

resultant effect *effect/result.* • Concern exists over the antiandrogenic activity of cimetidine and its resultant effect on feminization of male rats. *Concern exists over the antiandrogenic activity of cimetidine and its effect on feminization of male rats.*

(a/the) result of the fact that *because.* • Trepidation from Colts fans in the two weeks leading up to Super Bowl XLIV will be felt as a result of the fact that this run to the championship has come too easy. *Trepidation from Colts fans in the two weeks leading up to Super Bowl XLIV will be felt because this run to the championship has come too easy.* • The risk that bird flu will spread is also much reduced as a result of the fact that poultry production in Finland chiefly takes place under cover. *The risk that bird flu will spread is also much reduced because poultry production in Finland chiefly takes place under cover.* • PLN has been mired in red ink for years, mostly as a result of the fact that it has to supply electricity at below cost. *PLN has been mired in red ink for years, mostly because it has to supply electricity at below cost.*

resume again *resume.* • Perhaps the most positive outcome was that the talks were believed likely to resume again in late August or September. *Perhaps the most positive outcome was that the talks were believed likely to resume in late August or September.*

retain . . . position as *remain.* • I also will retain my position as the Secretary of Jones Family Farm, Inc. *I also will remain the Secretary of Jones Family Farm, Inc.*

retreat back *retreat.* • Having conquered consumer electronics, the Japanese firms are attacking in industrial electronics, and the American firms are once again in the process of retreating back to defense electronics to get those higher returns on investment. *Having conquered consumer electronics, the Japanese firms are attacking in industrial electronics, and the American firms are once again in the process of retreating to defense electronics to get those higher returns on investment.* • So he retreated back to his cisterns, there to sit for some days, drinking the bittersweet waters of sanity. *So he retreated to his cisterns, there to sit for some days, drinking the bittersweet waters of sanity.*

return back *return.* • In the 1980s, we're returning back to the cultural norm of marriage and family. *In the 1980s, we're returning to the cultural norm of marriage and family.* • The handler performs its job and finally executes the IRETD instruction to return back to the calling application. *The handler performs its job and finally executes the IRETD instruction to return to the calling application.*

reuse again *reuse.* • If you want to create more than one graph for a model so that you can reuse them again, what must you do? *If you want to create more than one graph for a model so that you can reuse them, what must you do?*

reverse back *reverse.* • If you so much as breathe funny, the TICK reverses back to the downside. *If you so much as breathe funny, the TICK reverses to the downside.*

revert back *revert.* • Some companies that encounter operational problems during an advanced stage may revert back to a previous stage. *Some companies that encounter operational problems during an advanced stage may revert to a previous stage.* • This way, if you ever need to revert back to the original version, you can simply open the original document. *This way, if you ever need to revert to the original version, you can simply open the original document.*

rise up (higher) *rise.* • If the river keeps on rising up higher, I'd be concerned. *If the river keeps on rising, I'd be concerned.* • The balloons rise up high into the atmosphere, taking measurements throughout. *The balloons rise into the atmosphere, taking measurements throughout.*

(the) role of delete. • The role of research and development is crucial to the future of a nation's economic growth and to the future of an industry and an individual business. *Research and development is crucial to the future of a nation's economic growth and to the future of an industry and an individual business.*

ROM memory *ROM.*

root cause *cause/reason/root/source.* • White-collar crimes, not poor economic conditions or deregulation, are the root cause of the S&L crisis. *White-collar crimes, not poor economic conditions or deregulation, are the root of the S&L crisis.*

rough sketch *sketch.* • A rough sketch is made to indicate the type of illustration required and the method of reproduction to be used. *A sketch is made to indicate the type of illustration required and the method of reproduction to be used.*

routine procedure *routine.* • There is a routine procedure that we follow. *There is a routine that we follow.*

rules and regulations *regulations/rules.* • Rules and regulations regarding the use of the library have been posted throughout the building. *Rules regarding the use of the library have been posted throughout the building.*

run of the mill *average/common/everyday/mediocre/ordinary/typical/usual.*

S

sad to relate/say *sadly.* • Sad to relate, some bicyclists have become a menace to pedestrian and motor vehicle traffic. *Sadly, some bicyclists have become a menace to pedestrian and motor vehicle traffic.*

safe haven *haven.*

(the) same (thing) as *equal to/like.* • Asserting that the deficit numbers "have no clothes" is not the same thing as saying that all is fine in the nation's economic affairs. *Asserting that the deficit numbers "have no clothes" is not like saying that all is fine in the nation's economic affairs.*

(the) same exact *just (the)/the exact/the same.* • These are high-grade municipal bonds, the same exact ones that the banks buy. *These are high-grade municipal bonds, the same ones that the banks buy.*

(the) same thing *as much/the same.* • Looking back, I find I did the same thing. *Looking back, I find I did the same.* • Other rivals have discovered the same thing. *Other rivals have discovered as much.*

(the) same way *as/like.* • Normally when you make a printout, it looks the same way it does when displayed on the screen. *Normally when you make a printout, it looks as it does when displayed on the screen.*

satirical *satiric.* • My neighbor often makes satirical remarks about the fanaticism with which people mow and rake their lawns. *My neighbor often makes satiric remarks about the fanaticism with which people mow and rake their lawns.*

save and except *except/save.* • I confirm that I have not engaged in Outside Professional Activities that use university resources save and except as set out on page 2 of this report. *I confirm that I have not engaged in Outside Professional Activities that use university resources except as set out on page 2 of this report.*

say, for example/for instance *for example/for instance/say.* • Say, for example, you use a 12 percent home equity loan to finance $10,000 of an automobile purchase. *Say you use a 12 percent home equity loan to finance $10,000 of an automobile purchase.*

scatter in all/every direction(s) *scatter.* • Do people scatter in all directions when they see you coming? *Do people scatter when they see you coming?*

(the) scope of *delete.* • The scope of the loss of control over one's body can only be understood through a personal experience. *The loss of control over one's body can only be understood through a personal experience.*

(a/the) score of *delete.* • Sweden is on top by a score of 6 to 1. *Sweden is on top by 6 to 1.*

scream and yell *scream/yell.*

seasoned veteran *veteran.*

secondarily *second.* • Secondarily, we serve the community beyond the Air Force Academy through a variety of programs. *Second, we serve the community beyond the Air Force Academy through a variety of programs.*

secondly *second.* • First, be correct in your vocabulary or word choices; secondly, use standard grammar in your speeches. *First, be correct in your vocabulary or word choices; second, use standard grammar in your speeches.*

second of all *second.*

seeing (as/as how/that) *because/considering/for/given/in that/since.* • Seeing as how I don't have any stamps, I'm going to deliver this myself. *Since I don't have any stamps, I'm going to deliver this myself.* • Seeing that I am feeling better about things than I was last week, I will answer the phone if you call. *Since I am feeling better about things than I was last week, I will answer the phone if you call.* • Perhaps this comes as no surprise seeing as how *Playboy* is the bellwether for an industry that sells itself. *Perhaps this comes as no surprise given that* Playboy *is the bellwether for an industry that sells itself.* • Although the book struck me as being somewhat juvenile, this shortcoming was perfectly forgivable, seeing as how the book was written when the author was only twelve years old. *Although the book struck me as being somewhat juvenile, this shortcoming was perfectly forgivable, since the book was written when the author was only twelve years old.*

seek out *seek.* • In most cases, we actively seek out foreign investment. *In most cases, we actively seek foreign investment.*

seesaw back and forth/up and down *seesaw.* • The Hang Seng index seesawed back and forth last week as student demonstrations fueled speculation. *The Hang Seng index seesawed last week as student demonstrations fueled speculation.*

select out *choose/pick out/select.* • The other approach, selecting out for doctors' treatment those at particularly high risk, is already well established, but it has limitations. *The other approach, selecting for doctors' treatment those at particularly high risk, is already well established, but it has limitations.*

(my)self *(I/me).* • Richard and myself are going to lunch. *Richard and I are going to lunch.* • Very large people like yourself can eat tiny amounts of food and not lose an ounce. *Very large people like you can eat tiny amounts of food and not lose an ounce.* • Let's hope someone comes along, like myself, to take his place. *Let's hope*

someone comes along, like me, to take his place. • We feel Mr. Roedler's comments do an injustice to collectors like ourselves who currently pay $1,500 to $2,000 for radios of this type. *We feel Mr. Roedler's comments do an injustice to collectors like us who currently pay $1,500 to $2,000 for radios of this type.* • Neither the mayor nor myself desires to comment on the status of the matter. *Neither the mayor nor I desire to comment on the status of the matter.*

selfsame *same.*

seminal fluid *semen.* • He provided a DNA sample for investigators to compare to seminal fluid found on her clothing. *He provided a DNA sample for investigators to compare to semen found on her clothing.* • The prostate is a walnut-shaped gland that helps make and store seminal fluid. *The prostate is a walnut-shaped gland that helps make and store semen.*

(a) sense of *delete.* • Our sense of foreboding grew as the afternoon wore on. *Our foreboding grew as the afternoon wore on.* • I felt a sense of helplessness when he beat me. *I felt helpless when he beat me.*

(five/many/several) separate *(five/many/several)/separate.* • The report cites 171 separate studies, most of them conducted during the past decade, as references. *The report cites 171 studies, most of them conducted during the past decade, as references.*

separate and apart *apart/separate.* • We agreed that these issues ought to be separate and apart from the treaty. *We agreed that these issues ought to be separate from the treaty.*

separate and autonomous *autonomous/separate.* • As separate and autonomous organizations, we are committed to "bridging education and the world of work" and agree to support and cooperate with each other. *As autonomous organizations, we are committed to "bridging* *education and the world of work" and agree to support and cooperate with each other.*

separate and discrete *discrete/separate.* • We found that 58 percent of respondent worksites had a separate and discrete unit that supports end-user computing. *We found that 58 percent of respondent worksites had a discrete unit that supports end-user computing.*

separate and distinct *distinct/separate.* • Each of us has four separate and distinct vocabularies: a written, a spoken, a heard, and a visual vocabulary. *Each of us has four distinct vocabularies: a written, a spoken, a heard, and a visual vocabulary.* • The creature, though separate and distinct, and having its own jurisdiction, cannot arise and consume its creator. *The creature, though separate, and having its own jurisdiction, cannot arise and consume its creator.*

separate and independent *independent/separate.* • Uncoupling is complete when the partners have defined themselves and are defined by others as separate and independent of each other. *Uncoupling is complete when the partners have defined themselves and are defined by others as independent of each other.*

separate and individual *individual/separate.* • A Covered Person will be fully insured for benefits under the Policy while taking an airline trip only when the fare has been charged separately and individually to the Basic or Additional Cardmember's enrolled account. *A Covered Person will be fully insured for benefits under the Policy while taking an airline trip only when the fare has been charged separately to the Basic or Additional Cardmember's enrolled account.*

separate apart *separate.* • Within each tetrad, the sister chromosomes begin to separate apart. *Within each tetrad, the sister chromosomes begin to separate.* • From Egypt to China to Australia to Alaska, cultures believed that each individual had not one, but two, souls which would per-manently separate apart at death unless steps were taken to prevent this division. *From Egypt to China to Australia to Alaska, cultures believed that each individual had not one, but two, souls which would permanently separate at death unless steps were taken to prevent this division.*

separate entity *entity/separate.* • The artificial separation of these three dimensions is confusing when they are seen as three separate entities. *The artificial separation of these three dimensions is confusing when they are seen as three entities.*

separate individual *individual/separate.* • The children were never seen and treated as separate individuals. *The children were never seen and treated as individuals.*

separate out *detach/disconnect/isolate/seclude/ segregate/separate.* • If length permits, we should separate out user input from other functions. *If length permits, we should separate user input from other functions.* • Find out as much as you can about the process used in industry to separate out crude oil. *Find out as much as you can about the process used in industry to isolate crude oil.* • Note that you will want to separate out test data from training data. *Note that you will want to separate test data from training data.* • These steps make it possible to separate out needed projects from unnecessary ones. *These steps make it possible to segregate needed projects from unnecessary ones.*

seriously addicted *addicted.* • I was never seriously addicted to heroin. *I was never addicted to heroin.*

serve up *serve.* • Can I serve you up some quiche? *Can I serve you some quiche?*

shaken up *shaken.*

share (a/the) common *share.* • Group action is possible in your meeting, even when everyone does not share a common understanding of the subject. *Group action is possible in your meeting, even when everyone does not share an understanding of the subject.* • Cattell and Galton shared a common interest in the measurement of human capacity. *Cattell and Galton shared an interest in the measurement of human capacity.*

share . . . in common/with *share.* • U.S. research on global change shares something in common with the legendary horseman who roamed the hills of Washington Irving's Sleepy Hollow: They both appear to lack heads. *U.S. research on global change shares something with the legendary horseman who roamed the hills of Washington Irving's Sleepy Hollow: They both appear to lack heads.* • Our research addresses issues related to corporate strategy, operations and general management, and we focus on identifying management initiatives, processes, tools and frameworks that will allow our clients to avoid reinventing the wheel in addressing problems they share in common with their peers. *Our research addresses issues related to corporate strategy, operations and general management, and we focus on identifying management initiatives, processes, tools and frameworks that will allow our clients to avoid reinventing the wheel in addressing problems they share with their peers.*

share together *share.* • If there is one commitment that defines him, it is the commitment that we share together. *If there is one commitment that defines him, it is the commitment that we share.* • Opa and I shared a bedroom together with adjoining twin beds. *Opa and I shared a bedroom with adjoining twin beds.*

short and sweet *brief/concise/pithy/short/succinct/terse.*

short and to the point *brief/concise/pithy/short/succinct/terse/to the point.*

should . . . then *should.* • Should the Department of Public Utilities concur that the blame

for these plant outages rests with Boston Edison, then the company's stockholders must absorb the costs. *Should the Department of Public Utilities concur that the blame for these plant outages rests with Boston Edison, the company's stockholders must absorb the costs.*

show (a/the) . . . (of/to) delete. • Figure 14.3 shows a comparison of dimensions in millimeters with those in inches. *Figure 14.3 compares dimensions in millimeters with those in inches.* • The respondents preferred to retain but not retrain obsolete older employees and showed a tendency to withhold promotions from older workers. *The respondents preferred to retain but not retrain obsolete older employees and tended to withhold promotions from older workers.*

shown at/in *at/in.* • Each of the sequences shown at the right is an arithmetic sequence. *Each of the sequences at the right is an arithmetic sequence.*

shrink down *shrink.* • First the leaves disappear; then the stems start to shrink down. *First the leaves disappear; then the stems start to shrink.* • Some Internet browsers will automatically shrink down pictures to fit your screen. *Some Internet browsers will automatically shrink pictures to fit your screen.*

shuttle back and forth between . . . and *shuttle between . . . and.* • He shuttles back and forth between his home in New Hampshire and his office in Washington. *He shuttles between his home in New Hampshire and his office in Washington.* • In 1982, Hans Toch described the largely ineffective practice of bus therapy, whereby disturbed inmates are shuttled back and forth between mental health centers and correctional facilities. *In 1982, Hans Toch described the largely ineffective practice of bus therapy, whereby disturbed inmates are shuttled between mental health centers and correctional facilities.*

sick and tired *annoyed/disgusted/sick/tired.*

side by side (with) *alongside/among/beside/ next to/with.*

significant/substantial *ample/big/grand/great/ heavy/huge/immense/large/many/most/much/ vast.* • The region began the decade with a significant surplus of power. *The region began the decade with a large surplus of power.*

(a/the) significant/substantial amount (of) *a good (great) deal (of)/a good (great) many (of)/ almost all (of)/considerable/many (of)/most (of)/ much (of)/nearly all (of)/vast.* • This difficulty is a major stumbling block, costing end users significant amounts of time and money. *This difficulty is a major stumbling block, costing end users much time and money.*

(a/the) significant/substantial degree (of) *a good (great) deal (of)/considerable/great/much (of)/vast.*

(a/the) significant/substantial element (of) *a good (great) deal (of)/a good (great) many (of)/ considerable/great/many (of)/much (of)/vast.*

(a/the) significant/substantial fraction (of) *a good (great) deal (of)/a good (great) many (of)/ almost all (of)/many (of)/most (of)/much (of)/ nearly all (of)/three-fourths (two-thirds) (of).* • A significant fraction of leading U.S. weapons production specialists met last weekend to discuss the proposal, with predictable results. *Six of ten leading U.S. weapons production specialists met last weekend to discuss the proposal, with predictable results.*

significant importance *consequence/importance/significance.* • Finally, and of significant importance, he was sensitive to our concerns for minimizing the disruption to our lives inherent to most renovation projects. *Finally, and of significance, he was sensitive to our concerns for minimizing the disruption to our lives inherent to most renovation projects.* • The recommendations included herein will respond

not only to those stated needs, but also to other significantly important requirements that emerged during the course of our proceedings. *The recommendations included herein will respond not only to those stated needs, but also to other significant requirements that emerged during the course of our proceedings.*

significantly/substantially *a good (great) deal/ amply/far/greatly/largely/mostly/much/vastly.* • Two of the 13 had slightly higher earnings; only three did substantially better. *Two of the 13 had slightly higher earnings; only three did far better.*

(a/the) significant/substantial majority (of) *a good (great) deal (of)/a good (great) many (of)/ almost all (of)/many (of)/most (of)/much (of)/ nearly all (of)/three-fourths (two-thirds) (of).* • A substantial majority think certain reforms would improve the present primary system. *Many think certain reforms would improve the present primary system.*

(a/the) significant/substantial minority (of) *almost half (of)/fewer than half (of)/(one) in (three) (of)/less than half (of)/nearly half (of)/ one-third (one-fifth) (of)/(20) percent (of).* • A significant minority of agents said that they would not sell the type of insurance our researchers requested in the amount they wanted to buy. *Eighteen of fifty agents said that they would not sell the type of insurance our researchers requested in the amount they wanted to buy.* • A new study indicates a significant minority of critical-care nurses are occasionally committing euthanasia. *A new study indicates one in six critical-care nurses are occasionally committing euthanasia.*

(a/the) significant/substantial number (of) *a good (great) many (of)/almost all (of)/countless/ dozens (of)/hundreds (of)/many (of)/millions (of)/most (of)/nearly all (of)/numerous/scores (of)/thousands (of).* • We did this because we received a substantial number of reports that the election was unfair. *We did this because we* *received hundreds of reports that the election was unfair.*

(a/the) significant/substantial part (of) *a good (great) deal (of)/a good (great) many (of)/almost all (of)/many (of)/most (of)/much (of)/nearly all (of)/three-fourths (two-thirds) (of).* • Businessland Inc. says mice represent a substantial part of its computer accessories sales. *Businessland Inc. says mice represent 8 percent of its computer accessories sales.*

(a/the) significant/substantial percentage (of) *a good (great) deal (of)/a good (great) many (of)/almost all (of)/many (of)/most (of)/much (of)/nearly all (of)/three-fourths (two-thirds) (of).* • The drug can cause serious kidney damage and other side effects, and a substantial percentage of patients cannot absorb it. *The drug can cause serious kidney damage and other side effects, and many patients cannot absorb it.*

(a/the) significant/substantial portion (of) *a good (great) deal (of)/a good (great) many (of)/almost all (of)/many (of)/most (of)/much (of)/nearly all (of)/three-fourths (two-thirds) (of).* • The company said that a significant portion of the cuts will be achieved through early retirement. *The company said that most of the cuts will be achieved through early retirement.*

(a/the) significant/substantial proportion (of) *a good (great) deal (of)/a good (great) many (of)/almost all (of)/many (of)/most (of)/much (of)/nearly all (of)/three-fourths (two-thirds) (of).* • West German and British firms also account for a significant proportion of U.S. patents. *West German and British firms also account for many U.S. patents.*

(a/the) significant/substantial quantity (of) *a good (great) deal (of)/a good (great) many (of)/almost all (of)/dozens (of)/hundreds (of)/many (of)/millions (of)/most (of)/nearly all (of)/scores (of)/thousands (of).*

simple (and) fundamental *fundamental/simple.* • We welcome the opportunity to present the following two descriptions of barriers and gateways to communication, in the thought that they may help to bring the problem down to earth and show what it means in terms of simple fundamentals. *We welcome the opportunity to present the following two descriptions of barriers and gateways to communication, in the thought that they may help to bring the problem down to earth and show what it means in terms of fundamentals.*

simply and solely *simply/solely.* • She was fired simply and solely on account of her sex. *She was fired solely on account of her sex.*

simultaneously *as one/at once/collectively/concurrently/jointly/together.* • A collaborative work group is several people working on the same document simultaneously. *A collaborative work group is several people working on the same document at once.*

simultaneously . . . at the same time *at the same time/simultaneously.* • We can be simultaneously hard like rock, firm, unmoving, and at the same time, soft and gentle, and flowing. *We can be hard like rock, firm, unmoving, and at the same time, soft and gentle, and flowing.* • All of these synchronous connections must be serviced by the program simultaneously, at the same time. *All of these synchronous connections must be serviced by the program simultaneously.*

simultaneously . . . while *while.* • A dissemination system must simultaneously develop the capability of people at several levels through staff development and ongoing support while it works to create a context in schools, districts, and states. *A dissemination system must develop the capability of people at several levels through staff development and ongoing support while it works to create a context in schools, districts, and states.*

simultaneous/simultaneously with *with.* • The selection of the media to be used for advertising campaigns needs to be done simultaneously with the development of message, theme, concepts, and copy. *The selection of the media to be used for advertising campaigns needs to be done with the development of message, theme, concepts, and copy.*

(ever) since that time *since/since then.* • Since that time, a lot has changed in my life. *A lot has since changed in my life.*

(ever) since then *since.* • Since then several states have passed laws against the misuse of sickle cell screening. *Several states have since passed laws against the misuse of sickle cell screening.*

since . . . then *since.* • Since the objective of unattended operation is quality, then the primary benefit is consistent, high-quality service. *Since the objective of unattended operation is quality, the primary benefit is consistent, high-quality service.* • Since each telephone call is sampled 8,000 times each second, then each time slot must contain a packet of 8 samples, each 8 bits in length. *Since each telephone call is sampled 8,000 times each second, each time slot must contain a packet of 8 samples, each 8 bits in length.*

(the) single best/biggest/fastest/greatest/largest/most/slowest *best/biggest/fastest/greatest/largest/most/slowest.* • Our single biggest concern is the capacity issue. *Our biggest concern is the capacity issue.* • The BSA does give its prestigious annual Harleston Parker Award for the single best new building in the Boston area. *The BSA does give its prestigious annual Harleston Parker Award for the best new building in the Boston area.* • The single most important issue for women is equal pay for equal work. *The most important issue for women is equal pay for equal work.* • It's probably the single slowest

day I've seen in four years. *It's probably the slowest day I've seen in four years.*

(a) single one *a single/one.* • Not a single one of the dire accusations or predictions made in that article has come true. *Not one of the dire accusations or predictions made in that article has come true.*

(a) single solitary (one) *a single/one.*

sink down *sink.*

(a/the) -sion/-tion of/that/to *-ing.* • Determination of consumer's needs requires greater attention. *Determining consumer's needs requires greater attention.* • Their subordinates are nonmanagement workers—the group on which management depends for the execution of their plans. *Their subordinates are nonmanagement workers—the group on which management depends for executing their plans.* • Self-improvement and career planning both begin with an identification of your skills. *Self-improvement and career planning both begin with identifying your skills.* • I would suggest that, given the importance of building confidence in these tradesmen-turned-entrepreneurs to the proposal, inclusion of more background on them would be a good idea. *I would suggest that, given the importance of building confidence in these tradesmen-turned-entrepreneurs to the proposal, including more background on them would be a good idea.*

situated *delete.* • Many of the hospital incinerators are situated in heavily populated areas. *Many of the hospital incinerators are in heavily populated areas.* • Dubai is situated in which country? *Dubai is in which country?*

(in) (a/the) . . . situation *delete.* • We are in a crisis situation. *We are in a crisis.* • If he doesn't do something, it could be an embarrassing situation for him. *If he doesn't do something, it* *could be embarrassing for him.* • Fortunately for almost all involved in restaurant and kitchen work, these shows do not portray what happens in a normal situation. *Fortunately for almost all involved in restaurant and kitchen work, these shows do not portray what normally happens.* • Authorities in Greenbrier County defused a potentially tragic situation last Monday evening. *Authorities in Greenbrier County defused a potential tragedy last Monday evening.*

(the) situation/with *right/so/the case/true* delete. • This is often the situation with inexperienced managers, but it can be remedied with management training. *This is often so with inexperienced managers, but it can be remedied with management training.*

skill set *skills.* • They get in each other's way most of the time, as they have the same skill set. *They get in each other's way most of the time, as they have the same skills.* • One of things you need to start thinking about is acquiring the skill set to manage those relationships. *One of things you need to start thinking about is acquiring the skills to manage those relationships.*

skirt around *skirt.*

slight trace *trace.*

(a/the) small/tiny amount/degree/part/percentage/portion/proportion/quantity (of) *a couple (of)/(a) few (of)/a handful (of)/fewer than half (of)/hardly any (of)/less than half (of)/not many (of)/ (of)/scarcely any (of).* • Only a small percentage of the state's bridges will be repaired. *Only one-fourth of the state's bridges will be repaired.*

(a/the) smaller/tinier amount/degree/part/percentage/portion/proportion/quantity (of) *less.* • Americans are spending a smaller percentage of their incomes on food than ever before. *Americans are spending less of their incomes on food than ever before.* • The result

will likely be more work done in a smaller amount of time. *The result will likely be more work done in less time.*

(a/the) smaller/tinier number (of) *fewer.* • The instructor would back off, slow down, and give students a chance to follow and absorb the development of a smaller number of scientific ideas. *The instructor would back off, slow down, and give students a chance to follow and absorb the development of fewer scientific ideas.*

(a/the) small/tiny fraction (of) *a couple (of)/(a) few (of)/a handful (of)/fewer than half (of)/hardly any (of)/less than half (of)/not many (of)/ (of)/scarcely any (of).* • His deputy sold only a small fraction of his stock, not one-third as reported. *His deputy sold only one-twelfth of his stock, not one-third as reported.*

(a/the) small/tiny minority (of) *a couple (of)/(a) few (of)/a handful (of)/fewer than half (of)/hardly any (of)/less than half (of)/not many (of)/ (of)/scarcely any (of).* • A small minority may be troubled or are troublemakers. *A few may be troubled or are troublemakers.*

(a/the) small/tiny number (of) *a couple/a few/hardly any/not many//scarcely any.* • Many observers believe that by the turn of the century only a small number of giant financial supermarkets will cover the range of financial services. *Many observers believe that by the turn of the century only eight giant financial supermarkets will cover the range of financial services.* • A relatively small number of the examples in this chapter have a direct engineering application. *Few of the examples in this chapter have a direct engineering application.*

small/tiny particle *particle.* • With the high speeds and small spaces involved, even a small particle can cause the readwrite head to crash. *With the high speeds and small spaces involved, even a particle can cause the readwrite head to crash.*

small/tiny peccadillo *peccadillo.* • But this is only a small peccadillo and we will continue to commit it unabashed. *But this is only a peccadillo and we will continue to commit it unabashed.*

small-size(d) *small.*

(feels) smooth/rough to the touch *(feels) smooth/rough.* • Rattan furniture is durable, smooth to the touch, and made from plants that grow quickly and replenish easily. *Rattan furniture is durable, smooth, and made from plants that grow quickly and replenish easily.* • A quality tie will feel smooth to the touch and will consist of three, not two, pieces sewn together. *A quality tie will feel smooth and will consist of three, not two, pieces sewn together.* • Warts are usually skin colored and feel rough to the touch. *Warts are usually skin colored and feel rough.*

so as to *to.* • Salespeople often make their estimates low so as to keep their sales quotas down and make them easier to attain. *Salespeople often make their estimates low to keep their sales quotas down and make them easier to attain.*

sociological *sociologic.*

so consequently *consequently/hence/so/then/therefore/thus.*

solicitate *solicit.* • Town officials say signs that solicitate negatively impact the quality of life in Little Ferry. *Town officials say signs that solicit negatively impact the quality of life in Little Ferry.* • In order to help young professionals to make an informed career decision I would like to solicitate information from you about postgraduate training. *In order to help young professionals to make an informed career decision I would like to solicit information from you about postgraduate training.*

some but not all *a few/several/some.* • Some studies, but not all, found cancerous tumors in rats and mice fed dye chemicals. *Some studies found cancerous tumors in rats and mice fed dye chemicals.*

some day/time in the future *at length/eventually/in due time/in the end/in time/later/one day/over the months (years)/over time/someday/sometime/ultimately/with time/yet.* • Some time in the future, the problems could precipitate a crisis—a run on the dollar, a decline in living standards—the price the United States must pay for its profligacy. *Eventually, the problems could precipitate a crisis—a run on the dollar, a decline in living standards—the price the United States must pay for its profligacy.*

somehow or other *in some way/somehow/someway(s).* • Somehow or other, people get used to a system, even if it takes a little time. *Somehow, people get used to a system, even if it takes a little time.*

someplace/somewhere else *elsewhere.* • The meeting should run no more than two or three hours and provide obvious benefits for being there instead of somewhere else. *The meeting should run no more than two or three hours and provide obvious benefits for being there instead of elsewhere.* • I will economize somewhere else. *I will economize elsewhere.*

something like *or so/some.* • Pensions and Social Security may provide, on average, something like 60 percent of the household's prior working income. *Pensions and Social Security may provide, on average, some 60 percent of the household's prior working income.*

somewhere along the line/the way *at some point/at some time.* • Somewhere along the way, people got the idea that biotechnology is a magic solution to the food problem. *At some point, people got the idea that biotechnology is a magic solution to the food problem.*

somewhere around/round *or so/some.*

sooner or later *eventually/ultimately/yet.*

sort of delete. • I'm sort of curious to find out what your thoughts are. *I'm curious to find out what your thoughts are.*

so therefore *hence/so/then/therefore/thus.*

(the) space of delete. • Within the space of a few minutes, he was dead. *Within a few minutes, he was dead.*

speciality *specialty.*

(a/the) spectrum of *assorted/countless/different/diverse/extensive/many/numerous/scores of/sundry/varied/various/varying* delete.

springtime *spring.*

(a/the) stage of delete. • Other products take a long time to gain acceptance and may never reach a stage of widespread adoption. *Other products take a long time to gain acceptance and may never reach widespread adoption.*

stall for time *stall.*

stand in (marked/sharp) contrast to *clash with/conflict with/contest/contradict/contrast with/differ from/disagree with/dispute/oppose.* • That view stands in sharp contrast to those expressed by legislators and state business leaders. *That view sharply differs from those expressed by legislators and state business leaders.*

stand in need of *need/require.* • The country stands in need of a strong gesture in support of both science and education. *The country needs a strong gesture in support of both science and education.*

stand in opposition to *conflict with/contest/disagree with/disapprove of/dispute/object to/oppose/protest/resist.*

stand in support of *back/endorse/favor/prefer/support.* • With only 8 of the 1,176 voting delegates refusing to stand in support of the election, it appears Lee may have won the mandate he has been seeking. *With only 8 of the 1,176 voting delegates refusing to support the election, it appears Lee may have won the mandate he has been seeking.*

stand in the way of *block/frustrate/hinder/impede/interfere with/obstruct/prevent/thwart.* • The public health threat posed by AIDS is so great that we must find ways to overcome social and cultural taboos that stand in the way of improved AIDS prevention. *The public health threat posed by AIDS is so great that we must find ways to overcome social and cultural taboos that thwart improved AIDS prevention.*

start off/out *start.* • Lotus 1-2-3 assumes that you would prefer to start off by typing information into the worksheet. *Lotus 1-2-3 assumes that you would prefer to start by typing information into the worksheet.* • She started off by showing a hilarious example of how her parents wrapped her Christmas gifts when she was a child. *She started by showing a hilarious example of how her parents wrapped her Christmas gifts when she was a child.*

starve to death *starve.* • A suburban Chicago woman who let her 18-month-old son starve to death in 2001 today received a 45-year prison sentence. *A suburban Chicago woman who let her 18-month-old son starve in 2001 today received a 45-year prison sentence.*

(a/the) . . . state of delete. • All cultural dimensions of a society and individuals are in a constant state of flux. *All cultural dimensions of a society and individuals are in constant flux.* • Although still in its infancy, and in a state of transition, the ASP market has been hopping for the past two years. *Although still in its* *infancy, and in transition, the ASP market has been hopping for the past two years.*

(the) state of delete. • The state of Massachusetts is considering a similar law. *Massachusetts is considering a similar law.*

(the) state of (the . . . state) *the* delete. • Consumers were more confident about the state of the economy in December than during the same month last year. *Consumers were more confident about the economy in December than during the same month last year.* • Many priests feel celibacy is no greater than the married state. *Many priests feel celibacy is no greater than marriage.*

stereotypical *stereotypic.* • These theorists believe women have been taught and conditioned in stereotypical role behavior that predisposes them to the development of agoraphobia. *These theorists believe women have been taught and conditioned in stereotypic role behavior that predisposes them to the development of agoraphobia.*

sticktoitiveness *determination/perseverance/ persistence/resolve/tenacity.* • Loyalty, empathy, diligence, and sticktoitiveness are highly regarded, whether in a co-worker or a friend. *Loyalty, empathy, diligence, and resolve are highly regarded, whether in a co-worker or a friend.*

still and all *even so/still/yet.*

still continue/endure/last/persevere/persist/ prevail/remain/survive *continue/endure/last/ persevere/persist/prevail/remain/survive/still.* • The department has set up an internal review process to deal with some of these cases, but problems still persist. *The department has set up an internal review process to deal with some of these cases, but problems persist.* • Unfortunately, that attitude still prevails today. *Unfortunately, that attitude prevails today.*

still in existence *current/extant/surviving.*

still yet *still/yet.* • We came across some of the containment buoys that are still yet to be deployed. *We came across some of the containment buoys that are still to be deployed.* • Essentially, the full pedagogical potential for mobile learning had still yet to be explored, the study found. *Essentially, the full pedagogical potential for mobile learning had yet to be explored, the study found.*

stoical *stoic.*

strange to relate/say *oddly/strangely.* • Strange to say, that interest does not seem to be more than a few hundred years old. *Strangely, that interest does not seem to be more than a few hundred years old.*

strangle to death *strangle.* • The ex-wife of South Africa's last apartheid president was stabbed and strangled to death in her luxury beachfront flat. *The ex-wife of South Africa's last apartheid president was stabbed and strangled in her luxury beachfront flat.*

strategical *strategic.* • Read the manual and the README file which contain essential strategical and tactical notes you should easily try. *Read the manual and the README file which contain essential strategic and tactical notes you should easily try.* • In some cases, you will only need to expand your outpost to gain strategical advantage. *In some cases, you will only need to expand your outpost to gain strategic advantage.*

stressed out *stressed.* • Parents get stressed out when they feel as though these demands never stop. *Parents get stressed when they feel as though these demands never stop.* • A lot of people are going to be stressed out and concerned. *A lot of people are going to be stressed and concerned.* • The military advises stressed-out soldiers to get help quickly, but there's a fear of being ostracized. *The military advises stressed soldiers to get help quickly, but there's a fear of being ostracized.*

strong point/suit *forte.*

study up *study.*

subject/topic area/field/matter *area/field/subject/theme/topic.* • Each new title is arranged by subject area. *Each new title is arranged by subject.*

subsequently *after/afterward/later/since (then)/then.* • He resigned his positions in 1963 and was subsequently jailed. *He resigned his positions in 1963 and was later jailed.* • I have subsequently learned the manner in which Mr. Satoh was chosen for the position. *I have since learned the manner in which Mr. Satoh was chosen for the position.*

subsequent to (that/this) *after/afterward/later/since (then)/then.* • Subsequent to that, I had surgery to remove half of my stomach. *Afterward, I had surgery to remove half of my stomach.*

subsequent to the time (of/that/when) *after/following.* • The stock can be transferred any time subsequent to the time that a person actually receives it. *The stock can be transferred any time after a person actually receives it.*

substantiality *substance.* • Jackson has exhibited a remarkable degree of substantiality and common sense. *Jackson has exhibited a remarkable degree of substance and common sense.*

substantiate *back up/confirm/prove/support/verify.* • Recent studies clearly substantiate the health and economic advantage of car safety seat belts. *Recent studies clearly confirm the health and economic advantage of car safety seat belts.*

substantive *ample/big/grand/great/heavy/huge/immense/large/many/most/much/vast.* • The recent improvement in the economic well-being of most nations occurred without substantive change in the physical bulk or weight of gross national product. *The recent improvement in the economic well-being of most nations occurred without much change in the physical bulk or weight of gross national product.*

substitute out *substitute.* • You can substitute out all the butter for avocado. *You can substitute all the butter for avocado.* • I'm hoping we can substitute out the biased language for unbiased language. *I'm hoping we can substitute the biased language for unbiased language.*

succumb to (the) illness/injuries *die.* • Shortly after Harold's return, his father succumbed to the illness. *Shortly after Harold's return, his father died.*

such as . . . and others/and so forth/and so on/and such/and the like/et al./etc./or whatever *and others/and so forth/and so on/and such/and the like/et al./etc./or/like/such as.* • In addition to individuals, you may select a topic that informs your audience about groups of people such as skinheads, the Mafia, Aborigines, Motown musicians, and others. *In addition to individuals, you may select a topic that informs your audience about groups of people such as skinheads, the Mafia, Aborigines, and Motown musicians.* • You can explore the results of various approaches such as gross margin, markup over cost, and so on. *You can explore the results of various approaches such as gross margin and markup over cost.* • Weevils are very destructive pests which can decimate stored whole grain products such as corn, wheat, barley, rice, etc. *Weevils are very destructive pests which can decimate stored whole grain products such as corn, wheat, barley, rice.*

such as . . . for example/for instance *as/for example/for instance/like/such as.* • One of the book's main themes is the "fact" that women were responsible for all the important contributions to the advancement of civilization (such as the development of agriculture, for instance), often despite the arrogance and stupidity of men. *One of the book's main themes is the "fact" that women were responsible for all the important contributions to the advancement of civilization (such as the development of agriculture), often despite the arrogance and stupidity of men.* • If a substance is not on our chart (such as vanadium, for example), it's not yet considered essential by the National Academy of Sciences. *If a substance is not on our chart (vanadium, for example), it's not yet considered essential by the National Academy of Sciences.* • They also don't support other advanced elements of FrontPage Web sites, such as input forms, for example. *They also don't support other advanced elements of FrontPage Web sites, such as input forms.*

such as (your)self *like (you).* • It's very rare that we have an opportunity to talk to someone such as yourself. *It's very rare that we have an opportunity to talk to someone like you.*

such is the case *so it is.* • Such is the case with an individual who is considered a high potential in a semiconductor firm. *So it is with an individual who is considered a high potential in a semiconductor firm.*

suddenly and without warning *suddenly/without warning.* • Survivors said the pier in Butterworth, 180 miles northwest of Kuala Lumpur, collapsed suddenly and without warning yesterday. *Survivors said the pier in Butterworth, 180 miles northwest of Kuala Lumpur, collapsed suddenly yesterday.* • Most workers seldom think about the financial consequences of long-term disability and that the disability can occur suddenly and without warning. *Most workers seldom think about the financial consequences of long-term disability and that the disability can occur without warning.*

sufficient/sufficiently *due/enough.* • Bright ideas alone are not sufficient. *Bright ideas alone*

are not enough. • Since responsibility is assigned not to individuals but to the group, members may not devote sufficient time and effort to the task. *Since responsibility is assigned not to individuals but to the group, members may not devote due time and effort to the task.*

(a/the) sufficient amount (of) *due/enough.* • It's time we include a sufficient amount of money in the state budget for snow removal. *It's time we include enough money in the state budget for snow removal.*

sufficient/sufficiently enough *duly/enough/sufficiently.* • There may be an economy of scale if the outcome is sufficiently rigorous enough to warrant the state's participation. *There may be an economy of scale if the outcome is sufficiently rigorous to warrant the state's participation.* • The evidence is sufficient enough to support what we're saying. *The evidence is sufficient to support what we're saying.*

(a/the) sufficient number (of) *enough.* • If it gains the sufficient number of signatures to qualify, we'll have to watch it even more carefully. *If it gains enough signatures to qualify, we'll have to watch it even more carefully.*

sum/summary and substance *center/core/crux/essence/gist/heart/pith/substance/sum/summary.* • He asked, in summary and substance, whether GAF wanted to have Union Carbide close at a specific price for several days in a row. *He asked, in essence, whether GAF wanted to have Union Carbide close at a specific price for several days in a row.*

summation *sum/total.* • The summation of these products is 4320.154. *The sum of these products is 4320.154.*

summertime *summer.* • Even in summertime, snow sometimes occurs high up in rain clouds, and the flakes can terminate the arc of a rainbow. *Even in summer, snow sometimes occurs* *high up in rain clouds, and the flakes can terminate the arc of a rainbow.*

summing up *in brief/in fine/in short/in sum.* • Summing up, I feel strongly that my criteria capture the characteristics of firms that are likely to be successful in the Information Age. *In sum, I feel strongly that my criteria capture the characteristics of firms that are likely to be successful in the Information Age.*

(the) sum of *all* delete.

sum total *sum/total.* • Women have always commanded over half the sum total of human intelligence and creativity. *Women have always commanded over half the total of human intelligence and creativity.*

sum up *add/sum/total.*

superimpose one . . . on top of/over another/ the other *superimpose.* • Overlays allow you to superimpose one data range on top of another. *Overlays allow you to superimpose data ranges.*

surrounded . . . on all (four) sides *surrounded.* • Cyclones are areas of low pressure that are surrounded on all sides by high pressure. *Cyclones are areas of low pressure that are surrounded by high pressure.* • This is a 9,000-square-foot house, surrounded by water on all four sides. *This is a 9,000-square-foot house, surrounded by water.*

swallow down *swallow.* • I nearly swallowed down a piece of sharp pointy plastic which was found in my sushi. *I nearly swallowed a piece of sharp pointy plastic which was found in my sushi.*

switch over *switch.* • School systems in Maryland and California tried to switch over after the 1975 legislation. *School systems in Maryland and California tried to switch after the 1975 legislation.*

sworn affidavit *affidavit.*

symbolical *symbolic.* • I think the present change is more symbolical than realistic. *I think the present change is more symbolic than realistic.*

symmetrical *symmetric.* • If one of the functions is symmetrical, then reflection is unnecessary. *If one of the functions is symmetric, then reflection is unnecessary.*

symptomatize *symptomize.*

systematic *systemic.*

systematical *systematic/systemic.*

T

tailor-made *custom/tailored.* • The event seemed tailor-made to give the vice president the upper hand. *The event seemed tailored to give the vice president the upper hand.*

take account for/of *allow for/consider/provide for/reckon with/regard/weigh.* • But HMO officials say that current reimbursements fail to take account for medical inflation. *But HMO officials say that current reimbursements fail to allow for medical inflation.*

take action (to) *act* delete. • If we are to save the right whales, we will have to take action. *If we are to save the right whales, we will have to act.*

take . . . action (on/to) *act -(al)ly* delete. • The operator has to determine the cause of the deviation and then take corrective action. *The operator has to determine the cause of the deviation and then correct it.* • He issued a statement calling on the NRC to take immediate action to correct deficiencies identified in the report. *He issued a statement calling on the NRC to act immediately to correct deficiencies identified in the report.*

take advantage of 1. *abuse/cheat/deceive/ exploit/ill treat/mistreat/misuse/use/victimize/ wrong.* • He took advantage of her good nature. *He exploited her good nature.* 2. *benefit from/ gain/profit by/reap.* • There are several easy ways to take advantage of Fidelity's expertise in retirement planning. *There are several easy ways to profit by Fidelity's expertise in retirement planning.*

take aim *aim.*

take a . . . look (at) *consider/look/regard/view.* • We need to examine each, but let's first take a brief look at the foundations of management theory. *We need to examine each, but let's first briefly look at the foundations of management theory.*

take a measure of *approximate/estimate.* • The balance sheet yields financial data that can be used in various ratio calculations to take a measure of the company's financial health. *The balance sheet yields financial data that can be used in various ratio calculations to estimate the company's financial health.*

take a stand against/in opposition to *contest/ contradict/contrast with/differ from/disagree with/dispute/oppose/resist.*

take a stand for/in favor of/in support of *back/ endorse/favor/prefer/support.* • Delegates at the annual meeting of the American Medical Association took a strong stand in favor of abortion rights this week. *Delegates at the annual meeting of the American Medical Association strongly backed abortion rights this week.*

take a vacation *vacation.* • I don't take a vacation during the golf season. *I don't vacation during the golf season.* • Eighty-one percent of consumers plan to take a vacation this year. *Eighty-one percent of consumers plan to vacation this year.*

take a/the . . . view (of) *consider/look/regard/ view.* • Financial institutions can no longer take a passive view of product development. *Financial institutions can no longer regard product development passively.*

take a wait-and-see attitude *wait and see/wait and watch.*

take cognizance of *attend to/consider/hearken/ heed/listen to/mind/note/notice/observe/regard/ see/tend to/watch/witness.* • We should take cognizance of the role of civil society, which for academic purposes, includes the Church. *We should note the role of civil society, which for academic purposes, includes the Church.*

take delivery of/on *accept/acquire/buy/collect/ confiscate/get/obtain/possess/procure/purchase/ receive/seize/take.* • When you take delivery of the phone it is immediately ready to use. *When you receive the phone it is immediately ready to use.*

take enjoyment in *admire/delight in/enjoy/ rejoice in/relish/savor.* • Team members take enjoyment in their work and in their interactions with others at work. *Team members enjoy their work and their interactions with others at work.*

take exception to *challenge/complain about/ criticize/demur/differ in/disagree with/dispute/ find fault with/object to/oppose/protest/question/ resent.* • I take exception to the statement "Angiography is not only expensive but also painful and risky." *I disagree with the statement "Angiography is not only expensive but also painful and risky."*

take (a) hold of *grasp/seize/take.*

take into account *allow for/consider/provide for/reckon with/regard/weigh.* • It fails to take into account the impact of the U.S. federal budget deficit on U.S. competitiveness. *It fails to* *regard the impact of the U.S. federal budget deficit on U.S. competitiveness.*

take into consideration *allow for/consider/provide for/reckon with/regard/weigh.* • His prior offenses, even though they were in a different state, can be taken into consideration by the court. *His prior offenses, even though they were in a different state, can be weighed by the court.*

take into custody *arrest/capture/catch/seize.*

take issue (with) *attack/challenge/contradict/demur/differ (with)/disagree (with)/dispute/object (to)/oppose/question.* • He also takes issue with the state plan to pay. *He also opposes the state plan to pay.*

take measures (to) *act (to)* delete.

taken by surprise *startled/surprised.* • Everyone I talked to today was taken by surprise by his announcement. *Everyone I talked to today was surprised by his announcement.*

take note of *attend to/consider/hearken to/heed/listen to/mind/note/notice/observe/regard/see/tend to/watch/witness.* • The United States should take note of the percentage of technical graduates and lawyers in Japan's population. *The United States should note the percentage of technical graduates and lawyers in Japan's population.*

take notice of *attend to/consider/hearken/heed/listen to/mind/note/notice/observe/regard/see/tend to/watch/witness.* • But the government has failed to take notice of the demands of the people and their aspirations. *But the government has failed to note the demands of the people and their aspirations*

take offense at *disagree with/dislike/object to/resent.* • I take offense at the *Globe*'s editorial ("Scorsese and the stone-casters") and will no longer sit by and watch the Christian-bashing continue. *I resent the* Globe's *editorial ("Scorsese*

and the stone-casters") and will no longer sit by and watch the Christian-bashing continue.

take pity on/upon *pity/sympathize (with).*

take place *happen/occur.*

take pleasure in *admire/appreciate/cherish/delight in/enjoy/like/love/rejoice in/relish (in)/savor/treasure/value.* • My seasoned psyche says I am foolish to imagine such a thing or to take pleasure in the fantasy. *My seasoned psyche says I am foolish to imagine such a thing or to enjoy the fantasy.* • People take pleasure in other people's faults and misfortunes. *People delight in other people's faults and misfortunes.* • Make it a priority to do the things you take pleasure in. *Make it a priority to do the things you like.*

take possession of *accept/acquire/buy/collect/confiscate/get/obtain/possess/procure/purchase/receive/seize/take.*

take precedence over *antecede/come before/exceed/forego/go before/outrank/precede/surpass/transcend.* • Criminals' rights take precedence over the victims'. *Criminals' rights come before the victims'.* • Generic standards take precedence over basic standards while product standards take precedence over generic standards. *Generic standards forego basic standards while product standards forego generic standards.*

take priority over *antecede/come before/forego/go before/precede.* • He says that in women's shoes, fashion always takes priority over comfort. *He says that in women's shoes, fashion always precedes comfort.*

take satisfaction in *admire/appreciate/be pleased with/delight in/enjoy/like/rejoice in/relish (in)/savor.* • Brown alumni can take satisfaction in the contributions their college has made during 175 years both in the sacrifices of war and the arts of peace. *Brown alumni can delight in the contributions their college has made during 175 years both in the sacrifices of war and* *the arts of peace.* • Encourage your child to compare recent achievements with earlier efforts and to take satisfaction in their progress. *Encourage your child to compare recent achievements with earlier efforts and to be pleased with their progress.*

take the place of *accede/displace/follow/replace/succeed/supersede/supplant.* • Fog will likely take the place of rain. *Fog will likely replace rain.* • We would like to see a qualified and enthusiastic parks director named to take the place of Raymond D. *We would like to see a qualified and enthusiastic parks director named to succeed Raymond D.* • Researchers hope that maybe someday a blood test will take the place of mammograms and colonoscopies. *Researchers hope that maybe someday a blood test will supersede mammograms and colonoscopies.*

take the position (that) *assert/believe/claim/consider/contend/feel/hold/judge/maintain/regard/say/think/to/view.* • He takes the position that, as a meeting leader, you will be more effective if you view yourself "as the servant of the group rather than as its master." *He maintains that, as a meeting leader, you will be more effective if you view yourself "as the servant of the group rather than as its master."*

take the view (that) *assert/believe/claim/consider/contend/feel/hold/judge/maintain/regard/say/think/to/view.*

take the wrong way *misinterpret/misunderstand.*

take to task *admonish/chide/criticize/rebuke/reprimand/reproach/reprove/scold.* • He took the project's tenant leaders to task for their selection of an architectural consultant for the remodeling job. *He admonished the project's tenant leaders for their selection of an architectural consultant for the remodeling job.*

take umbrage at/with *disagree with/dislike/object to/resent.* • Some people, such as the NRA, took umbrage with the message of the show. *Some people, such as the NRA, disliked the message of the show.*

take under advisement *consider/contemplate/reflect on/review/think about/weigh.* • Pillsbury's board is taking the franchisee group's protest under advisement. *Pillsbury's board is reviewing the franchisee group's protest.*

take under consideration *consider/contemplate/reflect on/review/think about/weigh.* • About 1 in 50 products is taken under consideration. *About 1 in 50 products is considered.*

tedious monotony *boredom/dullness/ennui/tedium/monotony.* • High intelligence is seen as a hindrance, because there's no way that intelligent people would tolerate 40 hours of tedious monotony every week. *High intelligence is seen as a hindrance, because there's no way that intelligent people would tolerate 40 hours of tedium every week.*

tell the difference *discriminate/distinguish/tell apart.* • The reality is that science and technology have made it almost impossible to tell the difference between telecommunications and computers. *The reality is that science and technology have made it almost impossible to distinguish between telecommunications and computers.*

temperature *fever.*

temporary stopgap *stopgap.* • A temporary stopgap measure currently funding the government is set to expire midnight on Saturday. *A stopgap measure currently funding the government is set to expire midnight on Saturday.*

(my) tendency is to *(I) tend to.* • Our tendency is to get up a little later each morning and go to sleep a little later each night. *We tend to get up a little later each morning and go to sleep a little later each night.*

tense up *tense.*

term as *term.* • They term agents whose behavior depends on past history as "hysteretic agents." *They term agents whose behavior depends on past history "hysteretic agents."* • In college, you will be primarily dealing with what is termed as expository writing. *In college, you will be primarily dealing with what is termed expository writing.*

terminate *cancel/cease/conclude/end/finish/halt/stop.* • Having no plan at all would be better than terminating one. *Having no plan at all would be better than canceling one.*

terms and conditions *conditions/terms.* • You are responsible for regularly reviewing these terms and conditions. *You are responsible for regularly reviewing these terms.*

test out *test.* • At this point, you might want to test out our map by trying the following experiment. *At this point, you might want to test our map by trying the following experiment.*

(of) that/these/this/those delete. • For those calculators that do not have a 10x key, the antilogarithm can be found by using the INV or 2nd key. *For calculators that do not have a 10x key, the antilogarithm can be found by using the INV or 2nd key.* • Those options with the word patch in their titles are especially complicated. *Options with the word patch in their titles are especially complicated.*

that/this being the case *consequently/hence/so/then/therefore/thus.* • That being the case, the only apparent remedy is for owners of family firms to begin early in earmarking shares of the business for their children. *The only apparent remedy, then, is for owners of family firms to begin early in earmarking shares of the business for their children.* • That being the case, many financial advisors recommend a technique called "laddering" CDs for those individuals willing to commit their funds for longer periods in order to earn a higher rate of return. *Thus, many financial advisors recom-*

mend a technique called "laddering" CDs for those individuals willing to commit their funds for longer periods in order to earn a higher rate of return.

that/the/this business of *that/this* delete. • We've got to get over this business of seeing everything in cartoon terms. *We've got to get over seeing everything in cartoon terms.*

that/this fact *that/this.* • The world beyond visual range is a haze of anxiety, and the most sophisticated radar sets in the world do not change that fact. *The world beyond visual range is a haze of anxiety, and the most sophisticated radar sets in the world do not change that.*

that/which happens/occurs/takes place when *when.* • What about the inevitable disappointment that happens when a child doesn't win a trophy? *What about the inevitable disappointment when a child doesn't win a trophy?*

that is delete. • This relates to the cost that is incurred by start-up firms. *This relates to the cost incurred by start-up firms.*

that is/this is/which is as much as to say (that) *namely/that is/to wit.* • That is as much as to say that it is perfectly natural while it is gloriously supernatural. *That is, it is perfectly natural while it is gloriously supernatural.*

that is/which is to say (that) *namely/that is/to wit.* • That is to say, the person named by the testator in his will will normally be appointed by the court, despite lack of great intelligence or experience. *That is, the person named by the testator in his will will normally be appointed by the court, despite lack of great intelligence or experience.*

that/this juncture/moment/period/point/stage in time *(just/right) now/that/this time/then.* • Not until that moment in time did I understand what being homeless meant. *Not until then did I understand what being homeless meant.*

that/this kind/sort/type of stuff/thing *it/that/this* delete. • If there's a lot of that kind of thing, I will try to figure out whether things will stay depressed forever. *If there's a lot of that, I will try to figure out whether things will stay depressed forever.*

that/these/this/those of delete. • Another exercise is that of completing the views when some or all of them have missing lines. *Another exercise is completing the views when some or all of them have missing lines.*

that/those of (the) *(the) -'s.* • Toronto's population is close to 3 million, which is slightly larger than that of Boston. *Toronto's population is close to 3 million, which is slightly larger than Boston's.* • As the more aggrieved party, the victim's rights must take precedence over those of the perpetrator. *As the more aggrieved party, the victim's rights must take precedence over the perpetrator's.*

that/this time around/round *that/this time/then (now).* • Such an outcome has a far higher probability this time around. *Such an outcome has a far higher probability now.*

theistical *theistic.*

then and only then *only then/then.* • I suggest that then and only then will people such as Mr. Becker realize that there really is no free lunch. *I suggest that only then will people such as Mr. Becker realize that there really is no free lunch.*

then at that/this juncture/juncture in time/ moment/moment in time/period/period of time/point/point in time/stage/stage in time/ time *then.*

then subsequently *then.* • Then subsequently he left Digital and started his own business. *Then he left Digital and started his own business.*

theocratical *theocratic.*

the . . . of *-'s.* • I needed the help of my mother to care for my child. *I needed my mother's help to care for my child.* • The task of the analyst is to find the coefficients a and b in Equation 2-2. *The analyst's task is to find the coefficients a and b in Equation 2-2.* • The failure to recognize expenses of this type can affect the profitability of a product. *The failure to recognize expenses of this type can affect a product's profitability.* • The president will be expected to secure the judgment of the Senate upon any proposed change in educational policy or any matter affecting faculty rights and responsibilities. *The president will be expected to secure the Senate's judgment upon any proposed change in educational policy or any matter affecting faculty rights and responsibilities.* • These were very important laws which advanced the rights of women. *These were very important laws which advanced women's rights.*

theological *theologic.*

theoretical *theoretic.*

therapeutical *therapeutic.*

thereafter *later/next/then.*

there exists . . . (that/who) *exists* delete. • This is true for current products where there exists a sales history. *This is true for current products where a sales history exists.* • There exist two kinds of photoreceptors in the retina. *Two kinds of photoreceptors exist in the retina.* • This means that either party has the right to terminate the relationship, whether or not there exists just cause for doing so. *This means that either party has the right to terminate the relationship, whether or not just cause for doing so exists.* • According to Figure 3.4, there exists a set of weights that classifies all of them correctly. *According to Figure 3.4, a set of weights exists that classifies all of them correctly.*

therefore *hence/so/then/thus.* • The front view is more descriptive than the top view; therefore, the front view should be dimensioned. *The front view is more descriptive than the top view, so the front view should be dimensioned.*

there is . . . (that/who) *is* delete. • There are fifteen people in the group. *Fifteen people are in the group.* • There are millions of people who feel the way you do. *Millions of people feel the way you do.* • For every discovery that scientists make about Egyptian antiquity, there are hundreds that remain unsolved. *For every discovery that scientists make about Egyptian antiquity, hundreds remain unsolved.* • There's a healthy percentage of public investors who are interested and participate in the market throughout their lives. *A healthy percentage of public investors are interested and participate in the market throughout their lives.*

(a/the) . . . thing delete. • Censorship is a very dangerous thing. *Censorship is very dangerous.* • It's a very difficult thing. *It's very difficult.*

thinking in (my) mind *thinking.* • What were you thinking in your mind when you bought the two guns and the knife? *What were you thinking when you bought the two guns and the knife?*

think to myself *think.* • As they were yelling at me, I thought to myself, "These can't be my parents." *As they were yelling at me, I thought, "These can't be my parents."*

thin veneer *veneer.* • This case of illegal wire tapping has revealed the thin veneer of security surrounding electronic communications. *This case of illegal wire tapping has revealed the veneer of security surrounding electronic communications.*

thirdly *third.*

third of all *third.*

this coming *next/this.* • This coming Wednesday we are having our town fair. *This Wednesday we are having our town fair.*

those individuals/people/persons *people/persons/those.* • Only those people authorized to have access to information are allowed to see it. *Only people authorized to have access to information are allowed to see it.*

through and through *all through/completely/entirely/thoroughly/throughout/totally/wholly.*

throughout . . . entire/whole *entire/whole/throughout.* • He was in trouble throughout his entire life. *He was in trouble his entire life.*

throughout the length and breadth (of) *all through/completely/entirely/thoroughly/throughout/totally/wholly.*

through/throughout the course/duration/length of *during/for/in/over/throughout/when/while/with.* • This report is our opportunity to share the insights we have gained throughout the course of the study. *This report is our opportunity to share the insights we have gained throughout the study.* • Throughout the duration of his ministering tour of duty, he found the time to teach at five different universities. *Throughout his ministering tour of duty, he found the time to teach at five different universities.*

through the medium of *by/from/in/on/over/through/with.* • My basic interest is the lucid communication of ideas through the medium of print. *My basic interest is the lucid communication of ideas through print.*

through the use of *by/in/through/with.* • Verbal reasoning is the ability to think, comprehend, and communicate effectively through the use of words. *Verbal reasoning is the ability to think, comprehend, and communicate effectively with words.*

through whatever/whichever manner/means *despite how/however.* • Through whatever manner we meet, this fact has always remained the same. *However we meet, this fact has always remained the same.*

through what/which means/mechanism *how.* • Through what means can Congress control the actions of a bureaucracy? *How can Congress control the actions of a bureaucracy?*

throw into a rage *enrage.* • Thrown into a rage, he attacked the abuser with a knife, and then confessed to the killing without mentioning the woman. *Enraged, he attacked the abuser with a knife, and then confessed to the killing without mentioning the woman.*

throw into doubt *challenge/contradict/dispute/doubt/question.*

throw into jeopardy *endanger/imperil/jeopardize.* • The sale was thrown into jeopardy Friday when an FTC request for more information for antitrust appraisal pushed the transaction into 1989. *The sale was jeopardized Friday when an FTC request for more information for antitrust appraisal pushed the transaction into 1989.*

throw into question *challenge/contradict/dispute/doubt/question.*

thusly *thus.* • I have no television at present and thusly have had to get all my news via the web-based media. *I have no television at present and thus have had to get all my news via the web-based media.*

till/until after *before/till/until.* • Do not delete the first code until after you have made the adjustments. *Do not delete the first code until you have made the adjustments.*

till/until the juncture/juncture in time/moment/moment in time/period/period in time/point/point in time/stage/stage in time/time (that/when) *till/until.* • Until the time that deposit interest rates were set free to seek levels dictated by the financial markets, the thrift business was uncomplicated. *Until deposit interest rates were set free to seek levels dictated by the financial markets, the thrift business was uncomplicated.*

till/until . . . then *till/until.* • Until we realize that all addictive chemical substances are fair game in the war on drugs, then the war cannot be won, much less fought. *Until we realize that all addictive chemical substances are fair game in the war on drugs, the war cannot be won, much less fought.*

till/until the recent past *till/until lately/till/until of late/till/until recently* delete. • Until the recent past, such courses were taken, often as electives, by advanced undergraduates who already had a certain degree of sophistication. *Until recently, such courses were taken, often as electives, by advanced undergraduates who already had a certain degree of sophistication.*

time after time *frequently/often/recurrently/regularly/repeatedly.* • Time after time, the Democrats have turned to the idea of raising taxes. *The Democrats have regularly turned to the idea of raising taxes.*

time and (time) again *frequently/often/recurrently/regularly/repeatedly.* • This has been demonstrated time and time again in their subsequent on-the-job experiences. *This has been repeatedly demonstrated in their subsequent on-the-job experiences.*

(a/the) time frame (of) *age/eon/epoch/era/interval/period/time* delete. • Outpacing both, however, were the regional banks, which moved up 29 percent over the same time frame. *Outpacing both, however, were the regional banks, which moved up 29 percent over the same period.* • Some automotive assemblers can make every car to order, at a reasonable price and in a reasonable time frame. *Some automotive assemblers can make every car to order, at a reasonable price and in a reasonable time.*

(a/the) time horizon (of) *age/eon/epoch/era/interval/period/time* delete. • Estimates are then made of the values of these factors over an appropriate time horizon. *Estimates are then* *made of the values of these factors over an appropriate time.*

(a/the) time interval (of) *interval/period/time.* • Float is the time interval between the time a check is written and the time it is finally taken from the check writer's account. *Float is the interval between the time a check is written and the time it is finally taken from the check writer's account.*

time of day *time.*

(a/the) time period (of) *age/eon/epoch/era/interval/period/time* delete. • The Greek material is similar to stone tools from Hungary and Bulgaria dated to about the same time period. *The Greek material is similar to stone tools from Hungary and Bulgaria dated to about the same age.*

(five) times over *(five)fold.* • He was able to increase the conviction of drug traffickers five times over. *He was able to increase the conviction of drug traffickers fivefold.*

(a/the) time span (of) *age/eon/epoch/era/interval/period/time* delete. • Over the same time span, the savings rate rose from 4.1 to 5.4 percent. *Over the same period, the savings rate rose from 4.1 to 5.4 percent.*

time was when *formerly/long ago/once.*

(the) time will come when *at length/eventually/in due time/in the end/in time/later/one day/over the months (years)/over time/someday/sometime/ultimately/with time/yet.* • The time will come when you will appreciate all I've done for you. *One day you will appreciate all I've done for you.*

tiny/little bit *bit/fragment/hint/piece/shred/speck/trace.* • I think Kroger management is just a tiny bit more relaxed than they were yesterday. *I think Kroger management is just a bit more relaxed than they were yesterday.*

tiny little *little/tiny.*

(in order) to accomplish/achieve that/this aim/end/goal/objective *to that/this end/toward that/this end.* • To accomplish this goal, two special task forces were established. *To this end, two special task forces were established.* • In order to achieve that objective, Congress in 1985 authorized the Peace Corps to double its volunteers to 10,000. *Toward that end, Congress in 1985 authorized the Peace Corps to double its volunteers to 10,000.*

to a certain/limited/some degree *in a sense/in part/less often/less so/more or less/partially/partly/rather/some/somewhat* delete. • This depends to a limited degree on whether the company follows a global or a national strategy focus. *This partly depends on whether the company follows a global or a national strategy focus.* • You can intimidate umpires to a certain degree. *You can intimidate umpires somewhat.*

to a certain/limited/some extent *in a sense/in part/less so/more or less/partially/partly/rather/some/somewhat* delete. • These are two factors that women can control to some extent. *These are two factors that women can somewhat control.* • In Germany, and to some extent in Japan, our products are now priced competitively. *In Germany, and less so in Japan, our products are now priced competitively.*

to a degree *in part/more or less/partially/partly/rather/some/somewhat* delete. • Any choice would have been controversial to a degree. *Any choice would have been somewhat controversial.*

to a/the . . . degree *-(al)ly* delete. • We have reduced our nuclear weaponry to a significant degree. *We have significantly reduced our nuclear weaponry.* • To a surprising degree, we find the outlook hopeful. *We find the outlook surprisingly hopeful.*

to a/the . . . extent *-(al)ly* delete. • It's a change that's already been worked out to a considerable extent at the local level. *It's a change that's already been considerably worked out at the local level.* • To a sad extent, this development has hastened the dismantling of important Wright interiors. *Sadly, this development has hastened the dismantling of important Wright interiors.*

to a great/large degree *almost all/chiefly/commonly/generally/greatly/in general/largely/mainly/most/mostly/most often/much/nearly all/normally/overall/typically/usually/well.* • Because the state will pay for the bulk of building and running the school, it will naturally be involved in the project to a large degree. *Because the state will pay for the bulk of building and running the school, it will naturally be much involved in the project.* • In Malaysia, imports are controlled to a great degree by a handful of European commission houses. *In Malaysia, imports are mostly controlled by a handful of European commission houses.*

to a greater/larger degree/extent *more/more often/more so.* • The risks of radiation are understood to a much greater degree than many other risks we take for granted. *The risks of radiation are understood much more than many other risks we take for granted.* • Black males suffer from debilitating health problems to a greater degree than males in other ethnic and racial groups. *More black males suffer from debilitating health problems than males in other ethnic and racial groups.*

to a greater or lesser degree/extent *in part/in some way/more or less/partially/partly/rather/some/somehow/someway(s)/somewhat/to some degree/extent/various/variously/varying/varyingly* delete. • When people leave an organization, their departure results in a disruption that affects the remaining people to a greater or lesser degree. *When people leave an organization, their departure results in a disruption that variously affects the remaining people.*

to a great/large extent *almost all/chiefly/commonly/generally/greatly/in general/largely/mainly/most/mostly/most often/much/nearly all/normally/overall/typically/usually/well.* • To a large extent, the success of any business venture depends on planning. *The success of any business venture chiefly depends on planning.*

to a lesser/lower/smaller degree/extent *less/less often/less so.* • Some have been dramatically affected by this pilgrimage; others to a lesser degree. *Some have been dramatically affected by this pilgrimage; others less so.* • It is only in Iowa and, to a lesser extent, in New Hampshire, that candidates meet so many rural Americans. *It is only in Iowa and, less often, in New Hampshire that candidates meet so many rural Americans.*

to all appearances *apparently/appear (to)/outwardly/seem (to)/seemingly/superficially.*

to all appearances . . . appear/seem *appear/seem.* • To all appearances, he seems to be a brilliant career executive. *He seems to be a brilliant career executive.* • To all appearances, the market's outlook appears to be very bright as year-end institutional buying is likely to surface in a big way. *The market's outlook appears to be very bright as year-end institutional buying is likely to surface in a big way.*

to all intents and purposes *effectively/essentially/in effect/in essence/practically/virtually.* • To all intents and purposes, their revenue possibilities are now extremely limited. *In effect, their revenue possibilities are now extremely limited.* • This is to all intents and purposes an inertial force. *This is essentially an inertial force.*

to all practical purposes *effectively/essentially/in effect/in essence/practically/virtually.* • As you may recall, the natural regeneration of trees in the Pennypack is, to all practical purposes, nonexistent. *As you may recall, the natural regeneration of trees in the Pennypack is, virtually, nonexistent.*

to a major or minor degree/extent *in part/in some way/more or less/partially/partly/rather/some/somehow/someway(s)/somewhat/to some degree/extent/various/variously/varying/varyingly* delete. • All of us are involved in the writing of the shows to a major or minor degree. *All of us are somehow involved in the writing of the shows.*

to an extent *in part/more or less/partially/partly/rather/some/somewhat* delete.

to an increasing degree/extent *increasingly/more and more.*

to a/the point of *to.* • The business is very close to the point of breaking even. *The business is very close to breaking even.*

to a/the point/stage that/when/where *so (that)/so far (that)/so much (that)/so that/to/to when/to where* delete. • It got to the point where I didn't leave the house at all for fear of missing her phone call. *It got so that I didn't leave the house at all for fear of missing her phone call.* • Because of the mathematics involved, forecasting intimidates some managers to the point that they accept projections at face value. *Because of the mathematics involved, forecasting so intimidates some managers that they accept projections at face value.* • Her Parkinson's disease has progressed to a point where she is now semipsychotic. *Her Parkinson's disease has progressed to where she is now semipsychotic.*

to be *-(al)ly/to* delete. • To be frank, I think their products are inferior to ours. *Frankly, I think their products are inferior to ours.* • To be successful, you must work furiously. *To succeed, you must work furiously.* • If tobacco were to be declared illegal, I would feel comfortable in predicting a black market in nicotine smuggling. *If tobacco were declared illegal, I would feel comfortable in predicting a black market in nicotine smuggling.*

to begin/start with *first.* • To begin with, I never thought so many people would respond to such an intimate question. *First, I never thought so many people would respond to such an intimate question.*

to be sure *certainly/of course/surely.*

to do delete. • Saving money can be difficult to do. *Saving money can be difficult.* • I have to decide if I should retrace Sherman's route to the South as I originally planned to do. *I have to decide if I should retrace Sherman's route to the South as I originally planned.*

to find (a) fault in/with *blame/criticize/fault.*

together as a team/unit *as a team/as a unit/together.* • Here, in one location, specialists work together as a team to fulfill all aspects of a patient's needs. *Here, in one location, specialists work together to fulfill all aspects of a patient's needs.*

together . . . in combination *in combination/together.* • They can even be used together in combination. *They can even be used in combination.*

together . . . in groups *in groups/together.* • Although people around the world live together in groups and create their own cultures, in few cases does the intensity of human interaction approach the level found in prisons. *Although people around the world live in groups and create their own cultures, in few cases does the intensity of human interaction approach the level found in prisons.*

together with *along with/and/as well as/combined with/coupled with/joined with/paired with/with.* • Morgan proposed construction of a system of five reservoirs together with substantial channel improvements. *Morgan proposed construction of a system of five reservoirs coupled with substantial channel improvements.*

toggle back and forth between *toggle between.* • If you choose to have the puzzle solved for you, this will lock the puzzle and then allow you to toggle back and forth between your answers and the provided answers by pressing letter edit keys. *If you choose to have the puzzle solved for you, this will lock the puzzle and then allow you to toggle between your answers and the provided answers by pressing letter edit keys.* • You can use the F11 key to toggle back and forth between normal and full screen view. *You can use the F11 key to toggle between normal and full screen view.* • Moreover, it has special value to NBC because it allows its news division to toggle back and forth between its network and cable news outlets. *Moreover, it has special value to NBC because it allows its news division to toggle between its network and cable news outlets.*

to make (a/the) . . . (about/of/on/with) *to/to-(al)ly.* • I need to make a correction about something I said yesterday. *I need to correct something I said yesterday.* • I wanted to make a comment on his appearance. *I wanted to comment on his appearance.* • We will give the audience a chance to make inquiries about this. *We will give the audience a chance to inquire about this.* • I will do everything possible to make a thorough evaluation of your application. *I will do everything possible to thoroughly evaluate your application.* • I am eager to make a deal. *I am eager to deal.*

to one degree/extent or another *in part/in some way/more or less/partially/partly/rather/some/somehow/someway(s)/somewhat/to some degree/extent/various/variously/varying/varyingly* delete. • Competition is present in nearly all of our markets to one extent or another. *Competition is present to some extent in nearly all of our markets.*

(the) topic of delete. • He spoke on the topic of probate lawyers and fiduciaries at the recent ABA convention in Toronto. *He spoke on pro-bate lawyers and fiduciaries at the recent ABA convention in Toronto.*

to such a degree *so/so far/so much/so well/such.* • Never have so many crucial issues confronting a president depended to such a degree on science and technology. *Never have so many crucial issues confronting a president depended so much on science and technology.* • The writings of Thoreau retain importance and vitality to such a degree that a century later they have had significant influence on the greatest leaders of our time. *The writings of Thoreau retain such importance and vitality that a century later they have had significant influence on the greatest leaders of our time.*

to such an extent *so/so far/so much/so well/such.* • He believes Americans are deluged to such an extent with health messages that they exist in a state of heightened health consciousness all the time. *He believes Americans are so deluged with health messages that they exist in a state of heightened health consciousness all the time.* • Young Sioux boys literally lived with their favorite horse and came to know it to such an extent that they commonly talked with their animals. *Young Sioux boys literally lived with their favorite horse and came to know it so well that they commonly talked with their animals.*

to summarize/sum up *in brief/in fine/in short/in sum.*

to take this opportunity delete. • I'd like to take this opportunity to commend these women for their courage in sharing their stories. *I'd like to commend these women for their courage in sharing their stories.* • We would like to take this opportunity to update you on the status of our investigation. *We would like to update you on the status of our investigation.*

total/totally delete. • He went totally bankrupt. *He went bankrupt.* • This person totally destroyed my career. *This person destroyed my* career. • I'm the total antithesis of my mother. *I'm the antithesis of my mother.*

(a/the) total . . . (of) delete. • The United States sent a total of 3.4 million men and women to serve in Southeast Asia during the period. *The United States sent 3.4 million men and women to serve in Southeast Asia during the period.* • The status line displays the total number of words that were checked. *The status line displays the number of words that were checked.*

(the) totality of *all* delete. • If you look at the totality of votes cast, Jackson is very well off. *If you look at all the votes cast, Jackson is very well off.*

total up *add/sum/total.* • When you total up the outside and inside executives, you get an overwhelming preponderance of board members with a managerial mindset. *When you total the outside and inside executives, you get an overwhelming preponderance of board members with a managerial mindset.*

to tell (you) the truth *actually/candidly/ frankly/honestly/truthfully* delete. • She was a very sweet, kind woman, but to tell you the truth, a few of us worried about her. *She was a very sweet, kind woman, but frankly a few of us worried about her.*

to that/this degree/extent *so/so far/so much/ such.* • I didn't realize women could lose hair to that extent. *I didn't realize women could lose so much hair.*

(something) to that/the/this effect (that) *affirming/claiming/conveying/declaring/profess-ing/purporting/saying/suggesting.* • A call to its former office in Dallas resulted in a telephone company answer to the effect that "service has been disconnected." *A call to its former office in Dallas resulted in a telephone company answer declaring "service has been disconnected."* • He has never met him, and he produced witnesses

to that effect. *He has never met him, and he pro-duced witnesses professing that.*

. . . to the contrary *after all/apart/aside/despite/ even with/for all/with all.* • Appearances to the contrary, he insists he doesn't plan to run for office. *Despite appearances, he insists he doesn't plan to run for office.*

to the contrary *but/conversely/however/instead/ no/not so/rather.* • To the contrary, we found there's a strong tendency for counties that have high radon levels to have low lung-cancer rates. *Instead, we found there's a strong tendency for counties that have high radon levels to have low lung-cancer rates.*

to the degree (that/to which) *as far as/as much as/so far as/so much as.* • To the degree that Divi Hotels can do so, it has purchased distressed properties at discount prices and has then ren-ovated them. *So far as Divi Hotels can do so, it has purchased distressed properties at discount prices and has then renovated them.* • Volume markdowns did not occur to the degree they did last year. *Volume markdowns did not occur as much as they did last year.*

to the degree/extent of *up to.* • In the event of either a partial or total loss, the person is self-insured to the extent of one-third of the damage. *In the event of either a partial or total loss, the person is self-insured up to one-third of the damage.*

to the extent (that/to which) *as far as/as much as/so far as/so much as.* • To the extent that the distribution of income and wealth goes to the heart of a country's political ethic, the United States has grown unfair. *So far as the distribu-tion of income and wealth goes to the heart of a country's political ethic, the United States has grown unfair.* • I help out here and there, but maybe not to the extent that she'd like me to. *I help out here and there, but maybe not as much as she'd like me to.*

to the greatest/largest degree/extent *as far as/as much as/so far as/so much as.* • Nynex asked the judge to expedite consideration of the request to the greatest extent possible by ordering the DOJ to submit its response within 14 days under special procedures. *Nynex asked the judge to expedite consideration of the request as much as possible by ordering the DOJ to submit its response within 14 days under special procedures.*

to the point *apt/pertinent/relevant.*

to the purpose *apt/pertinent/relevant.*

to the tune of delete. • It's the lagniappe that members of Congress collect (to the tune of $9.8 million in 1987) in return for talking to special interest groups with money to spend on them. *It's the lagniappe that members of Congress collect ($9.8 million in 1987) in return for talking to special interest groups with money to spend on them.*

toward the direction of *toward.* • Take the highway A86 toward the direction of CRETEIL. *Take the highway A86 toward CRETEIL.* • This lesson plan reinforces the importance for proper food, nutrition, and a balanced diet in all living things by incorporating an activity that illustrates how plants grow toward the direction of a given light source. *This lesson plan reinforces the importance for proper food, nutrition, and a balanced diet in all living things by incorporating an activity that illustrates how plants grow toward a given light source.*

toward the east (north/south/west) *eastward (northward/southward/westward).*

to what degree *how/how far/how much/how often.* • Privacy provisions in current law leave ambiguous to what degree such information can be shared. *Privacy provisions in current law leave ambiguous how much such information can be shared.* • To what degree are you con-scious of the theme as you write? *How conscious of the theme are you as you write?*

to whatever degree/extent *however/however far/however much/however often.* • You can learn to develop your psychic ability to whatever degree you wish. *You can learn to develop your psychic ability however much you wish.* • The mentor will assist the company to whatever degree the client wishes. *The mentor will assist the company however the client wishes.*

to what extent *how/how far/how much/how often.* • What I would like to know is to what extent this is the result of reduced parental involvement in the child's upbringing. *What I would like to know is how much this is the result of reduced parental involvement in the child's upbringing.* • To what extent they carried that admiration, only they know. *How far they carried that admiration, only they know.*

to what length *how far/how much.* • Apart from other fascinating aspects of the ménage à trois, we are shown to what lengths some will go to further their objectives. *Apart from other fascinating aspects of the ménage à trois, we are shown how far some will go to further their objectives.*

trace amount *trace.* • He found trace amounts of chemicals in unrinsed containers, probably from the glue used to keep felt on the balls. *He found traces of chemicals in unrinsed containers, probably from the glue used to keep felt on the balls.*

trace back *trace.* • From dinosaurs to dogs, all land vertebrates trace their ancestry back to the water. *From dinosaurs to dogs, all land vertebrates trace their ancestry to the water.* • Think about those people and then pick out the most memorable five people of all and trace back the steps to where you first met. *Think about those people and then pick out the most memorable five people of all and trace the steps to where you first met.*

track record *record.* • He built the company into a fine organization with an excellent track record, until the last three or four years. *He built the company into a fine organization with an excellent record, until the last three or four years.*

tragical *tragic.*

trained expert *expert.*

transvestitism *transvestism.*

trivial details/facts/ideas/information/matters/ things *trivia.* • While withholding such seemingly trivial information as the astronauts' in-orbit menus might appear ridiculous, even that might provide some clues as to the timing of the launch. *While withholding such seeming trivia as the astronauts' in-orbit menus might appear ridiculous, even that might provide some clues as to the timing of the launch.*

(a/the) true fact *a fact/factual/the truth/true/ truthful.* • That's a true fact. *That's a fact.*

true to fact *fact/factual/the truth/true/truthful.*

(the) truth is (that) *actually/indeed/in fact/in faith/in truth/really/truly* delete.

(the) truth of the matter is (that) *actually/ indeed/in fact/in faith/in reality/in truth/really/ truly* delete. • The truth of the matter is that glasnost and communism are incompatible. *In truth, glasnost and communism are incompatible.*

turn and turn about *by turns.*

twelve midnight *midnight.*

twelve noon *noon.*

two twins *twins.* • He fathered two twins and had two illegitimate other children. *He fathered twins and had two illegitimate other children.*

type (of) delete. • It was a small, compact type of car. *It was a small, compact car.* • It's not a premeditated type of act. *It's not a premeditated act.* • Dungeons and Dragons is a very seductive type of game. *Dungeons and Dragons is a very seductive game.* • I'm basically a creative type person. *I'm basically a creative person.* • Give young men some booze and boredom, and they may come up with some bizarre type behavior. *Give young men some booze and boredom, and they may come up with some bizarre behavior.*

U

unaccustomed to *not used to/unused to.* • Adults and children who are unaccustomed to caffeine are more likely to be affected than the habitual consumer. *Adults and children who are not used to caffeine are more likely to be affected than the habitual consumer.*

unbeknown/unbeknownst *unknown.* • Condominium loans were the favored product, but unbeknownst to the bank, the market for condos had already peaked. *Condominium loans were the favored product, but unknown to the bank, the market for condos had already peaked.*

unconfirmed/unfounded/unsubstantiated rumor *rumor.* • The Committee on Standards suspended him for two terms and permanently marred his academic record on the basis of innuendo and unfounded rumor. *The Committee on Standards suspended him for two terms and permanently marred his academic record on the basis of innuendo and rumor.* • Wall Street staged an explosive late recovery Thursday after unsubstantiated rumors of an imminent rate cut all but erased a 274-point loss in the Dow Jones industrial average. *Wall Street staged an explosive late recovery Thursday after rumors of an imminent rate cut all but erased a 274-point loss in the Dow Jones industrial average.*

under any circumstances/conditions *altogether/ at all/completely/entirely/ever/fully/never/no matter what/not ever/utterly/whatever/wholly.* • I will not see him under any circumstances. *I will not see him at all.*

under certain/some circumstances/conditions *at times/every so often/for (in/with) some (of us/ people)/from time to time/now and again/now and then/occasionally/once in a while/on occasion/some/sometimes* delete. • Why does fiber, which fights constipation, also cause constipation under some circumstances? *Why does fiber, which fights constipation, also at times cause constipation?*

under no circumstances/conditions *in no way/ never/not/not ever/not once.* • Under no circumstances is it to be used or considered as an offer to sell, or a solicitation of any offer to buy, any security. *Never is it to be used or considered as an offer to sell, or a solicitation of any offer to buy, any security.*

under obligation *bind/compel/force/obligate/ oblige/require/restrict.* • The lessee usually has the option to buy the auto at the end of the lease for the assumed residual value but is not under obligation to do so. *The lessee usually has the option to buy the auto at the end of the lease for the assumed residual value but is not obligated to do so.*

under the provisions of *under.* • Under the provisions of the free milk policy, the determining official or officials shall review applications and determine eligibility. *Under the free milk policy, the determining official or officials shall review applications and determine eligibility.*

under the weather *ill/sick/unwell.*

unfair and inequitable *inequitable/unfair.*

unite into one *unite.*

unite together *unite.* • The proper scholarly interpretation was for all Muslims to unite together and fight as one against those fighting them. *The proper scholarly interpretation was for all Muslims to unite and fight as one against those fighting them.*

universal panacea *panacea.*

unless and/or until *till/unless/until.* • Unless or until they know what is happening, they obviously cannot file complaints to trigger an investigation. *Unless they know what is happening, they obviously cannot file complaints to trigger an investigation.*

unless . . . then *unless.* • Unless we're prepared to say the Japanese are just smarter than we are, then we're looking at motivation and role models and parents encouraging kids to keep their options open. *Unless we're prepared to say the Japanese are just smarter than we are, we're looking at motivation and role models and parents encouraging kids to keep their options open.*

unnecessarily *needlessly.* • The Japanese countered that moving part of the wing production would unnecessarily drive up the costs. *The Japanese countered that moving part of the wing production would needlessly drive up the costs.*

unproved allegation *allegation.* • We don't have to label something every time somebody makes an unproved allegation that it is dangerous. *We don't have to label something every time somebody makes an allegation that it is dangerous.*

unproven *unproved.* • In the context of Western medicine, acupuncture is still unproven. *In the context of Western medicine, acupuncture is still unproved.*

unrealized potential *potential.* • Behind them is an experienced coaching staff, and a world of unrealized potential, good or bad. *Behind them* *is an experienced coaching staff, and a world of potential, good or bad.*

unsubstantiated *baseless/groundless/unfounded.*

until and/or unless *till/unless/until.*

until such point/time as *until.* • Instead of a 50-percent pay raise, they should have a 50-percent pay cut until such time as they rule with honesty, integrity, and compassion. *Instead of a 50-percent pay raise, they should have a 50-percent pay cut until they rule with honesty, integrity, and compassion.* • Discussions will continue until such point as I have something to show on paper. *Discussions will continue until I have something to show on paper.*

(an/the) untold number (of) *countless/endless/ infinite/millions (of)/myriad/numberless/untold.* • If state government fails to actively support one of the world's most promising industries, it will be letting an untold number of jobs and revenue dollars slip through its fingers. *If state government fails to actively support one of the world's most promising industries, it will be letting untold jobs and revenue dollars slip through its fingers.*

up in the air *unanswered/uncertain/unclear/ undecided/unresolved/unsettled/unsure.* • Plans for an interview with Castro himself remain up in the air, according to a CBS News spokesperson. *Plans for an interview with Castro himself remain uncertain, according to a CBS News spokesperson.*

upon *on.* • Do you wish something of the sort had happened when the Senate was called upon to ratify ABM? *Do you wish something of the sort had happened when the Senate was called on to ratify ABM?*

up till/until *till/until.* • I was a model up until the age of 19. *I was a model until the age of 19.* • Up until now conflicting standards and prob-

lem hardware have kept plug and play from working properly. *Until now conflicting standards and problem hardware have kept plug and play from working properly.*

up till/until that/this juncture/juncture in time/ moment/moment in time/period/period in time/point/point in time/stage/stage in time/ time *so far/thus far/till/until now (then)/to date/ up to now (then)/(as) yet.* • Up until this point, he hasn't been able to show what he stands for. *Until now, he hasn't been able to show what he stands for.* • Up until this time, we have had one personnel director who took care of everybody. *To date, we have had one personnel director who took care of everybody.*

up to a maximum of *up to.* • If set to Yes, text wraps around the box (up to a maximum of 20 boxes per page). *If set to Yes, text wraps around the box (up to 20 boxes per page).*

up to and including *through.* • Every WordStar Professional command, feature, and function up to and including Release 5 is listed and described in detail. *Every WordStar Professional command, feature, and function through Release 5 is listed and described in detail.*

up to a point *rather/somewhat.*

up to that/this juncture/juncture in time/ moment/moment in time/period/period in time/point/point in time/stage/stage in time/ time *so far/thus far/till now (then)/to date/until now (then)/up to now (then)/(as) yet.* • Up to this point, we have discussed these motivation theories relating to the needs of the individual. *Until now, we have discussed these motivation theories relating to the needs of the individual.*

up to the current/present (time) *so far/thus far/ till now/to date/until now/up to now/(as) yet.*

upward(s) of *more than/over.* • In 1984, Peru had upwards of 40,000 acres of coca plants/

today, it has 600,000 acres. *In 1984, Peru had more than 40,000 acres of coca plants/today, it has 600,000 acres.*

usage *use.* • We project that ATM usage will increase to nearly 60 percent by 1995. *We project that ATM use will increase to nearly 60 percent by 1995.* • The usage of credit cards to fund small businesses seems to be the method of choice these days. *The use of credit cards to fund small businesses seems to be the method of choice these days.*

(the) . . . use of *using* delete. • Would the use of these exacerbate the situation? *Would using these exacerbate the situation?* • This construction is performed with the use of a compass and a straightedge. *This construction is performed with a compass and a straightedge.*

usually but not always *almost always/most often/nearly always/often/usually.*

utility *use/usefulness.* • This has resulted in the much needed return to utility of our long-idled bridge. *This has resulted in the much needed return to use of our long-idled bridge.*

utilization *use.* • Utilization of existing schools in a region could be optimized to reduce variances caused by local population fluctuations. *Use of existing schools in a region could be optimized to reduce variances caused by local population fluctuations.*

utilize *employ/use.* • If utilizing the master antenna system is impossible, we will devise a plan for running the cable within the building. *If using the master antenna system is impossible, we will devise a plan for running the cable within the building.*

V

vacillate back and forth *vacillate.* • Until we change how we think about ourselves, we will likely continue to vacillate back and forth between various states of health and illness. *Until we change how we think about ourselves, we will likely continue to vacillate between various states of health and illness.*

(a) valuable asset *(an) asset/valuable.* • The wasting of this valuable national asset, through neglect and privation, makes no sense. *The wasting of this national asset, through neglect and privation, makes no sense.*

vantage point *vantage.* • That it should do so is hardly surprising when one considers the unique vantage point from which he is able to view the historical scene. *That it should do so is hardly surprising when one considers the unique vantage from which he is able to view the historical scene.*

(a) variety of *assorted/countless/different/ diverse/extensive/many/numerous/scores of/sundry/varied/various/varying* delete. • Today, a variety of pricing approaches are used. *Today, various pricing approaches are used.*

(a/the) variety of different *assorted/a variety of/countless/different/diverse/extensive/many/ numerous/scores of/sundry/varied/various/varying.* • The children's museum will have a variety of different events. *The children's museum will have a variety of events.*

various and sundry *assorted/diverse/sundry/ varied/various/varying* delete. • There was a huge group of kids there of various and sundry ages. *There was a huge group of kids there of various ages.*

various different *assorted/countless/different/ diverse/extensive/many/numerous/scores of/sun-*

dry/varied/various/varying. • Couples have various different ways of splitting their money. *Couples have various ways of splitting their money.*

verbalization *discussion/speaking/talk.*

verbalize *speak/talk/write.* • Request that those who call you regularly put their thoughts in writing instead of verbalizing on the phone. *Request that those who call you regularly put their thoughts in writing instead of talking on the phone.*

very delete. • It's a very tragic story. *It's a tragic story.* • The driving conditions are very treacherous. *The driving conditions are treacherous.* • I thought her performance was very spectacular. *I thought her performance was spectacular.* • Last year's event was a very huge success. *Last year's event was a huge success.* • Moreover, the wind at the peak can be very deadly. *Moreover, the wind at the peak can be deadly.*

very much -ed/-en *much -ed/much -en.* • I was very much concerned about that. *I was much concerned about that.* • Their efficacy as classroom texts would be very much improved if their pedagogical features were more plentiful. *Their efficacy as classroom texts would be much improved if their pedagogical features were more plentiful.*

vestigial remnant *remnant/vestige.* • We Americans have only a vestigial remnant of several basic industries—consumer electronics, photography, toymaking, and office equipment to name a few. *We Americans have only a remnant of several basic industries—consumer electronics, photography, toymaking, and office equipment to name a few.*

viable delete. • Having an affair is not a viable solution. *Having an affair is not a solution.*

VIN number *VIN.*

violent explosion *explosion.* • A violent explosion destroyed a Los Lunas mobile home and sent the couple living inside to the hospital. *An explosion destroyed a Los Lunas mobile home and sent the couple living inside to the hospital.*

(a/the) vital . . . in/of/to *vital in/to.* • We have been very pleased with their performance and have found them to be a vital part of our operation. *We have been very pleased with their performance and have found them to be vital to our operation.*

vital necessity *necessity/vital.*

vocalize *express/say/state/tell/voice.*

voice . . . (about/for/of/to) delete. • They voiced doubt that trees will prove to be a bigger source of hydrocarbons than cars in most cities. *They doubted that trees will prove to be a bigger source of hydrocarbons than cars in most cities.* • He voiced strong support for the international effort to make ISDN the universally accepted worldwide network of the future. *He strongly supported the international effort to make ISDN the universally accepted worldwide network of the future.*

voice approval of *agree with/approve (of)/authorize/back/consent to/endorse/sanction/support.* • Previously, Blacks, more than any other group, had been reluctant to voice approval of the president. *Previously, Blacks, more than any other group, had been reluctant to back the president.* • Composed of four City Council members and fifteen citizens, this committee will review and voice approval of all aspects of projects prior to implementation. *Composed of four City Council members and fifteen citizens, this committee will review and approve all aspects of projects prior to implementation.*

voice concern (about/over) *1. agonize (about/over)/brood (on/over)/dread/fear/fret (about/over)/regret/stew (about/over)/worry (about/*

over). 2. *distrust/mistrust/question.* • U.S. officials have voiced concern about possible Chinese sales of newly developed short-range M-9 missiles elsewhere in the Middle East. *U.S. officials have worried about possible Chinese sales of newly developed short-range M-9 missiles elsewhere in the Middle East.* • He was fired after voicing concern over the company's direction. *He was fired after questioning the company's direction.*

voice criticism of *contest/criticize/disagree with/disapprove of/dispute/object to/oppose/protest.* • Some of the Christian representatives find it difficult to voice criticism of Israel. *Some of the Christian representatives find it difficult to criticize Israel.*

voice disapproval of *contest/criticize/disagree with/disapprove of/dispute/object to/oppose/protest.* • In the last two weeks, I've heard several students voice disapproval of the sentiments expressed. *In the last two weeks, I've heard several students disapprove of the sentiments expressed.*

voice objection to *contest/criticize/disagree with/disapprove of/dispute/object to/oppose/protest.* • No one appeared at a public hearing conducted prior to the regular board meeting to voice objections to the budget for fiscal year 2003. *No one appeared at a public hearing conducted prior to the regular board meeting to object to the budget for fiscal year 2003.*

voice opposition to *contest/criticize/disagree with/disapprove of/dispute/object to/oppose/protest.* • Congress in 1986 passed the Montgomery Amendment after several governors voiced opposition to the Reagan administration's Central American policy. *Congress in 1986 passed the Montgomery Amendment after several governors opposed the Reagan administration's Central American policy.*

voice skepticism (about) *disbelieve/distrust/doubt/mistrust/question.*

voice sorrow (about) *bemoan/deplore/grieve/lament/moan/mourn/regret.*

voice support for *agree with/approve (of)/authorize/back/consent to/endorse/sanction/support.* • Several university professors voiced support for the Nader campaign. *Several university professors endorsed the Nader campaign.* • Still, influential Republicans continue to voice support for the embattled regulator. *Still, influential Republicans continue to support the embattled regulator.*

W

waffle back and forth *waffle.* • If a person is plagued with this mind-set, he will waffle back and forth between the fear of failure and quitting constantly. *If a person is plagued with this mind-set, he will waffle between the fear of failure and quitting constantly.*

wage (a/the) . . . delete. • The report notes that the state has been waging a battle against drugs for several years. *The report notes that the state has been battling against drugs for several years.*

wait around *wait.* • The key customers are not going to wait around while those issues get resolved. *The key customers are not going to wait while those issues get resolved.*

want to have *want.* • We don't want to have the drug in our formulary unless it has a superior patient care advantage. *We don't want the drug in our formulary unless it has a superior patient care advantage.*

warn . . . in advance *warn.* • Warn them in advance that anyone who comes into your house will have to remove their shoes. *Warn them that anyone who comes into your house will have to remove their shoes.*

(the) way *as.* • Look carefully at the results, and try to determine why they behave the way they do. *Look carefully at the results, and try to determine why they behave as they do.*

(the) way (in which) *how* delete. • This overview should give you a feel for the way these programs work and the way you can use them. *This overview should give you a feel for how these programs work and how you can use them.* • That's the way people can reduce their blood pressure. *That's how people can reduce their blood pressure.*

ways and means *means/methods/ways.*

weather conditions *climate/weather.* • The adverse weather conditions on Saturday postponed the running of the race until a day later. *The adverse weather on Saturday postponed the running of the race until a day later.*

weld together *weld.* • They manufactured their samples by welding together two single-crystal gold films. *They manufactured their samples by welding two single-crystal gold films.*

(all) well and fine/good *all right/fine/good/ great/nice/pleasant/pleasing/welcome/well.* • Variety and customization are well and good, but they are low on most consumers' lists of priorities. *Variety and customization are nice, but they are low on most consumers' lists of priorities.*

were it not for *but for/except for.*

what appears/seems to be *apparent/seeming.* • Manchester police also said a bottle of nonprescription pills was found in the room along with what appeared to be a suicide note. *Manchester police also said a bottle of nonprescription pills was found in the room along with an apparent suicide note.*

what ... does is. delete. • What they do is provide repair and replacement of Sun and HP products. *They provide repair and replacement of Sun and HP products.*

what ... for *why.* • What did you do that for? *Why did you do that?*

what ... happens/occurs/results/takes place is (that) delete. • What happens with motherhood is you rarely repeat the problems of your own mother. *With motherhood you rarely repeat the problems of your own mother.* • What happens, again and again, is that people with good intentions falter. *Again and again, people with good intentions falter.*

what have you *whatnot.*

what in God's/heaven's name *whatever/what ever.* • What in God's name does it have to do with the subject of business? *Whatever does it have to do with the subject of business?*

what in the world/on earth *whatever/what ever.* • What on earth are you talking about? *Whatever are you talking about?*

what is ... (is that) *-(al)ly* delete. • What we need is a way to go directly to the partition block. *We need a way to go directly to the partition block.* • What we hope to do is increase our inventory and decrease our costs. *We hope to increase our inventory and decrease our costs.* • What we have described is a typical, hierarchical, central-processor-based, online architecture. *We have described a typical, hierarchical, central-processor-based, online architecture.* • What is not so clear or commonly accepted is the scope and nature of these obligations. *Not so clear or commonly accepted is the scope and nature of these obligations.* • What is more alarming is that Black women made up less than 25 percent of the city's population. *More alarming is that Black women made up less than 25 percent of the city's population.* • What create static electricity are different potentials. *Different potentials create static electricity.* • I am not religious, so I would not know what others' thoughts on this are. *I am not religious, so I would not know others' thoughts on this.*

what is called/known as/named/referred to as/termed delete. • Many municipal and rural developments are located within what is referred to as the flood plain. *Many municipal and rural developments are located within the flood plain.*

what is the likelihood/probability (of) *how likely/ how probable.* • What is the likelihood of that? *How likely is that?*

what is the time frame/time horizon/time period/time span in which (of) *when.* • What was the time frame in which you had your relationship with President Kennedy? *When did you have your relationship with President Kennedy?*

what it is (that/who) *what.* • I took it upon myself to research what it was that made this matter such a hot commodity. *I took it upon myself to research what made this matter such a hot commodity.* • It's time for us to rethink what it is we are asking of our employees. *It's time for us to rethink what we are asking of our employees.*

what it/he/she is is *it (he/she) is.* • What it is is a sequence of events that have brought us into crash mode. *It is a sequence of events that have brought us into crash mode.* • What it is, is race-baiting. *It's race-baiting.* • What it is is a charming night out full of all the teenage optimism without the condescending tone that too often comes with it in Hollywood. *It is a charming night out full of all the teenage optimism without the condescending tone that too often comes with it in Hollywood.* • What she is, is relatable to the vast majority of Americans, and especially American women. *She is relatable to the vast majority of Americans, and especially American women.*

what/whatever/which/whichever one(s) *what/whatever/which/whichever.* • Which one would be accomplished better or faster with the help of a computer? *Which would be accomplished better or faster with the help of a computer?* • Whichever one you select, it will be an improvement on the one you now have. *Whichever you select, it will be an improvement on the one you now have.*

whatsoever *at all/whatever.* • As far as I'm concerned, twins have no ESP ability whatsoever. *As far as I'm concerned, twins have no ESP ability whatever.*

what with *given/since/with.* • What with the constant change in today's world, financial plans must be continually updated. *With the constant change in today's world, financial plans must be continually updated.* • You might think the MTV generation would be too jaded to notice, what with Mariah Carey's washcloth-size skirts and Janet Jackson also in the buff. *You might think the MTV generation would be too jaded to notice, given Mariah Carey's washcloth-size skirts and Janet Jackson also in the buff.* • There's going to have to be a lot of support to get Gore elected what with Bush in there. *There's going to have to be a lot of support to get Gore elected with Bush in there.* • It's getting harder to make a living as an editor of the printed word, what with newspapers and other publications cutting staff. *It's getting harder to make a living as an editor of the printed word with newspapers and other publications cutting staff.*

when all is said and done *all in all/all told/altogether/finally/in all/in the end/overall/ultimately.* • When all is said and done, Mr. Marshall emerges as a monster by anyone's standards. *All in all, Mr. Marshall emerges as a monster by anyone's standards.*

when and as *as/when.* • Late payments are subject to a late-payment charge of 1½ percent per month, and the advertisers agree to pay any such late-payment penalty when and as billed by the publisher. *Late payments are subject to a late-payment charge of 1½ percent per month, and the advertisers agree to pay any such late-payment penalty when billed by the publisher.*

when and/or if *if/when.* • So when and if the discount rate is charged, it could well be interpreted on Wall Street as nothing more than a "catch-up" move. *So if the discount rate is charged, it could well be interpreted on Wall Street as nothing more than a "catch-up" move.*

when and/or whether *if/when/whether.*

when, as, and if *if/when.*

when compared to/with *against/alongside/beside/compared to/with/-(i)er than/less/less than/more/more than/next to/over/than/to/versus/vis-à-vis.* • There is a 23 percent higher suicide rate of Vietnam veterans when compared to other persons in the same age group. *There is a 23 percent higher suicide rate of Vietnam veterans compared to other persons in the same age group.* • IBM is expected to price the line aggressively, when compared to the competition. *IBM is expected to price the line more aggressively than the competition.*

when compared to/with . . . relatively *compared to/with/-(i)er than/less than/more than/than.* • Although the UK is relatively small when compared with the United States, its landscape and people are varied and dramatic; what it lacks in physical size it makes up for in culture, history etc. *Although the UK is small when compared with the United States, its landscape and people are varied and dramatic; what it lacks in physical size it makes up for in culture, history etc.*

when (a/the) . . . done/finished/over/through *after.*

when it/you comes/gets right down to it *all in all/all told/altogether/in all/overall.*

when it comes to *about/as for/as to/concerning/for/in/of/on/over/regarding/respecting/to/toward/when/with* delete. • She's very shy when it comes to performing in front of an audience. *She's very shy about performing in front of an audience.* • Employers, employees, and society are often in conflict when it comes to dealing with five key issues facing them today in the workplace. *Employers, employees, and society are often in conflict over dealing with five key issues facing them today in the workplace.* • Being terrible with names is not an option when it comes to naming your book. *Being terrible with names is not an option when naming your book.*

when measured against *against/alongside/beside/compared to/with/-(i)er than/less/less than/more/more than/next to/over/than/to/versus/vis-à-vis.* • The size of the Pennwalt takeover offer isn't large when measured against the multibillion-dollar bidding wars that have reshaped 1988 as the year of unprecedented megadeals. *The size of the Pennwalt takeover offer isn't large alongside the multibillion-dollar bidding wars that have reshaped 1988 as the year of unprecedented megadeals.*

whensoever *whenever.*

when . . . then *when.* • When the detector no longer sounds, then you know you have reached safety. *When the detector no longer sounds, you know you have reached safety.* • When the reference count is zero, then the control can destroy itself and free memory for other purposes. *When the reference count is zero, the control can destroy itself and free memory for other purposes.*

whereabouts *where.*

where . . . at *where.* • We don't really know where we are at. *We don't really know where we are.* • What was that like and where was it held at? *What was that like and where was it held?*

wherefore *why.*

where . . . is concerned *about/as for/as to/concerning/for/in/of/on/over/regarding/respecting/to/toward/with* delete. • Bank customers are often less venturesome where their money is concerned. *Bank customers are often less venturesome with their money.* • Keep in mind that bigger isn't necessarily better where information is concerned. *Regarding information, keep in mind that bigger isn't necessarily better.* • It's beginning to show signs of weakness where demand is concerned, but that's true everywhere. *It's beginning to show signs of weakness in demand, but that's true everywhere.* • Most investigators use one of three primary methods where sketching is concerned. *Most investigators use one of three primary methods of sketching.* • Geller is notoriously tight-lipped where matters of sex and romance are concerned. *Geller is notoriously tight-lipped about matters of sex and romance.*

wheresoever *wherever.*

where . . . to *where.* • Where are you going to? *Where are you going?*

whereupon *whereon.*

wherewithal *assets/cash/funds/means/money/supplies.* • He added that the Minnesotan also has the wherewithal to shore up finances during bad times. *He added that the Minnesotan also has the cash to shore up finances during bad times.*

whether *if.* • A patent can be granted only after the PTO examiners have searched existing patents to determine whether the invention has been previously patented. *A patent can be granted only after the PTO examiners have searched existing patents to determine if the invention has been previously patented.*

whether and/or when *if/when/whether.*

whether or not *if/whether.* • With so many choices, the question is not whether or not to buy a server but what to implement as a server. *With so many choices, the question is not whether to buy a server but what to implement as a server.*

which is delete. • There's a certain enzyme which is lacking in their systems. *There's a certain enzyme lacking in their systems.* • Tandy Corp., which is probably the largest U.S. distributor of small business systems, also sells personal computers in its stores. *Tandy Corp., probably the largest U.S. distributor of small business systems, also sells personal computers in its stores.* • The Moscow Papyrus dealt with solving practical problems which are related to geometry, food preparation, and grain allowance. *The Moscow Papyrus dealt with solving practical problems related to geometry, food preparation, and grain allowance.*

whichsoever *whichever.*

while at the same time *as/at the same time/while.* • So the objective of the game within the Administration was to finesse the longer-term implications of SDI while at the same time manipulating the shorter-term impact of the program in such a way as either to advance arms control or to stop it in its tracks. *So the objective of the game within the Administration was to finesse the longer-term implications of SDI while manipulating the shorter-term impact of the program in such a way as either to advance arms control or to stop it in its tracks.* • Women's colleges are offering women innovative programs, while at the same time they are opening doors for minorities. *Women's colleges are offering women innovative programs, while they are opening doors for minorities.*

while concurrently *as/while.* • Researchers joined development projects for one month and participated in interface design while concurrently interviewing other project participants and employees. *Researchers joined development projects for one month and participated in interface design while interviewing other project participants and employees.* • A message can be sent to the driver vectoring her to a repair center, while concurrently a message is sent to the repair center alerting it to the car's arrival. *A message can be sent to the driver vectoring her to a repair center, as a message is sent to the repair center alerting it to the car's arrival.*

while/whereas on the contrary *whereas.* • The logical conclusion of the contest does not interest the wrestling-fan, while on the contrary a boxing-match always implies a science of the future. *The logical conclusion of the contest does not interest the wrestling-fan, whereas a boxing-match always implies a science of the future.* • Hasdrubal, Hannibal's brother, is portrayed as an effeminate and castrated man, while on the contrary Silius' representation of Asbyte, a woman warrior, shows a female with masculine traits. *Hasdrubal, Hannibal's brother, is portrayed as an effeminate and castrated man, whereas Silius' representation of Asbyte, a woman warrior, shows a female with masculine traits.*

while simultaneously *as/while.* • While getting signatures, volunteers were simultaneously assessing the degree of support for my candidacy. *While getting signatures, volunteers were assessing the degree of support for my candidacy.* • Our aim is to help professional and semi-professional freelance writers promote their work to thousands of publications worldwide, while simultaneously providing editors with a valuable resource for written material. *Our aim is to help professional and semi-professional freelance writers promote their work to thousands of publications worldwide, while providing editors with a valuable resource for written material.*

who in the world/on earth *whoever/who ever.* • Who in the world is that? *Who ever is that?*

who is delete. • The groups can vary from project associates to laymen who are unfamiliar with the project and its objectives. *The groups can vary from project associates to laymen unfamiliar with the project and its objectives.* • Leanne Deacon, who is 16 and British, suffered a cardiac arrest while on one of the rides in Disney World, Florida. *Leanne Deacon, 16 and British, suffered a cardiac arrest while on one of the rides in Disney World, Florida.*

whole/wholly delete. • Never in my whole life have I ever seen such a thing. *Never in my life have I ever seen such a thing.* • There's a whole plethora of new technologies emerging. *There's a plethora of new technologies emerging.*

whole, entire *entire/whole* delete. • It wasn't her whole, entire face; it was just part of it. *It wasn't her entire face; it was just part of it.* • She is Emily, my best friend in the whole, entire world. *She is Emily, my best friend in the whole world.* • What he did, and what Barack Obama is doing now, is going to change the whole entire world. *What he did, and what Barack Obama is doing now, is going to change the world.*

wholly and completely *completely/utterly/wholly.* • A member of group C, for example, remains wholly and completely a C. *A member of group C, for example, remains wholly a C.*

whomsoever *whomever.* • If Bush orders an invasion of Venezuela to remove whomsoever the CIA has labeled as the left-wing, radical regime of President Hugo Chavez Frias, the losses will be catastrophic. *If Bush orders an invasion of Venezuela to remove whomever the CIA has labeled as the left-wing, radical regime of President Hugo Chavez Frias, the losses will be catastrophic.*

whosoever *whoever.* • Perhaps our city fathers, or whosoever decides on street names, do care about these things. *Perhaps our city fathers, or whoever decides on street names, do care about these things.*

why in the world/on earth *why ever.* • Why in the world would liberals oppose the idea? *Why would liberals ever oppose the idea?*

(the) whys and (the) wherefores (of) *aim/cause/ explanation/goal/grounds/motive/purpose/reason.* • We're going to be talking about the whys and the wherefores of his lead. *We're going to be talking about the reasons for his lead.* • But for those who'd like to know what to do before hearing all the whys and wherefores, I start with the three main CORBA "developer action items." *But for those who'd like to know what to do before hearing all the reasons, I start with the three main CORBA "developer action items."*

(many) widely varying *assorted/broad/countless/different/diverse/extensive/many/numerous/scores of/sundry/varied/various/varying.* • If a distributor bases its application programs on the Unix operating system, it can choose among many widely varying computers. *If a distributor bases its application programs on the Unix operating system, it can choose among various computers.*

widow/widower of the late *widow/widower.*

widow woman *widow.*

window of opportunity *chance/opportunity.* • Interviews with government scientists and physicians suggest a critical window of opportunity was missed. *Interviews with government scientists and physicians suggest a critical opportunity was missed.*

wintertime *winter.* • In the wintertime, however, the sun's weaker rays generate less heat energy near the Earth's surface. *In the winter, however, the sun's weaker rays generate less heat energy near the Earth's surface.*

-wise delete. • He has a lot of sense, businesswise. *He has a lot of business sense.* • I don't know that that would be very effective, costwise.

I don't know that that would be very cost effective. • What do you look like, facewise? *What does your face look like?* • Make sure it is as close as possible to perfect, spelling and grammar wise, as you are able to make it. *Make sure it is as close as possible to perfect spelling and grammar as you are able to make it.*

with a/the thought of/to (-ing) *for (-ing)/so as to/to.* • We assume that they wish to examine their consumption patterns with a thought to increase their savings rate. *We assume that they wish to examine their consumption patterns so as to increase their savings rate.*

with a/the view of/to (-ing) *for (-ing)/so as to/ to.* • All categories of terms have been reviewed and in some areas an entirely new approach has been adopted with a view to making the book more useful for the reader. *All categories of terms have been reviewed and in some areas an entirely new approach has been adopted to make the book more useful for the reader.* • She is also co-chairing an important panel looking at cutting spending with a view toward reducing the government's $24.7-billion deficit. *She is also co-chairing an important panel looking at cutting spending so as to reduce the government's $24.7-billion deficit.*

with few/rare exception(s) *almost all/almost every/most/nearly all/nearly every.* • With few exceptions, federal and state policies are not aimed at upgrading the technology of existing firms. *Almost all federal and state policies are not aimed at upgrading the technology of existing firms.*

with increasing frequency *increasingly/more and more.* • Women are dating younger men with increasing frequency. *More and more women are dating younger men.*

without (a/any) question/shadow of a doubt *certainly/doubtless/no doubt/surely/without (a/ any) doubt.*

without basis in fact *baseless/groundless/ unfounded.* • The imputation was totally without basis in fact, and was in no way a fair comment, and was motivated purely by malice. *The imputation was totally groundless, and was in no way a fair comment, and was motivated purely by malice.*

without (a/any) doubt *certainly/doubtless/no doubt/surely.*

without equal *matchless/novel/peerless/singular/special/unequaled/unique/unmatched/ unrivaled.*

without exception *all/always/consistently/constantly/every/everybody/everyone/every time/ invariably/unfailingly* delete. • Without exception, consumers should be aware that caveat emptor is an understatement in this field. *Consumers should always be aware that caveat emptor is an understatement in this field.*

without foundation *baseless/groundless/ unfounded.* • Most allegations of men abusing their children are totally without foundation. *Most allegations of men abusing their children are totally unfounded.*

without number *countless/endless/infinite/millions (of)/myriad/numberless/untold.*

without peer *matchless/novel/peerless/singular/special/unequaled/unique/unmatched/unrivaled.* • He is the entrepreneur extraordinaire/ he is without peer. *He is the entrepreneur extraordinaire/he is peerless.*

without (a) question *certainly/doubtless/no doubt/surely.*

with reference to *about/as for/as to/concerning/ for/in/of/on/over/regarding/respecting/to/toward/ with* delete. • With reference to the stereo, I think she should have put it in storage. *Concerning the stereo, I think she should have put it in storage.* • With reference to your article on the World Bank, the Bank has no plans to issue commodity bonds or to make commodity-indexed loans. *As for your article on the World Bank, the Bank has no plans to issue commodity bonds or to make commodity-indexed loans.*

with regard to *about/as for/as to/concerning/ for/in/of/on/over/regarding/respecting/to/ toward/with* delete. • The evidence is mixed with regard to the existence of an optimal capital structure. *The evidence is mixed on the existence of an optimal capital structure.* • With regard to the first rationalization, how can a manager know how far is too far? *As to the first rationalization, how can a manager know how far is too far?*

with relation to *about/as for/as to/concerning/ for/in/of/on/over/regarding/respecting/to/ toward/with* delete. • There are conflicting reports with relation to the altitude of the Iranian airliner. *There are conflicting reports about the altitude of the Iranian airliner.*

with respect to *about/as for/as to/concerning/ for/in/of/on/over/regarding/respecting/to/ toward/with* delete. • Something very interesting was said with respect to gender differences. *Something very interesting was said about gender differences.* • Each Licensee hereunder shall have the following rights with respect to the Licensed Software. *Each Licensee hereunder shall have the following rights concerning the Licensed Software.* • The floodway within communities that have adopted flood-plain regulations is usually subject to strong restrictions with respect to building. *The floodway within communities that have adopted flood-plain regulations is usually subject to strong building restrictions.*

with the exception of/that *apart from/aside from/barring/besides/but for/except/except for/*

excepting/excluding/other than/outside of. • With the exception of their paper, these studies found a link between financial structure and industry class. *Except for their paper, these studies found a link between financial structure and industry class.* • Overall, bears and other stuffed animals, with the exception of dinosaurs, are out. *Overall, bears and other stuffed animals, other than dinosaurs, are out.*

with the exclusion of/that *apart from/aside from/barring/besides/but for/except/except for/ excepting/excluding/other than/outside of.*

with the intent of -ing (to) *for (-ing)/so as to/ to.* • The Intra-Arterial Cardiac Support System 8000 is being designed with the intent to expand the use of nonsurgical cardiac support systems by providing significantly greater support to the heart than is possible with clinically available non-surgical systems. *The Intra-Arterial Cardiac Support System 8000 is being designed to expand the use of non-surgical cardiac support systems by providing significantly greater support to the heart than is possible with clinically available nonsurgical systems.*

with the passage of time *at length/eventually/ in due time/in the end/in time/later/one day/over the months (years)/over time/someday/sometime/ ultimately/with time/yet.* • The distinctions that now exist between stationary and mobile communications will disappear with the passage of time. *The distinctions that now exist between stationary and mobile communications will ultimately disappear.* • He did not improve with the passage of time. *He did not improve over time.*

with the purpose of -ing *for (-ing)/so as to/to.* • The writer wrote the article with the purpose of teaching American businesspeople about Japanese gifts. *The writer wrote the article to teach American businesspeople about Japanese gifts.* • The first common schools were opened with the purpose of preparing the population for citizenship. *The first common schools were opened so as to prepare the population for citizenship.* • The same technology was used in a civilian application with the purpose of saving lives. *The same technology was used in a civilian application for saving lives.*

with the result (that) *so (that).* • All graven images were banned by the new Protestant Church, with the result that only a shadow of the Chapel's Medieval glory remains. *All graven images were banned by the new Protestant Church, so that only a shadow of the Chapel's Medieval glory remains.*

worthy of attention *considerable/newsworthy/ noteworthy.* • To give the media pride of place reinforces the impression that any event is worthy of attention only to the extent that a cameraman is blocking our view. *To give the media pride of place reinforces the impression that any event is noteworthy only to the extent that a cameraman is blocking our view.*

worthy of blame *blamable/blameworthy.*

worthy of commendation *admirable/com- mendable/praiseworthy.* • The fact that her article presents the Palestinian as well as the Israeli viewpoint is worthy of commendation. *The fact that her article presents the Palestinian as well as the Israeli viewpoint is commendable.*

worthy of (my) consideration *considerable/ newsworthy/noteworthy.* • As a critical reader and listener, you will be able to recognize ideas that are accurate, logical, and worthy of consideration. *As a critical reader and listener, you will be able to recognize ideas that are accurate, logical, and considerable.*

worthy of gratitude/thanks *thankworthy.*

worthy of note *considerable/newsworthy/note- worthy/outstanding.* • One change worthy of note has been made in the condominium form. *One noteworthy change has been made in the condominium form.*

worthy of praise *admirable/commendable/ praiseworthy.*

worthy of trust *honest/trustworthy.*

would appear/guess/hope/imagine/seem/submit/suggest/suspect/think *appear/guess/hope/ imagine/seem/submit/suggest/suspect/think.* • I would suspect that the greatest gains would be from teaching the existing users to make even better use of current machines. *I suspect that the greatest gains would be from teaching the existing users to make even better use of current machines.* • I would hope that's what he meant. *I hope that's what he meant.* • I would submit that a number of shaky S&Ls could be salvaged over the next few years. *I submit that a number of shaky S&Ls could be salvaged over the next few years.*

would have *had.* • Tiger's dad wishes he would have known one startling fact. *Tiger's dad wishes he had known one startling fact.* • I wish I would have been there with them. *I wish I had been there with them.* •

I wish I would have known that. *I wish I had known that.*

written communication/correspondence *correspondence/letter/memo/note/report.* • Written correspondence is answered within a week, and phone calls are returned within 24 hours. *Letters are answered within a week, and phone calls are returned within 24 hours.*

X Y Z

X-ray photograph *X-ray.*

(the) year (of) delete. • Nearly 2,500 years ago, in the year 500 B.C., the first object which could project an image was made in ancient China. *Nearly 2,500 years ago, in 500 B.C., the first object which could project an image was made in ancient China.*

year in (and) year out *annually/always/ceaselessly/consistently/constantly/endlessly/eternally/ everlastingly/every year/forever/invariably/never ending/perpetually/routinely/unfailingly/yearly.* • Eighty percent of what retailers are ordering are classic lines whose demand is stable year in and year out. *Eighty percent of what retailers are ordering are classic lines whose demand is always stable.*

years (old) delete. • The study began in 1981–82 with a statewide survey of a sample of women 45 to 55 years old. *The study began in 1981–82 with a statewide survey of a sample of women 45 to 55.*

years of age delete. • I have committed my life to public service since I was 29 years of age. *I have committed my life to public service since I was 29.*

yell and scream *scream/yell.* • My wife and I yell and scream at each other about a lot of things, and we have a very healthy marriage. *My wife and I yell at each other about a lot of things, and we have a very healthy marriage.*

you know? delete.

you know what I mean? delete.

you know what I'm saying? delete.

young child/infant *child/infant/young.*

zero in on *focus on/pinpoint.* • It zeroes in on the problem of how expectations are formed—and changed. *It pinpoints the problem of how expectations are formed—and changed.*

zoological *zoologic.*

zoological garden *zoo.*

PART THREE

Guide to Obfuscation: A Reverse Dictionary

H ere is another view of perfecting words: a reverse dictionary. Looking at concision from the opposite direction will also help you recognize wordiness.

CONCISE	WORDY

A

a	(a) matter of
	per
a/the	(a/the) . . . point
	(a/the) point of
abating	on the decline
	on the decrease
abet	aid and abet
abide	put up with
ability	capability
	intellectual ability/capacity
ability/capacity	mental ability/capacity
a bit	(a) little bit
able to	in a position to
about	about/concerning/in/on/regarding the matter/subject of
	(for) approximately
	around about
	as . . . apply to
	as concerns
	as/so far as . . . (goes/is concerned)
	as regards
	as to
	concerning
	(an) estimated
	in (the) . . . case (of)
	in connection with
	in point of
	in reference to
	in regard to
	in relation to
	in respect of/to
	in terms of
	in the area of
	(something/somewhere) in the area (of)
	(something/somewhere) in the nature (of)

CONCISE	WORDY
	(something/somewhere) in the neighborhood (of)
	(something/somewhere) in the . . . range (of)
	in the realm of
	(something/somewhere) in the realm (of)
	(something/somewhere) in the region (of)
	(something/somewhere) in the vicinity (of)
	insofar as . . . (goes/is concerned)
	just about
	on . . . grounds
	(something/somewhere) on the order (of)
	pertain/pertaining to
	regard/regarding
	relate/relating to
	relative to
	when it comes to
	where . . . is concerned
	with reference to
	with regard to
	with relation to
	with respect to
about/around	about/around . . . to
	at about/around
about/for/in/on/to that/this	along that/this line
	in that/this connection
	in/on that/this matter
	in that/this regard
	in that/this respect
about to	at/on the brink of
	at/on the point of
	on the threshold of
	on the verge of
above	above and beyond
	in excess of
above all	most important
abruptly	at/in the blink of an eye
	expeditiously
	in quick/short order
ABS	ABS system
absent	in the absence of
absolutely	absolutely positively
	ifs, ands, or buts
abundant	(an/the) abundance of
	(a/the) high degree (of)
	(a/the) high level (of)

CONCISE	WORDY
abuse	take advantage of
abuses	is exploitative/exploitive of
AC	AC current
accurate	accurate and factual
accept	come to grips with
	come to terms with
	place/put credence in
	take delivery of/on
	take possession of
acclimate	acclimatize
accomplished/established	an accomplished/established fact
accomplishment	past/previous/prior accomplishment
according to	in accord/accordance with
	in agreement with
	in compliance with
	in conformance to/with
	in conformity to/with
	in consonance to/with
	in correspondence to/with
accredits to	is accredited/credited to
	is attributable to
a certain	(a/a certain/some) degree (of)
	(an/a certain/some) extent of
	(a/a certain/some) measure (of)
achieve	accomplish
	effectuate
	implement
achievement	past/previous/prior achievement
acknowledged/known	an acknowledged/known fact
a couple (of)	(a) couple three/two/two or three
	(a/the) limited number of
	(a/the) limited selection (of)
	(a/the) minimal number (of)
	(a/the) minority (of)
	(a/the) small/tiny amount/degree/part/percentage/portion/proportion/quantity (of)
	(a/the) small/tiny fraction (of)
	(a/the) small/tiny minority (of)
	(a/the) small/tiny number (of)
acquire	take delivery of/on
	take possession of
across	all across
act	render
	take action (to)

CONCISE	WORDY
act (to)	take measures (to)
action	course of action
	plan of action/attack/battle
active	in force and effect
	in operation
	operational
	operative
act -(al)ly	take . . . action (on/to)
act on	act in accord/accordance with
	impact (on/upon)
acts on	has (a) . . . effect on/upon
	has (a) . . . impact on/upon
	has (a) . . . influence on/upon
	has a bearing on/upon
actually	as a matter of fact
	(the) fact is (that)
	(the) (simple) fact of the matter is (that)
	in actual fact
	in actuality
	in point of fact
	in reality
	really (and) truly
	to tell (you) the truth
	(the) truth is (that)
	(the) truth of the matter is (that)
adage	old adage
add	add . . . additional/further/more
	add together
	incorporate in(to)
	sum up
	total up
added	(an) additional . . . added/extra/further/more/other
addicted	seriously addicted
add to	contribute to
	maximize
adequate	adequate enough
	good and sufficient
admirable	worthy of commendation
	worthy of praise
admiration	positive feelings
admire	appreciate
	derive enjoyment from
	derive pleasure from
	derive satisfaction from

CONCISE	WORDY
	take enjoyment in
	take pleasure in
	take satisfaction in
admit	admit to
admonish	take to task
advance	advance ahead/forth/forward/on/onward
	advance up
	go forward
	move forward
	move forward into the future
	proceed ahead/forth/forward/on/onward
	progress ahead/forward/on/onward
	put forth
	put forward
advertise	bring attention to
	bring into the open
	bring to . . . attention (of)
	bring to light
	call . . . attention to
	call to . . . attention (of)
	concentrate (media/people's/public) attention on/upon
	direct . . . attention to
	draw attention to
	focus (media/people's/public) attention on/upon
a fact	(an) accomplished/established fact
	(an) acknowledged/known fact
	(a/the) true fact
a few (of)	(a) couple of
	(a) couple three/two/two or three
	(a/the) limited number of
	(a/the) limited selection (of)
	(a) matter of
	(a/the) minimal number (of)
	(a/the) minority (of)
	(a/a fair/any) number (of)
	(a/the) small/tiny amount/degree/part/percentage/ portion/proportion/quantity (of)
	(a/the) small/tiny fraction (of)
	(a/the) small/tiny minority (of)
	(a/the) small/tiny number (of)
	some but not all
a few months (years) ago	in the immediate past
	in the (very) near past
	in the not-so-distant/not-too-distant past

CONCISE	WORDY
	in/within the recent past
a few times	on a couple of/a few occasions
	on more than one occasion
	on one/two/three occasion(s)
affect	impact (on/upon)
affection	positive feelings
affects	has a bearing on/upon
	has (a) . . . effect on/upon
	has (a) . . . impact on/upon
	has (a) . . . influence on/upon
	is influential in (-ing)
affidavit	sworn affidavit
affirm	according to
	bear witness to
affirmatively	in the affirmative
affirms	is (a) testament to
	is (a) testimony to
	is witness to
afford	make available
afresh	over again
after	after . . . first
	after . . . later/subsequently
	after . . . next
	after the conclusion/end of
	after the event/incident/occurrence
	after . . . then
	as a consequence of
	as a result of
	based on/upon
	because of
	by consequence of
	by reason of
	by the result of
	by/in virtue of
	for reasons of
	in back of
	in consequence of
	in honor of
	in imitation of
	in reaction to
	in response to
	on account of
	on the basis of
	posterior to

CONCISE	WORDY
	subsequently
	subsequent to (that/this)
	subsequent to the time (of/that/when)
	when (a/the) . . . done/finished/over/through
(just/right) after	in the aftermath of
	in the wake of
	on/upon the heels of
after all	contrary to
	in despite of
	in (the) face of
	in spite of
	notwithstanding
	. . . to the contrary
afternoon/evening/night	(3:00) p.m. . . . afternoon/evening/night
afterward	after the event/incident/occurrence
	subsequently
	subsequent to (that/this)
again	a second time
	in repetition
	one more time
	over again
against	as against
	as compared to/with
	as contrasted to/with
	as opposed to
	by comparison to/with
	by contrast to/with
	compared to/with
	contrasted to/with
	in comparison to/with
	in contrast to/with
	in defiance of
	in opposition to
	in relation/relationship to
	in resistance to
	in the face of
	in the opposite direction from/of
	measured against
	relative to
	when compared to/with
	when measured against
age	(a/the) time frame (of)
	(a/the) time horizon (of)
	(a/the) time period (of)

CONCISE	WORDY
	(a/the) time span (of)
aged	advanced/along in years
aggregate	aggregate together
ago	previous/previously
agonize (about/over)	voice concern (about)
	express concern (about)
a good (great) deal (of)	(a/the) considerable/good/great/huge/large/sizable/vast amount (of)
	(a/the) considerable/good/great/huge/large/sizable/vast degree (of)
	(a/the) considerable/good/great/huge/large/sizable/vast element (of)
	(a/the) considerable/good/great/huge/large/ overwhelming/sizable/vast/wide majority (of)
	(a/the) considerable/good/great/huge/large/sizable/vast part (of)
	(a/the) considerable/good/great/huge/large/ overwhelming/sizable/vast percentage (of)
	(a/the) considerable/good/great/huge/large/sizable/vast portion (of)
	(a/the) considerable/good/great/huge/large/sizable/vast proportion (of)
	(a/the) considerable/good/great/huge/large/sizable/vast quantity (of)
	considerably
	(a/the) great/large fraction (of)
	(a/the) high degree (of)
	(a/the) high level (of)
	(a/the) high percentage (of)
	(a/the) high proportion (of)
	in great/large quantities
	(a/the) large/overwhelming/sizable/vast plurality (of)
	(a/the) major part/percentage/portion/proportion (of)
	(a/the) overwhelming/vast preponderance (of)
	(a/the) significant/substantial amount (of)
	(a/the) significant/substantial degree (of)
	(a/the) significant/substantial element (of)
	(a/the) significant/substantial fraction (of)
	significantly/substantially
	(a/the) significant/substantial majority (of)
	(a/the) significant/substantial part (of)
	(a/the) significant/substantial percentage (of)

CONCISE	WORDY
	(a/the) significant/substantial portion (of)
	(a/the) significant/substantial proportion (of)
	(a/the) significant/substantial quantity (of)
a good (great) many (of)	(a/the) considerable/good/great/huge/large/sizable/vast amount (of)
	(a/the) considerable/good/great/huge/large/overwhelming/sizable/vast/wide majority (of)
	(a/the) considerable/good/great/huge/large/overwhelming/sizable/vast number (of)
	(a/the) considerable/good/great/huge/large/sizable/vast part (of)
	(a/the) considerable/good/great/huge/large/overwhelming/sizable/vast percentage (of)
	(a/the) considerable/good/great/huge/large/sizable/vast portion (of)
	(a/the) considerable/good/great/huge/large/sizable/vast proportion (of)
	(a/the) considerable/good/great/huge/large/sizable/vast quantity (of)
	(a/the) great/large fraction (of)
	(a/the) high degree (of)
	(a/the) high level (of)
	(a/the) high number (of)
	(a/the) high percentage (of)
	(a/the) high proportion (of)
	in big/great/high/huge/large/overwhelming/sizable/vast numbers
	in great/large quantities
	(a/the) large/overwhelming/sizable/vast plurality (of)
	(a/the) major part/percentage/portion/proportion (of)
	(a/the) multiplicity of
	(a/the) multitude of
	multitudinous
	(a/the) overwhelming/vast preponderance (of)
	(a/the) significant/substantial amount (of)
	(a/the) significant/substantial element (of)
	(a/the) significant/substantial fraction (of)
	(a/the) significant/substantial majority (of)
	(a/the) significant/substantial number (of)
	(a/the) significant/substantial part (of)
	(a/the) significant/substantial percentage (of)

CONCISE	WORDY
	(a/the) significant/substantial portion (of)
	(a/the) significant/substantial proportion (of)
	(a/the) significant/substantial quantity (of)
agree	arrive at (an/the) accord (about/as to/concerning/of/on/regarding)
	arrive at (an/the) agreement (about/as to/concerning/of/on/regarding)
	arrive at (a/the) compromise (about/as to/concerning/of/on/regarding)
	arrive at (a/the) resolution (about/as to/concerning/of/on/regarding)
	arrive at (a/the) settlement (about/as to/concerning/of/on/regarding)
	arrive at (an/the) understanding (about/as to/concerning/of/on/regarding)
	come to a/the compromise (about/as to/concerning/of/on/regarding)
	come to an accord (about/as to/concerning/of/on/regarding)
	come to an agreement (about/as to/concerning/of/on/regarding)
	come to an/the understanding
	come to a/the resolution (about/as to/concerning/of/on/regarding)
	come to a/the settlement (about/as to/concerning/of/on/regarding)
	come to terms (about/as to/concerning/of/on/regarding)
	enter into an agreement/contract
	reach (an/the) accord (about/of/on/upon/with)
	reach (an/the) agreement (about/of/on/upon/with)
	reach (a/the) compromise (about/of/on/upon/with)
	reach (a/the) resolution (about/of/on/upon/with)
	reach (a/the) settlement (about/of/on/upon/with)
	reach (an/the) understanding (about/of/on/upon/with)
	respond in the affirmative
agreement	contractual agreement
	joint agreement
agreement/agree	mutual agreement/mutually agree
agrees (on/with)	is in agreement (on/with)
agrees (with)	is coherent with
	is compatible with
	is consistent with
	is in accord/accordance on/with
	is in concurrence with

CONCISE	WORDY
	is in conformance to/with
	is in conformity to/with
	is in harmony with
	is in keeping with
	is in line with
	is in step with
	is of the same opinion (as)
agree with	go along with
	voice approval of
	voice support for
a handful (of)	(a/the) minimal number (of)
	(a/the) minority (of)
	(a/the) small/tiny amount/degree/part/percentage/portion/proportion/quantity (of)
	(a/the) small/tiny fraction (of)
	(a/the) small/tiny minority (of)
ahead of	in advance of
aid	aid and abet
	assistance
	render assistance to
AIDS	AIDS syndrome
aids	is advantageous for (to)
	is beneficial to
	is favorable to
	is of benefit to
aids in	is helpful in (-ing)
	is instrumental in (-ing)
	is instrumental in helping
aids in (-ing)	is of assistance in (-ing)
aim	take aim
	(the) whys and (the) wherefores (of)
aims	(the) hows and (the) whys
akin to	along the lines of
	in the nature of
	on the order of
alike	along the same line
	both . . . alike
	in a/the fashion/manner/way characteristic of
	in a/the fashion/manner/way similar to
	in a similar fashion/manner/way (to)
a little	(a) little bit
all	all and sundry
	all . . . long
	any and all

CONCISE	WORDY
	anybody (anyone) and everybody (everyone)
	anything and everything
	each and every (one)
	every single (solitary)
	in (almost) all/every cases/circumstances/instances/ situations
	in each/every case/circumstance/instance/situation
	on each/every occasion
	one and all
	the sum of
	the total (of)
	the totality of
	without exception
(we) all	all of (us)
	in its/their entirety
all (the)	all of (the)
allegation	unproved allegation
allege	according to
all in all	all things considered
	at the end of the day
	in the final/last analysis
	in the overall scope/sphere of things
	when all is said and done
	when it/you comes/gets right down to it
all over	present everywhere
allow	afford (give/offer/present/provide) . . . (an/the) opportunity (to)
	allow of
	make allowance for
	make concession for
	make provision for
	take account for/of
	take into account
	take into consideration
all right	(all) fine/good and good/well
	(all) well and fine/good
all/just the same	be that as it may
	but all/just the same
	in any case/event
all things	anything and everything
all through	extensively throughout
	from beginning to end
	from start to finish
	through and through

CONCISE	WORDY
	throughout the length and breadth (of)
all told	all in all
	all things considered
	at the end of the day
	in the final/last analysis
	in the overall scope/sphere of things
	on the whole
	when all is said and done
	when it/you comes/gets right down to it
ally	bring together
almost	almost without exception
	as a general rule
	as a rule
	(the) better part (of)
	(the) bulk (of)
	for the most part
	(a/the) high number (of)
	in (almost) all/every cases/circumstances/instances/ situations
	in big/great/high/huge/large/overwhelming/sizable/vast numbers
	in great/large measure
	in great/large part
	in great/large quantities
	in many/most cases
	in many/most circumstances
	in many/most instances
	in many/most situations
	in no small measure
	in no small part
	in the main
	just about
	(the) lion's share
	most but not all
	(a/a fair/any) number (of)
	on/upon the whole
	predominant/predominantly
	primary/primarily
	principal/principally
	to a great/large degree
	to a great/large extent
	with few/rare exception(s)
almost all (of)	(a/the) considerable/good/great/huge/large/sizable/vast amount (of)

CONCISE	WORDY
	(a/the) considerable (good/great/huge/large/ overwhelming/sizable/vast/wide) majority (of)
	(a/the) considerable/good/great/huge/large/ overwhelming/sizable/vast number (of)
	(a/the) considerable/good/great/huge/large/sizable/vast part (of)
	(a/the) considerable/good/great/huge/large/ overwhelming/sizable/vast percentage (of)
	(a/the) considerable/good/great/huge/large/sizable/vast portion (of)
	(a/the) considerable/good/great/huge/large/sizable/vast proportion (of)
	(a/the) considerable/good/great/huge/large/sizable/vast quantity (of)
	(a/the) great/large fraction (of)
	(a/the) high percentage (of)
	(a/the) high proportion (of)
	(a/the) large/overwhelming/sizable/vast plurality (of)
	(a/the) majority (of)
	(a/the) major part/percentage/portion/proportion (of)
	(a/the) overwhelming/vast preponderance (of)
	(a/the) plurality (of)
	(a/the) significant/substantial amount (of)
	(a/the) significant/substantial fraction (of)
	(a/the) significant/substantial majority (of)
	(a/the) significant/substantial number (of)
	(a/the) significant/substantial part (of)
	(a/the) significant/substantial percentage (of)
	(a/the) significant/substantial portion (of)
	(a/the) significant/substantial proportion (of)
	(a/the) significant/substantial quantity (of)
	(a/a certain/some) part (of)
	(a/a certain/some) percentage (of)
	(a/a certain/some) portion (of)
	(a/a certain/some) proportion (of)
	(a/a certain/some) quantity (of)
	(a/the) preponderance (of)
almost always	in (almost) all/every cases/circumstances/instances/ situations
	in many/most cases
	in many/most circumstances

CONCISE	WORDY
	in many/most instances
	in many/most regards
	in many/most respects
	in many/most situations
	more often than not
	most (of the) time(s)
	usually but not always
almost every	almost without exception
	with few/rare exception(s)
almost half (of)	(a/the) significant/substantial minority (of)
alone	(all) alone by himself/herself
	(all) by itself/themselves
	(all) by -self/-selves)
	high and dry
	in isolation (from)
alongside	alongside of
	as compared to/with
	as contrasted to/with
	as opposed to
	by comparison to/with
	by contrast to/with
	compared to/with
	contrasted to/with
	in comparison to/with
	in contrast to/with
	in relation/relationship to
	in the company of
	in the presence of
	measured against
	relative to
	side by side (with)
	when compared to/with
	when measured against
along with	accompanied by
	in association with
	in combination with
	in company with
	in conjunction with
	in connection with
	together with
aloud	out loud
alphabetic	alphabetical
alphabetize	put in alphabetical order
alphameric	alphanumerical

CONCISE	WORDY
alphanumeric	alphanumerical
also	additionally
	also . . . as well
	also . . . too
	and . . . also
	and . . . further/furthermore/in addition/moreover/ what's more
	as a matter of fact
	by the same token
	for that matter
	furthermore
	in addition
	in the next place
	in the second place
	in the third place
	next of all
	on top of (that/this)
alternative	alternative choice
although	albeit
	despite the fact that
	in spite of the fact that
	irregardless of the fact that
	irrespective of the fact that
	notwithstanding the fact that
	regardless of the fact that
altogether	all things considered
	at the end of the day
	in the final/last analysis
	under any circumstances/conditions
	when all is said and done
	when it/you comes/gets right down to it
always	all the time
	always and forever
	at every turn
	day in (and) day out
	for ever and a day
	forevermore
	from the beginning (start)
	in (almost) all/every cases/circumstances/instances/ situations
	in each/every case/circumstance/instance/situation
	in perpetuity
	on each/every occasion
	without exception

CONCISE	WORDY
	year in (and) year out
(8:00) a.m.	(8:00) a.m. . . . morning
amass	bring together
ambit	breadth and depth
amiable	kinder (and) gentler
amid	in (the) time(s) of
	in the middle of
	in the midst of
among	alongside of
	in the company of
	in the middle of
	in the midst of
	in the presence of
	on . . . part
	on the . . . side
	on the part of
	side by side (with)
among (us)	in (our) midst
amounts to	is (the) equal to
	is (the) equivalent of/to
	is identical to/with
	is tantamount to
ample	(a/the) high degree (of)
	(a/the) high level (of)
	(an/the) abundance of
	significant/substantial
	substantive
amply	considerably
	significantly/substantially
an array of	(a/the) broad/extensive/great/vast/wide array of
analysis	detailed/in-depth analysis
analytic	analytical
analyze	analyze in depth/in detail
and	accompanied by
	additionally
	and . . . also
	and . . . as well
	and . . . further/furthermore/in addition/moreover/ what's more
	and . . . too
	and so
	and yet
	as a matter of fact
	as well as

CONCISE	WORDY
	by the same token
	for that matter
	furthermore
	in addition
	in association with
	in combination with
	in company with
	in conjunction with
	in connection with
	in the next place
	in the second place
	in the third place
	next of all
	on top of (that/this)
	together with

and/between/both/
    each other/one another/two
	mutual . . . and/between/both/each other/
	                       one another/two

and others/and so forth/
    and so on/and such/
    and the like/et al./etc.
	e.g. . . . and others/and so forth/and so on/and such/
	                 and the like/et al./etc.
	like . . . and others/and so forth/and so on/and such/and
	                 the like/et al./etc.

and others/and so forth/
    and so on/and such/
    and the like/et al./etc./or
	for example . . . and others/and so forth/and so on/and
	                 such/and the like/et al./etc./or
	                 whatever
	for instance . . . and others/and so forth/and so on/and
	                 such/and the like/et al./etc./or
	                 whatever
	such as . . . and others/and so forth/and so on/and such/
	                 and the like/et al./etc./or whatever

and so forth	and etc./et cetera and everything/stuff/things like that and so on and so forth et cetera, et cetera, et cetera (etc., etc., etc.)
and so on	and etc./et cetera/ and everything/stuff/things like that and so on and so forth et cetera, et cetera, et cetera (etc., etc., etc.)
and that	along with/and/combined with/coupled with/plus/ together with . . . the fact that

CONCISE	WORDY
and the like	and etc./et cetera
	and everything/stuff/things like that
	and so on and so forth
	et cetera, et cetera, et cetera (etc., etc., etc.)
anew	over again
an/one example	(a) case in point
(be) an example/an instance	for one . . . (be) an example/an instance
anger	negative feelings
angry	furiously angry
	in a bad mood
anniversary	annual anniversary
announce	according to
	bring attention to
	bring into the open
	bring to . . . attention (of)
	bring to light
	call . . . attention to
	call to . . . attention (of)
	concentrate (media/people's/public) attention on/upon
	direct . . . attention to
	draw attention to
	focus (media/people's/public) attention on/upon
annoyance	negative feelings
annoyed	sick and tired
annually	year in (and) year out
antecede	take precedence over
	take priority over
anticipate	anticipate ahead
	anticipate ahead of time
	anticipate in advance
anxiety	fear and trembling
any	any and all
	anything/something in the way of
anybody	individual(s)
anybody/anyone	anybody/anyone and everybody/everyone
anyhow	all/just the same
	at any rate
	be that as it may
	by one means or another
	in any case/event
	nevertheless
	nonetheless
	(in) one way or another
anyone	individual(s)

CONCISE	WORDY
anyplace	at/from/in/on/to any/each/every/some area/locale/ locality/location/place/point/ position/region/site/spot
	at/from/in/on/to any/each/every/some area/locale/ locality/location/place/point/ position/region/site/spot where
anything	anything and everything
anything at all	anything and everything
any time	at any date/hour/time
anyway	by one means or another
	(in) one way or another
anywhere	at/from/in/on/to any/each/every/some area/locale/ locality/location/place/point/ position/region/site/spot
	at/from/in/on/to any/each/every/some area/locale/ locality/location/place/point/ position/region/site/spot where
apace	at/in the blink of an eye
	expeditiously
	in quick/short order
apart	in despite of
	in (the) face of
	in spite of
	notwithstanding
	separate and apart
	. . . to the contrary
apart (from)	contrary to
	in isolation (from)
	apart from . . . also/as well
	with the exception of/that
	with the exclusion of/that
a part of	(an) integral part of
apparent	in evidence
	what appears/seems to be
apparently	it is apparent that
	it is evident that
	on its (the) face (of it/of things)
	on the surface (of it/of things)
	to all appearances
appeals to	is of interest to
appear	come into being
	come into existence
	come into play
	make an appearance

CONCISE	WORDY
	put in an appearance
appear (to)	on its (the) face (of it/of things)
	on the surface (of it/of things)
	to all appearances
appear/arrive	appear/arrive on/upon the scene
appear/guess/hope/imagine/seem/ submit/suggest/suspect/think	would appear/guess/hope/imagine/seem/submit/suggest/ suspect/think
appear/seem	on its (the) face (of it/of things) . . . appear/seem
	on the surface (of it/of things) . . . appear/seem
	to all appearances . . . appear/seem
applaud	appreciate
applies in/to	is applicable in/to
	is appropriate in/to
applies to	is pertinent to
	is relevant to
	is suitable to
apply	bring to bear (on/upon)
appoint	appoint as
appreciate	appreciate in value
	come to an/the understanding (about/as to/concerning/ of/on/regarding)
	derive pleasure from
	derive satisfaction from
	place/put a premium on/upon
	place/put a priority on/upon
	place/put a value on/upon
	take satisfaction in
appreciates	has (an/the) appreciation for
	is appreciative of
approach	come close/near to
approaching	at/on the brink of
	at/on the point of
	on the threshold of
	on the verge of
approval	approbation
approval/consent	prior approval/consent
approve (of)	meet with (our) approval
	voice approval of
	voice support for
approves of	has (an/the) appreciation for
	is appreciative of
approximate	arrive at (an/the) estimate/estimation (about/as to/ concerning/of/on/regarding)

CONCISE	WORDY
	come to an/the estimate/estimation (about/as to/concerning/of/on/regarding)
	reach (an/the) estimate/estimation (about/of/on/upon/with)
	take a measure of
approximation/estimate/estimation	close/near/rough approximation/ estimate/estimation
apt	to the point
	to the purpose
a/the question	(an/the) open question
a range of	(a/the) broad/extensive/great/vast/wide range of
arbitrate	come to terms (about/as to/concerning/of/on/regarding)
area	breadth and depth
	general vicinity
	locality
	subject/topic area/field/matter
arguable	(an/the) open question
	open to doubt
	open to question
argues	is an indication/indicator of
	is indicative of
	is suggestive of
argument	argumentation
arise	come into being
	come into existence
	come into play
	eventuate
	first come into being
arises from	is a consequence of
	is a result of
ARM	ARM mortgage
around	(for) approximately
	around about
	(an) estimated
	(something/somewhere) in the area (of)
	(something/somewhere) in the nature (of)
	(something/somewhere) in the neighborhood (of)
	(something/somewhere) in the . . . range (of)
	(something/somewhere) in the realm (of)
	(something/somewhere) in the region (of)
	(something/somewhere) in the vicinity (of)
	(something/somewhere) on the order (of)
around/near here/there	in that/this general vicinity
arrange	prioritize
arrange for	make allowance for

CONCISE	WORDY
	make concession for
	make provision for
arrest	apprehend
	take into custody
arrive	make an appearance
	put in an appearance
arrive when	arrive at a time when
arrogant	high and mighty
as	as and when
	as . . . for example/for instance
	as is the case
	(and) at the same time (as/that)
	equally as
	in a/the fashion/manner/way (in which/that)
	in a/the fashion/manner/way characteristic of
	in a/the fashion/manner/way similar to
	in a similar fashion/manner/way (to)
	in terms of
	in the capacity of
	in the form of
	in the function of
	in the position of
	in the role of
	like . . . for example/for instance
	such as . . . for example/for instance
	the same way
	the way
	when and as
	while at the same time
	while concurrently
	while simultaneously
as (a/the)	in (a/the) . . . capacity/function/position/role (as/of)
as (be)	in the same fashion/manner/way (as/that)
as (does)	from (a/the) . . . aspect (of)
	from (a/the) . . . perspective (of)
	from (a/the) . . . point of view (of)
	from (a/the) . . . standpoint (of)
	from (a/the) . . . viewpoint (of)
as a result	and so as a result
as a rule	as a general rule
as a team/unit	together as a team/unit
ascend	ascend up
ascribes to	is accredited/credited to
	is attributable to

CONCISE	WORDY
as far as	inasmuch/insomuch as
	insofar as
	to the degree (that/to which)
	to the extent (that/to which)
	to the greatest/largest degree/extent
as follows	in the following fashion/manner/way
as for	about/concerning/in/on/regarding the matter/subject of
	as . . . apply to
	as concerns
	as/so far as . . . (goes/is concerned)
	as regards
	concerning
	from (a/the) . . . aspect (of)
	from (a/the) . . . perspective (of)
	from (a/the) . . . point of view (of)
	from (a/the) . . . standpoint (of)
	from (a/the) . . . viewpoint (of)
	in (the) . . . case (of)
	in connection with
	in point of
	in reference to
	in regard to
	in relation to
	in respect of/to
	insofar as . . . (goes/is concerned)
	in terms of
	in the area of
	in the realm of
	pertain/pertaining to
	regard/regarding
	relate/relating to
	when it comes to
	where . . . is concerned
	with reference to
	with regard to
	with relation to
	with respect to
as for/in/with	as for/in/with the case of
aside	in (the) face of
	in despite of
	in spite of
	notwithstanding
	. . . to the contrary
aside (from)	aside from . . . also/as well

CONCISE	WORDY
	contrary to
	with the exception of/that
	with the exclusion of/that
as it were	figuratively speaking
	in a manner of speaking
	metaphorically speaking
ask	ask (a/the) question (on)
	inquire (about/of)
as long as	on (the) condition (of/that)
	on (the) understanding (of/that)
as much	the same thing
as much as	inasmuch/insomuch as
	insofar as
	to the degree (that/to which)
	to the extent (that/to which)
	to the greatest/largest degree/extent
as needed	as the need arises/develops
as one	at the same time
	concurrently
	simultaneously
a spectrum of	(a/the) broad/extensive/great/vast/wide spectrum of
as planned/projected	according to plan/projections
assail	attack by assailants
assault	attack by assailants
assemble	assemble in a group
	assemble together
	bring together
	come together
	put together
assert	according to
	hold (to) the opinion (that)
	hold (to) the view (that)
	in the assessment of
	in the estimation of
	in the judgment of
	in the opinion of
	in the view of
	take the position (that)
	take the view (that)
asserts	is inclined to believe (that)
	is inclined to think (that)
	is of the belief (that)
	is of the opinion (that)
	is of the view (that)

CONCISE	WORDY
assess	arrive at (an/the) estimate/estimation (about/as to/concerning/of/on/regarding)
	come to an/the estimate/estimation (about/as to/concerning/of/on/regarding)
	form (a/the) judgment (about/as to/concerning/of/on/regarding)
	form (an/the) opinion (about/as to/concerning/of/on/regarding)
	reach (an/the) estimate/estimation (about/of/on/upon/with)
(an) asset	(a) valuable asset
assets	financial/monetary resources
	financial wherewithal
	wherewithal
assigns to	is accredited/credited to
	is attributable to
assist	help assist
	render assistance to
assists in	is helpful in (-ing)
	is instrumental in (-ing)
	is instrumental in helping
assists in (-ing)	is of assistance in (-ing)
	(many) widely varying
as soon as possible	at your earliest convenience
assorted	(an) array of
	(a/the) broad/extensive/great/vast/wide array of
	(a/the) broad/extensive/great/vast/wide range of
	(a/the) broad/extensive/great/vast/wide spectrum of
	(a/the) broad/extensive/great/vast/wide variety of
	(a/the) diversity of different
	(a) range of
	(a/the) spectrum of
	(a) variety of
	(a/the) variety of different
	various and sundry
	various different
as such	in and of itself
assumes	is based on the assumption
	is predicated on the assumption (that)
	is under the assumption (that)
	is under the impression (that)
assuming (that)	if by way of hypothesis/supposition
assurance	positive assurance
assuredly	beyond a/the shadow of a doubt

CONCISE	WORDY
as to	about/concerning/in/on/regarding the matter/subject of
	as . . . apply to
	as concerns
	as/so far as . . . (goes/is concerned)
	as regards
	concerning
	from (a/the) . . . aspect (of)
	from (a/the) . . . perspective (of)
	from (a/the) . . . point of view (of)
	from (a/the) . . . standpoint (of)
	from (a/the) . . . viewpoint (of)
	in (the) . . . case (of)
	in connection with
	in point of
	in reference to
	in regard to
	in relation to
	in respect of/to
	insofar as . . . (goes/is concerned)
	in terms of
	in the area of
	in the realm of
	pertain/pertaining to
	regard/regarding
	relate/relating to
	when it comes to
	where . . . is concerned
	with reference to
	with regard to
	with relation to
	with respect to
as usual	in the normal/ordinary/typical/usual course of business/events/things
as well	additionally
	also . . . as well
	and . . . as well
	and . . . further/furthermore/in addition/moreover/what's more
	as a matter of fact
	by the same token
	for that matter
	furthermore
	in addition
	in the next place

CONCISE	WORDY
	in the second place
	in the third place
	next of all
	on top of (that/this)
as well as	accompanied by
	both . . . as well as
	in association with
	in combination with
	in company with
	in conjunction with
	in connection with
	together with
at	at (a/the) . . . pace (of)
	at (a/the) . . . rate (of)
	at (a/the) . . . speed (of)
	at the corner/intersection of
	in the direction of/toward
at/for	at/for a/the cost/price/sum of
at/in	given at/in
	shown at/in
at all	absolutely
	by any means
	in any fashion/manner/way
	in any way, shape, or form (or fashion)
	(in) one way or the other
	under any circumstances/conditions
	whatsoever
at first	in/over the near term
	in/over the short run
	in/over the short term
	initial/initially
	over the short haul
at last	at long last
	(after/for/in/over/within) (an) extended/lengthy/long/prolonged/protracted amount of time/length of time/period/period of time/span of time/time/while
at least	at the (very) minimum
	(a/the) minimum (of)
at length	(after/for/in/over/within) (an) extended/lengthy/long/prolonged/protracted amount of time/length of time/period/period of time/span of time/time/while
	as (the) days/decades/months/weeks/years go on

CONCISE	WORDY
	as time goes on
	as time progresses/forward/on/onward
	at a/some future/later/subsequent date/time
	down the line/pike/road/way
	in/over (the) coming days/decades/months/weeks/years
	in/over (the) days/decades/months/weeks/years ahead
	in/over (the) days/decades/months/weeks/years to come
	in due course/time
	in good time
	in/into the future
	in the course of events/things/time
	in/over the long run
	in/over the long term
	later in time
	later on down the line/pike/road/way
	over the long haul
	some day/time in the future
	(the) time will come when
	with the passage of time
ATM	ATM machine
at odds	at the same time
	at your earliest convenience
	concurrently
	instantaneous/instantaneously
	in the immediate future
	of (a) different opinion
	simultaneously
at one	of the same opinion
at one time	at a certain/any/one/some point in my history/point in my life/point in the history of my life/point in time
atop	atop of
	at/on (the) top (of)
	on (the) top of
at present	at that/this juncture
	at that/this juncture/juncture in time/moment/moment in time/period/period in time/point/point in time/stage/stage in time/time in my history/in my life/in the history of my life
	at that/this juncture/moment/period/point/stage in time
	at that/this moment
	at that/this point
	at that/this stage

CONCISE	WORDY
	at that/this time
	at the current/present time
	at the (current/present) moment
	in/over the near term
	in/over the short run
	in/over the short term
	on that/this (particular) occasion
	over the short haul
at some point	at some point/time along the line/the way
	somewhere along the line/the way
at some time	somewhere along the line/the way
at that/this time	at that/this juncture
	at that/this juncture/juncture in time/moment/moment in time/period/period in time/point/point in time/stage/stage in time/time in my history/in my life/in the history of my life
	at that/this juncture/moment/period/point/stage in time
	at that/this moment
	at that/this stage
	on that/this (particular) occasion
at the same time	simultaneously . . . at the same time
	while at the same time
at this time	at the current/present time
at times	ever and anon
	every now and then
	every once in a while
	in certain/some cases
	in certain/some circumstances
	in certain/some instances
	in certain/some situations
	in other cases/circumstances/instances/situations
	occasionally
	once in a (great) while
	on certain/some occasions
	under certain/some circumstances/conditions
attach	attach together
attack	attack by assailants
	take issue (with)
attend	make an appearance
	put in an appearance
attend to	pay attention to
	pay heed to
	take cognizance of

CONCISE	WORDY
	take note of
	take notice of
attends	is in attendance (at)
attends to	is attentive to
attention on	attention . . . focused on/upon
attest	according to
	attest to the fact (that)
attests	(just) goes to show
attests to	is an indication/indicator of
	is indicative of
	is suggestive of
	is (a) testament to
	is (a) testimony to
	is witness to
attest to	bear witness to
attitude	frame of mind
	point of view
attraction	positive feelings
attracts	is of interest to
attributes to	is accredited/credited to
	is attributable to
at work	in force and effect
	operative
audible	audible to the ear
author	authoress
authorities	law enforcement officers
authorize	voice approval of
	voice support for
autonomous	separate and autonomous
a variety of	(a/the) broad/extensive/great/vast/wide variety of
	(a/the) diversity of different
	(a/the) variety of different
aver	according to
average	run of the mill
avow	according to
awhile	for a while
	for awhile
	for (an) extended/prolonged/protracted amount of time/ length of time/period/period of time/ span of time/time/while

CONCISE	WORDY

B

baby	(brand) new baby
back	go along with
	stand in support of
	take a stand for/in favor of/in support of
	voice approval of
	voice support for
background	background (of) experience
backs	is in favor of
	is in support of
back up	substantiate
balance	balance out
bald	bald-headed
bare	(very) limited
barring	with the exception of/that
	with the exclusion of/that
based on	by the result of
	on the basis of
base on	predicate on/upon
baseless	no basis in fact
	unsubstantiated
	without basis in fact
	without foundation
basic	basic (and) fundamental
	fundamental
	fundamental (and) basic
basis	basis in fact/reality/truth
	factual basis
	fundamental basis
bathroom	bathroom facilities
	comfort facilities
	facility
be	constitute
bear	bring/give forth
	bring into the world
	give birth to
	give rise to
	put up with
bear on	impact (on/upon)
bears on	has (a) . . . effect on/upon

CONCISE	WORDY
	has (a) . . . impact on/upon
	has (a) . . . influence on/upon
	has a bearing on/upon
	is applicable in/to
	is appropriate in/to
	is pertinent to
	is relevant to
	is suitable to
because	about the fact that
	as a consequence of the fact that
	as a result of the fact that
	attributable to the fact that
	based on the fact that
	because of the fact that
	being (as/as how/that)
	by reason of the fact that
	by the fact that
	by/in virtue of the fact that
	considering the fact that
	due to the fact that
	forasmuch as
	for the (simple) reason that
	from the fact that
	given the fact that
	inasmuch/insomuch as
	in consequence of the fact that
	in consideration of the fact that
	in (the) light of the fact that
	insofar as
	in the sense that
	in view of the fact that
	on account of the fact that
	on (the) grounds that
	on the basis of the fact that
	over the fact that
	owing to the fact that
	(the) reason (why) . . . is because
	reason (why) . . . is that
	seeing (as/as how/that)
because of	as a consequence of
	as a result of
	ascribable to
	attributable to
	by consequence of

CONCISE	WORDY
	by reason of
	by the result of
	by/in virtue of
	caused because of/due to/owing to
	(a/the) consequence of
	for reasons of
	in consequence of
	in consideration of (payment of/sum of)
	in reaction to
	in response to
	in the wake of
	on account of
	on the basis of
	reason (why) . . . is due to (the fact that)
beer	liquid refreshment
befall	come about
	come to pass
	eventuate
before	ahead of
	ahead of time
	anterior to
	at an/some earlier/former/past/previous date/time
	back/before in the past
	before . . . first
	first . . . before
	in advance
	in advance of
	in (the) days/decades/months/weeks/years gone by
	in (the) days/decades/months/weeks/years of old
	in (the) days/decades/months/weeks/years past
	in earlier/former/prior times
	in front of
	in (the) olden days
	in/over (the) past days/decades/months/weeks/years
	in the days/decades/months/weeks/years before/prior to
	in the distant past
	in the face of
	in the (very) near past
	in the not-so-distant/not-too-distant past
	in the past
	in (within) the recent past
	on earlier/former/previous/prior occasions
	preliminary to
	previous/previously

CONCISE	WORDY
	previous to
	prior to
	prior to . . . first
	prior to that/the/this time (of)
	till/until after
beforehand	ahead of time
	in advance
before long	(after/for/in/over/within) a brief/limited/little/short amount of time/length of time/ moment of time/period/period of time/span of time/time/while
	in/into the future
	in/over (the) coming days/decades/months/weeks/years
	in/over (the) days/decades/months/weeks/years ahead
	in/over (the) days/decades/months/weeks/years to come
	in the foreseeable future
	in the immediate future
	in the (very) near future
	in/over the near term
	in the not-so-distant/not-too-distant future
	in/over the short run
	in/over the short term
	over the short haul
before now/then	prior to that/the/this time (of)
begin	begin and commence
	begin . . . first
	bring about
	bring to pass
	commence
	first begin
	first come into being
	first start
begin/start	initially . . . begin/start
beginnings	early beginnings
behavior	behavior pattern
behead	decapitate . . . (the) head (of)
behind	in back of
	posterior to
(close) behind	in the aftermath of
	in the wake of
	on/upon the heels of
being	human being
be killed	made/paid the ultimate sacrifice
belief	belief/opinion/point of view/view/viewpoint

CONCISE	WORDY
	frame of mind
	personal belief/opinion/point of view/view/viewpoint
	point of view
believe	hold (to) the opinion (that)
	hold (to) the view (that)
	in the assessment of
	in the estimation of
	in the judgment of
	in the opinion of
	in the view of
	place/put credence in
	take the position (that)
	take the view (that)
believes	is inclined to believe (that)
	is inclined to think (that)
	is of the belief (that)
	is of the opinion (that)
	is of the view (that)
	is under the assumption (that)
	is under the impression (that)
be like	bear (a/the) . . . resemblance/similarity to
bellow/holler/howl/roar/ scream/shout/shriek/yell	loudly bellow/holler/howl/roar/scream/shout/shriek/yell
belongs to	affiliated with
	associated with
below	follow . . . below
	on the bottom of
	underneath
bemoan	express sorrow (about)
	voice sorrow (about)
beneath	on the bottom of
	underneath
benefit	derive benefit (from)
	positive benefit
	prove of benefit to
benefit from	take advantage of
benefits	is advantageous for (to)
	is beneficial to
	is favorable to
	is of benefit to
be pleased with	take satisfaction in
beside	adjacent to
	alongside of
	as compared to/with

CONCISE	WORDY
	as contrasted to/with
	as opposed to
	by comparison to/with
	by contrast to/with
	compared to/with
	contrasted to/with
	in comparison to/with
	in contrast to/with
	in relation/relationship to
	in the company of
	in the presence of
	measured against
	relative to
	side by side (with)
	when compared to/with
	when measured against
besides	above and beyond
	additionally
	and . . . further/furthermore/in addition/moreover/what's more
	apart from
	apart from . . . also/as well
	as a matter of fact
	aside from
	aside from . . . also/as well
	besides . . . also/as well
	by the same token
	for that matter
	furthermore
	in addition
	in addition to
	in addition to . . . additionally/also/as well/too
	in the next place
	in the second place
	in the third place
	next of all
	on top of (that/this)
	other than
	other than . . . also/as well
	over and above
	with the exception of/that
	with the exclusion of/that
be similar to	bear (a/the) . . . resemblance/similarity to
bespeaks	is an indication/indicator of

CONCISE	WORDY
	is indicative of
	is suggestive of
best	no better (than)
	of the first magnitude
	of the first/highest order
	optimal/optimum
best/biggest/fastest/greatest/ largest/most/slowest	
	best/biggest/fastest/greatest/largest/most/slowest . . . single
	(the) single best/biggest/fastest/greatest/largest/most/ slowest
best/most	one best/most
be still	continue to be
	continue to remain
best known	most well known
betokens	is an indication/indicator of
	is indicative of
	is suggestive of
better than	in excess of
between	(something/somewhere) in between
	from one . . . to another
between . . . and	anywhere/somewhere between . . . and
	between . . . as compared to/as opposed to/compared to/ versus
	(the) decade/period/period of time/span of time/time/ years between . . . and
	(the) decade/period/period of time/span of time/time/ years (from) . . . through/till/to/until
	during/for/over the decade/period/period of time/span of time/time/years (from) . . . through/ till/to/until
	(something/somewhere) in the range from (of) . . . through/to
	in the . . . through/to . . . range
(be) between . . . and	begin/start at . . . and end/finish at
between them/us	between the two of them/us
between us	between you and me/us
beyond	above and beyond
	apart from
	apart from . . . also/as well
	aside from
	aside from . . . also/as well
	besides . . . also/as well
	in addition to

CONCISE	WORDY
	in addition to . . . additionally/also/as well/too
	in excess of
	other than . . . also/as well
	over and above
beyond that/this	additionally
	and . . . further/furthermore/in addition/moreover/ what's more
	as a matter of fact
	by the same token
	for that matter
	in addition
	in the next place
	in the second place
	in the third place
	on top of (that/this)
bias	biased opinion
	personal bias
	prejudicial opinion
bid	enter a bid
big	big, huge/large
	humongous
	significant/substantial
	substantive
biggest	maximal
	(a/the) maximum amount (of)
	(a/the) maximum number (of)
	(a/the) maximum . . . of
bimonthly	on a regular basis
bind	place/put restrictions on/upon
	place/put under obligation
	under obligation
biographic	biographical
biologic	biological
biometric	biometrical
biophysiologic	biophysiological
bit	tiny/little bit
bits	bits and pieces
biweekly	on a regular basis
blamable	worthy of blame
blame	to find (a) fault in/with
blameworthy	worthy of blame
blazon	bring attention to
	bring into the open
	bring to . . . attention (of)

CONCISE	WORDY
	bring to light
	call . . . attention to
	call to . . . attention (of)
	concentrate (media/people's/public) attention on/upon
	direct . . . attention to
	draw attention to
	focus (media/people's/public) attention on/upon
blend	blend of both
	blend together
block	block out
	stand in the way of
blocks	is a deterrent to
	is a hindrance to
	is an impediment to
	is an obstacle to
blurred	out of focus
bode ill/well	bode ill/well for the future
body	dead body
bond	bring together
	relationship
bonus	added bonus
booming	on the increase
	on the rise
boredom	tedious monotony
botch	botch up
both	both . . . alike
	both equally
	both . . . in combination
	both of (the)
	(the) both of
	both share
	both together
	in both cases/circumstances/instances/situations
	(a/the) combination (of)
both (of them)	(a/the) combination of both
	(a/the) combination of the two
both . . . and	both . . . as well as
bothers	is of concern to
boundary	parameter
bouquet	bouquet of flowers
breadth	breadth and depth
break	fail to comply with
brewing	in the making
bridge	build a bridge across/between

CONCISE	WORDY
brief	minimal
	short and sweet
	short and to the point
briefly	(after/for/in/over/within) a brief/limited/little/short amount of time/length of time/ moment of time/period/period of time/span of time/time/while
	briefly in passing
	for (an) indefinite/indeterminate amount of time/length of time/period/period of time/span of time/time/while
	in a few minutes/moments/seconds
	in a minute/moment/second
	in a nutshell
briefly/concisely/succinctly	in brief/concise/succinct summary
bring about	cause to happen/occur/take place
	effectuate
briskly	at/in the blink of an eye
	expeditiously
	in quick/short order
broad	(a/the) broad/extensive/great/vast/wide array of
	(a/the) broad/extensive/great/vast/wide range of
	(a/the) broad/extensive/great/vast/wide spectrum of
	(a/the) broad/extensive/great/vast/wide variety of
	(a/the) diversity of different
	(a/the) high degree (of)
	(a/the) high level (of)
	(many) widely varying
broadcast	bring attention to
	bring into the open
	bring to . . . attention (of)
	bring to light
	call . . . attention to
	call to . . . attention (of)
	concentrate (media/people's/public) attention on/upon
	direct . . . attention to
	draw attention to
	focus (media/people's/public) attention on/upon
broaden	maximize
broadly	far and wide
brood (on/over)	express concern (about)
	is concerned (about)
	voice concern (about)
build	put together

CONCISE	WORDY
building	edifice
	facility
	institution
	premises
burden	place/put a burden on/upon
	place/put a strain on/upon
business	establishment
	official business
	place of business/employment/work
businesslike	matter-of-fact
but	but all/just the same
	but however
	but instead
	but nevertheless
	but nonetheless
	but on the other hand
	but rather
	but whereas
	by/in comparison
	by/in contrast
	by way of comparison/contrast
	contrariwise
	despite the fact that
	in spite of the fact that
	irregardless of the fact that
	irrespective of the fact that
	no more than
	notwithstanding the fact that
	on the contrary
	on the other hand
	regardless of the fact that
	to the contrary
but for	if it were not for
	were it not for
	with the exception of/that
	with the exclusion of/that
but to	other than to
buy	purchase
	take delivery of/on
	take possession of
by	according to
	as a consequence of
	as a result of
	as to

CONCISE	WORDY
	at (a/the) . . . pace (of)
	at (a/the) . . . rate (of)
	at (a/the) . . . speed (of)
	at the hands of
	based on/upon
	because of
	by (a/the) . . . margin (of)
	by (the) means of
	by/in virtue of
	by (the) way of
	by consequence of
	by reason of
	by the result of
	for reasons of
	in accord/accordance with
	in agreement with
	in . . . behalf (of)
	in compliance with
	in conformance to/with
	in conformity to/with
	in consequence of
	in consonance to/with
	in correspondence to/with
	in reaction to
	in response to
	in terms of
	on account of
	on . . . part
	on the basis of
	on the part of
	pursuant to
	through the medium of
	through the use of
by (-ing)	by way of (-ing)
by being	by way of being
by chance	as it turned out
	as luck would have it
	it (just) so happens
by/in contrast	on the other hand
by far	by (a/the) considerable/good/great/huge/large/ overwhelming/sizable/vast/wide margin
	far and away
by hand	manually by hand

CONCISE	WORDY
by himself/herself	alone
by itself	in isolation (from)
by next week/tomorrow	(after/for/in/over/within) a reasonable amount of time/ length of time/period/period of time/ span of time/time/while
	in a timely fashion/manner/way
	on a timely basis
by no means	absolutely not
by some means	by one means or another
	(in) one way or another
by turns	turn and turn about

C

cachet	badge/mark/sign/symbol of authenticity/distinction/ honor/prestige/rank
cacophony	cacophony of noise/sound
call	call up
	characterize as
	communicate (with)
	contact
	get in touch with
	make contact (with)
	pick up the phone/telephone and call
	refer to as
called	known as
call or write	communicate (with)
calm	calm, cool, and collected
can	has (an/the) ability to
	has a/the capability to
	is able to
	is capable of -ing
	is it possible for
cancel	do away with
	terminate
candidly	to tell (you) the truth
candor	candor and frankness
cannot	is incapable of -ing
capacity	full capacity
	intellectual ability/capacity
capital	capital city
	financial/monetary resources

CONCISE	WORDY
	financial wherewithal
capitol	capitol building
capture	apprehend
	take into custody
carry out	effectuate
cash	compensation
	financial wherewithal
	remittance
	remuneration
	wherewithal
catch	apprehend
	take into custody
cause	bring about
	bring to pass
	cause to happen/occur/take place
	give rise to
	root cause
	(the) whys and (the) wherefores (of)
caused by	ascribable to
	attributable to
	caused because of/due to/owing to
	(a/the) consequence of
causes	(the) hows and (the) whys
CD-ROM	CD-ROM disc
cease	bring (to) a close (to)
	bring (to) a completion (to)
	bring (to) a conclusion (to)
	bring (to) a halt (to)
	bring (to) an end (to)
	bring to a standstill
	call a halt to
	call an end to
	call a stop to
	cease and desist
	come to a close
	come to a/the conclusion (about/as to/concerning/of/on/ regarding)
	come to a halt
	come to an end
	come to a standstill
	draw to a close/end
	draw to a conclusion
	put a halt to
	put a stop to

CONCISE	WORDY
	put an end to
	terminate
ceaselessly	all the time
	at every turn
	day in (and) day out
	for ever and a day
	in perpetuity
	year in (and) year out
center	focal point
	(the) heart of the matter
	sum/summary and substance
	(the) long and (the) short
center on	center around
central	(of) central/critical/vital importance
	most important
	number-one
	of the first magnitude
	of the first/highest order
central to	(a/the) central . . . in/of/to
certainly	beyond a/the shadow of a doubt
	to be sure
	without (a/any) doubt
	without (a) question
	without (a/any) question/shadow of a doubt
certifies to	is (a) testament to
	is (a) testimony to
	is witness to
certify to	bear witness to
challenge	bring into question
	call into question
	cast doubt on/upon
	fly in the face of
	place/put into question
	raise doubts about/on
	raise objections about/on/to
	raise opposition about/on/to
	raise questions about/on
	take exception to
	take issue (with)
	throw into doubt
	throw into question
chance	probability
	window of opportunity
characterizes	is characteristic of

CONCISE	WORDY
	is descriptive of
	is illustrative of
charges to	is accredited/credited to
	is attributable to
charge with	charge with the responsibility for/of
charm	personal charm
chat	have a conversation (about)
	make conversation
cheat	take advantage of
cheats	is exploitative/exploitive of
check	check to see
	look/observe to see
cheerful	in a good mood
cherish	place/put a premium on/upon
	place/put a priority on/upon
	place/put a value on/upon
cherishes	has (an/the) appreciation for
	is appreciative of
chide	take to task
chief	first and foremost
	most important
	number-one
	of the first magnitude
	of the first/highest order
	predominant/predominantly
	primary/primarily
	principal/principally
chiefly	as a general rule
	as a rule
	basically
	by and large
	first and foremost
	for the most part
	in great/large measure
	in great/large part
	in no small measure
	in no small part
	in the main
	on/upon the whole
	predominant/predominantly
	primary/primarily
	principal/principally
	to a great/large degree
	to a great/large extent

CONCISE	WORDY
child	little/small child
	young child
choose	pick and choose
	select out
christen	christen as
circle	encircle
city	locality
	metropolis
claim	according to
	hold (to) the opinion (that)
	hold (to) the view (that)
	in the assessment of
	in the estimation of
	in the judgment of
	in the opinion of
	in the view of
	take the position (that)
	take the view (that)
claiming	(something) to that/the/this effect (that)
claims	is inclined to believe (that)
	is inclined to think (that)
	is of the belief (that)
	is of the opinion (that)
	is of the view (that)
clamor	hue and cry
clashes with	is at loggerheads (with)
	is at odds over/with
	is at variance with
	is in conflict with
	is in (marked/sharp) contrast to
	is in disagreement (about/on/with)
clash with	stand in (marked/sharp) contrast to
clean	neat and tidy
clear	clear, free, and unencumbered
	free and clear
	plain and simple
clearly	(it) goes without saying (that)
	it is apparent that
	it is evident that
	needless to say
	needs hardly be said
cliché	old cliché
climate	weather conditions
climb	climb up

CONCISE	WORDY
close	bring (to) a close (to)
	bring (to) a completion (to)
	bring (to) a conclusion (to)
	bring (to) a halt (to)
	bring (to) an end (to)
	bring to a standstill
	call a halt to
	call an end to
	call a stop to
	close down
	come to a close
	come to a/the conclusion (about/as to/concerning/of/on/ regarding)
	come to a halt
	come to an end
	come to a standstill
	draw to a close/end
	draw to a conclusion
	put a halt to
	put an end to
	put a stop to
	close/near at hand
	close by
	in close proximity (to)
	in proximity (to)
	in the neighborhood (of)
	in the proximity (of)
	in the vicinity (of)
close (to)	adjacent to
	along the lines of
	(for) approximately
	at/on the brink of
	at/on the point of
	(the) better part (of)
	close/near at hand
	(an) estimated
	in close proximity (to)
	in proximity (to)
	(something/somewhere) in the area (of)
	in the nature of
	(something/somewhere) in the nature (of)
	in the neighborhood (of)
	(something/somewhere) in the neighborhood (of)
	in the proximity (of)

CONCISE	WORDY
	(something/somewhere) in the . . . range (of)
	(something/somewhere) in the realm (of)
	(something/somewhere) in the region (of)
	in the vicinity (of)
	(something/somewhere) in the vicinity (of)
	on the order of
	(something/somewhere) on the order (of)
	on the threshold of
	on the verge of
closeness	proximity
clout	input
club	establishment
clue	indication
cluster	cluster together
cobble	cobble together
coerce	bring pressure to bear on/upon
coffee	liquid refreshment
cohabit	cohabitate
	cohabit together
coheres with	is coherent with
	is compatible with
	is consistent with
	is in concurrence with
	is in harmony with
	is in keeping with
	is in line with
	is in step with
coincides (with)	is in accord/accordance on/with
	is in agreement (on/with)
	is in conformance to/with
	is in conformity to/with
coined	first/initially coined
coiner/coined	original coiner/originally coined
cold	freezing cold
collaborate	collaborate together
collect	bring together
	collect together
	take delivery of/on
	take possession of
collected	calm, cool, and collected
collectively	at the same time
	simultaneously
college	educational institution
	institution of higher learning

CONCISE	WORDY
combination	(a/the) combination of both
	(a/the) combination of the two
combine	combine both
	combine into one
	combine together
combined	in conjunction
combined with	accompanied by
	in association with
	in combination with
	in conjunction with
	in connection with
	together with
come	make an appearance
	put in an appearance
come about	come into play
	eventuate
come across	come in contact (with)
come before	take precedence over
	take priority over
comes with	is equipped/furnished with
come when	come at a time when
come with	come equipped/furnished with
comic	comical
commence	begin and commence
commendable	worthy of commendation
	worthy of praise
comment	according to
	make (a/the) statement saying/stating
commitment	firm/strong commitment
common	common (and) everyday
	matter-of-course
	run of the mill
commonly	as a general rule
	as a matter of course
	as a rule
	as often as not
	by and large
	for the most part
	in great/large measure
	in great/large part
	in many/most cases
	in many/most circumstances
	in many/most instances
	in many/most situations

CONCISE	WORDY
	in normal/ordinary/typical/usual practice
	in no small measure
	in no small part
	in the main
	in the normal/ordinary/typical/usual course of business/ events/things
	more often than not
	most (of the) time(s)
	on (an/the) average
	on/upon the whole
	to a great/large degree
	to a great/large extent
communicate	communicate in writing
	have a conversation (about)
	make conversation
communication	mutual communication
company	establishment
	place of business/employment/work
compare (to)	compare and contrast (versus)
compared/contrasted to/with	comparatively . . . compared/contrasted to/with
	compared/contrasted to/with . . . relatively
	in comparison/in contrast to/with . . . relatively
	relatively . . . compared/contrasted to/with
	relatively . . . in comparison/in contrast to/with
	relatively . . . in relation to
	relatively . . . relative to
compared to/with	as compared to/with
	as compared to/with . . . relatively
	as contrasted to/with
	as opposed to
	as opposed to . . . relatively
	by comparison (to/with) . . . relatively
	by comparison to/with
	by contrast to/with
	contrasted to/with
	in comparison to/with
	in contrast to/with
	in relation/relationship to
	measured against
	relative to
	relatively . . . as/when compared to/with
	when compared to/with
	when compared to/with . . . relatively
	when measured against

CONCISE	WORDY
compares to/with	is comparable to/with
	is similar to/with
compare to/with	compare against (versus)
compartment	compartmentalize
compass	breadth and depth
compassionate	kinder (and) gentler
compel	bring pressure to bear on/upon
	place/put restrictions on/upon
	place/put under obligation
	under obligation
competence	competency
competes with	is competitive with
	is in competition with
compile	compile together
complain/to	lodge a complaint (with)
complain about	raise objections about/on/to
	raise opposition about/on/to
	take exception to
complains about	is critical of
complements	is complementary to
complete	all done/finished
	as a whole
	at an end
	bring (to) a close (to)
	bring (to) a completion (to)
	bring (to) a conclusion (to)
	bring (to) a halt (to)
	bring (to) an end (to)
	bring to a standstill
	call a halt to
	call an end to
	call a stop to
	come to a close
	come to a/the conclusion (about/as to/concerning/of/on/ regarding)
	come to a halt
	come to an end
	come to a standstill
	complete and utter
	draw to a close/end
	draw to a conclusion
	finalize
	implement
	over and done with

CONCISE	WORDY
	(all) over with
	put a halt to
	put an end to
	put a stop to
(the) complete	in its/their entirety
completely	backward and forward
	completely and utterly
	from beginning to end
	from start to finish
	in its/their entirety
	inside (and) out
	through and through
	throughout the length and breadth (of)
	under any circumstances/conditions
	wholly and completely
completion	final/ultimate completion
complies (with)	is compliant with
	is in accord/accordance on/with
	is in agreement (on/with)
	is in compliance with
	is in conformance to/with
	is in conformity to/with
complimentary	free, complimentary
comply with	act in accord/accordance with
component	component (and) part/piece
compose	constitute
comprehend	come to an/the understanding (about/as to/concerning/of/on/regarding)
	come to grips with
	come to terms with
comprehends	is aware of/that
	is cognizant of/that
	is conscious of/that
	is knowledgeable about/in/of
	is mindful of/that
comprises	is composed of
	is comprised of
compromise	arrive at (an/the) accord (about/as to/concerning/of/on/regarding)
	arrive at (an/the) agreement (about/as to/concerning/of/on/regarding)
	arrive at (a/the) compromise (about/as to/concerning/of/on/regarding)
	arrive at (an/the) understanding (about/as to/concerning/of/on/regarding)

CONCISE	WORDY
	come to a/the compromise (about/as to/concerning/of/ on/regarding)
	come to an accord (about/as to/concerning/of/on/ regarding)
	come to an agreement (about/as to/concerning/of/on/ regarding)
	come to an/the understanding
	come to terms (about/as to/concerning/of/on/regarding)
	reach (an/the) accord (about/of/on/upon/with)
	reach (an/the) agreement (about/of/on/upon/with)
	reach (a/the) compromise (about/of/on/upon/with)
	reach (an/the) understanding (about/of/on/upon/with)
concatenate	concatenate together
conceivable	in (within) the realm of possibility
conceive	bring into being/existence
	call into being/existence
concentrate on	concentrate .... attention on/upon
	concentrate . . . effort on/upon
	concentrate . . . energy on/upon
	concentrate . . . time and energy on/upon
	focus . . . attention on/upon
	focus . . . effort on/upon
	focus . . . energy on/upon
	focus . . . time and energy on/upon
concerning	about/concerning/in/on/regarding the matter/subject of
	as . . . apply to
	as concerns
	as/so far as . . . (goes/is concerned)
	as regards
	in (the) . . . case (of)
	in connection with
	in point of
	in reference to
	in regard to
	in relation to
	in respect of/to
	insofar as . . . (goes/is concerned)
	in terms of
	in the area of
	in the realm of
	pertain/pertaining to
	relate/relating to
	relative to
	when it comes to
	where . . . is concerned

CONCISE	WORDY
	with reference to
	with regard to
	with relation to
	with respect to
concerns	has reference to
	(that) has to do with
	is applicable in/to
	is appropriate in/to
	is concerned with
	is of concern to
	is of interest to
	is pertinent to
	is relevant to
	is suitable to
concise	short and sweet
	short and to the point
concisely	in a nutshell
conclude	arrive at (a/the) conclusion (about/as to/concerning/of/on/regarding)
	arrive at (a/the) decision (about/as to/concerning/of/on/regarding)
	arrive at (a/the) determination (about/as to/concerning/of/on/regarding)
	arrive at (an/the) opinion (about/as to/concerning/of/on/regarding)
	arrive at (a/the) resolution (about/as to/concerning/of/on/regarding)
	arrive at (a/the) settlement (about/as to/concerning/of/on/regarding)
	bring (to) a close (to)
	bring (to) a completion (to)
	bring (to) a conclusion (to)
	bring (to) a halt (to)
	bring (to) an end (to)
	bring to a standstill
	call a halt to
	call an end to
	call a stop to
	come to a close
	come to a/the conclusion (about/as to/concerning/of/on/regarding)
	come to a/the decision (about/as to/concerning/of/on/regarding)
	come to a/the determination (about/as to/concerning/of/on/regarding)

CONCISE	WORDY
	come to a halt
	come to an end
	come to an/the opinion (about/as to/concerning/of/on/ regarding)
	come to a/the resolution (about/as to/concerning/of/on/ regarding)
	come to a/the settlement (about/as to/concerning/of/on/ regarding)
	come to a standstill
	draw (a/the) conclusion (of)
	draw (a/the) inference (of)
	draw to a close (end)
	draw to a conclusion
	finalize
	form (a/the) judgment (about/as to/concerning/of/on/ regarding)
	form (a/the) resolution (about/as to/concerning/of/on/ regarding)
	form (an/the) opinion (about/as to/concerning/of/on/ regarding)
	make (a/the) decision/determination (about/as to/ concerning/of/on/regarding)
	make (a/the) determined decision (about/as to/ concerning/of/on/regarding)
	put a halt to
	put an end to
	put a stop to
	put two and two together
	reach (a/the) conclusion (about/of/on/upon/with)
	reach (a/the) decision (about/of/on/upon/with)
	reach (a/the) determination (about/of/on/upon/with)
	reach (an/the) opinion (about/of/on/upon/with)
	reach (a/the) resolution (about/of/on/upon/with)
	reach (a/the) settlement (about/of/on/upon/with)
	terminate
conclusion	conclusive end
	final/ultimate conclusion
conclusively	once (and) for all
concur	arrive at (an/the) accord (about/as to/concerning/of/on/ regarding)
	arrive at (an/the) agreement (about/as to/concerning/of/ on/regarding)
	arrive at (a/the) compromise (about/as to/concerning/of/ on/regarding)

CONCISE	WORDY
	arrive at (an/the) understanding (about/as to/concerning/of/on/regarding)
	come to a/the compromise (about/as to/concerning/of/on/regarding)
	come to an accord (about/as to/concerning/of/on/regarding)
	come to an agreement (about/as to/concerning/of/on/regarding)
	come to terms (about/as to/concerning/of/on/regarding)
	come to a/the understanding
	reach (an/the) accord (about/of/on/upon/with)
	reach (an/the) agreement (about/of/on/upon/with)
	reach (a/the) compromise (about/of/on/upon/with)
	reach (an/the) understanding (about/of/on/upon/with)
concurrently	at the same time
	simultaneously
concurs (with)	is in agreement (on/with)
	is coherent with
	is compatible with
	is consistent with
	is in accord/accordance on/with
	is in concurrence with
	is in conformance to/with
	is in conformity to/with
	is in harmony with
	is in keeping with
	is in line with
	is in step with
	is of the same opinion (as)
condemns	is critical of
conditions	ifs, ands, or buts
conduces to	is conducive to
confer	confer together
	have a conversation (about)
confidence	positive feelings
confirm	attest to the fact (that)
	substantiate
confirms	is proof of/that
confiscate	take delivery of/on
	take possession of
conflagration	fiery conflagration
conflicts with	is at loggerheads (with)
	is at odds over/with

CONCISE	WORDY
	is at variance with
	is in conflict with
	is in (marked/sharp) contrast to
	is in disagreement (about/on/with)
	is in opposition to
	is opposed to
conflict with	stand in (marked/sharp) contrast to
	stand in opposition to
conform to	act in accord/accordance with
conforms to/with	is coherent with
	is compatible with
	is consistent with
	is in accord/accordance on/with
	is in agreement with
	is in compliance with
	is in concurrence with
	is in conformance to/with
	is in conformity to/with
	is in harmony with
	is in keeping with
	is in line with
	is in step with
confronted by/with	in the face of
confronting	in the face of
congregate	come together
	congregate together
conjure	bring into being/existence
connect	bring together
	concatenate together
	connect together
	link together
connection	association
	relationship
connote	connotate
consecutive	consecutive/continuous days/weeks/months in a row
consensus	consensus (of) opinion
	general consensus
	(a/the) overwhelming/vast consensus (of opinion)
	popular consensus
consent to	voice approval of
	voice support for
consequence	significant importance
consequence/effect/outcome of	consequence/effect/outcome resulting from
consequential	fraught with meaning/significance

CONCISE	WORDY
consequently	and so as a result
	as a consequence
	as a result
	for that/this reason
	in consequence
	so consequently
	that/this being the case
consider	(please) bear in mind
	consider as
	consider as being
	hold (to) the opinion (that)
	hold (to) the view (that)
	in the assessment of
	in the estimation of
	in the judgment of
	in the opinion of
	in the view of
	make allowance for
	make concession for
	make provision for
	pay attention to
	pay heed to
	take account for/of
	take a . . . look (at)
	take a/the . . . view (of)
	take cognizance of
	take into account
	take into consideration
	take note of
	take notice of
	take the position (that)
	take the view (that)
	take under advisement
	take under consideration
considerable	(a/the) considerable/good/great/huge/large/sizable/vast amount (of)
	(a/the) considerable/good/great/huge/large/sizable/vast degree (of)
	(a/the) considerable/good/great/huge/large/sizable/vast element (of)
	(a/the) significant/substantial amount (of)
	(a/the) significant/substantial degree (of)
	(a/the) significant/substantial element (of)
	worthy of attention

CONCISE	WORDY
	worthy of (my) consideration
	worthy of note
considering	as a consequence of the fact that
	as a result of the fact that
	attributable to the fact that
	based on the fact that
	because of the fact that
	being (as/as how/that)
	by reason of the fact that
	by the fact that
	by/in virtue of the fact that
	considering the fact that
	due to the fact that
	forasmuch as
	for the (simple) reason that
	from the fact that
	given the fact that
	inasmuch/insomuch as
	in consequence of the fact that
	in consideration of the fact that
	in (the) light of the fact that
	insofar as
	in the sense that
	in view of the fact that
	on account of the fact that
	on (the) grounds that
	on the basis of the fact that
	owing to the fact that
	seeing (as/as how/that)
consistently	at every turn
	day in (and) day out
	for ever and a day
	in (almost) all/every cases/circumstances/instances/situations
	in each/every case/circumstance/instance/situation
	on each/every occasion
	without exception
	year in (and) year out
consists of	is composed of
	is comprised of
consolidate	consolidate together
conspicuous	in evidence
constantly	all the time
	at every turn

CONCISE	WORDY
	day in (and) day out
	for ever and a day
	in (almost) all/every cases/circumstances/instances/ situations
	in each/every case/circumstance/instance/situation
	in perpetuity
	on each/every occasion
	without exception
	year in (and) year out
construct	put together
construction	new construction
consult	consult with
contact	come in contact (with)
	get in touch with
	make contact (with)
contain	incorporate in(to)
contains	is composed of
	is comprised of
contemplate	take under advisement
	take under consideration
contend	according to
	hold (to) the opinion (that)
	hold (to) the view (that)
	in the assessment of
	in the estimation of
	in the judgment of
	in the opinion of
	in the view of
	take the position (that)
	take the view (that)
contends	is inclined to believe (that)
	is inclined to think (that)
	is of the belief (that)
	is of the opinion (that)
	is of the view (that)
contest	express opposition to
	stand in (marked/sharp) contrast to
	stand in opposition to
	take a stand against/in opposition to
	voice criticism of
	voice disapproval of
	voice objection to
	voice opposition to
contests	is in (marked/sharp) contrast to

CONCISE	WORDY
	is in opposition to
	is opposed to
	is resistant to
continue	advance ahead/forward/on/onward
	continue in existence/to exist
	continue into the future
	continue on
	go forward
	move forward
	move forward into the future
	proceed ahead/forth/forward/on/onward
	progress ahead/forward/on/onward
continue/endure/last/ persevere/persist/prevail/ remain/survive	still continue/endure/last/persevere/persist/prevail/ remain/survive
continuous	consecutive/continuous days/weeks/months in a row
continuously	continuously/incessantly and without interruption
contract	contractual agreement
	enter into an agreement/contract
contradict	bring into question
	call into question
	cast doubt on/upon
	fly in the face of
	place/put into question
	raise doubts about/on
	raise questions about/on
	stand in (marked/sharp) contrast to
	take a stand against/in opposition to
	take issue (with)
	throw into doubt
	throw into question
contradicts	is at loggerheads (with)
	is at odds over/with
	is at variance with
	is in (marked/sharp) contrast to
	is in conflict with
	is in disagreement (about/on/with)
contrast (to)	compare and contrast (versus)
contrast to/with	is comparable to/with
	stand in (marked/sharp) contrast to
	take a stand against/in opposition to
contrasts with	is in (marked/sharp) contrast to
contributes	is contributory to

CONCISE	WORDY
contributes to	is a contribution to
controls	is in charge of
	is in control of
converge	come together
	converge together
converse	have a conversation (about)
	make conversation
conversely	contrariwise
	on the contrary
	on the other hand
	to the contrary
conversing with	in conversation with
convey	get across
conveying	(something) to that/the/this effect (that)
conviction	firm/strong conviction
cool	calm, cool, and collected
cooperate	cooperate together
cooperation	joint cooperation
	mutual cooperation
cope with	come to grips with
	come to terms with
copious	(an/the) abundance of
copiously	in copious profusion
cops	law enforcement officers
copy	duplicate copy
core	core essence
	essential core
	(the) heart of the matter
	sum/summary and substance
	(the) long and (the) short
correct	rectify
correlates to/with	is associated to/with
	is connected to/with
	is related to
correspond	correspond back and forth
correspondence	written communication/correspondence
corresponds (to/with)	is in agreement (on/with)
	is coherent with
	is comparable to/with
	is compatible with
	is consistent with
	is in accord/accordance on/with
	is in concurrence with
	is in conformance to/with

CONCISE	WORDY
	is in conformity to/with
	is in harmony with
	is in keeping with
	is in line with
	is in step with
	is similar to/with
corroborate	attest to the fact (that)
cost	expenditure (of money)
costs	expenses and costs
count	enumerate
countless	(an/the) abundance of
	(an) array of
	(a) range of
	(a/the) spectrum of
	(a) variety of
	beyond number (a/the) broad/extensive/great/vast/wide array of
	(a/the) broad/extensive/great/vast/wide range of
	(a/the) broad/extensive/great/vast/wide spectrum of
	(a/the) broad/extensive/great/vast/wide variety of
	(a/the) considerable/good/great/huge/large/ overwhelming/sizable/vast number (of)
	(a/the) countless number (of)
	(a/the) diversity of different
	(a/the) high number (of)
	(an/the) infinite number (of)
	innumerable
	(a/the) multiplicity of
	(a/the) multitude of
	multitudinous
	numerous in number
	(a/the) significant/substantial number (of)
	(an/the) untold number (of)
	(a/the) variety of different
	various different
	(many) widely varying
	without number
counts on	is reliant on/upon
couple	couple together
coupled with	accompanied by
	in association with
	in combination with
	in conjunction with

CONCISE	WORDY
	in connection with
	together with
course	action/attack/battle/game plan
	course of action
	plan of action/attack/battle
cover	cover over
craft	come up with
craftsman/craftswoman	skilled craftsman/craftswoman
craze/fad/fancy	passing craze/fad/fancy
create	bring into being/existence
	call into being/existence
	come up with
	put together
created	first created
creation	new creation
creator/created	original creator/originally created
credit	place/put credence in
crime	criminal act
	criminal offense
	criminal wrongdoing
critical	(of) central/critical/vital importance
	critically/crucially/vitally important
	most important
critical to	(a/the) critical . . . in/of/to
criticize	express opposition to
	raise objections about/on/to
	raise opposition about/on/to
	take exception to
	take to task
	to find (a) fault in/with
	voice criticism of
	voice disapproval of
	voice objection to
	voice opposition to
criticizes	is critical of
crucial	critically/crucially/vitally important
	most important
crucial to	(a/the) crucial . . . in/of/to
crux	core essence
	essential core
	(the) heart of the matter
	(the) long and (the) short
	sum/summary and substance
cue	indication

CONCISE	WORDY
cull	pick and choose
culmination	final/ultimate culmination
cumulative	accumulative
curious	(something) out of the ordinary
current	at that/this juncture
	at that/this juncture/juncture in time/moment/moment in time/period/period in time/point/point in time/stage/stage in time/time in my history/in my life/in the history of my life
	at that/this juncture/moment/period/point/stage in time
	at that/this moment
	at that/this point
	at that/this stage
	at that/this time
	at the current/present time
	at the (current/present) moment
	still in existence
currently	at that/this juncture
	at that/this juncture/juncture in time/moment/moment in time/period/period in time/point/point in time/stage/stage in time/time in my history/in my life/in the history of my life
	at that/this juncture/moment/period/point/stage in time
	at that/this moment
	at that/this point
	at that/this stage
	at that/this time
	at the current/present time
	at the (current/present) moment
	in/over the near term
	in/over the short run
	in/over the short term
	on that/this (particular) occasion
	over the short haul
custom	custom-built
	custom-made
	custom-tailored
	made to measure
	made to order
	tailor-made
customarily	as a general rule
	as a matter of course

CONCISE	WORDY
	as often as not
	in normal/ordinary/typical/usual practice
	in the normal/ordinary/typical/usual course of business/events/things
	more often than not
	on (an/the) average
customary	matter-of-course
	par for the course
customized	custom-tailored
	made to measure
	made to order
custom-made	made to measure
	made to order
cute/handsome/pretty/ugly	cute/handsome/pretty/ugly looking
cyclic	cyclical
cynosure	center of attention/attraction
	focus of attention

D

CONCISE	WORDY
$ ...	$ ... dollars
daily	day in (and) day out
	on a regular basis
damages	is deleterious to
	is destructive of/to
	is detrimental to
	is harmful to
	is injurious to
	is ruinous to
date from	date back to
date to	date back to
-day	on -day
DC	DC current
dead	no longer in existence
	no longer with us
deals with	has reference to
	(that) has to do with
	is concerned with
deal with	come to grips with
	come to terms with
death	demise
debatable	(an/the) open question

CONCISE	WORDY
	open to doubt
	open to question
debate	argumentation
debt(s)	indebtedness
(a) decade/year of	(a) decade's/year's history of
decapitate	decapitate . . . (the) head (of)
deceased	no longer in existence
deceive	take advantage of
deceives	is exploitative/exploitive of
deceptive	false and misleading
decide	arrive at (an/the) accord (about/as to/concerning/of/on/ regarding)
	arrive at (an/the) agreement (about/as to/concerning/of/ on/regarding)
	arrive at (a/the) compromise (about/as to/concerning/of/ on/regarding)
	arrive at (a/the) conclusion (about/as to/concerning/of/ on/regarding)
	arrive at (a/the) decision (about/as to/concerning/of/on/ regarding)
	arrive at (a/the) determination (about/as to/concerning/ of/on/regarding)
	arrive at (an/the) opinion (about/as to/concerning/of/on/ regarding)
	arrive at (a/the) resolution (about/as to/concerning/of/on/ regarding)
	arrive at (a/the) settlement (about/as to/concerning/of/ on/regarding)
	arrive at (an/the) understanding (about/as to/concerning/ of/on/regarding)
	come to a/the compromise (about/as to/concerning/of/ on/regarding)
	come to a/the conclusion (about/as to/concerning/of/on/ regarding)
	come to a/the decision (about/as to/concerning/of/on/ regarding)
	come to a/the determination (about/as to/concerning/of/ on/regarding)
	come to an accord (about/as to/concerning/of/on/ regarding)
	come to an agreement (about/as to/concerning/of/on/ regarding)
	come to an/the opinion (about/as to/concerning/of/on/ regarding)

CONCISE	WORDY
	come to an/the understanding
	come to a/the resolution (about/as to/concerning/of/on/ regarding)
	come to a/the settlement (about/as to/concerning/of/on/ regarding)
	come to terms (about/as to/concerning/of/on/regarding)
	form (a/the) judgment (about/as to/concerning/of/on/ regarding)
	form (an/the) opinion (about/as to/concerning/of/on/ regarding)
	form (a/the) resolution (about/as to/concerning/of/on/ regarding)
	make (a/the) decision/determination (about/as to/ concerning/of/on/regarding)
	make (a/the) determined decision (about/as to/ concerning/of/on/regarding)
	make up (my) mind
	reach (a/the) compromise (about/of/on/upon/with)
	reach (a/the) conclusion (about/of/on/upon/with)
	reach (a/the) decision (about/of/on/upon/with)
	reach (a/the) determination (about/of/on/upon/with)
	reach (a/the) resolution (about/of/on/upon/with)
	reach (a/the) settlement (about/of/on/upon/with)
	reach (an/the) accord (about/of/on/upon/with)
	reach (an/the) agreement (about/of/on/upon/with)
	reach (an/the) opinion (about/of/on/upon/with)
	reach (an/the) understanding (about/of/on/upon/with)
decide what/when/where/ whether/which/why	decide on what/when/where/whether/which/why
decisively	once (and) for all
declare	according to
	bear witness to
declares	is (a) testament to
	is (a) testimony to
	is witness to
declaring	(something) to that/the/this effect (that)
decline	respond in the negative
declining	on the decline
	on the decrease
decrease	decrease down
	minimize
decreasing	on the decline
	on the decrease

CONCISE	WORDY
decreasingly	(a/the) declining/decreasing/diminishing/dwindling amount/degree/extent/part/ percentage/portion/proportion (of)
	(a/the) declining/decreasing/diminishing/dwindling number/quantity (of)
	decreasing in
dedicated to	completely entirely/exclusively/fully/solely/thoroughly/ totally/utterly/wholly dedicated to
deduce	arrive at (a/the) conclusion (about/as to/concerning/of/ on/regarding)
	arrive at (a/the) decision (about/as to/concerning/of/on/ regarding)
	arrive at (a/the) determination (about/as to/concerning/ of/on/regarding)
	arrive at (an/the) opinion (about/as to/concerning/of/on/ regarding)
	come to a/the conclusion (about/as to/concerning/of/on/ regarding)
	come to a/the decision (about/as to/concerning/of/on/ regarding)
	come to at/the determination (about/as to/concerning/of/ on/regarding)
	come to an/the opinion (about/as to/concerning/of/on/ regarding)
	draw (a/the) conclusion (of)
	draw (a/the) inference (of)
	form (a/the) judgment (about/as to/concerning/of/on/ regarding)
	form (an/the) opinion (about/as to/concerning/of/on/ regarding)
	put two and two together
	reach (a/the) conclusion (about/of/on/upon/with)
	reach (a/the) decision (about/of/on/upon/with)
	reach (a/the) determination (about/of/on/upon/with)
	reach (an/the) opinion (about/of/on/upon/with)
deduction	deductive reasoning
deem	deem as
deep	in depth
defends	is protective against (of)
defer	defer back
defies	is in contempt of
	is in defiance of
defunct	no longer in existence

CONCISE	WORDY
defy	fly in the face of
degree	breadth and depth
dejected	in a bad mood
delight in	derive enjoyment from
	derive pleasure from
	derive satisfaction from
	take enjoyment in
	take pleasure in
	take satisfaction in
delimit	delimitate
demand	necessitate
demands on	is insistent on
demolish	level to the ground
	raze to the ground
demonstrate	attest to the fact (that)
demonstrates	is a demonstration of
	is illustrative of
demur	raise objections about/on/to
	raise opposition about/on/to
	take exception to
	take issue (with)
denote	denotate
departed	no longer in existence
departs from	is a variant of
	is different from/than
	is distinguished from
departure	new departure
dependence	dependency
depends on	is a function of
	is conditional/conditioned on/upon
	is contingent on/upon
	is dependent on/upon
	is reliant on/upon
	is subject to
depicts	is characteristic of
	is descriptive of
	is illustrative of
deplore	express sorrow (about)
	voice sorrow (about)
deprecate	depreciate in value
	out of favor
	raise objections about/on/to
	raise opposition about/on/to
depressed	in a bad mood

CONCISE	WORDY
descend	descend down
describes	is a description of
	is characteristic of
	is descriptive of
	is illustrative of
desecrates	is in violation of
deserves	is deserving of
design	come up with
designate	designate as
designates	is characteristic of
	is descriptive of
	is illustrative of
desires to	is desirous of -ing
desist	cease and desist
despises	is contemptuous of
	is scornful of
despite	contrary to
	in defiance of
	in despite of
	in (the) face of
	in spite of
	notwithstanding
	. . . to the contrary
despite (what)	irregardless of
	irrespective of (what)
	no matter (what)
	regardless of (what)
despite how	by whatever/whichever manner/means
	in whatever/whichever fashion/manner/way
	irrespective of how
	no matter how
	regardless of how
	through whatever/whichever manner/means
despite when	irrespective of when
	no matter when
	regardless of when
despite where	irrespective of where
	no matter where
	regardless of where
despite whether	irrespective of (the fact) whether . . . (or)
	no matter whether . . . (or)
	regardless of whether . . . (or)
despite which	irrespective of which
	no matter which

CONCISE	WORDY
	regardless of which
despite who	irrespective of who
	no matter who
	regardless of who
despite whom	irrespective of whom
	no matter whom
	regardless of whom
destroy	do away with
	level to the ground
	put to sleep
	raze to the ground
destroys	is destructive of/to
	is ruinous to
detach	separate out
detail	analyze in depth/in detail
	describe/explain in . . . detail
	detailed/in-depth analysis
	minutely detail
details	(the) ins and (the) outs
determination	sticktoitiveness
determine	arrive at (a/the) conclusion (about/as to/concerning/of/ on/regarding)
	arrive at (a/the) decision (about/as to/concerning/of/on/ regarding)
	arrive at (a/the) determination (about/as to/concerning/ of/on/regarding)
	arrive at (an/the) opinion (about/as to/concerning/of/on/ regarding)
	come to a/the conclusion (about/as to/concerning/of/on/ regarding)
	come to a/the decision (about/as to/concerning/of/on/ regarding)
	come to a/the determination (about/as to/concerning/of/ on/regarding)
	come to an/the opinion (about/as to/concerning/of/on/ regarding)
	come to a/the resolution (about/as to/concerning/of/on/ regarding)
	form (a/the) judgment (about/as to/concerning/of/on/ regarding)
	form (an/the) opinion (about/as to/concerning/of/on/ regarding)
	form (a/the) resolution (about/as to/concerning/of/on/ regarding)

CONCISE	WORDY
	make (a/the) decision/determination (about/as to/ concerning/of/on/regarding)
	make (a/the) determined decision (about/as to/ concerning/of/on/regarding)
	reach (a/the) conclusion (about/of/on/upon/with)
	reach (a/the) decision (about/of/on/upon/with)
	reach (a/the) determination (about/of/on/upon/with)
	reach (an/the) opinion (about/of/on/upon/with)
	reach (a/the) resolution (about/of/on/upon/with)
determined	bound and determined
deters	is a deterrent to
	is a hindrance to
	is an impediment to
	is an obstacle to
develop	come into play
	materialize
developing	in the making
developments	future developments
deviates from	is a variant of
	is different from/than
	is distinguished from
devise	bring into being/existence
	call into being/existence
	come up with
	formulate
	put together
devoted to	completely/entirely/exclusively/fully/solely/thoroughly/ totally/utterly/wholly devoted to
dialogue	communication
diametral	diametrical
die	pass away/on/over
	succumb to (the) illness/injuries
died	made/paid the ultimate sacrifice
differ (with)	take issue (with)
differ from	stand in (marked/sharp) contrast to
	take a stand against/in opposition to
differ in	raise objections about/on/to
	raise opposition about/on/to
	take exception to
different	(an) array of
	(a/the) broad/extensive/great/vast/wide array of
	(a/the) broad/extensive/great/vast/wide range of
	(a/the) broad/extensive/great/vast/wide spectrum of
	(a/the) broad/extensive/great/vast/wide variety of

CONCISE	WORDY
	(five/many/several) different
	different and distinct
	distinct difference/distinctly different
	(a/the) diversity of different
	(something) out of the ordinary
	(a) range of
	(a/the) spectrum of
	(a) variety of
	(a/the) variety of different
	various different
	(many) widely varying
differs	has a difference of opinion with
differs from	is a variant of
	is at loggerheads (with)
	is at odds over/with
	is at variance with
	is different from/than
	is distinguished from
	is in conflict with
	is in (marked/sharp) contrast to
	is in disagreement (about/on/with)
difficult	(a/the) difficult task
difficulty -ing	difficulty in/of -ing
diminish	diminish down
direct	head up
direction	course of action
	plan of action/attack/battle
directly	(after/for/in/over/within) a brief/limited/little/short amount of time/length of time/moment of time/period/period of time/span of time/time/while
	at/in the blink of an eye
	at any minute/moment/second
	expeditiously
	from minute/moment/second to minute/moment/second
	in/over the near term
	in/over the short run
	in/over the short term
	in a few minutes/moments/seconds
	in a minute/moment/second
	in quick/short order
	in the foreseeable future
	in the immediate future
	in the (very) near future

CONCISE	WORDY
	in the not-so-distant/not-too-distant future
	over the short haul
directs	is in charge of
	is in control of
dirty	filthy dirty
dis-	(a/the) absence of
	(a/the) lack of
	devoid of
	insufficient
	lacking in
	less than (enthusiastic)
disagree	respond in the negative
disagrees with	has a difference of opinion with
	is at loggerheads (with)
	is at odds over/with
	is at variance with
	is in conflict with
	is in (marked/sharp) contrast to
	is in disagreement (about/on/with)
	is in opposition to
	is resistant to
disagree with	express opposition to
	not in favor of
	take issue (with)
	raise objections about/on/to
	raise opposition about/on/to
	stand in (marked/sharp) contrast to
	stand in opposition to
	take a stand against/in opposition to
	take exception to
	take offense at
	take umbrage at/with
	voice criticism of
	voice disapproval of
	voice objection to
	voice opposition to
disappoint	come as a disappointment (to)
disapprove	out of favor
disapprove of	express opposition to
	raise objections about/on/to
	raise opposition about/on/to
	stand in opposition to
	voice criticism of
	voice disapproval of

CONCISE	WORDY
	voice objection to
	voice opposition to
disapproves of	is in opposition to
	is opposed to
	is resistant to
disbelieve	express skepticism (about)
	voice skepticism (about)
disbelieves	is distrustful about/of
	is doubtful about/of
	is dubious about/of
	is in doubt about/of
	is mistrustful about/of
	is skeptical about/of/that
disclose	bring attention to
	bring into the open
	bring to . . . attention (of)
	bring to light
	call . . . attention to
	call to . . . attention (of)
	concentrate (media/people's/public) attention on/upon
	direct . . . attention to
	draw attention to
	focus (media/people's/public) attention on/upon
discomfit	discomfiture
discomfort	discomfiture
	negative feelings
disconnect	separate out
discover	come in contact (with)
	make contact (with)
discrete	separate and discrete
discriminate	tell the difference
discrimination	invidious discrimination
discuss	have a conversation (about)
disdainful	high and mighty
disdains	is contemptuous of
	is scornful of
disease	pathological disease
disesteems	is disrespectful of/toward
disfavor	negative feelings
	out of favor
disgusted	sick and tired
dislike	bear/have/hold a grudge (against)
	negative feelings
	out of favor

CONCISE	WORDY
	take offense at
	take umbrage at/with
dismay	fear and trembling
dismisses	is dismissive of
disobey	fail to comply with
disparage	out of favor
displeased	in a bad mood
displeasure	negative feelings
disputable	(an/the) open question
	open to doubt
	open to question
dispute	argumentation
	bring into question
	call into question
	cast doubt on/upon
	express opposition to
	fly in the face of
	place/put into question
	raise doubts about/on
	raise objections about/on/to
	raise opposition about/on/to
	raise questions about/on
	stand in (marked/sharp) contrast to
	stand in opposition to
	take a stand against/in opposition to
	take exception to
	take issue (with)
	throw into doubt
	throw into question
	voice criticism of
	voice disapproval of
	voice objection to
	voice opposition to
disputes	has a difference of opinion with
	is in (marked/sharp) contrast to
	is in opposition to
	is opposed to
	is resistant to
disregard	fly in the face of
	negative feelings
disrespects	is disrespectful of/toward
disrupts	is disruptive of
dissociate	disassociate
distaste	negative feelings

CONCISE	WORDY
distinct	different and distinct
	distinct difference/distinctly different
	separate and distinct
distinction	distinct difference/distinctly different
distinguish	make (a/the) distinction
	tell the difference
district	locality
distrust	express skepticism (about)
	voice skepticism (about)
distrusts	is distrustful about/of
	is doubtful about/of
	is dubious about/of
	is in doubt about/of
	is mistrustful about/of
	is skeptical about/of/that
disturbs	is of concern to
diverges from	is a variant of
	is different from/than
	is distinguished from
diverse	(an) array of
	(a/the) broad/extensive/great/vast/wide array of
	(a/the) broad/extensive/great/vast/wide range of
	(a/the) broad/extensive/great/vast/wide spectrum of
	(a/the) broad/extensive/great/vast/wide variety of
	(a/the) diversity of different
	many and varied
	(a) range of
	(a/the) spectrum of
	(a) variety of
	(a/the) variety of different
	various and sundry
	various different
	(many) widely varying
divide	divide up
divulge	bring attention to
	bring into the open
	bring to . . . attention (of)
	bring to light
	call . . . attention to
	call to . . . attention (of)
	concentrate (media/people's/public) attention on/upon
	direct . . . attention to
	draw attention to
	focus (media/people's/public) attention on/upon

CONCISE	WORDY
do	accomplish
	perform (a/the) . . . of
	render
doable	in/within the realm of possibility
doctorate	doctorate degree
dogmatic	high and mighty
domineering	high and mighty
done	all done/finished
	at an end
	over and done with
	(all) over with
done/finished/over	done/finished/over with
do not know	is still to be seen
	remains to be seen
doomed	doomed to fail/failure
dose	dosage
doubt	bring into question
	call into question
	cast doubt on/upon
	express skepticism (about)
	place/put into question
	raise doubts about/on
	raise questions about/on
	throw into doubt
	throw into question
	voice skepticism (about)
doubtful	(an/the) open question
	open to doubt
	open to question
doubtless	beyond a/the shadow of a doubt
	without (a/any) doubt
	without (a) question
	without (a/any) question/shadow of a doubt
doubts	is distrustful about/of
	is doubtful about/of
	is dubious about/of
	is in doubt about/of
	is mistrustful about/of
	is skeptical about/of/that
doubt that	doubt but that
down	drop down
	plummet down
	plunge down
downcast	in a bad mood

CONCISE	WORDY
down to	down to a minimum of

dozens (of)	(a/the) considerable/good/great/huge/large/
	        overwhelming/sizable/vast
	        number (of)

	(a/the) considerable/good/great/huge/large/sizable/vast quantity (of)
	(a/the) high number (of)
	(a/a fair/any) number (of)
	(a/the) significant/substantial number (of)
	(a/the) significant/substantial quantity (of)
	in big/great/high/huge/large/overwhelming/sizable/vast numbers
	in great/large quantities
draft	come up with
	preliminary draft
dramatic	dramatical
draw	draw (a/the) conclusion (of)
	draw (a/the) inference (of)
	put two and two together
dread	express concern (about)
	fear and trembling
	is concerned (about)
	voice concern (about)
dreads	is afraid of/to
	is apprehensive of
	is fearful (about/of/that)
	is frightened of/to
	is in fear for/of
	is scared (to)
dressed	attired
drink	beverage
	liquid refreshment
drive	driving force
	motivating force
driving	make (my) way
drop	drop down
dual	dualistic
dubious	(an/the) open question
	open to doubt
	open to question
due	due and payable
	(a/the) sufficient amount (of)
	sufficient/sufficiently
due to	as a consequence of

CONCISE	WORDY
	as a result of
	ascribable to
	attributable to
	by consequence of
	by reason of
	by the result of
	by/in virtue of
	caused because of/due to/owing to
	(a/the) consequence of
	in consequence of
	in consideration of (payment of/sum of)
	in reaction to
	in response to
	in the wake of
	on account of
	on the basis of
	reason (why) . . . is due to (the fact that)
dullness	tedious monotony
duly	duplicate copy
	exact/exactly duplicate
	exact/exactly equivalent
	exact/exactly identical
	exact/exactly match
	exact/exactly (the) same
	follow along the lines of
	(an) identical/identically match
	identical/identically (the) same
	match exactly
	match perfectly
	perfect/perfectly match
	sufficient/sufficiently enough
duplicates	is duplicative of
	is (the) equal to
	is (the) equivalent of/to
	is identical to/with
	is tantamount to
during	during the course/length of
	for the duration/length of
	(somewhere) in the course of
	in the company of
	in the middle of
	in the midst of
	in the presence of
	in (the) time(s) of

CONCISE	WORDY
	over the course/duration/length of
	through/throughout the course/duration/length of
dwell	domicile
	reside
dwindle	dwindle down
dynamic	dynamical

E

each	each and every (one)
	each one
	in each/every case/circumstance/instance/situation
	on each/every occasion
each time	in each/every case/circumstance/instance/situation
	on each/every occasion
earlier	ahead of time
	at an/some earlier/former/past/previous date (time)
	back/before in the past
	in advance
	in (the) days/decades/months/weeks/years gone by
	in (the) days/decades/months/weeks/years of old
	in (the) days/decades/months/weeks/years past
	in earlier/former/prior times
	in (the) olden days
	in/over (the) past days/decades/months/weeks/years
	in the distant past
	in the (very) near past
	in the not-so-distant/not-too-distant past
	in the past
	in/within the recent past
	on earlier/former/previous/prior occasions
	previous/previously
earlier than	anterior to
early	ahead of schedule
ease	facilitate
eastward/northward/southward/ westward	toward the east/north/south/west
-ed/-en	before/earlier/previously -ed/-en
	-ed/-en before/earlier/previously
effect	bring/give forth
	bring about
	cause to happen/occur/take place

CONCISE	WORDY
	consequence
	effectuate
	implement
	put into effect
	resultant
	resultant effect
effective	in force and effect
	operative
effectively	for all intents and purposes
	for all practical purposes
	to all intents and purposes
	to all practical purposes
efficacy	efficacity
e.g.	e.g. . . . and others/and so forth/and so on/and such/and the like/et al./etc.
	for example . . . and others/and so forth/and so on/and such/and the like/et al./etc./or whatever
	for instance . . . and others/and so forth/and so on/and such/and the like/et al./etc./or whatever
egoistic	egoistical/egotistical
egotistic	egoistical/egotistical
either	either one
either/neither way	in either/neither case/circumstance/instance/situation
	in either/neither event
either way	(in) one way or the other
elderly	advanced/along in years
elect	elect as
electric	electrical
eliminate	completely/entirely/fully/thoroughly/totally/utterly/wholly eliminate
elliptic	elliptical
elsewhere	anyplace/anywhere else
	someplace/somewhere else
emblematic	emblematical
emblemizes	is emblematic of
	is representative of
	is symbolic/symbolical of
emerge	become known
	come into play
	come to light
	emerge out
empathic	empathetic

CONCISE	WORDY
employ	bring to bear (on/upon)
	utilize
employed by	affiliated with
	associated with
employees	human resources
encapsule	encapsulate
enclosed is	enclosed herein/herewith is/please find
encounter	come in contact (with)
	make contact (with)
encumber	place/put a burden on/upon
	place/put a strain on/upon
end	bring (to) a close (to)
	bring (to) a completion (to)
	bring (to) a conclusion (to)
	bring (to) a halt (to)
	bring (to) an end (to)
	bring to a standstill
	call a halt to
	call an end to
	call a stop to
	come to a close
	come to a/the conclusion (about/as to/concerning/of/on/ regarding)
	come to a halt
	come to an end
	come to a standstill
	conclusive end
	demise
	do away with
	draw to a close/end
	draw to a conclusion
	put a halt to
	put an end to
	put a stop to
	terminate
endanger	place/put . . . in danger
	place/put . . . in jeopardy
	place/put . . . in/into peril
	throw into jeopardy
endangered	(be) in jeopardy
endangers	is dangerous to
ended	all done/finished
	at an end
	over and done with

CONCISE	WORDY
	(all) over with
endless	(a/the) countless number (of)
	(a/the) multiplicity of
	(a/the) multitude of
	(an/the) infinite number (of)
	(an/the) untold number (of)
	beyond number
	innumerable
	multitudinous
	numerous in number
	without number
endlessly	all the time
	at every turn
	day in (and) day out
	for ever and a day
	in perpetuity
	year in (and) year out
endorse	endorse on the back (of)
	go along with
	stand in support of
	take a stand for/in favor of/in support of
	voice approval of
	voice support for
endorses	is in favor of
	is in support of
	is supportive of
endure	continue in existence/to exist
	put up with
energy	driving force
	motivating force
enigma	question mark
enjoy	appreciate
	derive enjoyment from
	derive pleasure from
	derive satisfaction from
	take enjoyment in
	take pleasure in
	take satisfaction in
enjoys	has (an/the) appreciation for
	is appreciative of
enlarge	maximize
ennui	tedious monotony
enormous	(a/the) high degree (of)
	(a/the) high level (of)

CONCISE	WORDY
enough	adequate enough
	(an/the) adequate number (of)
	in sufficient amount
	in sufficient number
	in sufficient quantity
	(a/the) sufficient amount (of)
	(a/the) sufficient number (of)
	sufficient/sufficiently
	sufficient/sufficiently enough
enrage	throw into a rage
ensconced	comfortably ensconced
ensuing	in the aftermath of
	in the wake of
	on/upon the heels of
ensure	assure/ensure/insure . . . guarantee
entire	as a whole
(the) entire	in its/their entirety
entire/whole	throughout . . . entire/whole
entirely	backward and forward
	from beginning to end
	from start to finish
	in its/their entirety
	through and through
	throughout the length and breadth (of)
	under any circumstances/conditions
entity	separate entity
envisage	(to) . . . in my (own) mind's eye
envision	(to) . . . in my (own) mind's eye
eon	(a/the) time frame (of)
	(a/the) time horizon (of)
	(a/the) time period (of)
	(a/the) time span (of)
epidemic	epidemical
epidemiologic	epidemiological
epigrammatic	epigrammatical
epigraphic	epigraphical
epitomizes	is reflective of
epoch	(a/the) time frame (of)
	(a/the) time horizon (of)
	(a/the) time period (of)
	(a/the) time span (of)
equal/equivalent to	the equal/equivalent of
equal to	the same (thing) as
equally	both equally

CONCISE	WORDY
	equally as
equals	is (the) equal to
	is (the) equivalent of/to
	is identical to/with
	is on (a) par (with)
	is tantamount to
equates with	is associated to/with
	is comparable to/with
	is connected to/with
	is related to
	is similar to/with
equitable	fair/just and equitable
equivalent	exact/exactly equivalent
-(i)er	comparatively
	more -(i)er
	relatively
(the) -(i)er	(the) -(i)er . . . of the two
	(the) more . . . of the two
era	(a/the) time frame (of)
	(a/the) time horizon (of)
	(a/the) time period (of)
	(a/the) time span (of)
eradicate	completely/entirely/fully/thoroughly/totally/utterly/ wholly eradicate
errs	is in error
-(i)er than	as compared to/with
	as contrasted to/with
	as opposed to
	by comparison to/with
	by contrast to/with
	compared to/with
	contrasted to/with
	in comparison to/with
	in contrast to/with
	in relation/relationship to
	measured against
	relative to
	when compared to/with
	when measured against
-(i)er than/less than/more than	as compared to/with . . . relatively
	as opposed to . . . relatively
	by comparison (to/with) . . . relatively
	compared/contrasted to/with . . . relatively
	comparatively -(i)er than/less than/more than

CONCISE	WORDY
	relatively . . . as/when compared to/with
	relatively . . . compared/contrasted to/with
	relatively -(i)er than/less than/more than
	relatively . . . in relation to
	relatively . . . relative to
	when compared to/with . . . relatively
-(i)er . . . than	-(i)er . . . rather than
essence	core essence
	essential core
	(the) heart of the matter
	(the) long and (the) short
	sum/summary and substance
essential	essential prerequisite
	necessary essential
essential/indispensable	absolutely essential/indispensable
essentially	for all intents and purposes
	for all practical purposes
	to all intents and purposes
	to all practical purposes
essentials	important essentials
essential to	(an/the) essential . . . for/in/of/to
-est	-est ever
-(i)est	most -(i)est
establish	firmly establish
esteem	place/put a premium on/upon
	place/put a priority on/upon
	place/put a value on/upon
	positive feelings
esteems	has (an/the) appreciation for
	is appreciative of
estimate	arrive at (an/the) estimate/estimation (about/as to/ concerning/of/on/regarding)
	come to an/the estimate/estimation (about/as to/ concerning/of/on/regarding)
	reach (an/the) estimate/estimation (about/of/on/upon/ with)
	take a measure of
etc.	et cetera, et cetera, et cetera (etc., etc., etc.)
	and etc./et cetera
	and everything/stuff/things like that
	and so on and so forth
eternally	at every turn
	day in (and) day out
	for ever and a day

CONCISE	WORDY
	in perpetuity
	year in (and) year out
euphemism	polite euphemism
evaluate	arrive at (an/the) estimate/estimation (about/as to/concerning/of/on/regarding)
	come to an/the estimate/estimation (about/as to/concerning/of/on/regarding)
	form (a/the) judgment (about/as to/concerning/of/on/regarding)
	form (an/the) opinion (about/as to/concerning/of/on/regarding)
	reach (an/the) estimate/estimation (about/of/on/upon/with)
even	additionally
	and . . . further/furthermore/in addition/moreover/what's more
	as a matter of fact
	by the same token
	for that matter
	furthermore
	in addition
	on top of (that/this)
even so	after all is said and done
	all (just) the same
	at any rate
	be that as it may
	in any case/event
	nevertheless
	nonetheless
	still and all
even though	despite the fact that
	in spite of the fact that
	irregardless of the fact that
	irrespective of the fact that
	notwithstanding the fact that
	regardless of the fact that
even with	contrary to
	in despite of
	in (the) face of
	in spite of
	notwithstanding
	. . . to the contrary
event	eventuality
eventual	in the distant future

CONCISE	WORDY
eventually	as (the) days/decades/months/weeks/years go on
	as time progresses (forward/on/onward)
	at a/some future/later/subsequent date/time
	(after/for/in/over/within) (an) extended/lengthy/long/ prolonged/protracted amount of time/length of time/period/period of time/span of time/time/while
	in/over (the) coming days/decades/months/weeks/years
	in/over (the) days/decades/months/weeks/years ahead
	in/over (the) days/decades/months/weeks/years to come
	in the course of events/things/time
	in the distant future
	in/into the future
	in/over the long run
	in/over the long term
	later in time
	later on down the line/pike/road/way
	over the long haul
	some day/time in the future
	sooner or later
	(the) time will come when
	with the passage of time
ever	at a certain/any/one/some point in my history/point in my life/point in the history of my life/ point in time
	at/from/in/on/to any/each/every/some area/locale/ locality/location/place/point/ position/region/site/spot
	at/from/in/on/to any/each/every/some area/locale/ locality/location/place/point/ position/region/site/spot where in (the) history (of the world)
	under any circumstances/conditions
everlastingly	day in (and) day out
	for ever and a day
	in perpetuity
	year in (and) year out
evermore	forevermore
every	every single (solitary)
	in its/their entirety
	without exception
every (one)	each and every (one)
everybody	all and sundry
	individual(s)

CONCISE	WORDY
	without exception
everybody/everyone	anybody/anyone and everybody/everyone
everyday	all the time
	at every turn
	common (and) everyday
	for ever and a day
	run of the mill
	all and sundry
every day	day in (and) day out
every one	in each/every case/circumstance/instance/situation
everyplace	at/from/in/on/to any/each/every/some area/locale/ locality/location/place/point/ position/region/site/spot
	at/from/in/on/to any/each/every/some area/locale/ locality/location/place/point/ position/region/site/spot where
every so often	in certain/some circumstances
	in certain/some instances
	in certain/some situations
	under certain/some circumstances/conditions
everything	all and sundry
	anything and everything
every time	in each/every case/circumstance/instance/situation
	on each/every occasion
	without exception
everywhere	at/from/in/on/to any/each/every/some area/locale/ locality/location/place/point/ position/region/site/spot
	at/from/in/on/to any/each/every/some area/locale/ locality/location/place/point/ position/region/site/spot where
every year	year in (and) year out
	high and low
	present everywhere
evidence for/of/that	evidence in/to support of/that
evident	in evidence
	it is apparent that
	it is evident that
evinces	is evidence of/that
	is proof of/that
evolve	come into being
	come into existence
	evolve over time
	materialize

CONCISE	WORDY
exact	exact/exactly (the) same
	exact/exactly duplicate
	exact/exactly equivalent
	exact/exactly identical
	exact/exactly match
	(an) identical/identically match
	identical/identically (the) same
	necessitate
	perfect/perfectly match
exactly	just exactly
	no more (and) no less
exaggerate	overexaggerate
exam	examination
examine	check to see
	look/observe to see
example	illustrative example
example (of)	(an) example that illustrates/to illustrate
exceed	take precedence over
exceeded/surpassed	more than exceeded/surpassed
exceeds	is in excess of
except	save and except
	with the exception of/that
	with the exclusion of/that
except for	if it were not for
	were it not for
	with the exception of/that
	with the exclusion of/that
excepting	with the exception of/that
	with the exclusion of/that
exceptional	(something) out of the ordinary
excerpt	excerption
excessive	(a/the) excessive amount (of)
	(a/the) excessive number (of)
excites	is of interest to
excluding	with the exception of/that
	with the exclusion of/that
excruciating	excruciatingly painful
execute	effectuate
exemplifies	is illustrative of
	is reflective of
	is typical of
exercise	bring to bear (on/upon)
exert	bring to bear (on/upon)
	put forth

CONCISE	WORDY
exiguous	few and far between
	few/small in number
exist	come into being
	come into existence
	continue in existence/to exist
exists	is in existence
	there exists . . . (that/who)
exodus	mass exodus
expect/expectation	expect/expectation and hope
	hope and expect/expectation
expects	is hopeful
expedience	expediency
expedite	quickly expedite
expense	expenditure (of money)
expenses	expenses and costs
experience	background (of) experience
	go through . . . experience
	historical experience
	past/previous/prior experience
expert	qualified expert
	trained expert
explain	get across
explain (how)	account for the fact (that)
explanation	(the) whys and (the) wherefores (of)
exploit	take advantage of
exploitive	exploitative
exploits	is exploitative/exploitive of
exploring	in pursuit of
explosion	violent explosion
expose	bring attention to
	bring into the open
	bring to . . . attention (of)
	bring to light
	call . . . attention to
	call to . . . attention (of)
	concentrate (media/people's/public) attention on/upon
	direct . . . attention to
	draw attention to
	focus (media/people's/public) attention on/upon
express	vocalize
extant	still in existence
extend	extend out
extensive	(an) array of
	(a/the) broad/extensive/great/vast/wide array of

CONCISE	WORDY
	(a/the) broad/extensive/great/vast/wide range of
	(a/the) broad/extensive/great/vast/wide spectrum of
	(a/the) broad/extensive/great/vast/wide variety of
	(a/the) diversity of different
	(a/the) high degree (of)
	(a/the) high level (of)
	(a) range of
	(a/the) spectrum of
	(a) variety of
	(a/the) variety of different
	various different
	(many) widely varying
extensively in/through	extensively throughout
extent	breadth and depth
extinct	no longer in existence
extinction	mass extinction
extra	added extra
	(an) additional
extraordinary	(something) out of the ordinary
extremely	in the extreme
extricate	extricate out

F

face	come to grips with
	come to terms with
	face up to
faced with	in the face of
faces	is faced with
facing	in the face of
fact	basis in fact/reality/truth
	factual basis
	proven fact
	(a/the) real fact
	true to fact
factory	facility
	institution
facts	facts and information
factual	accurate and factual
	matter-of-fact
	(a/the) true fact
	true to fact

CONCISE	WORDY
failing	in the absence of
fair	equitable
	fair/just and equitable
	fair and square
fairly	(a) little bit
faith	positive feelings
false	false and misleading
familiar	intimately familiar
far	considerably
	significantly/substantially
far and away	by (a/the) considerable/good/great/huge/large/ overwhelming/sizable/vast/wide margin
far from	by no means
	far away from
fashion	bring into being/existence
	call into being/existence
	come up with
	put together
fast	(after/for/in/over/within) a reasonable amount of time/ length of time/period/period of time/ span of time/time/while
	at/in the blink of an eye
	expeditiously
	in a timely fashion/manner/way
	in quick/short order
	on a timely basis
fasten	fasten together
faster than	in excess of
fault	to find (a) fault in/with
favor	go along with
	place/put a premium on/upon
	place/put a priority on/upon
	positive feelings
	stand in support of
	take a stand for/in favor of/in support of
favor . . . over	favor . . . as opposed to (instead of/rather than)
favor . . . to	favor . . . as opposed to (instead of/rather than)
favorably	in the affirmative
favorite	most favorite
favors	has a/the preference for
	is advantageous for (to)
	is beneficial to
	is favorable to

CONCISE	WORDY
	is in favor of
	is in support of
	is of benefit to
fear	express concern (about)
	fear and trembling
	is concerned (about)
	voice concern (about)
fears	is afraid of/to
	is apprehensive of
	is fearful (about/of/that)
	is frightened of/to
	is scared of/to
fears (for)	is in fear for/of
features	(the) ins and (the) outs
fee	compensation
	remittance
	remuneration
feel	experience
	feel inside
	hold (to) the opinion (that)
	hold (to) the view (that)
	indicate
	in the assessment of
	in the estimation of
	in the judgment of
	in the opinion of
	in the view of
	take the position (that)
	take the view (that)
feeling	personal feeling
feels	is inclined to believe (that)
	is inclined to think (that)
	is of the belief (that)
	is of the opinion (that)
	is of the view (that)
	is under the assumption (that)
	is under the impression (that)
feign	make believe
	put on an act
felon	convicted felon
female/male	human being
	(of) (the) opposite sex
females/males	(the) female/male gender/sex

CONCISE	WORDY
fervor	fervency
fever	temperature
few	(a/the) declining/decreasing/diminishing/dwindling number/quantity (of)
	few and far between
	few/small in number
	(a/the) lack of
	(very) limited
	(a/the) modicum of
fewer	(a/the) decreased/decreasing number of
	(a/the) smaller/tinier number (of)
fewer and fewer	(a/the) declining/decreasing/diminishing/dwindling number/quantity (of)
fewer than half (of)	(a/the) minimal number (of)
	(a/the) minority (of)
	(a/the) significant/substantial minority (of)
	(a/the) small/tiny amount/degree/part/percentage/ portion/proportion/quantity (of)
	(a/the) small/tiny fraction (of)
	(a/the) small/tiny minority (of)
field	breadth and depth
	subject/topic area/field/matter
fill	fill to capacity
	fill up
fillip	added fillip
film	motion picture
filter	filter out
filthy	filthy dirty
final	final and irrevocable
finally	after all is said and done
	at long last
	at the end of the day
	(after/for/in/over/within) (an) extended/lengthy/long/ prolonged/protracted amount of time/length of time/period/period of time/span of time/time/while
	in conclusion
	in the final/last analysis
	once (and) for all
	when all is said and done
finances	financial/monetary resources
	financial wherewithal
find	come in contact (with)

CONCISE	WORDY
	come up with
	encounter
	experience
	find out
	make contact (with)
find fault with	raise objections about/on/to
	raise opposition about/on/to
	take exception to
fine	(all) fine/good and well
	(all) well and fine/good
finest	of the first magnitude
	of the first/highest order
finish	bring (to) a close (to)
	bring (to) a completion (to)
	bring (to) a conclusion (to)
	bring (to) a halt (to)
	bring (to) an end (to)
	bring to a standstill
	call a halt to
	call an end to
	call a stop to
	come to a close
	come to a/the conclusion (about/as to/concerning/of/on/ regarding)
	come to a halt
	come to an end
	come to a standstill
	draw to a close/end
	draw to a conclusion
	finalize
	finish off
	finish up
	put a halt to
	put an end to
	put a stop to
	terminate
finished	all done/finished
	at an end
	over and done with
	(all) over with
fire	fiery conflagration
fired	no longer with us
firm	establishment
	firmly establish

CONCISE	WORDY
	hard and fast
	place of business/employment/work
first	first and foremost
	first ever
	first initially
	firstly
	first of all
	first off
	for one (thing)
	initial/initially
	in the first place
	to begin/start with
first/last	for the first/last time
first-class	of the first/highest order
first of all	in the first place
first time	first time ever
fix	rectify
fixed	hard and fast
flammable	inflammable
flourishing	on the increase
	on the rise
focus	center of attention/attraction
	focal point
	focus in
	focus of attention
focus on	attention . . . focused on/upon
	concentrate . . . attention on/upon
	concentrate . . . effort on/upon
	concentrate . . . energy on/upon
	concentrate . . . time and energy on/upon
	focus . . . attention on/upon
	focus . . . effort on/upon
	focus . . . energy on/upon
	focus . . . time and energy on/upon
	zero in on
focuses on	is focused on/upon
(five)fold	(five) times over
fold	fold up
follow	act in accord/accordance with
	follow after
	follow . . . below
following	according to
	after the conclusion/end of
	as a consequence of

CONCISE	WORDY
	as a result of
	by consequence of
	by reason of
	by the result of
	by/in virtue of
	in accord/accordance with
	in agreement with
	in compliance with
	in conformance to/with
	in conformity to/with
	in consequence of
	in consonance to/with
	in correspondence to/with
	in imitation of
	in reaction to
	in response to
	in the aftermath of
	in the wake of
	on account of
	on the basis of
	on/upon the heels of
	posterior to
	pursuant to
	subsequent to the time (of/that/when)
fondness	positive feelings
for	about the fact that
	about/concerning/in/on/regarding the matter/subject of
	as a consequence of
	as a consequence of the fact that
	as . . . apply to
	as a result of
	as a result of the fact that
	as concerns
	as/so far as . . . (goes/is concerned)
	as regards
	associated with
	as to
	attributable to the fact that
	based on/upon
	based on the fact that
	because of
	because of the fact that
	being (as/as how/that)

CONCISE	WORDY
	by consequence of
	by reason of
	by reason of the fact that
	by the fact that
	by the result of
	by/in virtue of
	by/in virtue of the fact that
	concerning
	connected with
	considering the fact that
	due to the fact that
	during the course/length of
	forasmuch as
	for (in/to) (the) furtherance of
	for . . . purposes (of)
	for reasons of
	for the (simple) reason that
	for the sake of
	for . . . to come
	from (a/the) . . . aspect (of)
	from (a/the) . . . perspective (of)
	from (a/the) . . . point of view (of)
	from (a/the) . . . standpoint (of)
	from (a/the) . . . viewpoint (of)
	from the fact that
	given the fact that
	inasmuch/insomuch as
	in (the) . . . case (of)
	in connection with
	in consequence of
	in consequence of the fact that
	in consideration of (payment of/sum of)
	in consideration of the fact that
	in defense of
	in exchange (for)
	in favor (of)
	in honor of
	in (the) light of the fact that
	in order for
	in order that
	in payment for/of
	in place of
	in point of

CONCISE	WORDY
	in proportion to
	in punishment for/of
	in reaction to
	in reference to
	in regard to
	in relation to
	in respect of/to
	in response to
	in return for
	insofar as
	insofar as . . . (goes/is concerned)in support of
	in terms of
	in the amount/sum of
	in the area of
	(somewhere) in the course of
	in the direction of/toward
	in the interest of (-ing)
	in the realm of
	in the sense that
	in the support of (-ing)
	in trade (for)
	in view of the fact that
	involve in . . . behalf (of)
	on account of
	on account of the fact that
	on . . . behalf (of)
	on (the) grounds that
	on . . . part
	on the basis of
	on the basis of the fact that
	on the part of
	on the side of
	over the course/duration/length of
	over the fact that
	owing to the fact that
	pertain/pertaining to
	regard/regarding
	relate/relating to
	relative to
	seeing (as/as how/that)
	through/throughout the course/duration/length of
	when it comes to
	where . . . is concerned
	with reference to

CONCISE	WORDY
	with regard to
	with relation to
	with respect to
for (-ing)	as a means for/of/to (-ing)
	as a way for/of/to (-ing)
	as the basis for (-ing)
	by way of (-ing)
	for the purpose of (-ing)
	with a/the thought of/to (-ing)
	with a/the view of/to (-ing)
	with the intent of -ing (to)
	with the purpose of -ing
for all	contrary to
	in despite of
	in (the) face of
	in spite of
	notwithstanding
	. . . to the contrary
for a long time/while	for (an) extended/prolonged/protracted amount of time/length of time/period/period of time/span of time/time/while
for a time	for (an) indefinite/indeterminate amount of time/length of time/period/period of time/span of time/time/while
	for the foreseeable future
	for the immediate future
	for the (very) near future
	for the not-so-distant/not-too-distant future
for a time/while	for (an) extended/prolonged/protracted amount of time/length of time/period/period of time/span of time/time/while
for a while	for (an) indefinite/indeterminate amount of time/length of time/period/period of time/span of time/time/while
	for the immediate future
	for the (very) near future
	for the not-so-distant/not-too-distant future
for being	by way of being
for (in) both	in both cases/circumstances/instances/situations
force	bring pressure to bear on/upon
	driving force
	(with) might and main
	motivating force
	place/put restrictions on/upon

CONCISE	WORDY
	place/put under obligation
	under obligation
for days/hours/months	for (an) extended/prolonged/protracted amount of time/ length of time/period/period of time/ span of time/time/while
for (in) each	in each/every case/circumstance/instance/situation
	on each/every occasion
forebear	forebearer
foreboding	fear and trembling
forecast	forecast . . . future
	foretell . . . future
	predict . . . future
forecasts	is predictive of
forego	take precedence over
	take priority over
forge	bring into being/existence
	call into being/existence
forgets	does not remember
foremost	first and foremost
	most important
	number-one
	of the first magnitude
	of the first/highest order
foretell	forecast . . . future
	foretell . . . future
	predict . . . future
foretells	is predictive of
forever	all the time
	always and forever
	at every turn
	day in (and) day out
	for ever and a day
	forevermore
	in perpetuity
	year in (and) year out
for (in) every	in each/every case/circumstance/instance/situation
	on each/every occasion
for example/for instance	as an example
	as . . . for example/for instance
	by way of example/illustration
	(a) case in point
	e.g. . . . and others/and so forth/and so on/and such/and the like/et al./etc.

CONCISE	WORDY
	for example . . . and others/and so forth/and so on/and such/and the like/et al./etc./or whatever
	for instance . . . and others/and so forth/and so on/and such/and the like/et al./etc./or whatever
	like . . . for example/for instance
	say, for example/for instance
	such as . . . for example/for instance
form	bring into being/existence
	call into being/existence
	come up with
	constitute
	formulate
	materialize
	put together
for many/several months/years	
	for the foreseeable future
	for the immediate future
	for the (very) near future
	for the not-so-distant/not-too-distant future
formerly	at an/some earlier/former/past/previous date/time
	back/before in the past
	in (the) days/decades/months/weeks/years gone by
	in (the) days/decades/months/weeks/years of old
	in (the) days/decades/months/weeks/years past
	in earlier/former/prior times
	in the (very) near past
	in (the) olden days
	in/over (the) past days/decades/months/weeks/years
	in the distant past
	in the immediate past
	in the not-so-distant/not-too-distant past
	in the past
	in/within the recent past
	on earlier/former/previous/prior occasions
	time was when
forming	in the making
formula	action/attack/battle/game plan
for myself	in my (own) mind(s)
for now	for the foreseeable future
	for the immediate future
	for the (very) near future

CONCISE	WORDY
	for the not-so-distant/not-too-distant future
	for the present
	for the time/while being
	in/over the near term
	in/over the short run
	in/over the short term
	over the short haul
for one	for one . . . (be) an example/an instance
for (in/with) some (of us)	under certain/some circumstances/conditions
for some time	for the foreseeable future
	for the immediate future
	for the (very) near future
	for the not-so-distant/not-too-distant future
forte	long suit
	strong point/suit
for the moment	for the time/while being
for the present	for the foreseeable future
	for the immediate future
	for the (very) near future
	for the not-so-distant/not-too-distant future
	for the time/while being
for the time being	for the foreseeable future
	for the immediate future
	for the (very) near future
	for the not-so-distant/not-too-distant future
	in quick/short order
forthwith	at/in the blink of an eye
	expeditiously
forward	forward in/into the future
fosters	is supportive of
founder/founded	original founder/originally founded
fourth	fourthly
fragment	tiny/little bit
frankly	to tell (you) the truth
frankness	candor and frankness
free	at/for no charge/cost
	clear, free, and unencumbered
	for free
	free and clear
	free and gratis
	free, complimentary
	free of charge
	free up
freezing	freezing cold

CONCISE	WORDY
frequently	again and again
	at frequent/periodic/regular intervals/periods
	in a lot of cases/circumstances/instances/situations
	in a/the majority of cases/circumstances/instances/ situations
	in many/most cases
	in many/most circumstances
	in many/most instances
	in many/most situations
	it is often the case/circumstance/situation (that)
	(a) lot of (the) time
	many times over
	on a number of /any number of/frequent/many/ numerous/several occasions
	on more than one occasion
	over and over (again)
	time after time
	time and (time) again
fret (about/over)	express concern (about)
	is concerned (about)
	voice concern (about)
frets (about/over)	is afraid of/to
	is apprehensive of
	is fearful (about/of/that)
	is frightened of/to
	is in fear for/of
	is scared of/to
friend/friendship	personal friend/friendship
friendship	mutual friendship
from	as a consequence of
	as a result of
	as to
	at the hands of
	-based
	based in
	based on/upon
	because of
	by (the) means of
	by/in virtue of
	by (the) way of
	by consequence of
	by reason of
	by the result of
	for reasons of

CONCISE	WORDY
	from (a/the) . . . aspect (of)
	from (a/the) . . . distance of
	from (a/the) . . . perspective (of)
	from (a/the) . . . point of view (of)
	from (a/the) . . . standpoint (of)
	from (a/the) . . . viewpoint (of)
	in consequence of
	in reaction to
	in response to
	in the wake of
	off of
	on account of
	on . . . part
	on the basis of
	on the part of
	through the medium of
from/in (1989)	from/in the following year
	from/in the preceding year
from . . . away	from (a/the) . . . distance of
	of from . . . to
from now	down the line/pike/road/way
	in . . . from now
	later in time
	later on down the line/pike/road/way
from now (on)	from this day/moment/point/time (forward/on/onward)
from then (on)	from that day/moment/point/time (forward/on/onward)
from the start	instantaneous/instantaneously
from . . . through/to	(the) decade/period/period of time/span of time/time/ years (from) . . . through/till/to/until
	(the) decade/period/period of time/span of time/time/ years between . . . and
	during/for/over the decade/period/period of time/span of time/time/years (from) . . . through/ till/to/until
from time to time	every now and then
	every once in a while
	under certain/some circumstances/conditions
from . . . to	from . . . until
	(something/somewhere) in the range from (of) . . . through/to
	in the . . . through/to . . . range
frustrate	stand in the way of
frustration	negative feelings
fulfill	implement

CONCISE	WORDY
(the) full	in its/their entirety
fully	backward and forward
	in its/their entirety
	under any circumstances/conditions
functioning	in operation
fundamental	basic (and) fundamental
	fundamental (and) basic
	simple (and) fundamental
funds	financial/monetary resources
	financial wherewithal
	wherewithal
furious	furiously angry
furnish	make available
further	(a) bigger/greater/higher/larger degree/extent (of)
	(an) additional
	additionally
	and . . . further/furthermore/in addition/moreover/what's more
	as a matter of fact
	by the same token
	for that matter
	furthermore
	in addition
	in the next place
	in the second place
	in the third place
	next of all
	on top of (that/this)
furthermore	additionally
	and . . . further/furthermore/in addition/moreover/what's more
	as a matter of fact
	by the same token
	for that matter
	in addition
	in the next place
	in the second place
	in the third place
	next of all
	on top of (that/this)
fuse	fuse together
future	in the distant future

CONCISE	WORDY

G

gain	take advantage of
gather	bring together
	come together
	gather together
generally	as a general rule
	as a rule
	as often as not
	by and large
	for the most part
	in great/large measure
	in great/large part
	in no small measure
	in no small part
	in the main
	more often than not
	most (of the) time(s)
	on (an/the) average
	on/upon the whole
	predominant/predominantly
	to a great/large degree
	to a great/large extent
gentle	kinder (and) gentler
geographic	geographical
geologic	geological
geometric	geometrical
get	procure
	take delivery of/on
	take possession of
giant	humongous
gibberish	meaningless gibberish
gift	free gift
gist	core essence
	essential core
	(the) heart of the matter
	(the) long and (the) short
	sum/summary and substance
give	present with
	proffer
	provide . . . with

CONCISE	WORDY
	put forth
	put forward
	render
give birth to	bring into the world
give . . . (the) chance	afford/give/offer/present/provide . . . (an/the) opportunity (to)
given	as a consequence of the fact that
	as a result of the fact that
	attributable to the fact that
	based on the fact that
	because of the fact that
	being (as/as how/that)
	by reason of the fact that
	by the fact that
	by/in virtue of the fact that
	considering the fact that
	due to the fact that
	forasmuch as
	for the (simple) reason that
	from the fact that
	given the fact that
	inasmuch/insomuch as
	in consequence of the fact that
	in consideration of the fact that
	insofar as
	in the sense that
	in view of the fact that
	on account of the fact that
	on (the) grounds that
	on the basis of the fact that
	owing to the fact that
	seeing (as/as how/that)
	what with
given that	in (the) light of the fact that
glad	in a good mood
gladly	of . . . own accord/free will
gleeful	in a good mood
glum	in a bad mood
go	proceed
go against	fly in the face of
goal	(the) whys and (the) wherefores (of)
goals	(the) hows and (the) whys
go before	take precedence over
	take priority over

CONCISE	WORDY
gone	no longer with us
good	good and sufficient
	(all) fine/good and well
	(all) well and fine/good
go on	advance ahead/forward/on/onward
	go forward
	move forward
	move forward into the future
	proceed ahead/forth/forward/on/onward
	progress ahead/forward/on/onward
go through	experience
	go through . . . experience
governs	is in charge of
	is in control of
GPS	GPS system
gradually	bit by bit
	little by little
grand	humongous
	significant/substantial
	substantive
grasp	come to an/the understanding (about/as to/concerning/of/on/regarding)
	take (a) hold of
(be) grateful (for)	appreciate
gratefulness	appreciation
gratitude	appreciation
	grateful thanks
great	(a/the) considerable/good/great/huge/large/sizable/vast degree (of)
	(a/the) considerable/good/great/huge/large/sizable/vast element (of)
	(all) fine/good and well
	(a/the) high degree (of)
	(a/the) high level (of)
	humongous
	of the first/highest order
	significant/substantial
	(a/the) significant/substantial degree (of)
	(a/the) significant/substantial element (of)
	substantive
	(all) well and fine/good
greaten	maximize
greater than	in excess of
greatest	maximal

CONCISE	WORDY
	(a/the) maximum amount (of)
	(a/the) maximum number (of)
	(a/the) maximum . . . of
greatly	as a general rule
	as a rule
	considerably
	for the most part
	in great/large measure
	in great/large part
	in no small measure
	in no small part
	in the main
	on/upon the whole
	significantly/substantially
	to a great/large degree
	to a great/large extent
grieve	express sorrow (about)
	voice sorrow (about)
grouchy	in a bad mood
groundless	no basis in fact
	unsubstantiated
	without basis in fact
	without foundation
grounds	(the) whys and (the) wherefores (of)
group	group together
growing	on the increase
	on the rise
guarantee	assure (ensure/insure) . . . guarantee
guards	is protective against (of)
guest	invited guest
gunman	armed gunman

H

habitual	matter-of-course
habitually	as a matter of course
had	had . . . then
	if . . . had
hale	hale and hearty
half	half of
half (of)	fifty (50) percent (of)
half/third	one-half/one-third

CONCISE	WORDY
halt	bring (to) a close (to)
	bring (to) a completion (to)
	bring (to) a conclusion (to)
	bring (to) a halt (to)
	bring (to) an end (to)
	bring to a standstill
	call an end to
	call a halt to
	call a stop to
	come to a close
	come to a/the conclusion (about/as to/concerning/of/on/ regarding)
	come to a halt
	come to an end
	come to a standstill
	draw to a close/end
	draw to a conclusion
	put a halt to
	put an end to
	put a stop to
	terminate
halve	cut by/in half
	divide in half
	reduce by/to half
hamper	place/put a burden on/upon
	place/put a strain on/upon
happen	come about
	come into play
	come to pass
	eventuate
	go forward
	materialize
	move forward
	take place
happy	in a good mood
harbinger	harbinger of the future (of things to come)
hardly	by no means
hardly/scarcely	not hardly/scarcely
hardly any (of)	(a/the) minimal number (of)
	(a/the) minority (of)
	(a/the) small/tiny amount/degree/part/percentage/ portion/proportion/quantity (of)
	(a/the) small/tiny fraction (of)
	(a/the) small/tiny minority (of)

CONCISE	WORDY
	(a/the) small/tiny number (of)
harms	is deleterious to
	is destructive of/to
	is detrimental to
	is harmful to
	is injurious to
	is ruinous to
has	has got
	is in possession of
hastily	at/in the blink of an eye
	expeditiously
	in quick/short order
has to	is required to
hate	negative feelings
hatred	negative feelings
haughty	high and mighty
have	encounter
	experience
	have . . . in (my) possession
	incorporate in(to)
	possess (a/the) . . . (about/for/of/on/over)
(I) have been told	it has been called to (my) attention
	it has come to (my) attention
(I) have learned	it has been called to (my) attention
	it has come to (my) attention
haven	safe haven
have to	necessarily have to
having no	(a/the) absence of
	in the absence of
head	head up
heal	ameliorate
healthy	hale and hearty
hearken	take notice of
hearken to	pay attention to
	pay heed to
	take cognizance of
	take note of
hearsay	baseless/groundless/unfounded/unsubstantiated rumor
heart	(the) heart of the matter
	(the) long and (the) short
	sum/summary and substance
hearty	hale and hearty
heat	heat up
heavy	significant/substantial

CONCISE	WORDY
	substantive
heed	(please) bear in mind
	pay attention to
	pay heed to
	take cognizance of
	take note of
	take notice of
heeds	is attentive to
help	aid and abet
	aid in -ing
	ameliorate
	assistance
	assist in -ing
	facilitate
	help assist
	help out
	help . . . to
	render assistance to
help (-ing)	help in/of -ing
helpless	high and dry
helps	is advantageous for (to)
	is beneficial to
	is favorable to
	is helpful in (-ing)
	is instrumental in (-ing)
	is instrumental in helping
	is of assistance in (-ing)
	is of benefit to
hence	accordingly
	and so as a result
	as a consequence
	as a result
	consequently
	for that/this reason
	from hence
	from now (on)
	from this day/moment/point/time (forward/on/onward)
	henceforth/henceforward
	hereafter
	in consequence
	so consequently
	so therefore
	that/this being the case
	therefore

CONCISE	WORDY
henceforth	from this day/moment/point/time (forward/on/onward)
henceforward	from this day/moment/point/time (forward/on/onward)
herald	bring attention to
	bring into the open
	bring to . . . attention (of)
	bring to light
	call . . . attention to
	call to . . . attention (of)
	concentrate (media/people's/public) attention on/upon
	direct . . . attention to
	draw attention to
	focus (media/people's/public) attention on/upon
here	in that/this case/circumstance/instance/situation
	(of) the present . . .
here is	enclosed herein/herewith is (please find)
	enclosed is
high	(a/the) high degree (of)
	(a/the) high level (of)
	. . . in height
highest	maximal
	(a/the) maximum amount (of)
	(a/the) maximum number (of)
	(a/the) maximum . . . of
highly	in the extreme
highly regard	place/put a premium on/upon
	place/put a priority on/upon
hinder	place/put a burden on/upon
	place/put a strain on/upon
	stand in the way of
hinders	is a deterrent to
	is a hindrance to
	is an impediment to
	is an obstacle to
hinges on	is conditional/conditioned on/upon
	is contingent on/upon
	is dependent on/upon
	is subject to
hint	indicate
	indication
	tiny/little bit
historically	historically . . . in the past
history	historical experience
	historical precedent
	historical record

CONCISE	WORDY
	past/previous/prior history
HIV	HIV virus
hoist	hoist up
hold	hold (to) the opinion (that)
	hold (to) the view (that)
	hold true
	in the assessment of
	in the estimation of
	in the judgment of
	in the opinion of
	in the view of
	take the position (that)
	take the view (that)
holds	is inclined to believe (that)
	is inclined to think (that)
	is of the belief (that)
	is of the opinion (that)
	is of the view (that)
holdup	armed holdup
home	domicile
	residence
honest	fair and square
	worthy of trust
honestly	(the) honest truth
	honestly and truly/truthfully
	to tell (you) the truth
hope	expect/expectation and hope
	hope and expect/expectation
	positive feelings
(I/we) hope	hopefully
hopes	is hopeful
horror	fear and trembling
hospital	facility
	institution
hourly	on a regular basis
hours	in/over . . . days/decades/hours/minutes/months/weeks/ years time
house	domicile
	premises
	residence
how	by what/which means/mechanism
	in what/which fashion/manner/way
	in what/which regard/respect
	(what is) (a/the) manner/means/mechanism/method/ procedure/process/technique by which

CONCISE	WORDY
	(what is) the fashion/manner/way (in which/that)
	(the) degree to which
	(the) extent to which
	through what/which means/mechanism
	to what degree
	to what extent
	(the) way (in which)
how come	how is it (that)
how do (you)	how do (you) go about (-ing)
how ever	how in God's/heaven's name
	how in the world/on earth
however	(in) one way or another
	but however
	by/in comparison
	by/in contrast
	by one means or another
	by way of comparison/contrast
	by whatever/whichever manner/means
	contrariwise
	how in God's/heaven's name
	how in the world/on earth
	howsoever
	in whatever/whichever fashion/manner/way
	irrespective of how
	no matter how
	on the contrary
	on the other hand
	regardless of how
	through whatever/whichever manner/means
	to the contrary
	to whatever degree/extent
however far	to whatever degree/extent
however much	to whatever degree/extent
however often	to whatever degree/extent
how far	(the) degree to which
	(the) extent to which
	to what degree
	to what extent
	to what length
how likely/probable	what is the likelihood/probability (of)
how long	the length of time
how much	the degree of
	(the) degree to which
	the extent of
	(the) extent to which

CONCISE	WORDY
	to what degree
	to what extent
	to what length
how often	(the) degree to which
	(the) extent to which
	to what degree
	to what extent
HTML	HTML language
hubbub	hue and cry
huge	big, huge (large)
	(a/the) high degree (of)
	(a/the) high level (of)
	humongous
	significant/substantial
	substantive
hugely	in the extreme
human	human being
humane	kinder (and) gentler
hundreds (of)	(a/the) considerable/good/great/huge/large/ overwhelming/sizable/vast number (of)
	(a/the) considerable/good/great/huge/large/sizable/vast quantity (of)
	(a/the) high number (of)
	in big/great/high/huge/large/overwhelming/sizable/vast numbers
	in great/large quantities
	(a/a fair/any) number (of)
	(a/the) significant/substantial number (of)
	(a/the) significant/substantial quantity (of)
hundreds/thousands	many hundreds/thousands
hurriedly	at/in the blink of an eye
	expeditiously
	in quick/short order
hurry	hurry up
hurts	is deleterious to
	is destructive of/to
	is detrimental to
	is harmful to
	is injurious to
	is ruinous to

CONCISE	WORDY

I/he/her/him/me/she/ them/they/us/we	the/this author/reader/writer
I advise	it is my recommendation (that)
	it is my suggestion (that)
I advocate	it is my recommendation (that)
	it is my suggestion (that)
I anticipate	it is my expectation (that)
I appreciate	it is my understanding (that)
I assert	based on/upon my personal judgment/opinion
	in my assessment
	in my estimation
	in my judgment
	in my opinion
	in my view
	it is my assessment (that)
	it is my belief (that)
	it is my estimation (that)
	it is my judgment (that)
	it is my opinion (that)
	it is my view (that)
I believe	based on/upon my personal judgment/opinion
	in my assessment
	in my estimation
	in my judgment
	in my opinion
	in my view
	it is my assessment (that)
	it is my belief (that)
	it is my estimation (that)
	it is my judgment (that)
	it is my opinion (that)
	it is my view (that)
I claim	based on/upon my personal judgment/opinion
	in my assessment
	in my estimation
	in my judgment
	in my opinion
	in my view
	it is my assessment (that)

CONCISE	WORDY
	it is my belief (that)
	it is my estimation (that)
	it is my judgment (that)
	it is my opinion (that)
	it is my view (that)
I comprehend	it is my understanding (that)
I consider	based on/upon my personal judgment/opinion
	in my assessment
	in my estimation
	in my judgment
	in my opinion
	in my view
	it is my assessment (that)
	it is my belief (that)
	it is my estimation (that)
	it is my judgment (that)
	it is my opinion (that)
	it is my view (that)
I contend	based on/upon my personal judgment/opinion
	in my assessment
	in my estimation
	in my judgment
	in my opinion
	in my view
	it is my assessment (that)
	it is my belief (that)
	it is my estimation (that)
	it is my judgment (that)
	it is my opinion (that)
	it is my view (that)
I declare	in my assessment
	in my estimation
	in my judgment
	in my opinion
	in my view
	it is my assessment (that)
	it is my belief (that)
	it is my estimation (that)
	it is my judgment (that)
	it is my opinion (that)
	it is my view (that)
identical	exact/exactly duplicate
	exact/exactly equivalent
	exact/exactly identical

CONCISE	WORDY
	exact/exactly match
	exact/exactly (the) same
	(an) identical/identically match
	identical/identically (the) same
	one and the same
	perfect/perfectly match
identify	put . . . finger on/upon
I discern	it is my observation (that)
idle	lackadaisical
I doubt	I don't think
I expect	it is my expectation (that)
if	as, if, and when
	as long as/so long as (that)
	if and only if
	if and/or when
	if . . . then
	in case
	in cases/circumstances/instances/situations in which
	in cases when/where
	in circumstances when/where
	in instances when/where
	in situations when/where
	on (the) condition (of/that)
	on (the) understanding (of/that)
	provided/providing (that)
	when and/or if
	when and/or whether
	when, as, and if
	whether
	whether and/or when
	whether or not
if (there were)	in (the) event (of/that)
	in the eventuality of (that/this)
	in the unexpected/unlikely event of/that
	on the occasion of
I fancy	it is my preference (that)
I favor	it is my preference (that)
I feel	based on/upon my personal judgment/opinion
	in my assessment
	in my estimation
	in my judgment
	in my opinion
	in my view
	it is my assessment (that)

CONCISE	WORDY
	it is my belief (that)
	it is my estimation (that)
	it is my judgment (that)
	it is my opinion (that)
	it is my view (that)
if . . . should	in (the) event (of/that)
	in the eventuality of (that/this)
	in the unexpected/unlikely event of/that
	on the occasion of
if so	if that/this is the case/situation
	if that/this is true
ignore	fly in the face of
ignores	does not pay attention to
I grasp	it is my understanding (that)
I hold	based on/upon my personal judgment/opinion
	in my assessment
	in my estimation
	in my judgment
	in my opinion
	in my view
	it is my assessment (that)
	it is my belief (that)
	it is my estimation (that)
	it is my judgment (that)
	it is my opinion (that)
	it is my view (that)
I (we) hope	it is (to be) hoped
I intend	it is my intention (that)
I judge	based on/upon my personal judgment/opinion
	in my assessment
	in my estimation
	in my judgment
	in my opinion
	in my view
	it is my assessment (that)
	it is my belief (that)
	it is my estimation (that)
	it is my judgment (that)
	it is my opinion (that)
	it is my view (that)
il-	(a/the) absence of
	(a/the) lack of
	devoid of
	insufficient

CONCISE	WORDY
	lacking in
	less than (enthusiastic)
ill	under the weather
ill treat	take advantage of
ill treats	is exploitative/exploitive of
illusion	false illusion
(to) illustrate	(an) example that illustrates/to illustrate
illustrates	is an illustration of
	is characteristic of
	is descriptive of
	is illustrative of
illustration	illustrative example
im-	(a/the) absence of
	(a/the) lack of
	devoid of
	insufficient
	lacking in
	less than (enthusiastic)
imagine	(to) . . . in my (own) mind's eye
I maintain	based on/upon my personal judgment/opinion
	in my assessment
	in my estimation
	in my judgment
	in my opinion
	in my view
	it is my assessment (that)
	it is my belief (that)
	it is my estimation (that)
	it is my judgment (that)
	it is my opinion (that)
	it is my view (that)
imitate	follow along the lines of
imitates	is imitative of
immaterial	beside the point
	neither here nor there
immediately	in the immediate future
immense	humongous
	significant/substantial
	substantive
immunologic	immunological
impairs	is deleterious to
	is destructive of/to
	is detrimental to
	is harmful to

CONCISE	WORDY
	is injurious to
	is ruinous to
impede	stand in the way of
impedes	is a deterrent to
	is a hindrance to
	is an impediment to
	is an obstacle to
imperil	place/put . . . in/into peril
	place/put . . . in danger
	place/put . . . in jeopardy
	throw into jeopardy
imperiled	(be) in jeopardy
imperils	is dangerous to
impetus	driving force
	motivating force
implode	implode on itself
import	consequence
	importance
	magnitude
importance	significant importance
important	(of) central/critical/vital importance
	critically/crucially/vitally important
	of (a/the) . . . importance (that/to)
important for/to	(an/the) important . . . for (in/of/to)
impossible	beyond (outside) the realm of possibility
	out of the question
	out/outside (of) the realm of possibility
improbable	out/outside (of) the realm of possibility
improve	ameliorate
	rectify
improved	more improved
	new and improved
imputes to	is accredited/credited to
	is attributable to
in	about/concerning/in/on/regarding the matter/subject of
	as a consequence of
	as . . . apply to
	as a result of as/so far as . . . (goes/is concerned)
	as concerns
	as regards
	associated with
	as to
	back in
	-based

CONCISE	WORDY
	based in
	based on/upon
	because of
	by consequence of
	by (the) means of
	by reason of
	by the result of
	by/in virtue of
	by (the) way of
	concerning
	connected with
	during the course/length of
	for reasons of
	from (a/the) . . . aspect (of)
	from (a/the) . . . perspective (of)
	from (a/the) . . . point of view (of)
	from (a/the) . . . standpoint (of)
	from (a/the) . . . viewpoint (of)
	in a/the . . . state (of) . . .
	(something/somewhere) in between
	in (the) . . . case (of)
	in connection with
	in consequence of
	in (a/the) . . . form
	in . . . from now
	in point of
	in reaction to
	in reference to
	in regard to
	in relation to
	in respect of/to
	in response to
	insofar as . . . (goes/is concerned)
	in terms of
	in the area of
	in the company of
	in the context of
	(somewhere) in the course of
	in the direction of/toward
	in the middle of
	in the midst of
	in the presence of
	in the process of
	in the realm of

CONCISE	WORDY
	in (the) time(s) of
	involve
	involved in
	on account of
	on the basis of
	on the part of
	on the . . . side
	out in
	out of
	over the course/duration/length of
	pertain/pertaining to
	regard/regarding
	relate/relating to
	through/throughout the course/duration/length of
	through the medium of
	through the use of
	when it comes to
	where . . . is concerned
	with reference to
	with regard to
	with relation to
	with respect to
in-	(a/the) absence of
	(a/the) lack of
	devoid of
	insufficient
	lacking in
	less than (enthusiastic)
in (March) (1992)	in (March) of (1992)
in/within	in/within the boundaries/limits/parameters of
in action	in force and effect
	operative
in/within a day/year	(after/for/in/over/within) (a) reasonable amount of time/ length of time/period/period of time/ span of time/time/while
	in a timely fashion/manner/way
	on a timely basis
in addition	and . . . further/furthermore/in addition/moreover/what's more
	in the next place
	in the second place
	in the third place
in addition to	in addition to . . . additionally/also/as well/too
in advance	ahead of time

CONCISE	WORDY
in all	all in all
	all things considered
	at the end of the day
	including everything
	in the final/last analysis
	in the overall scope/sphere of things
	on the whole
	when all is said and done
	when it/you comes/gets right down to it
in a month/week	in the foreseeable future
	in/into the future
	in the immediate future
	in the (very) near future
	in the not-so-distant/not-too-distant future
in/over a month/week	in/over the near term
	in/over the short run
	in/over the short term
	over the short haul
in any way	by one means or another
	in any way, shape, or form (or fashion)
	(in) one way or another
inapt	beside the point
	neither here nor there
in a sense	figuratively speaking
	in a manner of speaking
	metaphorically speaking
	to a certain/limited/some degree
	to a certain/limited/some extent
in a way	figuratively speaking
	in a manner of speaking
	metaphorically speaking
in between	betwixt and between
	in the middle of
	in the midst of
in brief	in brief/concise/succinct summary
	in summary/summation
	summing up
	to summarize/sum up
in case (of)	in (the) event (of/that)
	in the eventuality of (that/this)
	in the unexpected/unlikely event of/that
	on the occasion of
incessantly	continuously/incessantly and without interruption
in closing	in conclusion

CONCISE	WORDY
include	incorporate in(to)
includes	is composed of
	is comprised of
in combination	both . . . in combination
	together . . . in combination
in comparison to/with	in comparison/in contrast to/with . . . relatively
incompetence	incompetency
inconceivable	beyond/outside the realm of possibility
	out of the question
	out/outside (of) the realm of possibility
in contrast to/with	in comparison/in contrast to/with . . . relatively
increase	maximize
increasing	(an/the) increased/increasing amount of
	(an/the) increased/increasing number of
	on the increase
	on the rise
increasingly	(a/the) burgeoning/growing/increasing/rising amount/ degree/extent/number/part/ percentage/portion/proportion/ quantity (of)
	increasing in
	increasingly more
	to an increasing degree/extent
	with increasing frequency
incumbent	current/present incumbent
in/over . . . days/decades	in/over . . . days/decades/hours/minutes/months/weeks/ years time
in days/months/weeks/years	in recent history/memory/times
indeed	as a matter of fact
	(the) fact is (that)
	(the) (simple) fact of the matter is (that)
	in actual fact
	in actuality
	in point of fact
	in reality
	really (and) truly
	(the) truth is (that)
	(the) truth of the matter is (that)
indefinitely	for (an) indefinite/indeterminate amount of time/length of time/period/period of time/span of time/time/while
independent	separate and independent
indicate	bring attention to
	bring into the open

CONCISE	WORDY
	bring to . . . attention (of)
	bring to light
	call . . . attention to
	call to . . . attention (of)
	concentrate (media/people's/public) attention on/upon
	direct . . . attention to
	draw attention to
	focus (media/people's/public) attention on/upon
	point to the conclusion
indicates	is an indication/indicator of
	is emblematic of
	is evidence of/that
	is indicative of
	is proof of/that
	is representative of
	is suggestive of
	is symbolic/symbolical of
	is symptomatic of
indifference	negative feelings
indisputably	beyond a/the shadow of a doubt
indistinct	out of focus
individual	separate and individual
	separate individual
in doubt	(an/the) open question
	open to doubt
	open to question
induction	inductive reasoning
in due time	as time goes on
	as time progresses (forward/on/onward)
	at a/some future/later/subsequent date/time
	(after/for/in/over/within) (an) extended/lengthy/long/ prolonged/protracted amount of time/length of time/period/period of time/span of time/time/while
	in the course of events/things/time
	in/into the future
	some day/time in the future
	(the) time will come when
	with the passage of time
in effect	for all intents and purposes
	for all practical purposes
	in force and effect
	operative
	to all intents and purposes

CONCISE	WORDY
	to all practical purposes
in essence	for all intents and purposes
	for all practical purposes
	to all intents and purposes
	to all practical purposes
inequitable	unfair and inequitable
inevitably	must necessarily/of necessity
in fact	as a matter of fact
	(the) fact is (that)
	(the) (simple) fact of the matter is (that)
	in actual fact
	in actuality
	in point of fact
	in reality
	really (and) truly
	(the) truth is (that)
	(the) truth of the matter is (that)
in faith	as a matter of fact
	(the) fact is (that)
	(the) (simple) fact of the matter is (that)
	in actual fact
	in actuality
	in point of fact
	in reality
	really (and) truly
	(the) truth is (that)
	(the) truth of the matter is (that)
infant	young infant
infer	arrive at (a/the) conclusion (about/as to/concerning/of/on/regarding)
	arrive at (a/the) decision (about/as to/concerning/of/on/regarding)
	arrive at (a/the) determination (about/as to/concerning/of/on/regarding)
	arrive at (an/the) opinion (about/as to/concerning/of/on/regarding)
	come to a/the conclusion (about/as to/concerning/of/on/regarding)
	come to a/the decision (about/as to/concerning/of/on/regarding)
	come to a/the determination (about/as to/concerning/of/on/regarding)
	come to an/the opinion (about/as to/concerning/of/on/regarding)

CONCISE	WORDY
	draw (a/the) conclusion (of)
	draw (a/the) inference (of)
	form (a/the) judgment (about/as to/concerning/of/on/ regarding)
	form (an/the) opinion (about/as to/concerning/of/on/ regarding)
	put two and two together
	reach (a/the) conclusion (about/of/on/upon/with)
	reach (a/the) decision (about/of/on/upon/with)
	reach (a/the) determination (about/of/on/upon/with)
	reach (an/the) opinion (about/of/on/upon/with)
inferior	more inferior
infest	infestate
in fine	in brief/concise/succinct summary
	in summary/summation
	summing up
	to summarize/sum up
infinite	beyond number
	(a/the) countless number (of)
	(an/the) infinite number (of)
	innumerable
	(a/the) multiplicity of
	(a/the) multitude of
	multitudinous
	(an/the) untold number (of)
	without number
influence	bring to bear (on/upon)
	impact (on/upon)
influences	has a bearing on/upon
	has (a) . . . effect on/upon
	has (a) . . . impact on/upon
	has (a) . . . influence on/upon
	is influential in (-ing)
in force	in force and effect
	operative
information	facts and information
infrequent	few and far between
	few/small in number
infringes on	is in violation of
-ing	(a/the) -ance (-ence) of
	(a/the) -ing of
	in the act of -ing
	in the middle/midst of -ing
	in the process of –ing

CONCISE	WORDY
	(a/the) -ment of
	(a/the) . . . of
	(a/the) -sion (-tion) of (that/to)
-ing (that)	in (on/with) (a/the) . . . (of/that)
in general	as a general rule
	as a rule
	for the most part
	in great/large measure
	in great/large part
	in no small measure
	in no small part
	in the main
	on/upon the whole
	predominant/predominantly
	to a great/large degree
	to a great/large extent
in groups	together . . . in groups
initially	first initially
	in/over the near term
	in/over the short run
	in/over the short term
	over the short haul
in itself	in and of itself
injures	is deleterious to
	is destructive of/to
	is detrimental to
	is harmful to
	is injurious to
	is ruinous to
in keeping with	in accord/accordance with
	in agreement with
	in compliance with
	in conformance to/with
	in conformity to/with
	in consonance to/with
	in correspondence to/with
inkling	indication
in line with	in accord/accordance with
	in agreement with
	in compliance with
	in conformance to/with
	in conformity to/with
	in consonance to/with

CONCISE	WORDY
	in correspondence to/with
in many months/years	in the distant future
innovation	new innovation
innovative	innovative new
	new and innovative
in no way	in no way, shape, or form
	under no circumstances/conditions
I note	it is my observation (that)
I notice	it is my observation (that)
in parentheses	enclosed in parentheses
in part	in/on/to/with various/varying degrees/extents
	to a certain/limited/some degree
	to a certain/limited/some extent
	to a degree
	to a greater or lesser degree/extent
	to a major or minor degree/extent
	to an extent
	to one degree/extent or another
in passing	briefly in passing
in place	in operation
in play	in force and effect
	operative
in profusion	in copious profusion
in proximity	in close proximity (to)
in question	(an/the) open question
	open to doubt
	open to question
in reality	as a matter of fact
	(the) (simple) fact of the matter is (that)
	in actual fact
	in point of fact
	really (and) truly
	(the) truth of the matter is (that)
in relation to	relatively . . . in relation to
in return for	in consideration of (payment of/sum of)
in short	in brief/concise/succinct summary
	in summary/summation
	summing up
	to summarize/sum up
inside	in the middle of
	in the midst of
	inside of
	on the inside of

CONCISE	WORDY
insists on	is insistent on
in some way	by one means or another
	in/on/to/with various/varying degrees/extents
	of one form/kind/sort/type or another
	(in) one way or another
	somehow or other
	to a greater or lesser degree/extent
	to a major or minor degree/extent
	to one degree/extent or another
inspect	check to see
	look/observe to see
instant/instantly	instantaneous/instantaneously
instead	but instead
	contrariwise
	on the contrary
	to the contrary
instead of	as opposed to
in step with	in accord/accordance with
	in agreement with
	in compliance with
	in conformance to/with
	in conformity to/with
	in consonance to/with
	in correspondence to/with
institute	institution
insulates	is protective against (of)
insults	is offensive to
in sum	in brief/concise/succinct summary
	in summary/summation
	summing up
	to summarize/sum up
integral to	(an) integral part of
integrate	integrate together
intellect	intellectual ability/capacity
intelligence	intellectual ability/capacity
intention	course of action
	plan of action/attack/battle
interact	interact with each other/one another
interdependence	interdependency
interest	positive feelings
interestingly	(the) interesting thing is (that)
	it is interesting to note
interests	is of concern to
	is of interest to

CONCISE	WORDY
interfere with	stand in the way of
interpret	interpretate
interpret as	interpret to mean
interpretive	interpretative
interval	(a/the) time frame (of)
	(a/the) time horizon (of)
	(a/the) time interval (of)
	(a/the) time period (of)
	(a/the) time span (of)
in that	about the fact that
	as a consequence of the fact that
	as a result of the fact that
	attributable to the fact that
	based on the fact that
	because of the fact that
	being (as/as how/that)
	by/in virtue of the fact that
	by reason of the fact that
	by the fact that
	considering the fact that
	due to the fact that
	forasmuch as
	for the (simple) reason that
	from (a/the) . . . aspect (of)
	from (a/the) . . . perspective (of)
	from (a/the) . . . point of view (of)
	from (a/the) . . . standpoint (of)
	from (a/the) . . . viewpoint (of)
	from the fact that
	given the fact that
	inasmuch/insomuch as
	in consequence of the fact that
	in consideration of the fact that
	in (the) light of the fact that
	insofar as
	in the sense that
	in view of the fact that
	on account of the fact that
	on (the) grounds that
	on the basis of the fact that
	over the fact that
	owing to the fact that
	seeing (as/as how/that)
in that/this age	in that/this day and age

CONCISE	WORDY
in the end	after all is said and done
	at the end of the day
	in the course of events/things/time
	in the final/last analysis
	in/over the long run
	in/over the long term
	over the long haul
	some day/time in the future
	(the) time will come when
	when all is said and done
	with the passage of time
in/into the future	forward in/into the future
in the future	in the future going/moving forward
in the least	in any fashion/manner/way
	in any way, shape, or form (or fashion)
	(in) one way or the other
in the morning	(8:00) a.m. . . . morning
in the past	back/before in the past
	historically . . . in the past
in the range of . . . to	anywhere/somewhere in the range of . . . to
in the slightest	in any way, shape, or form (or fashion)
	(in) one way or the other
intimate	intimately familiar
in time	as (the) days/decades/months/weeks/years go on
	as time goes on
	as time progresses (forward/on/onward)
	at a/some future/later/subsequent date/time
	down the line/pike/road/way
	(after/for/in/over/within) (an) extended/lengthy/long/ prolonged/protracted amount of time/length of time/period/period of time/span of time/time/while
	in/over (the) coming days/decades/months/weeks/years
	in/over (the) days/decades/months/weeks/years ahead
	in/over (the) days/decades/months/weeks/years to come
	in due course/time
	in good time
	in the course of events/things/time
	in the distant future
	in/into the future
	in/over the long run
	in/over the long term later in time
	later on down the line/pike/road/way
	over the long haul

CONCISE	WORDY
	some day/time in the future
	(the) time will come when
	with the passage of time
in/on time	in a timely fashion/manner/way
	on a timely basis
introduce	introduce (a/the) new
introduced	first introduced
introduction	new introduction
in truth	as a matter of fact
	(the) fact is (that)
	(the) (simple) fact of the matter is (that)
	in actual fact
	in actuality
	in point of fact
	in reality
	really (and) truly
	(the) truth is (that)
	(the) truth of the matter is (that)
in trying to	in an attempt/effort/endeavor to
	in an attempt/effort/endeavor to try to
in two/ten months/years	in the distant future
inure to	inure to the benefit of
inured to	accustomed to
invalid	null and void
invariably	day in (and) day out
	for ever and a day
	in (almost) all/every cases/circumstances/instances/ situations
	in each/every case/circumstance/instance/situation
	on each/every occasion
	without exception
	year in (and) year out
invent	bring into being/existence
	call into being/existence
invented	first invented
invention/inventor	original invention/inventor
invidiousness	invidious discrimination
in view of	in consideration of (payment of/sum of)
invite	extend (issue) an invitation to
in whatever way	by one means or another
	(in) one way or another
I observe	it is my observation (that)
iota	little/small/tiny iota
I perceive	it is my observation (that)

CONCISE	WORDY
I plan	it is my intention (that)
I propose	it is my recommendation (that)
	it is my suggestion (that)
ir-	(a/the) absence of
	(a/the) lack of
	devoid of
	insufficient
	lacking in
	less than (enthusiastic)
IRA	IRA account
I realize	it is my understanding (that)
I recognize	it is my understanding (that)
I recommend	it is my recommendation (that)
	it is my suggestion (that)
I regard	based on/upon my personal judgment/opinion
	in my assessment
	in my estimation
	in my judgment
	in my opinion
	in my view
	it is my assessment (that)
	it is my belief (that)
	it is my estimation (that)
	it is my judgment (that)
	it is my opinion (that)
	it is my view (that)
ironic	ironical
irrefutably	beyond a/the shadow of a doubt
irregular	(something) out of the ordinary
irrelevance	irrelevancy
irrelevant	beside the point
	neither here nor there
irrevocable	final and irrevocable
is	amounts to
	happens to be
	has occasion to be
	is defined as
	is (the) equal to
	is (the) equivalent of/to
	is identical to/with
	is tantamount to
	is there ... (that/who)
	it is ... (that/who)
	represents

CONCISE	WORDY
	there is . . . (that/who)
is able to	has (an/the) ability to
	has a/the capability to
	is capable of -ing
is about	has reference to
	(that) has to do with
	is concerned with
I say	based on/upon my personal judgment/opinion
	in my assessment
	in my estimation
	in my judgment
	in my opinion
	in my view
	it is my assessment (that)
	it is my belief (that)
	it is my estimation (that)
	it is my judgment (that)
	it is my opinion (that)
	it is my view (that)
ISBN	ISBN number
is certain/sure	is for certain/sure
I see	it is my observation (that)
island	island (completely) surrounded by water
is not (now/yet) known	is still to be seen
	remains to be seen
isolate	separate out
issue	issuance
I suggest	it is my recommendation (that)
	it is my suggestion (that)
is unable to	is incapable of -ing
is uncertain	is still to be seen
	remains to be seen
is unclear	is still to be seen
	remains to be seen
is unknown	is still to be seen
	remains to be seen
is unsure	is still to be seen
	remains to be seen
it	that/this kind/sort/type of stuff/thing
iterate	reiterate
	reiterate again (and again)
I think	based on/upon my personal judgment/opinion
	I don't think
	in my assessment

CONCISE	WORDY
	in my estimation
	in my judgment
	in my opinion
	in my view
	it is my assessment (that)
	it is my belief (that)
	it is my estimation (that)
	it is my judgment (that)
	it is my opinion (that)
	it is my view (that)
I think not	I do not think so
I understand	it is my understanding (that)
I urge	it is my recommendation (that)
	it is my suggestion (that)
I view	based on/upon my personal judgment/opinion
	in my assessment
	in my estimation
	in my judgment
	in my opinion
	in my view
	it is my assessment (that)
	it is my belief (that)
	it is my estimation (that)
	it is my judgment (that)
	it is my opinion (that)
	it is my view (that)

J

jail	correctional/prison facility
	facility
	incarcerate
	institution
jeopardize	place/put . . . in danger
	place/put . . . in jeopardy
	place/put . . . in/into peril
	throw into jeopardy
jeopardized	(be) in jeopardy
jeopardizes	is dangerous to
job	capacity
	place of business/employment/work
	position

CONCISE	WORDY
jobs	employment opportunities
john	bathroom facilities
	comfort facilities
join	bring together
	integrate together
	join together
joined with	accompanied by
	in association with
	in combination with
	in conjunction with
	in connection with
	together with
jointly	at the same time
	concurrently
	simultaneously
joyful	in a good mood
joyous	in a good mood
judge	arrive at (a/the) conclusion (about/as to/concerning/of/on/regarding)
	arrive at (a/the) decision (about/as to/concerning/of/on/regarding)
	arrive at (a/the) determination (about/as to/concerning/of/on/regarding)
	arrive at (an/the) opinion (about/as to/concerning/of/on/regarding)
	come to a/the conclusion (about/as to/concerning/of/on/regarding)
	come to a/the decision (about/as to/concerning/of/on/regarding)
	come to a/the determination (about/as to/concerning/of/on/regarding)
	come to an/the opinion (about/as to/concerning/of/on/regarding)
	form (a/the) judgment (about/as to/concerning/of/on/regarding)
	form (an/the) opinion (about/as to/concerning/of/on/regarding)
	hold (to) the opinion (that)
	hold (to) the view (that)
	in the assessment of
	in the estimation of
	in the judgment of
	in the opinion of
	in the view of

CONCISE	WORDY
	judge as
	reach (a/the) conclusion (about/of/on/upon/with)
	reach (a/the) decision (about/of/on/upon/with)
	reach (a/the) determination (about/of/on/upon/with)
	reach (an/the) opinion (about/of/on/upon/with)
	take the position (that)
	take the view (that)
judge/sentence	pass judgment/sentence on/upon
juice	liquid refreshment
just	exact/exactly (the) same
	fair (just) and equitable
	fair and square
	just exactly
	just recently
	just simply
	no more (and) no less
just (the)	the same exact
just as (more/most) important	just as (more/most) importantly
	just as (more/most) significantly
just like	just the same as

K

keep in mind	it is important to keep in mind
	it is important to remember
	it must/should be remembered
key	most important
	number-one
	of the first magnitude
	of the first/highest order
(a) key to	(a/the) key . . . in/of/to
kill	do away with
	put to sleep
killer	deadly killer
kind	kinder (and) gentler
know	experience
	know for a fact
knowledge	knowledge base
knows	is acquainted with
	is an acquaintance of
	is aware of/that
	is cognizant of/that

CONCISE	WORDY
	is conscious of/that
	is conversant with
	is familiar with
	is knowledgeable about/in/of
	is mindful of/that

L

label	label as
lack	devoid of
	lack for
	lacking in
lacking	(a/the) absence of
lack of	insufficient
	in the absence of
lacks	is deficient in
lament	express sorrow (about)
	voice sorrow (about)
languid	lackadaisical
large	big, huge (large)
	(a/the) high degree (of)
	(a/the) high level (of)
	humongous
	large-size(d)
	significant/substantial
	substantive
largely	as a general rule
	as a rule
	basically
	by and large
	considerably
	for the most part
	in great/large measure
	in great/large part
	in many/most regards
	in many/most respects
	in no small measure
	in no small part
	in the main
	on/upon the whole
	predominant/predominantly
	primary/primarily

CONCISE	WORDY
	principal/principally
	significantly/substantially
	to a great/large degree
	to a great/large extent
larger than	in excess of
	maximal
	(a/the) maximum amount (of)
	(a/the) maximum number (of)
	(a/the) maximum . . . of
last	back in
	continue in existence/to exist
	in duration
	in length
	last of all
	the last time
last half of	latter part of
lastly	in conclusion
late	in arrears
	latter part of
lately	in recent days/decades/months/weeks/years
	in recent history/memory/times
	in the immediate past
	in the (very) near past
	in the not-so-distant/not-too-distant past
	in/over the past few/several days/decades/months/weeks/years
	in/within the recent past
later	after the event/incident/occurrence
	as (the) days/decades/months/weeks/years go on
	as time goes on
	as time progresses (forward/on/onward)
	at a/some future/later/subsequent date/time
	down the line/pike/road/way
	in/over (the) coming days/decades/months/weeks/years
	in/over (the) days/decades/months/weeks/years ahead
	in/over (the) days/decades/months/weeks/years to come
	in due course/time
	in good time
	in the course of events/things/time
	in the distant future
	in/into the future
	in/over the long run
	in/over the long term
	later in time

CONCISE	WORDY
	later on
	later on down the line/pike/road/way
	over the long haul
	posterior to
	(then) . . . proceed (to)
	some day/time in the future
	subsequent to (that/this)
	subsequently
	(the) time will come when
	thereafter
	thereupon
	with the passage of time
latest	most recent
laugh	laugh out loud
lazy	lackadaisical
lead	head up
leading	most important
	number-one
	of the first magnitude
	of the first/highest order
learn	find out
least	minimal
(the) least	(a/the) minimum (of)
leave	depart
legion	(an/the) abundance of
legitimate	legitimatize
legitimize	legitimatize
lend	lend out
less	as contrasted to/with
	as opposed to
	by comparison to/with
	by contrast to/with
	comparatively
	compared to/with
	contrasted to/with
	(a/the) declining/decreasing/diminishing/dwindling amount/degree/extent/part/percentage/portion/proportion (of)
	(a/the) decreased/decreasing amount of
	in comparison to/with
	in contrast to/with
	in relation/relationship to
	(a) lesser/lower/smaller degree/extent (of)
	measured against

CONCISE	WORDY
	relative to
	relatively
	(a/the) smaller/tinier amount/degree/part/percentage/ portion/proportion/quantity (of)
	as compared to/with
	to a lesser/lower/smaller degree/extent
	when compared to/with
	when measured against
-less(ness)	(a/the) absence of
	(a/the) lack of
	devoid of
	insufficient
	lacking in
less and less	(a/the) declining/decreasing/diminishing/dwindling amount/degree/extent/part/ percentage/portion/proportion (of)
lessen	alleviate
less often	to a certain/limited/some degree
	to a lesser/lower/smaller degree/extent
less so	to a certain/limited/some degree
	to a certain/limited/some extent
	to a lesser/lower/smaller degree/extent
less than	as compared to/with
	as contrasted to/with
	as opposed to
	by comparison to/with
	by contrast to/with
	compared to/with
	contrasted to/with
	in comparison to/with
	in contrast to/with
	in relation/relationship to
	measured against
	relative to
	when compared to/with
	when measured against
less than half (of)	(a/the) minimal number (of)
	(a/the) minority (of)
	(a/the) significant/substantial minority (of)
	(a/the) small/tiny amount/degree/part/percentage/ portion/proportion/quantity (of)
	(a/the) small/tiny fraction (of)
	(a/the) small/tiny minority (of)

CONCISE	WORDY
lest	for fear (that/of) . . . can/could/may/might/shall/should/ will/would
	in case
	out of fear (of/that) . . . can/could/may/might/shall/ should/will/would
let	afford/give/offer/present/provide . . . (an/the) opportunity (to)
	allow . . . to
	enable . . . to
	permit . . . to
let's hope	it is (to be) hoped
	hopefully
letter	communication
	correspondence
	written communication/correspondence
level	level to the ground
	raze to the ground
liberal	(an/the) abundance of
lie	make false statements
lift	along the lines of
	appreciate
	as . . . for example/for instance
	as for (in/with) the case of
	as is the case
	in a/the fashion/manner/way (in which/that)
	in a/the fashion/manner/way characteristic of
	in a/the fashion/manner/way similar to
	in a similar fashion/manner/way (to)
	in common with
	in the nature of
	in the same fashion/manner/way (as/that)
	(a) . . . kind/sort/type (of) thing
	lift up
	like . . . also/as well
	like . . . and others/and so forth/and so on/and such/and the like/et al./etc.
	like . . . for example/for instance
	on the order of
	such as . . . and others/and so forth/and so on/and such/ and the like/et al./etc./or whatever
	such as . . . for example/for instance
	take satisfaction in
	the equal/equivalent of

CONCISE	WORDY
	the nature of
	the same (thing) as
	the same way
like (you)	such as (your)self
likelihood	probability
likely	in all likelihood
	in all probability
likens to	is comparable to/with
likes	has (an/the) appreciation for
	is appreciative of
like that/this	along that/this line
	in that/this fashion/manner/way
	of that/this kind/sort/type
	of that/this nature
likewise	along the same line
	by the same token
	in like fashion/manner
	in the same fashion/manner/way (as/that)
liking	positive feelings
limit	limitation
	parameter
limited	few/small in number
linger	linger on
link	association
	concatenate together
	connect together
	linkage
	link together
	relationship
linked to	associated with
	connected with
list	enumerate
	prioritize
listen	have/take a listen
	listen in
listen to	pay attention to
	pay heed to
	take cognizance of
	take note of
	take notice of
listless	lackadaisical
literal	matter-of-fact
little	(very) limited
	(a/the) limited number of

CONCISE	WORDY
	(a/the) limited selection (of)
	(a/the) minimum (of)
	(a/the) modicum of
	tiny little
live	domicile
	operational
	reside
loan	borrowed loan
locale	locality
locate	come in contact (with)
	make contact (with)
long	(for) a long time/while
	for (an) extended/prolonged/protracted amount of time/ length of time/period/period of time/ span of time/time/while
	for long
	for some time (now)
	for (many/several) years (now)
	in duration
	in length
	lengthy
long ago	in the distant past
	(a) long time/while ago
	time was when
longer	more extended/lengthy/prolonged/protracted
longest	maximal
	(a/the) maximum amount (of)
	(a/the) maximum number (of)
	(a/the) maximum . . . of
long since	in the distant past
long-term	in/over the long run
	in/over the long term
	over the long haul
loo	bathroom facilities
	comfort facilities
look	check to see
	have/take a look
	look/observe to see
	take a . . . look (at)
	take a/the . . . view (of)
look ahead	look ahead/forward to the future
look for	cast about for
look forward	look ahead/forward to the future
look like	bear (a/the) . . . resemblance/similarity to

CONCISE	WORDY
look to the future	look ahead/forward to the future
lose	lose out on
love	positive feelings
lower	minimize
lowest	minimal
	(a/the) minimum (of)
luckily	as it turned out
	as luck would have it
	it (just) so happens
-(al)ly	at (a/the) . . . level
	at (a/the) . . . pace (of)
	at (a/the) . . . rate (of)
	at (a/the) . . . speed (of)
	by (a/the) . . . margin (of)
	by . . . standards
	do (a/the) . . . (about/in/of/on/to)
	from (a/the) . . . aspect (of)
	from (a/the) . . . perspective (of)
	from (a/the) . . . point of view (of)
	from (a/the) . . . standpoint (of)
	from (a/the) . . . viewpoint (of)
	in (a/the) . . . case/circumstance/instance/situation
	in (a/the) . . . fashion
	in (a/the) . . . form
	in (a/the) . . . manner
	in (a/the) . . . way
	in . . . circumstances/conditions
	in . . . order
	in (a/the) . . . sense
	in . . . terms
	in . . . tones
	it is . . . (that/who)
	-(al)ly enough
	-(al)ly speaking
	on a/the . . . basis
	on a/the . . . note
	on a/the . . . scale/scope
	on a/the . . . scene
	on . . . grounds
	on (a/the) . . . level
	on the . . . side
	regular -(al)ly
	to a/the . . . degree

CONCISE	WORDY
	to a/the . . . extent
	to be
	what is . . . (is that)
-(al)ly important	of (a/the) . . . importance (that/to)

M

made of	made up out of
magnitude	breadth and depth
main	first and foremost
	most important
	number-one
	of the first magnitude
	of the first/highest order
	predominant/predominantly
	primary/primarily
	principal/principally
mainly	as a general rule
	as a rule
	basically
	by and large
	first and foremost
	for the most part
	in great/large measure
	in great/large part
	in no small measure
	in no small part
	in the main
	on/upon the whole
	predominant/predominantly
	primary/primarily
	principal/principally
	to a great/large degree
	to a great/large extent
maintain	according to
	hold (to) the opinion (that)
	hold (to) the view (that)
	in the assessment of
	in the estimation of
	in the judgment of
	in the opinion of

CONCISE	WORDY
	in the view of
	take the position (that)
	take the view (that)
maintains	is inclined to believe (that)
	is inclined to think (that)
	is of the belief (that)
	is of the opinion (that)
	is of the view (that)
major	most important
	number-one
	of the first magnitude
	of the first/highest order
make	bring into being/existence
	call into being/existence
	cause . . . to be/become
	come up with
	formulate
	implement
	put into effect
	render
make better	ameliorate
make known	bring attention to
	bring into the open
	bring to . . . attention (of)
	bring to light
	call . . . attention to
	call to . . . attention (of)
	concentrate (media/people's/public) attention on/upon
	direct . . . attention to
	draw attention to
	focus (media/people's/public) attention on/upon
make public	bring attention to
	bring into the open
	bring to . . . attention (of)
	bring to light
	call . . . attention to
	call to . . . attention (of)
	concentrate (media/people's/public) attention on/upon
	direct . . . attention to
	draw attention to
	focus (media/people's/public) attention on/upon
make up	constitute
mammoth	humongous

CONCISE	WORDY
man	gentleman
man/woman	(of) (the) opposite sex
	human being
	individual(s)
manages	is in charge of
	is in control of
manifestly	it is apparent that
	it is evident that
manifold	many and varied
manually	manually by hand
many	(an/the) abundance of
	(an) array of
	(a/the) broad/extensive/great/vast/wide array of
	(a/the) broad/extensive/great/vast/wide range of
	(a/the) broad/extensive/great/vast/wide spectrum of
	(a/the) broad/extensive/great/vast/wide variety of
	(a/the) diversity of different
	(a) (whole) host of
	in big/great/high/huge/large/overwhelming/sizable/vast numbers
	in great/large quantities
	in many/most cases
	in many/most circumstances
	in many/most instances
	in many/most regards
	in many/most respects
	in many/most situations
	(a) lot of
	many but not all
	most but not all
	multiple
	(a/the) multiplicity of
	(a/the) multitude of
	multitudinous
	(a/a fair/any) number (of)
	numerous in number
	(a) range of
	significant/substantial
	(a/the) spectrum of
	substantive
	(a) variety of
	(a/the) variety of different
	various different

CONCISE	WORDY
	(many) widely varying
many (of)	(a/the) considerable/good/great/huge/large/sizable/vast amount (of)
	(a/the) considerable/good/great/huge/large/overwhelming/sizable/vast/wide majority (of)
	(a/the) considerable/good/great/huge/large/overwhelming/sizable/vast number (of)
	(a/the) considerable/good/great/huge/large/sizable/vast part (of)
	(a/the) considerable/good/great/huge/large/overwhelming/sizable/vast percentage (of)
	(a/the) considerable/good/great/huge/large/sizable/vast portion (of)
	(a/the) considerable/good/great/huge/large/sizable/vast proportion (of)
	(a/the) considerable/good/great/huge/large/sizable/vast quantity (of)
	(a/the) great/large fraction (of)
	(a/the) high degree (of)
	(a/the) high level (of)
	(a/the) high number (of)
	(a/the) high percentage (of)
	(a/the) high proportion (of)
	(a/the) large/overwhelming/sizable/vast plurality (of)
	(a/the) major part/percentage/portion/proportion (of)
	(a/the) majority (of)
	(a/the) overwhelming/vast preponderance (of)
	(a/a certain/some) part (of)
	(a/a certain/some) percentage (of)
	(a/the) plurality (of)
	(a/a certain/some) portion (of)
	(a/the) preponderance (of)
	(a/a certain/some) proportion (of)
	(a/a certain/some) quantity (of)
	(a/the) significant/substantial amount (of)
	(a/the) significant/substantial element (of)
	(a/the) significant/substantial fraction (of)
	(a/the) significant/substantial majority (of)
	(a/the) significant/substantial number (of)
	(a/the) significant/substantial part (of)
	(a/the) significant/substantial percentage (of)

CONCISE	WORDY
	(a/the) significant/substantial portion (of)
	(a/the) significant/substantial proportion (of)
	(a/the) significant/substantial quantity (of)
many months/years ago	in the distant past
many times	in many/most cases
	in many/most circumstances
	in many/most instances
	in many/most situations
	on a number of /any number of/frequent/many/ numerous/several occasions
	on more than one occasion
map (out)	come up with
marginally	by (a/the) little/narrow/nominal/slender/slight/slim/ small/tiny margin
marked	(a/the) high degree (of)
	(a/the) high level (of)
marry	get married
mars	is deleterious to
	is destructive of/to
	is detrimental to
	is harmful to
	is injurious to
	is ruinous to
match	(an) identical/identically match
	exact/exactly duplicate
	exact/exactly (the) same
	exact/exactly equivalent
	exact/exactly identical
	exact/exactly match
	follow along the lines of
	identical/identically (the) same
	match exactly
	match perfectly
	match up
	perfect/perfectly match
matches	is (the) equal to
	is (the) equivalent of/to
	is identical to/with
	is tantamount to
matchless	in a class by herself/itself
	one-of-a-kind
	without equal
	without peer
maxim	old maxim

CONCISE	WORDY
may	may or may not
may/might	may/might perhaps
	may/might possibly
	perhaps . . . may/might
	possibly may/might
may not	may or may not
meager	(a/the) limited number of
	(a/the) limited selection (of)
	(very) limited
	few and far between
	few/small in number
	in short supply
mean	involve
meander	meander back and forth
meaningful	fraught with meaning/significance
means	financial wherewithal
	is defined as
	ways and means
	wherewithal
meantime	in the interim
	in the interval
	in the meantime
meanwhile	in the interim
	in the interval
	in the meantime
mechanical	mechanical mechanism
mechanism	mechanical mechanism
mediocre	run of the mill
meet	encounter
	hold a meeting
	make . . . acquaintance
	measure up to
	meet together
meet (with)	come in contact (with)
	make contact (with)
memo	correspondence
	memorandum
	notation
	written communication/correspondence
men/women	(the) female/male gender/sex
	individual(s)
	like-gender individuals/people/persons
mention	bring attention to
	bring into the open

CONCISE	WORDY
	bring to . . . attention (of)
	bring to light
	call . . . attention to
	call to . . . attention (of)
	concentrate (media/people's/public) attention on/upon
	direct . . . attention to
	draw attention to
	focus (media/people's/public) attention on/upon
	indicate
	make mention of
mercenary	hired mercenary
merely	no more than
merge	merge into one (company)
	merge together
merry	in a good mood
mesh	mesh together
message	communication
method	action/attack/battle/game plan
	course of action
	methodology
	plan of action/attack/battle
methods	ways and means
midnight	twelve midnight
might	might or might not
mightily	humongous
	in the extreme
might not	might or might not
milk	liquid refreshment
millions (of)	beyond number
	(a/the) considerable/good/great/huge/large/ overwhelming/sizable/vast number (of)
	(a/the) considerable/good/great/huge/large/sizable/vast quantity (of)
	(a/the) countless number (of)
	(a/the) high number (of)
	in big/great/high/huge/large/overwhelming/sizable/vast numbers
	(an/the) infinite number (of)
	in great/large quantities
	innumerable
	(a/the) multiplicity of
	(a/the) multitude of
	multitudinous

CONCISE	WORDY
	(a/the) significant/substantial number (of)
	(a/the) significant/substantial quantity (of)
	(an/the) untold number (of)
	without number
mind	pay attention to
	pay heed to
	take cognizance of
	take note of
	take notice of
mingle	mingle together
	mix and mingle
minimum	(a/the) minimum (of)
minor	minimal
minus	in the absence of
minutes	in/over . . . days/decades/hours/minutes/months/weeks/ years time
mirrors	is reflective of
mis-	(a/the) absence of
	devoid of
	insufficient
	lacking in
	(a/the) lack of
	less than (enthusiastic)
misinterpret	take the wrong way
misleading	false and misleading
missing	(a/the) absence of
	in the absence of
mistreat	take advantage of
mistreats	is exploitative/exploitive of
mistrust	express skepticism (about)
	voice skepticism (about)
mistrusts	is distrustful about/of
	is doubtful about/of
	is dubious about/of
	is in doubt about/of
	is mistrustful about/of
	is skeptical about/of/that
misunderstand	take the wrong way
misuse	take advantage of
misuses	is exploitative/exploitive of
mix	mix and mingle
	mix together
moan	express sorrow (about)
	voice sorrow (about)
modern	modern, state-of-the-art

CONCISE	WORDY
mold	bring into being/existence
	call into being/existence
	come up with
	put together
moment	consequence
	importance
	magnitude
momentarily	(after/for/in/over/within) a brief/limited/little/short amount of time/length of time/moment of time/period/period of time/span of time/time/while
	at any minute/moment/second
	from minute/moment/second to minute/moment/second
	in the immediate future
momently	at any minute/moment/second
	from minute/moment/second to minute/moment/second
	in a few minutes/moments/seconds
	in a minute/moment/second
momentous	fraught with meaning/significance
money	compensation
	financial/monetary resources
	financial wherewithal
	remittance
	remuneration
	wherewithal
monopoly	complete monopoly
monotony	tedious monotony
monstrous	humongous
monthly	on a regular basis
months	in/over . . . days/decades/hours/minutes/months/weeks/years time
	months of age
moot	(an/the) open question
	open to doubt
	open to question
more	(an) additional
	as compared to/with
	as contrasted to/with
	as opposed to
	(a) bigger/greater/higher/larger degree/extent (of)
	(a/the) burgeoning/growing/increasing/rising amount/degree/extent/number/part/percentage/portion/proportion/quantity (of)
	by comparison to/with

CONCISE	WORDY
	by contrast to/with
	comparatively
	compared to/with
	contrasted to/with (a/the) greater/larger number (of)
	further
	in (a/the) bigger/greater/higher/larger amount/degree/ number/quantity
	in comparison to/with
	in contrast to/with
	(an/the) increased/increasing amount of
	(an/the) increased/increasing number of
	increasingly more
	in relation/relationship to
	measured against
	more -(i)er
	relative to
	relatively
	to a greater/larger degree/extent
	when compared to/with
	when measured against
(the) more	(the) -(i)er . . . of the two
	(the) more . . . of the two
more (of)	(a/the) majority (of)
	(a/the) major part/percentage/portion/proportion (of)
	(a/the) plurality (of)
	(a/the) preponderance (of)
more/most	the more/most
more and more	(a/the) burgeoning/growing/increasing/rising amount/ degree/extent/number/part/ percentage/portion/proportion/ quantity (of)
	increasingly more
	to an increasing degree/extent
	with increasing frequency
more often	in (a/the) bigger/greater/higher/larger amount/degree/ number/quantity
	to a greater/larger degree/extent
more or less	(for) approximately
	(an) estimated
	(something/somewhere) in the area (of)
	(something/somewhere) in the nature (of)
	(something/somewhere) in the neighborhood (of)
	(something/somewhere) in the . . . range (of)
	(something/somewhere) in the realm (of)

CONCISE	WORDY
	(something/somewhere) in the region (of)
	(something/somewhere) in the vicinity (of)
	in/on/to/with various/varying degrees/extents
	(something/somewhere) on the order (of)
	to a certain/limited/some degree
	to a certain/limited/some extent
	to a degree
	to a greater or lesser degree/extent
	to a major or minor degree/extent
	to an extent
	to one degree/extent or another
more so	in (a/the) bigger/greater/higher/larger amount/degree/ number/quantity
	to a greater/larger degree/extent
more than	above and beyond
	as compared to/with
	as contrasted to/with
	as opposed to
	by comparison to/with
	by contrast to/with
	compared to/with
	contrasted to/with
	in comparison to/with
	in contrast to/with
	(a) . . . increase over
	in excess of
	in relation/relationship to
	measured against
	over and above
	relative to
	upward(s) of
	when compared to/with
	when measured against
more than once	on more than one occasion
more than that/this	additionally
	and . . . further/furthermore/in addition/moreover/ what's more
	as a matter of fact
	by the same token
	for that matter
	in addition
	in the next place
	in the second place
	in the third place

CONCISE	WORDY
	on top of (that/this)
moreover	additionally
	and . . . further/furthermore/in addition/moreover/ what's more
	as a matter of fact
	by the same token
	for that matter
	in addition
	in the next place
	in the second place
	in the third place
	next of all
	on top of (that/this)
(the) most	the biggest/greatest/highest/largest amount/degree/ extent/number/part/percentage/ portion/proportion/quantity (of)
most (of)	almost without exception
	as a general rule
	as a rule
	basically
	(the) better part (of)
	(the) bulk (of)
	by and large
	(a/the) considerable/good/great/huge/large/sizable/vast amount (of)
	(a/the) considerable/good/great/huge/large/ overwhelming/sizable/vast/wide majority (of)
	(a/the) considerable/good/great/huge/large/ overwhelming/sizable/vast number (of)
	(a/the) considerable/good/great/huge/large/sizable/vast part (of)
	(a/the) considerable/good/great/huge/large/ overwhelming/sizable/vast percentage (of)
	(a/the) considerable/good/great/huge/large/sizable/vast portion (of)
	(a/the) considerable/good/great/huge/large/sizable/vast proportion (of)
	(a/the) considerable/good/great/huge/large/sizable/vast quantity (of)
	for the most part
	(a/the) great/large fraction (of)

CONCISE	WORDY
	(a/the) high degree (of)
	(a/the) high level (of)
	(a/the) high number (of)
	(a/the) high percentage (of)
	(a/the) high proportion (of)
	in big/great/high/huge/large/overwhelming/sizable/ vast numbers
	in great/large measure
	in great/large part
	in great/large quantities
	in many/most cases
	in many/most circumstances
	in many/most instances
	in many/most regards
	in many/most respects
	in many/most situations
	in no small measure
	in no small part
	in the main
	(a/the) large/overwhelming/sizable/vast plurality (of)
	(the) lion's share
	(a/the) majority (of)
	(a/the) major part/percentage/portion/proportion (of)
	maximal
	(a/the) maximum amount (of)
	(a/the) maximum number (of)
	(a/the) maximum . . . of
	most but not all
	most -(i)est
	most . . . one
	(a/a fair/any) number (of)
	on/upon the whole
	(a/the) overwhelming/vast preponderance (of)
	(a/a certain/some) part (of)
	(a/a certain/some) percentage (of)
	(a/the) plurality (of)
	(a/a certain/some) portion (of)
	predominant/predominantly
	(a/the) preponderance (of)
	primary/primarily
	principal/principally
	(a/a certain/some) proportion (of)
	(a/a certain/some) quantity (of)
	significant/substantial

CONCISE	WORDY
	(a/the) significant/substantial amount (of)
	(a/the) significant/substantial fraction (of)
	(a/the) significant/substantial majority (of)
	(a/the) significant/substantial number (of)
	(a/the) significant/substantial part (of)
	(a/the) significant/substantial percentage (of)
	(a/the) significant/substantial portion (of)
	(a/the) significant/substantial proportion (of)
	(a/the) significant/substantial quantity (of)
	substantive
	to a great/large degree
	to a great/large extent
	with few/rare exception(s)
most favored	most favorite
most important	of the first/highest order
	of the first magnitude
most/very likely	in all likelihood
	in all probability
mostly	as a general rule
	as a rule
	basically
	by and large
	considerably
	first and foremost
	for the most part
	in great/large measure
	in great/large part
	in many/most regards
	in many/most respects
	in no small measure
	in no small part
	in the main
	on/upon the whole
	predominant/predominantly
	primary/primarily
	principal/principally
	significantly/substantially
	to a great/large degree
	to a great/large extent
most often	as a general rule
	as a rule
	for the most part
	in a lot of cases/circumstances/instances/situations

CONCISE	WORDY
	in a/the majority of cases/circumstances/instances/ situations
	in great/large measure
	in great/large part
	in many/most cases
	in many/most circumstances
	in many/most instances
	in many/most regards
	in many/most respects
	in many/most situations
	in no small measure
	in no small part
	in the main
	it is often the case/circumstance/situation (that)
	more often than not
	most (of the) time(s)
	on/upon the whole
	predominant/predominantly
	primary/primarily
	principal/principally
	to a great/large degree
	to a great/large extent
	usually but not always
most/very probably	in all likelihood
	in all probability
motivation	driving force
	motivating force
motive	motivation
	(the) whys and (the) wherefores (of)
motives	(the) hows and (the) whys
mourn	express sorrow (about)
	voice sorrow (about)
move	course of action
	plan of action/attack/battle
	proceed
move on	advance ahead/forward/on/onward
	go forward
	move forward
	move forward into the future
	proceed ahead/forth/forward/on/onward
	progress ahead/forward/on/onward
movie	motion picture
much (of)	as a general rule

CONCISE	WORDY
	as a rule
	by (a/the) considerable/good/great/huge/large/over-whelming/sizable/vast/wide margin
	(a) certain amount of
	(a/the) considerable/good/great/huge/large/sizable/vast amount (of)
	(a/the) considerable/good/great/huge/large/sizable/vast degree (of)
	(a/the) considerable/good/great/huge/large/sizable/vast element (of)
	(a/the) considerable/good/great/huge/large/overwhelming/sizable/vast/wide majority (of)
	(a/the) considerable/good/great/huge/large/sizable/vast part (of)
	(a/the) considerable/good/great/huge/large/overwhelming/sizable/vast percentage (of)
	(a/the) considerable/good/great/huge/large/sizable/vast portion (of)
	(a/the) considerable/good/great/huge/large/sizable/vast proportion (of)
	(a/the) considerable/good/great/huge/large/sizable/vast quantity (of)
	considerably
	(a/a certain/some) degree (of)
	(an/a certain/some) extent of
	far and away
	for the most part
	(a/the) great/large fraction (of)
	(a/the) high degree (of)
	(a/the) high level (of)
	(a/the) high percentage (of)
	(a/the) high proportion (of)
	in great/large measure
	in great/large part
	in many/most cases
	in many/most circumstances
	in many/most instances
	in many/most situations
	in no small measure
	in no small part
	in the main
	(a/the) large/overwhelming/sizable/vast plurality (of)

CONCISE	WORDY
	(a) lot
	(a) lot of
	(a/a certain/some) measure (of)
	muchly
	on/upon the whole
	(a/the) overwhelming/vast preponderance (of)
	(a/a certain/some) part (of)
	(a/a certain/some) percentage (of)
	(a/a certain/some) portion (of)
	(a/a certain/some) proportion (of)
	(a/a certain/some) quantity (of)
	significant/substantial
	(a/the) significant/substantial amount (of)
	(a/the) significant/substantial degree (of)
	(a/the) significant/substantial element (of)
	(a/the) significant/substantial fraction (of)
	significantly/substantially
	(a/the) significant/substantial majority (of)
	(a/the) significant/substantial part (of)
	(a/the) significant/substantial percentage (of)
	(a/the) significant/substantial portion (of)
	(a/the) significant/substantial proportion (of)
	substantive
	to a great/large degree
	to a great/large extent
much as	in a/the fashion/manner/way characteristic of
	in a/the fashion/manner/way similar to
	in a similar fashion/manner/way (to)
	in much the same fashion/manner/way (as/that)
much -ed/-en	very much -ed/-en
much later	in the distant future
much like	in a/the fashion/manner/way characteristic of
	in a/the fashion/manner/way similar to
	in a similar fashion/manner/way (to)
	in much the same fashion/manner/way (as/that)
	in the same fashion/manner/way (as/that)
much the same (as)	along the same line
	in a/the fashion/manner/way characteristic of
	in a/the fashion/manner/way similar to
	in a similar fashion/manner/way (to)
multifaceted	many and varied
multifarious	many and varied
multifold	many and varied
multiform	many and varied

CONCISE	WORDY
multiple	many and varied
must	has (got) to
	is required to
	it is essential that
	it is imperative that
	it is necessary (for/that/to)
	must necessarily/of necessity
	necessitate
myriad	(an/the) abundance of
	beyond number
	(a/the) countless number (of)
	(an/the) infinite number (of)
	innumerable
	(an/the) untold number (of)
	without number
mystery	question mark

N

naked	in the altogether
name	appellation
	characterize as
	enumerate
	name as
	refer to as
named	known as
namely	in other words
	(to) put (it) another way
	that is/this is/which is as much as to say (that)
	that is/which is to say (that)
narrowly	by (a/the) little/narrow/nominal/slender/slight/slim/small/tiny margin
nationwide	(all) across/throughout the country/nation
natural	matter-of-course
naturally	as a matter of course
	(it) goes without saying (that)
	needless to say
	needs hardly be said
near	adjacent to
	(for) approximately
	(the) better part (of)
	at/on the brink of

CONCISE	WORDY
	at/on the point of
	close/near at hand
	(an) estimated
	in close proximity (to)
	in proximity (to)
	(something/somewhere) in the area (of)
	(something/somewhere) in the nature (of)
	in the neighborhood (of)
	(something/somewhere) in the neighborhood (of)
	in the proximity (of)
	(something/somewhere) in the realm (of)
	(something/somewhere) in the . . . range (of)
	(something/somewhere) in the region (of)
	in the vicinity (of)
	(something/somewhere) in the vicinity (of)
	(something/somewhere) on the order (of)
	on the threshold of
	on the verge of
nearby	anywhere near
	(for) approximately
	at/on the brink of
	at/on the point of
	close/near at hand
	(an) estimated
	in close proximity (to)
	in proximity (to)
	(something/somewhere) in the area (of)
	(something/somewhere) in the nature (of)
	in the neighborhood (of)
	(something/somewhere) in the neighborhood (of)
	in the proximity (of)
	(something/somewhere) in the . . . range (of)
	(something/somewhere) in the realm (of)
	(something/somewhere) in the region (of)
	in the vicinity (of)
	(something/somewhere) in the vicinity (of)
	just about
	(something/somewhere) on the order (of)
	on the threshold of
	on the verge of
nearly all (of)	almost without exception
	as a general rule
	as a rule
	(the) better part (of)

CONCISE	WORDY
	(the) bulk (of)
	(a/the) considerable/good/great/huge/large/sizable/vast amount (of)
	(a/the) considerable/good/great/huge/large/overwhelming/sizable/vast/wide majority (of)
	(a/the) considerable/good/great/huge/large/overwhelming/sizable/vast number (of)
	(a/the) considerable/good/great/huge/large/sizable/vast part (of)
	(a/the) considerable/good/great/huge/large/overwhelming/sizable/vast percentage (of)
	(a/the) considerable/good/great/huge/large/sizable/vast portion (of)
	(a/the) considerable/good/great/huge/large/sizable/vast proportion (of)
	(a/the) considerable/good/great/huge/large/sizable/vast quantity (of)
	for the most part
	(a/the) great/large fraction (of)
	(a/the) high number (of)
	(a/the) high percentage (of)
	(a/the) high proportion (of)
	in (almost) all/every cases/circumstances/instances/situations
	in big/great/high/huge/large/overwhelming/sizable/vast numbers
	in great/large measure
	in great/large part
	in great/large quantities
	in many/most cases
	in many/most circumstances
	in many/most instances
	in many/most situations
	in no small measure
	in no small part
	in the main
	(a/the) large/overwhelming/sizable/vast plurality (of)
	(the) lion's share
	(a/the) majority (of)
	(a/the) major part/percentage/portion/proportion (of)
	most but not all

CONCISE	WORDY
	(a/a fair/any) number (of)
	on/upon the whole
	(a/the) overwhelming/vast preponderance (of)
	(a/a certain/some) part (of)
	(a/a certain/some) percentage (of)
	(a/the) plurality (of)
	(a/a certain/some) portion (of)
	predominant/predominantly
	(a/the) preponderance (of)
	primary/primarily
	principal/principally
	(a/a certain/some) proportion (of)
	(a/a certain/some) quantity (of)
	(a/the) significant/substantial amount (of)
	(a/the) significant/substantial fraction (of)
	(a/the) significant/substantial majority (of)
	(a/the) significant/substantial number (of)
	(a/the) significant/substantial part (of)
	(a/the) significant/substantial percentage (of)
	(a/the) significant/substantial portion (of)
	(a/the) significant/substantial proportion (of)
	(a/the) significant/substantial quantity (of)
	to a great/large degree
	to a great/large extent
	with few/rare exception(s)
nearly always	in (almost) all/every cases/circumstances/instances/ situations
	in many/most cases
	in many/most circumstances
	in many/most instances
	in many/most regards
	in many/most respects
	in many/most situations
	more often than not
	most (of the) time(s)
	usually but not always
nearly every	almost without exception
	with few/rare exception(s)
nearly half (of)	(a/the) significant/substantial minority (of)
nearness	proximity
neat	neat and tidy
necessarily	must necessarily/of necessity
necessary	necessary essential
	necessary prerequisite

CONCISE	WORDY
	necessary requirement
	necessary requisite
	vital necessity
need	desideratum
	necessitate
	necessity
	need to have
	require
	requirement
	requisite
	stand in need of
needed	necessary
needful	necessary
needlessly	unnecessarily
need not	need not necessarily/of necessity
need only	has only to
needs	is in need of
	is in want of
	is needful of
needs not	does not have to
	does not necessarily
need to	it is necessary (for/that/to)
negatively	in the negative
neglect	fly in the face of
neighboring	in the neighborhood (of)
neither	neither one
never	at no time
	in no case
	in no way
	in no way, shape, or form
	never at any time
	never ever
	not . . . at any time
	(does) not ever
	on no consideration
	on no occasion
	under any circumstances/conditions
	under no circumstances/conditions
never ending	day in (and) day out
	for ever and a day
	in perpetuity
	year in (and) year out
nevertheless	but nevertheless
new	brand new

CONCISE	WORDY
	innovative new
	new and improved
	new and innovative
newest	most recent
newsworthy	worthy of (my) consideration
	worthy of attention
	worthy of note
next	after the event/incident/occurrence
	in the next place
	in the second place
	in the third place
	next of all
	(then) . . . proceed (to)
	thereafter
	thereupon
	this coming
next month/year	in the distant future
	in the foreseeable future
	in/into the future
	in the immediate future
	in the (very) near future
	in/over the near term
	in the not-so-distant/not-too-distant future
	in/over the short run
	in/over the short term
	over the short haul
next to	adjacent to
	alongside of
	as compared to/with
	as contrasted to/with
	as opposed to
	by comparison to/with
	by contrast to/with
	compared to/with
	contrasted to/with
	in comparison to/with
	in contrast to/with
	in relation/relationship to
	measured against
	relative to
	side by side (with)
	when compared to/with
	when measured against
nice	(all) fine/good and well

CONCISE	WORDY
	(all) well and fine/good
no	(a/the) absence of
	absolutely not
	devoid of
	does not . . . any
	in the negative
	insufficient
	lacking in
	(a/the) lack of
	to the contrary
nod	nod (her) head
no doubt	beyond a/the shadow of a doubt
	without (a/any) doubt
	without (a) question
	without (a/any) question/shadow of a doubt
no matter how	irrespective of how
	regardless of how
no matter what	irregardless of
	irrespective of (what)
	regardless of (what)
	under any circumstances/conditions
no matter when	irrespective of when
	regardless of when
no matter where	irrespective of where
	regardless of where
no matter whether	irrespective of (the fact) whether . . . (or)
	regardless of whether . . . (or)
no matter which	irrespective of which
	regardless of which
no matter who	irrespective of who
	regardless of who
no matter whom	irrespective of whom
	regardless of whom
nominally	by (a/the) little/narrow/nominal/slender/slight/slim/ small/tiny margin
non-	(a/the) absence of
	devoid of
	insufficient
	lacking in
	(a/the) lack of
	less than (enthusiastic)
none	does not . . . any
	not a one
nonetheless	but nonetheless

CONCISE	WORDY
noon	noontime
	twelve noon
no one	not a one
normal	matter-of-course
	par for the course
normally	as a general rule
	as a matter of course
	as a rule
	as often as not
	by and large
	for the most part
	in great/large measure
	in great/large part
	in many/most cases
	in many/most circumstances
	in many/most instances
	in many/most situations
	in no small measure
	in no small part
	in normal/ordinary/typical/usual practice
	in the main
	in the normal/ordinary/typical/usual course of business/events/things
	more often than not
	most (of the) time(s)
	on (an/the) average
	on/upon the whole
	to a great/large degree
	to a great/large extent
not	(a/the) absence of
	as opposed to
	devoid of
	in no case
	in no way
	in no way, shape, or form
	insufficient
	lacking in
	(a/the) lack of
	under no circumstances/conditions
not any	(a/the) absence of
not at all	absolutely not
not binding	null and void
note	according to
	(please) bear in mind

CONCISE	WORDY
	communication
	correspondence
	it is important to note
	it is interesting to note
	it is significant to note
	it must/should be noted
	memorandum
	notation
	pay attention to
	pay heed to
	take cognizance of
	take note of
	take notice of
	written communication/correspondence
not enough	insufficient
	(a/the) insufficient amount (of)
	(a/the) insufficient number (of)
not ever	in no case
	in no way
	in no way, shape, or form
	never at any time
	never ever
	not . . . at any time
	on no consideration
	on no occasion
	under any circumstances/conditions
	under no circumstances/conditions
noteworthy	worthy of attention
	worthy of (my) consideration
	worthy of note
not having	(a/the) absence of
	in the absence of
nothing	does not . . . any
	not anything
notice	advance/prior notice
	notification
	pay attention to
	pay heed to
	take cognizance of
	take note of
	take notice of
not long ago	in the immediate past
	in the (very) near past
	in the not-so-distant/not-too-distant past
	in/within the recent past

CONCISE	WORDY
not many (of)	few/small in number
	(a/the) limited number of
	(a/the) limited selection (of)
	(a/the) minimal number (of)
	(a/the) minority (of)
	(a/the) small/tiny amount/degree/part/percentage/ portion/proportion/quantity (of)
	(a/the) small/tiny fraction (of)
	(a/the) small/tiny minority (of)
	(a/the) small/tiny number (of)
not much	minimal
not once	in no case
	in no way
	in no way, shape, or form
	never at any time
	never ever
	not . . . at any time
	on no consideration
	on no occasion
	under no circumstances/conditions
not pertinent	beside the point
	neither here nor there
not so	contrariwise
	on the contrary
	to the contrary
not used to	unaccustomed to
novel	fictional novel
	in a class by herself/itself
	one-of-a-kind
	(something) out of the ordinary
	without equal
	without peer
now	in/over the near term
	in/over the short run
	in/over the short term
	in that/this case/circumstance/instance/situation
(just/right) now	(even) as I (we) speak
	at (the) present
	at that/this juncture
	at that/this juncture/juncture in time/moment/moment in time/period/period in time/point/ point in time/stage/stage in time/time in my history/in my life/in the history of my life
	at that/this juncture/moment/period/point/stage in time

CONCISE	WORDY
	at that/this moment
	at that/this point
	at that/this stage
	at that/this time
	at the current/present time
	at the (current/present) moment
	currently
	(the) here and now
	in that/this day and age
	in the immediate future
	on that/this (particular) occasion
	over the short haul
	presently
	that/this juncture/moment/period/point/stage in time
	the present day
nowadays	at (the) present
	at that/this juncture
	at that/this juncture/juncture in time/moment/moment in time/period/period in time/point/point in time/stage/stage in time/time in my history/in my life/in the history of my life
	at that/this juncture/moment/period/point/stage in time
	at that/this moment
	at that/this point
	at that/this stage
	at that/this time
	at the current/present time
	at the (current/present) moment
	in that/this day and age
	the present day
nowaday's	(the) present-day
now and again	ever and anon
	every now and then
	every once in a while
	in certain/some circumstances
	in certain/some instances
	in certain/some situations
	occasionally
	once in a (great) while
	on certain/some occasions
	under certain/some circumstances/conditions
now and then	ever and anon
	every now and then

CONCISE	WORDY
	every once in a while
	in certain/some cases
	in certain/some circumstances
	in certain/some instances
	in certain/some situations
	occasionally
	once in a (great) while
	on certain/some occasions
	under certain/some circumstances/conditions
nowhere	not anywhere
nude	in the altogether
null	null and void
numberless	beyond number
	(a/the) countless number (of)
	(an/the) infinite number (of)
	innumerable
	(a/the) multiplicity of
	(a/the) multitude of
	multitudinous
	(an/the) untold number (of)
	without number
numerate	enumerate
numeric	numerical
numerous	(an/the) abundance of
	(an) array of
	(a/the) broad/extensive/great/vast/wide array of
	(a/the) broad/extensive/great/vast/wide range of
	(a/the) broad/extensive/great/vast/wide spectrum of
	(a/the) broad/extensive/great/vast/wide variety of
	(a/the) considerable/good/great/huge/large/over-whelming/sizable/vast number (of)
	(a/the) diversity of different
	(a/the) high number (of)
	(a) (whole) host of
	(a) lot of
	(a/the) multiplicity of
	(a/the) multitude of
	multitudinous
	numerous in number
	(a) range of
	(a/the) significant/substantial number (of)
	(a/the) spectrum of
	(a) variety of
	(a/the) variety of different

CONCISE	WORDY
	various different
	(many) widely varying
numerous times	on a number of /any number of/frequent/many/ numerous/several occasions
nurtures	is supportive of

O

obey	act in accord/accordance with
object (to)	express opposition to
	has a difference of opinion with
	is in opposition to
	is opposed to
	is resistant to
	raise objections about/on/to
	raise opposition about/on/to
	stand in opposition to
	take exception to
	take issue (with)
	take offense at
	take umbrage at/with
	voice criticism of
	voice disapproval of
	voice objection to
	voice opposition to
obligate	place/put restrictions on/upon
	place/put under obligation
	under obligation
oblige	under obligation
observe	pay attention to
	pay heed to
	take cognizance of
	take note of
	take notice of
obstruct	stand in the way of
obtain	take delivery of/on
	take possession of
obviate (-ing)	obviate the necessity/need for/of/to
obvious	in evidence
	plain and simple
obviously	for obvious reasons
	(it) goes without saying (that)

CONCISE	WORDY
	it is apparent that
	it is evident that
	needless to say
	needs hardly be said
occasion	bring about
occasionally	ever and anon
	every now and then
	every once in a while
	in certain/some cases
	in certain/some circumstances
	in certain/some instances
	in certain/some situations
	on certain/some occasions
	under certain/some circumstances/conditions
occur	come about
	come into play
	come to pass
	eventuate
	go forward
	materialize
	move forward
	take place
occurrence	eventuality
occur when	occur at a time when
odd	(something) out of the ordinary
oddly	strange to relate/say
of	about/concerning/in/on/regarding the matter/subject of
	as . . . apply to
	as concerns
	as/so far as . . . (goes/is concerned)
	as regards
	associated with
	as to
	-based
	based in
	concerning
	connected with
	in (the) . . . case (of)
	in connection with
	in point of
	in reference to
	in regard to
	in relation to
	in respect of/to

CONCISE	WORDY
	insofar as . . . (goes/is concerned)
	in terms of
	in the amount/sum of
	in the area of
	in the realm of
	involve
	involved in
	on . . . part
	on the part of
	out of
	pertain/pertaining to
	regard/regarding
	relate/relating to
	when it comes to
	where . . . is concerned
	with reference to
	with regard to
	with relation to
	with respect to
of course	(it) goes without saying (that)
	needless to say
	needs hardly be said
	to be sure
of late	in recent days/decades/months/weeks/years
	in recent history/memory/times
	in the immediate past
	in the (very) near past
	in the not-so-distant/not-too-distant past
	in/over the past few/several days/decades/months/weeks/years
	in/within the recent past
off	off of
offend	give offense to
offends	is offensive to
offense	criminal offense
offer	proffer
	put forth
	put forward
office	facility
	institution
	place of business/employment/work
	premises
officers	law enforcement officers
of necessity	must necessarily/of necessity

CONCISE	WORDY
often	again and again
	as often as not
	in a lot of cases/circumstances/instances/situations
	in a/the majority of cases/circumstances/instances/ situations
	in many/most cases
	in many/most circumstances
	in many/most instances
	in many/most regards
	in many/most respects
	in many/most situations
	it is often the case/circumstance/situation (that)
	(a) lot of (the) time
	many times over
	oftentimes/ofttimes
	on (an/the) average
	on a number of /any number of/frequent/many/ numerous/several occasions
	on more than one occasion
	over and over (again)
	time after time
	time and (time) again
	usually but not always
of . . . to	of from . . . to
old	advanced/along in years
omen	harbinger of the future (of things to come)
omnipresent	present everywhere
on	about/concerning/in/on/regarding the matter/subject of
	as . . . apply to
	as concerns
	as/so far as . . . (goes/is concerned)
	as of
	as regards
	as to
	at/on (the) top (of)
	based on/upon
	by (the) means of
	by (the) way of
	by the result of
	concerning
	in (the) . . . case (of)
	in connection with
	in point of
	in reference to

CONCISE	WORDY
	in regard to
	in relation to
	in respect of/to
	insofar as . . . (goes/is concerned)
	in terms of
	in the area of
	in the direction of/toward
	in the realm of
	on . . . grounds
	on the basis of
	on the surface of
	pertain/pertaining to
	regard/regarding
	relate/relating to
	relative to
	through the medium of
	upon
	when it comes to
	where . . . is concerned
	with reference to
	with regard to
	with relation to
	with respect to
on account of	in consideration of (payment of/sum of)
once	as soon as
	at a certain/any/one/some point in my history/point in my life/point in the history of my life/point in time
	at an/some earlier/former/past/previous date/time
	at one time (in the past)
	back/before in the past
	in (the) days/decades/months/weeks/years gone by
	in (the) days/decades/months/weeks/years of old
	in (the) days/decades/months/weeks/years past
	in (the) olden days
	in/over (the) past days/decades/months/weeks/years
	in earlier/former/prior times
	in the (very) near past
	in the distant past
	in the not-so-distant/not-too-distant past
	in the past
	in/within the recent past
	once . . . then
	on one/two/three occasion(s)

CONCISE	WORDY
	time was when
once (twice)	one (two) time(s)
once in a while	ever and anon
	every now and then
	every once in a while
	under certain/some circumstances/conditions
once more	a second time
	one more time
	over again
once or twice	on a couple of/a few occasions
	on one/two/three occasion(s)
one	a single one
	a single solitary (one)
	one and only
	one and the same
	one single
one day	as (the) days/decades/months/weeks/years go on
	as time goes on
	as time progresses (forward/on/onward)
	at a certain/any/one/some point in my history (point in my life/point in the history of my life/point in time)
	at a/some future/later/subsequent date/time
	at/from/in/on/to any/each/every/some area/locale/locality/location/place/point/position/region/site/spot
	at/from/in/on/to any/each/every/some area/locale/locality/location/place/point/position/region/site/spot where
	in/over (the) coming days/decades/months/weeks/years
	in/over (the) days/decades/months/weeks/years ahead
	in/over (the) days/decades/months/weeks/years to come
	in due course/time
	in good time
	in the course of events/things/time
	in the distant future
	in/into the future
	over the long haul
	in/over the long run
	in/over the long term
	some day/time in the future
	(the) time will come when
	with the passage of time
one example/one instance	for one . . . (be) an example/an instance

CONCISE	WORDY
one-half (of)	fifty (50) percent (of)
one time	on one/two/three occasion(s)
only	first and last
	first and only
	no more than
	one and only
only if	if and only if
only then	then and only then
on occasion	ever and anon
	every now and then
	every once in a while
	in certain/some cases
	in certain/some circumstances
	in certain/some instances
	in certain/some situations
	once in a (great) while
	under certain/some circumstances/conditions
on record	in recorded history
on the other hand	but on the other hand
OPEC	OPEC countries
open	(an/the) open question
	open up
opinion	frame of mind
	point of view
opportunity	window of opportunity
oppose	express opposition to
	not in favor of
	raise objections about/on/to
	raise opposition about/on/to
	stand in (marked/sharp) contrast to
	stand in opposition to
	take a stand against/in opposition to
	take exception to
	take issue (with)
	voice criticism of
	voice disapproval of
	voice objection to
	voice opposition to
opposed to	in opposition to
opposes	has a difference of opinion with
	is in (marked/sharp) contrast to
	is in opposition to
	is opposed to

CONCISE	WORDY
	is resistant to
oppress	place/put a burden on/upon
	place/put a strain on/upon
optimism	positive optimism
optimist	hopeful optimist
or	or else
order	prioritize
orderly	neat and tidy
ordinarily	as a matter of course
	as often as not
	in many/most circumstances
	in many/most instances
	in many/most situations
	in normal/ordinary/typical/usual practice
	in the normal/ordinary/typical/usual course of business/ events/things
	on (an/the) average
ordinary	matter-of-course
	run of the mill
organized	neat and tidy
orient(ed)	orientate(d)
origin	origination
or so	(for) approximately
	(an) estimated
	(something/somewhere) in the area (of)
	(something/somewhere) in the nature (of)
	(something/somewhere) in the neighborhood (of)
	(something/somewhere) in the . . . range (of)
	(something/somewhere) in the realm (of)
	(something/somewhere) in the region (of)
	(something/somewhere) in the vicinity (of)
	(something/somewhere) on the order (of)
	or thereabouts
	something like
	somewhere around/round
oscillate	oscillate back and forth
other	(an) additional
	in other cases/circumstances/instances/situations
	otherwise
others	other people/persons
other than	other than . . . also/as well
	with the exception of/that
	with the exclusion of/that

CONCISE	WORDY
(at) other times	in other cases/circumstances/instances/situations
out of	as a consequence of
	as a result of
	because of
	by consequence of
	by reason of
	by/in virtue of
	for reasons of
	in consequence of
	in reaction to
	in response to
	on account of
outcome	consequence
	eventuality
	final/ultimate outcome
outcry	hue and cry
outrages	is outrageous to
outrank	take precedence over
outside (of)	on the outside of
	outside of
	with the exception of/that
	with the exclusion of/that
outstanding	worthy of note
outwardly	on its (the) face (of it/of things)
	on the surface (of it/of things)
	to all appearances
over	about/concerning/in/on/regarding the matter/subject of
	above and beyond
	all done/finished
	as . . . apply to
	as compared to/with
	as concerns
	as contrasted to/with
	as/so far as . . . (goes/is concerned)
	as opposed to
	as regards
	as to
	at an end
	by comparison to/with
	by contrast to/with
	by (the) means of
	by (the) way of
	compared to/with

CONCISE	WORDY
	concerning
	contrasted to/with
	during the course/length of
	in (the) . . . case (of)
	in comparison to/with
	in connection with
	in contrast to/with
	in excess of
	in point of
	in preference to
	in reference to
	in regard to
	in relation to
	in relation/relationship to
	in repetition
	in respect of/to
	insofar as . . . (goes/is concerned)
	in the area of
	(somewhere) in the course of
	in the realm of
	in (the) time(s) of
	measured against
	over again
	over and above
	over and done with
	over the course/duration/length of
	(all) over with
	pertain/pertaining to
	regard/regarding
	relate/relating to
	relative to
	through/throughout the course/duration/length of
	through the medium of
	upward(s) of
	when compared to/with
	when it comes to
	when measured against
	where . . . is concerned
	with reference to
	with regard to
	with relation to
	with respect to
over-	overly
overall	all in all

CONCISE	WORDY
	all things considered
	as a general rule
	as a rule
	at the end of the day
	for the most part
	including everything
	in great/large measure
	in great/large part
	in no small measure
	in no small part
	in the final/last analysis
	in the main
	in the overall scope/sphere of things
	on/upon the whole
	on the whole
	to a great/large degree
	to a great/large extent
	when all is said and done
	when it/you comes/gets right down to it
overdue	in arrears
overlook	fly in the face of
oversight	inadvertent/unintended/unintentional oversight
overtax	place/put a burden on/upon
	place/put a strain on/upon
over the (years)	in (the) days/decades/months/weeks/years gone by
	in (the) days/decades/months/weeks/years of old
	in (the) days/decades/months/weeks/years past
over the months/years	as (the) days/decades/months/weeks/years go on
	as time progresses (forward/on/onward)
	at a/some future/later/subsequent date/time
	(after/for/in/over/within) (an) extended/lengthy/long/ prolonged/protracted amount of time/length of time/period/period of time/span of time/time/while
	in the course of events/things/time
	in/over the long run
	in/over the long term
	over the long haul
	some day/time in the future
	(the) time will come when
	with the passage of time
over time	as (the) days/decades/months/weeks/years go on
	as time goes on
	as time progresses (forward/on/onward)

CONCISE	WORDY
	at a/some future/later/subsequent date/time
	(after/for/in/over/within) (an) extended/lengthy/long/ prolonged/protracted amount of time/length of time/period/period of time/span of time/time/while
	in/over (the) coming days/decades/months/weeks/years
	in/over (the) days/decades/months/weeks/years ahead
	in (the) days/decades/months/weeks/years gone by
	in (the) days/decades/months/weeks/years of old
	in (the) days/decades/months/weeks/years past
	in/over (the) days/decades/months/weeks/years to come
	in due course/time
	in good time
	in the course of events/things/time
	in the distant future
	in/into the future
	in/over the long run
	in/over the long term
	over the long haul
	some day/time in the future
	(the) time will come when
	with the passage of time
overview	overall look/view
owing to	as a consequence of
	as a result of
	ascribable to
	attributable to
	by consequence of
	by reason of
	by the result of
	by/in virtue of
	caused because of/due to/owing to
	(a/the) consequence of
	in consequence of
	in consideration of (payment of/sum of)
	in reaction to
	in response to
	in the wake of
	on account of
	on the basis of
own	possess (a/the) . . . (about/for/of/on/over)

CONCISE	WORDY

P

pack	pack together
painful	excruciatingly painful
paired	paired in twos
paired with	accompanied by
	in association with
	in combination with
	in conjunction with
	in connection with
	together with
panacea	panacea for all ills
	universal panacea
paradisal	paradisiacal
	paradisiac
	paradisiacal
part	component
	component (and) part/piece
	part and parcel
(a) part (of)	(a/a certain/some) part (of)
	(a/a certain/some) percentage (of)
	(a/a certain/some) portion (of)
	(a/a certain/some) proportion (of)
	(a/a certain/some) quantity (of)
partially	in a (some) measure
	in/on/to/with various/varying degrees/extents
	to a certain/limited/some degree
	to a certain/limited/some extent
	to a degree
	to a greater or lesser degree/extent
	to a major or minor degree/extent
	to an extent
	to one degree/extent or another
particle	small/tiny particle
particulars	(the) ins and (the) outs
partly	in a (some) measure
	in/on/to/with various/varying degrees/extents
	partially
	to a certain/limited/some degree
	to a certain/limited/some extent
	to a degree

CONCISE	WORDY
	to a greater or lesser degree/extent
	to a major or minor degree/extent
	to an extent
	to one degree/extent or another
pass	free pass
past	all done/finished
	at an end
	over and done with
	(all) over with
patchquilt	patchwork quilt
patchwork	patchwork quilt
patently	it is apparent that
	it is evident that
pathetic	pathetical
pathologic	pathological
pathology	pathological disease
pay	compensate
	compensation
	remittance
	remunerate
	remuneration
payable	due and payable
payment	compensation
	remittance
	remuneration
peace	peace and quiet
peccadillo	small/tiny peccadillo
pedal	foot pedal
peerless	in a class by herself/itself
	one-of-a-kind
	without equal
	without peer
penetrate	penetrate into
people	human resources
	individual(s)
per	per each/every
percent	percentage point/unit
perform	accomplish
	implement
	put into effect
performance	past/previous/prior performance
perhaps	perhaps . . . may/might
period	(a/the) . . . amount of time/length of time/period of time/ span of time

CONCISE	WORDY
	(a/the) time frame (of)
	(a/the) time horizon (of)
	(a/the) time interval (of)
	(a/the) time period (of)
	(a/the) time span (of)
periodic	periodical
periodically	at frequent/periodic/regular intervals/periods
	at specific/specified/timed intervals/periods
perk	added perk
permit	afford/give/offer/present/provide . . . (an/the) opportunity (to)
	allow of
perpetually	day in (and) day out
	for ever and a day
	in perpetuity
	year in (and) year out
perseverance	sticktoitiveness
persevere	continue in existence/to exist
perseveres in	is persistent in
persist	continue in existence/to exist
persistence	sticktoitiveness
persists in	is persistent in
person	human being
	individual(s)
persons	human resources
pertains to	has reference to
	(that) has to do with
	is applicable in/to
	is appropriate in/to
	is concerned with
	is pertinent to
	is relevant to
	is suitable to
pertain to	appertain/appertaining to
pertinent	to the point
	to the purpose
pharmacologic	pharmacological
phase	passing phase
phone	communicate (with)
	contact
	get in touch with
	make contact (with)
	phone up
	pick up the phone/telephone and call

CONCISE	WORDY
physiologic	physiological
pick	pick and choose
pick out	select out
pictures	is characteristic of
	is descriptive of
	is illustrative of
piece	component (and) part/piece
	tiny/little bit
pieces	bits and pieces
PIN	PIN number
pinpoint	zero in on
pith	core essence
	essential core
	(the) heart of the matter
	(the) long and (the) short
	sum/summary and substance
pithy	short and sweet
	short and to the point
pity	take pity on/upon
pivotal	most important
place	facility
	institution
	locality
plain	in evidence
	matter-of-fact
	plain and simple
plainly	(it) goes without saying (that)
	it is apparent that
	it is evident that
	needless to say
	needs hardly be said
plan	action/attack/battle/game plan
	bring into being/existence
	call into being/existence
	come up with
	course of action
	plan ahead
	plan in advance
	plan of action/attack/battle
	plan out
	preplan
planning	forward planning
planning/plans	advance planning/plans
plans	future plans

CONCISE	WORDY
	plans and specifications
plant	facility
	institution
pleasant	(all) fine/good and well
	(all) well and fine/good
please	I (we) would appreciate it if
pleased	in a good mood
pleasing	(all) fine/good and well
	(all) well and fine/good
plentiful	(an/the) abundance of
plenty of	(an/the) abundance of
plot	come up with
plummet	plummet down
plunge	plunge down
(3:00) p.m.	(3:00) p.m. . . . afternoon/evening/night
poetic	poetical
point	locality
point/unit	percentage point/unit
point out	bring attention to
	bring into the open
	bring to . . . attention (of)
	bring to light
	call . . . attention to
	call to . . . attention (of)
	concentrate (media/people's/public) attention on/upon
	direct . . . attention to
	draw attention to
	focus (media/people's/public) attention on/upon
point to	bring attention to
	bring into the open
	bring to . . . attention (of)
	bring to light
	call . . . attention to
	call to . . . attention (of)
	concentrate (media/people's/public) attention on/upon
	direct . . . attention to
	draw attention to
	focus (media/people's/public) attention on/upon
police	law enforcement/police officers
policy	action/attack/battle/game plan
	course of action
	plan of action/attack/battle
polish	polish up
portends	is predictive of

CONCISE	WORDY
portrays	is characteristic of
	is descriptive of
	is illustrative of
position	capacity
	frame of mind
	point of view
positively	absolutely positively
	in the affirmative
possess	have . . . in (my) possession
	take delivery of/on
	take possession of
possesses	is in possession of
possible	in/within the realm of possibility
posthaste	at/in the blink of an eye
	expeditiously
	in quick/short order
postpone	postpone until later
posture	frame of mind
	point of view
potential	potentiality
	unrealized potential
potential/potentiality	full/maximum potential/potentiality
pouring	pouring (down) rain
power	driving force
	(with) might and main
	motivating force
powerless	high and dry
practically	for all intents and purposes
	for all practical purposes
	to all intents and purposes
	to all practical purposes
practice	past/previous/prior practice
praise	approbation
praiseworthy	worthy of commendation
	worthy of praise
precede	take precedence over
	take priority over
precedent	historical precedent
	past/previous/prior precedent
precisely	no more (and) no less
predict	forecast . . . future
	foretell . . . future
	predict ahead of time/beforehand/in advance
	predict . . . future

CONCISE	WORDY
predicts	is predictive of
prefer	it is my preference (that)
	place/put a premium on/upon
	place/put a priority on/upon
	stand in support of
	take a stand for/in favor of/in support of
preferable	more preferable
prefer . . . over	prefer . . . as opposed to/instead of/rather than
prefers	has a/the preference for
	is in favor of
	is in support of
prefer . . . to	prefer . . . as opposed to/instead of/rather than
prejudice	biased opinion
	prejudicial opinion
preparation	advance preparation
preparation/prepare . . . for	preparation/prepare . . . ahead of time/before/ beforehand/in advance
prepare	come up with
prepare (for)	make allowance for
	make concession for
	make provision for
	prepare (for) . . . ahead of time/before/beforehand/in advance
prerequisite	essential prerequisite
	necessary prerequisite
presages	is predictive of
present	at that/this juncture
	at that/this juncture/juncture in time/moment/moment in time/period/period in time/point/ point in time/stage/stage in time/time in my history/in my life/in the history of my life
	at that/this juncture/moment/period/point/stage in time
	at that/this moment
	at that/this point
	at that/this stage
	at that/this time
	at the current/present time
	at the (current/present) moment
	bring attention to
	bring into the open
	bring to . . . attention (of)
	bring to light
	call . . . attention to

CONCISE	WORDY
	call to . . . attention (of)
	concentrate (media/people's/public) attention on/upon
	direct . . . attention to
	draw attention to
	focus (media/people's/public) attention on/upon
	in attendance
	put forth
	put forward
presently	(after/for/in/over/within) a brief/limited/little/short amount of time/length of time/moment of time/period/period of time/span of time/time/while
	at any minute/moment/second
	at that/this juncture
	at that/this juncture/juncture in time/moment/moment in time/period/period in time/point/point in time/stage/stage in time/time in my history/in my life/in the history of my life
	at that/this juncture/moment/period/point/stage in time
	at that/this moment
	at that/this point
	at that/this stage
	at that/this time
	at/in the blink of an eye
	at the current/present time
	at the (current/present) moment
	at your earliest convenience
	expeditiously
	from minute/moment/second to minute/moment/second
	(the) here and now
	in a few minutes/moments/seconds
	in a minute/moment/second
	in/over (the) coming days/decades/months/weeks/years
	in/over (the) days/decades/months/weeks/years ahead
	in/over (the) days/decades/months/weeks/years to come
	in/over the near term
	in/over the short run
	in/over the short term
	in quick/short order
	in the foreseeable future
	in the immediate future
	in the (very) near future
	in the not-so-distant/not-too-distant future

CONCISE	WORDY
	on that/this (particular) occasion
	over the short haul
press	bring pressure to bear on/upon
pressing	necessary
pressure	bring pressure to bear on/upon
	pressurize
pretend	make believe
	put on an act
pretense	false pretense
prevail	continue in existence/to exist
prevent	stand in the way of
preventive	preventative
prevents	is a deterrent to
	is a hindrance to
	is an impediment to
	is an obstacle to
previously	in (the) days/decades/months/weeks/years past
	in/over (the) past days/decades/months/weeks/years
	in the distant past
	in the immediate past
	in the (very) near past
	in the not-so-distant/not-too-distant past
	in the past
	in/within the recent past
	on earlier/former/previous/prior occasions
primarily	first and foremost
primary	first and foremost
principal	first and foremost
	most important
	of the first magnitude
	of the first/highest order
principally	first and foremost
principle	basic principle
	fundamental principle
prior to	prior to . . . first
prison	correctional/prison facility
	facility
	institution
prize	appreciate
	place/put a premium on/upon
	place/put a priority on/upon
	place/put a value on/upon
prizes	has (an/the) appreciation for
	is appreciative of

CONCISE	WORDY
probably	in all likelihood
	in all probability
probing	in pursuit of
problematic	problematical
procedure	action/attack/battle/game plan
	course of action
	plan of action/attack/battle
proceed	advance ahead/forward/on/onward
	go forward
	move forward
	move forward into the future
	proceed ahead/forth/forward/on/onward
	progress ahead/forward/on/onward
proceeding	make (my) way
proclaim	bring attention to
	bring into the open
	bring to . . . attention (of)
	bring to light
	call . . . attention to
	call to . . . attention (of)
	concentrate (media/people's/public) attention on/upon
	direct . . . attention to
	draw attention to
	focus (media/people's/public) attention on/upon
procure	take delivery of/on
	take possession of
produce	bring about
	bring (give) forth
	bring into being/existence
	bring into the world
	call into being/existence
	cause to happen/occur/take place
	come up with
	implement
	put into effect
product	end product
professing	(something) to that/the/this effect (that)
profit by	take advantage of
profits	profitability/profitableness
profuse	(an/the) abundance of
progress	advance ahead/forward/on/onward
	forward progress
	go forward
	move forward

CONCISE	WORDY
	move forward into the future
	proceed ahead/forth/forward/on/onward
	progress ahead/forward/on/onward
project	project out
projections	future projections
promote	bring attention to
	bring into the open
	bring to . . . attention (of)
	bring to light
	call . . . attention to
	call to . . . attention (of)
	concentrate (media/people's/public) attention on/upon
	direct . . . attention to
	draw attention to
	facilitate
	focus (media/people's/public) attention on/upon
promptly	(after/for/in/over/within) a reasonable amount of time/ length of time/period/period of time/ span of time/time/while
	at/in the blink of an eye
	expeditiously
	in a timely fashion/manner/way
	in no time (at all)
	in quick/short order
	on a timely basis
proof	proven fact
propose	come up with
	put forth
	put forward
prosaic	matter-of-fact
prospect	probability
prospects	future prospects
protects	is protective against (of)
protest	express opposition to
	protestation
	raise objections about/on/to
	raise opposition about/on/to
	stand in opposition to
	take exception to
	voice criticism of
	voice disapproval of
	voice objection to
	voice opposition to

CONCISE	WORDY
protests	is in opposition to
	is opposed to
	is resistant to
protrude	protrude out
prove	attest to the fact (that)
	establish conclusive evidence/proof of
	substantiate
proved	proven
proverb	old proverb
proves	(just) goes to show
	is a demonstration of
	is evidence of/that
	is proof of/that
provide	make available
provided	on (the) condition (of/that)
	on (the) understanding (of/that)
provide for	make allowance for
	make concession for
	make provision for
	take account for/of
	take into account
	take into consideration
psychiatric	psychiatrical
psychic	psychical
psychoanalytic	psychoanalytical
psychobiologic	psychobiological
psychometric	psychometrical
psychopathologic	psychopathological
psychophysiologic	psychophysiological
public	general public
publicize	bring attention to
	bring into the open
	bring to . . . attention (of)
	bring to light
	call . . . attention to
	call to . . . attention (of)
	concentrate (media/people's/public) attention on/upon
	direct . . . attention to
	draw attention to
	focus (media/people's/public) attention on/upon
pull	input
purchase	take delivery of/on
	take possession of

CONCISE	WORDY
pure	pure (and) unadulterated
	pure and simple
purporting	(something) to that/the/this effect (that)
purpose	(the) whys and (the) wherefores (of)
purposes	(the) hows and (the) whys
pursuing	in pursuit of
puzzle	puzzlement
	question mark

Q

quarrels (with)	is at loggerheads (with)
	is at odds over/with
	is at variance with
	is in conflict with
	is in disagreement (about/on/with)
question	bring into question
	call into question
	cast doubt on/upon
	express skepticism (about)
	place/put into question
	question mark
	(a/the) question to answer
	raise doubts about/on
	raise objections about/on/to
	raise opposition about/on/to
	raise questions about/on
	take exception to
	take issue (with)
	throw into doubt
	throw into question
	voice skepticism (about)
questionable	(an/the) open question
	open to doubt
	open to question
questions	is distrustful about/of
	is doubtful about/of
	is dubious about/of
	is in doubt about/of
	is mistrustful about/of
	is skeptical about/of/that

CONCISE	WORDY
quickly	(after/for/in/over/within) a brief/limited/little/short amount of time/length of time/ moment of time/period/period of time/span of time/time/while
	(after/for/in/over/within) a reasonable amount of time/ length of time/period/period of time/ span of time/time/while
	at/in the blink of an eye
	at your earliest convenience
	expeditiously
	in a few minutes/moments/seconds
	in a minute/moment/second
	in a timely fashion/manner/way
	in/over (the) coming days/decades/months/weeks/years
	in/over (the) days/decades/months/weeks/years ahead
	in/over (the) days/decades/months/weeks/years to come
	in no time (at all)
	in quick/short order
	in the foreseeable future
	in the immediate future
	in the (very) near future
	in the not-so-distant/not-too-distant future
	on a timely basis
	over the short haul
	presently
quiet	peace and quiet
quixotic	quixotical

R

radiate	radiate out
raise	maximize
	raise up
RAM	RAM memory
range	breadth and depth
range from . . . to	begin/start at . . . and end/finish at
	range anywhere/somewhere from . . . to
	range from . . . all the way to/all the way up to/up to
	range from a low of . . . to a high of
rank	prioritize
rant	rant and rave

CONCISE	WORDY
rapidly	(after/for/in/over/within) a reasonable amount of time/ length of time/period/period of time/ span of time/time/while
	at/in the blink of an eye
	expeditiously
	in a timely fashion/manner/way
	in no time (at all)
	in quick/short order
	on a timely basis
rapport	personal rapport
rare	few and far between
	few/small in number
	in short supply
	(very) limited
	(something) out of the ordinary
rarely/seldom	rarely/seldom ever
rate	arrive at (an/the) estimate/estimation (about/as to/ concerning/of/on/regarding)
	come to an/the estimate/estimation (about/as to/ concerning/of/on/regarding)
	prioritize
	reach (an/the) estimate/estimation (about/of/on/upon/ with)
rate highly	place/put a premium on/upon
	place/put a priority on/upon
rather	but rather
	contrariwise
	in a way
	in certain/some regards
	in certain/some respects
	in/on/to/with various/varying degrees/extents
	(a) little bit
	on the contrary
	to a certain/limited/some degree
	to a certain/limited/some extent
	to a degree
	to a greater or lesser degree/extent
	to a major or minor degree/extent
	to an extent
	to one degree/extent or another
	to the contrary
	up to a point
rather like	in a/the fashion/manner/way characteristic of
	in a/the fashion/manner/way similar to

CONCISE	WORDY
	in a similar fashion/manner/way (to)
rather than	as opposed to
rave	rant and rave
raze	level to the ground
	raze to the ground
re-	again re-
	one more time
	over again
	re- again
reach	breadth and depth
	contact
	get in touch with
	make contact (with)
readily	of . . . own accord/free will
ready to	in a position to
reality	basis in fact/reality/truth
realize	(please) bear in mind
	effectuate
	implement
realize/recognize	it is important to realize/recognize
realizes	is aware of/that
	is cognizant of/that
	is conscious of/that
	is mindful of/that
really	as a matter of fact
	(the) fact is (that)
	(the) (simple) fact of the matter is (that)
	in actual fact
	in actuality
	in point of fact
	in reality
	really (and) truly
	(the) truth is (that)
	(the) truth of the matter is (that)
reap	take advantage of
reason	arrive at (a/the) conclusion (about/as to/concerning/of/on/regarding)
	arrive at (a/the) decision (about/as to/concerning/of/on/regarding)
	arrive at (a/the) determination (about/as to/concerning/of/on/regarding)
	arrive at (an/the) opinion (about/as to/concerning/of/on/regarding)
	basis in fact/reality/truth

CONCISE	WORDY
	come to a/the conclusion (about/as to/concerning/of/on/regarding)
	come to a/the decision (about/as to/concerning/of/on/regarding)
	come to a/the determination (about/as to/concerning/of/on/regarding)
	come to a/the opinion (about/as to/concerning/of/on/regarding)
	draw (a/the) conclusion (of)
	draw (a/the) inference (of)
	factual basis
	form (a/the) judgment (about/as to/concerning/of/on/regarding)
	form (an/the) opinion (about/as to/concerning/of/on/regarding)
	logical reason
	put two and two together
	rationale
	rational reason
	reach (a/the) conclusion (about/of/on/upon/with)
	reach (a/the) decision (about/of/on/upon/with)
	reach (a/the) determination (about/of/on/upon/with)
	reach (an/the) opinion (about/of/on/upon/with)
	reason why
	root cause
	(the) whys and (the) wherefores (of)
reason is (that)	reason being is
	(the) reason (why) . . . is because
	reason (why) . . . is due to (the fact that)
reasons	(the) hows and (the) whys
rebound	rebound back
rebuke	take to task
recall	bring (back) to mind
	call to mind
	recall back
recalls	is reminiscent of
recede	recede back
receive	receive back
	take delivery of/on
	take possession of
receives	is in receipt of
	is (a/the) recipient of
recent	in recent days/decades/months/weeks/years
	in recent history/memory/times

CONCISE	WORDY
	in the immediate past
	in the (very) near past
	in the not-so-distant/not-too-distant past
	in/over the past few/several days/decades/months/weeks/ years
	in/within the recent past
recently	in recent days/decades/months/weeks/years
	in recent history/memory/times
	in the immediate past
	in the (very) near past
	in the not-so-distant/not-too-distant past
	in/over the past few/several days/decades/months/weeks/ years
	in/within the recent past
	just recently
recite	recite back
reckon with	take account for/of
	take into account
	take into consideration
recognizes	is aware of/that
	is cognizant of/that
	is conscious of/that
	is mindful of/that
recoil	recoil back
recollect	bring (back) to mind
	call to mind
record	all-time record (high)
	criminal record
	historical record
	new (high) record
	past/previous/prior record
	record-breaking (high)
	record high
	record-setting
	record size
	track record
recorded	in recorded history
record low	all-time record low
recruit	new recruit
recur	occur again
	recur again (and again)
	reoccur
recurrence	reoccurrence
	repeat occurrence

CONCISE	WORDY
recurrently	again and again
	many times over
	over and over (again)
	time after time
	time and (time) again
reduce	alleviate
	minimize
	reduce down
refer	refer back
reflect	reflect back
reflect on	take under advisement
	take under consideration
reflects	is reflective of
reflects (on)	is a reflection of/on/upon
regard	hold (to) the opinion (that)
	hold (to) the view (that)
	in the assessment of
	in the estimation of
	in the judgment of
	in the opinion of
	in the view of
	pay attention to
	pay heed to
	positive feelings
	take account for/of
	take a . . . look (at)
	take a/the . . . view (of)
	take cognizance of
	take into account
	take into consideration
	take note of
	take notice of
	take the position (that)
	take the view (that)
regard as	regard as being
regarding	about/concerning/in/on/regarding the matter/ subject of
	as . . . apply to
	as concerns
	as/so far as . . . (goes/is concerned)
	as regards
	in (the) . . . case (of)
	in connection with
	in point of

CONCISE	WORDY
	in reference to
	in regard to
	in relation to
	in respect of/to
	insofar as . . . (goes/is concerned)
	in terms of
	in the area of
	in the realm of
	pertain/pertaining to
	relate/relating to
	relative to
	when it comes to
	where . . . is concerned
	with reference to
	with regard to
	with relation to
	with respect to
regardless of	irregardless of
	irrespective of (what)
regardless of how	irrespective of how
regardless of when	irrespective of when
regardless of where	irrespective of where
regardless of whether	irrespective of (the fact) whether . . . (or)
regardless of which	irrespective of which
regardless of who	irrespective of who
regardless of whom	irrespective of whom
regards	has reference to
	(that) has to do with
	is concerned with
	is pertinent to
	is relevant to
	is suitable to
region	locality
regress	regress back
regret	express concern (about)
	express sorrow (about)
	is concerned (about)
	voice concern (about)
	voice sorrow (about)
regrets	is regretful about/of/that
regrettably	alas and alack
regular	matter-of-course
regularly	again and again
	as a matter of course

CONCISE	WORDY
	at frequent/periodic/regular intervals/periods
	at specific/specified/timed intervals/periods
	many times over
	on a number of /any number of/frequent/many/ numerous/several occasions
	on a regular basis
	over and over (again)
	time after time
	time and (time) again
regulations	rules and regulations
reiterate	reiterate again (and again)
rejects	is dismissive of
rejoice in	derive enjoyment from
	derive pleasure from
	derive satisfaction from
	take enjoyment in
	take pleasure in
	take satisfaction in
relate	relate back
related to	associated with
relates to	has reference to
	(that) has to do with
	is a function of
	is applicable in/to
	is appropriate in/to
	is associated to/with
	is comparable to/with
	is concerned with
	is connected to/with
	is pertinent to
	is related to
	is relevant to
	is similar to/with
	is suitable to
relate to	appertain/appertaining to
relation	association
	relationship
relatively	in comparison/in contrast to/with . . . relatively
relative to	relatively . . . relative to
relevance	relevancy
relevant	to the point
	to the purpose
relic	old relic
	relic of the past

CONCISE	WORDY
relies on	is hopeful
	is reliant on/upon
relieve	come as a relief (to)
relish (in)	derive enjoyment from
	derive pleasure from
	derive satisfaction from
	take enjoyment in
	take pleasure in
	take satisfaction in
remain	continue in existence/to exist
	continue to be
	continue to remain
	retain . . . position as
remains	remainder
remand	remand back
remark	make (a/the) statement saying/stating
remember	it is important to keep in mind
	it is important to remember
	it must/should be remembered
	keep in mind
	remember again
	remember back
reminisce	reminisce about the past
remit	remit back
remnant	vestigial remnant
render	cause . . . to be/become
repay	repay back
repeat	reiterate
	reiterate again (and again)
	repeat again (and again)
	repeat back
	repeat over (and over)
repeatedly	again and again
	many times over
	on a number of /any number of/frequent/many/ numerous/several occasions
	over and over (again)
	time after time
	time and (time) again
replica	authentic replica
reply	reply back
report	communication
	correspondence
	report back

CONCISE	WORDY
	written communication/correspondence
represents	is a representation of
	is emblematic of
	is illustrative of
	is representative of
	is symbolic/symbolical of
reprieve	temporary reprieve
reprimand	take to task
reproach	take to task
reprove	take to task
require	necessitate
	stand in need of
	under obligation
requirement	necessary requirement
requisite	necessary requisite
resemble	bear (a/the) . . . resemblance/similarity to
	come close/near to
	follow along the lines of
resembles	is comparable to/with
	is similar to/with
resembling	along the lines of
	in a/the fashion/manner/way characteristic of
	in a/the fashion/manner/way similar to
	in a similar fashion/manner/way (to)
	in the nature of
	on the order of
resent	bear/have/hold a grudge (against)
	raise objections about/on/to
	raise opposition about/on/to
	take exception to
	take offense at
	take umbrage at/with
resentment	negative feelings
resents	is resentful of
reservations	advance reservations
reside	domicile
resilience	resiliency
resist	stand in opposition to
	take a stand against/in opposition to
resists	is in opposition to
	is opposed to
	is resistant to
resolute	bound and determined
resolution	final/ultimate resolution

CONCISE	WORDY
	firm/strong resolution
resolve	arrive at (an/the) accord (about/as to/concerning/of/on/regarding)
	arrive at (an/the) agreement (about/as to/concerning/of/on/regarding)
	arrive at (a/the) compromise (about/as to/concerning/of/on/regarding)
	arrive at (a/the) conclusion (about/as to/concerning/of/on/regarding)
	arrive at (a/the) decision (about/as to/concerning/of/on/regarding)
	arrive at (a/the) determination (about/as to/concerning/of/on/regarding)
	arrive at (a/the) resolution (about/as to/concerning/of/on/regarding)
	arrive at (a/the) settlement (about/as to/concerning/of/on/regarding)
	arrive at (an/the) opinion (about/as to/concerning/of/on/regarding)
	arrive at (an/the) understanding (about/as to/concerning/of/on/regarding)
	come to a/the compromise (about/as to/concerning/of/on/regarding)
	come to a/the conclusion (about/as to/concerning/of/on/regarding)
	come to a/the decision (about/as to/concerning/of/on/regarding)
	come to a/the determination (about/as to/concerning/of/on/regarding)
	come to an accord (about/as to/concerning/of/on/regarding)
	come to an agreement (about/as to/concerning/of/on/regarding)
	come to an/the opinion (about/as to/concerning/of/on/regarding)
	come to an/the understanding
	come to a/the resolution (about/as to/concerning/of/on/regarding)
	come to a/the settlement (about/as to/concerning/of/on/regarding)
	form (a/the) judgment (about/as to/concerning/of/on/regarding)
	form (a/the) resolution (about/as to/concerning/of/on/regarding)

CONCISE	WORDY
	form (an/the) opinion (about/as to/concerning/of/on/regarding)
	make (a/the) decision/determination (about/as to/concerning/of/on/regarding)
	make (a/the) determined decision (about/as to/concerning/of/on/regarding)
	reach (an/the) accord (about/of/on/upon/with)
	reach (an/the) agreement (about/of/on/upon/with)
	reach (a/the) compromise (about/of/on/upon/with)
	reach (a/the) conclusion (about/of/on/upon/with)
	reach (a/the) decision (about/of/on/upon/with)
	reach (a/the) determination (about/of/on/upon/with)
	reach (a/the) resolution (about/of/on/upon/with)
	reach (a/the) settlement (about/of/on/upon/with)
	reach (an/the) opinion (about/of/on/upon/with)
	reach (an/the) understanding (about/of/on/upon/with)
	sticktoitiveness
resolved	bound and determined
resources	financial/monetary resources
respect	place/put a premium on/upon
	place/put a priority on/upon
	place/put a value on/upon
	positive feelings
respecting	about/concerning/in/on/regarding the matter/subject of
	as . . . apply to
	as concerns
	as/so far as . . . (goes/is concerned)
	as regards
	in (the) . . . case (of)
	in connection with
	in point of
	in reference to
	in regard to
	in relation to
	in respect of/to
	insofar as . . . (goes/is concerned)
	in terms of
	in the area of
	in the realm of
	when it comes to
	where . . . is concerned
	with reference to
	with regard to
	with relation to

CONCISE	WORDY
	with respect to
respects	is respectful of/toward
respond	respond back
responsible for	charge with the responsibility for/of
rest	remainder
	rest up
restore	restore back
restrict	place/put restrictions on/upon
	place/put under obligation
	under obligation
restricts	is restrictive in/to
rests on	is based on/upon
	is founded on/upon
result	come about
	come into play
	come to pass
	consequence
	end/final/net/ultimate result
	eventuate
	materialize
	resultant
	resultant effect
result from	attributable to
resulting from	(a/the) consequence of
	ascribable to
result of	consequence/effect/outcome resulting from
results from	is a consequence of
	is a result of
resume	resume again
retreat	retreat back
return	return back
reuse	reuse again
reveal	bring attention to
	bring into the open
	bring to . . . attention (of)
	bring to light
	call . . . attention to
	call to . . . attention (of)
	concentrate (media/people's/public) attention on/upon
	direct . . . attention to
	draw attention to
	focus (media/people's/public) attention on/upon
reveals	(just) goes to show
	is evidence of/that

CONCISE	WORDY
	is proof of/that
	is revealing of
	reverse back
revert	revert back
review	take under advisement
	take under consideration
reward	compensation
	remuneration
right	the case
	the situation/with
right away	at/in the blink of an eye
	at your earliest convenience
	expeditiously
	in a timely fashion/manner/way
	in no time (at all)
	in quick/short order
	on a timely basis
rising	on the increase
	on the rise
rivals	is (the) equal to
	is (the) equivalent of/to
	is identical to/with
	is tantamount to
ROM	ROM memory
rooms	accommodations
root	root cause
roughly	(for) approximately
	(an) estimated
	(something/somewhere) in the area (of)
	(something/somewhere) in the nature (of)
	(something/somewhere) in the neighborhood (of)
	(something/somewhere) in the . . . range (of)
	(something/somewhere) in the realm (of)
	(something/somewhere) in the region (of)
	(something/somewhere) in the vicinity (of)
	(something/somewhere) on the order (of)
route	course of action
	plan of action/attack/battle
routine	day-to-day routine
	matter-of-course
	regular routine
	routine procedure
routinely	as a matter of course
	day in (and) day out

CONCISE	WORDY
	for ever and a day
	year in (and) year out
ruin	level to the ground
	raze to the ground
ruins	is destructive of/to
	is ruinous to
rules	rules and regulations
rumor	baseless/groundless/unfounded/unsubstantiated rumor
	unconfirmed/unfounded/unsubstantiated rumor
run	proceed
running	in operation
	make (my) way
	operational

S

-s	has the effect of -ing
-'s	associated with
	-based
	based in
	connected with
	on . . . part
	on the part of
	that/those of
	the . . . of
sad	in a bad mood
sadly	alas and alack
	sad to relate/say
salient	(a/the) high degree (of)
	(a/the) high level (of)
same	selfsame
(the) same	(an) identical/identically match
	exact/exactly duplicate
	exact/exactly equivalent
	exact/exactly identical
	exact/exactly match
	exact/exactly (the) same
	identical/identically (the) same
	perfect/perfectly match
sanction	voice approval of
	voice support for
satiric	satirical

CONCISE	WORDY
satisfaction	full satisfaction
save	save and except
savor	derive enjoyment from
	derive pleasure from
	derive satisfaction from
	take enjoyment in
	take pleasure in
	take satisfaction in
saw	old saw
say	according to
	(for) approximately
	as . . . for example/for instance
	for example/for instance
	hold (to) the opinion (that)
	hold (to) the view (that)
	in the assessment of
	in the estimation of
	in the judgment of
	in the opinion of
	in the view of
	indicate
	input
	make (a/the) statement saying/stating
	relate (to)
	say, for example/for instance
	take the position (that)
	take the view (that)
	vocalize
saying	(something) to that/the/this effect (that)
	old saying
say no	respond in the negative
says	is inclined to believe (that)
	is inclined to think (that)
	is of the belief (that)
	is of the opinion (that)
	is of the view (that)
say yes	respond in the affirmative
scant	(a/the) absence of
	few and far between
	few/small in number
	in short supply
	insufficient
	(a/the) lack of
	(very) limited

CONCISE	WORDY
	(a/the) limited number of
	(a/the) limited selection (of)
	minimal
	(a/the) minimum (of)
scanty	few and far between
	few/small in number
	(very) limited
	(a/the) limited number of
	(a/the) limited selection (of)
scarce	few and far between
	few/small in number
	in short supply
	(very) limited
scarcely	by no means
scarcely any (of)	(a/the) minimal number (of)
	(a/the) minority (of)
	(a/the) small/tiny amount/degree/part/percentage/ portion/proportion/quantity (of)
	(a/the) small/tiny fraction (of)
	(a/the) small/tiny minority (of)
	(a/the) small/tiny number (of)
scare	frightening scare
scatter	scatter in all/every direction(s)
scattered	few and far between
scheme	action/attack/battle/game plan
	course of action
	plan of action/attack/battle
school	educational institution
	facility
	institution
	institution of higher learning
scold	take to task
scope	breadth and depth
	magnitude
scores (of)	(an) array of
	(a/the) broad/extensive/great/vast/wide array of
	(a/the) broad/extensive/great/vast/wide range of
	(a/the) broad/extensive/great/vast/wide spectrum of
	(a/the) broad/extensive/great/vast/wide variety of
	(a/the) considerable/good/great/huge/large/ overwhelming/sizable/vast number (of)
	(a/the) considerable/good/great/huge/large/sizable/vast quantity (of)

CONCISE	WORDY
	(a/the) diversity of different
	(a/the) high number (of)
	in big/great/high/huge/large/overwhelming/sizable/vast numbers
	in great/large quantities
	(a/a fair/any) number (of)
	(a) range of
	(a/the) significant/substantial number (of)
	(a/the) significant/substantial quantity (of)
	(a/the) spectrum of
	(a) variety of
	(a/the) variety of different
	various different
	(many) widely varying
scorns	is contemptuous of
	is scornful of
scream	scream and yell
	yell and scream
scrutiny	close scrutiny
search for	cast about for
searching	in pursuit of
seclude	separate out
second	for another (thing)
	in the next place
	in the second place
	next of all
	second of all
	secondarily
	secondly
see	check to see
	experience
	look/observe to see
	observe
	pay attention to
	pay heed to
	take cognizance of
	take note of
	take notice of
seek	cast about for
	seek out
seeking	in pursuit of
seem (to)	on its (the) face (of it/of things)
	on the surface (of it/of things)
	to all appearances

CONCISE	WORDY
seeming	what appears/seems to be
seemingly	on its (the) face (of it/of things)
	on the surface (of it/of things)
	to all appearances
sees	is aware of/that
	is cognizant of/that
	is conscious of/that
	is mindful of/that
	is (a) witness to
seesaw	seesaw back and forth/up and down
segregate	separate out
seize	apprehend
	take delivery of/on
	take (a) hold of
	take into custody
	take possession of
seldom	few and far between
select	pick and choose
	select out
semen	seminal fluid
seminal	most important
sense	experience
separate	(five/many/several) separate
	separate and apart
	separate and autonomous
	separate and discrete
	separate and distinct
	separate and independent
	separate and individual
	separate apart
	separate entity
	separate individual
	separate out
separate (from)	in isolation (from)
serve	serve up
set	implement
set up	establish
	in operation
	institute
	put together
settle	arrive at (an/the) accord (about/as to/concerning/of/on/ regarding)
	arrive at (an/the) agreement (about/as to/concerning/of/ on/regarding)

CONCISE	WORDY
	arrive at (a/the) compromise (about/as to/concerning/of/ on/regarding)
	arrive at (a/the) conclusion (about/as to/concerning/of/ on/regarding)
	arrive at (a/the) decision (about/as to/concerning/of/on/ regarding)
	arrive at (a/the) determination (about/as to/concerning/ of/on/regarding)
	arrive at (an/the) opinion (about/as to/concerning/of/on/ regarding)
	arrive at (a/the) resolution (about/as to/concerning/of/on/ regarding)
	arrive at (a/the) settlement (about/as to/concerning/of/ on/regarding)
	arrive at (an/the) understanding (about/as to/concerning/ of/on/regarding)
	bring (to) a close (to)
	bring (to) a completion (to)
	bring (to) a conclusion (to)
	bring (to) a halt (to)
	bring (to) an end (to)
	bring to a standstill
	call a halt to
	call an end to
	call a stop to
	come to a/the compromise (about/as to/concerning/of/ on/regarding)
	come to a/the conclusion (about/as to/concerning/of/on/ regarding)
	come to a/the decision (about/as to/concerning/of/on/ regarding)
	come to a/the determination (about/as to/concerning/of/ on/regarding)
	come to an accord (about/as to/concerning/of/on/ regarding)
	come to an agreement (about/as to/concerning/of/on/ regarding)
	come to an/the opinion (about/as to/concerning/of/on/ regarding)
	come to an/the understanding
	come to a/the resolution (about/as to/concerning/of/on/ regarding)
	come to a/the settlement (about/as to/concerning/of/on/ regarding)

CONCISE	WORDY
	come to terms (about/as to/concerning/of/on/regarding)
	form (a/the) judgment (about/as to/concerning/of/on/ regarding)
	form (an/the) opinion (about/as to/concerning/of/on/ regarding)
	form (a/the) resolution (about/as to/concerning/of/on/ regarding)
	put a halt to
	put an end to
	put a stop to
	reach (an/the) accord (about/of/on/upon/with)
	reach (an/the) agreement (about/of/on/upon/with)
	reach (a/the) compromise (about/of/on/upon/with)
	reach (a/the) conclusion (about/of/on/upon/with)
	reach (a/the) decision (about/of/on/upon/with)
	reach (a/the) determination (about/of/on/upon/with)
	reach (an/the) opinion (about/of/on/upon/with)
	reach (a/the) resolution (about/of/on/upon/with)
	reach (a/the) settlement (about/of/on/upon/with)
	reach (an/the) understanding (about/of/on/upon/with)
settlement	final/ultimate settlement
several	multiple
	(a/a fair/any) number (of)
	some but not all
several times	on a number of /any number of/frequent/many/ numerous/several occasions
	on more than one occasion
	on one/two/three occasion(s)
shaken	shaken up
shall	is going to
shape	bring into being/existence
	call into being/existence
	come up with
	put together
share	both share
	have/possess . . . in common
	share (a/the) common
	share . . . in common/with
	share together
shelters	is protective against (of)
shields	is protective against (of)
shop	establishment
short	(very) limited
	minimal

CONCISE	WORDY
	short and sweet
	short and to the point
short-term	in/over the near term
	in/over the short run
	in/over the short term
	over the short haul
shortest	(a/the) minimum (of)
shortly	(after/for/in/over/within) a brief/limited/little/short amount of time/length of time/ moment of time/period/period of time/span of time/time/while
	(after/for/in/over/within) a reasonable amount of time/ length of time/period/period of time/ span of time/time/while
	at/in the blink of an eye
	at your earliest convenience
	before (very) long
	expeditiously
	in a few minutes/moments/seconds
	in a minute/moment/second
	in a timely fashion/manner/way
	in/over (the) coming days/decades/months/weeks/years
	in/over (the) days/decades/months/weeks/years ahead
	in/over (the) days/decades/months/weeks/years to come
	in no time (at all)
	in quick/short order
	in the foreseeable future
	in the immediate future
	in the (very) near future
	in the not-so-distant/not-too-distant future
	on a timely basis
	over the short haul
	presently
should	if . . . should
	if . . . were
	in case
	it is essential that
	it is imperative that
	should . . . then
should (there)	in (the) event (of/that)
	in the eventuality of (that/this)
	in the unexpected/unlikely event of/that
	on the occasion of
show	bring attention to

CONCISE	WORDY
	bring into the open
	bring to . . . attention (of)
	bring to light
	call . . . attention to
	call to . . . attention (of)
	concentrate (media/people's/public) attention on/upon
	direct . . . attention to
	draw attention to
	focus (media/people's/public) attention on/upon
	indicate
	point to the conclusion
shows	(just) goes to show
	is a demonstration of
	is an indication/indicator of
	is evidence of/that
	is indicative of
	is proof of/that
	is suggestive of
show up	make an appearance
	put in an appearance
shred	tiny/little bit
shuttle between . . . and	shuttle back and forth between . . . and
sick	sick and tired
	under the weather
sign	harbinger of the future (of things to come)
	indication
signal	(a/the) high degree (of)
	(a/the) high level (of)
	point to the conclusion
signals	is an indication/indicator of
	is indicative of
	is suggestive of
	is symptomatic of
significance	significant importance
significant	(a/the) high degree (of)
	(a/the) high level (of)
	fraught with meaning/significance
signifies	is an indication/indicator of
	is emblematic of
	is evidence of/that
	is indicative of
	is proof of/that
	is representative of
	is suggestive of

CONCISE	WORDY
	is symbolic/symbolical of
	is symptomatic of
signify	point to the conclusion
similar (to)	along the lines of
	along the same line
	in a/the fashion/manner/way characteristic of
	in a/the fashion/manner/way similar to
	in a similar fashion/manner/way (to)
	in the nature of
	on the order of
	other similar
similarly	along the same line
	by the same token
	in like fashion/manner
similarly (to)	in a/the fashion/manner/way characteristic of
	in a/the fashion/manner/way similar to
	in a similar fashion/manner/way (to)
simple	plain and simple
	pure and simple
	pure (and) unadulterated
	simple (and) fundamental
simplify	facilitate
simply	just simply
	simply and solely
simultaneously	simultaneously . . . at the same time
since	about the fact that
	as a consequence of the fact that
	as a result of the fact that
	attributable to the fact that
	based on the fact that
	because of the fact that
	being (as/as how/that)
	by reason of the fact that
	by the fact that
	by/in virtue of the fact that
	considering the fact that
	due to the fact that
	forasmuch as
	for the (simple) reason that
	from (a/the) . . . aspect (of)
	from . . . on/onward
	from (a/the) . . . perspective (of)
	from (a/the) . . . point of view (of)
	from (a/the) . . . standpoint (of)

CONCISE	WORDY
	from that day/moment/point/time (forward/on/onward)
	from the fact that
	from the time of ... (on)
	from (a/the) ... viewpoint (of)
	given the fact that
	inasmuch/insomuch as
	in consequence of the fact that
	in consideration of the fact that
	in (the) days/decades/months/weeks/years since
	in (the) light of the fact that
	in the sense that
	insofar as
	in view of the fact that
	on account of the fact that
	on (the) grounds that
	on the basis of the fact that
	over the fact that
	owing to the fact that
	seeing (as/as how/that)
	(ever) since that time
	(ever) since then
	since ... then
	what with
since (then)	from that day/moment/point/time (forward/on/onward)
	in (the) days/decades/months/weeks/years since
	(ever) since that time
	subsequently
	subsequent to (that/this)
(a) single	(a) single one
	(a) single solitary (one)
	one single
singular	in a class by herself/itself
	one-of-a-kind
	(something) out of the ordinary
	without equal
	without peer
sink	sink down
site	locality
six	half (a) dozen
sizable	(a/the) high degree (of)
	(a/the) high level (of)
size	magnitude
sketch	come up with
	rough sketch

CONCISE	WORDY
skills	skill set
skirt	skirt around
slight	(very) limited
	minimal
slightest	(a/the) minimum (of)
slightly	by (a/the) little/narrow/nominal/slender/slight/slim/ small/tiny margin
	(a) little bit
slowly	bit by bit
	little by little
small	(very) limited
	small-size(d)
smallest	minimal
	(a/the) minimum (of)
(feels) smooth/rough	(feels) smooth/rough to the touch
so	accordingly
	and so
	and so as a result
	as a consequence
	as a result
	consequently
	for that/this reason
	in consequence
	in order that
	in such a fashion/manner/way so/so that
	in such a fashion/manner/way that
	in that/this fashion/manner/way
	in the same fashion/manner/way (as/that)
	of such
	so consequently
	so therefore
	that/this being the case
	the case
	the situation/with
	therefore
	to such a degree
	to such an extent
	to that/this degree/extent
so (that)	to a/the point/stage that/when/where
	with the result (that)
so as to	as a means for/of/to (-ing)
	as a way for/of/to (-ing)
	as the basis for (-ing)
	by way of (-ing)

CONCISE	WORDY
	for . . . purposes (of)
	for the purpose of (-ing)
	for the sake of
	in order to
	in such a fashion/manner/way as to/so as to
	in the interest of (-ing)
	in the support of (-ing)
	with a/the thought of/to (-ing)
	with a/the view of/to (-ing)
	with the intent of -ing (to)
	with the purpose of -ing
so as to be	by way of being
so far	to such a degree
	to such an extent
	to that/this degree/extent
	up till/until that/this juncture/juncture in time/moment/ moment in time/period/period in time/point/point in time/stage/stage in time/time
	up to that/this juncture/juncture in time/moment/ moment in time/period/period in time/point/point in time/stage/stage in time/time
	up to the current/present (time)
so far (that)	to a/the point/stage that/when/where
so far as	inasmuch/insomuch as
	insofar as
	to the degree (that/to which)
	to the extent (that/to which)
	to the greatest/largest degree/extent
so it is	such is the case
so long as	on (the) condition (of/that)
	on (the) understanding (of/that)
so -(al)ly	in such (a/the) . . . fashion/manner/way
(only) so many	(a/the) limited number of
	(a/the) limited selection (of)
so much	to such a degree
	to such an extent
	to that/this degree/extent
so much (that)	to a/the point/stage that/when/where
so much as	inasmuch/insomuch as
	insofar as
	to the degree (that/to which)
	to the extent (that/to which)

CONCISE	WORDY
	to the greatest/largest degree/extent
so that	in order that
	in such a fashion/manner/way so/so that
	in such a fashion/manner/way that
	to a/the point/stage that/when/where
so to speak	figuratively speaking
	in a manner of speaking
	metaphorically speaking
so well	to such a degree
	to such an extent
sociologic	sociological
soda	liquid refreshment
sole	first and last
	first and only
	one and only
solely	simply and solely
solicit	solicitate
some	anything/something in the way of
	(for) approximately
	(a) certain amount of
	(a/the) . . . element (in/of/to)
	(an) estimated
	(an/a certain/some) extent of
	in certain/some cases
	in certain/some circumstances
	in certain/some instances
	in certain/some situations
	in other cases/circumstances/instances/situations
	(something/somewhere) in the area (of)
	(something/somewhere) in the nature (of)
	(something/somewhere) in the neighborhood (of)
	(something/somewhere) in the . . . range (of)
	(something/somewhere) in the realm (of)
	(something/somewhere) in the region (of)
	(something/somewhere) in the vicinity (of)
	in/on/to/with various/varying degrees/extents
	(a/the) limited number of
	(a/the) limited selection (of)
	(a) matter of
	(a/a certain/some) measure (of)
	(a/the) modicum of
	(a/a fair/any) number (of)
	(something/somewhere) on the order (of)
	some but not all

CONCISE	WORDY
	something like
	somewhere around/round
	to a certain/limited/some degree
	to a certain/limited/some extent
	to a degree
	to a greater or lesser degree/extent
	to a major or minor degree/extent
	to an extent
	to one degree/extent or another
	under certain/some circumstances/conditions
some (of)	(a/a certain/some) degree (of)
	(a/a certain/some) part (of)
	(a/a certain/some) percentage (of)
	(a/a certain/some) portion (of)
	(a/a certain/some) proportion (of)
	(a/a certain/some) quantity (of)
somebody	individual(s)
someday	as (the) days/decades/months/weeks/years go on
	as time goes on
	as time progresses (forward/on/onward)
	at a certain/any/one/some point in my history/point in my life/point in the history of my life/point in time
	at a/some future/later/subsequent date/time
	at/from/in/on/to any/each/every/some area/locale/locality/location/place/point/position/region/site/spot
	at/from/in/on/to any/each/every/some area/locale/locality/location/place/point/position/region/site/spot where
	in/over (the) coming days/decades/months/weeks/years
	in/over (the) days/decades/months/weeks/years ahead
	in/over (the) days/decades/months/weeks/years to come
	in due course/time
	in good time
	in the course of events/things/time
	in the distant future
	in/into the future
	in/over the long run
	in/over the long term
	over the long haul
	some day/time in the future
	(the) time will come when
	with the passage of time

CONCISE	WORDY
some form/kind/sort/type of	of one form/kind/sort/type or another
somehow	by one means or another
	in a way
	in/on/to/with various/varying degrees/extents
	in certain/some regards
	in certain/some respects
	in some fashion/manner/way
	of one form/kind/sort/type or another
	(in) one way or another
	somehow or other
	to a greater or lesser degree/extent
	to a major or minor degree/extent
	to one degree/extent or another
somehow or another	by one means or another
	(in) one way or another
someone	individual(s)
someplace	at/from/in/on/to any/each/every/some area/locale/locality/location/place/point/position/region/site/spot
	at/from/in/on/to any/each/every/some area/locale/locality/location/place/point/position/region/site/spot where
sometime	as (the) days/decades/months/weeks/years go on
	as time goes on
	as time progresses (forward/on/onward)
	at a certain/any/one/some point in my history/point in my life/point in the history of my life/point in time
	at a/some future/later/subsequent date/time
	at/from/in/on/to any/each/every/some area/locale/locality/location/place/point/position/region/site/spot
	at/from/in/on/to any/each/every/some area/locale/locality/location/place/point/position/region/site/spot where
	in/over (the) coming days/decades/months/weeks/years
	in/over (the) days/decades/months/weeks/years ahead
	in/over (the) days/decades/months/weeks/years to come
	in due course/time
	in good time
	in the course of events/things/time
	in the distant future
	in/into the future
	in/over the long run

CONCISE	WORDY
	in/over the long term
	over the long haul
	some day/time in the future
	(the) time will come when
	with the passage of time
sometimes	ever and anon
	every now and then
	every once in a while
	in a lot of cases/circumstances/instances/situations
	in certain/some cases
	in certain/some circumstances
	in certain/some instances
	in certain/some situations
	in other cases/circumstances/instances/situations
	it is often the case/circumstance/situation (that)
	occasionally
	once in a (great) while
	on certain/some occasions
	under certain/some circumstances/conditions
someway(s)	by one means or another
	in a way
	in certain/some regards
	in certain/some respects
	in some fashion/manner/way
	in/on/to/with various/varying degrees/extents
	of one form/kind/sort/type or another
	(in) one way or another
	somehow or other
	to a greater or lesser degree/extent
	to a major or minor degree/extent
	to one degree/extent or another
somewhat	(a/a certain/some) degree (of)
	(an/a certain/some) extent of
	in a (some) measure
	in a way
	in certain/some regards
	in certain/some respects
	in/on/to/with various/varying degrees/extents
	(a) little bit
	to a certain/limited/some degree
	to a certain/limited/some extent
	to a degree
	to a greater or lesser degree/extent
	to a major or minor degree/extent

CONCISE	WORDY
	to an extent
	to one degree/extent or another
	up to a point
somewhere	at/from/in/on/to any/each/every/some area/locale/locality/location/place/point/position/region/site/spot
	at/from/in/on/to any/each/every/some area/locale/locality/location/place/point/position/region/site/spot where
soon	(after/for/in/over/within) a brief/limited/little/short amount of time/length of time/moment of time/period/period of time/span of time/time/while
	(after/for/in/over/within) a reasonable amount of time/length of time/period/period of time/span of time/time/while
	at any minute/moment/second
	at/in the blink of an eye
	at your earliest convenience
	before (very) long
	expeditiously
	from minute/moment/second to minute/moment/second
	in a few minutes/moments/seconds
	in a minute/moment/second
	in a timely fashion/manner/way
	in/over (the) coming days/decades/months/weeks/years
	in/over (the) days/decades/months/weeks/years ahead
	in/over (the) days/decades/months/weeks/years to come
	in no time (at all)
	in quick/short order
	in the foreseeable future
	in the immediate future
	in the (very) near future
	in the not-so-distant/not-too-distant future
	on a timely basis
	over the short haul
	presently
sooner	ahead of time
	in advance
sorrowfully	alas and alack
source	original source
	root cause
spare	(very) limited
	(a/the) limited number of

CONCISE	WORDY
	(a/the) limited selection (of)
sparse	few and far between
	few/small in number
	in short supply
	(very) limited
	(a/the) limited number of
	(a/the) limited selection (of)
speak	converse
	have a conversation (about)
	make conversation
	verbalize
speak (to)	make contact (with)
speak (with)	communicate (with)
speaker	interlocutor
speaking	(in) discussion
speaking to/with	in conversation with
special	in a class by herself/itself
	one-of-a-kind
	without equal
	without peer
specialty	speciality
specifications	plans and specifications
specifics	(the) ins and (the) outs
speck	tiny/little bit
speech	communication
	verbalization
speedily	(after/for/in/over/within) a reasonable amount of time/ length of time/period/period of time/ span of time/time/while
	at/in the blink of an eye
	expeditiously
	in a timely fashion/manner/way
	in no time (at all)
	in quick/short order
	on a timely basis
sphere	breadth and depth
spot	come in contact (with)
	locality
spring	springtime
square	fair and square
stall	stall for time
stand	frame of mind
	point of view
	put up with

CONCISE	WORDY
standard	established standard
	par for the course
standpoint	frame of mind
	point of view
stands for	is emblematic of
	is representative of
	is symbolic/symbolical of
start	bring to pass
	commence
	commencement
	first begin
	first come into being
	first start
	start off/out
starting point	point of departure
startle	catch by surprise
	come as a surprise (to)
startled	taken by surprise
starve	starve to death
state	according to
	locality
	make (a/the) statement saying/stating
	vocalize
state-of-the-art	modern, state-of-the-art
status	current/present status
stay	continue to be
	continue to remain
steadfast	hard and fast
stems from	is a consequence of
	is a result of
stereotypic	stereotypical
stew (about/over)	express concern (about)
	is concerned (about)
	voice concern (about)
stews (about/over)	is afraid of/to
	is apprehensive of
	is fearful (about/of/that)
	is frightened of/to
	is in fear for/of
	is scared of/to
still	after all is said and done
	all (just) the same
	at any rate
	be that as it may

CONCISE	WORDY
	contrariwise
	despite the fact that
	in any case/event
	in spite of the fact that
	irregardless of the fact that
	irrespective of the fact that
	nevertheless
	nonetheless
	notwithstanding the fact that
	on the contrary
	regardless of the fact that
	still and all
	still continue/endure/last/persevere/persist/prevail/ remain/survive
still and all	be that as it may
	in any case/event
still more	additionally
	and . . . further/furthermore/in addition/moreover/ what's more
	as a matter of fact
	by the same token
	for that matter
	furthermore
	in addition
	in the next place
	in the second place
	in the third place
	next of all
	on top of (that/this)
stirring	in the making
stoic	stoical
stop	bring (to) a close (to)
	bring (to) a completion (to)
	bring (to) a conclusion (to)
	bring (to) a halt (to)
	bring (to) an end (to)
	bring to a standstill
	call a halt to
	call an end to
	call a stop to
	come to a close
	come to a/the conclusion (about/as to/concerning/of/on/ regarding)
	come to a halt

CONCISE	WORDY
	come to an end
	come to a standstill
	do away with
	draw to a close/end
	draw to a conclusion
	put a halt to
	put an end to
	put a stop to
	terminate
stopgap	temporary stopgap
stops	is a deterrent to
	is a hindrance to
	is an impediment to
	is an obstacle to
store	establishment
	premises
straight	consecutive
	in a row
straightaway	(after/for/in/over/within) a brief/limited/little/short amount of time/length of time/moment of time/period/period of time/span of time/time/while
	at/in the blink of an eye
	expeditiously
	in a few minutes/moments/seconds
	in a minute/moment/second
	in quick/short order
	instantaneous/instantaneously
	in the immediate future
	over the short haul
straightforward	matter-of-fact
strain	place/put a burden on/upon
	place/put a strain on/upon
	place/put stress on/upon
strange	(something) out of the ordinary
strangely	strange to relate/say
strangle	strangle to death
strategic	strategical
strategy	action/attack/battle/game plan
	course of action
	plan of action/attack/battle
strength	(with) might and main
stress	place/put stress on/upon
stressed	stressed out

CONCISE	WORDY
strict	hard and fast
striking	(a/the) high degree (of)
	(a/the) high level (of)
stronger than	in excess of
struggle with	come to grips with
	come to terms with
study	study up
subject	subject/topic area/field/matter
submit	put forth
	put forward
substance	core essence
	essential core
	substantiality
	sum/summary and substance
	(the) heart of the matter
	(the) long and (the) short
substantial	(a/the) high degree (of)
	(a/the) high level (of)
substantiate	attest to the fact (that)
substitute	substitute out
succeeding	in the aftermath of
	in the wake of
	on/upon the heels of
succinct	short and sweet
	short and to the point
succinctly	in a nutshell
succor	assistance
such	to such a degree
	to such an extent
	to that/this degree/extent
such as	along the lines of
	as . . . for example/for instance
	in the nature of
	like . . . and others/and so forth/and so on/and such/and the like/et al./etc.
	like . . . for example/for instance
	on the order of
	such as . . . and others/and so forth/and so on/and such/and the like/et al./etc./or whatever
	such as . . . for example/for instance
such that	in such a fashion/manner/way so/so that
suddenly	all of a sudden
	suddenly and without warning
suffer	experience

CONCISE	WORDY
	put up with
sufficient	good and sufficient
sufficiently	sufficient/sufficiently enough
suggest	according to
	come up with
	indicate
	point to the conclusion
	put forth
	put forward
suggesting	(something) to that/the/this effect (that)
suggests	is an indication/indicator of
	is indicative of
	is suggestive of
sum	amount/quantity/sum of cash/money
	(the) heart of the matter
	(the) long and (the) short
	sum/summary and substance
	summation
	sum total
	sum up
	total up
summary	brief/concise/short/succinct summary
	sum/summary and substance
summer	summertime
sundry	(an) array of
	(a/the) broad/extensive/great/vast/wide array of
	(a/the) broad/extensive/great/vast/wide range of
	(a/the) broad/extensive/great/vast/wide spectrum of
	(a/the) broad/extensive/great/vast/wide variety of
	(a/the) diversity of different
	(a) range of
	(a/the) spectrum of
	(a) variety of
	(a/the) variety of different
	various and sundry
	various different
	(many) widely varying
superficially	on its (the) face (of it/of things)
	on the surface (of it/of things)
	to all appearances
superimpose	superimpose one . . . on top of/over another/the other
superior	more superior
	of the first magnitude
	of the first/highest order

CONCISE	WORDY
supplies	wherewithal
supply	make available
support	go along with
	stand in support of
	substantiate
	take a stand for/in favor of/in support of
	voice approval of
	voice support for
supports	(just) goes to show
	is in favor of
	is in support of
	is supportive of
supposes	is predicated on the assumption (that)
	is under the assumption (that)
	is under the impression (that)
supposing (that)	if by way of hypothesis/supposition
sure	exactly sure
surely	beyond a/the shadow of a doubt
	to be sure
	without (a/any) doubt
	without (a) question
	without (a/any) question/shadow of a doubt
surface	become known
	come into play
	come to light
surpass	take precedence over
	catch by surprise
	come as a surprise (to)
surprised	taken by surprise
surrounded	surrounded on all sides
survive	continue in existence/to exist
surviving	still in existence
suspect	alleged suspect
swallow	swallow down
sweep	breadth and depth
swiftly	(after/for/in/over/within) a reasonable amount of time/length of time/period/period of time/span of time/time/while
	at/in the blink of an eye
	expeditiously
	in a timely fashion/manner/way
	in no time (at all)
	in quick/short order
	on a timely basis

CONCISE	WORDY
switch	switch over
symbolic	symbolical
symbolizes	is emblematic of
	is representative of
	is symbolic/symbolical of
	is typical of
symmetric	symmetrical
sympathize (with)	take pity on/upon
symptomize	symptomatize
symptomizes	is symptomatic of
synopsis	brief/concise/short/succinct synopsis
systematic	systematical
systemic	systematic
	systematical

T

tailored	custom-built
	custom-made
	custom-tailored
	made to measure
	made to order
	tailor-made
tailor-made	made to measure
	made to order
take	take delivery of/on
	take (a) hold of
	take possession of
take place	come about
	come into play
	come to pass
	eventuate
	materialize
talk	communication
	(in) conversation
	converse
	have a conversation (about)
	make conversation
	verbalization
	verbalize
talk (to)	communicate (with)
	make contact (with)

CONCISE	WORDY
talker	interlocutor
talking	(in) discussion
talking to/with	in conversation with
task	(a/the) difficult task
tax	place/put a burden on/upon
	place/put a strain on/upon
tea	liquid refreshment
tedium	tedious monotony
telepathy	mental telepathy
tell	bring attention to
	bring into the open
	bring to . . . attention (of)
	bring to light
	call . . . attention to
	call to . . . attention (of)
	concentrate (media/people's/public) attention on/upon
	direct . . . attention to
	draw attention to
	focus (media/people's/public) attention on/upon
	indicate
	inform
	relate (to)
	vocalize
tell apart	tell the difference
temporarily	for (an) indefinite/indeterminate amount of time/length of time/period/period of time/span of time/time/while
	for the foreseeable future
	for the immediate future
	for the (very) near future
	for the not-so-distant/not-too-distant future
tenacity	sticktoitiveness
tender	kinder (and) gentler
tenderness	positive feelings
tends to	has a/the habit of (-ing)
	has a/the tendency (to)
	is disposed to
	is inclined to
	is prone to
tend to	pay attention to
	pay heed to
	take cognizance of
	take note of
	take notice of

CONCISE	WORDY
(I) tend to	(my) tendency is to
tense	tense up
term	characterize as
	refer to as
	term as
termed	known as
terror	fear and trembling
terse	short and sweet
	short and to the point
tersely	in a nutshell
test	test out
testifies (to)	is an indication/indicator of
	is evidence of/that
	is proof of/that
	is indicative of
	is suggestive of
	is (a) testament to
	is (a) testimony to
	is witness to
testify to	bear witness to
text	communication
than	as compared to/with
	as contrasted to/with
	as opposed to
	by comparison to/with
	by contrast to/with
	compared to/with
	contrasted to/with
	in comparison to/with
	in contrast to/with
	in relation/relationship to
	measured against
	relative to
	when compared to/with
	when measured against
(be) thankful (for)	appreciate
thanks	grateful thanks
thankworthy	worthy of gratitude/thanks
thank you (for)	appreciate
that	(the) . . . in question
	about the fact that
	as how
	in order that
	of the fact that

CONCISE	WORDY
	over the fact that
	the above
	the fact that
that/this	that/the/this business of
	that/this fact
	that/this kind/sort/type of stuff/thing
that/those	the above-mentioned
	the aforementioned
	the aforesaid
	the foregoing
	the forenamed
that is	in other words
	in the sense of
	(to) put (it) another way
	that is/this is/which is as much as to say (that)
	that is/which is to say (that)
that/this time	that/this juncture/moment/period/point/stage in time
	that/this time around/round
the	(the) . . . in question
	the above
	the above-mentioned
	the aforementioned
	the aforesaid
	the degree of
	the extent of
	the foregoing
	the forenamed
	the state of (the . . . state)
the best	(the) one best
the best/biggest/ greatest/largest/most	(the) single best/biggest/greatest/largest/most
the case	the situation/with
the exact	the same exact
theistic	theistical
theme	subject/topic area/field/matter
then	accordingly
	additionally
	after the event/incident/occurrence
	and . . . further/furthermore/in addition/moreover/ what's more
	and so as a result
	as a consequence
	as a matter of fact
	as a result

CONCISE	WORDY
	at that/this juncture
	at that/this juncture/juncture in time/moment/moment in time/period/period in time/point/point in time/stage/stage in time/time in my history/in my life/in the history of my life
	at that/this juncture/moment/period/point/stage in time
	at that/this moment
	at that/this point
	at that/this stage
	at that/this time
	by the same token
	consequently
	for that/this reason
	for that matter
	furthermore
	in addition
	in consequence
	in that/this case/circumstance/instance/situation
	in that/this day and age
	on that/this (particular) occasion
	on top of (that/this)
	(then) . . . proceed (to)
	so consequently
	so therefore
	subsequently
	subsequent to (that/this)
	that/this being the case
	that/this juncture/moment/period/point/stage in time
	then and only then
	then at that/this juncture/juncture in time/moment/moment in time/period/period of time/point/point in time/stage/stage in time/time
	then subsequently
	thereafter
	therefore
	thereupon
then (now)	that/this time around/round
theocratic	theocratical
theologic	theological
the opposite	the other way around/round
theoretic	theoretical
the present	(the) here and now

CONCISE	WORDY
	the present day
the present's	the present-day
therapeutic	therapeutical
there	in that/this case/circumstance/instance/situation
	therein
thereabouts/hereabouts	in that/this general vicinity
therefore	accordingly
	and so as a result
	as a consequence
	as a result
	consequently
	for that/this reason
	in consequence
	so consequently
	so therefore
	that/this being the case
the reverse	the other way around/round
the same	one and the same
	the same exact
	the same thing
the same as	in the same fashion/manner/way (as/that)
	just the same as
these days	at (the) present
	at that/this juncture/juncture in time/moment/moment in time/period/period in time/point/ point in time/stage/stage in time/time in my history/in my life/in the history of my life
	at that/this juncture/moment/period/point/stage in time
	at that/this moment
	at that/this point
	at that/this stage
	at that/this time
	at the current/present time
	at the (current/present) moment
	the present day
these/those days	in that/this day and age
the time	the length of time
the truth	(a/the) true fact
	true to fact
thick	in thickness
think	hold (to) the opinion (that)
	hold (to) the view (that)
	in the assessment of

CONCISE	WORDY
	in the estimation of
	in the judgment of
	in the opinion of
	in the view of
	take the position (that)
	take the view (that)
	think to myself
thinkable	in/within the realm of possibility
think about	take under advisement
	take under consideration
thinking	rationale
	thinking in (my) mind
thinks	is inclined to believe (that)
	is inclined to think (that)
	is of the belief (that)
	is of the opinion (that)
	is of the view (that)
	is under the assumption (that)
	is under the impression (that)
third	in the third place
	thirdly
	third of all
this	the above
	(of) the present . . .
	(the) . . . in question
	this coming
this (these)	the above-mentioned
	the aforementioned
	the aforesaid
	the foregoing
	the forenamed
this month/year	in the foreseeable future
	in the immediate future
	in the (very) near future
	in/over the near term
	in the not-so-distant/not-too-distant future
	in/over the short run
	in/over the short term
	over the short haul
thoroughly	backward and forward
	from beginning to end
	from start to finish
	inside (and) out
	through and through

CONCISE	WORDY
	throughout the length and breadth (of)
those	individual(s)
	those individuals/people/persons
though	albeit
	despite the fact that
	in spite of the fact that
	irregardless of the fact that
	irrespective of the fact that
	notwithstanding the fact that
	regardless of the fact that
thoughts	input
thousands (of)	(a/the) considerable/good/great/huge/large/overwhelming/sizable/vast number (of)
	(a/the) considerable/good/great/huge/large/sizable/vast quantity (of)
	(a/the) high number (of)
	in big/great/high/huge/large/overwhelming/sizable/vast numbers
	in great/large quantities
	(a/the) multiplicity of
	(a/the) multitude of
	multitudinous
	(a/the) significant/substantial number (of)
	(a/the) significant/substantial quantity (of)
three	(a) couple three/two/two or three
three-fourths/two-thirds (of)	(a/the) considerable/good/great/huge/large/overwhelming/sizable/vast/wide majority (of)
	(a/the) considerable/good/great/huge/large/sizable/vast part (of)
	(a/the) considerable/good/great/huge/large/overwhelming/sizable/vast percentage (of)
	(a/the) considerable/good/great/huge/large/sizable/vast portion (of)
	(a/the) considerable/good/great/huge/large/sizable/vast proportion (of)
	(a/the) great/large fraction (of)
	(a/the) high percentage (of)
	(a/the) high proportion (of)
	(a/the) large/overwhelming/sizable/vast plurality (of)
	(a/the) majority (of)
	(a/the) major part/percentage/portion/proportion (of)
	most but not all

CONCISE	WORDY
	(a/the) overwhelming/vast preponderance (of)
	(a/the) plurality (of)
	(a/the) significant/substantial fraction (of)
	(a/the) significant/substantial majority (of)
	(a/the) significant/substantial part (of)
	(a/the) significant/substantial percentage (of)
	(a/the) significant/substantial portion (of)
	(a/the) significant/substantial proportion (of)
three times	on one/two/three occasion(s)
throng	huge (large) throng
through	as a consequence of
	as a result of
	at the hands of
	based on/upon
	because of
	by consequence of
	by (the) means of
	by reason of
	by the result of
	by/in virtue of
	by (the) way of
	for reasons of
	in consequence of
	in consideration of (payment of/sum of)
	in reaction to
	in response to
	in terms of
	in the direction of/toward
	in the middle of
	in the midst of
	on account of
	on the basis of
	through the medium of
	through the use of
	up to and including
through (-ing)	by way of (-ing)
through being	by way of being
throughout	during the course/length of
	extensively throughout
	for the duration/length of
	from beginning to end
	from start to finish
	(somewhere) in the course of
	in (the) time(s) of

CONCISE	WORDY
	over the course/duration/length of
	through and through
	throughout . . . entire/whole
	through/throughout the course/duration/length of
	throughout the length and breadth (of)
thus	accordingly
	and so as a result
	as a consequence
	as a result
	consequently
	for that/this reason
	in consequence
	in that/this fashion/manner/way
	so consequently
	so therefore
	that/this being the case
	therefore
	thusly
thus far	up till/until that/this juncture/juncture in time/moment/ moment in time/period/period in time/point/point in time/stage/stage in time/time
	up to that/this juncture/juncture in time/moment/ moment in time/period/period in time/point/point in time/stage/stage in time/time
	up to the current/present (time)
thwart	stand in the way of
thwarts	is a deterrent to
	is a hindrance to
	is an impediment to
	is an obstacle to
tidy	neat and tidy
tie	association
	relationship
till	unless and/or until
	until and/or unless
till/until	till/until after
	till/until the juncture/juncture in time/moment/moment in time/period/period in time/point/ point in time/stage/stage in time/time (that/when)
	till/until . . . then
	up till/until

CONCISE	WORDY
till/until lately	till/until the recent past
till now	up to the current/present (time)
till now/then	up to that/this juncture/juncture in time/moment/moment in time/period/period in time/point/point in time/stage/stage in time/time
till/until now/then	up till/until that/this juncture/juncture in time/moment/moment in time/period/period in time/point/point in time/stage/stage in time/time
till/until of late	till/until the recent past
till/until recently	till/until the recent past
time	(a/the) . . . amount of time/length of time/period of time/span of time
	(the) passage of time
	(a/the) time frame (of)
	(a/the) time horizon (of)
	(a/the) time interval (of)
	time of day
	(a/the) time period (of)
	(a/the) time span (of)
timely	in a timely fashion/manner/way
	on a timely basis
tiniest	(a/the) minimum (of)
tiny	(a/the) modicum of
	tiny little
tired	sick and tired
title	appellation
	entitle
to	about/concerning/in/on/regarding the matter/subject of
	about (around) . . . to
	according to
	as against
	as a means for/of/to (-ing)
	as . . . apply to
	as a way for/of/to (-ing)
	as compared to/with
	as concerns
	as contrasted to/with
	as/so far as . . . (goes/is concerned)
	as opposed to
	as regards
	as the basis for (-ing)

CONCISE	WORDY
	as to
	by comparison to/with
	by contrast to/with
	by way of (-ing)
	compared to/with
	concerning
	contrasted to/with
	(the) decade/period/period of time/span of time/time/ years between . . . and
	(the) decade/period/period of time/span of time/time/ years (from) . . . through/till/to/until
	for . . . purposes (of)
	for the purpose of (-ing)
	for the sake of
	from (a/the) . . . aspect (of)
	from (a/the) . . . perspective (of)
	from (a/the) . . . point of view (of)
	from (a/the) . . . standpoint (of)
	from (a/the) . . . viewpoint (of)
	hold (to) the opinion (that)
	hold (to) the view (that)
	in accord/accordance with
	in agreement with
	in (the) . . . case (of)
	in comparison to/with
	in compliance with
	in conformance to/with
	in conformity to/with
	in connection with
	in consonance to/with
	in contrast to/with
	in correspondence to/with
	in honor of
	in order to
	in point of
	in reference to
	in regard to
	in relation/relationship to
	in relation to
	in respect of/to
	insofar as . . . (goes/is concerned)
	in such a fashion/manner/way as to/so as to
	in the area of

CONCISE	WORDY
	in the assessment of
	in the direction of/toward
	in the estimation of
	in the interest of (-ing)
	in the judgment of
	in the opinion of
	(something/somewhere) in the range from (of) . . . through/to
	in the realm of
	in the support of (-ing)
	in the . . . through/to . . . range
	in the view of
	is inclined to believe (that)
	is inclined to think (that)
	is of the belief (that)
	is of the opinion (that)
	is of the view (that)
	measured against
	pertain/pertaining to
	regard/regarding
	relate/relating to
	relative to
	so as to
	take the position (that)
	take the view (that)
	to a/the point of
	to a/the point/stage that/when/where
	to be
	to make (a/the) . . . (about/of/on/with)
	when compared to/with
	when it comes to
	when measured against
	where . . . is concerned
	with a/the thought of/to (-ing)
	with a/the view of/to (-ing)
	with reference to
	with regard to
	with relation to
	with respect to
	with the intent of -ing (to)
	with the purpose of -ing
to advance	for (in/to) (the) furtherance of
	in furtherance of
	in partial fulfillment of

CONCISE	WORDY
to be	by way of being
to complete	in fulfillment of
to date	up till/until that/this juncture/juncture in time/moment/moment in time/period/period in time/point/point in time/stage/stage in time/time
	up to that/this juncture/juncture in time/moment/moment in time/period/period in time/point/point in time/stage/stage in time/time
	up to the current/present (time)
today	at (the) present
	at that/this juncture
	at that/this juncture/juncture in time/moment/moment in time/period/period in time/point/point in time/stage/stage in time/time in my history/in my life/in the history of my life
	at that/this juncture/moment/period/point/stage in time
	at that/this moment
	at that/this point
	at that/this stage
	at that/this time
	at the current/present time
	at the (current/present) moment
	currently
	in that/this day and age
	on that/this (particular) occasion
	presently
	the present day
today's	the present-day
to finish	in fulfillment of
to foster	for (in/to) (the) furtherance of
to fulfill	in fulfillment of
to further	for (in/to) (the) furtherance of
	in furtherance of
	in partial fulfillment of
together	at the same time
	both together
	concurrently
	in conjunction
	simultaneously
	together as a team/unit
	together . . . in combination

CONCISE	WORDY
	together . . . in groups
together with	accompanied by
	in association with
	in combination with
	in company with
	in conjunction with
	in connection with
to help	in furtherance of
	in partial fulfillment of
toilet	bathroom facilities
	comfort facilities
to illustrate	by way of example/illustration
tolerant	kinder (and) gentler
	put up with
to -(al)ly	to make (a/the) . . . (about/of/on/with)
to me	based on/upon my personal judgment/opinion
	in my assessment
	in my estimation
	in my judgment
	in my opinion
	in my view
tomorrow	in the foreseeable future
	in the immediate future
	in the (very) near future
	in the not-so-distant/not-too-distant future
	over the short haul
too	additionally
	also . . . too
	and . . . further/furthermore/in addition/moreover/ what's more
	and . . . too
	as a matter of fact
	by the same token
	for that matter
	furthermore
	in addition
	in the next place
	in the second place
	in the third place
	next of all
	on top of (that/this)
too few	insufficient
	(a/the) insufficient number (of)
too little	insufficient

CONCISE	WORDY
	(a/the) insufficient amount (of)
too many	(a/the) excessive number (of)
too much	(a/the) excessive amount (of)
too soon	ahead of schedule
top	maximal
	(a/the) maximum amount (of)
	(a/the) maximum number (of)
	(a/the) maximum . . . of
topic	subject/topic area/field/matter
to promote	for (in/to) (the) furtherance of
to satisfy	in fulfillment of
to some degree/extent	in/on/to/with various/varying degrees/extents
	to a greater or lesser degree/extent
	to a major or minor degree/extent
	to one degree/extent or another
total	add together
	summation
	sum total
	sum up
	total up
totally	backward and forward
	from beginning to end
	from start to finish
	through and through
	throughout the length and breadth (of)
totals	amounts to
to that/this end	(in order) to accomplish/achieve that/this aim/end/goal/ objective
to the point	short and to the point
to try to	in an attempt/effort/endeavor to
	in an attempt/effort/endeavor to try to
touch	come in contact (with)
toward	about/concerning/in/on/regarding the matter/subject of
	as . . . apply to
	as concerns
	as/so far as . . . (goes/is concerned)
	as regards
	concerning
	in (the) . . . case (of)
	in connection with
	in furtherance of
	in partial fulfillment of
	in point of
	in reference to

CONCISE	WORDY
	in regard to
	in relation to
	in respect of/to
	insofar as . . . (goes/is concerned)
	in the area of
	in the direction of/toward
	in the realm of
	pertain/pertaining to
	regard/regarding
	relate/relating to
	toward the direction of
	when it comes to
	where . . . is concerned
	with reference to
	with regard to
	with relation to
	with respect to
toward that/this	in that/this direction
toward that/this end	(in order) to accomplish/achieve that/this aim/end/goal/ objective
to when	to a/the point/stage that/when/where
to where	to a/the point/stage that/when/where
to wit	in other words
	(to) put (it) another way
	that is/this is/which is as much as to say (that)
	that is/which is to say (that)
town	locality
trace	residual trace
	slight trace
	tiny/little bit
	trace amount
	trace back
tradition	established tradition
tragic	tragical
transcend	take precedence over
transpire	become known
	come to light
transvestism	transvestitism
treasure	place/put a premium on/upon
	place/put a priority on/upon
	place/put a value on/upon
treasures	has (an/the) appreciation for
	is appreciative of
trembling	fear and trembling

CONCISE	WORDY
trifle	(a/the) modicum of
trivia	trivial details/facts/ideas/information/matters/things
true	the case
	the situation/with
	(a/the) true fact
	true to fact
truly	as a matter of fact
	(the) fact is (that)
	(the) (simple) fact of the matter is (that)
	honestly and truly/truthfully
	(the) honest truth
	in actual fact
	in actuality
	in point of fact
	in reality
	really (and) truly
	(the) truth is (that)
	(the) truth of the matter is (that)
trust	expect/expectation and hope
	hope and expect/expectation
	positive feelings
trusts	is hopeful
	is trustful of
trustworthy	worthy of trust
truth	basis in fact/reality/truth
	factual basis
	(a/the) real fact
(the) truth	(the) honest truth
truthful	(a/the) true fact
	true to fact
truthfully	honestly and truly/truthfully
	(the) honest truth
	to tell (you) the truth
try	attempt
	endeavor
	make an attempt/effort/endeavor
tube	hollow tube
turn up	come into play
twice	on a couple of/a few occasions
	on one/two/three occasion(s)
twins	(a) pair of twins
	two twins
two	(a) couple of
	(a) couple three (two/two or three)

CONCISE	WORDY
two or three	(a) couple three (two/two or three)
two or three times	on a couple of/a few occasions
two times	on one/two/three occasion(s)
typical	matter-of-course
	par for the course
	run of the mill
typically	as a general rule
	as a matter of course
	as a rule
	as often as not
	by and large
	for the most part
	in great/large measure
	in great/large part
	in many/most cases
	in many/most circumstances
	in many/most instances
	in many/most situations
	in normal/ordinary/typical/usual practice
	in no small measure
	in no small part
	in the main
	in the normal/ordinary/typical/usual course of business/ events/things
	more often than not
	most (of the) time(s)
	on (an/the) average
	on/upon the whole
	to a great/large degree
	to a great/large extent
typifies	is emblematic of
	is reflective of
	is representative of
	is symbolic/symbolical of
	is typical of

U

ubiquitous	present everywhere
ultimately	after all is said and done
	as (the) days/decades/months/weeks/years go on
	as time goes on

CONCISE	WORDY
	as time progresses (forward/on/onward)
	at a/some future/later/subsequent date/time
	at the end of the day
	(after/for/in/over/within) (an) extended/lengthy/long/ prolonged/protracted amount of time/length of time/period/period of time/span of time/time/while in/into the future
	in/over (the) coming days/decades/months/weeks/years
	in/over (the) days/decades/months/weeks/years ahead
	in/over (the) days/decades/months/weeks/years to come
	in the course of events/things/time
	in the distant future
	in the final/last analysis
	in/over the long run
	in/over the long term
	later in time
	later on down the line/pike/road/way
	over the long haul
	some day/time in the future
	sooner or later
	(the) time will come when
	when all is said and done
	with the passage of time
un-	(a/the) absence of
	devoid of
	insufficient
	lacking in
	(a/the) lack of
	less than (enthusiastic)
unadulterated	pure (and) unadulterated
unanimous	completely/entirely/fully/thoroughly/totally/utterly/ wholly unanimous
unanswered	up in the air
unavoidably	must necessarily/of necessity
uncertain	(an/the) open question
	open to question
	question mark
	up in the air
unclear	(an/the) open question
	open to question
	up in the air
uncommon	few/small in number
	few and far between

CONCISE	WORDY
	(something) out of the ordinary
uncover	bring attention to
	bring into the open
	bring to . . . attention (of)
	bring to light
	call . . . attention to
	call to . . . attention (of)
	concentrate (media/people's/public) attention on/upon
	direct . . . attention to
	draw attention to
	focus (media/people's/public) attention on/upon
undecided	(an/the) open question
	betwixt and between
	open to question
	up in the air
under	according to
	during the rule of
	in accord/accordance with
	in agreement with
	in compliance with
	in conformance to/with
	in conformity to/with
	in consonance to/with
	in correspondence to/with
	in terms of
	on the bottom of
	pursuant to
	underneath
	under the provisions of
underneath	on the bottom of
understand	come to an/the understanding (about/as to/concerning/of/on/regarding)
	come to grips with
	come to terms with
	it is important to understand
	it must/should be understood
(I) understand	it has been called to (my) attention
	it has come to (my) attention
understanding	mutual understanding
understands	has (an/the) appreciation for
	is appreciative of
	is aware of/that
	is cognizant of/that
	is conscious of/that

CONCISE	WORDY
	is knowledgeable about/in/of
	is mindful of/that
undoable	beyond/outside the realm of possibility
	out of the question
	out/outside (of) the realm of possibility
undoubtedly	beyond a/the shadow of a doubt
unencumbered	clear, free, and unencumbered
unequaled	in a class by herself/itself
	one-of-a-kind
	without equal
	without peer
unfailingly	at every turn
	day in (and) day out
	for ever and a day
	in (almost) all/every cases/circumstances/instances/ situations
	in each/every case/circumstance/instance/situation
	on each/every occasion
	without exception
	year in (and) year out
unfair	unfair and inequitable
unfavorably	in the negative
unfeasible	out/outside (of) the realm of possibility
unfeeling	matter-of-fact
unfold	come into play
unfortunately	alas and alack
unfounded	no basis in fact
	unsubstantiated
	without basis in fact
	without foundation
unhappily	alas and alack
unhappy	in a bad mood
unique	in a class by herself/itself
	one-of-a-kind
	without equal
	without peer
unite	bring together
	unite into one
	unite together
university	educational institution
	institution of higher learning
unknown	(an/the) open question
	open to question
	question mark

CONCISE	WORDY
	unbeknown/unbeknownst
unless	except when
	unless and/or until
	unless . . . then
	until and/or unless
unlike	as contrasted to/with
	as opposed to
	by contrast to/with
	contrasted to/with
	in contrast to/with
unluckily	as it turned out
	as luck would have it
	it (just) so happens
unmatched	in a class by herself/itself
	one-of-a-kind
	without equal
	without peer
unproved	unproven
unquestionably	beyond a/the shadow of a doubt
unreasonable	beyond/out of all reason
unresolved	up in the air
unrivaled	in a class by herself/itself
	one-of-a-kind
	without equal
	without peer
unsettled	(an/the) open question
	open to question
	up in the air
unsuccessful	of/to no avail
unsure	(an/the) open question
	open to question
	question mark
	up in the air
unthinkable	beyond/outside the realm of possibility
	out of the question
	out/outside (of) the realm of possibility
until	unless and/or until
	until and/or unless
	until such point/time as
until now	up to the current/present (time)
until now/then	up to that/this juncture/juncture in time/moment/ moment in time/period/period in time/point/point in time/stage/stage in time/time

CONCISE	WORDY
untold	beyond number
	(a/the) broad/extensive/great/vast/wide array of
	(a/the) broad/extensive/great/vast/wide range of
	(a/the) broad/extensive/great/vast/wide spectrum of
	(a/the) broad/extensive/great/vast/wide variety of
	(a/the) countless number (of)
	(an/the) infinite number (of)
	innumerable
	(a/the) multiplicity of
	(a/the) multitude of
	multitudinous
	numerous in number
	(an/the) untold number (of)
	without number
unused to	unaccustomed to
unusual	few and far between
	(something) out of the ordinary
unveil	bring attention to
	bring into the open
	bring to . . . attention (of)
	bring to light
	call . . . attention to
	call to . . . attention (of)
	concentrate (media/people's/public) attention on/upon
	direct . . . attention to
	draw attention to
	focus (media/people's/public) attention on/upon
	under the weather
up to	as many/much as
	to the degree/extent of
	up to a maximum of
up to now	up to the current/present (time)
up to now/then	up till/until that/this juncture/juncture in time/moment/ moment in time/period/period in time/point/point in time/stage/stage in time/time
	up to that/this juncture/juncture in time/moment/ moment in time/period/period in time/point/point in time/stage/stage in time/time
upholds	is supportive of
upsets	is of concern to
urgent	necessary
use	avail herself/themselves of

CONCISE	WORDY
	bring to bear (on/upon)
	employ
	employment
	take advantage of
	usage
	utility
	utilization
	utilize
used to	accustomed to
usefulness	utility
uses	is exploitative/exploitive of
using	the . . . use of
usual	matter-of-course
	par for the course
	run of the mill
usually	as a general rule
	as a matter of course
	as often as not
	by and large
	for the most part
	in a lot of cases/circumstances/instances/situations
	in a/the majority of cases/circumstances/instances/ situations
	in great/large measure
	in great/large part
	in many/most cases
	in many/most circumstances
	in many/most instances
	in many/most regards
	in many/most respects
	in many/most situations
	in normal/ordinary/typical/usual practice
	in no small measure
	in no small part
	in the main
	in the normal/ordinary/typical/usual course of business/ events/things
	it is often the case/circumstance/situation (that)
	more often than not
	most (of the) time(s)
	on/upon the whole
	to a great/large degree
	to a great/large extent
	usually but not always

CONCISE	WORDY
utter	complete and utter
utterly	backward and forward
	completely and utterly
	under any circumstances/conditions
	wholly and completely

V

vacillate	vacillate back and forth
valuable	(a) valuable asset
value	appreciate
	dollar value
	place/put a premium on/upon
	place/put a priority on/upon
	place/put a value on/upon
values	has (an/the) appreciation for
	is appreciative of
vantage	frame of mind
	point of view
	vantage point
varied	(an) array of
	(a/the) broad/extensive/great/vast/wide array of
	(a/the) broad/extensive/great/vast/wide range of
	(a/the) broad/extensive/great/vast/wide spectrum of
	(a/the) broad/extensive/great/vast/wide variety of
	(a/the) diversity of different
	many and varied
	(a) range of
	(a/the) spectrum of
	(a) variety of
	(a/the) variety of different
	various and sundry
	various different
	(many) widely varying
varies from	is a variant of
	is different from/than
	is distinguished from
varies with	is at loggerheads (with)
	is at odds over/with
	is at variance with
	is in conflict with
	is in disagreement (about/on/with)

CONCISE	WORDY
various	(an) array of
	(a/the) broad/extensive/great/vast/wide array of
	(a/the) broad/extensive/great/vast/wide range of
	(a/the) broad/extensive/great/vast/wide spectrum of
	(a/the) broad/extensive/great/vast/wide variety of
	(a/the) diversity of different
	in/on/to/with various/varying degrees/extents
	many and varied
	to a greater or lesser degree/extent
	to a major or minor degree/extent
	to one degree/extent or another
	(a/the) variety of different
	(a) range of
	(a/the) spectrum of
	(a) variety of
	various and sundry
	various different
	(many) widely varying
variously	in/on/to/with various/varying degrees/extents
	to a greater or lesser degree/extent
	to a major or minor degree/extent
	to one degree/extent or another
varying	(an) array of
	(a/the) broad/extensive/great/vast/wide array of
	(a/the) broad/extensive/great/vast/wide range of
	(a/the) broad/extensive/great/vast/wide spectrum of
	(a/the) broad/extensive/great/vast/wide variety of
	(a/the) diversity of different
	(a) range of
	(a/the) spectrum of
	(a) variety of
	(a/the) variety of different
	in/on/to/with various/varying degrees/extents
	to a greater or lesser degree/extent
	to a major or minor degree/extent
	to one degree/extent or another
	various and sundry
	various different
	(many) widely varying
varyingly	in/on/to/with various/varying degrees/extents
	to a greater or lesser degree/extent
	to a major or minor degree/extent
	to one degree/extent or another
vast	(a/the) broad/extensive/great/vast/wide array of

CONCISE	WORDY
	(a/the) broad/extensive/great/vast/wide range of
	(a/the) broad/extensive/great/vast/wide spectrum of
	(a/the) broad/extensive/great/vast/wide variety of
	(a/the) considerable/good/great/huge/large/sizable/vast amount (of)
	(a/the) considerable/good/great/huge/large/sizable/vast degree (of)
	(a/the) considerable/good/great/huge/large/sizable/vast element (of)
	(a/the) high degree (of)
	(a/the) high level (of)
	significant/substantial
	(a/the) significant/substantial amount (of)
	(a/the) significant/substantial degree (of)
	(a/the) significant/substantial element (of)
	substantive
vastly	considerably
	significantly/substantially
veracity	basis in fact/reality/truth
verbiage	excess verbiage
verging on	at/on the brink of
	at/on the point of
	on the threshold of
	on the verge of
verifies	(just) goes to show
	is (a) testament to
	is (a) testimony to
	is witness to
verify	bear witness to
	determine the truth/truthfulness/validity/veracity of
	substantiate
versus	as compared to/with
	as contrasted to/with
	as opposed to
	by comparison to/with
	by contrast to/with
	compared to/with
	contrasted to/with
	in comparison to/with
	in contrast to/with
	in relation/relationship to
	measured against
	relative to
	when compared to/with

CONCISE	WORDY
	when measured against
vestige	vestigial remnant
veteran	seasoned veteran
vexed	in a bad mood
vicinity	general vicinity
victimize	take advantage of
victimizes	is exploitative/exploitive of
view	frame of mind
	hold (to) the opinion (that)
	hold (to) the view (that)
	in the assessment of
	in the estimation of
	in the judgment of
	in the opinion of
	in the view of
	point of view
	take a . . . look (at)
	take a/the . . . view (of)
	take the position (that)
	take the view (that)
viewpoint	frame of mind
	point of view
views	input
VIN	VIN number
violate	fail to comply with
violates	is in violation of
virtually	for all intents and purposes
	for all practical purposes
	to all intents and purposes
	to all practical purposes
vis-à-vis	as compared to/with
	as contrasted to/with
	as opposed to
	by comparison to/with
	by contrast to/with
	contrasted to/with
	in comparison to/with
	in contrast to/with
	in relation/relationship to
	measured against
	relative to
	when compared to/with
	when measured against
visit	get in touch with

CONCISE	WORDY
	make an appearance
	make contact (with)
	pay a visit to
	put in an appearance
visualize	(to) . . . in my (own) mind's eye
vital	(of) central/critical/vital importance
	critically/crucially/vitally important
	necessary
	vital necessity
vital in/to	(a/the) vital . . . in/of/to
voice	input
	vocalize
void	null and void
vouch	according to

W

waffle	waffle back and forth
wage	compensation
	remittance
	remuneration
wait	wait around
wait and see	take a wait-and-see attitude
wait and watch	take a wait-and-see attitude
walk	proceed
walking	make (my) way
waning	on the decline
	on the decrease
want	devoid of
	lacking in
	want to have
wants	is deficient in
	is in need of
	is in want of
	is needful of
wants to	is desirous of -ing
warn	forewarn
	warn in advance
warning	advance warning
watch	pay attention to
	pay heed to
	take cognizance of

CONCISE	WORDY
	take note of
	take notice of
water	liquid refreshment
ways	ways and means
weather	weather conditions
weekly	on a regular basis
weeks	for (an) extended/prolonged/protracted amount of time/ length of time/period/period of time/ span of time/time/while
	in/over . . . days/decades/hours/minutes/months/weeks/ years time
weigh	take account for/of
	take into account
	take into consideration
	take under advisement
	take under consideration
weigh down	place/put a burden on/upon
	place/put a strain on/upon
welcome	appreciate
	(all) fine/good and well
	(all) well and fine/good
welcomes	is appreciative of
	is receptive to
weld	weld together
well	(all) fine/good and well
	hale and hearty
	to a great/large degree
	to a great/large extent
	(all) well and fine/good
were	if . . . were
were (there)	in (the) event (of/that)
	in the eventuality of (that/this)
	in the unexpected/unlikely event of/that
	on the occasion of
what	what it is (that/who)
what/whatever/which/ whichever	what/whatever/which/whichever one(s)
whatever	irregardless of
	irrespective of (what)
	no matter (what)
	regardless of (what)
	under any circumstances/conditions
	what in God's/heaven's name
	what in the world/on earth

CONCISE	WORDY
	whatsoever
what ever	what in God's/heaven's name
	what in the world/on earth
whatnot	what have you
what's more	additionally
	and . . . further/furthermore/in addition/moreover/what is more
	as a matter of fact
	by the same token
	for that matter
	in addition
	in the next place
	in the second place
	on top of (that/this)
what's worse	(to) make matters worse
when	as and when
	as, if, and when
	as soon as
	at a/the juncture/juncture in time/moment/moment in time/period/period in time/point/point in time/stage/stage in time/time
	at a/the juncture/juncture in time/moment/moment in time/period/period in time/point/point in time/stage/stage in time/time when
	at what/which juncture/juncture in time/moment/moment in time/period/period in time/point/point in time/stage/stage in time/time
	considering the fact that
	during a/the juncture/juncture in time/moment/moment in time/period/period in time/point/point in time/stage/stage in time/time when
	during the course/length of
	given the fact that
	if and/or when
	in cases/circumstances/instances/situations in which
	in cases when/where
	in circumstances when/where
	in (the) event (of/that)
	in instances when/where
	in (the) light of the fact that
	in situations when/where

CONCISE	WORDY
	(somewhere) in the course of
	in the eventuality of (that/this)
	in view of the fact that
	on the occasion of
	over the course/duration/length of
	that/which happens/occurs/takes place when
	through/throughout the course/duration/length of
	what is the time frame/time horizon/time period/time span in which (of)
	when and as
	when and/or if
	when and/or whether
	when, as, and if
	when it comes to
	when . . . then
	whether and/or when
whence	from whence
whenever	irrespective of when
	no matter when
	regardless of when
	whensoever
where	(an/the) area/locale/locality/location/place/point/position/region/site/spot
	(an/the) area/locale/locality/location/place/point/position/region/site/spot where
	at/from/in/on/to an/the area/locale/locality/location/place/point/position/region/site/spot
	at/from/in/on/to an/the area/locale/locality/location/place/point/position/region/site/spot where
	at/from/in/on/to any/each/every/some area/locale/locality/location/place/point/position/region/site/spot
	at/from/in/on/to any/each/every/some area/locale/locality/location/place/point/position/region/site/spot where
	in cases/circumstances/instances/situations in which
	in cases when/where
	in circumstances when/where
	in instances when/where
	in situations when/where
	where . . . at
	where . . . to
	whereabouts

CONCISE	WORDY
whereas	as opposed to
	but whereas
	by/in comparison
	by/in contrast
	by way of comparison/contrast
	contrariwise
	in view of the fact that
	on the contrary
	on the other hand
	while/whereas on the contrary
whereon	whereupon
wherever	(an/the) area/locale/locality/location/place/point/position/region/site/spot
	(an/the) area/locale/locality/location/place/point/position/region/site/spot where
	at/from/in/on/to an/the area/locale/locality/location/place/point/position/region/site/spot
	at/from/in/on/to an/the area/locale/locality/location/place/point/position/region/site/spot where
	at/from/in/on/to any/each/every/some area/locale/locality/location/place/point/position/region/site/spot
	at/from/in/on/to any/each/every/some area/locale/locality/location/place/point/position/region/site/spot where
	irrespective of where
	no matter where
	regardless of where
	wheresoever
wherewithal	financial wherewithal
whether	as to whether
	when and/or whether
	whether and/or when
	whether or not
whether . . . or (not)	irrespective of (the fact) whether . . . (or)
	no matter whether . . . (or)
	regardless of whether . . . (or)
whichever	irrespective of which
	no matter which
	regardless of which
	whichsoever
while	(a/the) . . . amount of time/length of time/period of time/span of time

CONCISE	WORDY
	(and) at the same time (as/that)
	concurrently . . . while
	concurrent/concurrently with
	during the course/length of
	during the period/period of time/span of time/time/years (that)
	(somewhere) in the course of
	in the process of
	over the course/duration/length of
	simultaneously . . . while
	through/throughout the course/duration/length of
	while at the same time
	while concurrently
	while simultaneously
while -ing	in the act of -ing
whoever	irrespective of who
	no matter who
	regardless of who
	who in the world/on earth
	whosoever
who ever	who in the world/on earth
whole	as a whole
	backward and forward
	completely and utterly
	from beginning to end
	from start to finish
	in its/their entirety
	through and through
	throughout the length and breadth (of)
	under any circumstances/conditions
	wholly and completely
(the) whole	in its/their entirety
whomever	irrespective of whom
	no matter whom
	regardless of whom
	whomsoever
whose	(a/the) . . . of which
why	because why
	how is it (that)
	what . . . for
	wherefore
why (do)	I'm curious why
why ever	why in the world/on earth
wide	in width

CONCISE	WORDY
widely	far and wide
widespread	present everywhere
widow	widow woman
widow/widower	widow/widower of the late
will	has a/the habit of (-ing)
	has a/the tendency (to)
	is going to
will/would	(is) in the habit of
	is accustomed to (-ing)
willingly	of . . . own accord (free will)
wine	liquid refreshment
wingedly	at/in the blink of an eye
	expeditiously
	in quick/short order
winter	wintertime
wishes to	is desirous of -ing
with	about/concerning/in/on/regarding the matter/subject of
	accompanied by
	alongside of
	as a consequence of
	as . . . apply to
	as a result of
	as concerns
	as/so far as . . . (goes/is concerned)
	as regards
	associated with
	as to
	based on/upon
	because of
	by consequence of
	by (the) means of
	by reason of
	by the result of
	by/in virtue of
	by (the) way of
	concerning
	concurrent/concurrently with
	connected with
	during the course/length of
	in association with
	in (the) . . . case (of)
	in combination with
	in company with
	in conjunction with

CONCISE	WORDY
	in connection with
	in consequence of
	in defense of
	in favor (of)
	in opposition to
	in point of
	in proportion to
	in reaction to
	in reference to
	in regard to
	in relation to
	in resistance to
	in respect of/to
	in response to
	insofar as . . . (goes/is concerned)
	in support of
	in terms of
	in the area of
	in the assessment of
	in the company of
	(somewhere) in the course of
	in the direction of/toward
	in the estimation of
	in the judgment of
	in the opinion of
	in the presence of
	in the realm of
	in the view of
	involve
	on account of
	on the basis of
	on the side of
	over the course/duration/length of
	pertain/pertaining to
	regard/regarding
	relate/relating to
	side by side (with)
	simultaneous/simultaneously with
	through/throughout the course/duration/length of
	through the medium of
	through the use of
	together with
	what with
	when it comes to

CONCISE	WORDY
	where . . . is concerned
	with reference to
	with regard to
	with relation to
	with respect to
with all	contrary to
	in despite of
	in (the) face of
	in spite of
	notwithstanding
	. . . to the contrary
within	(something/somewhere) in between
	inside the boundaries/limits/parameters of
	in the middle of
	in the midst of
	involved in
with no	(a/the) absence of
	devoid of
	in the absence of
	lacking in
	(a/the) lack of
without	(a/the) absence of
	devoid of
	in the absence of
	lacking in
	(a/the) lack of
without delay	at your earliest convenience
without (a/any) doubt	without (a/any) question/shadow of a doubt
without equal	in a class by herself/itself
without interruption	continuously/incessantly and without interruption
without peer	in a class by herself/itself
without warning	suddenly and without warning
with time	as (the) days/decades/months/weeks/years go on
	as time goes on
	as time progresses (forward/on/onward)
	at a/some future/later/subsequent date/time
	(after/for/in/over/within) (an) extended/lengthy/long/ prolonged/protracted amount of time/length of time/period/period of time/span of time/time/while in/into the future
	in/over (the) coming days/decades/months/weeks/years
	in/over (the) days/decades/months/weeks/years ahead
	in/over (the) days/decades/months/weeks/years to come

CONCISE	WORDY
	in due course/time
	in good time
	in the course of events/things/time
	in the distant future
	in/over the long run
	in/over the long term
	over the long haul
	some day/time in the future
	(the) time will come when
	with the passage of time
witness	pay attention to
	pay heed to
	take cognizance of
	take note of
	take notice of
witnesses	is an indication/indicator of
	is indicative of
	is suggestive of
	is (a) witness to
words	communication
work	place of business/employment/work
workers	human resources
working	in force and effect
	in operation
	operational
	operative
workplace	place of business/employment/work
works for	affiliated with
	associated with
worldwide	(all) across/throughout the world
worries	is of concern to
worries (about/over)	is afraid of/to
	is apprehensive of
	is fearful (about/of/that)
	is frightened of/to
	is in fear for/of
	is scared of/to
worry (about/over)	express concern (about)
	is concerned (about)
	voice concern (about)
worse still/yet	(to) make matters worse
worthless	null and void
write	author
	communicate in writing

CONCISE	WORDY
	inform
	make contact (with)
	verbalize
write (to)	communicate (with)
	contact
	get in touch with
wrong	in error
	take advantage of
wrongdoing	criminal wrongdoing
wrongs	is deleterious to
	is detrimental to
	is exploitative/exploitive of
	is harmful to
	is injurious to

X Y Z

CONCISE	WORDY
X-ray	X-ray photograph
yearly	on a regular basis
	year in (and) year out
	yearly anniversary
yell	scream and yell
	yell and scream
yes	absolutely
	affirmative
	(most/very) assuredly
	(most/very) definitely
	in the affirmative
yet	after all is said and done
	all (just) the same
	and yet
	as (the) days/decades/months/weeks/years go on
	as time goes on
	as time progresses (forward/on/onward)
	as (of) yet
	at a/some future/later/subsequent date/time
	at any rate
	be that as it may
	by/in comparison
	by/in contrast
	by way of comparison/contrast
	contrariwise

CONCISE	WORDY
	despite the fact that
	in any case/event
	in/over (the) coming days/decades/months/weeks/years
	in/over (the) days/decades/months/weeks/years ahead
	in/over (the) days/decades/months/weeks/years to come
	in due course/time
	in good time
	in spite of the fact that
	in the course of events/things/time
	in the distant future
	in/into the future
	in/over the long run
	in/over the long term
	irregardless of the fact that
	irrespective of the fact that
	nevertheless
	nonetheless
	notwithstanding the fact that
	on the contrary
	on the other hand
	over the long haul
	regardless of the fact that
	some day/time in the future
	sooner or later
	still and all
	(the) time will come when
	with the passage of time
(as) yet	up till/until that/this juncture/juncture in time/moment/moment in time/period/period in time/point/point in time/stage/stage in time/time
	up to that/this juncture/juncture in time/moment/moment in time/period/period in time/point/point in time/stage/stage in time/time
	up to the current/present (time)
(just) yet	at (the) present
	at that/this juncture
	at that/this juncture/juncture in time/moment/moment in time/period/period in time/point/point in time/stage/stage in time/time in my history/in my life/in the history of my life
	at that/this juncture/moment/period/point/stage in time

CONCISE	WORDY
	at that/this moment
	at that/this point
	at that/this stage
	at that/this time
	at the current/present time
	at the (current/present) moment
	currently
	on that/this (particular) occasion
	presently
yield	bring (give) forth
you	individual(s)
young	young child/infant
zone	locality
zoo	zoological garden
zoologic	zoological

Acknowledgments

To the capable staff at W. W. Norton who worked on this book, thank you. Amy Cherry, my editor, and Anna Mageras, her editorial assistant, were especially helpful, indeed, indispensable to the publication and production of *To the Point*. Well done.

About the Author

ROBERT HARTWELL FISKE is the editor and publisher of *The Vocabula Review* (vocabula.com), a monthly online journal about the English language. He is the author of *The Dictionary of Unendurable English*, *The Dimwit's Dictionary*, and other books. He also publishes *Robert Hartwell Fiske's Disagreeable English*, a quarterly bulletin of misused, misspelled, and mispronounced English.